Sussex Depicted
Views and Descriptions 1600-1800

1901-2001

The Sussex Record Society's Centenary Volume

Sussex Depicted

Views and Descriptions 1600-1800

John H. Farrant

with the assistance of
John Bleach, Timothy J. McCann,
Christopher Whittick and Peter Wilkinson

Sussex Record Society
Volume 85

2001

Published 2001 by
Sussex Record Society
Barbican House
High Street
Lewes
East Sussex BN7 1YE
United Kingdom

and issued to members of the Society for the year 2001

Design by Andy Gammon, Dip. A. D. Graphics
Maps by Susan Rowland
Index by Ann Hudson
Printed by Hobbs the Printers, Totton, Hampshire

ISBN 0 85445 051 3

British Library Cataloguing in Publication Data
A catalogue record for this book is available from the British Library

This book is dedicated to the memory of

VERENA SMITH
1903 - 1993

Fellow of the Society of Antiquaries
Secretary and Vice-President of
the Sussex Record Society

For more than 30 years, she worked with
unstinting devotion and determination for
the Sussex Record Society; and ensured its
successful advance into its second century.
Her generous legacy has made this
Centenary Volume possible. Its theme and
content reflect her two ruling passions: her
lifelong study and delight in architecture
and the visual arts, and her enthusiasm for
research and publication devoted to the
history and topography of her county of
Sussex.

Contents

Colour Plates

between pages 140 and 141

The Views

Bibliography

The Sussex Record Society, 1901-2001

Index

Illustrations and figures in the text

Preface

The theme of this Centenary volume of the Sussex Record Society is the systematic depiction of Sussex, past and present, in words and pictures, over some 250 years before the publication of the first full 'county history' in 1835. Here are reproduced some 150 views of Sussex made in the last quarter of the 18th century - many of buildings then already old. The majority of the pictures are by S. H. Grimm and James Lambert, senior and junior, painted for their client, Sir William Burrell, the most eminent antiquary of Sussex before the 20th century. They complement the 192 pictures by Grimm and the Lamberts printed in the Society's Jubilee volume, *Sussex views* (Godfrey and Salzman 1951). The present volume also reproduces views taken by 40 other artists in the 17th, 18th and early 19th centuries; it gives a substantial commentary on each View; it prints the texts of two antiquarian tours and several documents relating to published pictures and to antiquarian research; and it includes a long introductory Essay on the lives of the writers and artists and on their working methods.

The texts and pictures embraced are those where the motive of the author or artist was to depict a locality or some aspect of it. In the 16th and 17th centuries such depiction, as a branch of intellectual activity, was called 'chorography', 'the art or practice of describing, or delineating on a map or chart, particular regions or districts.' Until the 1760s, the authors and artists were overwhelmingly visitors to Sussex, for the descriptions and pictures were products of a curiosity about the past and the present of the travellers' native land. Some travelled purely for pleasure or at least edification, others hoping to profit by publishing books to inform local residents, visitors and fireside travellers. From the later 17th century, travel in England (and not only the Grand Tour) was part of a gentleman's education. The visitors were indeed almost exclusively, by the standards of their time, of gentlemanly or higher status, either by birth or by office (for example, as an Anglican cleric or a herald). But some local authors, particularly non-clerical schoolmasters, would not have been so acknowledged, and the originators of the pictures included 'artisan' painters employed by gentlefolk to make portraits of their houses.

Sussex's proximity to London, and its landscape, with the backbone of the South Downs between the clay of the Weald to the north and the English Channel to the south, established an east-west route, from Rye to Chichester, or *vice versa*, which many early tourists took. Some writers were primarily interested in contemporary conditions, particularly from the later 18th century, and others in antiquities, the relics of medieval and earlier eras. In practice there was a continuum, with even the most devoted antiquary, for example, comparing the bathing machines at Brighton with those at Margate. But there is undoubtedly a bias in the production of pictures, particularly in those which were engraved, towards the medieval castles, churches and religious houses. And there is little evidence of the interest in natural history (the term embracing both the biological and the earth sciences) which was apparent in other parts of Britain in the later 17th century.

The selection of pictures for reproduction and the discussion of the artists in the Essay has been underpinned by an inventory of original pictures of Sussex made before about 1860, when photography became widespread. This I compiled from the indexes of museums, archives and libraries, from published books and from auction catalogues. The resulting Picture Database (PDB) contains over 7700 records of pictures by nearly 700 named artists and an unknown number of anonymous artists. It has been deposited on CD-ROM in the East and West Sussex Record Offices and the Sussex Archaeological Society Library, and will be accessible via the Internet. A few prolific artists, represented by large holdings in one or two repositories, account for the majority of the pictures. In the work of Henry Petrie (some 430 recorded pictures from 1802-9) and Adelaide Tracy (290 pictures from 1846-57), their subject matter, churches throughout Sussex and, by Petrie, castles as well, overlap that of the Lamberts (720 pictures) and Grimm (1060 pictures). In the work of W. H. Brooke (270 pictures from 1818-56) and W. A. Delamotte (200 pictures from the 1850s), their subject matter is concentrated in single towns, Hastings and Brighton respectively, the former including vernacular buildings. At the other extreme, some 570 artists are known by five or fewer Sussex views each, and their work is concentrated on a few localities which were relatively well-illustrated by contemporary engravings. In descending order the localities represented in the database are Hastings, Brighton, Lewes, Chichester, Pevensey, Battle, Arundel and Herstmonceux. By the later 18th century the Sussex coastal towns were well established as holiday resorts. The well-trodden tourist route east-west across the county linked, or ran close to, these localities, some with particular historical associations, and sketching was, in the 19th century, a genteel leisure pastime. Conversely, the exceptional geographical spread and scope of Grimm's 900 different views is clearly demonstrated and, as in the 1951 volume, Grimm provides the bulk of the views reproduced here.

The progress of publishing county and urban histories is followed through to 1835 when the first for the whole county appeared, under the name of T. W. Horsfield. But for the views selected, the terminal date is 1815 because many engravings were published in the following 50 years, because there is less diversity in the subject matter and because fewer artists producing topographical views were active in the county once Napoleon's defeat opened the Continent again to travellers. Brooke, Delamotte and Tracy are therefore excluded. Many pictures have been selected because the building depicted is no longer standing or has been substantially altered, and has not been illustrated in a readily available book or journal. Some have been chosen because they complement a published account of the building or other published views, others because the caption can incorporate new research. The pictures are therefore treated first and foremost as historical documents providing information for the student of Sussex, and the captions concentrate on the subject matter, rather than the artistic qualities. A few, though, have been selected to make a point about the development or production of topographical art. In several instances, two or more views of the same building or locality are included, to allow a fuller treatment of the subject. Consequently the result is not an illustrated guidebook to 18th-century Sussex, depicting the most noteworthy buildings by either 18th-century or today's criteria. The Royal Pavilion at Brighton, for example, does not feature because its building history is extensively documented in print (see Morley 1984), while Chichester Cathedral (see Hobbs 1994) appears only in a cartoon for Samuel Buck's prospect of Chichester published as an engraving in 1738.

What are strongly represented are the houses in the countryside of the gentry and substantial tenant farmers. These views and their captions, as case studies, suggest some themes which deserve further study, such as the phasing of investment in new building, and the down-sizing or demolition of houses following absorption into the great aristocratic estates. The Essay does not attempt to address such themes - for which further documented cases are required, perhaps starting with houses illustrated in *Sussex views*. A seminal work which gives a good context for such houses is Cooper 1999, which can be supplemented by Platt 1994, Cliffe 1999 and Wilson and Mackley 2000. In preparation is a major study of the west Sussex country houses: Weller and Warren forthcoming. Williamson 1995 gives an excellent context for the parks, pointing out that they were not only for pleasure and that their designers had to accommodate many other uses. For the background to the major designers' work, see Mowl 2000. Berry 2000 considers public pleasure gardens, while Strong 2000 offers useful insights into garden art.

The pictures here are in the main works of topographical art, the art of depicting accurate views of places. The concern for accuracy did not preclude the artist from a pleasing composition, perhaps omitting trees which blocked the view from the desired point, adding people and animals, or 'staffage', which were not actually there, or, particularly in distant prospects, including more in the view than could be seen from any one vantage-point. The Lamberts were described as landscape painters, and several of the other artists represented here would have accepted that label, but none the label of topographical artist. Yet topographical illustration, in England, had the older roots, despite being subsumed within landscape painting as it developed in the middle of the 18th century. However, in the early history of topographical and landscape painting, unlike say the Lake District or the Wye Valley, Sussex has no distinctive place.

William Burrell commissioned the views by Grimm and the Lamberts between 1774 and 1791 as part of the most ambitious project to study Sussex's history prior to the *Victoria History of the County of Sussex* - which was launched some 130 years later and after a further century is still incomplete. As described in the Essay, Burrell undertook extensive documentary research and fieldwork, directly and through intermediaries, and intended that some of the views should be engraved and published with his text. Though Burrell's project did not lead to publication, his materials underpinned the county histories which did appear between 1815 and 1835, and are used by students of Sussex to this day.

It is fitting to pay tribute here also to the Sussex historians of the generations between Horsfield's and my own, on whose work much of the research presented here builds. Many feature in the Bibliography, but a special place goes to L. F. Salzman (1878-1971), Walter H. Godfrey (1881-1961) and Francis W. Steer (1912-78). Their distinguished contributions to historical studies extended way beyond the county's borders yet they were pillars of the Sussex Record Society for most of its first century. Their biographies appear in Steer 1971 and DNB 1998; Stevens 1961 and DNB 1998; and Murray 1980.

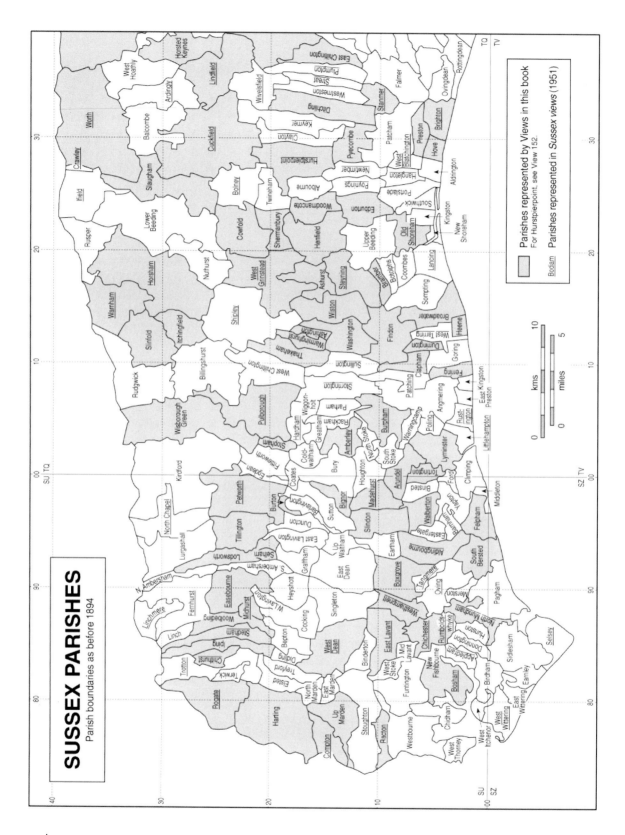

SUSSEX PARISHES

Parish boundaries as before 1894

Parishes represented by Views in this book
For Hurstpierpoint, see View 152.

Bodiam Parishes represented in *Sussex views* (1951)

kms 0 10

miles 0 5

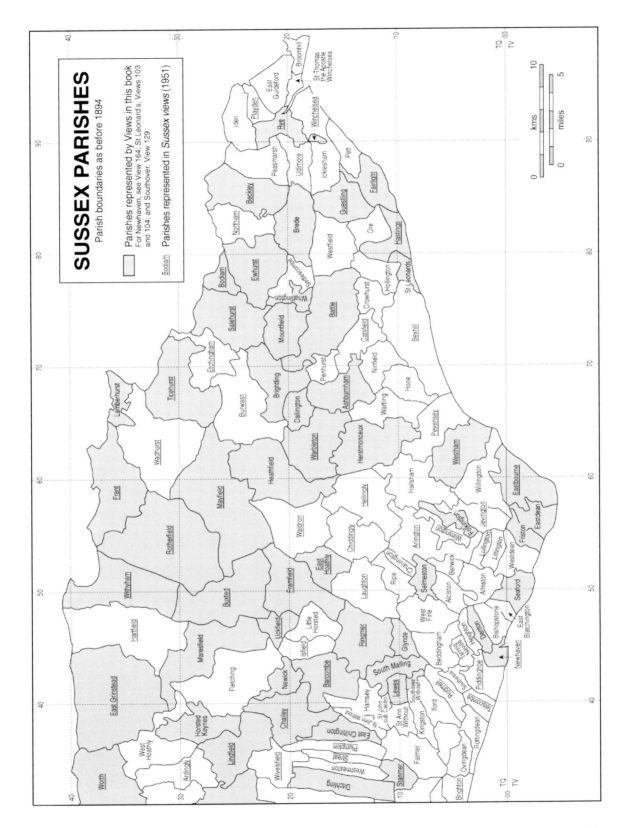

SUSSEX PARISHES

Parish boundaries as before 1894

Parishes represented by Views in this book
For Newhaven, see View 164; St Leonard's, Views 103 and 104; and Southover, View 129.

Bodiam Parishes represented in *Sussex views* (1951)

Acknowledgements

The idea for an illustrated volume for the Record Society's centenary was advanced by John Bleach, and he has been a tower of strength throughout its preparation, remaining calm and supportive as successive schemes were drafted and abandoned, making the initial selection of views from the Burrell collection, writing captions and offering freely of his wide-ranging knowledge of Sussex history. Tim McCann and Peter Wilkinson, both as members of the Society's Council and as staff of West Sussex Record Office, have given great help and have written most of the captions for the Rape of Chichester. Christopher Whittick of East Sussex Record Office has provided much constructive comment on drafts, numerous references from his deep knowledge of the archives of eastern Sussex and captions which are gems of research. My thanks go also to all the other authors of captions, Annabelle Hughes, Ron Iden, Richard Jones, Michael Leppard, Alison McCann, Janet Pennington and Joyce Sleight. Michael Hunter and Margaret Thorburn kindly commented on a late draft of the Essay.

Our debt to the *Victoria County History of Sussex* is much greater than the citations reveal, for several architectural descriptions come almost verbatim from the recent volumes edited by Tim Hudson. David and Barbara Martin have given valuable advice on building history, over and above their excellent survey reports which are cited under the reference ESRO, HBR. From the Sussex Gardens Trust, Barbara Abbs, Sharyn Hedge and Sue Berry (who also advised on the further reading suggested above) have assisted on garden history. Julia Abel-Smith, Marlis Bickersteth, Melanie Blake (Witt Library), John Burrowes (WSRO), John Cooper (Booth Museum), John Hardcastle, Ralph Hyde (Guildhall Library), Helen Jones (Adept Scientific plc), Laura Kidner (Worthing Museum & Art Gallery), Graham Marsh and Malcolm Marjoram (British Library), Tony Marr, Bernard Nurse (Society of Antiquaries), Henrietta Pattinson (Sotheby's), P. M. Reid, Brian Short, Brian Warner, Victoria Williams (Hastings Museum & Art Gallery) and Emma Young (SAS) provided references, access to material and technical assistance. On the production side, I have had the pleasure of working again with Ann Hudson and Susan Rowland as indexer and cartographer and above all with Andy Gammon as this volume's designer whose enthusiasm for the project I greatly appreciated.

The Essay draws on my research over thirty years, and I remain indebted to all those who helped me to write the articles listed in the Bibliography. I have consulted material in over sixty libraries, record offices, museums and private collections, and amongst those I record my special thanks to the British Library, the Bodleian Library, the East and West Sussex Record Offices, the Sussex Archaeological Society and the University of Sussex Library. I am grateful to *Sussex Archaeological Collections* for having published my work on John Norden, Francis Grose, the James Lamberts and the Arthur Youngs, which reappears here in abbreviated form.

The Sussex Record Society wishes to thank the following for their permission to reproduce pictures in their collections (the numbers refer to the Views, unless otherwise indicated):

Ashmolean Museum, Oxford: 130

By permission of The British Library: all Views and Colour plates not otherwise acknowledged

© Copyright The British Museum: 29, 164, 195

County Archivist, East Sussex Record Office: 12, 13, 42-49, 90, 97, 108, 114 (Colour plate XI), 158, 180 (Colour plate XVI)

East Sussex County Library (Eastbourne Reference Library): page 131

The Trustees of the Goodwood Collection. Photograph: Photographic Survey, Courtauld Institute of Art: 25

Hastings Museum & Art Gallery: 106, 107

Leeds Museums and Galleries (City Art Gallery). Photograph: Courtauld Institute of Art: 27, 80

Su concessione del Ministero per i Beni e le Attività Culturali, Italia: 161

MuseuMAfricA, Johannesburg: 31, 32

The National Gallery of Scotland: 9

By permission of the Duke of Northumberland. Photograph: Photographic Survey, Courtauld Institute of Art: 146

Private collection. Photograph courtesy of B. M. Short: 142, 143

Private collection. Photograph courtesy of Sotheby's: 8 (Colour plate I)

Photograph courtesy of Sotheby's: 61

Sussex Archaeological Society: 53, 91, 128, 129, page 362

The County Archivist of West Sussex: 51, 54, 58 (Colour plate III), 59, 76-78, 123, 176

West Sussex County Council Library Service (Worthing Library): 145

Worthing Museum & Art Gallery: 35-37, 82

Yale Center for British Art, Paul Mellon Collection: 93, 111, 157, 177, 197, 198

Editorial Conventions

In cross-references, the main components of the book are referred to as the Essay, the Documents, the Views and the Colour plates, followed by the relevant section, document or plate number.

Source references. The Essay and the Documents each has endnotes in a section entitled References. The caption to each View includes a list of Sources. The References and the Sources cite published works using the author-date system, and the Bibliography lists those works. In the author-date citations and in the Bibliography, the digits before a colon denote the volume number, with the page numbers following. Archival sources are cited by repository and reference, sometimes with a brief description of the document. The main repositories are abbreviated, as on page xx. Standard biographical sources which are not cited recurrently are DNB 1998, IGI, the dictionaries of Oxford and Cambridge alumni in Venn and Venn 1922-54 and Foster 1887-92, and of clergy in Le Neve 1964 and the Clergy Index in SAS Library, Waterhouse 1981 and Mallalieu 1976-90 on artists, Colvin 1995 on architects, Bendall 1997 on map-makers and Brent 1993, valuable in identifying Lewes residents. Nor are archive references always given for well-known sources mentioned in the text, such as the Hearth Tax.

The Documents. The editing principles in Hunnisett 1977 have been followed, and spelling, capitalisation and punctuation in the manuscript documents have been modernised, and obvious grammatical and scribal errors silently corrected. The originals do not call for deep exegesis and are readily accessible in public collections to anyone wishing to check my readings. Original spellings have been retained only in cases of doubt or where, for example, the form of a place-name may be of interest. The same applies to quotations in the Essay and the captions. But the original has been respected in the transcripts of printed documents (Documents 1 and 2, except that the titles of subscribers in 2.3 have been standardised) and in the Bibliography. [Square brackets] enclose significant editorial interpolations, and [*blank*] signifies a gap in the original which the author intended, but failed, to fill and which I have not been able to complete. In Document 7.2 <angle brackets> are used for material from other versions of the list, as explained there. To maintain consistency with the Documents and the other sources used, Imperial measurements are given throughout

the book. The relevant conversions to metric measures are:

12 in (inches) = 1 foot; 3 ft (feet) = 1 yard = 0.914 metre
1760 yards = 1 mile = 1.609 kilometres
1 acre = 4840 square yards = 0.405 hectares
12d. (pence) = 1s. (shilling)
20s. = £1; 21s = 1 gn. (guinea)

The Views. Each plate has a title with the following elements:

the *serial number* in this book.

the *subject of the picture*, starting with the ancient ecclesiastical parish (except for urban parishes where the town - Chichester, Hastings or Lewes - is given), which determines the order of the plates; the customary name of the subject is used, rather than, for example, the title given by the artist. Hence the title may contain a name which was not in use at the date immediately following it.

the *year* given on the picture or (if known to be different) the year in which the view was originally taken. If the picture is known to be a later copy, the date of the copy is given after the artist's name. '?1783' signifies 'probably 1783'. For example, a reproduced view by Grimm is undated, but his other views of the same site are dated. The date '*c.* 1783' signifies 'about 1783'. '1783-95' points to good evidence that the view was taken within those years. (Elsewhere in the text, with reference to probable birth and death dates, the form used is '1654?-1702?'.)

the *name of the artist*, followed by the date of the copy if different from that of original composition.

the *repository* in which the picture is now held, with the accession number or reference. Views in Burrell's collection in the British Library are cited by both folio and, in [square brackets], serial number.

(where appropriate) the number of the *Colour plate* in which the View is also reproduced.

As this is not an art-historical catalogue, the physical characteristics of the picture are omitted, though medium and size are recorded in the Picture Database. The media for the great majority are ink and grey wash and watercolour on paper. Many of the views by Grimm are about $7\frac{1}{2}$ in. by $10\frac{1}{2}$ in. (190 mm by 270 mm). His technique is described by Gilbert White in Essay 3.5. In some of these views reproduced here, foxing caused by the glue with which they have been mounted may show through.

Each plate has a caption. In 24 instances, two or more consecutive plates have a composite caption. The authors of captions have critically reviewed the existing secondary literature, and for a substantial minority of Views they have undertaken additional research in primary sources or on site. We acknowledge that we may not be aware of relevant unpublished research by local historians and may not have exploited the archival material fully. The author's initials appear at the end of the caption. The Views for which each author wrote the caption are also given below, * indicating joint authorship.

JB	John Bleach: 28, 30, 39-40, 55, 66-8,74*, 75-7, 79, 83, 89, 99, 103-4*, 109, 122, 125-6, 129, 133*, 134, 136-7, 147-8, 152, 156-8, 162-3, 166, 174, 183, 196, 199, 201-2
JHF	John H. Farrant: 3-11, 19*, 20, 22-6*, 27, 29, 31-8, 41-50, 51-2*, 57, 58-9*, 61, 62*, 65*, 70*, 72-3, 74*, 80, 82, 87-8, 90-1, 96, 103-4*, 105-8, 111, 114-18, 127*, 128, 130-2, 133*, 142-3, 145, 146*, 149-50, 159*, 161, 164-5, 171-2, 175, 178-9, 189, 191-2, 195*, 197-8, 203*
AFH	Annabelle F. Hughes: 2, 19*, 60, 110, 119-21, 124, 151, 169-70, 190, 204
RI	Ron Iden: 17-18, 81
RJ	Richard Jones: 78
MJL	Michael Leppard: 92-5
AMcC	Alison McCann: 51*, 53, 54, 71, 146*
TJMcC	Timothy J. McCann: 22-6*, 52*, 64, 65*, 69, 70*, 100-2, 127*, 135, 138, 141, 154-5*, 159*, 173, 184, 186, 195*, 203*
JP	Janet Pennington: 177*, 200
JS	Joyce Sleight: 177*
CHCW	Christopher Whittick: 12-16, 62*, 63, 84-6, 97-8, 112-13, 139, 140, 160, 167-8, 180-1, 185, 187-8, 193-4
PMW	Peter Wilkinson: 1, 21, 56, 58-9*, 123, 144, 153, 154-5*, 176, 182

Following the caption are given the Sources; the National Grid Reference (NGR) for the main or a prominent feature in the picture; and the picture's unique number in the Picture Database (PDB).

The Colour plates. The choice of the Views also to be reproduced in colour was determined by which justified reproduction in colour and then by whether copies in colour could be obtained at reasonable cost. Few met the first criterion because Grimm's views are usually in grey wash, with at most the addition of blue for the sky and green or brown for the foreground. Only a handful have some colour added to the building.

Bibliography. Modern editions of older published works are cited, and listed in the Bibliography, under the name of the original author, rather than of the editor, on the ground that the reader consulting the Bibliography independently of the text is more likely to know the author's than the editor's name. The same generally applies to editions of, or extracts from, manuscripts, if the author's name appears in the title, for example, *The book of John Rowe* or *The journals of Gilbert White*. For up-to-date references on many topics touched on in this book, see Leslie and Short 1999.

Abbreviations

b.	born or baptised
BL	British Library, London
Bodl.	Bodleian Library, Oxford
c.	*circa*, about
d.	died
ESRO	East Sussex Record Office, Lewes
fc.	facing
fl.	*floruit*, active at the given dates
GM	*Gentleman's Magazine*
NGR	National Grid Reference
PDB	Picture Database
PRO	Public Record Office, London
SA	Society of Antiquaries of London
SAS	Sussex Archaeological Society, Lewes
Sussex views or *SV*	Godfrey, W. H., and L. F. Salzman, eds 1951. *Sussex views selected from the Burrell Collections.* Sussex Record Society Jubilee volume
SWA	*Sussex Weekly Advertiser*
VAM	Victoria and Albert Museum, London
VCHS	*Victoria County History of Sussex*
WSRO	West Sussex Record Office, Chichester
YCBA	Yale Center for British Art, New Haven, CT

John Farrant
Lewes
February 2001

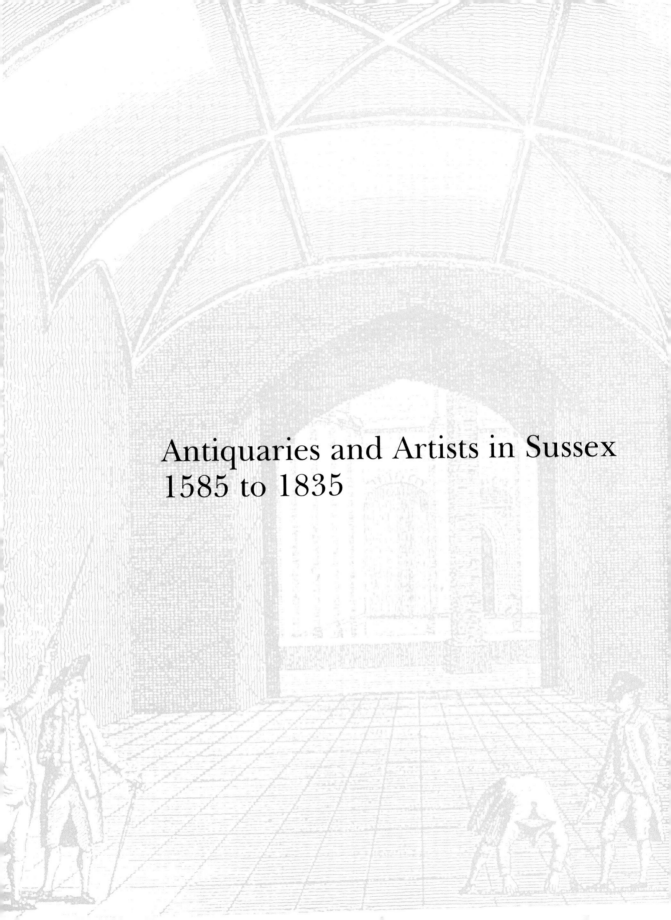

Antiquaries and Artists in Sussex
1585 to 1835

The first archaeological illustration in an English book depicted the inscription at Lewes which records how a Danish prince, Magnus, became an anchorite there. William Camden drew it in the early 1580s on his tour through Sussex, while collecting material for his *Britannia* which appeared in 1586. Two hundred and fifty years later, in 1835, the Lewes publisher John Baxter issued the two thick volumes of *The history, antiquities, and topography of the County of Sussex*, edited by T. W. Horsfield and illustrated by many engravings and woodcuts. The first history of the county had a long gestation.

Overleaf Antiquaries at work in the porter's lodge, Herstmonceux Castle, 1776. Engraving in Francis Grose, *The antiquities of England and Wales. Supplement* 2 (1786-7), from a picture by S. H. Grimm after James Lambert junior: see pages 44, 112-13.

1. Sussex chorography before 1700

1.1 The beginnings of county history

The dissolution of the monasteries under Henry VIII and the subsequent dispersal of many of their libraries meant that a mass of little-known historical material became accessible to those with antiquarian tastes. The breach with Rome enhanced national self-consciousness and the desire to demonstrate the scriptural (as distinct from Romish) foundations of [England's] ecclesiastical traditions. The expansion of the trades of printing, bookbinding, and bookselling facilitated communication of knowledge. And an age of victories abroad, rising prosperity for many, and pride in a great Queen tended to arouse new interest in family trees, appreciation of ancient monuments, curiosity about the lay-out of towns, woods and fields, about how Britain and British institutions came to be as they were.

So May McKisack summarises some of the factors which contributed to the Tudor renaissance of historical studies - which flourished at the levels both of the nation and of its constituent parts.[1] The county emerged as a major focus of interest. Although established as a unit of local government some 600 years earlier, it acquired under Queen Elizabeth a new significance through the duties placed on the gentry acting as justices of the peace, both individually and collectively in quarter sessions, and the emergence of the office of lord lieutenant. So was established the genre of the 'county history', a printed book dedicated to a varying range of topics related to its chosen territory, but always with a concentration on the past, whether the physical remains of human activity (the antiquities), the history of institutions such as the diocese or borough corporations, or the ancestry of the landowning families. The first of this genre came from Sussex's neighbour to the east: William Lambarde's *A perambulation of Kent* (1576). William Dugdale's *Antiquities of Warwickshire* (1656) became the model. Each parish was treated separately, with introductory remarks covering topography, etymology, archaeology and notable events, but most of the pages comprising detailed accounts of manors and their owners, advowsons and church monuments. Successor histories also had a general introduction to the county, usually speculating on its history before the Norman Conquest. Robert Plot's *Natural history of Oxfordshire* (1677) and *of Staffordshire* (1686) widened the range of subject matter studied within the frame of the county.

The period of the archetypal county studies was also that which produced a bedrock of printed primary sources for English history. For example, the narrative sources of English medieval history in the monastic chronicles were edited for the first time, by William Fulman and Thomas Gale, in three massive folio volumes appearing between 1684 and 1691, and then by Thomas Hearne in the early decades of the next century. Abraham Wheloc produced editions of Bede's *Ecclesiastical history* and the Anglo-Saxon Chronicle in 1643. Building on Roger Dodsworth's work, Sir William Dugdale's *Monasticon Anglicanum* (three volumes, 1655-73) made accessible a great corpus of monastic charters, while his *Baronage of England* (two volumes, 1675-6) was an invaluable compilation of pedigrees and heraldry. In 1703 the House of Lords appointed a committee to oversee the preservation and keeping of the nation's records, and Thomas Rymer was employed to edit important documents relating to foreign policy, published as *Foedera* in 20 volumes in 1726-35. Access to the public records was improved for those with the time and skills (or the money to pay record searchers), and that assisted studies such as Arthur Collins's *Peerage of England*, first published in 1709.

Other such publications are to be found in William Burrell's bibliography (Document 7.1). Together they provided a starting point for the student of a county's history, and the more assiduous acknowledged them in footnotes.[2]

The pace of the necessary research and of publication varied greatly from county to county, and one thread in this Essay is that Sussex waited for a history of the whole county until 1835. By then Kent had Edward Hasted's *History* in four volumes in its first edition (1778-99) and in eight in its second (1797-1801), to which there had been several precursors besides Lambarde. John Aubrey's *Natural history and antiquities of Surrey* drafted in the 1670s had appeared in five volumes in 1718, and Manning and Bray's *History and antiquities of Surrey* in three volumes in 1804-14. To Sussex's west, Hampshire, though, was faring no better, for D.Y.'s *Collections for a history of Hampshire* in five volumes (1795) were highly derivative, and basic coverage of each parish was achieved only by the *Victoria County History* for Hampshire and the Isle of Wight (five volumes, 1900-12).[3]

So it was that, in his bibliographical guide of 1720, Richard Rawlinson had to record of Sussex: 'of this county we have nought published, except the monumental inscriptions of the Cathedral Church of Chichester, with *The antiquities of Worcester*' by Thomas Habingdon (1717) - a mere 14 inscriptions in fact. With minor exceptions, until the second half of the 18th century Sussex featured only as part of projects with a nation-wide scope. One reason may be that the gentry network, which supported historical projects in other counties, was not so effective in Sussex, because quarter sessions sat as two separate benches, east and west, for three sessions a year, and only at Midsummer, in Lewes, did the gentry for the whole county assemble together - and that practice was discontinued in 1687. Furthermore the different pattern of landownership between the two ends of the county may have inhibited an antiquarian project: in the west great ducal estates whose owners, with lands also in other counties, had a weaker attachment to the soil of Sussex contrasted with the smaller gentry estates in the east. Yet, almost co-terminous with the Diocese of Chichester, the county was the obvious unit for study. The gentry nevertheless, as individuals, showed characteristic pride in ancestry, and heralds on visitations noted the arms on glass, for example, at Laughton Place in about 1608 and at Arundel in 1634, the latter copied by the herald painter John Withie, View 7. In the early-17th-century glass now in Stopham Church, the glazier, Roelant, portrayed the client's 13th-century ancestor in chain mail and surcoat, View 178. John Philipot, Somerset Herald, who conducted the 1634 visitation of Sussex, was not above encouraging the gentry's interest by fabricating documents and tales such as that of Sir John Pelham taking the French king prisoner at the battle of Poitiers in 1356.[4]

For many English counties, antiquarian descriptions begin with John Leland's. After nearly ten years in travelling and collecting materials, in 1546 he laid before Henry VIII his plan for a description and history of the Tudor nation. This was to include, for each shire separately, an account of its history and topography. The project was never realised, but Leland's manuscript notes first circulated amongst later antiquaries and then were printed in 1710-12. These, however, contain detailed descriptions only of Petworth and Winchelsea in Sussex, possibly surviving fragments of a journey along the south coast in 1540 or 1541.[5]

The first printed account of Sussex appeared in 1586 in William Camden's *Britannia*, with editions revised by the author down to 1607. Camden (1551-1623) conceived the *Britannia* as a tour of Roman Britain, with the consequent need to establish its geography, trace the Roman roads and identify the towns in the Antonine

Itinerary. The counties of England and Wales were grouped according to the supposed locations of the British tribes. 'Within each county Camden rambled from town to town, choosing his subjects by the availability of material first of all and then by the interest of the place. If there was a Roman or some other kind of interest, the description might be extended; if not that, then the interest might lie in some curiosity, a story, the home of a notable, even a fair. If nothing of the sort could be found, the place was best omitted.'[6] In Sussex he found no Roman remains, posited only one identification, that of Aldrington as *Portus Adurni*, and admitted that 'I shall confine myself to a survey of the coast from West to East. The inner parts of the county being thick set with villages have nothing very remarkable' - that is, there were no towns which might have Roman origins. The places which he named in the first edition indicate his route on a single transit of the county, which must have been made no later than 1585. These, with the antiquities noted, are: Bosham, Chichester, Selsey, Arundel with Cowdray and Petworth upstream, Offington near Tarring (with Cissbury hillfort nearby), Old Shoreham with Bramber (castle) and Steyning upstream, Portslade, Aldrington, Brighton, Lewes (the Magnus inscription at St John-sub-Castro), Beachy Head, Pevensey (castle), Battle (abbey), Hastings, Winchelsea and Rye with Bodiam (castle) upstream. The places noted as inland on the rivers were probably not visited. Despite its slight content, the Sussex section of the first edition does have a place in history, as the woodcut of the Magnus inscription is the first archaeological illustration in an English book.[7]

By showing Britain's place in the Roman Empire, the book sought to connect the island to the fountainhead of European culture, with its intended audience primarily the scholars of Europe. But it also found a popular readership, and Camden's revisions in five further Latin editions down to 1607 - and the English translation of 1610 - were mainly for the gentry and the urban middle class with a more insular interest in Britain's topography and the history of its noble families. By 1607 *Britannia* was some three times longer than in 1586. But, again, Sussex came out badly. The entry was roughly doubled, mainly with information on the nobility. Aside from a description of Chichester and a transcription and translation of the Magnus inscription, antiquities get short shrift: for example a long paragraph on the Fiennes and Dacre families of Herstmonceux makes no mention of the castle.

Sussex does however provide a nice illustration of how travel in Britain was part of a gentleman's education and how *Britannia* was used in that. Francis Willughby of Trinity College, Cambridge (1634/5-72) wrote to his pupil, only a few years his junior, Peter Courthope of Danny in Hurstpierpoint (1639-1725), having just returned from a tour together one spring in the later 1650s:

It has been part of my work since I came home to take exact notes out of Camden of all the monasteries, castles, families, old Roman towns and other remarkable things, which I would fain have you do too, and if ever we travel together again, it will be very profitable to confer notes. You may for shortness use *f:* for family, *f:o:* where there is a town of the same name, *me:* medals, *mo:* monastery etc. If you go about it, you must get the folio Camden and read it seriously from one end to t'other.

The Rye preacher and lawyer Samuel Jeake (1623-90) bought the 1639 epitome of *Britannia*, as well as Lambarde's *A perambulation of Kent* (1576) and Dugdale's *Antiquities of Warwickshire* (1656). We can image that his son, also Samuel (1652-99), consulted his father's *Britannia* for the holiday trips he made, to London and north Kent in the

1660s and '70s; he also visited northern France for pleasure.[8]

The last of the Latin editions contained county maps, and that of Sussex was by John Norden, reduced from the map he had published in 1595. Norden (1547?-1625), whose perspective view of Preston is reproduced here (View 149), had earlier spotted a market for more accessible texts, as in the late 1580s he planned 'Speculum Britanniae', a series of brief county chorographies illustrated by small maps, published in books easily carried in the pocket. Only those for Middlesex and Hertfordshire were published in his lifetime, but he did compile a 'Description of Sussex' which he presented in manuscript to the Queen in 1595, the same year as his map appeared. As Norden's explorations of the county were more thorough than Camden's, the 'Description' provides an insight into the perceived interest of visitors (and presumably locals as well) at the end of the 16th century.[9]

Over half the 'Description' is taken up by 'An alphabetical table of the cities, towns, parishes, chapels & hamlets within Sussex', containing 368 entries, excluding cross-references. All but four include references to the map's grid of two by two mile squares. Of those with grid references:

150 have grid references only;

86 also have one or more alternative place-names or spellings of the place-name;

44 also have place-name derivations;

27 also have both derivations and alternative names and spellings;

57 also have topographical and/or historical information, usually with derivations and alternative names and spellings.

Norden's place-name derivations do have a curiosity value as the first attempt to analyse Sussex names. His usual practice is to translate the place-name into Latin, thus illuminating the elements in it. Sometimes the Latin version is translated back into English. Several elements recur with the same Latin equivalent. Thus 'ton' is 'villa', as in Clayton, Hangleton, Houghton and (South) Heighton, which are, respectively, 'villa argillacea clayish or Lutosa dirtie, so rightly called', 'Anglorum villa' and the last two both are 'villa alta' (because they stand on spurs projecting into river valleys). Among the more fanciful derivations is 'forte a bibendo', or boozy, for Kingston Bowsey. In *Nordens preparative to his Speculum Britanniae* of 1596, he wrote at some length on place-name elements and explained the problems of their study arising from corruption of the pronunciation in common usage. He took many of his examples from Sussex, such as: 'Many words take name of the quality of the place, and mispronounced by custom, as Tarring for Terring, arrival or landing, Fering, transporting. Sometime we find names in England given of the French, and mispronounced, as Blackboys for Blancboys, white wood ....'

Most of Norden's topographical and historical information, other than that encompassed by place-name derivations, falls into five categories. First, there are references to events in 'national' history, especially the Saxon invasion (Almodington in Earnley, Chichester, Maresfield and Shoreham) and the Norman Conquest (Battle, Bulverhythe, Hastings and Pevensey). Secondly, events in their own history are mentioned for a few towns (Brighton, Chichester, Rye, Shoreham and Winchelsea). Thirdly, standing or ruined buildings in fourteen places are mentioned, often with the present or former owner named (Aldingbourne, Amberley, Arundel, Battle, Bramber, Broomhill, Bulverhythe, Camber, Chichester, Hastings, Lewes, South Malling, Pevensey and Winchelsea). Fourthly, monumental inscriptions from Arundel, Lewes and Wiston have been copied, along with seal inscriptions from Shoreham. Lastly the presence of markets is recorded. There is only one illustration, of Bevis's sword at Arundel Castle - a misfortune, as Norden was a skilled draughtsman and did illustrate other county descriptions.[10]

For historical information, Norden drew on Camden's *Britannia* which, for example, provided the references to Bede's Ecclesiastical history under Bosham and Selsey and a quotation about the site of Battle Abbey from William of Newburgh. Holinshed's *Chronicles* (published in 1587) were probably also used, for example, for Jack Cade's capture at Heathfield and French firings of Rye in 1377 and of Brighton in 1514 and 1545. For comments relating to his own day, Norden seems to have relied mainly on personal research and observation. The list of places for which he gave more than the slightest contemporary information leaves little doubt that he traversed the county from west to east or *vice versa*. If he entered from Hampshire, he did so at Emsworth and passed to Chichester, a plan of which was inset to the map of Sussex. From there he may have made a detour in the direction of the Selsey peninsula, Bognor and Aldingbourne, on his way to Arundel. He then took the downland ridgeway until he descended to Wiston, at the north foot. Passing through the Adur gap at Bramber, he came to Old and New Shoreham from where the road took him through Hangleton to Brighton. His route then lay inland to Lewes, where he noted down the Magnus inscription differently from Camden. After a visit to Malling he returned to the coast at Eastbourne and then Pevensey. Hastings was reached by riding along the beach. Winchelsea came next and, passing west of Camber Castle, he reached Rye. A boat across the Rother took him to East Guldeford and into Kent. The lack of evidence of travel through the Weald poses the question how he completed his map.

As he travelled he found some helpful informants. At Arundel, he had an enthusiastic guide to the sites of the town, while the inhabitants of Hastings impressed on him their need for a harbour. One of Lord Buckhurst's agents probably told him about the Sackville estates, and the information was carefully noted, for Buckhurst was a signatory of the Privy Council warrant of January 1594 ordering local officials to assist Norden. Buckhurst's arms appeared the following year on the map which was the only part of the 'Description' to be published. The map attracted sponsorship from William Sanderson who had already financed the production of the first English-made globes. But Norden was not so lucky with the text which probably rested in the royal library until plundered during the Civil War, and enjoyed only limited circulation thereafter.[11]

Having provided an overview for all Britain, Camden's *Britannia* is credited with encouraging other chorographers to describe their own part of the British Isles. None came forward in Sussex, though it happened that in 1587, the year after its publication, the chancel of Lewes St John-sub-Castro was demolished. The Magnus inscription was rescued from the debris and fixed in the south wall 'by such as were lovers and favourers of antiquities'. Those were the words, some years later, of the Lewes attorney, John Rowe (1560/1-1639), in his volume of rentals and customs for Lord Abergavenny's manors, where he also recorded his dissent from Camden's derivation of the name 'Lewes'. On this slender base, Rowe has been hailed 'the father of Sussex archaeology', ignoring his readiness to pay for flints to be removed from his home town's castle, for repairing a wall.[12] The purpose of such volumes prepared by manorial stewards was the protection of the lord's interests. Contemporary lawyers required the skills and expertise of the antiquary. As Richard Hoskyns of the Middle Temple put it to Sir John Gage of Firle in 1627, emphasising his 30 years in great men's estates, 'Changes of time and descents (honoured Sir) work alterations in rights and possessions, and searches into muniments and evidences, are works for men approved, for fear of danger, and of experience, for fear of error and mistaking.' John Smith of Nibley (1567-1641) was exceptional in how fully in 1637 he researched the descent of Bosham manor, citing entries in the courts of record in London. But his aim was still to inspire its then lord, young George Berkeley of Berkeley Castle, Gloucestershire, to care for his inheritance.[13]

Lieutenant Hammond was similarly exceptional in his detailed descriptions of Arundel Castle and Church, Chichester Cathedral and Petworth House (View 146), along with many other observations, on a tour from Norwich in 1635. John Taylor's tour in 1653, published in verse, gives little information by comparison. John Aubrey (1626-97) perambulated Surrey in 1672, collecting a wealth of material for John Ogilby's proposed *Britannia*, and was looking forward to doing the same in Sussex, when Ogilby cut back his plan. There was some antiquarian activity around Chichester Cathedral. In 1658, Daniel King drew an elevation which was engraved and published, and a plan marking some tombs which was not. Archdeacon Richard Bowchier (1661-1723), a canon residentiary, compiled notes on the lives of the bishops and deans which were of great help to John Le Neve for his *Fasti Ecclesiæ Anglicanæ* (1719). Nothing had appeared in print by the time Edmund Gibson assembled a team in the early 1690s to revise Camden's *Britannia*. John Harris (1667-1719) who was working on a history of Kent was given the task of revising Sussex, but found little, in a page and a half, to add.[14]

So, with the possible exception of Richard Budgen's county map dated 1724 but maybe issued several years later (discussed in Essay 2.1), there were no specifically Sussex publications on which the compilers could draw for *Magna Britannia et Hibernia, antiqua et nova. Or, a new survey of Great Britain, wherein to the topographical account given by Mr Cambden and the late editors of his Britannia is added a more large history, not only of the cities, boroughs, towns, and parishes mentioned by them, but also of many other places of note and antiquities since discovered*, six volumes (1720-31). It offered a survey of each English county, combining general history with a topographical gazetteer. As a part-work started by the Revd Anthony Hall, Fellow of Queen's College, Oxford (1679-1723), it was probably continued by the successive publishers employing hacks. Its traditional attribution, originated by Richard Gough, to an Essex clergyman, Thomas Cox, is spurious, but Thomas Cox of Cornhill, London, was publisher from 1724, so on that basis he may be named the 'author' of the Sussex section. That appeared in parts between November 1728 and May 1729, was bound into volume 5 (1730) and also was issued separately as *A compleat history of Sussex*. Cox acknowledged a few local correspondents: Mr Dendy and Mr Haylor wrote on Steyning in 1710 (probably a misprint for 1720), Mr Haylor also on Brighton and a physician (later identified as Thomas Mannington, Rector of Slinfold 1711-50) in 1725 on plants in the Arun valley. Mainly, though, Cox drew on the historical publications of the previous 70 years which were national in scope but local in some of their detail, such as Dugdale's *Monasticon Anglicanum* and *Baronage*, Collins's *Peerage of England* and Fuller's *Worthies of England*. In fact, a very substantial proportion of the text is biographical, with families' histories entered under the parishes in which they had property or notables' biographies under the parish where they were born. Very little is said about antiquities or local history or contemporary conditions. And it contains numerous errors from careless compilation. Nevertheless it was to be the only available 'history of Sussex' for over a century.[15]

1.2 Native mapmakers and foreign artists

There were very few pictorial representations of specific places in Sussex before the later 16th century. None of the buildings in the Bayeux Tapestry of about 1080 - the church and Harold Godwinson's house at Bosham, a motte under construction and several houses at Hastings - is likely to be an accurate representation of the structure as known to the artist. The same is probably true of the details of Brighton being raided by a French fleet in 1514, as it appeared in a picture map likely drawn for the survey of coastal defences which the Privy Council ordered in February 1539. Lambert Barnard's painting of about 1535, still in the south transept of Chichester Cathedral, may accurately depict Selsey Church and its detached bell-tower. Barnard (d. 1568), possibly an Englishman with some continental training, painted much else in the cathedral and also in the Bishop's Palace, Amberley Castle (View 2) and Boxgrove Priory - a reminder that painting was a long-established craft. Painters had decorated churches (and probably houses as well) and illuminated manuscripts since Saxon times. Clients' requirements included routine work such as, for Barnard at the cathedral in 1558-61, making and mending the wings of two angels, painting a clock and painting the Ten Commandments on a cloth behind the altar; but they rarely called for topographical views.[16]

Such work comprised one of four threads which can be identified in illustration from the late 16th century through to the early 18th century:
i.   heraldic and house painters, not of topographical views but using motifs in common with:
ii. cartographers who embellished their maps with motifs to be found in house decoration and also showed buildings in bird's-eye or perspective view which bear comparison with:
iii. estate prospects, initially by Dutch artists, which, by taking a bird's-eye view, brought in the gardens and the estate as well as the house; and
iv. in the 1630s and 40s a brief flourish of topographical illustration, both by immigrant artists and by a local artist trained as a military surveyor.

Barnard was the first of three generations of painters in Chichester, being succeeded by his son Anthony (d. 1619) and grandson Lambert (1582-1655); none of their work is known to survive. Painters working in and around Lewes can be identified from the late 16th century. Mr Dape painted the sentences of scripture in St Michael's Church in 1594. Mr Bugg of Lewes painted the gallery, ceiling, font and escutcheons in Cuckfield Church in 1633, and the king's arms and the Ten Commandments in Cliffe Church in 1661. For the 17th century, our knowledge of painting on the walls of domestic buildings comes from what survives rather than from documents, for example the Prodigal Son at Gallops, Albourne, and hunting at Friston Place (View 90). John Head painted the tablet of benefactors in the Sessions House at Lewes in 1709. Robert Smith and Benjamin Conley shared the local work around 1720, both being employed at St Anne's and St Michael's churches, on king's arms, commandments and an altar-piece. Conley also painted during the construction of Stanmer House and Compton Place (View 74). John Morris painted and gilded the face of the town clock in 1751. Further east, in 1721, Roger Mortimer, probably of Eastbourne, painted the altar-piece and ceiling of Hastings St Clement's.[17] As well as embellishing carvings, such as funerary monuments and plaster-work fashioned by other craftsmen, they used similar motifs, such as strapwork, in their own compositions.

The same decorative motifs are found on maps as borders and surrounding the title, but the cartographers went further, sometimes including the property owner's coat of arms and even his portrait. Their practice was to show buildings in profile or perspective, paying most attention, of course, to the client's house. From about the 1720s plan views progressively took over. Rye and Camber Castle are depicted on a map of the harbour by John Prowze in 1572, while in 1620 George Randoll drew the houses lining the main thoroughfare through Lewes and the significant buildings to either side.[18] Given the purpose for which they were drawn, these maps show humbler buildings than those depicted by later topographical artists, and such drawings have been used to study the evolution of vernacular buildings. Reproduced here are John Norden's plan of Preston Manor and village, near Brighton, in 1617 (View 149), and John Pattenden's view of Buxted Place and village in 1654 (View 42). William Gier, when mapping Wardsbrook in Ticehurst in 1612, placed an enlarged view of the house in a cartouche, supported by a putto leaning on a scull and blowing bubbles towards a flaming sun and a winged hour-glass, a motif from a Flemish engraving of 1594 and a common *memento mori* (View 180).[19]

The scale of mapmaking can be indicated as follows. At least 27 surveyors were producing maps of Sussex estates between 1597 and 1650. The entries for these men in Bendall's *Dictionary* show that six are known only from their Sussex work, ten from work in Sussex and Kent, and the remainder from more wide-ranging commissions. The overlap with Kent (but much less with Surrey and none with Hampshire) is notable, suggesting a relatively high demand for mapping on the small gentry estates of the Weald. Conversely the surveyors who were London-based, held Crown appointments and worked all over England, John Norden and Ralph Treswell, were employed on the large estates in the west of the county.[20]

Of some local surveyors, a little is known beyond their maps. Giles Burton, for example, was married in Sedlescombe in 1612 and featured in the registers and rate lists there for a few years. Thereafter he was of Battle, where for a time he was a general shopkeeper. He died at Ninfield in 1656. Burton's maps are dated between 1631 and 1656 and show lands in Sussex, Kent and Surrey. On one he described himself as 'practitioner in some of the sciences mathematical.' He was an early user of metal stamps to reproduce little pictures of animals, men and houses, and parts of the scrolls surrounding the field acreages.[21]

These estate maps not only helped the landowner to manage his estate; they also, especially if hung on the wall, served to 'demonstrate his standing amongst his peers, his influence and prestige to his visitors, and his authority over his tenants.'[22] In this they served the same purpose as the 'prospect': large oil paintings, centred on the house and gardens, with an extensive view of the rest of the estate from between 30 and 90 degrees above horizontal, with the perspective adjusted to maximise the view. This genre was popularised by Dutch artists, painting between the Restoration and about 1730; thereafter earth-bound viewpoints were more usual. Five Sussex examples are an anonymous view of Petworth before the rebuilding of 1688-96 (View 146); from the 1720s or early '30s, prospects of Uppark and Ashburnham Place (View 8) by Peter Tillemans (*c.* 1684-1734) - the latter some nine feet wide; the view of Whiligh in Ticehurst in 1722 (View 181); and George Lambert's Kidbrooke in the 1740s (View 93). Bernard Lens III (1682-1740) was active at Arundel at some date.[23] Three Sussex owners - of Folkington Place (Views 85 and 85), Stansted Park and Uppark - were prepared to pay for their newly built or enlarged houses to be engraved, from drawings by Leonard Knyff in bird's-eye view, for *Britannia illustrata or Views of several of the*

Queen's palaces also of the principal seats of the nobility and gentry of Great Britain (1707). A variant are views closer to the house and to ground level, with a 'hunting conversation' in the foreground, for example of Wiston (1668, with the owner leaning on the fence) and, by Gerald Van Edema in 1690, of Bayley Park in Heathfield.[24]

'Landscape' incorporating recognisable localities was established as a genre of painting in Flanders in the second half of the 16th century. Peter Paul Rubens (1577-1640) has been credited with bringing landscape painting to London when he came to the Court of Charles I in 1629, no doubt carrying examples of his own and others' work. But Sir Anthony Van Dyck (1599-1641), arriving in 1632, struck deeper roots in England and, though his reputation and fortune were founded on his portraits, he made landscape sketches, partly to provide material for the background of portraits and partly, one suspects, for relaxation. Of the 29 known landscape drawings by him, five at least are certainly of Rye, and the Ypres Tower also appears in the background to a portrait (View 161). Jacob Esselens (1626-87) also drew at least four views of Rye.[25]

A local artist was also at work in the 1630s. In 1612 John Dunstall (b. 1584?) was a military surveyor in Ireland, preparing a bird's-eye view of Carrickfergus Castle and the proposed harbour. The same distinctive signature appears on a deed of 1644, as that of John Dunstall the elder of Chichester, stationer, selling a tenement in North Street. Five small etchings of views in or near Chichester are inscribed 'J. Dunstall' or 'J. D.' None is dated, but two are of St Bartholomew's Church, Chichester, which was destroyed in the siege of December 1642, and the distant view of Chichester Cathedral appears to show as still standing the north-west tower which collapsed in 1635/6. In Leeds City Art Gallery are five unsigned views in pen and ink and grey wash, of Bramber and Pevensey Castles and Wiston Place (View 27). They are dated 18 August 1635 and between 12 and 22 February 1636. The style and lettering are compatible with Dunstall's Irish view, and castles would naturally be of interest to a former military surveyor. Dunstall senior may reasonably be identified as the artist of both the Chichester views and the Leeds drawings.[26]

Another John Dunstall, probably son and pupil, was the artist of the watercolour of a pollard oak with Westhampnett Place and a watermill on the Lavant in the background (View 195). The signature identifies him as the John Dunstall who by 1661 was a drawing master in London and was drawing, etching and engraving natural history plates for Peter Stent, a leading London print publisher. He married Margaret Lister at St Andrew's Chichester in 1655, and died in London in 1693. Recently identified as the first English artist who consistently attempted to make a living by teaching drawing, Dunstall junior published on his own account six sets of plates, as copybooks, with the subjects of geometry, faces, flowers, fruit, trees and houses. Further plates of his work appeared in a similar copybook, *A view of the Creation*, published in London in about 1666 by Robert Walton (1618-88). Dunstall was also the artist of a broadsheet of 'plague scenes' of about 1665. Walton is named as the publisher on one of the Chichester etchings, and Dunstall's name and initials are etched the same on them as on the copybooks. It is likely therefore that Dunstall junior made the etchings in the 1660s from drawings by Dunstall senior. The Westhampnett view need not have been painted before Dunstall junior left Chichester, for the tree is the central feature and the buildings may have been added as embellishment from his father's drawings.[27]

The artist most usually associated with views of Sussex in the 17th century is Wenceslaus Hollar from Prague (1607-77). His etchings have often been reproduced: four of the ruins of Bramber Castle, Wiston Place, Arundel (dated 1644), Pevensey

Castle, a prospect from the Downs behind Old Shoreham and Chichester Cathedral (published 1673). 'Much the most distinguished topographical draftsman working in seventeenth-century England and ... the dominant influence on English topographical drawing until the middle of the eighteenth century', Hollar arrived in England in December 1636, having joined the service of Thomas Howard, Earl of Arundel, while the latter was leading an embassy to Emperor Ferdinand II. His patron went into exile in 1642. Hollar himself was in Antwerp from 1644 to 1652. Two Sussex drawings survive: a slight and insecurely attributed sketch of the south-east elevation of Arundel Castle, and a draft after Van Dyck for the engraving of Rye on a map of Kent, 1659. The drawings attributed above to Dunstall senior were previously attributed to Hollar, but they are dated before his arrival in England. Hollar probably acquired them (and maybe others now lost) and based at least five etchings on them; those five drawings then passed with other items from Hollar's studio to his friend Francis Place (1647-1728), in whose family they descended. Perhaps Hollar took the drawings with him into exile and made the etchings before the Earl's death in 1646, on account of their association with the county of his ancestral home. Or, back in London, he may have had them from the younger Dunstall - who etched a plate after Hollar for a 1663 collection. It is likely that one drawing he acquired was a view of Chichester Cathedral from the north, because the etching he made in 1671 for Dugdale's *Monasticon* (1673) shows the north-west tower intact, although it had collapsed in 1635/6. A tentative conclusion is that Hollar never visited Sussex and that both his and the Chichester etchings - almost the sum total of Sussex views published in the 17th century - were based on drawings by Dunstall senior.[28]

At the same time as John Dunstall senior was sketching in west Sussex, the young John Evelyn (1620-1706) was living with his grandparents and attending school in Lewes, and taking 'an extraordinary ... fancy to drawing and designing.' A pen and ink washed landscape of the family home at Wotton in Surrey, made in 1640, shows a skilled amateur. His first attempts at landscape may have been of scenes in Lewes, though none is known to survive, and one wonders whether he had tuition from a local painter.[29]

2. Antiquarian study in the early 18th century

2.1 The discovery of Roman Sussex

The early 18th century saw some stirring of local interest in the physical remains of the past and in their recording. The stimulus was interest in Sussex under the Britons and the Romans. Sussex was found to have a Roman history. Of key importance were two archaeological discoveries.

The first was at Eastbourne. The locals said they were long familiar with crop-marks and with debris brought up in ploughing, when in 1712 the landowner, Thomas Willard (1654/5-1733), an attorney, took note of tesserae found when a fence was being erected. He sent for John Pursglove, an engineer formerly employed in mines in 'the north of England', probably Derbyshire, but then at Herstmonceux. Pursglove made borings and the floor was exposed. Richard Russell (1687-1759), recently established as a surgeon in Lewes and later famed for his sea-water treatments, measured it in plan and section, and forwarded his drawing and description to the Royal Society - Sussex's first excavation report. At the end of 1716, Dr John Tabor (1667-1729), physician of Lewes, reopened and extended the excavation to find a Roman bath. The Royal Society printed his report which was Sussex's first printed archaeological report and one of the earliest in Britain. The perspective drawing lacks scale and orientation, but these can be supplied from the text which noted a destruction level and the small finds (View 73). By the time Jeremiah Milles visited in 1743 (Document 3), 'one can only see the bed of plaster in which the mosaic was fixed, everybody that came to see it took away pieces of it, and no care was taken to preserve it.'[30]

Tabor reviewed the evidence from classical and medieval authors to argue that Eastbourne had been the Roman *Anderida*, and that Pevensey could not be because too much remained for a place razed by the invading Saxon, Ælla, in 491; but 'perhaps 'tis the greatest and most entire remain of Roman building, anywhere to be seen in Great Britain.' Jeremiah Milles in 1743 was content to accept that *Anderida* had been at Eastbourne. Tabor also undertook fieldwork on the Downs, there being 'few parts of them that I have not often viewed', by recording the shape and rough dimensions of 18 'camps' between the Trundle and Belle Tout. Camden in his *Britannia* had noted only Cissbury and Chanctonbury. Harris in the 1695 edition had drawn on John Aubrey's manuscript 'Monumenta Britannica' to add the Trundle and Goosehill (and a Roman camp, at the Broyle, north of Chichester). Tabor identified another 13. He reckoned that most dated from the Britons' resistance to the invading Saxons' eastwards advance which culminated in the Battle of *Mercredesburn* near Beachy Head in 485.[31]

The second discovery was at Chichester where, in April 1723, the Cogidubnus (or Togidubnus) inscription emerged from a cellar during demolition. The first to appreciate its significance was yet another medical man, Dr Edward Bayly of Havant, who sent an account to Thomas Hearne in Oxford. Dr William Stukeley and Roger Gale arrived to see it in September. At the end of the year Gale's reconstruction of the wording and a drawing were published by the Royal Society and in the following year in Stukeley's *Itinerarium curiosum*. As at Eastbourne, conservation was a problem: ''twas happy we took great care in transcribing the letters, for since it has been in the possession of the Duke of Richmond, I hear a workman who pretended to set the fragments together, has defaced it.' They were now in no doubt of Chichester's Roman origin, rather than Saxon, as Camden had supposed. Stukeley published his drawings of the inscription, Story's Cross and the prospect from the Trundle. It was perhaps to Bayly that Rawlinson referred in 1720: 'It is said that a learned physician of this place [Chichester] has made some progress towards a full description of this county.' When another inscription was found in August 1740, Stukeley's informant was the Revd Lucius Henry Hibbins (b. 1696), then living at Norton in Aldingbourne, for whom the Duke of Richmond was seeking a benefice, but who may have known Stukeley from living in south Lincolnshire in the 1720s. It is striking, though, how long it was before the walls of Chichester were recognised as Roman. A very knowledgeable visitor in 1740 reckoned that 'Chichester shows nothing Roman except a few bricks being probably used by them, having been an ancient British fortification.... The present wall and towers projecting from it seem to be no older than the Barons' War, being all built of flint, brick and some rubble stone.' It seems that herring-bone brick courses were considered essential evidence of Roman origin.[32]

It is notable that these discoveries in Chichester generated considerable interest amongst both locals and visiting antiquaries, but that it was not an interest which came from or fed into study of the locality as such. Leading players acted on a wider stage. That can be illustrated, first, by Charles Lennox, 2nd Duke of Richmond (1701-50), a man of wide cultural and intellectual interests, as a devotee of opera, patron of Canaletto in painting and Colen Campbell in architecture, and an active Fellow of the Royal Society. He had the Cogidubnus stone set up in a specially built temple, and a tall prehistoric monolith also graced his landscaping. In 1747 he commissioned George Vertue to make an engraving of Story's Cross, and, as newly-elected President of the Society of Antiquaries in 1750, he submitted a drawing of a Roman pavement uncovered a few days previous in the bishop's garden. These relics he must have valued as part of a wider British, rather than of a local, history.[33]

Secondly, many years later, in 1771, the Revd William Clarke (1695-1771) sent to William Burrell a copy of that drawing of the Roman pavement and the original copper plate of the Cogidubnus inscription. In the covering letter, he denied having ever thought of embarking on a county history, though was glad that Burrell should, and advised him on how to treat the Roman period. In Clarke, Chichester had a resident antiquary of much erudition. His published contributions to learning were the introduction to a collection of early Welsh laws (1730) and, the fruit of 20 years' study, *The connexion of the Roman, Saxon, and English coins deduced from observations on the Saxon weights and money* (1767), a 550-page tome based on printed editions of classical and later texts, with little attention to surviving artefacts. On graduating from Cambridge, he had been briefly chaplain to the Bishop of St David's and then to the Duke of Newcastle. He was collated to the rectory of Buxted in 1724 and to the prebend of Hova Villa in Chichester Cathedral in 1728. Newcastle secured his admission as a canon residentiary in 1739, and thereafter Clarke divided his time between Buxted (particularly in the summer) and Chichester. An enthusiastic advocate of outdoor exercise, he delighted in riding and indeed left in a letter of 1736 the earliest known account of both seabathing and sunbathing at Brighton. While he diligently supported Newcastle's interest in parliamentary elections, he was not deeply involved in the politics of either county or cathedral, though he was Chancellor during the last year of his life.[34]

Locally the focus of his scholarly efforts was the cathedral. As Canon Librarian from at least 1731 until his death, he supervised the removal of the library to the Lady Chapel in 1750, worked extensively on the catalogues and on listing the archives and made an orderly compilation of the cathedral's statutes, forms and customs, episcopal injunctions and chapter decrees. In 1753 at Bishop Mawson's request he compiled notes on the cathedral's history, commenting on the attempt to date the fabric which Charles Lyttelton, Dean of Exeter (1714-68), had made in the previous July. However, in the east of the county he did draw attention to two significant medieval artefacts. In 1748 he had George Vertue draw the painted glass in Bexhill Church, supposed portraits of Henry III and Queen Eleanor. Probably alerted by these drawings, Horace Walpole (1717-97) sought out the glass in 1760 to illustrate his *Anecdotes of painting* (1762) and in 1771 secured it for the east window of a new-built chapel at Strawberry Hill. The glass, of Christ and the Virgin Mary, was returned to Bexhill in 1921. And Clarke was the first to identify in Isfield Church the tombslab of Gundrada de Warenne, of which Burrell arranged the removal to Southover Church in 1775 (Document 6.1).[35]

There are also some glimmerings of concern in eastern Sussex to record and preserve medieval structures. The Lords of Lewes Borough made copyhold grants to Thomas Friend of the Barbican of Lewes Castle in 1733 on condition that it should not be altered, pulled down or destroyed, and of the interior of the Keep in 1750 on condition that he should repair it and not pull it down. He found a new use for the Keep, for Richard Gough wrote in 1757 that it 'is ascended to by a winding path planted with flowering shrubs and secured by Chinese railing; the area within is laid out in parterres, the apartments plastered with rough lime and pebbles and stuck about with prints, vases on brackets, and Chinese ornaments in the manner of a summer house.' Sir Thomas Webster (1677-1751), already well established on lands in Essex, may well have been motivated by antiquarian sentiment, in buying the Sussex estates which gave him Battle Abbey in 1721, where he came to reside, Bodiam Castle in 1723 and Robertsbridge Abbey in 1726. Indeed, in 1727 he had David Casley, the King's Librarian, transcribe for him not only the Battle Abbey cartularies which came with the estate, but also the Battle Abbey chronicle in the Cottonian Library. Richard Budgen's survey for him in 1724 included a bird's-eye view of Battle Abbey. Likewise in the margin to their maps for Spencer Compton both John Rowley in 1710 and Richard Budgen in 1725 drew Wilmington Court Farm including the remains of the Priory. But when the high tower of the inner castle at Pevensey fell down in 1735, the steward initially prohibited the locals from carrying away the debris, to assert Compton's rights to it as a quarry for use elsewhere.[36]

2.2 Medieval monuments popularised: the Bucks' engravings

A rising interest in Sussex's medieval monuments is demonstrated by the popularity of a dozen engravings published in 1737. They were part of the ambitious project to publish topographical views initiated by Samuel Buck. That the project was carried to fruition in some 500 plates, the great majority showing medieval buildings, testifies to the interest being taken in the architecture of the past by a wide section of the educated public and to the evaporation of residual popular objections to admiring monastic ruins on account of their associations with popery.[37]

Samuel Buck (1696/7-1779) started sketching antiquities for John Warburton's intended but abandoned history of Yorkshire in 1719-20. In April 1720 he was working on a prospect of Leeds which, with York, was probably published late in 1721. These were the first of 89 'town prospects' of which publication continued until 1753; the prospectus of 1736 is in Document 2.1. By February 1724 Buck was resident in London and immediately working with the Society of Antiquaries. William Stukeley whom he accompanied on antiquarian tours encouraged him to undertake the recording of antiquities nationwide, and his proposal for 24 plates of Yorkshire antiquities appeared in January 1725. He found that most religious houses were 'mouldering now in ruins, being no more than defaced remains of what they originally were, and in danger of being quite erazed' and his ambition was 'to rescue the mangled remains of these aged and venerable edifices from the inexorable jaws of time', by visiting them and making careful perspective drawings; see the prospectus of 1737 in Document 2.2. So began visits each summer to one or more counties to sketch antiquities and collect subscriptions for the engravings which appeared the following spring. The English tours were completed in 1738. Wales was covered over the next three years.

From 1727 Samuel Buck was accompanied by his brother Nathaniel (*fl.* 1727-53/9) and the plates were thereafter inscribed 'S.B. delin. N.B. sculp.' or *vice versa*, or, from 1729, 'Saml. & Nathl. Buck delin. & sculp.' Nevertheless other artists were employed 'to strengthen the outlines of the drawings made on the spot, to improve the appearance of the landscape, to people the foregrounds with figures and animals appropriate to the scenes depicted, and generally to bring the Bucks' awkward drawings to life'. In his detailed study of the town prospects, Hyde has detected three stages as the field-sketches were prepared for engraving. The Buck sketch was squared, and multiple copies made, with significant buildings and monuments strengthened in sepia ink. A second artist might take one or more copies and complete the town, foreground and the more distant landscape: View 51. If the Bucks were not satisfied, the sketch went back to the second artist (or a third one) to provide alternative staffage. Furthermore it is unlikely that the Bucks were the engravers. From the early 1730s Dutch engravers (or English adopting Dutch style) were employed, whose skill in staffage could transform a simple Buck drawing. From 1743 the style was more distinctly French.[38] The engravings of castles and abbeys were not, however, elaborated with staffage, so no other artist may have been involved and the Bucks may have been their own engravers: View 111.

The Bucks visited Sussex in 1736, and the '12th collection' of their engravings of castles and abbeys in England, was published on 25 March 1737, priced at two guineas. It comprised plates of twelve Sussex antiquities, eight Surrey, three Middlesex and one Hertfordshire. Document 2.2 is the prospectus for the 13th collection issued in 1738, the nearest surviving in date, and Document 2.3 is the subscription list for the 12th. The prospect of Chichester appeared in 1738 in the sixth set of town views, priced at 15 shillings, along with Canterbury, Chatham dockyard, Guildford, Maidstone and Rochester; the prospectus is Document 2.1. Listed, as they may have been visited in a tour beginning at Chichester and ending at Tunbridge Wells, the Sussex antiquities were Boxgrove Priory, Arundel Castle, Amberley Castle, Lewes Priory, Pevensey Castle (two views), Herstmonceux Castle, Battle Abbey, Winchelsea Greyfriars, Camber Castle, Bodiam Castle and Bayham Abbey. All but Winchelsea and Bayham were dedicated to the site's proprietor, whose readiness to pay for the privilege perhaps influenced the selection of views for engraving. Preparatory sketches survive for Amberley, Arundel (two), Battle, Bodiam, Boxgrove, Herstmonceux and Pevensey (both views), and also for Chichester (two) (Views 51 and 111).[39] Some carry pinholes, suggesting that they were the versions from which the engraver transferred the image to the copper plate. There are differences in detail, for example the engraving shows different numbers of crenellations on Amberley Castle and adds windows in the north gable of the guest-house at Boxgrove and shows its west windows blocked (View 22).

Each 'collection' or annual part of the antiquities was accompanied by a list of subscribers. The Bucks realised that, while some people would purchase all the parts, others would want only the part including their home county, at least in the first instance. Every year they must have expended considerable effort in canvassing for subscriptions as they sketched in the field - at a time when few parts of England were covered by newspapers which might be used for advertising. They can be seen at work in Sussex from the Earl of Wilmington's cash accounts which in June 1736 recorded one guinea 'subscription to prints of ruins in Sussex, 1st payment'.[40] The number of subscribers increased, for instance from 141 for the 1st collection (1726), to 228 for the 8th (1733), 239 for the 11th, Kent (1736), 385 for the 12th (1737) and 409 for the 13th, Essex, Norfolk and Suffolk (1738), though it had dropped back to 381 for the 14th (1739). The list for the 12th collection marked a sharp increase.[41]

Here is printed (Document 2.3) the subscription list for the 1737 collection which included the Sussex plates. To help distinguish the long-term subscribers from those interested only in the counties covered in that collection, those who also subscribed to the 1736 or 1738 collections, or both, are identified. Subscribers known to have Sussex connections are individually annotated. Of the 385 subscribers, 167 had already subscribed for the previous year's collection, and 211 were to subscribe to the following year's; 145, 38%, subscribed for all three years. For the 1737 collection the Bucks achieved an exceptional year-on-year increase in subscribers (from 239 to 385) and a useful increase in those who continued at least for a second collection, but they also picked up a larger increase in one-off subscriptions. Thus 70% of 1736's subscribers also subscribed for 1737, but only 55% of 1737's subscribers also subscribed for 1738. The 1737 collection included not only Sussex, but also Surrey and Middlesex which were home to many London merchants and professionals who would be a prime target for such a publication. Even so, of the 150 who subscribed for 1737 only, some 80, more than half, had Sussex connections. So the Bucks must have been pleased with their recruitment in Sussex.

Here we have evidence of widespread interest in Sussex's antiquities and history. That it found expression in subscribing to the Bucks' engravings suggests that it extended to an 'educated' as well as to a 'scholarly' readership. Of some 115 subscribers with known Sussex connections, 7 were peers, 12 baronets, 63 esquires, 22 clergy and 4 gentlemen.

2.3   A county map, poems and traveller's diaries

There were several other ways in which systematic interest in the contemporary scene and its antecedents were expressed in the earlier 18th century, through a county map, topographical poetry and more numerous descriptions.

Another publication by subscription was Richard Budgen's map of Sussex, the next Sussex survey based on original fieldwork after Norden's map of 1595, and indeed one of the first large-scale county surveys. It was probably completed and first printed in proof late in 1723, then published with the date of 1724 and the names and arms of 148 subscribers updated, though actual issue may have been several years later.[42] Within the limitations of its form, it aspired to range widely in the information incorporated. The prospectus (Document 1) anticipated, for example, that 'everything relating to Natural History of the County, whether Mines, Iron, Coal, or other Minerals, shall be inserted; as also the Manufactories; how far any River is navigable; Antiquities, where met with, whether *Roman*, *Saxon*, or *Danish*, to be noted', as well as 'the Value of Livings in the King's Books, whether Rectories or Vicarages, etc.' and 'that more especially, by giving remarkable Facts and Circumstances to Places in easy Characters to be explained by themselves, that thereby it may, in some measure give, an Historical as well as a Geographical Account of the County.' Roads are marked on the map, the principal ones with distances marked at one-mile intervals, as are the boundaries of the county, rapes, hundreds and deaneries. The representation of relief by oblique hachures is very tentative, and picks out with any accuracy only the scarp of the Downs. There are symbols for market towns, disused market towns, gentlemen's seats (with a coronet added for the nobility's seats), manor or farm houses, churches 'according to their several forms', parks, camps (i.e. prehistoric enclosures), castles, ruins of abbeys, priories, etc., furnaces, forges, smith's forges, windmills, watermills, mineral waters, woodlands, parts abounding most with oak timber, heaths, commons, marshland, stone quarries, rocks (on the coast), sands, and the limits of navigation on the rivers. 'Horse courses' feature on Waterdown Forest and above Lewes. Where space allows, and so mainly off the coast, a few observations are added, such as 'the south wall of Middleton Church stands about 60 feet from the full'. Budgen delivered only a little less than he promised in the prospectus: he did not differentiate the era of field monuments or the types of watermills nor incorporate the values of livings.

An interesting variant on topographical description is William Hay's poem, *Mount Caburn*, written to 'celebrate my native county' and published in 1730, which offered a potted local history inspired by the view (see View 91). William Hay of Glyndebourne (1695-1755) was to be MP for Seaford from 1734 to 1753, and then briefly held the sinecure of Keeper of the Records in the Tower when, most likely, he had 'Mr Conway' make the transcripts relating to Sussex which Burrell saw in the 1770s (see Document 7.2). One earlier topographical poem on Sussex was T. Chaloner's 'The description of New Shoreham' (1729). A couple eulogised Baldy's Garden in Lewes in 1746 and 1747, while 'A journey of pleasure to the Sea-Houses at Bourne in Sussex, July 1, 1749' was printed in 1787. Otherwise the next such poem recorded is Mr Bailey's 'Mount Caburn, the summer's day: a descriptive pastoral' in 1770. Thereafter they are more numerous, including efforts by Sophia, William Burrell's wife, and James Hurdis's *The village curate* (1788), written while he was at Burwash. Doubtless many more were written than were published.[43]

Thirdly, as the 18th century progressed, more and more people were travelling for recreation or curiosity - and with the intention of recording what they saw.[44] In parallel the publishers' market for descriptions of Britain expanded, best exemplified by Daniel Defoe's *Tour thro' the whole island of Great Britain*. The first volume appeared in May 1724 and contained an account of touring Kent, Sussex, Hampshire and Surrey, ostensibly in the autumn of 1722. While it was drafted then (and updated in proof a year or so later), Defoe is unlikely to have taken the route as given, though he probably had recently been in the parts of Surrey close to London. The paragraphs on Sussex with the greatest verisimilitude for personal observation at the given date are those for the Chichester area. The problems of the *Tour* as an historical source are well illustrated for Brighton. The statement that Brighton boats were going to Yarmouth Fair was some 30 years out of date, as the practice had ended in 1690s. But it is the sole source for the content of the church brief granted by February 1723 to raise funds for building groynes at Brighton - a printed document which would have circulated in London. Nevertheless, Defoe (?1660-1731) drew on a lifetime of sharp-eyed observation as merchant, government spy and journalist, and his text has a liveliness matched by few other 18th-century writers on Sussex.[45]

Only three other works on Sussex published before 1760 deserve note. The first was by John Macky who travelled across Sussex from east to west in September 1713. Macky had been (like Defoe) a government secret agent, particularly monitoring traffic across the Channel to the Low Countries, but came under suspicion in the later years of Anne's reign and was imprisoned. His published journey started on his release. His account of Petworth is now the most significant part of his Sussex narrative. The following paragraph illustrates his interest in the lifestyle of the nobility and gentry: [46]

Few subjects abroad have such palaces; those at Prague in Bohemia come the nearest to this; theirs indeed excel any of the Emperor's, their Master's. But what is particular in the Duke of Somerset is that all his palaces are completely furnished, and he moves to them without removing anything from his other seats. There are several other gentleman's seats in the village, which are very large, and where a stranger is as well lodged as he can wish. The country round it being fat and fertile makes the roads bad in winter; whereas the Downs, which are two hours from hence, are firm and solid all the year round; and to which his Grace must have the mortification to ride in the dirt when he goes ahunting.

Macky's *Letters* were widely read, going through several editions, and were a significant quarry for Defoe. The second published author was the Revd John Burton (1696-1771) who wrote accounts of two visits to Sussex which, we can be confident, were not as widely read, for they were written in Greek and Latin respectively. Published in 1752, the longer, Greek, account had been written in about 1730 and the Latin one in 1746-51.[47] As a fellow of Corpus Christi College, Oxford, 1721-33, Burton was an exceptionally dedicated tutor and an advocate for improving the study of Greek; indeed the tours were prefaced by 'A critical letter on certain elements of instruction in the Greek language' (in Latin), so their language had a didactic purpose. They were occasioned by visiting his mother and stepfather, the Revd John Bear, who was Rector of Shermanbury and who, at least between 1736 and 1744, ran a small boarding school for the sons of local gentry.[48] Burton's descriptions offer a good deal of unique topographical information, for example on Lewes Castle, on the groynes at Brighton and on Horsham:[49]

Thus after riding more than nine miles without dust indeed, but not without fatigue we discovered on our right, close by, the lofty spire of a church, constructed of wood, but painted so as to resemble stone. This was the large and populous town of Horsham, the chief place in the Weald (formerly called the forest of Anderida) for here is the county gaol and sessions house; the natives come hither to attend the assizes once a year and to the market once a week and here the Londoners purchase vast quantities of poultry. I should not forget to mention that, in the midst of this muddy soil, a sandy eminence rises and continues for three miles, which we rode over with pleasure. Here too is another treasure, whose value here is enhanced by its scarcity. Here are quarries where they procure slate which serves to cover their houses instead of tiles and gives the town a respectable appearance.

Thirdly may be noted Benjamin Martin's section on Sussex in *Martin's Magazine*, 3 (1756), reprinted in *Natural history of England*, 1 (1759). This brief gazetteer of places on the coastal route from Bosham to Rye may not be as derivative as other such publications (or indeed for other counties in the *Magazine*), as Martin (1705-82) married the daughter of a Chichester schoolmaster, set up his own school there by 1734 and continued it until about 1741. By then he was also an itinerant lecturer on scientific subjects; he moved to Reading in 1742. So he may have drawn on his own observations.[50]

Amongst the accounts of visits to Sussex in 1700-60, which were not written for publication but have survived in manuscript, five may be taken to show the range of motivation and subject matter, and to illustrate several aspects of the depiction of Sussex in that period. The first serves to underline the lack of local interest in natural history, despite the upsurge in its study, particularly following the foundation of the Royal Society in 1660.

James Petiver (1663-1718), apothecary to the Charterhouse and demonstrator of plants to the Society of Apothecaries, and James Sherard (1666-1738), also an apothecary, made a botanical tour into Sussex and Kent in August 1714. Departing from London, they called at Sevenoaks on Dr Thomas Fuller (1654-1734) who 'regaled us with cold venison, pastry and extraordinary good strong beer'; passing through Tunbridge Wells, they stayed with John Tilden, tenant of Brede Place (View 28). John was a brother of George Tilden who was of St Bride's, City of London, and the source of the introduction. 'After a plentiful breakfast on oysters and other good things' they set out for Hastings with both Tildens. At Hastings they collected specimens from the castle walls, by the Bourne stream and on the beach. At Pett they were entertained by John Martyn who had married the Tildens' sister Alice. They stayed at The Salutation inn at Winchelsea, kept by the Mayor, Thomas Jenkin, who produced 'so excellent punch that every bowl was better than its predecessor'. They forded the Rother below Rye and drove their chaise on the beach to Lydd. Their route thereafter was to Dover, Knowlton (to stay with Mr D'Eath), Deal, Sandwich, the Isle of Thanet, back to Knowlton, then Canterbury and the main road to London. They recorded about 35 species, many of them for the first time in Sussex.[51]

The Tilden family seem not to have been active collaborators in the plant collecting, in contrast to the parson at Knowlton 'who has a pretty good taste of botany'. Indeed, for their or any earlier period, there is little sign of local systematic study of natural history in Sussex, with the honourable exception, if he did live at Plumpton, of Leonard Mascall, the early writer of farming textbooks (d. 1589). The great naturalist John Ray (1627-1705) was hosted in at least 1662, 1666 and 1667-8 by two former Cambridge pupils, Peter Courthope of Danny in Hurstpierpoint (1639-1725) and his cousin Timothy Burrell of Ockenden in Cuckfield (1642-1717). Although Ray dedicated *Synopsis animalium quadrupedum et serpentini generis* (1693) to them as 'the last survivors of his early associates', neither showed much interest in natural history once they had left Cambridge. However Courthope did prompt Ray to compile *A collection of English words, not generally used, with their significations and origin* (1674) which, along with *Dictionariolum trilingue* (1675), was printed at the expense of Thomas Burrell, Timothy's brother. Ray's list of plants distinctive to Sussex appeared in the 1695 edition of Camden's *Britannia*. How different Sussex botany might have been if in 1662, as he contemplated forfeiting his Cambridge fellowship for not subscribing to the Act of Uniformity, Ray had pursued his interest in the mastership of Lewes grammar school. [52]

Courthope was elected, in 1668, a Fellow of the Royal Society - but paid his subscription only during the next two years. Several other Sussex gentlemen were FRS over the next couple of generations. But their and their contemporaries' scientific interests extended at most to curious natural phenomena, rather than systematic study. For example, John Holney, physician (d. 1706), had the huge horns of a moose on display in his house in Lewes. John Fuller of Brightling, ironmaster, FRS 1704 and son-in-law of its Secretary, Dr Hans Sloane, sought the Society's approbation of *Mathematicks made plain* (1708) by a local autodidact, Richard Neve, who dedicated it to Fuller as 'a general encourager of all ingenious studies'. Fuller kept Sloane informed of curious phenomena down in Sussex. Thus his account of the strange effects of the great storm of 1703 was published; and in April 1711 'I send you herewith a couple of monstrous pigs, one of them was farrowed alive the other dead, the sow had six pigs beside, all of them as they should be.' One wonders in what condition they reached London, for the same letter said that the fire-backs had all been cast and would be sent, as soon as the roads were passable. Amongst half-a-dozen other papers in the Society's *Philosophical Transactions* were reports by Dr Benjamin Langwith, Rector of Petworth, on an aurora borealis there in 1726 and by William Green of Lewes in 1774 and 1775, on bullocks which had been struck by lightning at Swanborough, with illustrations by James Lambert.[53]

The second traveller, John Warburton (1682-1759), was appointed Somerset Herald in 1720. Prior to that, while in the service of the Excise in Yorkshire, he had started to publish county maps based on new surveys, that of Northumberland appearing in 1716. Yorkshire was issued in early 1721. Having moved south, he issued a prospectus in October 1720 for a one-sheet map of Middlesex, Essex and Hertfordshire. For the actual fieldwork he employed Payler Smyth who completed the survey of those three counties in November 1723. The map was published in mid-1725, but only after his fellow heralds had challenged his practice of embellishing each map with numerous coats of arms, some of which were ascribed to people without the right to bear them and others of which were inaccurate represented. They also observed that he had not resided at the College of Arms for two years.

In February 1722 Warburton issued a prospectus for a further map, of Kent, Sussex and Surrey. He toured Sussex in late September and early October 1723. There is no clue in his fragmentary notes that he was travelling with the surveyor nor that he was soliciting subscriptions. His perambulations in Sussex and elsewhere may also have been intended to identify the upwardly mobile who might aspire to a coat of arms and so might be clients for his services; heraldic visitations had by that time been abandoned. This was not his only visit to Sussex, for he was involved in a campaign with Dr Thomas Fuller of Sevenoaks to create a harbour for ships in distress on the coast between Dover and Portsmouth. In March of the following year, he wrote to Captain William Markwick of Catsfield, an engineer, that he had ridden the coast (and indeed had recently been in France) and had fixed on Newhaven as the harbour to be improved. In his reply, Markwick pestered Warburton about the progress of his grant of arms. The map never appeared, but following another initiative an improved Newhaven harbour was opened in October 1733.

Warburton's route in 1723 took him from his home in Wimbledon through Horsham south to Arundel, east to Brighton and north to Preston; his notes were, in William Burrell's opinion, 'a few idle superficial observations in pencil and outlines of houses miserably sketched' (Document 7.2), but they are of interest in default of other evidence (View 96; also Views 3, 122 and 189). Warburton's account of Horsham may be compared with Burton's: [54]

[From Crawley I] passed through the Forest of St Leonard which brought me to Horsham, a large straggling borough and town corporate in the figure of a cross and the streets called by the names of East, West, North and South Streets. The church is at the south end of the town and is a large edifice but irregular built and in bad repair. The steeple is a spire of a good height and covered with slate [in fact, shingles]. The churchyard is near covered with frames of wood that are set over the graves and on them are various singular inscriptions. The Town House which stands in the Market Place is a good edifice of Portland stone supported by [14] arched columns of the [blank] order and over it is the chamber where [the borough courts, quarter sessions and assizes meet]. At the north end of the Market Place stands the gaol built of freestone and crenellated on the top. And the houses worthy of remark in the town are:

a goodly brick building of nine sash windows in front and adorned with a pediment of the [blank] order belonging to Philip Tredcroft Esq.

a neat new edifice of nine sash windows in front with freestone pilasters, etc., at the north end of the town the seat of John Wicker Esq.

a goodly edifice in the West Street belonging to Dr Norman an eminent surgeon

a neat edifice opposite to it not yet finished belonging to a minor.

The third traveller, George Vertue (1684-1756), was an altogether more significant figure. A portrait engraver of great distinction, he was also the official engraver to the Society of Antiquaries and travelled around England with noble patrons, visiting the great country houses, drawing and noting everything of artistic and antiquarian interest. These notes formed the basis of Horace Walpole's *Anecdotes of painting in England* (1762-71). In 1738 he accompanied Edward Harley, 2nd Earl of Oxford, his greatest patron, on a tour through Kent, Sussex and Hampshire, making notes on a few churches, but more on the grand houses, Cowdray, Goodwood, Petworth and Stansted, and the pictures in them. He seems to have already visited Petworth and Cowdray in 1730. A third visit in 1747 was to fulfil the Duke of Richmond's commission to engrave a plate of Story's Cross at Chichester. He viewed Goodwood House, where he listed the pictures in the dining room, and its gardens (Views 25 and 26), and the Duke took him to Boxgrove Priory (Views 22 and 23). In 1751 he accompanied William Hanbury to draw family monuments at Buriton, Hampshire, returning via Cowdray.[55]

Vertue was visiting the great country houses to see, or with, clients. But visiting the houses to view their interiors and contents, was a well-established practice for the tourist arriving without notice or invitation. So, in 1753, Charles Lyttelton was riding from Exeter to Tunbridge Wells and 'got four miles this side of Petersfield by 11 where I was directed to the parson of the parish for a key of Sir Matthew Fetherstonhaugh's gate at Uppark (late Lord Tankerville's). I found the parson was ... a genteel and well beneficed clerk, so I took a moonshine with him and accepted of him for my cicerone round Uppark.' The practice gained further point, as art collections were gradually dispersed from London to the country from the 1730s through to the 1760s. It was in south-west Sussex that there were houses with grand collections. The 2nd Duke of Richmond at Goodwood was also a patron. He enabled at least the elder Smith brother, William (c. 1707-64) to study with a portrait painter in London, and he commissioned John Wootton (1678?-1764) between 1730 and 1743 to paint a series of six equestrian portraits, each against the backdrop of the Goodwood estate. George Stubbs (1724-1806) completed a finer set of four for the 3rd Duke in 1759/60. Both sets reflect the demise of the bird's-eye view in preference for ground-level viewpoints.[56]

The last two travellers were cousins: the Revd Richard Pococke (1704-65) and the Revd Jeremiah Milles (1719-84). They were both undergraduates at Corpus Christi College, Oxford, while John Burton was a fellow. In 1733-6 they travelled together in France, Italy and other parts of Europe. Pococke also spent 1737-41 in Greece, the Near East and Egypt, and published *A description of the East* (1743-5). So they were well-experienced observers by the time they wrote their notes of travels in England.

Milles, who was later to be Dean of Exeter and President of the Society of

Antiquaries, made two excursions into Sussex in 1743 (Document 3). Ranged from west to east, the places of which he took substantial note were: Stansted, Chichester and the cathedral, Bosham, Goodwood, Cowdray (particularly the pictures), monuments in Midhurst Church, Petworth House (again, pictures), Arundel Castle and monuments in the church, the Magnus inscription at Lewes, barrows and camps on the Downs towards Eastbourne and Roman remains there, Pevensey Castle, Battle Abbey, Hastings Castle, Winchelsea, Camber Castle and monuments in Rye Church. Country-house visiting was combined with viewing ruins and funerary monuments. His accounts of these tours are printed here because they are the most detailed and carefully prepared for Sussex before the second half of the 18th century which have not been published. He had done his homework before departing, clearly having read Camden and other writers on the vexed issue of the location of the Roman *Anderida*, and carefully reviewed their arguments by observation in the field. His analysis of Pevensey Castle is significant for its date. He was interested in changes in the coastline from erosion and accretion.

He also appreciated the landscape of the Downs, for example: 'Eastward of [Sea Houses] you have a fine prospect of a level country with the sea forming a bay of 18 miles broad; behind it rise most beautiful downs. The sea is in the front, and westward rises Beachy Head with a gentle ascent for two or three miles agreeably interspersed with downs and arable land; from whence you have a most extensive prospect both eastward and westward.' Gilbert White quoted with approval John Ray who 'was so ravished with the prospect from Plumpton Plain [in the 1660s] … that he mentioned those scapes in his *Wisdom of God in the works of Creation* with the utmost satisfaction, and thinks them equal to anything he had seen in the finest parts of Europe.' William Clarke similarly admired the Downs from the beach at Brighton in 1736: 'such a tract of sea, such regions of corn, and such an extent of fine carpet, that gives your eye the command of it all.' But other writers of the period tended to emphasise the view *from*, rather than the view *of*, the Downs, for example Burton from Truleigh Hill: 'An almost boundless range is offered to the sight from west to east. We behold the whole neighbouring country beautifully covered with corn and feeding numerous herds, in some parts woody, in others adorned with churches and villages appearing here and there and decked with various kinds of crop such as add a grace to the county and infuse a delight into the beholder.' Warburton noted two houses and a village for their views over the Weald and one for its view *through* the Downs to the sea.[57]

At the time, 1754, that he wrote an account of travelling through Sussex (where he had evidently been before), Dr Richard Pococke was Precentor of Waterford and Archdeacon of Dublin in Ireland, and was to be appointed Bishop of Ossory two years later. Compared with his cousin's, this account (which was printed in 1888) shows less evidence of prior reading and is much more an immediate record of what he saw and what he must have heard from guides and other informants. His route was from Rye to Chichester and Stansted. Even in an area as populated with settlements as Sussex, guides were probably more relied on by strangers than is apparent from the travellers' diaries. Sir George Thompson, for example, had guides from Arundel to Brighton in 1760.[58]

Other visitors to Sussex before about 1760 who left written accounts are:
Celia Fiennes, but alas only by short incursions, to Chichester in about 1694 and to Rye and Winchelsea in August 1697 [59]
John Whaley (Fellow of King's College, Cambridge), as tutor to John Dodd, with

Francis Shepheard and his tutor George Riste, travelling widely through England during July to October 1735, and passing from Rye to Chichester [60]

anonymous, unusual for including geological observations in the Chichester and Hastings areas, 1740 [61]

Sophia, Lady Newdigate, visiting Cowdray, Goodwood (Views 25 and 26), Chichester and Stansted in 1747 [62]

Horace Walpole, who was at Arundel, Petworth and Cowdray in 1749 and Herstmonceux in 1752 (View 111) [63]

Sir Peter Thompson (1698-1770), MP and well-known antiquary forming a library and museum at his house in Poole, travelling from there to Brighton in September 1760.[64]

Dr William Burrell, by Andrew Plimer,
c. 1785-90. From Williamson 1903

3. William Burrell and his collaborators

3.1 Francis Grose's *Antiquities of England and Wales*

Francis Grose was a close contemporary of William Burrell's, and both being born into prosperous families in the City of London one can imagine that they knew each other from childhood. For Sussex in his *Antiquities of England and Wales*, Grose drew on the collections of Burrell and local antiquaries, but he is given precedence here because he was - in the early 1760s - the draughtsman to produce the largest body of Sussex views before the Lamberts and because in some respects he carried on where the Bucks left off. The Bucks claimed that their 'Perspective views of cities and towns of note … are not only designed to delight the eye with as beautiful pictures as the places will afford, but also to entertain the mind with some useful knowledge, by means of a summary of what authentic history affords relating thereunto; such as the date, remarkable periods and accidents; also the present state of each place' (Document 2.1). But no more than 200 words were squeezed into the bottom margin of both town prospects and antiquities, and it is fair to say that description of the county's past and present, on the one hand, and topographical illustration, on the other, proceeded until the second half of the 18th century on parallel tracks, with only occasional convergence or combination, such as the Magnus inscription in Camden's *Britannia* and Chichester Cathedral in Dugdale's *Monasticon*.[65]

That changed with the appearance of Francis Grose's *Antiquities of England and Wales*, which was issued in just over 100 parts between 1772 and 1787. Each of over 600 engravings was accompanied by text which, though brief in some cases, was typically, for the 50 Sussex plates, about 600 words in length and might incorporate some new material. With reissues from 1783 until about 1809, the engravings have become very well known.

Francis Grose (1731-91) was the son of a jeweller, an immigrant from Switzerland, who traded in the City of London and retired to Richmond in Surrey. He first looked to the Army for a career. In early 1747 he saw the final campaign of the War of the Austrian Succession in Flanders and obtained a commission in November 1748. This he resigned in October 1751, just as his regiment was ordered to Scotland, probably because he was by then married to the daughter of a vintner in Canterbury. In 1755 his father bought him the place of Richmond Herald, but Grose showed no great taste for heraldry and sold it in 1763. As early as 1749 he was sketching medieval buildings in Kent, and in the mid-1750s attended William Shipley's drawing school in London.

Embodiment of the militia enabled him again to don uniform while avoiding distant postings. In November 1759 he was commissioned as a lieutenant in the Surrey Regiment and appointed adjutant and paymaster of its 2nd (Western) Battalion. Before the battalion was disembodied in December 1762, Grose's movements were dominated (in Edward Gibbon's words) 'by the arbitrary and often capricious orders of the War Office', as the Surrey Militia marched to and fro across southern England. But he was afforded ample opportunity to sketch, with, unsurprisingly, a strong emphasis on castles. In May 1760 he probably marched from Portchester to the Maidstone area, allowing him to sketch Bramber, Pevensey and Hastings castles and Winchelsea Church. Following the same route through Sussex in June 1761, he sketched at Boxgrove Priory, Bramber Church, Brighton blockhouse, Lewes Priory, Battle Abbey, Winchelsea Greyfriars and Camber Castle. For the second half of 1762 the battalion was stationed at Lewes, except for a week at Brighton to free its billets during the horse races in August. Grose sketched in both Brighton, with a general view from the west, and Lewes: the castle, the priory (View 129) and the Lord's Place, St James's Hospital, St John-sub-Castro and its monuments, Mount Caburn (View 91). Short excursions took in Hove Church, Laughton Place, Battle Abbey, Pevensey Castle (possibly with Paul Sandby) and Beachy Head.

When Grose, by then living in Wandsworth in Surrey, conceived *The antiquities* in about 1770, he already had a stock of pictures to use. Of the 20 Sussex views which appeared in the parts making up the first four volumes, between about June 1772 and June 1776, he relied on his drawings of 1760-2 for 17 and borrowed from Captain William Green (Hastings Castle 1759), Theophilus Forrest (Bayham Abbey 1774) and Major Hayman Rooke (Knepp Castle 1775); Green also provided the plans of St James's Hospital Lewes, Hastings Castle and Lewes Castle which were issued in late summer 1776. To other parts of the country he had to make tours, with views taken appearing as engravings within a few months. He returned to Sussex only in May 1777, to make a 12-day tour with Dr William Burrell. His diary of this tour is printed below as Document 5. At that time the first part of the *Supplement to The antiquities* was in the press, but Grose used only two views from the tour, both of Bodiam Castle. For this there were two reasons. First, only three parts appeared before publication was much slowed, even halted, by embodiment of the militia from March 1778 to February 1783. When he resumed the project in earnest, Grose had a new source of Sussex views, the drawings by S. H. Grimm for Burrell, of which 22 were engraved. (Grimm was no stranger to *The antiquities*, as he drew 'History preserving the monuments of antiquity' for the 1773 frontispiece of the first volume.) Two views came from James Moore, two from Mr Kenyon and one from Mr Verner. Secondly, the tour reflected Burrell's interest in churches which Grose only exceptionally included in *The antiquities*. But it did provide a large proportion of the examples to illustrate Grose's essay on church architecture and fittings issued in the *Supplement* in 1787, as well as similar illustrations (and a view of Sheffield Park) for *The Antiquarian Repertory*. The publication history of the plates is complex, so a guide for the Sussex plates is provided as Document 4.

Assembling the pictures was only part of the task, as the accompanying text also had to be prepared. Sometimes the text came almost entirely from published books, such as Camden's *Britannia* or Tanner's *Notitia monastica*. In other cases Grose was in correspondence to collect material from which he could draft, making general acknowledgement in the prefaces. We have three examples of the letters he received from Sussex contacts. The first was from the Revd Robert Austen (on whom more in Essay 3.2), dated 22 July 1772. Austen was replying to at least six questions from Grose about Lewes Priory and the nearby St James's Hospital. Most of the information he provided appeared in the text with the three relevant plates. A month later Grose was lamenting to Burrell that he could not delay publishing the St James's plate, though the historical information was still partial; it probably appeared in September. To Austen Grose wrote in January 1776: 'The plate of St John's Lewes is newly engraved. I shall therefore be obliged to you for the promised account of the building as soon as convenient', the plate appearing in March with Grose acknowledging the text to Burrell, who probably had it from John Elliot. In other instances views were engraved and long delayed in publication. In August 1772 he asked Burrell for information about Bramber Church, which had been engraved in the previous February but appeared only three years later, with special acknowledgement to Richard Gough. Indeed, the description of the architecture came verbatim from Gough's diary of 1767.[66] The second letter, of 31 May 1773, complete with a sketch-plan of Brighton, was from Captain William Green of the Corps of Engineers (1734/5-1820), concerning the blockhouse and the erosion of the beach and cliff. In using the letter, Grose was scrupulous in differentiating between what was in Green's own knowledge and what was not. Green joined Grose and Burrell for part of their tour in 1777. The third letter, dated 4 April 1774 from an unnamed correspondent, gives a precise description of Herstmonceux Castle which was largely followed as the text with plate IV of the castle, the history of its owners having been given with plates I to III.[67]

Grose's project was a national one which later extended to Scotland and Ireland, but in preparing the text for the plates of Sussex antiquities he was in touch with several antiquaries whose focus of study was Sussex. To these we now turn.

3.2 Clerics, schoolmasters and lawyers

The 1737 subscription list for the Bucks' views of Sussex antiquities shows interest amongst the clergy and gentry in the history of their home county. But it is not until the 1760s that we can detect sustained local activity to add to the body of knowledge or understanding of that history. With the wisdom of hindsight we can see it funnelling into, and culminating in, the collection made by William Burrell from which come most of the pictures reproduced here.

Two publications, however, proved to represent a false dawn. Dr Anthony Relhan's *Short history of Brighthelmston* (1761) was by one of Dr Richard Russell's successors and promoted the curative properties of the town and neighbourhood. While giving some account of the contemporary town, it was distinctly short on history, though Relhan (1715-76) sought to establish that Brighton had been a Roman station by reference to the form of its streets, an urn of 1000 denarii found 'some time ago', and a Roman *via* between Shoreham and Lewes found by an ingenious gentleman. And he had consulted the 1580 customs and, among current documentary sources, the custom-house diaries, the poor-rate book and the parish register. In 1766, the appearance of *The antiquities of Arundel; the peculiar privilege of its castle and lordships; with an abstract of the lives of the earls of Arundel, from the Conquest to this time* promised from its title the first substantial monograph on a Sussex locality. But the great majority of its 276 pages are devoted to the lives of the earls ('most awkwardly compiled from printed books' in Gough's judgement), and Arundel's antiquities are dispatched in 22 pages, most of them given to the Empress Matilda's stay in 1138, Clarendon's account of the 1643-4 siege and a few remarks on the town's contemporary condition. The author and publisher, Charles Caraccioli, described as 'the Master of the Grammar School at Arundel', was a Frenchman recently arrived there, possibly via the East Indies and employed in a school maintained by the Duke of Norfolk for Catholic children. He named 77 subscribers to his book, but, despite its dedication to the Duke and his heir, none of the ducal family was among them. Of Caraccioli no more is known than authorship of a novel, a three-volume life of Clive of India, a history of Sturbridge Fair in Cambridgeshire, *Anecdotes of New Hall, in the county of Essex*, and (in French) a study of Imperial Russia.[68]

More substantial, albeit unpublished, activity was taking place in eastern Sussex, in the persons of Robert Austen, Stephen Vine, John Elliot and William Hayley. Austen (1709/10-86) matriculated from Merton College, Oxford, in 1725, was ordained deacon and licensed as curate at Burwash in 1733, with a stipend of £40. In 1739 and repeatedly thereafter he applied to the Duke of Newcastle for preferment. In 1751 he was presented to Berwick by Edward Hawes on the understanding that he would resign when Hawes's son was qualified to claim the living, which he dutifully did in 1768. In 1753 he was appointed the master of the grammar school at Lewes (with the salary of £58 and a commodious house), serving also as curate at St Michael's and St Anne's. From Lord Pelham he secured Laughton in 1778. Copies by the Lamberts of a drawing by him show the Westgate before its inner walls were removed for road widening in 1763 (View 128). The information he provided to Grose in 1772 on Lewes Priory and St James's Hospital demonstrates the same archaeological interest. He made 'considerable collections' on the town's antiquities, but 'through an excess of literary modesty, ordered them all to be destroyed after his death.'[69]

Another schoolmaster, Stephen Vine of Lindfield, showed archaeological interest, but in an earlier period. He was the first Sussex contributor to the *Gentleman's Magazine* on the county's antiquities, reporting finds from barrows on the Downs in 1763 (an excavation by Robert Lucas of Alfriston), 1765 and 1768, and the discovery of an old paved road at St John's Common in 1781, and contributing notes on Herstmonceux Castle and Mayfield Place in 1773 and 1776 (Views 111 and 140). These articles, thought M. A. Lower in 1862, 'entitle him to the distinction of the Father of Sussex Topographers.' He also loaned documents to Burrell, including the important decrees of 1691 and 1693 for the enclosure of Ashdown Forest.[70]

Unlike Austen, John Elliot (1724-82) sought to ensure the survival of his notes, bequeathing them to William Burrell. He was born in the parish of St Michael, Lewes, and baptised on 30 October 1724, the only son of Obadiah Elliot (d. 1775), brewer, and his wife Elizabeth Boarer (d. 1771). After attending Lewes grammar school he was articled to an attorney and built up a good practice in London, acting as agent for lawyers in his home county. He was admitted to the Society of the Inner Temple in 1779/80, having had chambers there by 1771. In June 1763 he married Margaret Cook of Berwick-upon-Tweed (d. 1791).[71]

According to Dunvan, Elliot's father discouraged his antiquarian pursuits, as detracting from training for his profession, and his wife, a strict Methodist, feared for their effect on his spiritual welfare. The earliest evidence for his scholarship are notes of churches visited in eastern Sussex in 1762-3.[72] His research otherwise dates from 1770 and was confined to Lewes, the borough, the priory and the barony, and focused on the parish of St John-sub-Castro, in which were the brewery his father had bought in 1743 and the house he inherited in 1775 and occupied thereafter.[73]

'Having accidentally looked into some of our most ancient history for other purposes,' probably to prove title to property, he wrote in 1773,[74]

curiosity led me farther than intended, 'til at length it was drawn off and narrowed to my native place of Lewes, and its neighbourhood; of which little has been said, and nothing purposely written to my knowledge, save only in scattering wise, or as connected with the general history of the Kingdom, whilst almost every other county, and even cities and towns, have had volumes dedicated to their particular history. But finding the county at large would take more time than could be spared to a mere amusement, the Town and Rape of Lewes confined my inquiries and observations, which so far as my small opportunities have enabled, are briefly penned in the following sheets, minuted down as they occurred promiscuously.

Elliot made extracts from medieval documents in the British Museum and the public records, particularly the cartulary of Lewes Priory in the Cottonian Library, though halted after transcribing the first third, as 'it would perhaps take up the better part of one man's life to read and digest the remaining two-thirds.'[75] He drafted an account of Lewes's origin within the bounds of a Roman camp, but his only printed works were two long letters to the *Sussex Weekly Advertiser*, 3 January 1774 and 16 January 1775, on St John-sub-Castro Church. He was a competent draughtsman, carefully drawing memorials in St John's and old gravestones discovered there and at Seaford. In December 1780 he was elected a Fellow of the Society of Antiquaries, to which he had sent, in 1775 and 1777, two communications on Lewes antiquities. He provided the Revd John Watson with information on the barony of Lewes for his *Memoirs of the ancient earls of Warren and Surrey* (1782, but privately circulated in draft in 1776) – as also J. C. Brooke for his research in 1778 on the Earl of Surrey's inherited estates. Elliot was probably James Lambert's first client for antiquarian pictures, and Lambert's views of Lewes which Watson had engraved by Basire must have come from him (Essay 3.4). He also bought from Dominic Serres (1722-93) a large prospect in oils of Lewes from the south, at a cost of £8 8s. plus £1 16s. for the gilt frame with Italian moulding.[76]

Elliot died suddenly at his house at 5 Southampton Row, Bloomsbury, on 28 February 1782, and was buried in St Michael's churchyard in Lewes. 'In person,' Dunvan said, 'he was tall, in manners unassuming and plain, in disposition gentle and disinterested, in his profession upright and candid, and in friendship liberal and sincere.' To Dr William Burrell Elliot bequeathed his notes, bound and unbound, although Burrell had already borrowed and copied from them. They did not pass with Burrell's own collection to the British Museum. Burrell's eldest son lent them to T. W. Horsfield when he was engaged upon *History and antiquities of Lewes and its vicinity*, 1 (1824); and the family disposed of them in the early 20th century. Three libraries between them hold six volumes. His picture by Serres and 'all my tinted drawings in my portfolio of subjects in and about Lewes and in Sussex' he bequeathed to his fellow townsman Henry Shelley.[77]

Like Elliot, the Revd William Hayley (1714/15-89) also thought to write a county history. He came from Bewdley in Worcestershire, matriculated from Exeter College, Oxford, in 1733 and graduated BA in 1739 from Merton College. He was inducted as Rector of Brightling in 1752, having married Anne Burrell (unrelated to Dr William Burrell) whose family had held the living for 70 years. He also held Preston and Hove in plurality from 1754. His meticulous nature is shown by the parish census of Brightling he undertook in 1756 and his close analysis of the parish register between 1754 and 1781, for example calculating how many of the marriages produced children who were baptised in the parish and how many of those baptised were from other couples. For his correspondence with Burrell, see Document 6.1.[78]

His executors sold his antiquarian notes to John Fuller of Rose Hill in Brightling (1757-1834, see View 29 and Essay 4.4), who presented them to the British Museum in 1820. He had started work by 1764 and was still adding material in 1785.[79] The manuscript sources he consulted were:

i.   Battle Abbey cartulary in the possession of Sir Whistler Webster;
ii. Battle Abbey documents in the British Museum;
iii. copy of the 1634 Visitation in possession of John Nicoll of Mountfield 1764;
iv. charters, deeds, etc., in the possession of John Hilder of Robertsbridge 1777, of Lord Pelham 1778, and of John Fuller of Rose Hill 1784, 1785;
v.   extracts by or for John Elliot, lent to Hayley by Robert Austen, from the British Museum, the Bodleian Library and the register of Kingston near Lewes;
vi. parish registers, probably mainly at Burrell's behest.

Hayley set down a plan for a history of Sussex, with the following headings:[80]

Book 1 The general history of the County of Sussex, or perhaps The civil and natural history of the County of Sussex in general
Ch. 1   Of the state of Sussex before the coming in of the Saxons
Ch. 2   Of the South Saxons
Ch. 3   Of the County of Sussex: e.g. the earls, sheriffs, knights of the shire, lords lieutenant, JPs, baronets, gentlemen etc.
Ch. 4   Of the nature and properties of the county: its face or appearance; soil; produce or natural commodities; manufactures
Ch. 5   Of the rivers
Ch. 6   Of the situation, extent and division of the county: natural, ecclesiastical, civil. List of parishes giving name, natural division (east, west), rape, hundred, longitude and latitude, archdeaconry, deanery, first fruits, tenths, clear yearly value of living

Book 2 The ecclesiastical history
Ch. 1   Of the conversion of the South Saxons
Ch. 2   Of the bishops of Selsey
Ch. 3   Of the bishops of Chichester
Ch. 4   Of the Cathedral Church of Chichester
Ch. 5   Of the deans of Chichester
Ch. 6   Of the canons residentiary, prebendaries, etc. of Chichester
Ch. 7   Of the archdeacons and chancellors of the diocese
Ch. 8   Of the peculiars in the diocese
Ch. 9   Of the religious houses in the diocese - in general, a more particular account being given under the parish

Book 3 The parochial (or topographical) history, taking in alphabetical order each rape:
An account of the rape in general and its lords etc.
An account of the hundreds
An account of each parish in alphabetical order and therein:
    1   name, ancient and modern, derivation and significance
    2   situation, extent and boundaries
    3   history preceding the Conquest
    4   description in Domesday book
    5   history of the descent and several owners of it or its principal manors
    6   account and descent of other manors therein, estates, houses of note, their past and present possessors, with anything remarkable relating to them, and their coats of arms
    7   castles or other ancient buildings
    8   religious houses
    9   lands belonging to religious houses in other parts, with a general account of those houses and their order
    10   the rectory or vicarage, the advowson or patronage, first fruits, tenths, procuration, etc. Its real or reputed value. The succession of its incumbents
    11   the church, of what sort and how many buildings, when and by whom founded, to whom dedicated, what free chapels or chantries founded therein,

what and what sort of monuments and tombs in it, what epitaphs or memorials of interment, what remains of painted glass, what inscriptions or coats of arms in the windows or on its walls

12   hospitals

13   schools

14   charitable benefactions of all sorts, to church, poor, highways, etc.

15   antiquities: British, Roman, Saxon, Danish, Norman

16   particular histories relating to it since the Conquest, and remarkable transactions that have happened there

17   eminent men born or bred up there

18   natural curiosities: medicinal waters, minerals, rare plants, etc.

19   manufacture, its rise, progress and improvement

20   taxation, ancient and modern.

This scheme was characteristic of its period, to which the county historian aspired, indeed even *Magna Britannia* had attempted similar coverage, at the level of the county. Dallaway's plan for his *History of the western division of the County of Sussex* was similar, and it is not greatly different to the plan for the *Victoria County History* at its inception. Hayley made a small start towards fulfilling this plan, in that into two volumes he collated his extracts by topic, following broadly the structure above and under some headings drafting text. He titled the volumes 'Notitia Sussexiensis sive Sussexiæ antiqua & nova, to wit, An account chorographical, genealogical, historical, of the County of Sussex, collected from records, charters, deeds, manuscripts, and other authorities, interspersed with epitaphs, inscriptions, arms.'[81]

Austen, Elliot, Vine and Hayley are the names which recur in their own and Burrell's papers as active Sussex antiquaries in the 1770s. There were connections between them, but they cannot be designated as an antiquarian 'circle' such as can be identified in neighbouring Kent. Hayley's notes include only three letters to Austen (in December 1772 and February 1773) and, even though he and Elliot had both been working on Sussex history for 15 years by 1778, they did not then know each other.

There were a few others in Sussex, less conspicuous. The house at Alfriston of Thomas Chowne (d. 1788), FSA, was consumed by fire in 1765, destroying 'some valuable MSS relating to the antiquities of the county' arising from studies in which he had long indulged. Their loss left him depressed and he quitted Sussex, hoping to find solace in the pleasures of London. John Luke Nicoll of Mountfield, sometime Deputy Paymaster General (d. 1767) owned the copy of the 1634 Visitation of Sussex which Hayley copied in 1764 and also 'Segar's Pedigrees of Sussex'. Thomas Wakeham (*c.* 1728-1803), an East Grinstead lawyer, was forming a collection from the late 1770s, acquiring drawings of Herstmonceux Castle in 1778, having a copy of the Book of John Rowe made in 1783/4 and recording the fall of East Grinstead Church's tower in 1785 (Views 92 and 95).[82]

One Richard Norris noted on the flyleaf of his copy of *A compleat history of Sussex*, in 1773: 'A good history of the County can be expected only from some gentleman long resident in it; and 'tis reported that the Revd Mr Hayley of Brightling has compiled one, the publication of which only waits the publication of Domesday Book, now in hand.' The report was mistaken, for Hayley must have been overwhelmed with the magnitude of the task which he had outlined, but ''tis also said,' - and this was true - 'Dr Burrell has formed a large collection of materials, with a view to publishing the History, or a Deduction of the landed property, of this county, from the Norman

Conquest, in the manner of Dugdale's Warwickshire; but 'tis said that work is not in any degree of forwardness.' [83]

3.3 William Burrell, antiquary

The efforts of Austen, Vine, Elliot and Hayley pale beside those of William Burrell, the most significant figure in Sussex antiquarianism before the generation which founded the Sussex Archaeological Society in 1846 or even that which founded the Sussex Record Society in 1901. While his fame rests on his bequest to the British Museum of his materials on the history of Sussex, little survives from which to write his biography. Few other working notes or private or business papers have survived, much probably being lost by fire in 1904 at Knepp Castle, Shipley, to which his eldest son had presumably removed his papers.[84]

William Burrell (1732-96) was born on 10 October 1732 in Leadenhall Street, in the City of London, the third son of Peter Burrell (1692-1756), also of Beckenham, Kent, and Amy (1699/1700-1789), daughter of Hugh Raymond of Saling Hall, Essex, and Langley, Kent. His father was a considerable merchant who held important contracts for remittances and the victualling of troops; a director of the South Sea Company, 1724-33, involved in the 'Bubble'; a director of the Royal Exchange Assurance Company, 1726-38; and MP for Haslemere, 1722-54, and for Dover, 1755-6, steadily supporting the Administration.[85]

William entered Westminster School in January 1743, proceeded to St John's College, Cambridge, in June 1749, and graduated LLB in 1755 and LLD in 1760. On 13 September 1760 he was admitted as an advocate in the Arches Court of Canterbury and on 3 November as a Fellow of the College of Advocates, colloquially known as Doctors' Commons. He practised in both the ecclesiastical courts and the Admiralty courts. He was appointed Chancellor of the Diocese of Worcester through the influence of the Duke of Newcastle in July 1764, and of Rochester in August 1771, continuing in both posts until his death.[86] His diligence as a lawyer is exemplified by several volumes of pleadings, judgements and opinions which he compiled. A volume of pleadings before the Court of Admiralty, 1764-74 (including four in which he appeared in 1768 and 1774), a volume on prize cases, 1757-66, and selected cases and opinions before Admiralty Courts, 1701-81, were considered of sufficient historical interest as to be printed in 1885. A volume of 173 ecclesiastical cases from 1769 to 1774 contains only one in which he appeared, but that was the celebrated case brought in 1769 by Sir Charles Bunbury against his wife Lady Sarah Lennox for adultery. Another volume includes about a dozen of his opinions and judgements as Chancellor of the Diocese of Worcester, down to 1778. That the two volumes of admiralty and ecclesiastical cases end in 1774 is significant, for it was in the spring of that year that Burrell retired from Doctors' Commons.[87] His duties as diocesan chancellor were presumably mainly thereafter discharged through deputies.

The circumstances of his appointment to Worcester are revealing. In 1758 the Duke of Newcastle had recommended Thomas Secker for appointment as Archbishop of Canterbury, for which Secker had promised him the gift of the Deanship of the Arches on its next vacancy. Newcastle appointed Dr George Hay (*c*. 1715-78) who thereby vacated his offices in the Diocese of Worcester; that of vicar-general Newcastle had given to Dr Peter Calvert of Trinity Hall, Cambridge (*c*. 1730-88). In June 1764 he begged the bishop to give the chancellorship to William Burrell, 'a very pretty deserving young man, amiable in himself, exemplary in his character, and very promising in his profession.' The bishop was happy to oblige, especially for one known so long and for whose family he had long had particular regard. Burrell returned his thanks to Newcastle in appropriately obsequious terms and, as the Duke's correspondence showed, furthered his interest on several occasions, such as the election of the vice-chancellor of the University of Cambridge later that year. As Burrell put it in 1767, 'I acknowledge my obligations to the Duke of Newcastle, and the right he has to command my services upon every occasion. Allow me to add, My Lord, that my voice is entirely at your disposal.' [88]

By 1764 Burrell, still unmarried, was living at the family's country seat at Beckenham which had passed on their father's death in 1756 to the eldest son, Peter. In London he lived at Peter's house, a rented one at 21 Berkeley Square. A letter of 11 July 1765 to Benjamin Way (1740-1808) shows him engaged in the socio-political London life of men of his class. He had come to town that morning on account of an ague and his duty to the Court of Directors (probably of the South Sea Company of which both men were directors). The rumoured appointments to the new Ministry are listed. Burrell had dined with Way's father in Richmond the previous Saturday and could report that his sister had gone to Blackheath and Greenwich, staying with Lady Northampton and, after meeting their father at Sir Gregory Page's, would be returning to Richmond that evening. Burrell hoped to see Way in the country for a day or two; he did not intend to leave England until the beginning of August. This last remark refers to his only known foreign trip which took him at least to Paris where he paid court to Horace Walpole and from which he departed for England on 26 October.[89]

A more active engagement in politics came on his election as MP for Haslemere in March 1768 on the family interest. Unsurprisingly Burrell steadily supported the Administration. He sat for six years, resigning on being appointed a commissioner of Excise in 1774. This office was not a sinecure, but well rewarded by £1250 a year. In offering to meet the Earl of Surrey in 1778, he proposed 'any other Saturday or Monday, as on other days he is generally engaged about public business', and indeed when in London he did attend each week three or four of the Excise Board's meetings. He was a director of the Sun Fire Insurance Company, 1773-95.[90]

That he left politics and active legal practice in 1774 and the South Sea Company in 1775 is probably related to his marriage in April 1773. His wife, a woman 20 years his junior, was Sophia (1753-1802), daughter of Charles Raymond of Valentines in Ilford, Essex, and Sarah, daughter of Thomas Webster of Bromley, Kent. Her father was a successful banker, and her marriage portion was said in the press to be £100,000. As the marriage settlement refers to only £10,000, what was meant was her fortune, and indeed when her father died in 1788, he was reported to be worth £200,000 (or perhaps only £150,000 because of some recent losses) with two daughters as sole heirs. Undoubtedly she was a wealthy bride. In the year of her marriage, her father was made a baronet with reversion to Burrell, so he gained prospects of both fortune and title. It is by reason of the reversion, in 1788, that Burrell was known as Sir William. They had five sons (of whom two died in infancy) and two daughters, born between 1774 and 1789, and lived in Harley Street, Marylebone.[91] Just before he died, his father-in-law bought Knepp Castle in Shipley. He bequeathed it to his two daughters, and Burrell bought his sister-in-law's share. That gave the Burrells a country residence, in Sussex, but they did not live there (as did their son after 1806). They took summer holidays at Felpham at least in 1776 and 1777. Sophia Burrell dabbled in literature. Volumes of poetry appeared in 1793 and 1794, and two tragedies in 1800. She was also a competent watercolour artist.[92]

Burrell now devoted his energies to the history of Sussex. His antiquarian interests had been evident at an early age. In September 1753, noting that Burrell was aiming for Doctors' Commons, his tutor at Cambridge, John Taylor, sought help in securing Burrell's election to the Society of Antiquaries from Andrew Coltee Ducarel (1713-85), an ecclesiastical lawyer, later librarian at Lambeth Palace, and a prominent member. Perhaps Ducarel was Burrell's mentor both in preparing for admission to Doctors' Commons and as an antiquary, though he was not one of Burrell's sponsors when he was elected, aged 22, the following April. As early as 1755 Burrell was collecting, for he provided William Clarke with a copy of the print of his coins.[93]

Burrell toured Scotland with a college contemporary in 1758. The account he prepared is striking for describing not only the ancient and modern 'sights', but also giving much information about crops, industries, trade, food, prices and living conditions in general. Perhaps this is the ambitious young lawyer preparing himself for a role in public affairs. As the account is the only surviving piece of sustained original writing by Burrell, it deserves some quotation; for example on Irvine:[94]

From Air to Irvine is 12 miles over the sands when the water is low. Here is a good harbour, to which between 70 and 80 sail belong. They trade with Ireland with coal (which the neighbouring hills abound with) and get money in return. To the West Indies they carry bale goods and bring back rum, sugar and mahogany. Over the River Irvine is a bridge of 4 arches. There is a good tollbooth. The country is flat, but rich; arable lets from £1 0s. 0d. to £2 0s. 0d. per acre, sells from 30 to 32 years' purchase. Manure is dung, lime and seaweed. Labour, 8d. [per day] the whole year when constantly employed, when accidentally, from 10d. to 1s. There are two rope walks and a sail cloth and handkerchief manufactory. A mile north east of Irvine stands Eglington Castle, a poor edifice, but the spacious plantations of firs that surround it are remarkably beautiful. A mile further is the village of Kilwinnen, noted for the large ruins of an abbey. The country about it is very fruitful and in general there are large crops of all sorts of grain, particularly oats.

and on Blair Castle:

In the old castle are a dining room 36 feet long 27 feet broad and 18 feet high, and on the second storey a magnificent ballroom 52 feet long, breath 30 feet, height 23 feet, furnished with crimson damask and most richly carved; the ceiling coved and elegantly stuccoed. The windows do not give sufficient light, the walls being 9 feet thick. There are few except family pictures, among which the most remarkable are The Prince of Orange and the Earl of Tullybardin, date 1606.... The kitchen garden is the best disposed I ever saw; it is situated on a declivity on both sides, between which is a canal the whole length of it, with several small islands.

The recording of distances travelled, rents, land-values and wages (tabulated at the end) is consistent. Internal dimensions are common, the descriptions rather pedestrian but very earnest.

Such was the cast of mind of the ecclesiastical lawyer who embarked on the history of Sussex. But why did he chooseSussex, where he never lived? His great-grandfather, Walter (1600-71), was one of Sussex's chief ironmasters who prospered and accumulated property in and around Cuckfield; he was 'my honoured friend' who provided John Ray with a description of ironworking and some observations on husbandry. There being nine sons and three daughters, the youngest son Peter (1649-1718) sought his fortune elsewhere, and having made it as a London merchant bought an estate at Beckenham in Kent. By the accident of all his elder brothers predeceasing him without direct heirs, in the year before his own death Peter inherited the Cuckfield lands and also property acquired around Lewes. The latter lands passed in 1756 to William Burrell.[95]

Work on the history was underway before his marriage, by February 1771. A letter from the Revd Edward Clarke (1730-86, a contemporary from St John's, Cambridge), on behalf of his father William (1695-1771), Rector of Buxted and Canon Residentiary of Chichester Cathedral (Essay 2.1), suggests that, as a preliminary, Burrell had been seeking to establish what other people had already done: [96]

My Father had never the least thought of engaging in such a work, as he is glad to hear you have undertaken. He had never either the fortune or abilities proper for it. The history of property alone in the County could not be collected without an expense of time and money which he could not answer. As to the natural history part of it, he had never premises sufficient to undertake it. He is glad it has fallen into your hands by inclination, as without that it would go on heavily. But with it must be a very agreeable amusement.... It would be a pretty thing to give the Roman history and antiquities of the County, then the history of the Cinque Ports, then the history of property from Domesday Book downwards in six chapters divided by the six rapes, then the natural history.

Work on archives was in progress in 1771. Visits to parish churches began in earnest in September 1772 and peaked in 1776. In 1775 he first commissioned pictures from James Lambert and his nephew James and in 1778 from S. H. Grimm.

Burrell suffered a stroke in August 1787 and, though he recovered his speech, he lost the use of his left arm. He nevertheless continued research until 1791: the last entry in his list of archives searched (Document 7.2) relates to material seen at Cowdray in 1790 and 1791, and the last dated visits to parish churches were in June 1791, to Funtington and East Lavant. In March 1790 he resigned from the commission of Excise and later that year bought from the Duke of Norfolk (the Earl of Surrey in Document 6.1) The Deepdene, a substantial house outside Dorking in Surrey, rebuilt in the early 1770s. He removed there from Harley Street in the following year. Grimm's last commission may have been of views in The Deepdene's gardens.[97] That his active researches were now ended is sadly reflected in the letter of June 1794 printed as Document 6.2: 'I have none of my Sussex Books here, ... and it would be a difficult task to decipher many parts of [them], even if my health permitted me to continue collecting information respecting antiquities in Sussex.' It was presumably in the late 1780s that he offered his collection to the publisher John Nichols (1745-1826), but Nichols declined to print them and the principal drawings at his own risk, for he was committed to his own history of Leicestershire. So Burrell bequeathed it, by his will of November 1790, to the British Museum.[98]

Burrell died at The Deepdene on 20 January 1796 and was buried at West Grinstead, his second surviving son having inherited West Grinstead Park from Burrell's uncle in 1789. Simple monuments by Flaxman are both there and at Cuckfield. His widow continued to live at The Deepdene which was sold after her death in 1802.[99]

His town library was auctioned on 2-5 May 1796 at the Turf Gallery, Hanover Square, and was described in the catalogue as 'an extraordinary choice collection of the Greek and Roman classics, with their lexicons, and many of the rarest collation; for the most part in large paper, and in Morocco and Russia bindings: together with a selection of British history, antiquities and topography; several beautiful manuscripts upon vellum, with illuminations; books of prints and drawings, and other literary curiosities; the whole in fine condition.' Presumably the 42 volumes bequeathed to the British Museum were transferred there at about the same date. They were soon being used. William Bray (1736-1832), the lawyer who later completed Manning's *History and antiquities of Surrey* (1804-14), consulted them while writing the history of the Sussex estates of Smith's Charity, of which he was clerk. His citations are the first printed acknowledgement to them; it was to be the first of many.[100]

Those volumes, now in the British Library, can be grouped as follows:

1. extracts and notes on the descent of property, arranged mainly by manor within rape, with two volumes for each rape (Add. MSS 5679-90)
2. 'the church notes', being copies of monumental inscriptions, extracts from parish registers and notes on incumbents, arranged by parish within rape, two rapes to a volume (Add. MSS 5697-9)
3. extracts and notes on religious houses (Add. MS. 5706)
4. one volume of pedigrees in draft (Add. MS. 5711) and six volumes prepared to receive fair copies, with coats of arms drawn in the top right corner of alternate folios, but only a few pedigrees entered (Add. MSS 5691-6)
5. watercolour views by the James Lamberts, uncle and nephew, and S. H. Grimm (Add. MSS 5670-8)
6. transcripts of records, most made by copyists (Add. MSS 5700-2, 5709)
7. Burrell's working papers and a few notes from fellow antiquaries (Add. MSS 5703-5, 5708)
8. non-Sussex material: catalogue of deeds in Lambeth Palace Library; debates in 1688 on abdication and vacancy of the throne (Add. MSS 5707, 5710).

One thing which makes Burrell's collection exceptional is its orderly presentation. J. C. Brooke visited Burrell in February 1778 'and was with him all the morning looking over his Sussex MSS, which are in [Brooke's] opinion the most copious and best arranged of any he has seen for any county.'[101] This is not a muddled accumulation of working papers, but an organised series of collated extracts from primary and secondary sources. Groups 1, 2 and 3 are written up from notes, of which few survive. They are not fair copies, as material was added over time to sections headed up with the names of manors, parishes and religious houses. Group 4 was prepared by a heraldic artist to take the pedigrees derived from the information in Groups 1 and 2. Given that in 1778 (Document 6.1) Burrell said that he 'collected materials for a History of Sussex with a view to publish them', and that he offered his collection to John Nichols for printing, we may surmise that he considered Groups 1, 2 and 3, illustrated from Group 5, to be ready for publication. They were indeed broadly similar to what Nichols was publishing as his *History of Leicestershire*, except that his topographical material was arranged entirely by parish and not split between parish and manor.

The neatness of the collection means that we have limited evidence of how Burrell approached his project, but five, overlapping, working methods can be identified:

i. taking notes from published sources
ii. taking notes and transcribing from manuscripts (or commissioning others to do so)
iii. making visits to churches
iv. making written enquiries of other antiquaries and parochial clergy

v.   commissioning artists to make pictures of buildings and monuments.

As to taking notes, Burrell maintained lists of books and of manuscripts which he had consulted. Two successive versions of the lists are found in two interleaved copies of *A compleat history of Sussex* (1730), the Sussex section reprinted from *Magna Britannia et Hibernia*. These lists are edited here as Documents 7.1 and 7.2. The list of books shows how reliant Burrell was on the nationwide studies of the 70 years between 1650 and 1720. The list of manuscripts shows him collecting material from libraries, landowners, their stewards, parochial clergy and other antiquaries. In some cases he was the recipient of copies, in other cases he examined the documents, either in the custodian's muniment-room or by borrowing them, showing that he had done so by the reprehensible habit of initialling them. A letter from J. C. Brooke in January 1786 affords a glimpse of him at work: 'I hope this letter will find you in good health, and that my long absence in the country has not prevented you prosecuting your researches at Norfolk House, if it has, I will now attend you when agreeable.' BL, Add. MS. 5705, is what may be called (to use an accounting analogy) his first 'day book', in that he wrote into it consecutively extracts from whatever manuscript he was studying. These extracts were later 'posted' to the 'ledger account' for the manor or parish mentioned. This volume was mostly filled in 1771-3, opening with extracts from surveys of Sussex lands borrowed from the office of the Surveyor General of Crown Lands - who between 1769 and 1775 was his elder brother Peter. Sometimes the volume was left with someone else to enter extracts.[102]

Initially, it seems, the extracts were posted to BL, Add. MS. 5708, the first interleaved copy of Thomas Cox's *A compleat history of Sussex*, but its structure was unsuitable for Burrell's intentions and the volume was soon outgrown. But in this early phase he compiled a list of manors and, probably around 1775, the sets of manorial and parishes volumes (Add. MSS 5679-90 and 5697-9) were ruled up, with a couple of folios allotted (as in a ledger) to each manor and parish. The material in Add. MS. 5708 was transferred to these and new material was added as it came to hand, so far as possible in chronological order in the manorial sections. Burrell may have done some of the posting himself, but he clearly employed clerks who mimicked his handwriting. The letter of 1794 (Document 6.2) refers to 'persons whom I employed in copying my memorandums'. The day book contains instructions to the clerk, for example, 'not to be entered' (so the material is not struck through with a vertical red line) and, with reference to part of John Rowe's book, 'NB The items marked | denote them to be entered in their particular places, though it may be proper to enter them altogether as the freelands belonging to the Manor of Keymer &c.' (ff. 69, 99).

In his 'church notes' (Add. MSS 5697-9), in the bottom margin of some 200 of over 300 parish entries, Burrell noted 'Visited' or 'Surveyed' followed by a date usually to the day. For dates before August 1773, 'surveyed' is used exclusively. The earliest, those in 1762 (2 churches), 1763 (3), 1768 (2) and 1769 (1), are dated only to year, and the description of Alfriston Church has been found in John Elliot's hand, indicating that Elliot was visiting churches in the 1760s and passed his notes to Burrell. Eleven churches on and south of the Downs between the Ouse and the Adur were 'surveyed' in September 1772. Chiddingly was 'surveyed' by a Mr Looker in June 1776. But in three cases (Bishopstone, Brede and Udimore, 1777) we know that Burrell was there, with Grose. If we allow occasional inconsistency, we can infer that 'surveyed' usually referred to someone else visiting the church, and that Burrell relied on others until 1773 and occasionally thereafter. Only after his marriage in April 1773, did he make summer tours. Seven churches were visited in 1773 and two in 1774, but 31 in 1775, rising to 80 in 1776, and then falling away to 28 in 1777, 17 in 1778, four in each of the following three years, eight in 1782, three in 1783, six in 1784, two in 1787 and two in 1791. Hayley in April 1777 referred to 'the line of your Whitsun route', and the dates on the church notes do confirm that Burrell made annual tours immediately after Whitsun from 1776 to 1784 and in 1787. The law calendar may still have regulated Burrell's year, and these Whitsun tours fell between the Easter and Trinity terms. In the busiest years there were also tours in July and September 1775, August to September 1776 and August and September 1777. S. H. Grimm accompanied him for at least part of the way on six tours in the 1780s. The Lamberts were with him only during his visit to Lewes and neighbourhood in September 1775. Francis Grose joined Burrell for the Whitsun tour of 1777 and his diary of it (Document 5) shows the pace: he visited 18 churches in five days.

Presumably the main purposes of the visits were to prepare a short description of the church and to copy monumental inscriptions and coats of arms. Whether Burrell sought systematically to collect information in advance of visits is unclear. There is no sign of his sending a standard questionnaire to the clergy, as antiquaries in some counties - such as Jeremiah Milles in Devon - did. The church notes for 47 parishes record that inscriptions and/or parish register extracts were sent by 23 clergy and a surveyor of customs, led by 'Mr Durnford' for ten parishes and Hayley for nine. But Hayley's and Burrell's letters show that Hayley helped on further parishes and the list of manuscript sources (Document 6.1) acknowledged five clergy who are not named in the notes. So there may have been more correspondence with clergy than is apparent. Parish registers were portable as monuments were not. In 1778 Hayley borrowed the Burwash registers (and offered to borrow the Salehurst ones), while in 1773 Stephen Vine apologised to James Lambert for not yet having sent a register, via Richard Pim, the Lindfield paper-maker, to John Elliot - who presumably was acting for Burrell, as the letter is amongst Burrell's notes. As to fellow antiquaries, Burrell corresponded with Austen, Elliot and Hayley, and with the herald J. C. Brooke (Document 6.1). The tone of Hayley's letters to Burrell is very deferential: 'If my house at Brightling be in the line of your Whitsun route, I shall be very happy to accommodate you as far as in my power, but if that happens not to be the case, I shall with great willingness follow your summons to Battle or whichever place will be most convenient to you.' But there may have been mutual advantage in the relationship, for Burrell lent books and may have provided information from archives, access to which inferior social status and relative penury may have denied Hayley.[103]

Purchasing and commissioning pictures was Burrell's final working method. The artists employed - James Lambert, uncle and nephew, and S. H. Grimm - are the subjects of the following sections. Burrell bequeathed 269 finished watercolours by the Lamberts who seem to have started working in earnest for him in 1775, continuing until 1784. Pictures bearing earlier dates may have been bought or copied from their shop stock. Grimm, coming from London, had no previous Sussex work to present. He was employed to copy the younger Lambert's views of Herstmonceux Castle in 1778, but otherwise was retained to tour Sussex sketching for about two weeks from Whitsun each year between 1780 and 1791 (except 1786), a programme yielding Burrell nearly 900 finished pictures.

Perhaps Burrell's intentions when he embarked on his project for a History of Sussex had been wider ranging than the volumes of notes and extracts now reflect: he may have had a scheme as extensive as Hayley's, which he was forced to scale down.

But his working methods suggest that the concentration on the descent of landed property and the genealogy of the landowning families was his aim from the outset. Richard Norris, in 1773, may have accurately made the distinction between 'a good history of the County' which Hayley was said to have compiled, and 'a Deduction of the landed property, of this county, from the Norman Conquest' on which Burrell had embarked.

Burrell's work was not highly regarded by those of the next generation who thought themselves the leaders in antiquarian study. Craven Ord (1756-1832) wrote to Richard Gough:[104]

By favour of Mr [Joseph] Planta [Principal Librarian of the British Museum] I have examined Sir William Burrell's three volumes of church notes and the folios of drawings. The list of patrons and incumbents is not complete by any means, the churches are but very scantily described 'the church is a good room', 'room very damp', 'holy water vase' constantly, in short he had never travelled with or read a church note taken by my Enfield friend [i.e. Gough] and does not know what to observe, the arms are all too much shaded and finished in formal shields of one pattern, the extracts from Registers have been made with much labour, as have been the terriers and other matters relating to tithes, the drawings in these volumes are too slight for engraving. ... seven folios of drawings by Grimm, two by Lambert, consist of views of churches, monuments, old and modern houses, some few of fonts and painted glass, but by no means such a collection as I would have made, many of them however are curious. In the vacation I mean going through the volumes of descents of property.

3.4 James Lambert, senior and junior, landscape painters

The Lamberts were the only Sussex-based artists within our period who produced a significant body of topographical illustrations of Sussex. James Lambert senior (1725-88) was baptised on 29 December 1725 at Willingdon, near Eastbourne, the youngest of the eight children of John Lambert (1690-1764) and Susan Bray (1687-1771). The family moved to Lewes in about 1730, the father working in the Cliffe as a flax-dresser. James's nephew, James Lambert junior (1744-99), was born on 21 September 1744.[105]

The known body of pictures by or associated with the Lamberts now exceeds 600 items, ranging from slight pencil sketches to large oils. The elder James Lambert was the more competent artist. The representation in several topographical views of two artists working together may be taken to be uncle and nephew, rather than just a conventional motif (see page 141). The signed work suggests that some pictures are the sole work of one or other, some are copies by one of the other's original and some are the joint efforts of both. One likely division of labour was that the nephew used a ruler to lay out the building which was the subject of the view, and his uncle added the foliage and the staffage in the foreground. The 1776/7 pictures of Herstmonceux Castle for Lord Dacre (described later) and a full-size drawing of Gundrada's tomb for Thomas Townsend, 1795, show the nephew at his best.[106] These were measured record drawings, but Lambert junior was more often the copyist. Appropriately he owned and bequeathed 'my case of drawing instruments, my drawing board square and parallel rule' and 'my pantagraft', a device of perforated rods for laying out copies to variable scales, as well as 'my best set of water colours'. In his will he described himself as 'coach-painter', rather than the grander 'herald and landscape painter' on his memorial. This account hereafter is concerned mainly with the uncle.

Dunvan said that Lambert had 'no more than the humble advantages of a common writing-school [and] applied to music and painting with the persevering enthusiasm of unassisted genius.... As he advanced towards maturity, he received some instructions from a music master; but in painting he had still to trust solely to his own taste and application.'[107]

It is of Lambert as a musician that we have the earlier record. The organ installed at St Thomas at Cliffe in 1739-40 was probably the only one in the district and he became organist in 1745, at the age of 20, continuing in office - with an annual fee of £5 - until his death in 1788. Perhaps the first organist, Mr Gibbs, was his music teacher. Lambert published volumes of psalms and of hymns for use in local churches, the second edition of each being dated 1760 and 1774. Between November 1756 and June 1758 he taught music to John Bridger of Coombe Place (1733-1816) for half a guinea a month, in succession to John Baptist Malchair. Later well known for his teaching of both music and drawing in Oxford, Malchair had passed a year or so in Lewes while attached as a musician to the King's Own Dragoons. He made a few drawings (View 130) and perhaps encouraged the church organist's natural talent for drawing.

Music provided Lambert with only a secondary income. Around 1760 he was in business primarily as 'coach and sign-painter at the Golden Head in the Cliffe, Lewes', offering for sale artist's colours and equipment, maps and prints, printed books, writing-paper and books, writing accessories, fans, musical instruments and sundries, and framing. An engraved trade card used in 1764 mentioned embroidery materials and a wider range of painting: 'coach and sign painting, gilding, writing, escutcheons for funerals and hatchments.' In 1776 he was selling tickets for a concert and in 1777 lottery tickets. The retail business was maintained throughout his life, perhaps under the direction of his wife whom he had married in 1760, she being Mary (1736-1810), daughter of Francis Winton of Sompting, farmer; their one child died in infancy. After his death it was the stock-in-trade of 'bookseller, stationer, print-seller, and landscape painter' which was auctioned. If the workshop which Lambert junior bequeathed in 1799 had been taken over from his uncle, then the latter's shop was facing the Fair Place by St Thomas's Church.

Lambert sold paint for decorating the new vicarage at Glynde in 1760 and for the bridge at the Hooke, Chailey (View 50), in 1766. He worked on renewing the pews in St Thomas's Church in about 1754 and probably gilded the weathervane as well. John Bridger's boat he painted in 1758. In 1759-61 he refurbished the crier's staff, the town arms, the royal arms and other items for the Borough of Lewes, and in 1776/7 did work on the market house and its clock; in 1764 he painted the clock face at East Hoathly Church, and in 1773 a constable's stave for Bishopstone hundred. In 1764 he gilded the golden ball above the stables at Glynde and in 1776 the weathercock at Coombe Place. At the Hooke in Chailey, he or his nephew painted a bookcase in 1783 and a coach in the following year. Sir George Shiffner sent the nephew his coach in 1792, and was chasing progress a month later.[108] Many of the old inn signs, which were still remembered by the older inhabitants of Lewes in 1905 as the best of such productions, had been painted by Lambert in his early days. The royal arms still hanging in Hamsey and Eastbourne churches are credited to Lambert junior and dated 1772 and 1791, as also are royal arms of 1773 which were removed from the old Sessions House to the new County Hall in 1812 and an altar piece of 1774 at Friston. Another form of public art were the 'elegant designed transparent paintings' which Lambert put up in his windows to celebrate the result of the County Election in November 1774, depicting the successful candidates, the freeholders of the Cliffe who ventured to Chichester to cast votes for them and emblematical figures of Liberty, Peace and Plenty. Exceptional commissions came from Bishop Trevor as he transformed Glynde Place, where in 1766 Lambert cleaned and repaired three portraits, a large still-life, a picture of fowls and one of Mars and Venus, gilding all the frames as well. Further pictures were cleaned in 1768.

Despite Dunvan's assertion, Lambert almost certainly received instruction in conventional 'academic' painting from George Smith of Chichester (1713/14-76; View 25). His elder brother William Smith (*c.* 1707-64) was enabled by the 2nd Duke of Richmond's patronage to study with a portrait painter in London, and if George and John (*c.* 1717-64) did not benefit similarly, they could have learned from him and from working in London. In about 1750 George and John returned to Chichester and successfully painted still-life portraits and imaginary landscapes, selling both locally and in London.[109] Lambert was distantly related to the Smiths, a connection kept fresh by three of his Lambert uncles (one of them, like his father, a flax-dresser) living in or by Chichester. In 1775 George Smith, the longest lived of the three brothers, made Lambert, 'landscape painter', his executor and guardian of his three children, and at his own death Lambert owned paintings by all three Smiths, including their portrait by George and John.

The first evidence of Lambert as artist as distinct from artisan painter (or musician or stationer) comes from May 1762, with a distant view from Sompting, over the Adur estuary to the cliffs as far as Seven Sisters. Several of his early pictures were of that area, so perhaps he met Smith for instruction at his father-in-law's farm at Sompting.[110] Smith's earliest dated landscape is from 1753, so it is reasonable to see Lambert as an early disciple, within a decade and relatively innovative. When Lambert first exhibited in London in 1768, he did so at the Free Society of Artists, where George Smith had exhibited since 1761, and gave the same London address. One and possibly two of his exhibits in that year were 'from a picture of Mr George Smith'. The 42 pictures which Lambert exhibited, at the Free Society in 1768-73 and then the Royal Academy in 1774-8, divide into sixteen of sheep, seven of named places in Sussex (most of which can be identified with watercolour versions; two, of Lewes Castle, 1775, are catalogued as 'drawings'), eighteen landscapes (of which eleven with cattle and/or sheep) and one drawing from nature in black lead. Between 1769 and 1778 Lambert junior exhibited 22 portraits of flowers, fruit or cabbage (a genre also practised by George Smith), three of birds (two in watercolour), and a view of Brambletye. Most of their pictures were offered for sale.

Several pictures of animals survive in watercolour, like the plates engraved in 1797/8 after Lambert for the 1808 edition of the Revd Arthur Young's *General view of the agriculture of the county of Sussex*. 'Mr Bakewell's famous ram' exhibited in 1774 must have been commissioned by John Baker Holroyd of Sheffield Place who had hired a Dishley ram from Robert Bakewell at 25 guineas for the 1772 season, to cross with South Downs. Portraits of animals rather than people may have been what Mary Capper saw at Lambert's shop in 1782 and caused her to call him a portrait as well as a landscape painter.

Eight pictures in oils which are first and foremost landscapes have been firmly attributed to Lambert. They are of imaginary scenes such as: a river scene with thatched huts by a bridge over a weir; travellers resting, others crossing a weir, with a castle on a hill above the wooded river; and a lake or river in a wooded landscape with a thatched, timbered cottage to the right and cows in the foreground.[111] Six of the eight are dated, between 1767 and 1770. These conform closely to the characterisation of George Smith's landscapes, a synthesis of styles uniting elements of the (Claudean) pastoral and the (Dutch) picturesquely conceived rustic imagery, in their own way unpretentiously original. One of them is identical in composition to George Smith's 'River landscape' at Goodwood.

All the buildings in his oils were composites of what Lambert could see in Sussex. The building on a promontory is inspired by Herstmonceux and Brambletye. The timbered and thatched houses are paralleled by sketches at Henfield (1765 - View 110) and Glynde (1775). The people Lambert could have observed any day in the countryside around Lewes. Amongst the trees oaks predominate. They are prominent features, in the foreground, and carefully observed. But in the disposition of the components the pictures are Claudean, with (for the Sussex landscape) exaggerated height of outcrops over large riverine vistas. All eight contain wide expanses of water. In contrast to George Smith, Lambert pays less attention to particular subjects. Smith's frost scenes are justly famed; and his pictures tend to have purposeful rural activity in progress - picking hops or apples, gathering wood, extinguishing a chimney fire - even if no moral or story is intended. Such points of interest are lacking from Lambert's pictures. The people are usually travelling or resting. One watercolour, though, which does approach, for example, Smith's 'The Hop Pickers' in composition, is that of Southerham chapel (1780) which had become a cottage, with flowering shrubs to the right and a shepherd and sheep under a tree to the left (View 136).

One pupil of Lambert's is known. William Groombridge (1748-1811) lived at Goudhurst in Kent until 1773, had addresses in London in 1775-83, and removed to Canterbury before emigrating to the United States, probably in the early 1790s. He was exhibiting both landscapes and portrait miniatures in London in 1773-6, but only landscapes thereafter. One of only three known oils is very similar to Lambert's work, and in 1782 he exhibited 'a view in Plashett Park', as had Lambert in 1776, and in 1784 'Lewes Castle, sunset'. Around 1776 is the most plausible date for Lambert giving instruction. A pencil sketch of Lewes from the Wallands signed 'H. B. 1766' has enough features characteristic of Lambert to be by a youngster under his instruction.[112]

For Lambert, the high point of his artistic career was the award of a premium of 15 guineas by the (later Royal) Society of Arts. But this was not quite the distinction it appeared. The competition was for premiums of 50 and 25 guineas for the two best original landscapes on canvas, painted in England during 1769. There were seven anonymous entries before the Society's Polite Arts Committee which started by agreeing that only 30 guineas should be awarded as the first premium, then selected Lambert's picture for it, by seven out of eleven votes, and recommended the second premium of 25 guineas to the runner-up. But the Society in general meeting reversed these recommendations and reduced the second premium to 15 guineas. When the committee set about identifying the artists, it found that the winner had not followed the instructions for putting a secret mark on his canvas and the accompanying envelope, and duly disqualified him. Lambert received his 15 guineas, as the only premium awarded in that year's competition. Clearly the Society was dissatisfied with the standard of entries because it had already determined that the 1770 competition for landscape oils should be the last (although in fact a final award was to be in 1771).

Lambert's exhibited landscapes and animal pictures in oils comprise much of his recorded early work. Thus of some 45 images from the first decade of dated activity (1762-71), half are exhibition works. But the balance of his dated work shifted decisively towards the topographical from 1772, and he did not exhibit after 1778. The earliest dated topographical pictures are among the sketches in BL, Add. MS. 71714, six being dated 1762-6, but these may have been notes for imaginary landscapes (View

110). The small, semi-ruined and ivy-clad St James's Hospital and St Nicholas's Hospital in Lewes, dated to 1762 on later copies, would also have served that purpose well. A clutch of topographical views, all of Lewes and South Malling, however, are dated 1772 and may have been commissions from John Elliot for whom Lambert was working in early 1771.

Descriptive topographical work was generally well-established as an important landscape genre and, indeed, was quantitatively the dominant one. Lambert's topographical pictures reflect a growing market which he exploited with some success. They can be divided into three overlapping groups: house portraits for proud owners; pictures, both watercolours and engravings, of local sites for visitors to take away or for residents to display; and record pictures for serious antiquaries.

Rather than oils for grandees, the Lamberts painted houses in watercolours for, in the main, the middling gentry. The example reproduced here is Delves in Ringmer, the house of Henry Blunt (Views 156 and 157). Lambert produced first a pencil version for the client's approval. Several of these survive for larger houses, more finished than the sketch of Newick Charity School (View 145, by the nephew). A letter to John Elliot in February 1771 reveals how Lambert adjusted the preliminary sketch before starting on the final version, in this case of the view of Lewes Castle from the north which was to be exhibited at the Free Society of Artists that summer:[113]

I went to the Wallands twice to correct the Drawing I had formerly made of the Castle etc. I have now taken in more each way (viz.) to the end of the wall, on the left - and a little above the White Lion Lane to the right - which I doubt not but you will think a great improvement as it still keeps the Castle in the middle but it would not have a good effect if extended high enough to take in Mr Shelley's - nor farther to the left. I have therefore fixed on the size and have made a beginning on a canvas three feet long and two feet one inch high - which you may be assured I will not neglect for any other work. I will take a sketch from St Michael's churchyard at the first opportunity.

The second category, pictures of local sites for visitors to take home or for residents to display, are evidenced by several copies surviving of 'sights', such as the castle, the priory and the bridge in Lewes. The studio copy of a prospect of Rottingdean from the east indicates how the Lamberts worked. It is endorsed with a note that the view was taken for Lady Vernon, copied in smaller size on 9 October 1786, and again for Miss Gwinnett.

Five of these standard views - Lewes Castle from St Michael's churchyard, the Barbican from the south, Lewes Priory from the west and from the east, the Priory gateway - and three others - Lewes Castle from the Wallands (as commissioned by Elliot), Gundrada's tombstone and Pevensey Castle - were acquired by John Watson so that Basire might engrave them for his *Memoirs of the ancient earls of Warren and Surrey.* Basire exhibited three of them at the Royal Academy in 1779. Lambert junior may have produced for sale much more modest etchings of Lewes views. Also for a more popular market were the ten views by Lambert which Jasper Sprange had engraved for his *Tunbridge Wells guide,* bearing dates between 1782 and 1791. The six views of buildings in Kent were probably commissioned by Sprange. Related sketches are dated between 1780 and 1783, and the panoramic view of Tunbridge Wells, 1783, and views of the Rocks made in 1785-6, must be associated.

On his own account Lambert made only one, apparently unsuccessful, venture into publishing an engraving. In August 1765 he issued a proposal for 'a print of a view of

Brighthelmston and the Sea Coast as far as the Isle of Wight', of which drawings might be inspected at Messrs Baker's Circulating Library on the Steine. The print was to be subscribed for at 5s., or at a guinea with the opportunity to win a painting of the view on canvas, about five feet by three feet. Over a year later, in October 1766, he announced the print's publication but begged to be excused awarding the painting until the following summer, because of 'the whole subscription falling greatly short of the expense he has already been at for engraving and publishing' it.[114]

The 269 finished watercolours in Burrell's collection can roughly be divided between pictures which the Lamberts were able to copy from stock (or which they worked up more fully, in the hope of further orders, or which Burrell acquired at second hand) and pictures which Burrell commissioned and for which they did not anticipate a wider market. The division is broadly by subject matter, in the former category (about 100) castles, major residences and religious houses (generally ruined), in the latter category (about 170) churches and chapels (generally not). The former are larger and more often coloured, the latter smaller and almost invariably in grey wash. Work for Burrell began in earnest in autumn 1775, continued until 1784 and was never intensive over a long period. Perhaps a maximum of 50 or 60 finished pictures were produced in any one year (1777, 1782 and 1783). It seems that the basic commission was to draw the churches and chapels of Sussex. For an experienced artist like Lambert, perhaps aided by a camera obscura, a wash drawing of a country church would have been quickly completed.[115] Dated pencil sketches from 1775-6 in BL, Add. MS. 71714 do not reveal any obvious pattern of tours made to cover a defined locality. Maybe Lambert was paid for each completed picture, as and when he was able to produce it, and he sketched while travelling on other business.

The commissions for Burrell were not the only systematic antiquarian work which the Lamberts undertook. In 1775 Robert Hare ordered the stripping and partial demolition of the interior of Herstmonceux Castle, leaving the exterior as a picturesque ruin (see Views 112 and 113). Faced by the destruction of his ancestral home, which the family had sold in 1708, Lord Dacre employed the Lamberts to record it in '13 most capital drawings', for the considerable fee of 110 guineas. Copies were made for Lord Sheffield (John Baker Holroyd of Sheffield Place) and Thomas Wakeham (of the Hermitage, East Grinstead – View 95) and also for Burrell, by Grimm - who charged Gilbert White of Selborne only two and a half guineas a week. The sketches are measured perspective drawings, often with the dimensions on them, and are the work of Lambert junior at his best (see page 1).

Lambert's training - and first love in painting - was in landscapes in oils. But he did not achieve what the Smiths did, for they sufficiently established themselves in the London market to return to and work from Chichester where they also enjoyed the patronage of the Duke of Richmond's family. Dunvan acknowledged that Lambert was not cut out for the London art scene of the later 18th century: 'His natural modesty, and early habits of taciturnity in the cultivation of his favourite arts, gave a slowness and hesitation to his language, that, in the company of strangers, bordered on embarrassment.... Constitutional diffidence, and his partiality to rural manners and scenery, restrained him from seeking due encouragement for his talents in the metropolis.'[116] Dunvan predicted, seven years after his death, that in view of 'the improving taste of the age', Lambert's landscapes 'will yet rise very considerably in the public estimation.' But they did not provide a sufficient living. Unsold landscape oils, including the premium picture of 1770, were what the visitor to his shop saw on the walls. The expanding market for topographical pictures, touristic and antiquarian, provided a better living in the 1770s and '80s, though still not good enough to prevent the administration of his estate being granted to his creditors. It was with the old-fashioned term for a watercolourist, a limner, that the parish clerk recorded his burial. But it was as 'landscape painter' that his nephew commemorated him on his memorial plaque.

3.5 S. H. Grimm, topographical artist

The pictures by S. H. Grimm are arguably Burrell's greatest contribution to Sussex history. A large proportion of the documents from which he took notes have survived today and can be checked by historians (Document 7.2), but if the views had not been captured by Grimm's brush they would have been lost to us beyond retrieval.[117]

Samuel Hieronymus Grimm (1733-94) was baptised on 18 January 1733 at Burgdorf, Switzerland, the youngest of three children of Johann Jakob Grimm (d. 1749), a notary. In the 1750s he was a pupil of the painter Johann L. Aberli in Berne. As his first known professional work, in 1758 Grimm prepared views of glaciers in the Bernese Oberland for G. S. Gruner's *Die eisgebirge des Schweizerlandes* (1760), and the associated tour gave rise to a long narrative poem. These and other poems were published in 1762, as had been a eulogy to Frederick the Great of Prussia which appeared in Berlin in 1758. Though that was the limit of his own published literary efforts, his next venture was illustrating other men's writings, by working for Swiss publishers for ten years from 1764.

In or soon after August 1765, Grimm moved to Paris where he joined the circle of J. G. Wille, a leading engraver, whose studio was a place of cheerful comradeship. With other artists he made excursions in the vicinity of Paris and in 1766 a walking tour to sketch in Normandy. The surviving pictures are in watercolour, and indeed by this date Grimm had ceased to work in oils. France was only a staging post, for in February 1768 he left Paris for London. There he took lodgings with Mrs Susanna Sledge, a printseller at 1 Henrietta Street, Covent Garden, where he remained for the rest of his life. He never married.[118]

Of his life in England the evidence is almost exclusively his pictures. Written documentation is negligible. Only three letters from him are know to survive. He directed that his own papers should be destroyed after his death - all the more to be regretted, as in one of those letters he revealed how he seldom destroyed letters and frequently noted down in his pocket book the transactions of the day, by retrieving the details of the dispatch of five drawings to Richard Gough six months previously.[119] The only other surviving personal document is his will, printed here as Document 8. As the grant of probate named him as Samuel Jerome and as one letter is signed S. J., he may have been known to his friends as Jerome. In other contexts he was referred to as H. Grimm. He signed his pictures S. H. Grimm. An engraving reputedly of him shows a thick-necked man with fleshly features and wavy hair (reproduced on page 50).[120]

On his arrival in London he was absorbed into its artistic circles, probably associating with other Swiss immigrants. He exhibited at the Society of Artists within months and at the Royal Academy from the following year, continuously until 1781 and then in 1783-4 and 1793. Elected to the Society of Arts in November 1773, he was an active member on its Polite Arts Committee until 1777. Teaching he mentioned in passing in a letter, and Sophia Burrell's style suggests she had lessons from him.[121]

His artistic output in England fell into three categories. First, there was commercial work for engraving. He continued to work for Swiss publishers, and in London six satirical mezzotints by him appeared in 1771-4, as well as, for example, the frontispiece and vignettes to Francis Grose's *Antiquities of England and Wales*, 1 (1773). Some of the mezzotints were printed for his landlady in Henrietta Street. Secondly, various watercolours of Shakespearean, classical and genre scenes, and also topographical views around London, may have been made in the hope of their being taken up by publishers or of attracting orders for copies from private collectors. Thirdly, and most important, were commissioned watercolours of antiquities, historic buildings and landscapes.

In this last field he was well established from 1773. Some commissions were very specific. The Society of Antiquaries retained him on four occasions between 1779 and 1791 to copy Tudor paintings. Two clients wanted illustrations for their books, Gilbert White for his *Natural history and antiquities of Selborne* (1789), a month's work in 1776, including small assignments for several neighbours, and Henry Penruddocke Wyndham (1736-1819), with whom he travelled for three months in 1777, for the second edition of *A gentleman's tour through Monmouthshire and Wales* (1781). Lord Scarborough evidently commissioned views of his Yorkshire estates in 1781. Three 'worthy friends and employers' of many years' standing were named by Grimm in his will. Cornelius Heathcote Rodes (1755-1825) of Barlborough Hall in Derbyshire knew Grimm in 1773 and employed him from at latest 1780 and for several months in 1785, to sketch in the Chesterfield area. His work in Sussex for Burrell, resulting in nearly 900 finished watercolours, is considered below. Most significant of the three was Dr Richard Kaye (1736-1809) who, as the King's Sub-Almoner, commissioned pictures of the Maundy Ceremony in 1773 and gave Grimm frequent employment for the rest of his life. Kaye's collection, in British Library, Add. MSS 15537-48, runs to some 2500 finished pictures. The counties most represented reflect Kaye's succession of ecclesiastical preferments, in Nottinghamshire, the north-east and Lincolnshire, and, in 1788-90, tours during summer sojourns at West Country health resorts when Grimm acted as artist-companion.

Gilbert White's letters give some insight into the working life and methods of the topographical artist, at the whim of his clients (in this case a well-pleased one), and into contemporary opinion of Grimm's work. [122]

August 1775: 'Mr Grimm, the Swiss, is still in Derbyshire; and is to continue there and in Staffordshire 'til the end of the month. I have made all the enquiry I can concerning this artist, as it much behoves me to. Mr Thomas Mulso, and brother Thomas, and Benjamin, and Mr Lort have been to his lodgings to see his performances. They all agree that he is a man of genius; but the two former say he does hardly seem to stick enough to nature; and that his trees are grotesque and strange. Brother Benjamin seems to approve of him. They all allow that he excels in grounds, water, and buildings. Friend Curtis recommends a Mr Mullins, a worker in oil-colours.[123] Grimm, it seems, has a way of staining his scapes with light water-colours, and seems disposed much in scapes for light sketchings; now I want *strong lights and shades* and good trees and foliage.'

May 1776: 'At present I think of sending for Grimm about the beginning of July: I may employ him for perhaps a month. Mr Yalden of Newton then talks of taking him for a week to draw his house, and outlet; and then he is to go to Penruddocke Wyndham Esquire at Warnford. So he will have a good stroke of work. His price is two guineas and a half per week. His buildings, human figures, quadrupeds, waters, perspective among trees, are good; but his trees are not so pleasing: he has also a vein of humour, but I shall not allow him to call it forth, as all my plates must be serious. At the last Exhibition he produced some very good drawings.'

August 1776: 'Mr Grimm was with me just 28 days; 24 of which he worked very hard, and showed good specimens of his genius, assiduity, and modest behaviour, much to my satisfaction. He finished for me 12 views. He first of all sketches his scapes in lead-pencil; then he *pens* them all over, as he calls it, with Indian-ink, rubbing out the superfluous pencil-strokes; then he gives a charming shading with a brush dipped in Indian-ink; and last he throws a light tinge of water-colours over the whole. The scapes, many of them at least, looked so lovely in their Indian-ink shading, that it was with difficulty the artist could prevail on me to permit him to tinge them; as I feared those colours might puzzle the engravers: but he assured me to the contrary.' 'From me my artist went to Mr Yalden; and took a view of his house and outlet from the edge of his chalk-pit. The employer wanted and intended a view from the alcove; but the draughtsman as well as myself, objected much to the uniformity of that scene; so I carried G. to the chalk-pit, on the west side of the house, from whence he took a charming view. From Newton I carried G. to Lord Clanricarde's at Warnford; where in the gardens he took a perspective internal view, section, and elevation of a very curious old hall, or church unknown to the antiquaries, for a gentleman visiting there [i.e. Wyndham], who will one day oblige the world with this neglected and obscure curiosity, now a barn. It is supposed to have been built by King John: the order is Saxon.[124] From hence G. went to Winton [Winchester], to work there for a week or ten days on his own account; and is to call at Hartley on his return.'

November 1776: 'You need not wonder that the drawings you saw by Grimm did not please you; for they were 3s. 6d. pieces done for a little ready money: so there was no room for softening his trees, etc. He is a most elegant colourist; and what is more, the use of these fine natural stainings is altogether his own; yet his pieces were so engaging in Indian-ink that it was with regret that I submitted to have some of them coloured. Mr Wyndham of Sarum [Salisbury] has engaged Grimm next summer for eight or nine weeks in a tour round north and south Wales.'

Trained by a Swiss miniaturist and drawing directly from nature, Grimm worked better in a free, exact but lively style with careful detailing. But as a journeyman artist Grimm had to satisfy a variety of clients, and some wanted the English stained topographical drawing. That is what White wanted, and four weeks were taken to produce 12 pictures. Similar were some of the pictures for Rodes. A 1785 view of Creswell Crags has been described as 'in many ways a classic example of the "stained" or "tinted" drawing produced by the late eighteenth century topographer, in which careful pencil underdrawing and layers of grey wash (to indicate light and shade) were superimposed with "local" colour and pen outlines to clarify form. This careful and restrained style had evolved especially to suit the needs of the reproductive printmaker.' But Grimm's studio work did not compete with that of contemporaries such as Paul Sandby and Michael Angelo Rooker.[125] Towards the other extreme were most pictures for Kaye, in that they are smaller in size, in grey wash only, and strictly topographical without staffage added; and they also include pictures of people and activities, such as local customs, seen on the road. The work for Burrell falls in between. Some are large and highly finished pieces, the majority small with at most blue and brown colour washes added, as views worked up from sketches in the field, including almost invariably one or two people at work.

Grimm died of a mortification of the bowels on 14 April 1794, at the house of William Wellings, engraver, in Tavistock Street, Covent Garden, and was interred on the 18th at St Paul's Covent Garden where Kaye conducted the funeral. His will

(Document 8) suggests thrifty and far from affluent living, perhaps in only one or two rooms. He was worth £300 in British funds, a family legacy which had been carefully conserved and was returned to the family in Berne. Whatever the sale of his drawings and few personal possessions yielded was to be divided between his landlady Susanna Sledge and, if he had lived, his executor John Webber RA (1752-93). His intense modesty was reflected in his instruction for his papers to be destroyed and for the plates of his engravings to be defaced and sold for the copper. Kaye had hoped to collect anecdotes of Grimm's life from his annual pocket books, but found that the person acting for Mrs Sledge had complied with 'Grimm's modest request'.[126]

About 500 of his drawings were sold by auction in July 1795. Presumably at that sale Richard Gough was the purchaser of the 'old book in folio bound in marbled paper with green strings, consisting mostly of sketches from nature, or copies from my sketches from nature, kept loose between the leaves ranged according to counties', and that was the source of the 236 Grimm drawings which Gough bequeathed to the Bodleian Library. The only other sizeable collection of Grimm's views are 120 at the University of Bristol, in a copy of the 1817-30 edition of Dugdale's *Monasticon* bearing the bookplate of John Jebb, DD, FRS, Bishop of Limerick (1775-1833). These views, however, carry cross-references, possibly in Burrell's hand, to the first edition of *Monasticon*, giving rise to the speculation that they were removed from Burrell's interleaved copy which had been auctioned after his death.[127]

Grimm was well-established when Burrell first employed him, as 'the very eminent artist' to copy the Lamberts' survey pictures of Herstmonceux (Document 6.1). That was in 1778. In 1775 Burrell had started to employ the Lamberts in earnest and continued to do so until 1784. From 1780 Burrell regularly employed Grimm as well. Necessarily the arrangements were different. The Lamberts were Sussex residents, working almost exclusively in the county for many clients, each on a small scale, and already with a stock of local views. The Lamberts may have worked for Burrell around other commissions. In 1780, when Burrell had done the great bulk of his reading, archival research and church visiting, he may have felt that the Lamberts' rate of progress was too slow and a more systematic approach was needed. So the Lamberts were allowed to continue for a few more years, but in addition Grimm was hired to tour the county for a fortnight or so each year from Whitsun, from 1780 until 1791, except 1786, though he happened to be at Cowdray that year, copying the Coronation Procession of Edward VI for the Society of Antiquaries. For at least part of each tour in 1780-4 and 1787 Grimm was accompanying Burrell.

This annual timing we know because, of the 236 drawings by Grimm in Gough's collection, 143 are of Sussex and 135 of those are dated to the day.[128] What Gough acquired were field-sketches, certainly started in the open air and presumably completed as far as necessary the same day. Some carry notes on the history and present use of the building, Brede Place, for example, 'formerly the mansion of the Oxenbrigge's, now inhabited by poor labourers' (View 28). The sketches were fair copied back in London and passed to Burrell. Burrell left 888 pictures (of monuments and architectural features, as well as of buildings), so Grimm was completing an average of 80 a year. Combining the drawings dated to the day in Gough's collection with those dated to the same year in Burrell's collection (and inferring the year for some undated) reveals his itinerary and allows an estimate of how many drawings he made. In 1781, for example, as shown on the map on page 108, Grimm travelled from London to Rusper (making 1 drawing; Burrell was also there) and Horsham (5 at the church) on Saturday 2 June, the following day being Whitsunday, to Steyning (5) and

Wiston (6) on Monday, returning to Steyning for the night, then through West Tarring (2), Goring (1) and Lyminster (1), to Arundel (10, continuing work on the castle started the previous year) where he stayed Tuesday and Wednesday nights, passing through Slindon (2) to reach Boxgrove Priory (15) on Thursday, continuing to sketch there on Friday. The next date is Thursday 14 June, but probably all that week was spent in Chichester (28), with a side-trip to Halnaker House (3) on the Friday, before departure north and east, perhaps on Monday 18 June through West Dean (2), Cowdray (2 of the exterior: the interior was to be drawn the following year) and Tillington (1) to Petworth (where he had sketched the previous year) - a total of 84 drawings over 13 working days. Ten of these are reproduced here.

With Grimm working at this pace and making fair copies later, without the opportunity to check details on site, he can be expected to have made mistakes. Thus, his views of the Great Court at Halland show that in his view of the north-west front a gable was misplaced from one side of the court to another (View 115). The spacing of the windows on Ditchling Church does not concur with later pictures by artists with a closer interest in church architecture (View 67). Several of his compass orientations have been found to be wrong (those for Herstmonceux Place have been corrected in Views 112 and 113). Another source of error arose when the finished pictures were mounted in volumes. Grimm's pictures for Dr Kaye show that he usually identified the subject on the back. Burrell had his pictures trimmed, pasted down and surrounded with watercolour borders, before any caption was added. The contents page in each volume was presumably a check list made before the information on the backs was hidden. Bridge House in Cuckfield, View 62, seems to have been the victim of Burrell's clerk reading 'Slough Green' as 'Slaugham Green', Slaugham being a name which he knew, of a parish adjacent to Cuckfield.

Churches and chapels made up a smaller proportion than in the Lamberts' work for Burrell, though still amounted to 282 out of 888 pictures. However, almost all the Lamberts' pictures were general exterior views, whereas Grimm's total is inflated by some 165 drawings of interior details and fittings, mainly funerary monuments, quite often with several views of the same one. Clearly Grimm knew which churches the Lamberts had already drawn, as there is little duplication. An instruction to draw any church not already in Burrell's collection would have been straightforward, as likewise the remains of religious houses known from Dugdale's *Monasticon* and the castles and hill-forts from other published literature. Major sites could receive careful attention. Pevensey Castle rated as many as 29 sectional views.

Houses were selected for drawing primarily because they were or had been occupied by landowning families. Who those families were, Burrell knew from his documentary research, from enquiry during his earlier tours and from correspondence with the clergy. When, for example, he met with Lewes lawyer William Michell in 1777, Burrell could doubtless have found out who were the landowners, and where they lived, for a goodly portion of eastern Sussex. For the south of the county, the four sheets of map by Thomas Yeakell and William Gardner published in 1778-83 must have helped in planning routes. Grimm produced pictures of some 200 country houses or large village houses, many of them belonging to middling landowners and professional gentlemen, of fairly recent build and aesthetically or architecturally of no particular distinction. Though the homes of the mass of people feature at most in the occasional view of a village street (such as Jevington, *Sussex views*, 88), the collection has a breadth of scope missing from the remaining body of pictorial material produced before the mid-19th century.

One suspects that Grimm was instructed to concentrate on the buildings - and that trees which obtruded into the view of the frontage were left out, and maybe the creepers on it as well. Trees and shrubs do tend neatly to frame Grimm's buildings, and formal gardens adjacent to the house are rarely to be seen. Although the fashion by the 1780s was for naturalistic layouts after the style of Capability Brown, it is hard to credit that the parterres and formal planting of earlier generations had been so extensively rooted out.

In Grimm's lifetime, 18 of his Sussex views (and four of his copies of Lambert's views of Herstmonceux Castle) were engraved and published in Grose's *Antiquities of England and Wales* (Document 4). A few days before his death the Society of Antiquaries bought his views of Cowdray, by then a charred ruin, and in 1796 it published six plates in *Vetusta monumenta*. Burrell allowed Grimm to make copies of views of Pevensey Castle for Edward King who included 10 in his *Munimenta antiqua; or, Observations on antient castles* in 1801.[129] Once Burrell's collections were in the British Museum the views were readily accessible to copyists and several were engraved for the county histories which appeared from 1815 onwards.

S. H. Grimm, from an engraving without title, signature or date. Courtauld Institute of Art, Witt Library

4. Sights for the tourist, tomes for the learned

4.1 The quest for scholarship, for the picturesque and for scientific knowledge

To some of Burrell's contemporaries, his efforts must have appeared deficient on one or other of three counts: either by falling short of the progressive scholarly standards and techniques, by lack of aesthetic awareness in perception of antiquities or by being narrowly antiquarian and genealogical.

As to scholarship, Craven Ord thought Burrell did not know what to observe in a church. In a similar vein, Gough's opinion of Francis Grose's drawings was reflected by the correspondent in 1772 for whom 'Mr Grose's first number had some picturesque merit; but his views are too small to give any satisfaction to the Gothic architect.' The point was that the majority of antiquaries had little interest in architectural analysis, but a few were attempting it from the 1760s. There had also been a drastic decline in the quality of topographical draughtsmanship since the mid-17th century, the engraved work of the Bucks, for example, being far inferior to that of Hollar.

As the Director of the Society of Antiquaries for 26 years from 1771 and a prolific writer, Richard Gough (1735-1809) was highly influential in the development of antiquarian studies. In 1769 he called for a closer study of the Gothic style, aided by accurate and detailed drawing, and carried forward this project through the Society.[130] He toured Sussex in 1757 and 1767. The list of sites he noted in the more extended, 1767, tour is close to Jeremiah Milles's: Chichester Cathedral, Cowdray and the pictures (Petworth's pictures he may have listed in 1757), monuments in Midhurst Church, Arundel Castle and monuments in the church, Steyning Church, Bramber Castle, at Lewes the castle, St Michael's, St Anne's, the Magnus inscription and the priory, Alfriston's Star Inn and barrows towards Eastbourne, Pevensey Castle, Battle Abbey and Rye Church. He published some notes on Alfriston in the *Gentleman's Magazine*. His descriptions are generally more detailed than earlier ones, and are notable for recording architectural features and building chronology, for example at Steyning: 'The church stands at some distance, completely Saxon in its exterior, consisting of a body with aisles, and a choir and west square thick embattled tower of square stones and flints alternately disposed in chequerwork. The clerestory windows of the nave round Saxon arches unornamented. The south aisle has a buttress quite of the Saxon style, a flat square pilaster with round pillars at the sides. In the point of the south porch an old head stuck in V under it "1766". Four round arches on each side of the nave with dentals and zigzag and these capitals [*sketch*]. The aisles and choir in a later style.' He also made observations of more contemporary matters, for example in 1757 that the bathing machines at Brighton were less commodious, and the way to them less private, than at Margate.

Gough summarised 'twenty years of journeying, and a longer term of reading and enquiry' in his edition of Camden's *Britannia* published in 1789. For his additions on Sussex to the 1607 edition he made no acknowledgement to others. Over 15 large folio pages he mixed historical and contemporary information, arranged topographically along the coast from west to east and then across the Weald to Horsham, but in the absence of a county history this was a more thorough collation of knowledge and opinion, carefully referenced, than anywhere else then in print. In the 1806 edition, the additions ran to 28 pages, not by reason of further personal observations, rather by the insertion of reference to recent research. 'A description of the Roman military works in the neighbourhood of Chichester in Sussex 1798' by William Sabatier is reproduced at length.[131]

Gough's text did not reflect any significant advance in Sussex archaeology. Roman discoveries at Chichester and Eastbourne early in the century have already been noticed, as have the finds from barrows on the Downs which Stephen Vine reported in the 1760s. Sussex seems not to have experienced the scale of excavation as eastern Kent did, where Brian Faussett (1720-76) opened over 600 graves and burial-mounds between 1757 and 1773. James Douglas (1753-1819) added another 100 which he opened while, as an Army captain, supervising construction of fortifications at Chatham Lines around 1780. These, however, he recorded much more carefully and, with access to Faussett's collections, he published in 1786-93 *Nenia Britannica or, A sepulchral history of Great Britain from the earliest period to its general conversion to Christianity*. This book constitutes a significant advance in archaeological technique, in its scientific consideration of the observed facts, but it was not readily accepted for what it was by contemporary antiquarian and literary opinion. It is T. W. Horsfield, in his *History of Sussex* (1835; Essay 4.4 below), who is credited with first announcing its true value: 'Up to this period no general attempt had been made to acquire the knowledge of the early inhabitants of our country which the tumuli were so likely to afford; and although accounts of particular barrows had been previously published, no extensive plan had been adopted by which the value of the discoveries and the generalisation of their results could be obtained.'

Nevertheless, Douglas having left the Army for the Church, it must have been his scholarly reputation - not just in antiquities but also in Flemish paintings - which caused the Earl of Egremont to present him to the (small) living at Middleton which he held from 1799. He lived at Petworth from 1799 to 1803, exploring 50 burial mounds on Bignor Hill and 15 above Lavington and uncovering a bath and part of a mosaic floor of the Roman villa at Bignor. He returned to Sussex under the patronage of the Duke of Norfolk in 1809, residing at Barnham and then at Arundel until 1812 when he accepted a curacy at Preston with the chaplaincy to the troops at Brighton. In 1809 he excavated a ship barrow on Rewell Hill. In June 1812, with several dilettante friends - and labourers from the 10th Royal Hussars - he explored 20 to 30 barrows at Saltdean near Brighton: 'The center I broke into; but time did not allow of a satisfactory ransack.' His excavation of a barrow near Brighton Church in August 1815 was witnessed by the artist Benjamin Robert Haydon (View 30), and of some others on 4 March by the Revd John Skinner:

Breakfasted with Rice, afterwards accompanied him, Mr Douglas, and Schofield to a spot about three miles from Brighton, in order to open some of the small barrows, having previously sent forward workmen for the purpose. In the course of the morning we laid open three, and found they contained, each, a skeleton of a large size. but no ornaments or warlike instruments. Returning at 5, I dressed, and went to dinner with Dr Holland.

Douglas's own notes identified these as amongst 17 barrows, at 'Balls down', presumably Balsdean in Rottingdean, seven of which he had opened two years earlier, and recorded that: 'Two soldiers of the 18th Dragoons quartered at [Rottingdean] on outpost duty in November 1814 opened two - one of the men having been my labourer, conceiving I had been digging for treasure, clandestinely opened one of the largest, which contained female ornaments of some value.' His final fieldwork was in 1818 on the Roman villa site at West Blatchington which he briefly reported in the *Gentleman's*

Magazine. In that year he published the only paper arising from his barrow digging on the Sussex Downs. It was the first synthetic study of Sussex archaeology since Tabor's paper of a century before, and he made important points about the relative dating of field monuments and about multi-period occupation of earthworks. But these observations were not appreciated for many years ahead. Returning to Brighton in 1821, Skinner could find no gentleman in the neighbourhood who took an interest in archaeological finds; rather he heard reports of how urns had been discarded after Douglas's death. Sussex's first major excavation was to be of the Bignor villa, started in 1811 under the direction of Samuel Lysons and lavishly published in 1815.[132]

But antiquities in general and ruined medieval buildings in particular evoked more widespread enthusiasm for an aesthetic response which was not necessarily compatible with a concern for stylistic and archaeological analysis. Here the arbiter of taste was the Revd William Gilpin (1724-1804), whose first discussion of landscape aesthetics, *Dialogue upon the gardens ... at Stow*, dated from 1748. This he followed with accounts of his tours through Britain in search of 'picturesque beauty', the best known being those through wild, 'sublime', scenery: the River Wye, the Lake District, the Highlands of Scotland. But he also travelled lowland England. His *Observations on the coasts of Hampshire, Sussex, and Kent* were made on a brief tour from his home in Cheam, Surrey, in late May 1774, though were only published 30 years later, with some softening of his judgements. He admired the wooded western Downs, but not the barren Downs further east: 'If the hills were not chalky, Lewes would be a pleasant town. It is clean and well-built: but the chalk disfigures any landscape.' In his *Essay on picturesque beauty* (1792), he illustrated two versions of landscape, one smoother and rounded, typical chalk scenery, which he pronounced 'ugly' and 'disgusting', while the other, broken and varied, was accounted admirable to the eye. One wonders whether he was deliberately contradicting Gilbert White's observation of 1773 from Ringmer, published in 1789: 'I think there is something peculiarly sweet and amusing in the shapely figured aspect of chalk-hills in preference of those of stone, which are rugged, broken, abrupt and shapeless.' The shift in perception had already been advanced by landscape gardening in the style of 'Capability' Brown which prompted planting on the Downs, as on Chanctonbury Ring in 1760 and in Stanmer Park. Such planting may also have met the objection voiced by Peter Oliver (1713-91), former Chief Justice of Massachusetts, visiting Brighton in 1776: there were fine walks for miles over the Downs, but 'trees are much wanted' as 'the sun beats too hot for a walk unless [one] could meet with cooling shades.'[133]

Lewes Castle (View 130) for Gilpin provided an object-lesson for the antiquary:

It is not in itself an unpicturesque fragment; but some busy hand has been employed in making hanging gardens around it, and adding other decorations, which only discover how much the improver missed his aim by trying to show his taste. It is among the first principles which should guide every improver, that all contiguous objects should suit each other, and likewise the situation in which they are placed. A modern building admits modern improvement, a ruin rejects them. This rule, though founded in nature, and obvious to sense, is scarcely ever observed. Wherever we see a ruin in the hands of improvement, we may be almost sure of seeing it deformed.

But you say, a ruin may stand as an ornament in an improved scene.

It may: but it must appear that the improved scene does not belong to the ruin, but the ruin got accidentally into the improvement. No improvement, however, should come within the precincts of the ruin. Deformities alone may be removed: and if the ruin retire into some sequestered place, and is seen only through trees, or rising above some screening wood, its situation would be better, than if it stood a glaring object in full sight.

The same applied to Battle Abbey: 'This abbey is converted into a modern dwelling (the seat of Sir W. Webster) which has been the cause of a second dissolution. The mixture of old building, and new, is something like the barbarous cruelty we read of uniting living bodies to the dead.' See View 3 for his comment on Arundel Castle.[134]

The third contemporary development to which Burrell did not respond was the quest for scientific knowledge, in relation to either contemporary conditions or natural history. It is striking that Burrell's Scottish tour reflects an interest in contemporary economic and social conditions and that William Hayley's scheme for a county history included 'the nature and properties of the county: its face or appearance; soil; produce or natural commodities; manufactures' and 'manufacture, its rise, progress and improvement' in each parish. Indeed the model for county histories from the later 17th century embraced those topics and 'natural history' in the widest sense. Yet Burrell's collection was narrowly focused on the antiquarian and genealogical - just at a time when there was a resurgence in interest in localised economic conditions. This interest is best represented in Sussex by the 'farmer's tours' of Arthur Young (1741-1820) and his son the Revd Arthur Young (1769-1827). Their principal interest was agricultural improvement, and that took them away from the coastal and river-gap towns and the conventional tourist route. The detailed diaries which they published amount to the largest body of printed descriptions of Sussex in the 18th century. In additional Young senior encouraged progressive farmers to report their observations in his periodical *The Annals of Agriculture*, in which appeared no fewer than 63 articles on Sussex topics between 1784 and 1806.[135]

Young senior's first recorded visit to Sussex, in 1770, was just when John Baker Holroyd was starting to improve his newly-purchased estate of Sheffield Place in Fletching - from which he took, in 1781, his title as Baron Sheffield. Their principal common interest was Southdown sheep. The other visits on that tour were to Newick Place (View 145); the Hooke in Chailey (View 50); Walberton; Bignor Park (View 19); the Chichester area; and Easton Farm near Sidlesham.

Returning from France in October 1788 Young senior stayed at Sheffield Place. He visited again, particularly to look at sheep and cattle, in December and January, received an introduction to John Ellman and met other farmers in and around Glynde. He then went east to Battle, Beauport Park and Hastings, presumably drumming up contributions to the *Annals*, as five from eastern Sussex appeared in 1789. Probably early in 1790 he stayed at Sheffield Place while buying cattle and visited Glynde and Beddingham again, and in October 1791 he was Ellman's guest at Lewes sheep fair where he met more of the progressive Sussex farmers and travelled as far west as Coombes in the Adur valley. On a visit in December 1792 Sheffield introduced him to George, 3rd Earl of Egremont (1751-1837) at Petworth. Egremont was extremely wealthy and, showing little interest in London political and social life, was all the better placed to spend heavily on improvements to his estates, on philanthropy and artistic patronage. Young met several tenant farmers in the neighbourhood, as well as two other noble proprietors, Lord Montague at Cowdray and the Duke of Richmond at Goodwood.

When the Board of Agriculture and Internal Improvement was established in 1793, the elder Young became its Secretary and secured for his son the commission to report on the agriculture of Sussex. Young junior graduated that year, was ordained deacon in May and found a curacy near the family home. His father's tours and contacts clearly moulded the route he took. Setting out from Bradfield in Suffolk he viewed Mr Clutton's farm at Cuckfield and reached Sheffield Place on 11 August 1793. As his arrival clashed with a militia review he was recommended immediately to Thomas Kemp of Conyboro in Barcombe (View 12) and George Allfrey of Friston (View 90), as well as to Ellman. He also visited Sir John Bridger at Hamsey and five other sheep-farmers on the Downs between Lewes and Eastbourne. Proceeding eastwards through Westham and Hellingly, he included (as had his father in 1789) visits to Mayo of Battle, Murray of Beauport Park and Milward of Hastings. Going as far as Winchelsea he collected data on flocks on Romney Marsh, then doubled back through Robertsbridge to visit Carr and Davies of Beddingham and other farmers in that vicinity. His next stop was some 20 miles west with Thomas Ellman (cousin of John) at New Shoreham and Francis Gell nearby. He called on William Frankland at Muntham in Findon (View 83); and though failing to find Sir Richard Hotham at Bognor (View 17) he visited several farms on the coastal plain and the Selsey peninsula. After an excursion to Portsmouth and the Isle of Wight, he visited Bosham, viewed the Duke of Richmond's farm at Goodwood and met several tenants before making a brief visit to the Earl of Egremont at Petworth which he left for home on 15 October.

His published account of the tour was dated five days later at Bradfield and extended to some 75,000 words or equivalent in tables. A summary appeared as the *General view of the agriculture of the county of Sussex, with observations on the means of its improvement*, along with a map and brief description of the soils of Sussex, the first to have been published, though, as he admitted, superficial and imperfect, as the subject required the attention of those with intimate local knowledge.

Authorised to prepare a revised report, he planned to describe Egremont's farming experiments, and was at Petworth in June 1793. He visited Glynde in January 1797 and published at least two flattering pieces on Egremont early that year. He attended the Petworth cattle show in November 1797. His father visited Sussex on at least five occasions in 1794-9, and in the autumn of 1800 he passed from Petworth through Horsham and Worth to Buxted and Mayfield collecting material on the effects of enclosure. Thereafter no further visits by either to Sussex are evident, and the son spent most of 1805-20 in Russia. The manuscript of the revised report probably left Young junior's hands in 1799. 'Corrected and improved' by his father, it was published in 1808.

Young junior was one of those frequent (or long-stay) guests to whom Egremont was so generous and of whom, 20 years later, the painter J. M. W. Turner was only the most famous. Another agricultural writer, William Marshall (1745-1818), had been one such in 1791. Receiving an unexpected invitation he was based at Petworth for several months making excursions to the near parts of Sussex, Surrey and Hampshire. These he wrote up in 1797 and published in 1798, with effusive tributes to Egremont. Egremont also enabled the Revd Robert Ferryman to set up at Petworth in 1796-7 his museum of British quadrupeds and birds which had previously been displayed in London. Two years later he equipped a scientific laboratory (as had Richmond at Goodwood in 1790), but the locality was neither a focus nor a source for these initiatives.[136]

While Sheffield and Egremont were leaders of agricultural improvement in east and west Sussex, the 3rd Duke of Richmond's distinctive contribution to useful knowledge at this period was the patronage of mapmaking. From 1758 he employed Thomas Yeakell (d. 1787), of Dutch or German origin, as a surveyor, and also gave much work to William Gardner (c. 1739-1800). From 1770 Yeakell and Gardner were in private practice together, and in 1778 they issued the first of eight planned sheets of a map of Sussex at two inches to the mile. It has been called 'the most important of all Sussex maps. It marks the start of the new era of scientific trigonometrical survey', and 'a masterpiece of cartographic design, representational method, and engraving.' Although only the four southerly sheets were issued over five years, that was due only partly to shortage of subscribers, for in 1784 both surveyors were in government service, Richmond by then being the Master-General of the Ordnance who oversaw the foundation of the Ordnance Survey in 1791. With Thomas Gream, in 1795 Gardner issued a simplified map for the whole county at one inch to the mile.[137]

Antiquarian activity came late to Sussex, and the same is even truer for natural history. Only in the person of William Markwick of Catsfield (1740-1813) do we first encounter systematic botanical and ornithological recording, from 1768 to 1793. That overlapped with the observations of Gilbert White (1720-93) when visiting his aunt Rebecca Snooke at Ringmer in most years between 1765 and 1779 (Views 156 and 157). Markwick's naturalist's calendars were used for comparison with White's in the 1802 edition of *The natural history of Selborne*. Before Markwick's 1791 paper on migration, there were only four published references to observations of birds in Sussex. His 'Aves Sussexiensis, or A catalogue of birds found in the county of Sussex' was read to Linnean Society in May 1795 and published in 1798.[138] At least from 1790, the Lewes draper Thomas Woollgar (1761-1821) was actively recording plants and contributed to C. Milne and A. Gordon's *Indigenous botany* (1793). The young gentleman William Borrer (1781-1862) was recording around Henfield and provided the list of Sussex species for Dawson Turner and Lewis Weston Dillwyn's *Botanist's guide* (1805); his herbarium is at Kew. Woollgar has been called 'Borrer's earliest assistant in botany', though he was clearly active before Borrer was. Thomas Furley Forster (1761-1825) and his two brothers from Walthamstow in Essex were collecting plants in the vicinity of Tunbridge Wells from the late 1780s, and they are said to have provided the lists of plants for Gough's edition of Camden's *Britannia* (1789). Records of climate were a component of the naturalist's calendar; a scarce instance of more extensive meteorological observations in 18th-century Sussex exists in a diary kept in 1769-70 by Dr John Bayly of Chichester (1735-1815).[139]

Nor was there any more activity in the field of geology. Only one informed observer has been identified before the end of the 18th century, an anonymous visitor in 1740 who wrote a few paragraphs while in Sussex, for example:[140]

At Godstone is got a very fine white hard free stone; and almost the same kind lies in a vast bed at East Grinstead but not so good. The same kind I saw in many places quite to Hastings where the cliffs are nearly perpendicular containing 5 strata of fine sandstone hard and very thick, 8, 10 or 12 foot apiece separated with a like quantity of smaller strata or rather more so as to make the large beds of stone farther asunder in some places than their own diameter. These when lying in the sea are much harder, and there lie several abrupt shelves of rocks in the sea dipping from the land, the more sloping the farther they are from the shore. The cliff seems about 60 yards high.

Gilbert White's observation in 1771 that there were 'few petrifactions [fossils] about Ringmer and Lewes' reflected the little attention given to Sussex's geology, and it was only in the early years of the next century that it was explored in any detail. That happened through the accident of the brothers Benjamin and John Farey being dismissed from their posts with the Duke of Bedford at Woburn, Bedfordshire, in 1802. Benjamin found employment with the Earl of Chichester at Stanmer (View 175) and

John (1766-1826) visited him there in the summer of 1806 and in February 1807. John Farey had met William Smith (1769-1839) in 1801 when Bedford engaged him to carry out drainage work and became interested in Smith's ideas on stratigraphy, the principles of which he applied in excursions from Stanmer. Sir Joseph Banks, President of the Royal Society, was convinced of the significance of Smith's methodology of correlating strata on the basis of unique fossils found within them, and paid Farey's expenses in preparing a section on the line of the road from London to Brighton; this was ready by August 1807. 'Farey recorded the stratigraphic sequence in incredible detail, as well as the anticlinal or "denuded" structure of the area and introduced a series of 25 faults between the North and South Downs, many of which have been confirmed by later geological surveying where he placed them.' Entering into public debate on the search for coal at Bexhill, he had less success in promoting the new science. His antagonist, Lewes schoolmaster and surveyor Cater Rand (1749-1825), had a wide interest in the sciences, as reflected in the books he owned and the Lewes Library Society bought at his suggestion. But he seems to have collected only chance observations of strata and not to have undertaken any systematic study.[141]

In May of the following year, 1808, William Smith was engaged as consultant surveyor to the Upper Ouse Navigation for its extension from Freshfield Bridge to Upper Ryelands Bridge. He also worked on the link to John Rennie's proposed Grand Southern Canal. Smith's diaries record over 20 visits to the works down to April 1812. Many years later he wrote that 'In searching for stone to build the locks and bridges, and by various geological excursions, I became acquainted with the strata, and collected many of the Sussex fossils.... [I was] sufficiently well acquainted with the stratification to draw its great outlines' on a county map published in 1819, the same year as his cross-section of the Wealden strata appeared. In the interval between his two periods of residence in Sussex, 1803-9, while Vicar of Kenton in Suffolk, James Douglas had been introduced to Smith and had been impressed by Smith's system. In late 1809, he was arranging from Barnham for fossils from Cuckfield to be sent to William Cunnington, another supporter of Smith, so it is likely that Douglas and Smith were in contact in Sussex. But the young surgeon Gideon Mantell (1790-1852) was the first Sussex resident to grasp the significance of Smith's ideas and also to apply them, publishing two articles in the *Sussex Weekly Advertiser* in 1812 and 1813 on strata around Lewes. His first major work, *The fossils of the South Downs*, appeared in 1822.[142]

4.2 Guidebooks and urban histories

The local historical research of the 1760s to 1780s had, in the short term, little impact beyond the circle of those directly involved and, after Burrell's collection was available there, readers in the British Museum Library. There were however other ways in which interest in Sussex and its history and antiquities was being expressed, particularly in connection with the burgeoning seaside resorts. These resorts created a market for guidebooks which not only extolled the attractions of the resort but also often described places to visit in the neighbourhood. They directed visitors into the interior, to sights and sites away from the well-established tour through the county following the coast, and, even if the information was slight, brought further antiquities to common knowledge.

The first such guide bearing on Sussex was Thomas Benge Burr, *The history of Tunbridge Wells* (1766), which described places of interest within 12 miles of the spa. Doubtless influenced by Gilpin, Burr was willing to make firmer aesthetic judgements than, for example, Jeremiah Milles in 1743 (Document 3), even if always favourable. For example, in a picturesque vein, he said of Bayham Abbey: 'the ruins of Bayham are kept in very good order by the present proprietor, John Pratt esquire, nephew of the Right Honourable Lord Camden. This gentleman has lately built a very neat house upon the spot in the gothic manner, which judiciously preserves an uniformity of effect, through the whole of this venerable scene.' Amongst sights newly introduced to the tourist was Buckhurst old mansion which 'has been so totally neglected, that it is now almost entirely gone to decay; though, it is said, its ruins are still well worth the inspection of the admirers of ancient architecture, and one tower in particular is much talked of in the country.' In his Tunbridge Wells guide first published in 1780, Jasper Sprange offered 'a short description of every place, building, or antiquity, within the circumference of sixteen miles. For the perfection of which, the most valuable materials have been collected from authentic records, the best esteemed authors, and the venerable repositories of ancient manuscripts searched, to present the public with a copious detail of historical facts.' Even if archival research is not much in evidence, he did cultivate the picturesque, on, for example, Rose Hill in Brightling (View 29): [143]

The house, which is ancient and large, is situated on a fine hill.... It is surrounded with woods and downs in a beautiful variety: from it you have a most extensive prospect, commanding a fine view of the Sussex coast, enriched by the constant motion of the vessels, whose swelling canvas courts the rising breeze, and delights the eye of the spectator.... The vales encompassing it are adorned with woods, meadows, hop-grounds, cornfields, towns and villages, so beautifully intermingled, as though art has conspired with nature to make everything appear grand and irregularly beautiful.

James Royer's guide to Eastbourne (1787) offered tours to Battle in one direction and to Newhaven in the other, which the author had clearly taken himself. To Pevensey Castle there was now organised guiding: 'The schoolmaster at Pevensey [John Christian] is a proper person to describe the particulars of this noble castle and country; but lest it should not be in his power to do so, or it may not be agreeable to have such kind of information, that description is given here.' Though by this time, authors were copying from existing guidebooks, J. Stell's *Hastings guide* of 1794 filled in the delights of the eastern corner of the county. The Revd John Evans, a resident of Islington but visitor to Worthing, covered the coast between Shoreham and Littlehampton and the adjoining Downland parishes. In the west of the county, Cowdray was the first stately home to have its own guide, in the form of a catalogue of the pictures published in 1777, and Alexander Hay produced the first edition of his *Chichester guide* in 1783, with expanded coverage of neighbouring places in the second edition of 1794.[144]

Easily the best early guide for the whole county with an antiquarian slant was the Sussex section by Frederic Shoberl (1775-1853) in *The beauties of England and Wales*, which appeared in 1813 and was also published separately as a 200-page book. Shoberl had recently travelled in Sussex, had consulted Burrell's notes and in his coverage of the towns and larger houses was more comprehensive and careful than any previous writer. He also included a thorough 'List of the principal books, maps, and views, that have been published in illustration of the topography, antiquities, &c. of the County of Sussex.'

The guidebooks cut into the market for travelogues such as had appeared in the earlier 18th century. Those of the later 18th century which are significant as historical records tend to be specialised, two of which have been mentioned in the previous section, the farmer's tours of the two Arthur Youngs and William Gilpin's picturesque tour. Thomas Pennant's *Journey from London to the Isle of Wight*, a composite of several tours, that through Sussex probably being in 1793, is slight, with little natural-history content, compared with his other tours. Stebbing Shaw's account of his 1790 sojourn has more original content and is mentioned further below. Similarly, the travel diaries kept for private delectation are less significant because they may regurgitate the guidebooks. The major exception are those of the Hon. John Byng (1743-1813) whose pithy remarks from his Sussex tour of 1788 are quoted in the captions to Views 20, 111, 112, 114 and 197, followed by John Skinner's journals for 1804, 1815 and 1821 which register a special interest in archaeology (View 30).[145]

Weightier fare than the guidebooks was provided by the first four substantive urban histories for Sussex. The *Ancient and modern history of Lewes and Brighthelmston* was published anonymously in twelve 48-page parts, starting in June/July 1792 and finishing in March/April 1795. The author was Paul Dunvan, a shadowy character with parallels with Charles Caraccioli, whose *The antiquities of Arundel* had appeared in 1766. Both were of French extraction and schoolmasters, Dunvan being usher at the Lewes grammar school. Only one contemporary documentary reference is known, to riotous behaviour at a Lewes town meeting in December 1792. He must have been commissioned by the printer William Lee (1747-1830), rather than have offered to Lee the fruits of many years' research. Lee attracted 278 subscribers, fairly typical for town histories of this sort and enough to make it a paying proposition, being without plates and in a modest format. The question then is how he was able to produce such a substantial tome - 555 pages - so quickly. He did not have access to Burrell's collection, that being at Burrell's house in Harley Street, nor to John Elliot's notes because they had been bequeathed to Burrell in 1782. Robert Austen, on Dunvan's statement, ordered his 'considerable collections' on Lewes to be destroyed after his death, which had occurred in 1786. Was Dunvan being less than honest when he said that 'a few memoranda which I happened to make from his papers before they were burnt were my first and best guides through the obscure maze into which I have ventured with more zeal than ability'? If Dunvan did indeed come to Lewes only shortly before 1792, then Austen's executors had not hastened to destroy the papers. Did he make much greater use than he implied, or was he working from copies which Lee had obtained? Was this one reason for the anonymity? It is hard to understand how, in the time and with facilities available to a school usher, he could have undertaken the research in the printed editions of the chronicles and the other scholarly texts which are cited in footnotes on Lewes before the 16th century.[146]

Another reason suggested for anonymity is Dunvan's radicalism. He subscribed strongly to the tradition of the 'Norman Yoke', that before 1066 the Anglo-Saxon inhabitants lived as free and equal citizens, governing themselves through representative institutions. The Norman Conquest deprived them of this liberty, and established the tyranny of an alien king and landlords. But the people did not forget the rights they had lost and fought continuously to recover them, with concessions from time to time extracted, such as after the Battle of Lewes. For Dunvan, Alfred ruled by 'national election, the only lawful base for kingly power', William the Conqueror imposed the 'intricate despotism of infeudation', William de Warenne was skilled in 'human butchery', and monks of the priory were 'holy despots' swollen with 'lust, hypocrisy, gluttony and pride.' More topically Dunvan denounced grasping landowners, neglect of female education, English contempt for Scotsmen and Irishmen, and colonial slavery.[147]

His history of Lewes falls into four main parts:

i.   the pre-Conquest history (pp. 1-38) which is overwhelmingly speculative.

ii. medieval Lewes (pp. 39-188) which gives much space to the histories of the lords of the barony of Lewes and to the circumstances of the Battle of Lewes, drawing on published sources and the register of Lewes Priory (perhaps from a copy of John Elliot's partial transcript). Two murage grants, of 1266 and 1334, from records in the Tower, were perhaps taken from the transcripts made for William Hay of Glyndebourne.

iii. Lewes from 1542 to 1794 (pp. 189-281) which was based on records locally available: the account of the Society of Twelve prepared by John Rowe in 1632 and preserved in his book of customs, in the keeping of George Medley of Buxted; and the town books of Lewes. He may have been helped by the collections on Lewes past and present which Thomas Woollgar began in 1790, at the same time as his botanical notes.[148]

iv. history and survey of the parishes within the borough and in the suburbs (pp. 282-431), drawing on the printed volumes on English medieval history, John Rowe's book, property deeds, personal observation and local enquiry, and probably greatly aided by Lee, a lifetime resident who also published the *Sussex Weekly Advertiser*.

The shorter history of Brighton (pp. 433-555) follows broadly the same structure. Here Dunvan was unable to build on any previous antiquary's work, and, excepting the manor court books, he consulted the main local records for Brighton before its development as a resort, namely the 1580 'ancient customs', deeds to town property, Charles Goodwyn's rental of 1665 and the vestry book started in 1682.[149]

The second urban history was the Revd Alexander Hay's *History of Chichester* (1804), with 163 subscribers. Born in about 1735, Hay is first found in Chichester in 1770, as a reader at St Mary's Hospital, an office he held until his death in 1806. From 1785 he was non-resident Vicar of Wisborough Green. He also ran a school. The first edition of his *Chichester guide* appeared in 1783. In the preface to the *History* he candidly admitted that prior to the coming of the Romans, 'Chichester, like every other part of the island, was hid in darkness.' From the Romans until several centuries after the Norman Conquest, the history 'of any particular place can be collected only by scraps and fragments from the general account of the historian.'

It appeared to me that the most effectual way to convey to the reader the justest idea that could be obtained, both of the city and county, would be to lay before him the state of society and religion, and the progress of arts and sciences, in England at that time, thus snatching a ray from general history to illuminate the particular objects I had in view; mixed with as much local history as could be procured, at least as I could collect.

Absence of evidence did not therefore prevent him from filling 335 out of 606 pages for the centuries down to the 16th. The history more specifically of Chichester from the Civil War to his own day took 170 pages, before 80 pages of ecclesiastical history, 50 of biographies of illustrious inhabitants, and lists of sheriffs, MPs and mayors. He did not make use of the City's archives, and William Clarke's notes which he had from his grandson may have been the source of any material from the Dean and Chapter's records. For recent changes in the fabric of the city, he may have made unacknowledged use of James Spershott's memoirs which had been written in about 1783.[150]

Two further urban histories appeared before the first comprehensive county history in 1835. William George Moss described himself as 'Draughtsman to His Royal Highness the Duke of Cambridge'. He had already illustrated and published Joseph Nightingale's 1818 history of Southwark parish church, which was near his home in Kennington in Surrey. His *History and antiquities of the town and port of Hastings* (1824) arose, he said, from occasional visits on account of ill-health; indeed, drawings in Hastings Museum carry dates back to 1821. His original intention was to provide authentic and correct views with a slight descriptive account, but the response to his prospectus induced him to make the work as complete as possible; acting as his own publisher, he named 171 subscribers. His four chapters comprised:

i.   The Cinque Ports, relying mainly on Samuel Jeake's *Charters of the Cinque Ports* (1728), but with some reference to Burrell's notes, pp. 1-38
ii. Military history, devoted mostly to the Battle of Hastings, pp. 39-75, 185-90
iii. Ecclesiastical history, including monuments in the churches, pp. 76-122
iv. Civil history, with lists of mayors and MPs, and a guide to the town, pp. 123-82

Moss acknowledged Edward Green who had 'attended different libraries to make researches' and 'without whose coadjutorship I should probably never have undertaken the task'. But there is no depth of original research to the book, except that on religious foundations he may have benefited from Herbert's work. For concurrently William Herbert (1771-1851) was being employed by the Earl of Chichester: 'It [had] become desirable, from numberless encroachments both of late and former years, made on the ground or precinct immediately surrounding the walls and site of the ancient castle of Hastings in Sussex, to ascertain what were the exact boundaries of such precinct; as well with a view to prevent further encroachments, as to facilitate the recovery' of land. Herbert was an antiquary with substantial publications on the history of London already to his credit, which doubtless helped to secure his appointment as Librarian of the Guildhall Library in 1828; his best-known book was to be the *History of the twelve great livery companies of London* (1836-7). His search of the Pelham family archives and of the Tower records was extensive. Chichester authorised Moss and Herbert to undertake an excavation within the castle, and Herbert's notes survive. Digging began on 9 September 1824; on the 11th Herbert drafted a report for the *Morning Herald* and from the 13th, to prevent hindrance to workmen, they had to refuse entry to visitors within the walls, except on Sundays: 'numbers went away disappointed but upon the whole pretty civilly.' The excavation was too late for Moss's book which had been completed in July. Herbert's fair copy report to Chichester on both the excavation and his documentary researches was given in 1897 to Charles Dawson who drew on it for his 1909 *History of Hastings Castle*. It is now lost, but Herbert's notes and drafts were used in the 1999 re-interpretation of the structure.[151]

Moss and Herbert embarked upon *The history and antiquities of the Rape of Hastings*, of which the first (and only) part, mainly on Battle Abbey, appeared in 1825. Moss's name was printed on the cover, but on his copy Herbert claimed authorship, leaving Moss responsible for the four plates. The scholarship of the text is Herbert's rather than Moss's, and perhaps they fell out over who was to be given credit.[152]

The Revd Mark Aloysius Tierney (1795-1862) was the most substantial scholar among the four urban historians. He was appointed (Catholic) chaplain to the Duke of Norfolk in 1824 and lived at Arundel for the rest of his life, with ample leisure for antiquarian studies. His *History and antiquities of the Castle and Town of Arundel; including the biography of its earls from the Conquest to the present time* appeared in 1834. It was also the longest of the four, at 772 pages. The Duke's patronage ensured that he did not need subscribers. As with his predecessor Charles Caraccioli, the earls' biographies took the bulk of the volume, 430 pages, with 110 pages on the castle and its privileges; another 110 pages were devoted to the ecclesiastical foundations, and only 35 to the Corporation of Arundel. He berated the latter for not replying to his request for access to its muniments - a request, though, he had made only 10 weeks before he penned the preface. Tierney made frequent reference to documents at Norfolk House, to the registers of the bishops of Chichester, to records in the Tower and to manuscript collections at the College of Arms. Tierney, alone among the Sussex antiquaries considered here, played a role in the new era of local studies which opened with the foundation of the Sussex Archaeological Society in 1846, for he was the first local secretary for Arundel, a member of the committee from 1850 to 1861 and author of several papers in the *Collections*.[153]

4.3 Touring artists

Every artist by whom views of Sussex can be firmly dated before 1777 has been named above, with the exception of most surveyors known only for perspective views on maps and of only four others, each with one Sussex picture: William James (the font in Brighton Church, 1767), William Michell (perhaps the Lewes attorney, 1708-71: Pevensey Castle, 1768), William Challen (an oil of the Miller's Tomb on Highdown Hill, 1770, View 82) and John Hamilton Mortimer (1741-79, born in Eastbourne: Pevensey Castle, 1774).[154] From 1777 the number of artists drawing Sussex scenes accelerated. The named artists, whose first dated work in Sussex falls in each decade, numbered: 1760s 6, 1770s 10, 1780s 18, 1790s 27 and 1800s 28. These figures reflect the growing popularity of drawing as a recreation for gentlefolk of both sexes and, of special signif-icance to Sussex, the rise of the seaside resort where such gentlefolk congregated along with professional artists anxious to instruct them and to sell them pictures. For about half the artists enumerated, the locale of their first dated view was at or close to a resort, Brighton being the foremost, followed by Hastings, Eastbourne, Worthing or Bognor. Many of these artists' work in Sussex amounts to only a handful of items, reflecting the fruits of a summer excursion.

The following discussion is based on the 30 or so artists whose first dated Sussex work falls between 1777 and 1810 and who are known by at least 10 views of Sussex. They are roughly classified as professional or amateur, according to whether or not they sought to make their living from painting. The amateurs are subdivided by their main motivation, antiquarian or artistic.

Amongst the five antiquaries, the only local may have been Thomas Smith. This artist of three sketchbooks containing 57 pedestrian views, mainly of churches in south-west Sussex in 1795, can be identified from several short articles in the *Gentleman's Magazine* between 1792 and 1816. Some were illustrated with plates, the first of Sussex in the magazine, except for a couple of Hastings in 1786.[155] Beyond that he is only a name. The Revd David Thomas Powell (1772/3-1848) was resident for only a few years, while curate at Wilmington and Ninfield around 1807-11, and he added to his notes for the rest of his life, forming also for other counties collections similar to those for Sussex, now with the Sussex Archaeological Society. Having served as an Army officer, he may have been trained in drawing, and his efforts are competent but limited in scope, concentrating on churches and their fittings. Latterly he lived as a recluse in

Tottenham and, unsurprisingly, he did not publish. When, in 1833, Frederic Madden of the British Museum intended to acknowledge his assistance on a point of heraldry, in which he had great expertise, he responded 'I have an unaccountable aversion to have my name handed to the public in matters of this sort … I think it beneath the dignity of an ecclesiastic to instruct the public in such matters.' To the remark, '… one like me who is totally unknown among antiquaries and men of letters and science, whose means are so confined', Madden added in the margin, years later: 'This miserly fellow when he died in 1848 left about £30,000 in hard cash to [the London] Hospital.'[156]

The Revd Stebbing Shaw (1762-1802) could have done with the cash. Eleven poor sketches now in Brighton Art Gallery date from travels in Sussex in 1790, from which several articles were published in *The Topographer*, and church notes in *Topographical Miscellanies* (see Views 39, 40, 82 and 151 for some of his observations). Having embarked on a history of his home county of Staffordshire in 1791 and published two volumes, he was driven to an early grave by the demands, intellectual, physical and financial, of the undertaking.[157] James Moore (1762-99) had no financial worries. A linen draper in Cheapside, he made several tours between 1785 and 1795, recording antiquities, probably in the last of those years on the coast of Kent and into Sussex as far as Pevensey. He employed professional artists to work up or redraw his pictures, and started publication of *Monastic remains* (1792-1816); see View 198.[158]

The most significant of the antiquaries was Henry Petrie (1772-1842). He did some teaching at his father's school in Stockwell in Surrey, but was otherwise a scholar pursuing his own, unpublished, researches, possibly with the support of the 2nd Earl Spencer who was collecting a fine library at Althorp. The exceptional knowledge he gained of the manuscript sources for English history secured his appointment as Keeper of the Records in the Tower in 1819. Between 1800 and 1809, he made several hundred watercolours, mostly of churches and castles in Bedfordshire, Kent, Surrey and Sussex. Those of Sussex, dated between 1802 and 1809, alone amount to over 400 views of which those of churches are in the possession of the Sussex Archaeological Society, and those of the religious houses and secular buildings were still (in 1999) with the dealer who had bought the entire collection in 1975.[159]

Amongst the amateurs, one stands out as semi-professional in that his work was exhibited and engraved, but he did not need to seek clients or patrons. This was John Nixon (*c.* 1750-1818), a convivial London merchant trading with Ireland, who made extensive sketching tours each summer, particularly in southern England (Views 35-37, 61). Sussex pictures date from 1783, 1787, 1789, 1791 and 1805-8. Of over 50 known pictures, nearly all were taken on or near the coast and include sketches of people at work: the crier at Worthing, a match maker in Brighton, a breeches-maker's shop at a Chichester fair. When Thomas Pennant's *Journey from London to the Isle of Wight* appeared in 1801, its illustrations included eight Sussex views from drawings by Nixon.[160]

Of the other amateurs, most were visitors to Brighton. Eleanor Lay is known for 14 views on and around the Steine, one dated 1777. William Burchell (1781-1863), the son of a nurseryman in Fulham, later achieved fame as a naturalist in South Africa and Brazil. His 23 Sussex sketches were made in 1799 to 1803, when he was aged between 18 and 21, having already received instruction in landscape drawing from Merigot (a Frenchman who had been a tutor in the Pugin family) and probably being taught drawing by the topographical draughtsman John Claude Nattes (1765-1839). He made sketches both at Brighton on holiday visits in 1799 and 1801 (Views 31 and 32), and on the road from or back to Fulham via Horsham and Henfield in the latter year. The Rocks at Eridge were visited in 1801 and East Grinstead in 1803. The Revd John Skinner (1772-1839), Rector of Camerton, Somerset, visited his sister in Brighton in 1815 and 1821, and made a tour through the county on the traditional south-coast route in 1804, preparing an illustrated journal on each occasion. These journals are notable for his interest in field archaeology and excavation (View 30).

The Revd Dr William Crotch (1775-1847) is best known as Oxford's Professor of Music for 50 years, but he was also competent in watercolours, having been taught by John Malchair. Sketches from a stay in Brighton in 1834 survive, and also a couple from visits to Heathfield Park in 1809 and 1811. The last are early examples of sketching at and around a Wealden country house, doubtless made in the company of William Newbery (1787-1838), also a pupil of Malchair's, whose father owned Heathfield Park (View 108). John Buckler (1770-1851) was making exemplary topographical drawings in Sussex between 1801 and 1830, probably in the first instance for his own pleasure.[161]

Several of the professional artists took annual holidays on which they sketched, collecting material for pictures which they worked up in their (usually) London studios. Joseph Farington (1747-1821) made his first stay at Hastings in 1785 (View 105). His famed diary, started in 1793, shows that he stayed for three weeks in September 1797, 11 weeks between November 1813 to January 1814 and two months September to November 1818. Michael Angelo Rooker (1743-1801) made walking tours from about 1788, covering 18 miles a day and spending two guineas a week.[162] He must have been in Sussex in 1791, as he exhibited four views of Sussex at the Royal Academy in the following year and two more in 1793, all of sites bounded by Pevensey, Battle and Rye (View 197). He may have been further west, in Lewes and Arundel, in 1795. At that time, he was well paid as the scene-painter at the Haymarket Theatre, so may not have been too concerned about buyers for his pictures. There is a noticeable clustering of professionals active in 1792-7 centred on Hastings, reflecting the wartime closure of the Continent and suggesting some joint expeditions: William Day (1764-1807), Thomas Underwood (1772-1836), J. M. W. Turner (1775-1851) and Thomas Girtin (1775-1802) (View 198), plus Edward Dayes (1764-1804) who also ranged into western Sussex. John Inigo Richards (1731-1810) made a view of Highdown Mill in Ferring, dated 1797; his other Sussex views are of Steyning (View 177) and Bodiam. John Russell, the portraitist (1745-1806) was sketching in and around Brighton in 1795, while Hendrick de Cort was active in the western Rother valley and around Edburton in several years between 1792 and 1799 (Views 76-8, 123, 176). Joshua Cristall (1768-1847) was active at Hastings from 1807.[163]

Of these, only Turner was to work on any scale in Sussex, his patrons being John Fuller of Rose Hill in Brightling (View 29 and Essay 4.4) and Lord Egremont of Petworth.[164] The frail Thomas Hearne (1744-1817) was received at Ashburnham Place in 1815 and 1816 for the benefit of his health (View 9). Others had Sussex clients in different capacities. Humphry Repton (1752-1818) prepared 'Red Books', with overlays to show the garden views before and after his proposed landscaping, for at least eight clients, and may have advised a further seven, between 1789 and 1812 (they are listed under Views 58 and 59; see also View 108). Thomas Poppleton worked in a humbler capacity, producing pictures of tenanted houses on the Buckhurst and Gilbert estates around 1800, as did the anonymous surveyor on the Buxted estate in 1798 (Views 43-9).

4.4 The county histories of the early 19th century

The second decade of the 19th century saw the first attempt to publish a county history which achieved any success. Shoberl reported in 1813 that 'A Mr Brown, formerly of New Shoreham, issued proposals for publishing a history of Sussex, in two octavo volumes, which never appeared. His widow still resides in Shoreham; but what progress he made, or whether his materials are yet in her possession, I have not learnt.' (A John Brown, Esq., attorney at Shoreham, was listed in the *Universal British directory* of 1798.) But he could say that 'under the patronage of the Duke of Norfolk, the Revd Mr Dallaway has been for a long time engaged upon an account of the three rapes comprising the western division of the county, which will be comprised in two quarto volumes, and two others devoted to the three eastern rapes, are preparing for publication, under the auspices of John Fuller, Esq. of Rose Hill.'[165]

Fuller's part of the project was enmeshed with his patronage of J. M. W. Turner. In early summer 1810 Fuller invited Turner to sketch in the vicinity of Rose Hill, and Turner was to return in several later years. Turner was already a highly successful artist, to whom Fuller paid £417 in 1811 alone. Four of the resulting watercolours, the views of the parks of Rose Hill, Beauport Park, Battle Abbey and Ashburnham Place, Fuller hired for 100 guineas so that they might be reproduced as coloured aquatints for private circulation. In 1815 Fuller agreed to pay William Bernard Cooke to engrave those four and further Sussex watercolours, for publication. Cooke explained to John Murray, the publisher, on 21 December 1818:

I have informed you some time ago that Mr Fuller of Rose Hill had employed me some years ago to engrave a set of plates for him from drawings by Turner. Mr Fuller has lent me two volumes of valuable MS copy on Sussex to extract from them the most interesting notices on the Rape of Hastings. It is on this rape that our present work will treat. The work is to be divided into three parts. The first part (plates and all) is ready for the press and Mr Fuller urges me to publish the first of March next. As the plates are done I see no reason for keeping the work back when it can be realising in cash. I shall therefore send you in the course of today a prospectus of the work also, to insert in your list of publications under the conviction that you will publish them.... Mr Fuller's work will be a splendid thing, and I trust will do credit to all the parties concerned.

Three days later Cooke confirmed that Fuller would meet the publication expenses. Murray agreed to publish, with sole rights of distribution and an extra 10% commission for advertising in all his lists and in his *Quarterly Review*; the first part was to be titled *Views in Sussex*. However, during 1819 Murray withdrew from another, long-running and much delayed, project with Cooke, *Picturesque views on the southern coast of England*, and the deal on *Views in Sussex* fell through in consequence. Murray's name, with the date 1819, was printed on the volume, but on many copies is struck through. Cooke was obliged to distribute the *Views* alone; his prospectus of 1820 announced a second part, for which three engravings were started, but it never appeared.[166]

The 'two volumes of valuable MS copy on Sussex' must have been William Hayley's 'Notitia Sussexiensis sive Sussexiæ antiqua et nova' (BL, Add. MSS 6343, 6344), which was scarcely suitable for rapid digesting by an overstretched engraver. The 'historical sketch' following the engravings runs to 20 pages, most of them given over to the Norman Conquest and the obligations and privileges of the Cinque Ports. A couple of pages may have drawn on Hayley's sections on 'Sussex before the coming in of the South Saxons' and 'The South Saxons'. Fuller was probably dissatisfied with the text, abandoned the project after the first part, presented Hayley's papers to the British Museum in 1820 - and in the early 1830s urged the Lewes printer and publisher, John Baxter, to take on the project - but did not live to see it achieved in 1835, the year after he died.

The Duke of Norfolk either had a concept of the project very different from Fuller's, or was better able to organise it. He had first approached the Revd James Douglas (1753-1819), the archaeologist already mentioned (Essay 4.1) who wrote to John Nichols from Barnham in March 1810:[167]

I have received an invitation from the Duke of Norfolk, and have dined with his Grace at his Castle.... I have been consulted about the history of this county; the compilation has been offered to me. Much assistance can be had from the manuscripts of the late Sir W. Burrell in the Museum; but the work being under the auspices of a nobleman of the highest consequence, who wishes it to be got up on the most elegant scale, I am afraid the expense will exceed all profit; what say you, my dear Sir? Is it likely for an individual, to obtain from the public, a recompense equal to the labour? I am afraid not.

So the Duke turned instead to his secretary in his capacity as Earl Marshal, the Revd James Dallaway (1763-1834). Dallaway was the son of a Gloucestershire banker. Following graduation from Oxford and ordination, he became curate in 1785 at Rodmarton, to Samuel Lysons (father of the antiquaries Daniel and Samuel), and then at Rodborough. He was engaged to assist Richard Bigland in editing his father's papers; before they parted acrimoniously in early 1794 he completed the first 22 parts of Ralph Bigland's *Historical, monumental, and genealogical collections, relative to the County of Gloucester* (1786-94) and gained a valuable introduction to the College of Arms. His *Inquiries into the origin and progress of the science of heraldry in England* (1793) was dedicated to the Earl Marshal. He was elected a Fellow of the Society of Antiquaries in 1789.

In 1793 he returned to Oxford, to attend the Radcliffe Infirmary and gain the degree of MB in December. He made a special study of 'the plague', for, through the 4th Earl of Bute's influence, Robert Liston had chosen him as physician and chaplain for his embassy to the Ottoman Empire. The party left in March 1794 and travelled overland to Constantinople. His *Itinerary* published in 1805 was one of the period's most detailed reports of the Balkans. Leaving for home in October 1795, Dallaway travelled via the Greek islands and Italy. Loss of most of his notes in transit precluded his planned continuation of Gibbon's *Decline and fall*, but his *Constantinople, ancient and modern, with excursions to the shores and islands of the Archipelago and to the Troad* (1797) was well regarded in its time, helped to awaken interest in the ancient manuscripts to be found there and contributed to the debate on the location of ancient Troy. The papers of an earlier ambassador's wife had passed to Bute, her grandson. When he reluctantly agreed to an authorised edition, he commissioned Dallaway to prepare *The works of ... Lady Mary Wortley Montagu* (5 vols, 1803), which a later editor described as 'shockingly incompetent'. Dallaway also reviewed books on Turkish topics for *The Monthly Review*.

Back in England, Dallaway was appointed by the 11th Duke of Norfolk, to be his secretary as Earl Marshal, from January 1797; he served for the rest of his life. The College of Arms became his regular place of work. Two years later the Duke presented him to the rectory of South Stoke, adjoining Arundel Park. This he resigned in 1803 on collation to the nearby vicarage of Slinfold which he held in plurality from 1804 with the vicarage of Leatherhead, Surrey, where he resided from 1805. His wife, daughter of a Gloucester alderman whom he married in 1800, shared his interests, writing *A manual of heraldry for amateurs* (1828). In 1811 he was given the Prebend of Hova Ecclesia in Chichester Cathedral, which he exchanged for that of Ferring in 1816; the latter he resigned in 1826.

His parochial duties and office as Earl Marshal's secretary left ample leisure for antiquarian studies. His journey through Italy had strengthened his interest in art history and he published *Anecdotes of the arts in England or comparative observations on architecture, sculpture, & painting, chiefly illustrated by specimens at Oxford* (1800); *Observations on English architecture, military, ecclesiastical, and civil* (1806; enlarged edition 1833, as *A series of discourses upon architecture in England*); *Of statuary and sculpture among the Ancients, with some account of specimens preserved in England* (1816); *Account of all the pictures exhibited in the rooms of the British Institution from 1813 to 1823, belonging to the nobility and gentry of England* (1824); and an edition with considerable additions of Horace Walpole's *Anecdotes of painting* (5 vols, 1826-8). He was a valuable continuater of Walpole's work, especially on Gothic architecture and medieval architects, while his attempt to divide the Gothic style into periods and to produce lists of contemporary buildings in each style deserves some of the credit commonly given to Thomas Rickman.

In April 1811 Dallaway agreed with the Duke to compile and prepare for the press a two-volume *History of the western division of Sussex*. Volume 1 in two parts containing 'preliminary observations' (176 pp.) and covering the City and Rape of Chichester appeared in 1815. Half of the 500 copies printed were still in stock when a fire at the printers destroyed them in June 1819. But part 1 of volume 2, on Arundel rape, was then just off the press and the entire impression of 500 copies, excepting only 20 at the binders, was lost.[168]

Besides Burrell's, Dallaway said in the Chichester volume that he knew of only two other collections on Sussex. The first was Hayley's, concerned mainly with the Rape of Hastings, 'the amusement of a long life', and especially his 'Notitia Sussexiensis sive Sussexiæ antiqua et nova'. The second, which he had been unable to trace, though Burrell and Hayley had mentioned it, was of five volumes of abstracts concerning lands in Sussex, by William Petyt (1689-1707), made while Keeper of the Records in the Tower of London, who had bequeathed them to the Inner Temple Library. But Dallaway had misread Burrell who had found from the general index to Petyt's large collection that there were references to Sussex in five volumes, and had had extracts made. Dallaway gave acknowledgement for his own access to the records in the Tower, at the College of Arms, and of the Bishop, the Dean and Chapter, and the City of Chichester. For subjects of statistical nature, he was indebted to the clergy, their exertions being sanctioned by the bishop. Several sections of the 'preliminary observations' are taken verbatim from published sources, for example Dawson Turner and Lewis Watson, *The botanist's guide* (1805) for plants, Gilbert White, *Natural history of Selborne* (1813 edn) for zoology and ornithology, and Arthur Young, *General view* (1808) for geology and minerals. The history of Chichester extends over 200 pages and indicates a considerable amount of archival research, Hay's *History* not providing much of a foundation, but Clarke's notes perhaps being a guide. The parochial topography for the rest of the rape fills 300 pages. When the parochial topography of the Rape of Arundel appeared in 1819, it was of similar length.[169]

Dallaway was ill at ease with the *History's* requirement for detailed archival research. His volumes were criticised on publication (and by later historians) for their numerous errors. M. A. Tierney found the account of Arundel 'neither full nor accurate in any one of its most essential and important points', and observed that 'His errors, indeed, are numerous - the consequences of negligence and inattention; but his habits of research have placed an immense fund of information at his command; and while the former necessarily escape the attention of all but the student, the latter invariably attract the regard, and win the confidence, of the general reader.'

By 1822 Dallaway had been stood down from the project. The 11th Duke had died in 1815 and left directions and funds for its completion. His executor Lord Henry Howard engaged the Revd Edmund Cartwright to write the volume on the Rape of Bramber, of which only 250 copies were printed in 1830. Cartwright (1773-1833) was the son of a Doncaster gentleman, who, after a precocious career at Oxford, obtained a commission in the West Yorkshire Militia in 1793. His enthusiasm was archaeology and while his regiment was stationed at Winchester he visited every antiquity within 20 miles. His colonel, the 11th Duke of Norfolk, induced him to relinquish his commission and to take holy orders. In his clerical career Cartwright had much in common with Dallaway. A fellow-pluralist, he held the livings of Earnley 1803-33, Storrington 1805-11, Parham 1819-25 and Lyminster 1825-33, the first two by the Duke's presentation. The Cathedral careers of both men were curiously intertwined: they served on the Chapter for 27 continuous years, yet never served together. Cartwright held the Prebend of Ferring 1806-11 and again (this time in succession to Dallaway) 1826-33; Dallaway held Hova Ecclesia followed by Ferring for the period 1811-26. Cartwright was perhaps outside the county in the years 1811-19, when he held only Earnley and served it by curates. His latter years were spent at Lyminster. He was probably more of a career cleric than Dallaway, with a high enough profile for his antiquarian neighbour John Hawkins to write of him in February 1830 as 'I believe to be the new Dean of Chichester', presumably in succession to Dean Slade who had died the previous December. But sadly he seems to have missed the boat both as a historian and a clergyman.

Having purchased the copyright and most of the plates of Dallaway's volumes, he planned to republish them but found the expense and risk too great. Because it effectively had not been published, in 1832 he reprinted the Rape of Arundel (200 copies, for which he had 150 subscribers), having added alterations to descents of property, extracts from Domesday, additions to the memoirs of the earls of Arundel, and indexes. Tierney, writing in October 1833, asserted that the publisher, John Gough Nichols (1806-73), was the real editor of the new edition. As regards Arundel, it did little more 'than engraft a fresh stock of errors on those of its predecessor.' His Bramber volume has similarly been found riddled with errors.[170]

The failure of Fuller's publication left the field in eastern Sussex open to another author, Thomas Walker Horsfield (1792-1837). Horsfield was the son of a book-keeper in Sheffield, trained at the Unitarian academy at Hackney and in 1817 came to Lewes as minister of the Westgate Chapel. It was probably the Lewes printer and publisher, John Baxter (1781-1858), who encouraged him to write *The history and antiquities of Lewes and its vicinity* which appear in 1824. Baxter had signed up as many as 700 subscribers and it was enough of a commercial success for a second volume covering 43 parishes within an eight to ten-mile radius to appear in 1827. Horsfield was elected a Fellow of the Society of Antiquaries in January 1825 on the strength of the first volume. Sir Charles Merrik Burrell, son of William, had lent John Elliot's manuscripts and allowed extracts from his father's collection. The Earl of Chichester and Viscount Gage had supplied scarce works from their libraries. The parish articles in the second volume followed much the same formula as Dallaway's *History*, giving a short account of the topography, the descent of the main landholdings, a brief description of the church, its monuments, the value of the living and the name of the incumbent, and a note of any exceptional antiquities. Both Horsfield and Cartwright had Gideon Mantell write a section on natural history.[171]

Late in 1832 Baxter sent to the subscribers a free 12-page supplement, describing recent events and improvements in Lewes, to draw their attention to the prospectus for a third uniform volume which would complete a 'History of Sussex'. It was to have three parts:

i.   the history of Brighton, past and present
ii.   the history and antiquities of the coast of Sussex, with the geology and natural history, the material being arranged by routes for the tourist
iii. those places not comprised under the previous heads, together with whatever may be worthy of notice as to trade, manufactures, agriculture, etc.

Baxter wanted to reach a wide readership:

It is not intended that this publication should be a dry topographical description of the places it may embrace; the author will endeavour to render it a volume abounding with information on subjects which do not commonly form part of local histories. The work will present great advantages to professional gentlemen and the trading interest, as the names of those who become subscribers will be arranged at the end of the work as a directory, affording the traveller and visitor a means of reference; it will also exhibit all matters of a commercial nature in each town in the county.

The author was again Horsfield - even though he had left Lewes in December 1827 to become minister at the Mary Street Chapel in Taunton, Somerset. The move had in part been precipitated by his support for Radical causes, including Catholic Emancipation, which had depleted numbers at his boarding school; he was to move again, in 1835 to Chowbent Chapel at Atheron, Lancashire, where he died in 1837. That support can be detected in *The history of Lewes*. For example, printing a 1283 manumission from Framfield allowed him to express the hope that similar documents would soon be granted to 'the sable inhabitants of Africa engaged in our West Indies plantations.' After completing *The history of Lewes*, he had nevertheless started composition of a similar work on 'The history of Brighton and the Sussex coast', at least to the extent of advertising in the *Brighton Herald* for material. The 1832 prospectus claimed that 'a great variety of scarce and valuable documents have long been in the hands of the author; and for several years he has been increasing his collection with whatever papers and facts will tend to illustrate and render interesting this projected work.' Noblemen and gentlemen with interesting details of any description were invited to send them to the publisher.

As 1832 turned to 1833, Baxter's opportunities changed. First, having bought Dallaway's copyrights, Cartwright announced a book on the three western rapes - but died early in 1833. Baxter bought from his executors the copyright, plates, wood-engravings and remaining stock of Dallaway's and Cartwright's volumes and also the manuscript of the book. Possibly at this stage a second (undated) prospectus was issued, for a two-volume 'History and topography of the County of Sussex', the first volume to cover Brighton and all places of interest or importance on the coast of Sussex, and the second all other places. It was now the publisher who had been enlarging his collection of documents. But then, secondly, *An historical and descriptive account of the coast of Sussex* was announced in September 1832 and appeared the following year from the pen of J. D. Parry who, so he said, had begun, completed and published the book inside six months; it does nevertheless contain substantial extracts from Burrell's and other manuscripts in the British Museum.[172]

Presumably at that point, Baxter feared that he had lost the visitor market and fell back to the less demanding production of a more conventional county history, which was ready for the press at the end of 1834 and appeared in 1835, in two volumes divided between the eastern and the western rapes. Baxter acknowledged that the late John Fuller, who had died in April 1834, had urged on him the work as 'the execution of his own earlier purpose'. Maybe, after the failure of 1820, Fuller wanted to emulate the western Sussex history now completed. An element of the original proposal, though, survived in that Brighton, rather than Lewes, comprised the first parochial article.[173]

Baxter, Horsfield wrote in the preface,

has sent intelligent agents into different parts of the county.... The places not visited by the Editor have thus furnished their respective share of interest.... The distance of the Editor's residence from the place of publication prevented his correction of the proof sheets, which were left to the care of competent readers.... [T]he Editor can be deemed responsible only for the use he has made of the many topographical facts of which he has thus been put in possession.... If the topographical portion of the second volume should be found a faithful condensation of the mass of facts derived chiefly from [Dallaway and Cartwright's work], it is all the praise which the Editor either anticipates or desires.

Baxter named 73 people who had kindly looked over the manuscripts of the different parishes. Horsfield acknowledged substantial contributions by William Durrant Cooper, including seven entire parish entries. Cooper wrote on parliamentary history, Thomas Henry Cooper on botany, Mantell on geology, John Ellman on agriculture, George Cooke on military and civil history, and William King on climate. Horsfield's radicalism came through at several points, for example in eulogising the poet Shelley and sympathising with Jack Cade.[174]

After *The history, antiquities, and topography of the County of Sussex* had appeared in 1835, Baxter mounted a set of the printed sheets in seven guard books to which were added the pages of manuscript which had been deleted as the copy was being prepared for setting.[175] These pages are in several different hands and, except for a section on the lordship of the barony of Chichester and Arundel, are entirely on the eastern rapes. This suggests that Cartwright's manuscript was set without alteration. However, the parish articles for the western rapes are not simply summaries of those in Dallaway and Cartwright, for small details are added and the phrasing is different. Furthermore, there is specific acknowledgement of, and quotation from, Cartwright's manuscript in the article on Chichester. Although we cannot determine at this distance of time who the authors were, there can be little doubt that the appellation 'Horsfield's *Sussex*' which has come down the years is too generous to Horsfield.

Baxter said that he had fixed the price (at £4 4s.) 'so low as to place it within the reach of a large class of persons to whom other county histories are sealed books.' His marketing was successful, as 1019 subscribers are listed alphabetically, of whom about 460 'professional gentlemen and tradesmen' were classified by their occupations, as proposed in 1832. The two lists show the subscribers to have included 29 nobility, 17 titled gentry (Sir and the Hon.), 12 other Members of Parliament, 53 other clergy and 12 other army and navy officers. Over 400 are identified only by surname, forename and parish, and presumably were mainly of independent means. The professions were represented by 57 solicitors and 47 physicians and surgeons, while the 13 proprietors of academies and schools, 37 booksellers and librarians and 44 hotel and innkeepers may have subscribed for the benefit of their customers. But some 250 - a quarter of the total - were tradesmen and craftsmen, from 26 architects and builders, through 24 brewers, maltsters and wine merchants, 25 drapers and tailors and 43 grocers, to 3 tanners and 2 wheelwrights. It is hard to believe that they paid their 4 guineas for a means of advertising. Perhaps we can see Baxter's marketing building a bridge between the traditional scholarly antiquarianism of the landed élite and the new popular antiquarianism pioneered by Walter Scott's verses and novels.[176]

5. References

[1] McKisack 1971, vii.

[2] Douglas 1951.

[3] See county articles in Currie and Lewis 1994. A helpful review of 18th-century local historical study is in Sweet 1997.

[4] Rawlinson 1720, 232. Fletcher 1975, 25, 134-6. Farrant et al. 1991, 149. BL, Add. MS. 5681, f. 426. Round 1929, 27-8. Salzman 1928, 60. London 1947, 44-5.

[5] Mendyk 1989, 44-6. Leland 1906-10, 4: 92-3, 113-14.

[6] Levy 1967, 152-3.

[7] Camden 1586, 154-63. Kendrick 1950, 151. Gilbert 1985, 269.

[8] Levy 1967, 152-5. Camden 1695, cols 165-84 and preface. Gunther 1937, 343. Jeake 1999, xliii, 58-9. Jeake 1988, 39.

[9] Farrant 1978, 269-75, for this and the following paragraphs. The MSS of the 'Description' are BL, Add. MS. 31853 (fragment only) and Northamptonshire Record Office, Finch-Hatton MS. 113 (photocopy in ESRO, AMS 5775). Extracts have been printed in Farrant 1977, Kitchen 1987a and Kitchen 1987b. The authoritative modern study of Norden is Kitchen 1992, summarised in Kitchen 1997.

[10] Kendrick 1950, pl. IX.

[11] Kingsley 1982, 13-16.

[12] Rowe 1928, 16. Turner 1872, 85. Farrant 1996a, 169.

[13] ESRO, SAS/G/ACC 921. Hall 1985, 257-68

[14] Hammond (Lieut.) 1936. Taylor 1940. Hunter 1975, 37, 72. Aubrey 1986. Welch 1956. Hobbs 1994, 143. Camden 1695.

[15] Hodson 1984-97, 1: 19-22. Hall 1720-31, 5: 477, 510, 537. Cox 1730. Dallaway 1815, 1: cxxxii.

[16] Wilson 1985. Beevers 1995, cat. 1. Harvey 1993, 44-7. Aldsworth 1979b, 103-4. Aldsworth and Garnett 1981. Croft-Murray 1956.

[17] ESRO, PAR 414/9/1/1a (Dape). Cooper 1902, 21, and ESRO, PAR 415/9/1a (Bugg). SAS, LEWSA 1997.7, 15 and ESRO, ACC 560/1 (Head). ESRO, PAR 411/9/1 and 414/9/1/2 (Smith and Conley). Brent 1993, 213 (Conley). ESRO, LEW/C2/1/1 (Morris). Moss 1824, 113-14 (Mortimer). Godfrey 1939. Godfrey 1942-3, 13-14.

[18] PRO, MPF 212, reproduced on paperback cover of Mayhew 1987. ESRO, ACC 3746. Bendall 1992, 46-50. Steer 1962, 1-70. Steer 1968, 1-18. Bendall 1997 for more on the surveyors.

[19] Yates 1982. Marchant 1986.

[20] Steer 1962 and Steer 1968, augmented by ESRO. Bendall 1997.

[21] East Sussex Record Office 1986.

[22] Bendall 1997, 1: 23. Bendall 1992, 177-84.

[23] Daniels 1990. Harris 1979, no. 255. Rees 1998, pl. v.

[24] Knyff 1984. Harris 1995, no. 4. Pryce 1996, fc. 72.

[25] Hardie 1966-8, 1: 56-7. Royalton-Kisch 1999, 86-93, 184-5.

[26] BL, Cotton MS. Aug. I.ii.41. WSRO, Chichester St Andrew register; Add. MS. 38403 (witnessed by another John Dunstall, but with a different signature from those on pictures by the younger Dunstall - and that of an older man, perhaps an uncle or cousin). Wellesley 1852, referring to the etchings in Bodl., Gough maps 31, ff. 1b,

42b; four are also in BL, K. Top. 42.19a. Morgan 1991, 254. Morgan 1992, 184.

27 Croft-Murray and Hulton 1960, 301-4. Griffiths 1998, 17, 138-40. Bridson and White 1990, nos B34-5, 37, 43-5; C105, 129-30; D142, 168, 221, 224. Sloan 2000, 23-4, 45, 58-60. WSRO, Cutten A1/1/3. BL, Add. MS. 5244. Litten 1991, 129-30, 145. Sotheby's, 9 March 1989 (lot 22) for a pen and ink study of walnuts and hazelnuts signed and dated 1666, now at YCBA.

28 Five of the etchings are in Camden 1977. Wark 1969, 30-1 (quoted). Sprinzels 1938, cat. 370, pl. 66, for Arundel, cats 353-6 for four of the Dunstalls. Croft-Murray and Hulton 1960, 302. Pennington 1982, xxii-xxiii, xlv-xlvi, nos 931, 944-6, 949, 951, 953, 955, 965, 965A; Pennington does not record the prospect of Chichester from the north, in Bodl., Gough maps 31, 1a. Hollar 1674. Welch 1956. Leeney 1947, 185-6. If the NW tower had recently collapsed, Hammond would surely have commented in August 1635: Hammond (Lieut.) 1936, 34-5.

29 Sloan 2000, 13. Evelyn 1955, 1: 7-12.

30 Royal Society archives, LBC.16, pp. 7-10 (dated 21 Oct. 1712). Tabor 1717. Hunter 1995, 187.

31 Tabor 1717, 791-9. Camden 1586. Camden 1695, col. 180. Aubrey's correspondents told him of earthworks elsewhere in Sussex: Aubrey 1980, 1: 280, 298, 318, 332, 376. Somner 1693, 104-5, who inclined to Pevensey as Anderida, pointed out that Camden had noticed in the castle walls 'great bricks' such as the Britons used, but in only the 1610 translation of *Britannia*.

32 Hearne 1727, 1: xxxvii-xl. Tomlin 1997, 129. Trail and Steer 1963, 1. Stukeley 1724, 1: 188-94 and pl. 49. Rawlinson 1720, 232. On Hibbins: Stukeley 1887, 227-30, 234; McCann 1984, 53, 59, 73-4; BL, Add. MS. 32696, f. 27; International Genealogical Index. Gough 1780, 2: 287. Warwickshire County Record Office, CR 2017/TP 1, p. 53.

33 McCann 1984, xxxii-xxxiv. Vertue 1930-55, 5: 89, 141-50. Society of Antiquaries, Minute Book V, 5 April 1750; this mosaic is not noted in the modern gazetteer of Roman finds in Chichester.

34 Farrant forthcoming. BL, Add. MS. 5703,

ff. 28-30. Nichols 1817-58, 3: 549-54. Cambridge Univ. Library, Add. MS. 7082, Newling family papers.

35 WSRO, Cap. I/1/5. Society of Antiquaries, MS. 153, ff. 39-42, Lyttelton's church notes in Sussex in July 1753. BL, Add. MS. 32123, ff. 31-2, for letter finished immediately before visiting the cathedral; 5706, ff. 131-3, for his observations and Clarke's report to the bishop, the latter printed in Hay 1804, 384, 408-15 and, addressed to Lyttelton, in Camden 1789, 1: 194-5. Bodl., Gough gen. top. 365, f. 490. Walpole 1937-83, 1: 244; 9: 326.

36 Bodl., MS. Top. gen. e.24, ff. 348-50. ESRO, BAT 4421, reproduced in Coad 1984, 10; ADA 159; PAR 510/7/1, probably copied from the original of AMS 5879/4, an incomplete photocopy. Devonshire Collections at Chatsworth House, CPP, box P, 15/33; Map 4108. Henry E. Huntington Library, Battle Abbey Papers, vols 31 and 32. SAS, Budgen Papers 125, 25 Jan. 1739.

37 Aston 1973, 253.

38 Hyde 1994, 8-28.

39 The engravings were issued without a title-page, but are often catalogued as *A collection of engravings of castles, and abbeys in England*. Brown 1982, no. 399; BM, P&D, 1981-12-12-33 (2), (4) and (7); Phimister, Wiles and Denison 1992, fig. 2; VAM, E.1005-1979; YCBA, B1977.14.1111; Towner Art Gallery, 1607 and 1608; Bodl., Gough maps 31, f. 2a; WSRO, F/PD 329.

40 SAS, Budgen Papers 86.

41 Guildhall Library, Gr 2.5.6, for all the subscription lists.

42 Facsimile with introduction in Skelton 1970. Kingsley 1982, 57-63.

43 Hay 1730. Taylor and Jones 1998, lxiii. Aubin 1936, 298-300, 321, 334. Royer 1787, 127-31.

44 Three collections of visitor's accounts, to Brighton, Chichester and Eastbourne, are in Farrant 1983, McCann 1995 and Farrant 1993b.

45 Defoe 1724-7, 1: letter II. Andrews 1960a. Andrews 1960b. Rogers 1975. Farrant 1985, 65. ESRO, PAR 420/7/1, Maresfield brief book.

46 Macky 1714, 1: letter VI. DNB 1998. Macky 1940, reprints the 2nd edn (1722).

47 Burton 1752. A manuscript translation of

the whole volume is in BL, Add. MS. 11571. Substantially complete translations of the Greek tour are in Burton 1856 and Burton 1916. Farrant 1976a.

48 Fant 1942. Sutherland and Mitchell 1986, 405, 495-7, 517-18. Caffyn 1998, 238, 283.

49 Farrant 1996a, 170-1. BL, Add. MS. 11571, ff. 117-18.

50 Millburn 1973. Caffyn 1998, 86-7, 317.

51 Petiver 1862-3, from BL, Sloane MS. 3340; the identification of their hosts I owe to Christopher Whittick, from ESRO, PAR 253/1/1/1; FRE 421, 7076, 7324-9, 7452; WIN 60, pp. 155, 158. The slight early notices of Sussex plants in published works, from 1568, are summarised in Wolley-Dod 1937, xxxv-xl.

52 Raven 1950, xvi-xvii, 52, 121, 142-3, 147, 169-71, 372. Cooper 1900, 14-18, 22, 24. Ray's letters to Courthope are now at ESRO, DAN 344-364; only nine have been properly edited, by Thompson 1974, but see Blencowe 1858, Gunther 1934 and Gunther 1937, 343-5, 352-4, 373-80. Burrell 1850. Ray 1674.

53 Hunter 1982, 206-7. Raven 1950, 382. Farrant 1988, 250. Lambert and Green 1776.

54 Godfrey, Wagner and London 1963, 160-1. Buck 1979. Hodson 1984-97, 1: 169-79. Centre for Kentish Studies, U129 Z17/8. Farrant 1972, 54, 57. BL, Lansdowne MS. 918, ff. 16-47, 18-19 quoted; 846, ff. 3-16 (extracts printed in Parry 1833, 183-6).

55 Autobiography: Vertue 1930-55, 1: 1-22. 1730: Vertue 1930-55, 5: 94-5, 2: 81-3. 1738: BL, LOAN 29/232, partly transcribed in Vertue 1930-55, 6: 88-90, also 4: 148-50. 1747: Vertue 1930-55, 5: 89, 141-50. 1751: Vertue 1930-55, 5: 84-5.

56 BL, Add. MS. 32123, f. 31 (reading of 'moonshine' is uncertain). Haskell 1985, 51. Rees 1998, pl. vi-xiv. Tate Gallery 1984, nos 28-31.

57 White 1981, 143 (Letter XVII). Nichols 1812-16, 4: 406. BL, Add. MS. 11571, f. 119; Lansdowne MS. 918, ff. 20-21, 24.

58 Pococke 1888-9, 2: 98-113.

59 Fiennes 1949, 39-41, 137-9.

60 Whaley 1945, from BL, Add. MS. 5842 which William Cole copied from BL, Add. MS. 5957. Also ESRO, AMS 5937, for a letter from Whaley to ?Walpole, printed in Walpole 1937-83, 40: 3-8.

61 Warwickshire County Record Office, CR 2017/TP 1.

62 Warwickshire County Record Office, CR 1841/7.

63 Walpole 1937-83, 9: 96-9, 35: 136-40.

64 Thompson 1885. Sedgwick 1970, 2: 466-7.

65 This section is based on Farrant 1993a and Farrant 1995b, which contain full references. Farrant 1996b. Hodson 1984-97, 3: 125-65.

66 Bodl., MS Top. gen. e.24, f. 287.

67 BL, Add. MS. 5679, f. 266, for the Herstmonceux letter.

68 Relhan 1761, 9. Caraccioli 1766. Whittick forthcoming. Gough 1780, 2: 288.

69 Dunvan 1795, 349, 358. Caffyn 1998, 281. Curtis 1966, 91-3, 96. Brent 1993, 96. He seems not to have left a will. Burrell was aware of Austen's collection but any extracts he made probably went into his 'Lewes papers' which have not survived: BL, Add. MS. 5705,ff. 126, 195.

70 Bodl., MS. Douce c.1, f. 42, for drawing of two urns found near Alfriston. Lower 1862, 227. Horsfield 1835, 1: 300-1, for a barrow dug west of Eastbourne in 1778, the urn presented to Burrell. Vine owned the first parish register of Kingston near Lewes: ESRO, PAR 408/1/1/1.

71 Dunvan 1795, 343-4. ESRO, Lewes St Anne's PR transcript; CHR 3/2/21; SAS/P 238; ACC 3632; AMS 6349/25. SAS, library accn 3718, Elliot Papers, letter of 28 Feb. 1771. Inderwick and Roberts 1896-1936, 5: 387.

72 Eastbourne Reference Library, Burrell's copy of *A compleat history of Sussex*, fc. 522. BL, Add. MS. 5697, f. 154.

73 ESRO, ADA 159, ff. 127-9; HIL 6/161/13-15. PRO, PROB 11/1088.

74 Eastbourne Reference Library, volume of notes by John Elliot, f. 173.

75 Brighton Reference Library, accn 33497R, p. 15.

76 Society of Antiquaries, Minute Book XVII, 7 Dec 1780; Ants Papers, 16 Nov 1775, 8 May 1777. Watson 1782, 2: 245. Bodl., MS. Eng. lett. e. 98, f. 29. Elliot's copy of the 1776 proof of Watson's book was, and may still be, in the Royal Institution Library: Horsfield 1832. The prospect by Serres, or another version of it, is at SAS: Poole 1993.

77 GM 1782, 52: 150. PRO, PROB 11/1088. Brighton Reference Library, accn 33497R (S9LEW EL5); Eastbourne Reference Library (Roman origins of Lewes); SAS Library (4 vols). Also ESRO, PAR 412/7/4, volume of inscriptions at St John-sub-Castro presented to the Rector. Challen 1952, 107.

78 ESRO, PAR 254/2/1 (parish register analysis); PAR 254/6/2 and ACC 165/60 (notes on prebendal manor).

79 BL, Add. MSS 6343-61. Dallaway 1815, 1: iv.

80 BL, Add. MS. 6355, ff. 13-14.

81 BL, Add. MSS 6343, 6344.

82 Sweet 1997, 60. BL, Add. MS. 6359, 27 Jan. 1778. Horsfield 1824-7, 2: 6. SAS, pic. coll. 3534. ESRO, ACC 386/1; ABE/D 560/1; SAS/ACC 1398. WSRO, Acc. 7986.

83 Brighton Reference Library, S9 C53, accn 85140. Domesday Book was published in Latin in 1783; an English translation of the Sussex section appeared in Henshall and Wilkinson 1799.

84 On the fire, see p. 131 below. For portraits: anon. 1927, 346, Horsfield 1824-7, 1: fc. 328, and Williamson 1903, 47 and plate.

85 BL, Add. MS. 5691, f. 50. Cooper 1900, 34. Namier and Brooke 1964, 2: 160.

86 Baker and Stenning 1928, 1: 145.

87 Burrell 1885. WSRO, Acc. 5979. Squibb 1977, 193.

88 BL, Add. MS. 32959, ff. 180, 357; 32963, ff. 119, 140; 32979, f.127.

89 See addresses from which letters already cited were written. Sheppard 1980, 230. BL, Add. MS. 21553, f. 117. Namier and Brooke 1964, 2: 163. Cole 1951, 56.

90 Namier and Brooke 1964, 2: 163. Bodl., MS. Eng. lett. e. 98, ff. 30, 79; 79, 85, for J. C. Brooke nominating a candidate for a place in the Rotation Office. The business of the Excise Board is indicated by Tom Paine's career: Keane 1995, 52-62, 72-5, 545-7. For Burrell's attendance in 1778: PRO, CUST 47/311-14; 48/19.

91 GM 1773, 43: 202 ('marriage portion'); GM 1796, 66 (1): 86 ('fortune'). WSRO, Acc. 921/XVIII/D/1. GM 1788, 58: 758, 834. Children: Cooper 1900, 39-40.

92 VCHS, 6 (2): 112. WSRO, MF 650. BL, Add. MS. 6359, nos 5, 6 and 9. Burrell 1793, 2: 97, 103-4. DNB 1998, Burrell, Lady Sophia.

93 Nichols 1812-16, 4: 665. DNB 1998, Ducarel, A. C. Society of Antiquaries, Minute Book VII, 28 Feb., 4 Apr. 1754. Nichols 1817-58, 3: 551.

94 National Library of Scotland, MS. 2911, edited as Burrell 1997, 7-8, quotations at 57 and 69. He transcribed an account of Iona by John Campbell in 1749; this he communicated to the Society of Antiquaries, probably in 1765 (Society of Antiquaries, Ants papers 115, Minute Book X, 5 Dec. 1765 and 13 Feb. 1766).

95 Ray 1674, 186-94. Property descent inferred from Cooper 1900, 29-30, and Davey 1991.

96 BL, Add. MS. 5703, f. 28.

97 GM 1796, 66 (1): 86. Mercer 1977, 117. Harris 1995, pl. 74, for a prospect of The Deepdene c. 1773 or 1783. Grimm's views sold at Sotheby's, 13 Jan. 1972.

98 Nichols 1812-16, 9: 797. PRO, PROB 11/1271.

99 VCHS, 6 (2): 90. Mercer 1977, 118.

100 BL, 269.c.5, auction catalogue. Bray 1800, 97; dedication dated Feb. 1799.

101 Bodl., MS. Eng. lett. e. 98, f. 30.

102 Bodl., MS. Eng. lett. e. 99, f. 34. WSRO, Acc. 2288, includes another early notebook, c. 1773.

103 Currie and Lewis 1994, 18, 156. BL, Add. MS. 6359, 29 Apr. 1777, 27 Jan. 1778. Eastbourne Reference Library, Burrell's copy of A compleat history, fc. 522; at 526-7 is Burrell's transcript of an anonymous account of the natural history of Maresfield and Uckfield, 1777, which reads as though answering 23 questions - but with no clue as who asked them. Thomas Durnford (1716/17-92) was incumbent at Harting and his son, also Thomas (1743/4-1801) of Kirdford and Middleton.

104 Bodl., Gough gen. top. 365, f. 473.

105 This section is based on Farrant 1997a which gives full references. Challen 1952 is an important source. Farrant 1997b.

106 SAS, LEWSA 2000.6.

107 Dunvan 1795, 323-4.

108 ESRO, SHR 820, 23 June, 23 July 1792.

109 Flower 1986, 16-34 for the Smiths.

110 VCHS 6 (1), 57.

111 YCBA, B1981.25.398 and 399 (repro. in Farrant 1997a, 267). Tate Gallery, ND 1658.

112 Pleasants 1943, 215-36. SAS, pic. coll. 5046.

113 SAS, library accn 3718, item 32.

114 On Sprange, see Freeman and Wells 1991. The draft for the Brighton view is now SAS, LEWSA 1995.9. An earlier prospect of Brighton, 1743, is from the sea and may have been for military purposes, being by Captain Clement Lemprière of the Board of Ordnance (d. 1746): Beevers 1995, no. 2, Bendall 1997, 2: 313.

115 Lambert sold such devices: Mallalieu 1976-90, 3: 198.

116 Dunvan 1795, 324-5.

117 This section is based, except as stated, on Clay 1941.

118 Royal Academy of Arts Library, catalogues of annual exhibitions, 1769-93 (except in 1793 the address is given as 26 Henrietta Street). Bodl., MS. Eng. lett. b. 11, f. 85, letter of Feb. 1792 is from no. 1.

119 BM, P&D 1958-7-12-3084, to James Tobin. Bodl., MS. Eng. lett. b. 11, ff. 84-5, to Richard Gough.

120 In the Witt Library, reproduced in Joyner 1983, pl. 1.

121 Allen 1992, 105-8, 116. BM, P&D 1958-7-12-3084. Eastbourne Reference Library, Burrell's copy of *A compleat history*, for finished watercolours by Sophia Burrell.

122 Holt-White 1901, 1: 288, 319-20, 326, 328; 2: 3.

123 Presumably George Mullins who came to London from Dublin in 1770 and probably died in 1775: Waterhouse 1981, 252.

124 Wyndham 1779. Lord Clanricarde was John Smith Bourke, 11th Earl, FRS, FSA (1720-82).

125 Lyles and Hamlyn 1997, 90. Joyner 1983, 7.

126 Hunt 1909, 174. Obituary in GM 1794, 64: 576. Nichols 1812-16, 6: 295.

127 Redgrave 1878, 188. University of Bristol Library, Special Collections, HAd. BL, 269.c.5, auction catalogue.

128 Listed in Wellesley 1850 who transcribed some of the notes.

129 King 1801, 1: Plates XXII, XXIII/2, XXV-XXVII/6.

130 Farrant 1995b, 370. Frew 1980, 174, 177.

131 Bodl., MS. Top. gen. e.24, ff. 236-332 (1767 tour), 344-59 (1757 tour), 363-76 (pictures at Petworth). GM 1767, 37: 443-4. Camden 1789, 1: 192-209. Camden 1806, 1: 275-302. Sabatier 1963.

132 Jessup 1975, 23-4, 49, 113, 123,160-5, 256-8, 272-3. Horsfield 1835, 1: 171. Douglas 1818. BL, Add. MS. 33649, 2, 4 Mar. 1815; 33658, 12 Feb. 1821. Steer 1966. National Monuments Record, BB 88/1915-1964, photographic copy of Douglas's notebook on excavations in 1814-16.

133 Gilpin 1804, 45. Brandon 1998, 146-50. White 1981, 143. BL, Egerton MS. 2672, f. 165. Garraty and Carnes 1999, 16: 691-3. On the 'Picturesque' generally, see Andrews 1989.

134 Gilpin 1804, 45. Bodl., MS. Eng. misc. f.194, ff. 93, 100-101. Farrant 1996a, 174.

135 These paragraphs on the Youngs are based on Farrant 1992 where full references are given. Their principal reports on Sussex are Young 1771, 3: 117-77, Young 1789, Young 1793, Young 1794 and Young 1808.

136 Marshall 1798, 2: passim. McCann 1983, 635, 638-9. Murphy 1959, 774.

137 Kingsley 1982, 91-6, 105-11. Skelton 1970. Holland 1957. Bendall 1997, 1: 53.

138 Mullens, Swann and Jourdain 1919. Markwick 1791. Markwick 1798. Mullens 1922. Harting 1890. Brighton Reference Library, accn 76520.

139 Bridson, Phillips and Harvey 1980 and Desmond 1994 under names. Trail and Steer 1963.

140 Warwickshire County Record Office, CR 2017/TP 1, pp. 59-60.

141 White 1931, 45. Ford and Torrens 1989, unpaginated; quoted. Torrens 1998, 182-6. Farrant 1973/4, 5.

142 Gibbs and Farrant 1970/1, 29. Oxford University Museum of Natural History, Smith Papers. Phillips 1844, 63. Kingsley 1982, 122. Jessup 1975, 259, 263, 269. Dean 1999, 38n, 23-5, 45. Mantell 1822.

143 Burr 1766, 249-50, 267. Sprange 1780, i-ii, 164.

144 Royer 1787, 47. Caffyn 1998, 290. Stell 1794. Evans 1805. anon. 1777. Hay 1783. Hay 1794. Heron-Allen and James 1940.

145 Pennant 1801. Byng 1934 is the main edition, but Byng 1933 contains more of the illustrations from the MS. in Brighton Reference Library. For Skinner, see note 161.

146 The attribution seems to rest on Charles Verral (1778-1843) in Horsfield 1835, 1: 52 and John Dudeney (1782-1842) in Blencowe 1849, 253. ESRO, SHR 820.

Announcement of first two parts in Delap 1792. Dunvan 1795, 344-5, 358. Sweet 1997, 29. The Revd John Mossop (1756-94) offered his collections for a history of Lewes to the publisher John Nichols: Bodl., Gough gen. top. 365, f. 481; Caffyn 1998, 321-2; Tibble 1989.

147 Hill 1994, 52. Brent 1993, 106-7.

148 Rowe 1928. Salzman 1946. Smith 1973. SAS, T. Woollgar, 'Spicilegia ... Lewensis', 4 vols.

149 Webb and Wilson 1952. North 1926. ESRO, SAS/C 1 (Goodwyn's rental); HOW 34/16 (vestry book).

150 Johnstone and Steer 1961. Hay 1804, ix-xi, 309-10. Spershott 1962. Wratten 1974.

151 Nightingale 1818. Moss 1824, xi-xiii. Dawson 1909, 1: viii; 2: 505-9. DNB 1998, Herbert, William. ESRO, AMS 6113. Martin and Martin 1999.

152 Moss 1825, of which the only recorded copy is in ESRO, AMS 6113/5.

153 DNB 1998. Tierney 1834, vi-vii. Arundel Castle Library has his manuscript and a corrected proof copy.

154 Bodl., Gough maps 32.17.b. Towner Art Gallery, 1609 (W.202). Worthing AG, X1975/382. YCBA, B1989.9.

155 Godfrey 1940; photocopies in WSRO, PD 2586; Easebourne repr. VCHS, 4: fc. 48. Kuist 1982, 144, 172.

156 SAS, library accn 9087-9. Farrant 1995a.

157 Brighton Museum, 101473-83. Shaw 1790a; also Shaw 1791b. Shaw 1792. Greenslade 1994, 20-21.

158 Brown 1982, nos 1386-1437, *passim*; Moore's view of Lewes Castle is paralleled by Girtin's, Sotheby's, 15 March 1990 (lot 63), copy at SAS.

159 Nurse forthcoming. GM 1842, 2nd s., 18: 661-2. Smith 1979.

160 Mallalieu 1977. Worthing Museum and YCBA each has several Nixons.

161 Lay: Brighton Museum, 101013-20, 101421-4, 102171, 102288. Burchell: Farrant 1999. Skinner: BL, Add. MSS 33637, 33649, 33658, 33670; Skinner 1984, 1-9. Crotch and Newbery: Rennert 1975, pl. xxii; Beevers 1995, 97-8; Pryce 1996, 93. Buckler: BL, Add. MSS 36389-90, 36404-5 (see Salzman 1952), K. Top. 42; Christie's 21 Mar. 1989.

162 Conner 1984, 39, 123.

163 See PDB. Turner's activity in Sussex in the 1790s requires further study: some of the pictures may be copies for Dr Munro. The seacoast view in the Fitzwilliam Museum is certainly not of Brighton: Beevers 1995, 32-9, 61-5.

164 Butler, Luther and Warrell 1989.

165 Shoberl 1813.

166 Shanes 1990, 8-10, 279-80. Finberg 1927, xii, 70-1. It was announced in the *Quarterly Review* for Jan. 1820, 'New publications', as *Views at Hastings and its vicinity*, pt 1, £3.

167 Nichols 1817-58, 6: 460-1.

168 Steer 1965. Steer 1967. Hope 1974b. Farrant forthcoming. WSRO, Add. MS. 46485. WSRO, Add. MSS 20186-259, Dallaway papers, include his Constantinople letters which await proper study: Hope 1974a does not use them.

169 Dallaway 1815, 1: iv; the geology section was rewritten by John Hawkins and issued on cancel leaves in 1819. Davies 1972. BL, Add. MS. 5702, ff. 132-3. Dallaway 1819.

170 Tierney 1834, ix-x. Hudson 1994b, 388-9. Lower 1865, 257-8. Hampshire Record Office, Top 343/2/12. Steer 1966, 7. Dallaway 1832, vi-vii. Cartwright 1830, preface.

171 Steer 1974b. Horsfield 1824-7, 1: [preface].

172 Horsfield 1832, photocopy at SAS Library. Devonshire Collections at Chatsworth House, CPP/L. SWA, 10 Sept. 1832.

173 Horsfield 1835, 1: i, vi; 2: 7.

174 Hudson 1994b, 389.

175 All except the first, covering Brighton, are in SAS Library: Salzman 1967.

176 Some of the duplicate entries for the same subscriber under different heads in the classified list may have been missed, so the counts here may not be exact. Mandler 1997, 22-38.

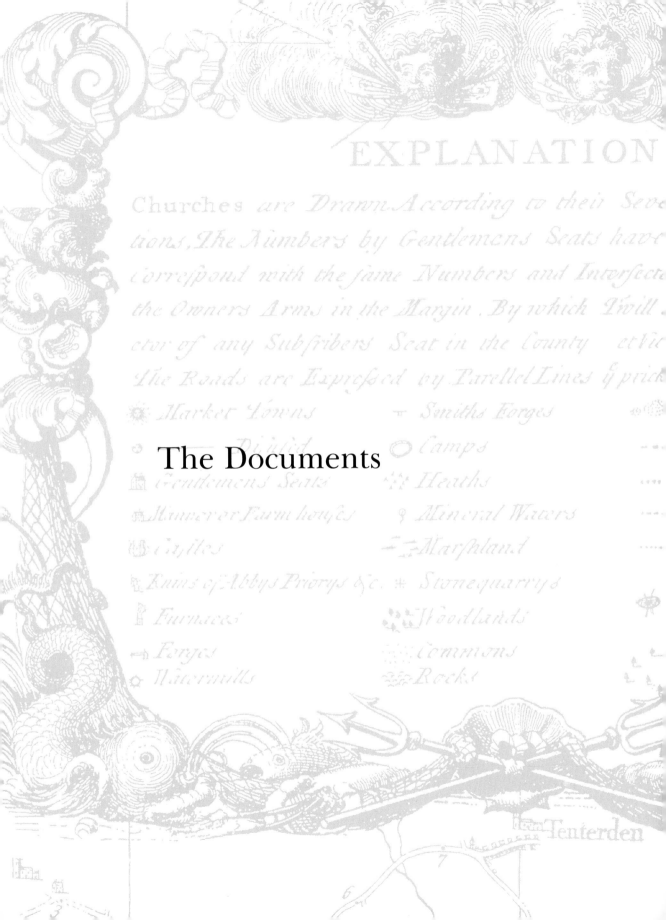

The Documents

PROPOSALS
By Way of
SUBSCRIPTION,
FOR
Making a new Survey, and publishing a most correct MAP, of the
County of Sussex.
By *RICHARD BUDGEN* Surveyor at *Frant* near *Tunbridge Wells*.

IT is proposed, I. That an actual Survey or Admeasurement be made of the whole County, divided into its Rapes and Hundreds; in which shall be described the Towns, Villages, Churches, Chapels, *&c.* according to their Forms and Situations; as likewise all Gentlemens Seats, Castles, Forests, Parks, Chaces, Creeks, Bays, Rocks, Shoals, Sands, Bridges, Lakes, Soil, (whether Woody, Heathy, Mountainous, or Champaign.) Also what belongs to the Iron Works, *viz.* Chief Mines, Furnaces, Forges, *&c.* Likewise Windmills, Watermills, whether for Corn, Gunpowder, *&c.*

II. That an actual Survey or Measurement be made, not only of the Post Roads that cross the County, but likewise all the principal Roads that are of Note or Use to Travellers, inserting the Names of all Commons, Downs, Forests, Greens, Cross-ways, Villages, Streets, *&c.* that shall lye in or near the Roads. Describing all Lanes and By-ways, that shall turn out of the Roads, to what Places they lead. To delineate and lay down the Roads thus survey'd exactly, according to their several Angles, Turnings, Bearings and Situations, noting the Miles between Town and Town, whereby the Distance, not only of the Towns, but also of other interjacent Places will appear by Inspection.

III. That every thing relating to Natural History of the County, whether Mines, Iron, Coal, or other Minerals, shall be inserted; as also the Manufactories; how far any River is navigable; Antiquities, where met with, whether *Roman*, *Saxon*, or *Danish*, to be noted.

IV. To give greater Advantages to this Map than any other yet published, not only as to the Roads, the true Longitude and Latitude of Places, the Value of Livings in the King's Books, whether Rectories or Vicaridges, *&c.* But also, and that more especially, by giving remarkable Facts and Circumstances to Places in easy Characters to be explain'd by themselves, that thereby it may, in some measure give, an Historical as well as a Geographical Account of the County.

Engraved by JOHN SENEX, and printed on the finest Imperial Paper, containing in length about five Foot, and in breadth about four; which will make the Scale so large as to contain a Mile in an Inch.

Those who are willing to have their Arms engrav'd are to pay half a Guinea in Hand, and half a Guinea more on the Delivery of a Map illuminated, pasted on Canvas with Rolls. Of this sort no more will be made up than are subscrib'd for: And those who are not willing to be at that Expence may have one in Sheets for half a Guinea.

SUBSCRIPTIONS will be taken in by RICHARD BUDGEN, at *Frant* near *Tunbridge Wells*; BERNARD LINTOT, at the *Cross Keys* between the *Temple Gates*, and by JOHN SENEX at *Salisbury Court*; by [blank] at *Chichester*; by [blank] at *Petworth*; by [blank] at *Horsham*; by [blank] at *East Grinstead*; by [blank] at *Arundel*; by [blank] at *Lewes*; and by [blank] at *Eastborne* in *Sussex*.

N.B. This Map is intended to be deliver'd at *Christmas* next.

Overleaf The key to the map as published and dated 1724

1. The prospectus for Richard Budgen's map of Sussex, 1723

Richard Budgen was born in 1695, the son of a Frant butcher with a shop in Tunbridge Wells. With whom he trained is not known. His career was short but considerable in achievement. The map of Sussex is his first known work and must have been a major undertaking. After it was completed, he is found doing more conventional work. He completed a survey of the Battle Abbey estate for Sir Thomas Webster in 1724, and was working for Sir Spencer Compton in and around Eastbourne between 1725 and 1730 and for Samuel Boys of Hawkhurst in 1728. The maps for all three clients included bird's-eye views of buildings which seem to be at least in part antiquarian in inspiration. In 1730 he published an account of the hurricane which tore through eastern Sussex in October 1729. The pamphlet also gave 'some account of a new engine to be worked by the wind' which he had 'perfected after a long time, a close and intent application of thoughts and a large expense in making and altering of models.' The costs of materials and, doubtless, of time taken from more profitable pursuits must have contributed to his indebtedness on his early death in 1731.[1]

Nevertheless, Richard Budgen was the founder of a dynasty of surveyors. His son Richard II (1730-89) was in practice as a surveyor at Frant by 1757 and had three sons who followed his profession. Richard III (b. 1760) took over the business in Frant, and was succeeded by two sons, William (b. 1790) and John (b. 1794). Thomas (1765-1832) was trained by Henry Hogben in Kent and was practising in Lewes by 1788 where he set up also as a printer, publishing the short-lived *Lewes and Brighthelmston Pacquet* newspaper in 1789. From the same year he worked for the Ordnance Survey first in Sussex and later in Wales and the West Country. He may have trained William Figg (1770-1833), from whose firm has descended the Lewes architects' practice, Fuller and Askew. Charles (1769-1838), of Barham in Kent in 1789, was a 'surveying draughtsman' with the Ordnance Survey from 1794, as was his sister Jane's husband, Robert Dawson of Dover (1771-1860) from 1791. Two of Dawson's sons entered the Ordnance Survey as well.[2]

This prospectus is dated to no later than 1723 on the strength of the last sentence, that the map was to be delivered at Christmas next, of a newspaper notice of 25 May 1723 announcing that the map was now finished and inviting subscribers to send in their arms for engraving, and of another notice of 21 December 1723, saying that it was available from Budgen, Bernard Lintot and booksellers in the county. Also in December 1723 Spencer Compton paid £21 for the privilege of the map being dedicated to him. However the map's publication history is unclear. All but one complete surviving copies are dated 1724, but may have been issued only some years later, as they were printed for Henry Lintot, Bernard's son who took over the business in the 1730s, and as some of the 148 subscribers' titles date from later. But one undated, though clearly earlier, copy was marked only as engraved by John Senex.[3] What at least the prospectus makes clear is that Bernard Lintot and Senex were partners in the project at the outset. See Essay 2.3 for discussion of the map's content. The only known copy of the prospectus is in the collection of papers on Sussex made by John Warburton who in February 1722 had issued his own prospectus for a map of Kent, Sussex and Surrey (Essay 2.3). The collection also contains a partial copy of the undated version of Budgen's map.

2. Two prospectuses and a subscription list for the Bucks' views

These documents are discussed in Essay 2.2; for pictures by Samuel Buck, see also Views 51 and 111. In Document 2.3, the list of subscribers, as printed in the subscription list to the 12th collection, has been augmented. In italics under the name is information to identify subscribers with known Sussex (and a few with Surrey) connections. 'P' or 'p' in the column at the left indicates a subscriber to the Sussex plates who was also a subscriber to the previous, 11th, collection issued in 1736 (views in Kent); and 'N' or 'n' a subscriber to the next, 13th, collection issued in 1738 (views in Norfolk, Suffolk and Essex), in order to isolate those other subscribers who may have been interested in only the plates for their home county. The capital letter, 'P' or 'N', indicates a subscriber to the 12th collection who was also named as a subscriber in the list on the reverse of the prospectus for the 6th set of *Perspective views of cities* (Document 2.1). That list has a different status to the list printed in Document 2.3: it was printed before the Bucks had canvassed the localities of which views were to be published and presumably comprised those people who had said that they wished to subscribe to all future sets. These subscribers included the core supporters of the Bucks' projects: of the 106 subscribers for the views of cities, 83 also subscribed to the 11th, 12th and 13th collections of antiquities, only 11 subscribed to none and 2 (indicated by *) subscribed to the 12th collection alone.

The identifications come from the indexes (and the knowledge of the archivists) at ESRO and WSRO, the poll book for the 1734 county election (ESRO, ASH 3225), the Sussex Clergy Index in SAS Library and the subscribers to Richard Budgen's Sussex map dated 1724, listed in Ellis 1873. Life dates are in (brackets); otherwise dates refer to the period in the office named.

To the Noble & Generous Encouragers of this Work by Subscri[...]

In SUSSEX.		
1. Battel Abby.	5. Winchelsea Monastery.	11. Winchelsea Castle.	16. G
2. Begeham Abby.	6. Arundel Castle	12. Hurstmonceux Castle.	17. B
3. {Lewis Priory and Castle.	7. Pevensey Castle N.E. View.	In SURRY.	18. L
	8. Pevensey Castle S.E. View.	13. Waverley Abby.	19. R
4. Boxgrove Priory.	9. Bodiham Castle	14. Newark Priory.	20. E
	10. Amberley Castle.	15. Farnham Castle.	

SUBSC

Duke of Ancaster.
Earl of Abingdon.
Earl of Arran.
Lord Visc. Andover.
Lord Abergavenny.
Rt. Hon.ble Tho. Auslabie Esq.r
Hon.ble Rich.d Arundell Esq.r
Sr. Will.m Ashburnham Bar.t
Sr. John St. Aubyn Bar.t
Swithin Adee M.D.
George Alderige M.D.
Edward Alexander Esq.r
Anthony Allen Esq.r
Thomas Attwood M.D.
Duke of Beaufort.
Duke of Bedford.

Late Ld. Archb.p of Canterbury.
Earl of Cholmondeley.
Lord Bp. of Chichester.
Lord Carteret.
Sr. William Carew Bar.t
Sr. Thomas Cave Bar.t
Sr. John Chester Bar.t
Sr. John Hynde Cotton Bar.t
Sr. William Courtenay Bar.t
Sr. Nathaniel Curzon Bar.t
Henry Campion Esq.r
Thomas Carew Esq.r
John Carew Esq.r
Henry Carleton Esq.r
John Caryll Esq.r
Arthur Champhernowne Esq.r

Earl of Effingham.
Earl of Exeter.
Sr. Jam.s Edwards B.t F.R.S.
Sr. Richard Ellys Bar.t
Sr. John Eyles Bar.t
Sr. Joseph Eyles K.t
Samuel Edwards Esq.r
Mrs. Mary Edwards.
George Egles Esq.r
Mrs. Elizabeth Eliot.
William Early Gent.
Lord Fairfax.
Hon.ble John Finch Esq.r
Hon.ble Hen. Finch Esq.r F.R.S.
Hon.ble Sr. And: Fountain. K.t

Earl of Harford.
Earl of Huntingdon.
Lord Harrington.
Hon.ble Geo. Hamilton Es[...]
Hon.ble Tho. Herbert Es[...]
James Hargrave D.D.
Brig. Gen.t Tho: Howa[...]
Francis Hamlin Esq.r
Col.t William Handasy[...]
James Harding Esq.r
Edward Harley Esq.r
Charles Harison Esq.r
William Hay Esq.r
Thomas Hayley Esq.r
Richard Heath Esq.r
Benjamin Heath Esq.r

2.1 Prospectus for *Perspective views of cities*, 1736

British Library, C.161.f.2
(49), printed

London, 1736

PROPOSALS

For Publishing by SUBSCRIPTION,

Six PERSPECTIVE VIEWS

VIZ. Of the

Cities of *CANTERBURY, ROCHESTER*, and *CHICHESTER*;

The Towns of *Guildford* and *Maidstone*:

AND OF

His Majesty's Dock-yard at *CHATHAM*,

In the Counties of *Kent, Sussex* and *Surrey*.

By SAMUEL and NATHANIEL BUCK.

According to Act of Parliament.

Perspective views of cities and towns of note are and always will be agreeable: But these are not only designed to delight the eye with as beautiful pictures as the places will afford, but also to entertain the mind with some useful knowledge, by means of a Summary of what authentick History affords relating thereunto; such as the *Date, remarkable Periods* and *accidents*; also the *present State* of each Place.

AND in particular regard to the promoters of this Undertaking, the Authors will persist in a rule, which they have hitherto in all their undertakings of this kind inviolably preserved; that is of parting with no prints but to *Subscribers only*.

THE size of each Print will be two Foot nine Inches in Length, and thirteen Inches in Depth; with proper *Explanations* and *References* to the places remarkable in each *View*.

THE drawings will be taken from the best Stations, and the *Plates* finished with the utmost care and expedition, that the *Prints* may be delivered as usual, to the satisfaction of the Subscribers, printed on the best Imperial Atlas paper.

THE price will be fifteen shillings a sett: five shillings to be paid at the time of subscribing, and the remainder on delivery.

THE Authors are obliged in gratitude to acknowledge the great encouragement their last five setts of perspective views of Cities and Towns met with, as well as their other labours of this kind, and are thereby emboldened to publish this Proposal, in order to go on with a sett annually, till they have perfected draughts of the most eminent Cities and Towns in the Kingdom.

THOSE prints already published are [*then follow the names of the cities and towns of which prints were published in the first five sets*].

ANY Gentlemen who subscribe to *these* now proposed, may (if they please) subscribe at the same time, and on the same terms (*i.e.* Fifteen Shillings) for the *whole*, or any single Sett of those already published; they being disposed of no other way nor by any other persons, than the *Undertakers*, who do *Themselves* design and draw the *Views* on the *Spot*, and engrave their own *Copper-Plates*.

SUBSCRIPTION-MONEY is taken in by the Authors, whose Chambers are in the Third Stair-case of No. 1 in *Garden-Court, Middle-Temple*.

[verso] Subscribers [106 names collated in Document 2.3]

PROPOSALS

London, 1737.

For Publishing by SUBSCRIPTION,
Twenty four perspective VIEWS,
Of the PRESENT STATE of the most Noted
Abbies, Religious Foundations, Castles,
And other REMAINS OF ANTIQUITY;
in NORFOLK, SUFFOLK, and ESSEX
By SAMUEL *and* NATHANIEL BUCK.

The Antiquity of such *Edifices*, together with the pious Intention of the *Founders*, having made the Memory of them justly venerable; and as most of those valuable *Structures* are now mould'ring in *Ruins*, they being already no more than the defac'd *Remains* of what they originally were: The best *Perspective Views* they are at this Day capable of, we find by Experience do not fail of being acceptable to this curious Age; as they greatly contribute to illustrate the History of the former State of this *Island*, and to transmit those things to Posterity, which must otherwise be irretrievably lost: The *Undertakers* have for these Reasons made it their principal Bussiness, at no small Expence, to visit them, and take *Perspective Views* of whatever remains remarkable.

THIS *Undertaking* they have pursued for twelve Years past with the desired success, and are therefore obliged in gratitude to acknowledge the Encouragement they have met with; having been honoured with the *subscriptions* of a great many of the *Nobility*, *Clergy*, and *Gentry*, which embolden them to proceed with their utmost Industry and Care, in their first Intention of going through the Kingdom.

THOSE which they now propose for the present year, will be *Twenty four Drawings*, collected from the abovesaid counties: which will be carefully taken upon the spot, engraved on the same Number of *Copper-Plates*, and printed each on a half sheet of *Royal Paper*. At the bottom of each Print, there will be a short Account of what *History* or the Information of curious learned Persons, concerned either with the *Date*, *Founders*, or notable *Accident*, relating thereunto, can afford: To which an Alphabetical List of *Subscribers* will be prefixed, and delivered by *Lady-Day* next.

THE SUBSCRIPTION will be *Two Guineas*, One to be paid down at the Time of Subscribing, and the other on the Delivery.

THEY have already been in the following *Counties*, and exhibited whatsoever is most deserving of Notice therein (viz) [*then a list of the counties in each of the first twelve sets, ending*] Sussex, Surrey, Middlesex, and Hertfordshire, the Twelfth.

ANY Gentlemen who subscribe for *these* now propos'd may (if they please) subscribe at the same Time and on the same Terms, (i.e. Two Guineas a Sett) for the *whole*, or any single *sett* of those already published; they being disposed of no other Way, nor by any other Persons, than the Undertakers, who do *themselves* design and draw the *Views* on the *spot*, and engrave their own *copper-plates*.

SUBSCRIPTION MONEY is taken in by the Authors, whose Chambers are in the Third Stair-Case of No. 1 in *Garden-Court, Middle-Temple*.

[verso: names of 240 subscribers printed and 15 in manuscript]

2.3 Subscribers to the 12th collection of *Perspective views of remains of antiquity*, 1737

Guildhall Library, City of London, Gr 2.5.6, printed

To the Noble & Generous Encouragers of this Work by Subscription This Twelfth Collection of Twenty four Views as follows

In SUSSEX
1. Battel Abby
2. Begeham Abby
3. Lewis Priory and Castle
4. Boxgrove Priory
5. Winchelsea Monastery
6. Arundel Castle
7. Pevensey Castle N.E. View
8. Pevensey Castle S.E. View
9. Bodiham Castle

10. Amberley Castle
11. Winchelsea Castle
12. Hurstmonceux Castle

In SURRY
13. Waverley Abby
14. Newark Priory
15. Farnham Castle
16. Guildford Castle
17. Betchworth Castle

18. Lambeth Palace
19. Richmond Palace
20. Esher Palace

In MIDDLESEX
21. Sion Abby
22. Tower of London S. View
23. Tower of London W. View

In HERTFORDSHIRE
24. St. Alban's Abby

is most gratefully Inscrib'd by Their most obed't hum'ble Serv's
SAMUEL & NATHANIEL BUCK

NB. The Generous Subscription this Twelfth Set of Prints has been honour'd with encouraging the Authors to proceed, They propose this Summer to take Drawings of the most remarkable Remains of ABBYS, CASTLES &c. to be found in Norfolk, Suffolk, & Essex, and to finish the Plates in Twelve Months time from the Date hereof.

No. 1 Garden Court Middle Temple London. Publish'd according to Act of Parliament by Samuel & Nathaniel Buck March 25th 1737.

	Subscriber
	Identification
PN	Duke of Ancaster
p n	Earl of Abingdon
PN	Earl of Arran
n	Lord Viscount Andover
n	Lord Abergavenny
	William Nevill of Kidbrooke Park (View 93)
PN	Rt Hon. John Aislabie esq
PN	Hon. Richard Arundell esq
	Sir William Ashburnham bt
	of Broomham in Guestling (View 98)
PN	Sir John St Aubyn bt
n	Swithin Adee MD

PN	George Alderige MD
p n	Edward Alexander esq
n	Anthony Allen esq
	of Guildford, Surrey
p	Thomas Attwood MD
PN	Duke of Beaufort
PN	Duke of Bedford
PN	Duke of Bolton
PN	Duke of Buccleuch
PN	Earl of Burlington
PN	Lord Brooke
	Sir Cecil Bishopp bt
	of Parham
PN	Sir Edward Blount bt
PN	Dean of Bristol
PN	John Burton DD
	perhaps the Fellow of Eton College whose travels in

Sussex are mentioned in Essay 2.3 - though his DD was not conferred until 1752
Archdeacon Ball
Thomas Ball, Archdeacon of Chichester, collated 7 Sept. 1736
Michael Baker esq
of Mayfield (View 140)
Edward Barker esq
of London, gent., with vote for land in West Tarring 1734
Revd Thomas Barton
Rector of Warbleton, 1732-61
p n John Basset esq
Edward Bathurst esq
of Goudhurst, Kent, with vote

for land in Lamberhurst 1734
William Battine esq
of East Marden
Thomas Beckford esq
Revd Mr Birch
John Board esq
of Paxhill in Lindfield (View 132)
p n Revd William Borlace
Thomas Borrett esq
p John Boulter esq
N Thomas Bradshawe esq
John Bridges esq
PN Marmaduke Buck MA
John Budgen MD
Thomas Budgen esq
of West Newdigate, Surrey
Robert Burnett esq
of Herrings in Dallington (View 63); Steward of the Household to the Duke of Newcastle
N George Bussel esq
James Butler esq
of Warminghurst (View 189)
n John Butler esq
of Warminghurst
P John Bodledge gent
John Browne gent
Late Lord Archbishop of Canterbury
p n Earl of Cholmondeley
Lord Bishop of Chichester
Francis Hare, 1731-40
p n Lord Carteret
PN Sir William Carew bt
p n Sir Thomas Cave bt
p n Sir John Chester bt
PN Sir John Hynde Cotton bt
PN Sir William Courtenay bt
n Sir Nathaniel Curzon bt
Henry Campion esq
of Danny in Hurstpierpoint
PN Thomas Carew esq
PN John Carew esq
Henry Carleton esq
p John Caryll esq
of Ladyholt in Harting, to whom plate 11 is dedicated (View 102)
PN Arthur Champernowne esq
Philip Cheale esq
of Henfield

n John Cheale esq
of Findon, Norroy King of Arms
Philip Cheale esq
of Shiprods in Henfield
n Thomas Chester esq
PN James Chetham esq
Charles Child esq
n Thomas Chowne esq
of Alfriston
Revd William Clarke
Rector of Buxted 1724-68; Prebendary of Hova Villa 1728-71 (Essay 2.1)
Revd John Clarke
PN Richard Cliff esq
p n Thomas Cokayne esq
John Collier esq
of Hastings
PN Thomas Coster esq
George Courthop esq
of Whiligh in Ticehurst (View 181)
p Alexander Courthope esq
of Sprivers in Horsmonden, Kent
p n John Crawley esq
p n John Creyk MA
Nathaniel Cruttenden esq
of Hastings
PN Duke of Devonshire
n Earl of Donegall
p Countess Dowager of Derby
Mary Stanley of Halnaker in Boxgrove (View 24), to whom plate 4 is dedicated
p Sir Basill Dixwell bt
of Broomehouse in Barham, Kent
p n Revd Sir John Doblin bt
Sir Thomas Dyke bt
of Horam in Waldron
George Darrell esq
of Scotney in Lamberhurst (Views 125 and 126)
Revd Charles Dixon
Rector of Newick 1734-54
William Dobell esq
of Folkington (Views 84 and 85)
John Dobson esq
Charles Docminique esq

of Chipstead, Surrey
p n John Douglas esq
Thomas D'oyly LLB
of a Chichester family, later Archdeacon of Lewes residing at Conyboro in Barcombe (View 12); graduated from Oxford BCL 1732 and DCL 1737
PN William Draper esq
of Addiscombe, Surrey
p n Earl of Effingham
Francis Howard 1st Earl
PN Earl of Exeter
n Sir James Edwards bt FRS
p n Sir Richard Ellys bt
PN Sir John Eyles bt
PN Sir Joseph Eyles kt
p n Samuel Edwards esq
PN Mrs Mary Edwards
George Egles esq
of Wadhurst
PN Mrs Elizabeth Eliot
William Early gent
p n Lord Fairfax
PN Lord Foley
p n Hon. John Finch esq
n Hon. Henry Finch esq FRS
p n Hon. Sir Andrew Fountain Kt
John Meres Fagge esq
of Glynleigh in Westham (View 193)
John Farhill esq
of Chichester, lawyer
N Cornelius Farr esq
Joseph Ferrers esq
of Oak Ferrers in Fletching (d. 1740), Colonel
p n John Fisher esq
Humphrey Fowle esq
of Rotherfield (1682-1756)
George Fox esq
James Fox esq
n Thomas Frederick esq
Revd John Frewen
Rector of Guestling 1736-43
John Fuller esq FRS
of Rose Hill in Brightling (View 29) (1680-1745)
John Fuller esq
of Rose Hill in Brightling (1706-55)

PN Earl of Godolphin
PN Lord Gower
 n Lord Guernsey
  Sir William Gage bt & kt
  of the Bath
  of Firle
 p Sir John Gifford bt
  Sir Charles Goring bt
  of Burton
PN Sir Robert Grosvenor bt
 n Sir Robert Godschall kt
 p n Roger Gale esq FRS
 n Nathaniel Garland esq
PN Charles Fleetwood
  Gerrard esq
  Richard Gilham esq
  Revd Daniel Gittins
  Rector of South Stoke 1733-61
 p n John Godfrey esq
  Thomas Godley esq
  John Goldham esq
  of Seaford
  Henry Gore esq
PN Thomas Green esq FRS
PN Richard Goeing gent
 p n Mr Richard Grimstead
PN Earl of Hartford
 p n Earl of Huntingdon
  Lord Harrington
  William Stanhope, MP for Steyning 1727
PN Hon. George Hamilton esq
 p n Hon. Thomas Herbert esq
  James Hargrave DD
  James Hargraves, Prebendary of Thorney, 1723-32 and Dean of Chichester 1739-41
  Brig Gen Thomas Howard
  Francis Hamlin esq
  of Ardingly?
 n Col William Handasyd
 n James Harding esq
PN Edward Harley esq
  Charles Harison esq
  of Sutton in Seaford
  William Hay esq
  of Glyndebourne
  Thomas Hayley esq
  Dean of Chichester 1735-9?
  Richard Heath esq
  of Hatchlands, East Clandon, Surrey?

 n Benjamin Heath esq
PN Anthony Henley esq
  Revd Edward Hill
  Chaplain to the Earl of Wilmington; Rector of St Clement's Hastings 1731-42 and Vicar of Fletching 1732-60
 n Robert Hinde esq
  Benjamin Hoadly MD FRS
  William Hodson esq
  Revd Thomas Hooper
  Rector of Beckley 1699-1752 (View 16); Vicar of Hailsham 1701-53
  Revd Robert Hooper
  Vicar of Mayfield 1733/4-46/7
 n Edward Hopson esq
 p Robert Humfreys esq
 p n John Hylton esq
  George Holmes gent
  of Burpham Place?
 n Charles Holwell gent
  Lord Viscount Irwin
  Henry Ingram, 7th Viscount; MP for Horsham 1722-36
  Hon. Col Charles Ingram
  of Hills near Horsham; MP for Horsham 1737-48
 p n Sir William Irby bt
 p n Sir Justinian Isham bt
PN Theodore Jacobsen esq
  FRS
  William James esq
  John Jewkes esq
  of Petworth, lawyer
 * Revd James Ingram
  Vicar of Oving 1725-46
 p n Maurice Johnson esq
 * Revd Chancellor Jordan
  George Jordan, Prebendary of Sidlesham, but not Chancellor of Chichester Cathedral?
 p n James Joye esq
 n Thomas Jenkins gent
  of Rampendene in Burwash
 p Duke of Kent
PN Duke of Kingston
PN Earl of Kinnoul
  Lord King
  John King, 2nd Baron of Ockham

PN Samuel Knight DD
 p Mrs Anne Knight
  William Kempe esq
  of Lewes or Slindon
 n George Kendall esq
PN Duke of Leeds
 n Earl of Leicester
  Lord Bishop of London
PN Lord Bishop of Lincoln
PN Sir Robert Lawley bt
PN Sir Thomas Lowther bt
 n Benjamin Langwith DD
  Rector of Petworth 1718-43
  John Lawton esq
  Percival Lewis esq
 p n George Liddell esq
  of Wakehurst?
  Mrs Anne Lintott
  widow of Thomas of Wallhurst in Cowfold
 p n Richard Long esq
 p Revd John Lloyd
  Rector of Maresfield 1728-39
  Revd Henry Lushington
  Vicar of Eastbourne 1734-79
 p Alexander Lutterell esq
 p Stephen Le Bass gent
PN Earl of Malton
PN Earl of Mountrath
 n Lord Viscount Midleton
 n Lady Rachel Morgan
  Hon. Christopher Mansel
  esq
  of Newick Place
  Sir Richard Mill bt
  of Stedham
  Sir John Miller bt
  of West Lavant Place in East Lavant (View 127)
 n Sir John Molesworth bt
PN Sir William Morice bt
 n Sir More Molyneux bt
  of Loseley in Guildford, Surrey
  Thomas Manningham DD
  Treasurer of Chichester Cathedral
  Simon Manningham LLD
  Rector of Jevington, Prebendary of Woodhorn
PN Richard Middleton Massey
  MD FRS
  Henry Mathew esq

PN Thomas May esq
of Mid Lavant?

PN Richard Mead MD FRS
Edward Medley esq
barrister, of Conyboro in Barcombe (View 12) (1680-1754)

p Revd Theobald Michell
of Horsham; Rector of Tarring Neville and South Heighton 1720-38
Edward Milward esq
of Hastings, Mayor 1721, lawyer

p n William Mitchell esq
p Peter Monins esq
PN Thomas Morgan esq
William Morland esq
of Court Lodge in Lamberhurst
William Michell esq
William Michell gent
of Lewes, lawyer (1708-81)

p n Duke of Norfolk
Edward Howard, 9th Duke, to whom plate 6 is dedicated; seat at Arundel (View 3)
Duke of Newcastle
seats at Halland (View 114) and Bishopstone

p n Earl of Northampton
Richard Newdegate esq
of the Inner Temple and Lewes

p Francis Hare Naylor esq
of Herstmonceux, to whom plate 12 is dedicated (View 111)
William Newnham esq
of Maresfield (View 139)
John Nicholas esq

n William Nicholas esq
PN Earl of Oxford
Lord Onslow
Richard, Baron Onslow, of Clandon, Surrey

n Rt Hon. Arthur Onslow
of Imber Court, Surrey. Speaker of the House of Commons 1728-61
Col Richard Onslow
MP for Guildford 1727-60
Revd Robert Offley
Rector of Abinger, Surrey,

1690-1743
James Ogle esq

PN Samuel Ongley esq
of Old Warden, Beds, MP for New Shoreham 1729-34

n William Oxenham esq
PN Lord Petre
p n Countess of Pomfret
p Rt Hon. Henry Pelham esq
brother of the Duke of Newcastle, with landholdings in east Sussex

p n Sir Herbert Pakington bt
PN Sir Henry Parker bt
Sir Walter Parker bt
of Ratton in Willingdon
Gen Thomas Panton
Col Thomas Pagett
Groom of the Bedchamber

p n Mrs Elizabeth Palmer
Humphrey Parsons esq
of the Priory, Reigate, Surrey
Miss Anne Parker
co-heiress of George Parker, to whom, with her sister, plate 10 is dedicated
Miss Jane Parker
ditto

n John Peachey esq
of West Dean (View 65)

n William Pearce esq
William Peckham esq
of Nyton in Aldingbourne (View 1), or of Iridge in Salehurst
Mrs Sarah Peckham
probably daughter and heiress of Robert Peckham, owner of the manor of Compton and of Littlegreen (View 58); she married Thomas Phipps in 1742
James Pelham esq
of Crowhurst
Thomas Pelham junr esq
of Stanmer (View 175)

PN Edward Penrose esq
p n John Periam esq
p n Zachariah Periam esq
n Micajah Perry esq
of Epsom, Surrey. MP for London 1727-41

p n John Pitt esq
PN Thomas Plampin esq
John Plummer esq
of Chailey and St Anne's Lewes
John Porter esq
Revd Richard Porter
Rector of Chailey 1713-53
Samuel Powell esq

p n Edmond Prideaux esq
PN Duke of Rutland
PN Earl of Rockingham
p n Lord Romney
p n Sir Thomas Robinson bt
p Dean of Rochester
Walter Roberts esq
of Stonehouse in Warbleton

PN Henry Rolle esq
p n James Rooke esq
Richard Russell MD
of South Malling

P Thomas Ross esq
Mr Charles Rivington

p n Earl of Shaftsbury
PN Earl of Strafford
Lady Elizabeth Seymour
of Petworth, daughter of the Duke of Somerset

PN Sir Jeremy Vanacker Sambrooke bt
PN Sir Thomas Samwell bt
P Sir Hans Sloane bt MD FRS
Charles Seagrave esq
Thomas Sergison esq
of Cuckfield Park

p n Edward Seymour esq
N William Sheldon esq
John Slaughter esq

p Revd Stephen Sleech
Rector of Farnham Royal, Surrey
Henry Smallbrook esq
George Smith esq

p n Powell Snell esq
Henry Snooke esq
of Delves in Ringmer (Views 156 and 157)
Revd John Sorsbie
Rector of Crowhurst 1730-64 and of Penhurst 1721-64
George Stovin esq

N Edward Stradling esq

Samuel Stringer MD
PN Alexander Stuart MD FRS
PN Revd William Stukeley MD FRS
PN William Scorborough gent
PN Enoch Seeman gent
p Mr Thomas Saunders
Mr James Small
p n Earl of Tankervile
Charles Bennett, 2nd Earl, of Uppark in Harting
PN Lord Viscount Tyrconnel
n Sir Robert Throckmorton bt
n Revd Sir John Tynte bt
p n John Talbot esq
p n Edward Tayler esq
n John Temple esq
PN Robert Thistlethwayte DD
n Philip Thomas esq
p n John Thorold esq
p n John Thorpe MD FRS
n William Toller esq
Edward Trayton esq
of Lewes, to whom plate 3 is dedicated
Edward Tredcroft esq
of Horsham
Abraham Tucker esq
n John Trevor esq
of Glynde
p n Chomley Turner esq
Jonathan Harris Turner esq
n James Turner esq
PN Lord Viscount Vane
p n George Venables Vernon esq
n Mrs Jane Vernon
P Earl of Wilmington
of Compton Place in Eastbourne (View 74), to whom plates 7 and 8 are dedicated
n Lord Bishop of Winchester
p Lord Bishop of Worcester
p n Hon. Thomas Willoughby esq
p n Sir Thomas Webster bt
of Battle Abbey, to whom plates 1 and 9 are dedicated
Sir Thomas Wilson bt

of Uckfield
p n Sir William Wyndham bt
married firstly daughter of 6th Duke of Somerset (of Petworth House)
n Edward Walpole esq
n Abel Walter esq
n Philip Ward esq
John Warden esq
of Cuckfield, d. 1766
p n William Warren LLD
Henry Weston esq
Mrs Melior Mary Weston
Granville Wheler esq FRS
p n Thomas Whitmore esq
John Wicker esq
of Horsham
Revd George Wilks LLB
Priest Vicar of Chichester Cathedral 1734-52
p n Brown Willis esq
George Worge esq
of Battle, attorney (View 14)
p John Worth esq
n Henry Worth esq
p n Watkin William Wynne esq
p n John Wood esq
George Woodroffe esq
Revd Francis Brown Wright
Rector of Sedlescombe 1730-46 and Vicar of Dallington 1732-43
Col John Wyvil
Joseph Weller esq
of Old Castle in Dallington
p John Weaver esq
p Henry Wilkins gent
PN Christ Church College Library Oxford
PN Clare Hall Library Cambridge
PN Library at Manchester
Lord Archbishop of Canterbury
n John Mills esq
n Edward Lisle esq
Thomas Ashby esq
James Cocks esq
n William Moore esq
William Coppard esq
PN Peter Monamy gent
PN John Devoto gent

Nicholas Maynard gent
of Hye House in Crowhurst, d. 1743
P Clement Lempriere gent
Army Captain; draughtsman to the Board of Ordnance; drew prospect of Brighton from the sea, 1743; perhaps related to a Lewes family
p John Merifield gent
N Mr Edward Cave
Mr Joseph Noble
William Morrice esq

The following 11 were subscribers to the *Views of cities*, but not to the *Views of remains of antiquity*
John Burd MD
Revd Samuel Caswell
Philip Cheadle gent
Mr Edward Cave
Mr James Cutler
Thomas Fane esq
Thomas Farr gent
Mr Fælix Farley
Isaac Gale gent
John Norman gent
Benjamin Travers gent

3. Jeremiah Milles's tours in Sussex, 1743

Jeremiah Milles was the son of the Revd Jeremiah Milles, Rector of Duloe, Cornwall, but was born at his grandfather's house, the rectory at Highclere, Hampshire, in 1714. He was educated at Eton College and Corpus Christi College, Oxford. In 1733-7 he travelled in Europe with his cousin Richard Pococke and kept journals of what he saw. On ordination he received preferment from his uncle Thomas Milles, Bishop of Waterford. Inheritance of the latter's considerable fortune in 1740 enabled him thereafter to live in England. In 1741 he was elected a Fellow of the Society of Antiquaries, and in the following year he became a Fellow of the Royal Society and a member of the Egyptian Club. In 1744 he was presented to the rectory of Saltwood with Hythe in Kent and in the following year he married the younger daughter of John Potter, Archbishop of Canterbury, from which alliance flowed ample preferments, including the rectory of West Tarring in Sussex. The office of Precentor of Exeter Cathedral in 1747 was followed by that of Dean in 1762.

His service as President of the Society of Antiquaries from 1768 until his death in 1784 was unremarkable, but he was supportive of the initiatives of Richard Gough, the Society's Director from 1771. His publications were not significant, but he did set out to write a parochial history of Devon, sending to every incumbent a lengthy questionnaire and compiling five volumes of notes from his own observations.[4]

Milles was therefore at the time of journeys through Sussex in August and September 1743 aged 29, unmarried and of independent means, with marked antiquarian interests and already well travelled. The initial form of the diary seems to have been letters written to Charles Lyttelton (1714-68), at that time Rector of Alvechurch in Worcestershire but later the Dean of Exeter and the President of the Antiquaries whom Milles succeeded. Two letters from Lyttelton in reply to ones written by Milles while on the road show them to be close friends, having been contemporaries at Eton and Oxford, collaborating on antiquarian matters: 'The ancient shields in church windows I would wish you to trick down whenever you meet with them except in those counties which are already published with the Church Notes preserved.' Regrettably for us Milles edited incidental comments out of the final document.[5] For example, Lyttelton replied, 'I am sorry your horse is in such pitious plight. The groom assures me that he was perfectly well when he was here, but not quite in so good care as when you brought him in the spring....' Some of Lyttelton's remarks are given in endnotes. See also Essay 2.3.

Milles's text is generally on the right-hand pages, but there are a few additions on the left-hand pages, as indicated. The manuscript was among the group of Milles's papers purchased by the British Museum from Thomas Thorpe on 25 April 1846. BL, Add. MS. 15777 contains a few rough notes made from published sources and while on the road in Sussex.

The routes of Milles's tours are shown on the map on page 108.

A journey from London to Tunbridge Wells, Rye, Winchelsea, Hastings, Battle and Lewes. Begun August 20th, finished September 2nd 1743.

[ff. 175-200: his journey from London to, and 10-day stay at, Tunbridge Wells, with several excursions. f. 201] I left Tunbridge Wells on Wednesday 31st of August in order to take the tour of the sea coast of Sussex, and passing through a woody country for five or six miles entered Sussex at a small town called Lamberhurst, from whence I continued about eight miles more through a sandy and heathy country intermixed with woods but thinly inhabited to Newenden [in Kent], a small village consisting of a few houses, the best of which is an ale house, and a small parish church. It is situated near the Rother, which is now a little rivulet, though formerly a navigable river, the tide coming (as is commonly reported) in Queen Elizabeth's time up to Bodiam Castle which is four miles above Newenden, and I am told that there are still to be seen iron rings there to which they used to moor their vessels.

Newenden by tradition was once a very considerable town which tradition, together with the situation of it on a navigable river, has induced Mr Camden to place the old Anderida here: a Roman fortress, which was garrisoned by a captain and band of Abulci, as the Notitia Imperii informs us, which calls it Anderidos, to stop and prevent the incursions of the Saxon pirates. From his authority, and from others since him the inhabitants confidently report it to have been Anderida, and I was informed there that, in digging the valley where the channel of the river ran formerly, they find anchors and vast quantities of decayed timber. But none of these circumstances are sufficient to prove Mr Camden's assertion, to which there are insuperable objections. First as this town is situated 10 miles inland and 15 by sea and consequently in a very improper place for a Roman fortress, as it neither could have any convenient communication with the rest of the Roman forts on the sea coast, nor could it at this distance from the sea be any guard against the pirates.

[f. 202] Secondly as this town was in all probability situated in the middle of the great forest of Anderida which extended from Kent all over Sussex into Hampshire, and by no means a likely or useful post for the Romans. The country is still very woody all round it.

Thirdly as I do not hear of any Roman antiquities being found there, though there is such a rumour in some authors, and what is a much stronger proof of all, namely that there is another place in Sussex, viz. Pevensey, which has all the likely circumstances that Anderida was there, as I shall mention hereafter, so that the only ground for Mr Camden's supposition seems to be the tradition that Newenden was once a great town: and so it might have been, and not have been Anderida.

[Following three paragraphs on verso of ff. 201 and 202.]

I observed in one of the windows of Newenden Church the following coat viz.
Party per pale ar: 3 Inn's Rampant Gules Ermine
Quartered with or a St Andrews cross gules between 4 birds.
The date of 1492 is on the painting of these windows.

Hereabouts I saw to the east at about 4 miles distance the beautiful steeple of a church in Kent [Wittersham] which according to the old proverb is said to have been the cause of the Goodwin sands, the meaning of which was that they expended the money on building this steeple which should have been employed in making good their fences against the sea, by which neglect the sea encroached upon the land, and destroyed that part of it, which is now called the Goodwin sands, having been formerly part of the ill-gotten estate of Earl Goodwin.

On the north side of the town are large remains of some religious house, which now I believe is turned into a warehouse [Lossenham, a house of Carmelite Friars, founded *c.* 1244?].

The country between Newenden and Rye, which is ten miles, is more fruitful and better cultivated.

The town of Rye is situated at the south-east corner of Sussex; on the west side of the river Rother which empties itself into the sea a little below the town. It stands on the rock of a steep ascent which was formerly a peninsula, though the river has retired from it in many places. Its situation on this eminence gives it a pleasing and an important look at a distance, though the town itself is neither large nor beautiful.

There is a large and handsome gothic church in the town, the west end of which has been lately repaired by their members of Parliament [View 161; *SV*, 142]. I saw nothing remarkable there but the following epitaph in the chancel of one Thomas Wilson [correctly, Hamon, who was mayor six times between 1595 and the year he died 1607].[6]

[f. 203]

> Loe Thomas Wilson here interrd doth lye
> Thrice Burgesse for the Parliament elected
> Six times by Freemens choice made Mayor of Rye
> And Captain longtime of the band selected
> whose Prudence, Justice, Courage, Gravitie
> Deserves a monument of memory.

A little beyond the church at the south-east corner of the town on an eminence overlooking the river is planted a small battery of guns on a platform, which are now of no use as the harbour is almost choked up. From thence you have a fine prospect over the grand level of Romney marsh for eight or ten miles, in which one sees the towns of Lydd and Romney though at a great distance. All the land for this length, and for about three or four miles in breadth, is addition made by the sea, which has caused great alterations on this coast.

It is said that formerly ships could come up to Appledore, and I think it appears so by the English history in the time of the Saxons, whereas it is now eight or ten miles within land. This great marsh feeds and fattens an immense number of cattle of all sorts for London market, both sheep and oxen. I could see few or no villages in the marsh, which must be a very unhealthy place, it being divided into portions by ditches and channels over which there are bridges. I saw very few trees or hedges growing there.

Rye is said to be a town of antiquity and to have been formerly of some consequence; it was walled round by King Edward III. It is a Cinque Port or rather a member to Hastings, not being one of the original ones. There was formerly a very good harbour, and a great trade in the town, but the sea has retired greatly from this coast, and has by degrees so choke up this harbour, that at present only [f. 204] very small vessels can go in and out, which has occasioned great decay of trade in the town. In order to remedy this they are making a new harbour, which is to open a little to the westward of the present harbour. They have already cut a great part of the way from the sea to the channel of the river, which is I believe above a mile in length.[7]

This harbour is of great importance especially in a French war: as it is the only one between Dover and Portsmouth where a ship may put in if pursued by the enemy. The late King [George I] was obliged to land here in January 1725-6, after a very dangerous passage from Holland. Rye sends two members to Parliament.

I left Rye on Thursday 1st September and having passed the channel which goes up towards Winchelsea I crossed a marsh three miles long, which brought me to that town. The greatest part if not all this marsh seems to have been an acquisition from the sea: which is very evident from an old castle on the south side of the road, about half way between Rye and Winchelsea which when built was at the mouth of Winchelsea river and stood on the sea shore, whereas now it is near a mile from the sea shore, and stands in the middle of a meadow. This addition must have been made since Henry VIII's time for this castle is supposed to have been built by him, and indeed its make, which very much resembles those of Deal, Sandown and Walmer on the Kentish coast, is a sufficient proof of it. It is still called Winchelsea [now Camber] Castle. I crossed over the end of the new cut that they are making to the sea, which when finished seems to be more convenient for the town of Winchelsea than for that of Rye.

[f. 205] New Winchelsea is beautifully situated on a hill pretty much like that of Rye, only it is larger and more lofty. It is called New Winchelsea, to distinguish it from the old town of the same name which is said to have been situated three miles more southward, and to have been swallowed up by the sea in the year 1250. I doubted very much whether the town could be situated so far or rather that the sea should have gained so much as two or three miles of the land hereabouts; but I was assured by some fishermen of the place, that they had often anchored their boats on the ruins of the old city and had brought up rubbish and mortar when they weighted their anchors. This town according to their description stood above a mile out in the sea directly south of the present town. It is said to have been a town of great trade, and to have had 18 parish churches in it.

There is one difficulty however in this account, which I think wants explanation, and which I do not well comprehend, which is that the sea should first of all encroach near two miles or perhaps more, as it did when it swallowed up the old town and came up pretty near to the present town, as we are told it did, and yet that the sea should after this retire again a mile backwards, as it certainly has done within these 2 or 3 last centuries.

However that be, New Winchelsea was built soon after the destruction of the old. Both the situation and the design in which it was laid out, would have made it one of the most beautiful places in England, if it had flourished. The whole hill was divided into, as they say, 32 squares by several streets crossing one another at right angles, and of a very convenient breadth. Of most of these streets there are still signs: I traced five in the length way and three or four that crossed them; the rest are turned into [f. 206] fields etc. The walls of the town surrounded almost all the hill and were of an oblong square figure; there are some remains of them, and of the four gates on the four sides of the town [View 198]. The hill towards the south, which looks to the sea is by much the steepest. Winchelsea at present is reduced to a miserable village consisting of only 10 or 12 houses; the people who live in them are very poor, as they have no manner of trade here, and I am told it is reckoned an unhealthy place and subject to agues on account of the marshes which are to the south of it. What is very remarkable in this town is the great number of noble gothic vaults which are under almost every house, and almost all over the site of the old town; they are very spacious, some of them being from 40 to 60 feet long, and from 12 to 20 feet wide and about 12 feet high; they are turned with gothic arches of hewn stone, ribbed across in as elegant a manner as the aisles of gothic churches. It was a noble design for a trading town, to build such spacious vaults, and if the superstructure was equal to them in beauty, Winchelsea must have been a noble town. But I doubt whether this design ever succeeded, and whether it was ever a town of any considerable trade. There remains the greatest part of a church, which was a light and beautiful gothic building [*SV*, 183]. It seems to have consisted only of a cross aisle and a chancel, for I could see no remains of a nave to the west of the cross aisle. The chancel is in repair, and that is as much as one can say of it. Against the north wall is the monument of a Knight Templar, one on grey marble of a lady, and a third of a man in a garment like a surplice. On the south side are two monuments of Knights Templars; on the shield of one are a lion rampant and scallop shells; the other has a fine gothic canopy over him of stone.[8] [f. 207] In the church yard on the west of the church is a large square tower which does not seem to be of any great antiquity.

Near the church they have a Town Hall and a gaol, the former of which they say is a handsome room; it might be so for Winchelsea, but I did not think it worth my seeing. A little southward of the parish church are some remains of a monastery [Greyfriars, View 197], a print of which is given by Mr Buck in his views of the monasteries. Near this is a field which they call Mondays market, where to be sure a market was held when this town was in its prosperity. It is now in the middle of a considerable farm, and not the sign of a house near it. There is a very fine prospect from the eminence, where this old monastery stands, which is (as it were) a natural terrace of a great height over the marsh.

Winchelsea is likewise a member of the Cinque Port of Hastings. It sends two members to Parliament, though there are not above 13 voters, and yet great sums of money have been expended on this occasion in this poor place. If the new cut which they are making towards the sea succeeds, there is some hopes that Winchelsea may revive, it lying nearer, and having more conveniences for a merchant, than Rye, by the number of its vaults. There are said to have been three churches formerly in Winchelsea.

From thence I went seven miles to Hastings crossing a high hill called Fairlight hill, from whence one has a very extensive prospect over the eastern part of Sussex [View 80].

[f. 208] Hastings is a middling town consisting of two long streets which run parallel to each other, and is situated in a narrow valley between two high hills. There are two good parish churches in the town. It was once a town of great trade, had a good harbour and was the first of the Cinque Ports, but the sea which is continually encroaching here has destroyed its harbour, having left only a beach on which they are obliged to draw up their fishing boats to secure them from the violence of the sea [View 106]. None but fishing boats belong to this town, but in the season they send a great fleet of these small craft to Yarmouth to be employed in the herring fishery. They were preparing for this voyage when I was at Hastings.

[This para. on f. 207v.] Hastings had several privileges granted to it by charters from William Rufus, Henry II, Richard I, Henry III, Edward I and Charles II. It was to furnish 14 ships of war to the King whenever he had occasion for them. Their Deputies bear up the canopy over the King's head at a coronation and dine at the uttermost table on the King's right hand, as do all the Deputies of the Cinque Ports.

On the summit of the hill, to the west of the town are some small remains of a castle, which by the manner of building I take to be very ancient [View 106]. It is built of small square stones about four times as large as common bricks, which are laid regularly along in rows. There is very little remaining of this castle at present, as it stands on the point of the hill, over the cliff great part of which together with the castle has fallen into the sea. The remaining part of it is of a semi-circular form. It is inaccessible on every side but that which joins to the hill, from which it is only separated by a fosse. I take this castle to have been built soon after the Conquest.

Some people have reported that William the Conqueror landed at Hastings, but the tradition of the country is much more probable, which fixes it at a small bay called Bulverhythe, about four or five miles west of Hastings, where they say there is a large stone, on which it is pretended he dined.

Hastings is supposed to have taken its name from Hastings a Danish pirate.

[f. 209] I went seven miles through a good country from Hastings to Battle, a pretty little town which received its name from the famous and decisive battle which was fought here between Harold the last Danish King and William the Conqueror, in which the former lost his life, as did also his two sons. The Conqueror in memory of this victory erected an abbey on the spot where Harold's body was found; it was afterwards enriched by many benefactions and was one of the most considerable in England. The building of the abbey occasioned afterwards the building of the town.

In this abbey was deposited the roll called Battle Abbey roll, which contained an account of the most considerable warriors who came over with William the Conqueror, many families of whom are still extant.

After the dissolution of the monasteries Sir Anthony Browne was possessed of this abbey. He began the shell of a noble old house here, but it was never finished, the back part of which commanded a fine prospect westward, being seated on an eminence. His descendants the Lords Viscount Montague, were in possession of it, 'til within these 20 years, when they sold it to Sir Thomas Webster who at present possesses it. He has made a habitable, though not a handsome, house out of some of the apartments of the old abbey, most of that part [the former guest-range] which was [re]built by Sir Anthony Browne being only bare walls not even covered with a roof [View 15]. There is a good old hall in the house. I observed in Sir Thomas's study two folio books, one of which contained the history and the other was the Register of Battle Abbey, but they were locked up so that I could not get a sight of them.[9]

All that remains at present of the old abbey is a large hall of which is now made use for a barn and stable, some part of the choir of the church, which is to be seen [f. 210] on the east side of the house, and a very handsome old gateway which fronts the street of Battle town [*Sussex views*, 16].

There is a very good parish church at Battle. In it on the north side is the monument of Sir Anthony Browne before mentioned with the following inscription, but the latter part cannot be read, because it is too close to the wall:

> Here lyeth the Right Honorable Sir Antony Brown Knyght of the Gartere, master of the Kings Majestes Horcys & one of the honorable Prive Cowncil of our most dread Sovraine Lord and Vice Kyng Henry the eight & Dame Alis his wyff which Alis deceeased the [31] day of Marche Ao Dni 1540 and the said Sir Anthony decesid the [ ] day of [ ] Ao Dni [ ] on whois sowls and all Cristen ihv have mercy[10]

[This para. on f. 209v.] Colonel [James] Pelham [1683-1761] has a house [at Crowhurst] with some very pretty improvements just before you come to Battle in the way from Hastings.

Battle is a rural Deanery and is famous for making gunpowder. I went from hence 10 miles further through a pleasant enclosed country to Pevensey. About four miles from Battle on the right hand of the road is a hill called Standard Hill, where it is said

William the Conqueror put up his standard of defiance the day before the battle. Lord Ashburnham's house and park is near this place [View 8].

About a mile or two before I came to Pevensey I entered on a marsh, which extends all the way to the town and seems to be so low that I should imagine the sea came up here formerly. Thus much is certain that Pevensey was formerly a very considerable harbour so that it is probable enough that the river extended all this breadth. It is now called Manxey level.

Pevensey is a miserable little village situated on a small rivulet about a mile from the sea. Its haven, as well as that which is called Sluice Haven about three or four miles to the eastward, is choked up. At present Pevensey has nothing to boast of but its castle, which is [f. 211] very remarkable not only for the thickness of its walls but also for its great antiquity [*Sussex views*, 124]. The inner castle which seems to have been either a pentagon or hexagon is faced with hewn stone, and the walls are of a prodigious solidity; there are round towers at the angles. This building I take to be much later than the Conquest. A great part of it towards the village is fallen down, but it is so well cemented together that it has fallen in prodigious large pieces.

This castle is surrounded with another wall of a considerable thickness, which is near half a mile in circumference. It is built with square stones regularly laid in rows and at the distance of every three or four feet two or three rows of Roman brick or tile. It is strengthened with semicircular towers at the distance of about 40 paces from each other; and I have all the reason in the world to think from the material, the manner of putting them together, the semicircular towers, the strength of the wall, which stands firm though is in some places entirely undermined, that this outer circumference is a Roman building, because it so exactly resembles almost in every particular the Roman walls which were made in England, and what confirmed me the more in this conjecture was that I observed about a certain height, which seems to have been the height of the wall all round, and of which height it still is in most places, that above this there seems to have been an additional wall of flints etc. made to raise it higher, which is of a quite different, and much more modern way of building. This wall for some paces on the north-west side is laid quite flat, being fallen altogether, which shows the compactness of it and the strength of the cement.

[f. 212] There is I own some difficulty in conceiving the outside to be so much more ancient than the inner castle, as it would be most natural to suppose them both built together, the outmost for the defence of the innermost, but whoever saw the difference in the building of the two, and the situation of the inner castle at one corner of the outer walls, may easily imagine that this inner castle was added since, as a greater strength and near the river in order to command the passage of it.

But supposing these outer walls are allowed to be Roman, what Roman town or castle shall we fix here? I own I cannot help supposing this to have been the old Anderida, which I am very sure was either here or at Bourne [Eastbourne] five miles further. Its situation on the sea shore, where there was a commodious harbour for shipping at a proper distance from the other Roman stations on the sea side; its lying not far from the Weald of Sussex which was the great wood called Anderida from whence it received its name, are so many proofs that it must have been hereabouts. And the historians who mention Ælla's expedition and the taking of Andreadceaster, or Anderida by Cissa, seem to fix the situation hereabouts, for they speak of it as not far from, though not in the forest of Anderida, and it is very natural to suppose that they marched all along the sea coast from Wittering, or Shoreham, whichever of the two it was that they landed at. But if it was at the latter, it is still more probable as this must have been then the first town they met with in their way. It likewise adds some weight to the argument that there was a castle here in the Conqueror's time, which strengthens the [f. 213] antiquity of it.

[This para. on f. 211v.] Gildas says expressly that Anderida was 'in littore Oceani ad Meridiem' and Henry of Huntingdon likewise says 'Saxones occuparunt littora maris in Sudsexe', that is the Saxons under Ælla marched all along the sea shore, which indeed was the only part of the country that was then inhabited, the rest being the Andreadsweld. It appears by the same author that Andreadceaster or Anderida was near to the wood.

There is however one objection, and a very strong one against this being Anderida, that is, that the city was razed to the ground by Ælla, and Henry of Huntingdon who wrote afterwards speaks as if the remains of it were hardly to be seen in his time, so that if that author may be depended upon, these walls cannot be those of Anderida.

Archbishop Usher [Ussher 1658] is of opinion that the town mentioned by the ancient English historians under the name of Pensavelcoit, must have been Pevensey and not Ivelchester as some imagine.

The Castle of Pevensey, or Pevensel as it was then called was in the possession of the Earl of Mortain at the time of the Conquest, that earl being half brother by the mother's side to William the Conqueror.

Adjoining to Pevensey Castle on the west side is a village called Westham, that is to say the western village.

From Pevensey I went the same evening five miles further pretty near the sea shore to the village of South Bourne, situated on the sea side, where there are some public houses, commonly known by the name of the Sea Houses, where gentlemen generally choose to bait, on account of the agreeableness of the situation and the good entertainment one meets with there. These public houses are situated on the sea shore, where they frequently catch good fish, and in the season, that is from June to September, are remarkable for wheatears, which I shall have occasion to mention hereafter [View 72].

Not far from the inn was discovered about [30] years since a mosaic pavement and bath of which an account was sent by a Mr [John Tabor] to the Royal Society, as may be seen in the Philosophical Transactions No. [351]; both one and the other are now entirely destroyed, so that one can only see the bed of plaster in which the mosaic was [f. 214] fixed. Everybody that came to see it took away pieces of it, and no care was taken to preserve it [View 73].

From hence to the sea side, and as I am told all the way to East Bourne, which is about a mile further [inland], they find foundations of Roman walls. I myself saw several on the cliff, a great part of which has been washed away by the sea, as appears very plainly by a camp which is about a mile or two further on Beachy Head and close to the seaside, a great part of which has been washed away by the sea [Belle Tout?].

If the testimony of Henry of Huntingdon will not allow us to fix Anderida at Pevensey, we must allow it to have been here. The situation near Beachy Head, one of the most southern promontories of England and a remarkable high land, and therefore the more proper for descrying the approach of vessels, seems to make this a very convenient place for the old Anderida. Mr [Nicholas] Mann [d. 1753], the Master of the Charterhouse, a gentleman of great learning who has often passed some time with the late Earl of Wilmington, is of the same opinion. At least if it was not the Roman station itself, both the pavement and bath make it evident that it was the situation of the country houses of the Romans, and indeed it is a proof of their good judgement, for it is one of the most delightful situations for the summer that ever I beheld. Eastward of it you have a fine prospect of a level country with the sea forming a bay of 18 miles broad; behind it rise most beautiful downs. The sea is in the front, and westward rises Beachy Head with a gentle ascent for two or three miles agreeably interspersed with downs and arable land; from whence you have a most extensive prospect both eastward and westward, and must see every ship almost that goes in or out of the Channel, this being the first land that they [ships] make, especially when they are homeward bound, and [they] keep generally pretty close to the shore unless the wind blow very hard at south. Then for sporting and fishing there are few places that can compare with it.

[f. 215] I left the Sea Houses next morning [2 September] and went through the village of South Bourne, leaving that of East Bourne about half a mile on my right hand. I passed by a country house which belonged to the late Earl of Wilmington [Compton Place, View 74]. The house though old has been fitted up and made very convenient, as I am told for I did not see the inside of it. It is most sweetly situated under the downs, from whence you have a pleasant prospect of the sea and yet it is greatly sheltered by woods from the violence of tempests. There is a pretty garden belonging to it, with a great deal of underwood in it, which so near the sea is somewhat extraordinary. The late Earl built a most compact little house near his own for his steward, in which I think one of the most agreeable situations for the summer, that one could wish for.

On the top of the downs fronting the Earl's house is a windmill, which as an addition to the prospect is built with a front in imitation of the gate of a gothic castle, but it is much too small in every way. [11]

This seat belongs now to the Earl of Northampton, to whom it devolved by the Earl of Wilmington's dying intestate [two months before, on 2 July 1743].

I ascended the downs on which I saw vast numbers of traps for wheatears. These birds are about the size of a lark with brown feathers, which have a streak of white in their wings and tails. They are a bird of passage, for they come in the month of June, and go away in September, during which time they are most prodigiously fat and are a most delicious morsel; they are supposed to be the same with the Beccafico's of Italy and Turkey. Their name of wheatears I take to be a corruption from white arse, the rumps of these birds being remarkably white and fat. There are but few parts of England where these birds come, for they frequent only the downs, and are supposed to live upon flies, because they never find anything in their [f. 216] stomachs, though I imagine they eat rape seed, because I saw many of them flying about it. They are a solitary bird, appearing always single, and are foolish enough to be easily ensnared. The manner of taking them is they. They cut up two oblong turfs out of the ground in the following shape ⌐; across one part of this cavity they fasten a small stick with two horse hair springs to it and then cover some part of the cavity with one of these turfs in this manner ✚ but so as the light may appear at each end. These birds hop about from turf to turf, and when the least cloud eclipses the sun, they run as if it were for shelter into the holes; where seeing the light appear at the other end, they make towards it and are caught in the springs. These traps are laid in rows all over the downs, at the distance of two or three yards from each other. The owner of them goes round twice a day to examine and take out what birds are caught. One man has oftentimes a hundred dozen of these traps, by which all the neighbouring country is supplied with birds. They are sold here picked and trussed for about one shilling a dozen.

Upon the down above the Earl of Wilmington's I observed many barrows. It is said that a battle [*Mercredesburn* in 485] was fought on these downs near a place called Burling [Birling] gap, which is a little to the westward of Beachy Head. From hence I rode eight miles over the downs through a very pleasant country to Seaford, a poor miserable village situated on the sea shore, but as there is no port to it the fisherboats are drawn up upon the beach for security [View 165]. Seaford is I think a member of the Cinque Port of Hastings. It sends two Barons to Parliament, for that is the name the representatives of the Cinque Ports bear.

[This para. on f. 216v.] About a mile to the east of Seaford is a hill called South Hill on which there is a camp but of what form I cannot exactly determine as I was not upon it.

[f. 217] From Seaford I went along the seaside for a mile, and then turning to the right passed by Bishopstone where the Duke of Newcastle has a small hunting seat which stands conveniently enough for that diversion, but otherwise its situation is disagreeable enough, being in a naked, open country, where there is hardly a tree to be seen.

From hence passing in sight of Newhaven, a small village and sea port at the mouth of the river Ouse which runs by Lewes, I crossed that river a little higher four miles from Seaford, and as many from Lewes, at a place called Stock Ferry, and came to Lewes.

Lewes, the capital town of Sussex, stands very pleasantly on a high ground at the edge of the downs, and on the banks of the river Ouse. It is not a large town but is very neat and pleasant and there are a good many well-built houses in it [View 131]. There is a suburb belongs to it on the other side of the river called Cliff, and the village of Southover joins to it on the south, where there are some remains of an abbey [the Priory of St Pancras]. I observed on a stone which is in the tower of the present parish church, a mitre and under these initial letters J.A./D.E. or J.A./E.D. I do not exactly remember which of the two it was [in fact, I.A.P.L., probably for John Ashdown, the penultimate Prior].

All that is remarkable in Lewes is the castle which is situated on an eminence above the town, at the extremities of which are two artificial round hills, where were placed two round towers. That to the westward has half of the tower remaining, but on that to the east only the foundations are visible. There is a very agreeable bowling green within the circumference of this castle [View 130; *Sussex views*, 94].

Near this town was fought a very bloody battle between King Henry III and the confederate Barons, in which [f. 218] King Henry together with Prince Edward and the King of the Romans were taken prisoners, and carried to the Priory of Lewes [noted, but not identified above], which as [Paul de] Rapin [in *The history of England*] says vol. 1st p. 338 folio edition was at the foot of the castle, of which I did not observe any remains unless it was where one of the parish churches now stands.

At a little church dedicated to St John on the north side of this castle [*Sussex views*, 95], I observed the following ancient inscription cut on two rows of stone in a semicircular form. It is probable they were formerly on the inside of the church, but now they are placed on the outside of the south wall. [Careful drawing of 15 stones] [12]

This [Magnus] inscription is copied in a different manner by Mr Camden, and it seems by his copy, as if the stones on which it is cut were not then in this shape, for he represented them as in this shape [inverted U] so that probably they have been put into the wall where they now are since his time. He likewise copies it wrong. Instead of <u>se</u> moribus, which I suppose is put for <u>sed</u> moribus; he writes it <u>prudentior</u>, but upon what authority I cannot tell for these words seem to be the ancient ones. Indeed there does seem to be a mixture of modern stones, amongst the old ones, [f. 219] for some of the letters are Roman, and others gothic. The three first stones and the twelfth seem to be modern, and probably they were copied from the old inscription which might have been decayed. But Mr Camden makes the letters in his inscription so imperfect that one can hardly guess from them what they meant, whereas all the letters appear now exceedingly plain and legible.

The inscription appears to have been erected to some officer of the Royal Danish blood, who retired into a convent. The lines are to be read thus.

Clauditur hic miles Danorum Regia Proles
Magnus nomen ei, magnae nota Progeniei,
Deponens magnum, sed moribus induit agnum
Præpete pro vita fit parvulus Anachorite

I dined at Lewes and in the afternoon set out for Tunbridge Wells. I observed two or three camps (Danish I suppose) on the downs near Lewes. I crossed the river Ouse, and having passed over the side of a down came into the deep enclosed flat country called the Weald of Sussex, which was the forest formerly called Anderida. The roads here are bad even in summer time and in winter they must be intolerable.

There are however some gentlemen's seats in this country. Sir William Gage has a house, park, and some fine fish ponds about four miles from Lewes [at Firle] on the right hand of the road to Tunbridge Wells [correctly, to Eastbourne].

About eight miles from Lewes I passed through a small town called Uckfield, and a little beyond it on the right hand Mr Medley is building a fine seat at a place called Buxted [View 43].[13] About two miles further I came to a great heath which is part of Ashdown forest, and ascending very gently for near a mile came to the summit of the hill, where there was formerly a beacon: it is still called Crowburrow [Crowborough] Beacon. From hence [f. 220] there is a most glorious and extensive prospect every way, eastward over the Weald of Sussex into Kent, southward as far as the sea, westward as far as Lewes and the downs about it, and northward of the forests of Ashdown and Waterdown and into Surrey. A gardener has built a little house on the very summit of this bleak hill and has found means to raise hedges and to make a most beautiful little garden, though the whole does not enclose an acre of ground. It must be a delightful place in summer, but it is most excessively bleak and exposed to the wind. This is about 14 miles from Lewes, and eight from Tunbridge Wells. Descending this hill I went in an enclosed country 'til I came within two miles of the Wells, when I came on the forest of Waterdown [View 87] , which brought me late that night to Tunbridge Wells. These 22 miles from Lewes are very long and tedious, especially the first fourteen.

I left Tunbridge Wells the next day being the 2nd of September and returned by the same road to London.

An Account of a Tour in Hampshire & Sussex. To Kingsclere, Basingstoke, Alton, Midhurst, Petworth, Arundel, Chichester, Portsmouth, Southampton, & Winchester. Begun on Thursday the 15th of September finished on Tuesday the 20th of September 1743

[ff. 221-4, 15 September, departed from Newtown, Hants, travelled via Kingsclere and Basingstoke to Alton.] I dined at Alton, and in the afternoon went about 14 miles to Midhurst. About half way between these two places I passed through Woolmer forest which extends about six or seven miles in length, part of it running into Sussex. [f. 225] Most of the woods are cut down, so that the greatest part of it is now a barren heath. I passed by one end of a large pond which, though there is not much water in it in summer, yet spreads over a great deal of ground in winter. It is called Woolmer pond; and what is very remarkable, in summer time when the pond is almost dry, the people hereabouts look for and often find Roman coins in the mud. How they should come there is difficult to imagine, for this was doubtless a forest in the times of the Romans, nor is it probable that they had any station or town in so deserted a place; and therefore the only way I can account for it is that in troublous times some people, either the Romans or others since their time, might have flung their money in here, in order to preserve it from their enemies. I observed near this pond some barrows, which make the supposition still more probable, as it is likely from them that there was some engagement in this place. This barren heath continues all the way to Midhurst, though I am not certain whether all of it is properly the forest of Woolmer. I entered Sussex at a place called Rake about five miles before I came to Midhurst.

Midhurst is a small market town situated on the river Arun [western Rother] which discharges itself into the sea below Arundel [*Sussex views*, 109]. It sends two members of Parliament who are chosen by the Duke of Somerset's interest.

About a quarter of a mile out of the town is a noble old Gothick seat belonging to the Lord Montacute, called Cowdray [View 70]. It is of hewn stone built round a square court with a square tower at each corner of the house. This edifice was erected (I believe) by Sir Anthony Browne, Master of the Horse to King Henry VIII; and one of the executors of his last will. He was the head of the present Lord Montague's family.

The apartments in this house are spacious and well furnished. There is a handsome old hall, which like all other old halls [f. 226] in England is said to be roofed with Irish oak. In the dining room, which is behind it, Hans Holbein has painted al fresco, the history of King Henry VIII's expedition to Flanders and his public entry into London on his return. This I suppose was done in compliment to Sir Anthony Browne who was at that time Master of the Horse to the King. The greatest merit of this picture is that it is the work of Holbein, for otherwise there is neither perspective drawing nor colouring in it that can please. The subject of the several pieces of painting is wrote over them as:

1. 'The meeting of the King by Sir Anthony Browne, upon the hill between Callis & Merguison'
2. 'The camping of the King at Merguison. The Kings Campe, Sir Anthony Browns camp'
3. 'The siege of Bulloigne, in which the tour d'ordre is represented & called there the olde man'
4. The King's landing at Portsmouth, but without any inscription.
5. His entry into London, the same.

In an apartment adjoining to this are some exceeding good family pictures, and amongst the rest an original of this Sir Anthony Browne with a long account of him under it. The stair case is beautifully painted by Pellegrini with a history out of Tasso (I believe). In the apartments above stairs are several old family pieces, as, Rauf Nevill, Alice daughter of the Lord Audley, Richard Nevill Earl of Salisbury and Alice daughter of Thomas Montague, Robert Nevill of Raby and Mary daughter of Raufe Lord of Medihm by his wife Anstace daughter of William Lord Percy. I observed one piece particularly, in which two persons were represented lying dead in their armour, one with a spear, the other with a sword through his body. Over the former is wrote 'Thomas Fitzwilliam', over the latter 'Jhoan Fitzwilliam', [f. 227] and under them, was wrote this motto: 'In doyng their Duty against the Scots'.

There is a very handsome gallery wainscotted with Dantrick oak, in which are two very good copies of Raphael's marriage of Cupid and Psyche, and the Assembly of the Gods, they are said to be done by Julio Romano: if they are not his, they are however done by some very good hand. There is another piece or two of Holbeins in this gallery, and some family pictures.

In the court of this house is a very handsome bronze fountain.

The situation of this house is by no means agreeable. It stands very low, in a watery meadow, by the side of a rivulet which must make it exceedingly damp. The park rises very beautifully behind it, and on the top of it are two or three clumps of well-grown oaks and beeches which look like the ancient luci.

In a chapel of the parish church of Midhurst [SV, 108] is a very sumptuous old monument erected to Sir Anthony Browne above mentioned [and buried at Battle, see previous tour], upon which he is represented kneeling before a desk, on each side of him are the couchant statues of two wives, the former of whom was Lady Jane Ratcliff, daughter to Robert Earl of Sussex, and died in 1552; the latter was Lady Magdalen Dacres, daughter of Sir Wm Dacres, Lord Dacres and Lord Warden of the West Marches of England for anempste Scotland. What these two words 'for anempste' signify I cannot tell, but they are part of the inscription over that lady [anenst, 'over against']. Sir Anthony's epitaph, which is in English, mentions that in 1553 he was employed in an embassy to Rome with Thirlby Bishop of Ely; [f. 228] that in the year 1559 he was Lieutenant of the Queen's forces at the siege of St Quintin, in 1565 he was Ambassador from Queen Elizabeth to the King of Spain and in 1566 to the Duke of Parma who was then Regent of the Low Countries.[14] There is another monument of a descendent of this Sir Anthony in the same chapel, but is not at all remarkable.

It is probable that all the country hereabouts was formerly a forest, for so the name of this town seems to import, Midhurst, signifying in the midst of the forest.

I lay at Midhurst on Wednesday night and the next day. Crossing Cowdray Park I went five miles to Petworth a small market town remarkable for a noble seat of the [6th] Duke of Somerset [1662-1748]; which together with a very great estate came to him by his first wife who was heiress to the family of Percys Earls of Northumberland. The Duke rebuilt the greatest part of the old house [View 146]; the front of which makes a grand appearance having 17 windows, on a storey; the misfortune is that the house is situated in a bad place, and fronted to a view that presents nothing but two or three fields, whereas had it been either placed a little higher in the Park, or fronted towards the summer house, it would have commanded a very fine prospect both of the town, and country, for it stands very high.

There is a very noble suite of apartments in the front of the house, and they are well furnished. The first room that you come into is beautifully adorned with a great quantity of [Grinling] Gibbons's [f. 229] carving of which there is more in this room than I ever saw in any one place before. It ranges round the frames of the family pictures with which this room is hung. In the next room there are several very valuable original pieces, and by the best hands. There is an Edward VI by Holbein, and a Henry VIII at full length by the same; and some good pieces of Guido [Reni] and others. There is likewise a picture representing the Tudor family, which of late has been engraved by [George] Vertue, though I am not sure whether this be the original from whence it was taken. On one side of an altar is represented King Henry VII, and opposite to him King Henry VIII, below them are King Edward and Queen Mary, and on one side Queen Elizabeth.

The stair case is painted very beautifully by [Louis] Laguerre [1663-1721], but I could not find out the history it is designed to represent; but it rather seems emblematical. The apartments above stairs are not furnished, at least not in a manner suitable to the house; but they are prodigiously numerous. There is a very handsome chapel in which there is constant service when the Duke is in the country. On the windows are painted the arms of all the Percy family and their alliances.

I observed on the back stairs some very good pictures, to which the Duke in his whimsies will not allow a better place, particularly a portrait of the Duke and Duchess of Brunswick done in the taste of Rubens, at the bottom of the stairs, and at the top of the stairs is an incomparable piece representing five or six of the Apostles (as I take them to be) in conference together, and pointing to a golden vase that stands on an altar at a little distance. I could not learn the name of the painter nor the history; the former I am told the Duke studiously conceals as he does that of most of his pictures, out of an unusual and ridiculous whimsy.

The gardens do not seem to be large nor in good taste; they are laid out in terraces one over the other; and the park rises behind them commanding a very good prospect.

[f. 230] The Duke spends most of his time here, in a grand retirement peculiar and agreeable only to himself. He comes down to breakfast at 8 of the clock of the morning in his full dress, with his blue ribbon [of the Garter]; after breakfast he goes into his offices, scolds and bullies his servants and steward, 'til dinner time, then very formally hands his Duchess down stairs. His table, though spread in a grand manner as if company was expected, always consists of his own family, the Duchess and his two daughters; and when he has a mind to be gracious the chaplain is admitted. He treats all his country neighbours and indeed every body else with such uncommon pride and distance, that none of them visit them.[15]

There is nothing worthy of remark in the town of Petworth unless it may be in the church which I did not see. Sir John Peachey [2nd bt, c. 1680-1744] has a house very prettily situated on the other side of the town [probably Newgrove which he inherited from his brother Henry in 1737, rather than West Dean House, View 65].

From Petworth I descended into a valley and crossed the river Arun [western Rother] which empties itself into the sea about a mile below Arundel; a little beyond this I ascended the downs on which I rode four miles to Arundel.

Arundel is a small town that sends two members to Parliament. It is situated on the side of a hill, on the west side of the river Arun, which gives name to the town, Arundel signifying the vale of the river Arun. This river empties itself into the sea about a mile or two lower at a place called [Little]Hampton, where there is a tolerable harbour for shipping; but only small vessels can come up as high as Arundel. This town or rather this coast was formerly famous for very fine mullets, but I think of late years they catch but few.

At the upper end of the town are the remains of Arundel Castle, a great part of which is still kept in repair and increased with additional buildings by the Duke of Norfolk, the owner of it, who passes a few days here sometimes [Views 3 and 4]. [f. 231] There are several good rooms in it, and an old gallery. The former command a very good prospect of the country southward to the mouth of the Arun and of the sea. The walls of the chapel are standing, which I suppose was dedicated to St Denis, by the reliefs which I observed in several places of that saint. This lower castle is built round a court. Above it on the top of a round mount are the remains of a large round tower which is about 80 feet in diameter; behind that in the enclosure of the castle is a small garden.

This castle or at least the foundation of it is of great antiquity. The manor of Erundele is given in King Alfred's will to Athelm his brother's son. After the Conquest William the Conqueror gave this castle to his kinsman Roger de Mongomery who repaired it and was called Earl of Arundel. But his son Robert de Beleasmo forfeited it to King Henry I, by his rebellion against that prince who besieged and took the castle. King Henry I gave it to his second wife Adeliza daughter of Geoffrey of Louvain, Duke of Lorraine and Brabant, who after his death married William de Albiny who held out this castle in favour of the Empress Maud against King Stephen, for which she created him Earl of Arundel. The fourth earl of this family dying without issue male, the estate came to Richard Fitzalan who married the heiress of that family and was made Earl of Arundel by Edward II. [This sentence on f. 231v.] It seems to have been from Edward II's time that this earldom was made local, when that prince made Richard Fitzalan Earl of Arundel, who married the heiress of the Albiny family. There were 11 earls of that family. The last of them Henry Fitzalan (whose epitaph I shall mention hereafter) leaving an only daughter, the estate and honour descended by her in 1579 to Thomas Howard, Duke of Norfolk, whose family enjoy it still.

The castle of Arundel has the singular privilege that whoever is in possession of it is Earl of Arundel, without the King's patent, so that it is in the power of [f. 232] the Duke of Norfolk to make any person Earl of Arundel that he pleases by putting them in possession of this place. There were and I believe are still great jurisdiction and many privileges belonging to this manor, which is called the Honour of Arundel; and they extend to several places in both Sussex and Hampshire.

It is said that they keep here the sword of Bevis, Earl of Southampton, concerning whom they have so many legends in this country, but I did not enquire for it.

The parish church is a good Gothick building and was formerly collegiate; there are some remains of the cloisters still remaining on the south side of the chancel [View 5]. It is now as I apprehend an impropriation and the entire tithes are in the hands of the Duke of Norfolk who allows a curate a salary for taking care of the parish.

The chancel was the burying place of the Earls of Arundel as it is now of the Duke of Norfolk's family. But the Duke not content with that shuts it up from the church entirely and refuses both the ministers and bishop admittance into it, but with what authority I cannot tell. Bishop Hare once caused the doors to be broke open and held his visitation in the chancel, but the present Bishop of Chichester has acquiesced in the thing.[16]

In the middle of the chancel is a monument of fine white marble, of exquisite workmanship, on which are the couchant statues of Thomas [5th] Earl of Arundel [d. 1415] and Beatrix, his wife, daughter of John King of Portugal [d. 1439]. The coronets on their heads are carved very beautifully and round the body of the monument are carved monks holding shields in their hands, on two of which I observed the following coats. [f. 233][sketches of 2 arms]

A little above this between the chancel and north aisle is a monument in white alabaster of a knight in armour, but there is no inscription on it; I suppose it however to be some of the Earls of Arundel [7th Earl, John Fitzalan, d. 1435]. It is open below on which is represented a body emaciated of which according to custom they tell you a story, that the person was shot with a poisoned arrow which emaciated him so.

Beyond this in the north aisle is a plain tomb of grey marble which by the inscription round it seems to have belonged to one of the Earls of Arundel [John, 6th Earl, d. 1435], though it is imperfect in some places. What remains of it is as follows: ..Gallia Normanniae.....issime floruit obiit autem anno Dni Millesimo CCCCXXI et mens Aprilis die 21 Hec Aliennia.....thumbrorum Comitissam Anno Dni Millo....[17] [Elevation of tomb]

[f. 233v] Over this inscription is the following coat of arms [sketch]

[f. 235] Towards the north-east end of the chancel is a noble gothic monument of Thomas [10th] Earl of Arundel [d. 1524, and of his son William, 11th Earl, d. 1544] in grey marble. [Elevation drawn on f. 234v. *Sussex views*, 11] It projects like a canopy and the front of it is supported by four gothic pillars adorned with sculpture, as the whole monument is. On the front of it are three coats of arms. Those in the middle are of a Knight of the Garter, with a horse and a stag for supporters. That on the left hand are the arms of the Percy and if I remember right without any supporters; but on one side of this coat I observed a key with a crown over it, and a little higher something like a horn; and on the other side a hog all carved very small. These I suppose were some emblem of honour that belonged to the Percy family, whose arms are in this shield. The shield on the other side has the Percy arms and some other quartered with it which I do not remember; the supporters are a stag and a unicorn. Against the back of this monument is the following inscription on a small brass tablet [omitted here].[18]

[f. 236] Opposite to this against the south wall of the chancel is another noble gothic monument in the same taste but rather larger and of more elegant workmanship. It is adorned in front with four taper wreathed pillars which are very beautiful. Under it on a raised monument are two couchant statues of an Earl of Arundel and his Countess [William Fitzalan, 9th Earl, d. 1487, and Joan], both which appear to have been gilt all over; but it is now almost worn off and the statues themselves broke. There are some signs of a gothic inscription, but so defaced with time that it is impossible to read one word of it. There are no arms on this monument or at least none that can be made out.

A little above it nearer the altar, on a marble tablet fastened against the wall is a long inscription to Henry Fitzalan, [12th] Earl of Arundel [d. 1580], and the last of that family, who is mentioned likewise in the epitaph of Thomas, Earl of Arundel. The inscription is as follows [omitted here].[19]

[f. 237] This Henry Earl of Arundel was a great friend to Queen Mary and instrumental in bringing her to the throne. He afterwards flattered himself that Queen Elizabeth was fond of him and endeavoured at a great expense to gain her affections, but not finding the success he expected he went abroad soon after.

The epitaph makes mention of his portrait and of an equestrian statue made by Lord Lumley in memory of him, out of his own armour, but I could not see nor learn any account what has become of either, for by the epitaph they seem to have been designed at least, if they were not actually erected in the church. [Milles does not mention the roof bosses or the painted glass: Views 6 and 7.]

[f. 238] From Arundel I went 10 miles to Chichester through a flat gravelly country, enclosed and abounding with wood, part of which is the forest of Arundel. [f. 237v]

About a mile before I came to Chichester I observed the Roman road now called Stanestreet Causeway coming from Billingshurst for the most part I believe in a straight line, at least it is so here, where it joins the Arundel road.

Chichester, called by the Britons Caercei and by the Saxons Cissanceaster, was founded by Cissa the second king of the South Saxons, who made it the place of his residence, though Mr Camden says that it was an obscure place until the Norman conquest, before which time it had only a monastery dedicated to St Peter and a nunnery in it. But the episcopal see being removed hither from Selsey in William the Conqueror's time increased it considerably.

It is now a pretty town well built of a circular form, the walls or at least remains of them are still standing. It is divided into four parts, by four handsome streets which lead from the middle of the town to the four gates [View 54]. At the place where these four streets meet is a very handsome old Gothick cross built upon arches and said to have been erected by Bishop Reed about the year 1400 though an inscription in the cathedral ascribe it to one Bishop Story who was bishop here about 1478. This difference may be determined I suppose by the coat of arms which is on the cross which are a cross between four cranes, and I suppose was the coat of the founder.

The Cathedral, Bishop's Palace and Prebendaries' houses take up one fourth part of the town [View 51; *Sussex views*, 37-9]. The cathedral is not a light Gothick building nor is it very large. Its greatest beauty is the spire which is inferior to none in England except Salisbury for height and beauty. Some years ago the lightening drove several stones out of the upper end of it; notwithstanding which the steeple stood firm. The body of the church is but indifferent; the choir is handsome and kept very neat. [f. 239] In the south aisle on one side are painted [by Lambert Barnard] the portraits of all the bishops of this see from Wilfred, Bishop of Selsey, to Robert Sherborne who was bishop about the year 1508 and had them painted, as he did on the opposite side the foundation of the see at Selsey, the removal of it to Chichester, and the portraits of all the Kings of England from the time of Cissa, which have been continued down to the present King.

Selsey where this see was first erected is in an peninsula on the seashore about six miles south of Chichester. Adelwalch who succeeded Cissa in the Kingdom of the South Saxons gave this place to Wilfrid, Archbishop of York, who being banished from his diocese by Eigfrith, King of the Northumbrians, took refuge here, built a monastery on the spot and planted Christianity in these parts; but after five years' stay here he returned to his diocese, and the see of Selsey then became subject to the Bishop of Winchester 'til the year 711, when it was made a separate diocese by itself. This is the account given by most of the historians, but the history painted at Chichester seems to differ from it, and to make the foundation of this see owing to Cedwalla, King of the West Saxons, who vanquished and killed Adelwalch, and whose zeal against the idolatrous inhabitants of the Isle of Wight whom he had conquered carried him so far as to threaten to destroy them, if he had not been dissuaded from it by Wilfrid who was then with him and to whom he gave the fourth part of that Island. It was about the year 682 when Selsey was given to Wilfrid, from whence we may date the rise of that see; it continued there, through a succession of 22 bishops 'til after the Conquest, [margin: Le Neve; Camden] but there then being an order to remove the bishop's sees into the most considerable towns, this was removed to Chichester in the time of Stigand, Bishop of Selsey [margin: Le Neve's Fasti] and about or at least [f. 240] after the year 1082.

There are in this church the monuments of several of their bishops, most of whom were persons of considerable figure and reputation in their time, the first of whom is Bishop Ralph who is buried at the east end of the choir before the door of St Mary's chapel. He was made bishop here in 1091 and died in 1123. He was the third bishop of this see after its removal from Selsey and was chaplain to William the Conqueror. He built a cathedral here in 1108, which was burnt down in 1114, but rebuilt again by him. He was of remarkable large stature and said to be a very good man.[20]

The next bishop in point of time whose monument is in this church is Seffrid II who was made bishop in 1180 in the time of Henry II and Richard I. In the year 1185 the cathedral was a second time burnt down together with the city. The former he rebuilt in the manner it now is, which was finished in less than 14 years and consecrated in 1199, besides which he built the episcopal palace and canons' houses, and died in 1204. His monument is in the north aisle behind the choir.

In the south cross aisle is the monument of Ralph Nevil, who was Lord Chancellor of England and made bishop of this see in 1223; he died in 1244. He was elected to the see of Canterbury and approved by the King but set aside by the Pope.

And under the south window in the same isle is the monument of John de Langton who was made bishop of this see in the year 1305. He was twice Lord Chancellor of England namely first in 1293 (before he was made bishop of this see) in which post he continued nine years. He was a second time made Chancellor of the Kingdom in 1308 which was the first of King Edward II, and enjoyed it [f. 241] for four years. He was at the same time one of those grave and great men who was appointed to be near the person of Edward II in order to prevent the ill effects of his favourite Gaveston's counsels, and again in the year 1319 he was amongst those who executed the same office with regard to the Spensers. He is said to have been a prelate of great wisdom and prudence, was a great benefactor to this church, and likewise to the University of Oxford to whom he bequeathed £100 to be deposited in a chest for the use of any poor members of the University who might borrow the whole or any part thereof without interest. He died in 1337.

There was about this time one of the same name namely Walter de Langton who was Bishop of Lichfield whom King Edward II on coming to the throne caused to be imprisoned for a long time in Wallingford castle, because both that Prince and his favourite Piers Gaveston had been imprisoned in his father's lifetime for breaking the pales of the bishop's park and killing his deer. I cannot say whether these two contemporary bishops were related or no. Besides these there were two of the same name Archbishops of Canterbury viz. Stephen Langton in 1206 and Thomas Langton in 1500 who was elected from the see of Winchester but died before his translation could be perfected.

Robert Stratford whose monument is in the south cross aisle succeeded John de Langton in 1337 [View 52]. He was Chancellor of the Exchequer, kept the great seal of England several times, went abroad with King Edward III when he besieged Tournai, but afterwards fell into the King's displeasure and was sent to the Tower, I suppose at the same time that the King was incensed against his brother John de Stratford, then Archbishop of Canterbury. [f. 242] The Bishop of Chichester however was soon released out of the Tower but lost his office. He was a great benefactor to the town of Stratford-upon-Avon, where he was born, and built the handsome church which is now standing there. He died in 1362.

Under the south arches in the nave of the church is the monument of Bishop John Arundel, Doctor of Physic, who was physician to King Henry VI, and made bishop of this see in 1459 and died in 1478.

To him succeeded Edward Story whose monument is in the north aisle, who was translated from Carlisle hither in 1478. He was a favourite of Edward IV and appointed by that prince one of the executors of his will. He was a great and good prelate; he built the Gothick cross that is in the town, and left an estate at a place called Amberley 11 miles from Chichester for the repair of it, which estate now brings in near £25 a year; but I think this estate was changed for some other which was appropriated to this use. He died in 1502.

Robert Sherborne who caused the portraits of the kings of England and bishops of Chichester to be painted is likewise buried in the south aisle; he was bishop here in 1508 and died 1536. He repaired and beautified this cathedral very much, as appears by his mottoes in every part of it, which are 'Credite operibus' and 'Dileti decorem domus mei Domine'.

Besides these there is in the north aisle the monument of Thomas Bickley bishop of this see in 1585, and at the upper end of the choir on each side of the altar those of Henry King, Guy Carleton and Robert Grove, bishops of this see, the first elected in 1641, died in 1669, the second elected in 1678, died in 1685 and the last elected 1691 and died in 1696.

[f. 243] Bishop Waddington [died 1731] is likewise buried in the east chapel of the south aisle but there is no monument over him, though his memory is much honoured in this place.

In the cloisters I observed on a plain marble stone against the wall the epitaph of the learned Mr [William] Chillingworth [1602-44] which is as follows: [not copied]²¹ Mr Chillingworth was taken prisoner in Arundel Castle where he served as an engineer, when that place was taken by the Parliament army. He was sent to Chichester (and not to London with the rest of the prisoners) where he was confined for some time in the Bishop's Palace and died. Lord Clarendon attributes his death to the barbarous usage of the clergy that attended the Parliament army, and Dr Walker in his Sufferings of the Clergy says that though he desired to be buried by the common prayer, it was not only denied him, but that his burial was attended with the most ridiculous and malicious invectives of Rump [f. 244] clergy both against him and his excellent book which he wrote against the Papists, which they flung into the grave with his corpse together with a thousand maledictions.

The episcopal palace since it was repaired at a great expense by Bishop Waddington seems to be a very good house; before it is a large and pleasant garden. The Deanery is likewise a good house; but there are but two houses more in all the close for prebends [View 51]. There are four residentaries, two archdeacons, and prebendaries that belong to this church.

Chichester was doubtless a Roman town; the Roman inscription which was dug up there some years ago is a convincing proof of it and that there was in it a temple dedicated to Neptune and Minerva. It could be no other place but Regnum of the [Antonine] Itinerary. That stone is now at the Duke of Richmond's seat of Goodwood, of which I shall make mention hereafter.

On Saturday morning the 17th of September I left Chichester and went three miles northwards to see Goodwood, the seat of the Duke of Richmond, which is pleasantly situated at the foot of the downs. The house is old and belonged formerly to the family of the Percys; the Duke has had design for some years to rebuild it, according to a design of Colen Campbell in the *Vitruvius Britannicus* [vol. 3 (1725), plates 51-4], and has already built up one of the offices, but I believe he will never do any more, because he is fitting up the old house and endeavouring to make it as convenient and comfortable as he can. The house has a regular old front towards the park, though there is no regularity at all in the apartments, nor anything remarkable in them. The park is but small. It rises behind the house up the side of the downs, from whence [f. 245] there is a most beautiful view of Portsmouth, St Helens, the Isle of Wight and Chichester. The Duke is now building a pretty summer house here.

The gardens consist of a little wood taken out of the park in which are two or three pleasant vistas [Views 25 and 26]. In the middle of the wood is a thatched hut where the Duke dines sometimes in summer. In a summer house not far from this, the Duke has fixed up the Roman inscription which was found at Chichester and which I mentioned before. On each side of it he has placed the statues of Neptune and Minerva and over it the bust of King Cogidubnus mentioned in the inscription. One end of the stone is broke off and lost, so that the beginning of the lines are wanting, but the defect may be easily supplied in all except the last line but one which is not so easily to be guessed. [Sketch of stone and supplied wording.]

[f. 246] The Duke had formerly a good menagerie at Goodwood, but within these few years he has disposed of almost all his beasts. One of his lionesses he has buried in his garden at the end of one of the walks and has erected a monument of Portland stone over her.

The park is but a barren spot of ground, and very indifferently planted. Just behind it is St Rooks Hill on the top of which is a large Danish camp, and not far from thence is a village called Charlton remarkable for the great resort of nobility in the hunting season, many of whom have little hunting houses there.

About two miles south of Chichester is the little village of Bosham, a place remarkable in ancient times [View 21]. For here, as Bede tells us, one Dicul a Scotch monk, erected a little monastery before the conversion of the South Saxons by Wilfrid, in which were five or six monks, but they were not able to convert their idolatrous countrymen. This village in Edward the Confessor's time belonged to the Archbishop of Canterbury, from whom Earl Godwin got it, by a most ridiculous stratagem, which is mentioned by all the historians of that time.

King Edward being at Bosham, together with the Archbishop of Canterbury, Earl Godwin and the rest of his court, the Earl having laid the scheme before hand comes up to the Archbishop attended with many of the nobility and gentry who were his followers, and in a jesting manner said to him 'Da mihi Boseam' ['Give me Bosham'], intending thereby that the Archbishop should think he said 'Da mihi Basium' ['Give me a kiss', in the sense 'Bless me as I kiss your hand']. And in effect the Archbishop either thinking that he did say so, or at least not knowing the meaning of his request, answered him 'Do tibi Boseam' ['I give you Bosham']. Upon which the Earl and his followers according to his direction prostrated themselves before the Archbishop in token of homage. The Earl very artfully expressing all [f. 247] the while his acknowledgements to the Archbishop for the favour and commending his generosity to the King and, in order to make sure of his new grant, went with a numerous attendance immediately to Bosham and there kept possession, the Archbishop not daring to dispute it with him.

It continued in Earl Godwin's and his son Harold's possession, the latter of whom used to divert himself there in fishing. It happened one day that he was drove from hence in a fishing boat over to the coast of Normandy, where he was taken prisoner by the Earl of Ponthieu, but he [the Earl] dispatched a messenger to William, Duke of Normandy, to let him know of this confinement and that he [Harold] came thither by the King of England's orders to assure him of his being designed by the Prince for his

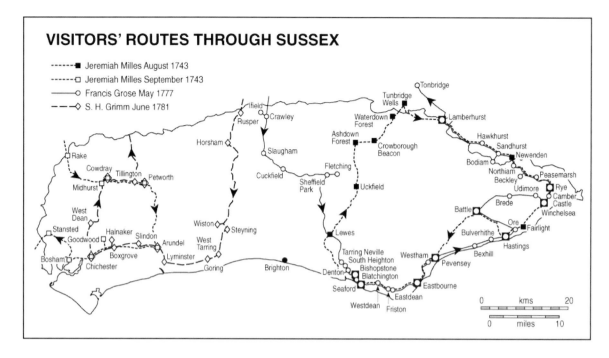

VISITORS' ROUTES THROUGH SUSSEX

------■ Jeremiah Milles August 1743
------□ Jeremiah Milles September 1743
————○ Francis Grose May 1777
— — ◇ S. H. Grimm June 1781

successor; who [William] immediately sent for him, and by degrees took such a fancy to him that he contracted him to his daughter, and Harold in return promised to put William in possession of the Castle of Dover (which he then had), upon the death of King Edward, and to assist him to the utmost of his power in getting the Crown of England. Not long after the Duke sent him honourably back to England; but King Edward told him at his return that this expedition of his would be of great prejudice to the nation and of reproach to himself, as in effect it proved to be.

Selsey is about four miles south of Bosham. It is now only a poor fishing village, the remains of the ancient town, where the episcopal see was, being covered with the sea, but are to be seen at low water.

From Chichester I went eight miles to Stansted, the seat of Mr [James] Lumley, which was left him by his brother the late Earl of Scarborough. It is situated in the middle of a little park, in a very woody country on the borders of the Forest of Bere. The house was built by the late Earl of Scarborough's father. It is a handsome brick building with a double front, and seven windows in front. [f. 248] The apartments are large, well proportioned and very well furnished, with exceeding good tapestry. The great staircase is of Virginia walnut, and very beautiful.

The park is a dead flat, and so much surrounded with woods that it has little or no prospect, though the upper rooms of the house command a very pleasant one of Portsmouth and the Isle of Wight. There is a fine avenue in the front of the house which is near two miles long, and there is a pretty good one of chestnut trees at the back front of the house. Stansted is in Sussex, but on the borders of Hampshire.

From Stansted I went five miles through the Forest of Bere to Havant, a small market town situated near a bay of the sea in which are two large islands, the names of which are Haling, & Thorney .... [thence to Portsmouth, Portchester (identified as the Roman Port Peris where Vespasian landed), Southampton, Winchester, Whitchurch, Highclere and Newtown, arriving on 20 September 1743].

4. Sussex views in Francis Grose's *Antiquities of England and Wales*

The purposes of the following table are to assist identification of Sussex engravings removed from Francis Grose's *Antiquities of England and Wales* and to illustrate the complexity of the history of the plates in such a publication. What became the first four volumes of the first edition were published in 60 parts, of which the first appeared in late February or early March 1772 and the last in June 1776, plus a supplement of 33 plans of monuments and an index giving the order (by county) in which the views and plans should be bound up. The price per part was 3s. Each part normally comprised six plates and the associated text on the same page, and included plates which were ready for publication. Hence the order of publication was different to the order, as given in the index, in which subscribers were advised to bind up the views and plans. However, as the parts appeared, successive volumes were deemed to be completed (or started) and title pages and introductions were issued. So, for example, the acknowledgements in volume 3 relate to the plates and text in parts 31 to 45 and not to the plates and text for the counties from Northumberland to Sussex.

Soon after completing the first four volumes, Grose started on a *Supplement*, of which the first part appeared in June or July 1777. Three parts had appeared by mid-1778, but thereafter Grose's militia service caused publication to cease until 1783, with the two volumes completed in Autumn 1787. There were 43 or 44 parts, priced again at 3s. each. Their composition is not known.

The antiquities was reissued in a cheaper (here called second) edition of eight volumes, in sequence by county, beginning in August 1783 in 168 fortnightly parts of four plates with the letterpress on separate sheets, at 1s. 6d. a part. The demand was sufficient to justify re-engraving many of the plates. Views from the *Supplement* were incorporated at the correct point if they were ready; volume 8 was a repeat sequence of counties for views appearing too late. The final part appeared in 1787, at about the same time as the last part of the *Supplement* to the first edition. So latterly some plates were published for the first time simultaneously in different formats for the two editions. For more on *The antiquities'* publication, see Hodson 1984-97, 3: 125-65.

The list contains the engravings of Sussex views, church monuments and fonts. For each plate the following information, as available, is given in the columns, from the left:

View This is not necessarily the title as given in *The antiquities*. The parish of the monument is given first, and spellings have been modernised.

Date The date at which the view was drawn is taken from the text accompanying the plate, in preference to the index. Several of the views by Grimm have dates before his employment by Burrell and the dates on the corresponding views in the British Library have been added in square brackets.

Artist The name of the artist responsible for the original view from which the plate derived is usually taken from the index, but if another name is given in an introduction it is preferred. The views of Herstmonceux Castle are attributed to Grimm, but he had made copies for Burrell from originals by James Lambert junior commissioned by Lord Dacre (see Document 6.1).

Engraver As given in the margin of the plate.

Engraved The date engraved in the margin of the plate in the first edition.

Re-engraved The date in the margin of the plate in the second edition, if different from the first edition.

(continued on page 114)

View	Date	Artist	Engraver	Engraved	Re-engraved
Arlington, Michelham Priory 1	1784	S. H. Grimm	Newton	1 Jul 85	
Arlington, Michelham Priory 2	1784	S. H. Grimm	Newton	1 Sep 85	
Arundel Castle, the Keep	1782	S. H. Grimm	T. Bonnor	10 Jan 83	
Battle Abbey 1, from W	1761	F. Grose	Godfrey	8 Jul 72	1 Jun 85
Battle Abbey 2, from SE	1762	F. Grose	Godfrey	1 Mar 73	1 Jun 85
Battle Church, brass of John Wythines	[1777]	F. Grose	N. C. Goodnight	9 Jul 87	
Bishopstone Church, font	[1777]	F. Grose	James Sparrow	18 Sep 87	
Bodiam Castle 1, from SW	1777	F. Grose	Sparrow	6 Jul 77	1 Jun 85
Bodiam Castle 2, from N	[1777]	F. Grose	D. L.	7 Jan 78	1 Jun 85
Bodiam Castle, interior looking N	1784	S. H. Grimm	Newton	27 May 85	
Bodiam Church, brass of woman in shroud	[1777]	F. Grose		9 Sep 87	
Bosham Church, crypt	1778 [1782?]	S. H. Grimm	T. Bonnor	10 Jan 83	
Boxgrove Priory	1761	F. Grose	Sparrow	1 Oct 72	7 Jun 85
Boxgrove, Halnaker House from SW	1782	S. H. Grimm	Sparrow	30 Aug 83	
Bramber Castle	1760	F. Grose	Sparrow	6 Feb 75	15 Jun 85
Bramber Church	1761	F. Grose	Godfrey	2 Feb 72	7 Jun 85
Brede Place	1774 [1784?]	S. H. Grimm	Sparrow	14 Jun 85	
Brighton, blockhouse	1761	F. Grose	Godfrey	10 Sep 73	1 Jun 85
Chichester, Town Hall, formerly Greyfriars, interior	1780 [1781?]	S. H. Grimm	Sparrow	28 Jul 84	
Chichester, Vicars' Close	1778 [1782?]	S. H. Grimm	T. Bonnor	10 Jan 83	
Crowhurst, ruins at	1785	James Moore	J. Newton	20 Apr 87	
Denton Church, font	[1777]	F. Grose	James Sparrow	18 Sep 87	
Easebourne Priory	1782 [1780?]	S. H. Grimm	T. Bonnor	10 Jan 83	
Fernhurst, Verdley Castle	[1782]	S. H. Grimm	Sparrow	13 Jun 85	
Fernhurst, Verdley Castle, plan	[1782]	S. H. Grimm			
Frant, Bayham abbey	1760	Theophilus Forrest	Godfrey	1 Mar 74	1 Jun 85
Hastings Castle 1, distant, from W	1760	F. Grose	B. Godfrey	1 Mar 72	15 Jun 85
Hastings Castle 2, from NW	1759	William Green	Godfrey	23 Feb 73	15 Jun 85
Hastings Castle, plan		William Green		20 Jan 76	
Herstmonceux Castle 1, from SE	[1776]	S. H. Grimm [after James Lambert jnr]	Godfrey	18 Jun 79	15 Jun 85
Herstmonceux Castle 2, Great Hall	[1776]	ditto	Godfrey	1 Jun 79	22 Jun 85

Issued	Part	Part vol.	1st edn.	2nd edn.	GFS	Original	Cartoon
			s2	8			
			s2	8			SA, Grose 3 258
			s2	5		BL, Add. MS. 5674, f. 30 [54]	
Jul 72	5	1	3	5	754	private coll.	
Mar 76	56	4	3	5			private coll.
			s1	1		BL, Add. MS. 17398, ff. 117-8	SA, Grose 4 404
			s1	1			SA, Grose 4 405(d)
			s2	5			
			s2	5			
			s2	5		BL, Add. MS. 5690, f. 9 [17]	
			s1	1		BL, Add. MS. 17398, f. 124	SA, Grose 4 401(b)
			s2	5		BL, Add. MS. 5672, f. 47 [86]	SA, Grose 3 250
Jan 73	11	1	3	5	480		
			s2	5		BL, Add. MS. 5675, f. 75 [141]	formerly A. W. F. Fuller and Randall Davies
Feb 75	40	3	3	5			Brighton Art Gallery 100670
Apr 75	42	3	3	5		Sotheby's 19 Dec 1992 (252)	Brighton Art Gallery 100674
			s2	8			
Oct 73	22	2	3	5			Brighton Art Gallery 100668
			s2	5		BL, Add. MS. 5675, f. 50 [92]	SA, Grose 3 251
			s2	5		BL, Add. MS. 5675, f. 53 [97]	SA, Grose 3 252
			s2	8			SA, Grose 3 253
			s1	1			SA, Grose 4 405(c)
			s2	5		BL, Add. MS. 5675, f. 7 [12]	SA, Grose 3 254
			s2	8		BL, Add. MS. 5675, f. 5 [8]	SA, Grose 3 263
			s2	8		BL, Add. MS. 5675, f. 6 [10]	SA, Grose 3 263
Apr 75	44	3	3	5			
Mar 75	28	2	3	5	693		
Jul 75	29	2	3	5	1094		
Sep 76	plan		3	5			
			s2	5		YCBA, B1977.14.1095	
			s2	5		YCBA, B1977.14.1106	SA, Grose 3 255

View	Date	Artist	Engraver	Engraved	Re-engraved
Herstmonceux Castle 3, Green Court from S	[1776]	ditto		1 Jun 79	22 Jun 85
Herstmonceux Castle 4, porter's lodge	[1776]	ditto	Sparrow	7 Oct 80	22 Jun 85
Lamberhurst, Scotney Castle	1783	Verner	Sparrow	12 Jun 86	
Lewes Castle	1762	F. Grose	D.L.	27 Apr 76	22 Jun 85
Lewes Castle, plan	1762	William Green			
Lewes Priory 1, with castle in distance, from S	1761	F. Grose	Sparrow	1 May 73	8 Jun 85
Lewes Priory 2	1761	F. Grose	Godfrey	10 Sep 73	8 Jun 85
Lewes, St James's Hospital	1762	F. Grose	L. Peake	1 Aug 72	8 Jun 85
Lewes, St James's hospital, plan		William Green			
Lewes, St John-sub-Castro Church from S		F. Grose	Godfrey	2 Mar 76	8 Jun 85
Linchmere, Shulbrede Priory		F. Grose	T. Bonnor	1 Dec 82	
map of Sussex		John Seller			
Mayfield Place 1, from NW	1778	Kenyon, author of Antiquities of Herefordshire	T. Bonnor	26 Dec 83	
Mayfield Place 2, from S	1778	Kenyon, author of Antiquities of Herefordshire	T. Bonnor	10 Jan 83	
Mayfield Place, Great Hall	1784	S. H. Grimm	Jas Newton	22 Jun 85	
Northiam Church, brass of Nicholas Tufton	[1777]	F. Grose		7 Sep 87	
Pevensey Castle 1, from W	1760	F. Grose	Sparrow	10 Jul 74	8 Jun 85
Pevensey Castle 2, with Westham Church, from S	1760	F. Grose	B. Godfrey	1 Mar 72	22 Jun 85
Pevensey Castle, bird's eye view		[S. H. Grimm]		20 Aug 85	
Pevensey Church, gravestone near chancel door	[1777]	F. Grose		7 Sep 87	
Rye, Ypres Tower	1784	S. H. Grimm	Newton	14 May 85	
Salehurst, Robertsbridge Abbey	1785	James Moore	Sparrow	May 87	
Shipley, Knepp Castle	1775	Major Hayman Rooke	D.L.	6 Feb 76	22 Jun 85
Stoughton, Stansted Place, inner court, E side	1778 [1782?]	S. H. Grimm	T. Bonnor	26 Dec 83	
Tarring Neville Church, font	[1777]	F. Grose	James Sparrow	18 Sep 87	
Westham Church, gravestone in S cross	[1777]	F. Grose		7 Sep 87	
Winchelsea Church	1760	F. Grose	Godfrey	20 Jun 74	8 Jun 85
Winchelsea, Camber Castle, interior	1761	F. Grose	R. Godfrey	1 May 72	8 Jun 85
Winchelsea, Greyfriars	1761	F. Grose	Canot	2 Jun 72	15 Jun 85
Winchelsea, NW gate	1784	S. H. Grimm	Sparrow	7 May 85	

Issued	Part	Part vol.	1st edn.	2nd edn.	GFS	Original	Cartoon
			s2	5		YCBA, B1977.14.1098	SA, Grose 3 256
			s2	5		YCBA, B1977.14.1097	SA, Grose 3 257
			s2	8			
Jun 76	60	4	3	5		SAS, pic. coll. 93	private coll.
Sep 76	plan		3	5			
May 73	16	2	3	5	394		Brighton Art Gallery 100671
Oct 73	22	2	3	5	885	SAS, pic. coll. 3590	
Sep 72	7	1	3	5	776		Brighton Art Gallery 100672
Sep 76	plan		3	5			
Apr 76	57	4	3	5		Bodl., Gough maps 31, f. 14	
			s2	5			
			s2	5		see Kingsley 1982, 46-8	
			s2	5			SA, Grose 3 259
			s2	5			SA, Grose 3 260
			s2	8		BL, Add. MS. 5671, f. 32 [53]	SA, Grose 3 261
						BL, Add. MS. 17398, f. 123	SA, Grose 4 403(b)
May 75	43	3	3	5		BL, K Top. 42.58f	Brighton Art Gallery 100673
Apr 76	57	4	3	5			
			s2	8		BL, Add. MS. 5671, f. 58 [103]	SA, Grose 3 262
			s1	1		Bodl., MS. Top. gen. e.70, f. 46	SA, Grose 4 398(c)
			s2	5		BL, Add. MS. 5670, f. 15 [28]	
			s2	8			Sotheby's 19 Dec 1992 (252)
Feb 76	54	4	3	5			
			s2	5		BL, Add. MS. 5675, f. 39 [71]	
			s1	1		Sotheby's 19 Dec 1992 (252)	SA, Grose 4 405(a)
			s1	1		Bodl., MS. Top. gen. e.70, f. 46	SA, Grose 4 398(d)
Jul 74	33	3	3	5	1174	private coll.	
Jun 72	4	1	3	5	483	Rye Museum	Rye Museum
Jul 72	5	1	3	5	421		
			s2	5		BL, Add. MS. 5670, f. 20 [37]	SA, Grose 3 265

Issued The estimated month in which the part (next column) was issued to subscribers.

Part The part in which the plate was issued for the first edition, according to the manuscript list presumably made up as a working index, by a subscriber as the parts arrived (now Bodl., MS. Top. gen. f. 30). As the parts were being issued, the volumes were formed as follows:

vol. 1	parts 1-12, 15, 18, 19
vol. 2	parts 13, 14, 16, 17, 20-30
vol. 3	parts 31-45
vol. 4	parts 46-60

1st edn The volume of the first edition (1 to 4) or of the supplement (s1, s2) into which the subscriber was advised to bind up the plates, in the index to the respective sets of volumes.

2nd edn The volume of the second edition (1 to 8) into which the subscriber was advised to bind up the plates.

GFS In 1774 Thomas Bentley, partner of Josiah Wedgwood and in charge of the design studio in London, drew extensively on Grose's views for decorating the 'Green Frog Service' of tableware commissioned by Catherine the Great of Russia and now in the State Hermitage, St Petersburg. On 2 February 1774 Wedgwood was invoiced for parts 1 to 25, less three parts (probably 15, 18 and 19, the introduction) which he had returned. The latest date on any plate (in part 25) was 13 January 1774. Of the 132 views in the 22 parts retained, 97 were used for the service. Bentley took subsequent parts as they were issued. Work on the service was completed on 6 August. The latest date on part 33 was 11 July 1774. Of the 48 views in parts 26 to 33, 25 were used. Grose or his publisher, Samuel Hooper, seems also to have allowed Bentley access to views engraved but awaiting publication or to cartoons awaiting engraving. Several of the plates were among those long delayed in issue; others bore dates after the service was completed. Two views on the service come from cartoons which were never engraved and published. Here are given the 'Bentley' numbers to the ten pieces of tableware bearing Sussex views after Grose. All the other eight Sussex views used were taken from the Bucks' views of 1737: Amberley (but omitted from the service as shipped), Arundel, Battle, Bodiam, Camber, Herstmonceux, Lewes, Pevensey.[22]

Original This gives the location of the artist's 'original' picture, either a field sketch or worked-up version of field sketches or a copy of that.

Cartoon This gives the location of the 'cartoon' Grose prepared from the original, to the size required, for the engraver to work from. He either copied from his own original views or from views by other artists (as indicated by the **Artist** column), with the sole exception that Burrell had Grimm prepare the cartoons from his own pictures. 'SA' stands for Society of Antiquaries of London.

5. Francis Grose's tour in Sussex with William Burrell, May 1777

Francis Grose's diary of his tour in Sussex with Dr William Burrell is now in British Library, Add. MS. 17398, ff. 103-26, numbered '5' among six notebooks bound up by Grose or soon after his death. Each notebook contains notes and sketches made while touring. The volume was purchased by the British Museum from Thomas Rodd on 8 July 1848. The Sussex tour has previously been printed as Grose 1934, but with some omissions and errors and little annotation.[23] See Essay 3.1 on Francis Grose.

The buildings visited reflected Burrell's interest in churches. He had visited the churches at Crawley, Ifield and Slaugham in 1774, at Lewes in 1775 and at Hastings, Ore, Battle, Winchelsea and Rye in 1776, and he did not record the visits of 1777 in his church notes. But the churches south of Lewes in the lower Ouse valley and eastwards through Seaford to Bexhill were in new territory, and the visits are recorded (though curiously the dates differ by a couple of days in five of twelve cases), all in BL, Add. MS. 5697. The notes on Fletching include no date of a visit. A church note contained several standard items: dedication, patron, deanery, appropriation, value in Pope Nicholas's Taxation and in the King's Books, date of visit, very short description of the fabric, parish register extracts, monumental inscriptions, drawings of coats of arms and names of incumbents (largely relying on the registers). Extracts from books and documents, and drawings, were added, where available. Most of the drawings have been made straight onto the same page as the text, so Burrell must have had a copyist (sometimes his wife) working directly into his volumes, the originals being lent by Grose. Document 5.2 is a list of the surviving pictures which probably originated on this tour. One of these, of Denton, is reproduced in this volume, View 66; the other cross-references to Views in the text are to pictures by other artists.

Examples of church descriptions are:

Denton: This church consists of a small nave, a chancel paved with brick except the west end of the church which is not paved; the roof is not ceiled and wants repairs. There are 2 bells. No parsonage house.

Westdean: This church consists of a small nave and chancel, ceiled and in good repair, has one bell in the turret, is paved with brick. Visited again 10 Sept 81: when I found the roof and ceiling out of repair and the floor decayed in several parts. The arch which separated the belfry from the body is circular and very ancient.

Grose only exceptionally included churches in *The antiquities of England and Wales*, but the tour did provide a large proportion of the examples to illustrate Grose's essay on church architecture and fittings issued in the *Supplement* in 1787, as well as similar illustrations (and a view of Sheffield Park) for *The Antiquarian Repertory*.

Only at one church, Ifield, did Grose record making extracts from the parish register. However, the speed at which they were visiting, and the evidence of Burrell gathering extracts from incumbents, suggest that this was the exception. It was presumably in 1777 that Grose acquired the 14th-century ivory plaque of the Assumption of Blessed Virgin Mary, said to have been found in the ruins of Hastings Castle, which he gave to Burrell and which, his family having acquired it in 1811, Lord Chichester gave to the Sussex Archaeological Society in 1886.[24]

The route of Grose's tour is shown on the map on page 108.

5.1 The diary

British Library, Add. MS. 17398, ff. 103-26

[f. 103] Saturday [17 May 1777] set off half after 3, went over Wandsworth Common, the lower end of which was very bad owing to the late rains, went through Streatham to Waddon Court, slept there.[25]

[Sunday 18 May] Mounted at $1/2$ after six, passed through Beddington, Carshalton and Sutton for Potters Lane where, for about an hundred yards, found the road almost impassable owing partly to the wet weather and partly to its having been just widened. Eight miles from Reigate an eminence and a fine prospect, passed by a fine house the owner's name as I think Hudson [Robert Hudson of Tadworth Court in Banstead];[26] passed by a public house called Tangier House. At about two miles from Reigate descend a steep and winding chalk hill from whence there is a beautiful prospect. Leave Gatton Park on the left. Inned at the Swan which is the post and excise office. Here are several good public houses, particularly the White Hart which seems a new building. Here is a market house but an indifferent street. Here joined Dr Burrell and got into his chaise for Crawley, distant ten miles. [f. 103v] Stopped at the first inn at Crawley, and having procured a boy to guide us walked directly for Ifield, said to be a mile and a half but really measuring two. The horse road almost impassable for a carriage, the footway tolerably good, though in winter that as well as the other must be execrable.

On our arrival near the church Dr Burrell went to Ifield Court expecting to see something antique, but when he joined me said he had met with nothing worth his notice.

The boy, my guide, applied to Mr Spenser [Nicholas Spencer, d. 1783], a gentleman who is the proprietor of the great tithes and lives near the churchyard, for the key which, being given us, I went in and drew two monuments and a font. Of these one is a man in ancient armour in the attitude of praying, cross legged on an altar or table monument with a lion at his feet, and on the south side of the church the figure of a woman with a lion at her feet, also with her hands joined in a praying posture. The font is evidently antique and of singular construction. [f. 104] Both these monuments are so surrounded and encumbered by pews that I could only see them close over the figures; they were supposed to be man and wife of the name of Poynings [Sir John and Lady Margaret de Ifelde, d. *c.* 1340 and 1350].[27] Behind the woman, or in the next pew east of it, under the cover of some boards about three feet below the surface are several leaden coffins, one in particular for a child and another hammered to the shape of the human body. Drew also a view of the church.

Mr Spenser, to whom Mr Burrell was known, kindly pressed us to dinner, or rather to take a scrap of the remaining victuals, they having dined. Here met Mr Jackson, parson of Ifield [a curate, as the vicar was John Allen] and who has a living in Derbyshire, and Mr Spenser's son named Godfrey, an undertaker in Palace Yard [Westminster]. Returned to the inn and dined.[28]

Dr Burrell on his way visited Ewhurst [Place in Ifield, *Sussex views*, 84] but found nothing particular. Ifield register was shown us in which were the following entries. [*No entries quoted, diary proceeds.*]

Set forwards for Cuckfield, passed by several fine prospects, particularly the ruins of [Slaugham, View 172], an ancient seat now in ruins, passed by Handcross and Hoadlands. Inned at the King's Head, Cuckfield [View 61]. [f. 104v] Walked in the evening to see Cuckfield Church in which some monuments of the Burrells, but nothing else worthy of notice. The steeple of this church has been struck by lightening.

[Monday 19 May] Set out about twelve and came to Sheffield House the seat of [John Baker] Holroyd Esq., formerly belonging to Lord de la Warr, an handsome gothic building with grounds most beautifully diversified. Dined and slept there. Met there a Doctor Foster, of the Kingdom of Ireland. Went on Tuesday morning to see Fletching Church, in which is an ancient table monument with two brass plates representing a knight and his lady.[29] An ancient monument of the reign of James I and another brass plate of a glovemaker ornamented with a pair of gloves in brass. The church here remarkably damp. The parson upwards of 80 [Michael Baynes, vicar, died aged 89 in May 1786]. The church door very ancient.

[f. 105] Wednesday [21 May] about 11 set off for Lewes distant about 12 miles. Arrived about one and went to dinner at Mr Jas Mitchell's [James Michell, 1721-80, Lewes attorney holding many public offices, including Clerk of the Peace and Registrar for the ecclesiastical courts]. Dr Ducarel [recently appointed as Commissary for the sub-deaneries of South Malling, Pagham and Tarring] dined with us. Slept at the Star, walked after dinner to Southover Church to see Gundrada's Stone [Document 6.1]; on the steeple the mitre and initials of the last abbot.

22 [May] Thursday dined at the Bear with the clergy; supped at Mr Mitchell's.[30] WB breakfasted with Mr Green.[31]

Set off on horseback with Dr Burrell and Mr Green on Friday 23 [May] through Southbourne [Southease] and over ferry, which is pulled by a rope, saw Tarring Church [*blank*] and the ruins of the church at Upper Denton [South Heighton]. This church being struck by lightening [in 1769] and so much injured as to make rebuilding necessary, it was thought most advisable to unite the parish with that of Lower Denton. The church therefore was sold by auction and taken down for the sake of the materials. At Lower Denton [i.e. Denton] there is a church but no parsonage house, that being quite in ruins and seemingly of great antiquity [View 66]. The font here seemed very ancient.

Saw Bishopstone Church of which I drew a south view. Drew the font which seemed the only thing remarkable, as also a south view of the church which appears ancient. The brackets on the steeple are grotesque heads and the door of the porch circular ornamented with zigzags. From thence mounted and went to Bleckington [Blatchington] Church where I drew a font and saw Major Boardman who had retired thither from the 4th Regiment. He had fitted up a tower house from whence a beautiful prospect of Seaford. The parsonage at Blatchington is a very ancient building.

Rode to Mr [Lancelot] Harison's who lives 3/4 of a mile N.E. of Seaford [at Sutton]. Mr Burrell went thither immediately and into the church. At his return he mentioned to me a curious column whose frieze was ornamented with strange figures rudely representing the Crucifixion; of this I made an accurate view. N.B. Height of the frieze in Seaford Church eight inches 3/8. Set off for East Dean [correctly, Westdean]. Saw [Westdean] Church in which several monuments of the family of Thomas. Mem. In our way to and from [Westdean] passed over Excete Bridge and a high narrow causey. Visited the old manor house once the seat of Sir [*blank*] Thomas.[32] By the remains it seems to have been a large mansion. A small stone gate of the style of James I is still remaining; the house was built with brick and stone. Returned to Mr Harison's where we slept.

[f. 106] [Saturday 24 May] Got up at 6 and after breakfast proceeded in our chaise to Friston Church of which I made a drawing [View 89]. There was no font but some fine monuments of the Selwyns. From thence walked to Eastdean a small neat church where I drew a head of an angel in the window. From thence proceeded through Southbourne [in the vicinity of today's Eastbourne Town Hall] in the chaise to Westham; the road chalky and very slippery.

Saw Westham where I drew the font and some gravestones. It is a large and seemingly a very ancient building, but much out of repair. Walked to Pevensey, a strange rude church; here where I drew the font and a gravestone, also a slight view of the church.

The way to Pevensey lies through the castle, the shape of the external walls near oval, the keep which is moated round, stands on the east side of the outer area; part of it has lately fallen down. Returned and dined at the King's Head, Mr Harison with us. After dinner we were joined by Mr Baker the curate. A vault lately fell in at the castle, but it contained only ashes and other rubbish.

[f. 106v] Set out in the chaise for Hastings, but the road proving extremely bad at about five miles from Pevensey mounted our horses and rode by the sluice houses to Bexhill, which is a strong clumsy church with circular arches and massive columns, one of which with the font I drew [*Sussex views*, 18]. From thence proceeded by Bulverhythe. Just close to the road at Bulverhythe, saw the ruins of a small chapel of some form like what is hereunder delineated, some broken masses of stones lying at a good distance to the west as at x. [Very rough sketch of ruined wall with 'x' to the left.]

From Bulverhythe over a tolerable gravelly road to Hastings Mill. Here missing our road and turning up to the left by the mill, we passed a dreadful piece of road like a step ladder consisting of huge loose stones buried in mud. At length at the close of day arrived safe at the Swan. Distant from Pevensey only 15 miles, [f. 107] total distance from Mr Harison's 24 miles.

25 [May] Sunday. Breakfasted at 8. Walked up the hill to see the castle, of which I made two drawings [View 106]. On the west side is a sally port of singular construction as under: [sketch]

No marks of the staircase now remain in the tower described by Mr Green.[33] The shape of the castle seemingly oval; descended by a lane on the west side which leads to the lime kilns; from thence walked to the rock near the priory [White Rock, View 107], under which a fair called Rock Fair is annually held.

A farm house is built on the site of the priory and only a few walls above five feet high now remain; these seem to be ruins of part of a gate. Here drew a view of the rock and returned to the inn.

[f. 107v] Walked in the afternoon to the castle with Mr Burrell when I made another view and we took the following measurements:

Diameter of the twisting stair case 4 feet 4 inches and a half.
Inside door of the sally port 2 feet 9 inches wide, 6 feet 6 inches high.
Width of the passage 2 feet five. Outside door 2 feet 8 1/2 by six feet.
Diameter of the Square Tower 7 feet 4.
Breadth of the stone over the door of the sally port on the outside 3 feet five.
Length 5 feet.

The top or roof of the passage is formed by stones laid across instead of being arched.

No trace of buildings in the castle.

26 [May] Monday. Left Hastings at seven o'clock, and ascend a gentle rise, from which there is an extensive prospect towards the sea.

Passed by Ore Church, adjoining to which is a once capital brick mansion, seemingly built about the reign of King James, now degraded to a farm house. [f. 108] On the right pass by a house [Beauport Park] belonging to General [James] Murray [Governor of Minorca] and on the left by Crowhurst the seat of Mr [John] Pelham, from whence there is a very extensive prospect, which with the beauty of the plantations for the foreground make it a most delightful spot. A little further see Battle and over and about it a rich and beautiful country [View 15]. Arrive at Battle and inn at the George. The road from Hastings good. Distance 7 miles and 1/2.

On our arrival we found the Revd Mr [William] Hayley who waited for us. After breakfast, repaired to the church which is a large handsome building consisting of three aisles. The arches pointed but supported by very massive columns alternately round and octagonal. Here is a fine alabaster monument of Sir Thomas [i.e. Anthony] Browne and his wife, half placed in the north wall. Here are also several ancient brasses, and marks on stones of several others taken away. In the north window are some paintings on glass representing a bishop with his crosier and saints male and female, but could not find the tablet recording the battle fought here, mentioned by Browne Willis.[34]

[f. 108v] After having finished some sketches I made in the church, we were joined by Mr [Godfrey] Webster,[35] who afterwards took us to the Abbey and showed us an ancient building of great length, traditionally reported to have been the refectory [i.e. the dorter range: *Sussex views*, 15]. The windows are all pointed. Saw likewise the place where it is said the high altar stood where Harold fell and the battle raged most furiously. Called Lac de Sang. Saw also divers vaulted rooms supported by one pillar serving for steward's room and other offices [in the gatehouse]. The stable is a very handsome building the arches all very sharp and elegant. Saw the [abbot's] great hall, a very lofty building, with a carved oak roof in the manner of Westminster Hall. A kind of chest used for repairing it remains drawn up by ropes; this is occasionally lowered to receive workmen.

[f. 109] Dined at the George, the Revd Mr Hayley with us. After dinner we went to the Abbey in pursuance of an invitation to drink tea there. Lady Webster [wife of Sir Whistler, 2nd bt] showed us the house. Most of the lodging rooms were originally used as an infirmary and this is sufficiently evinced by the passage which is extremely long and narrow, the rooms all opening into it. The present library was the infirmary chapel; it is remarkable that most of the arches are of the pointed kind even in the vaulted or groined rooms, which run thus [sketch], the arches x being pointed.

On the south side there are remains of some beautiful arcades, worked, particularly two roses [the remains of the claustral vaulting on the east face of the abbot's hall?]. [f. 109v] In the Abbey are some tolerable pictures, particularly one of a young man having a white sash cross his shoulders seemingly in calm but considerably musing, about him are toads and serpents and at a distance houses burning, storms at sea and all possible scenes of distress. Over his head this motto 'Rien mettone'. Tradition makes this one of the family of Digby.

Part of the house next the park is said to have been built by an Irishman who let it run to ruin almost as soon as it was finished.

[f. 110] Tuesday 27th [May]. Rose at six and, after a hasty breakfast in which we were favoured with the company of Mr Webster who agreed to meet us at Winchelsea, we set off about a quarter after seven in the chaise, the weather and road both exceeding fine, the prospects on both hands extensive and pleasing. At [Broad Oak] turned to the right for Breeding [Brede] Church. Leaving our chaise we mounted our horses and plunging through a long mile and a half of miry road came to that church which is no inelegant building. It had formerly some fine painted glass; in the great window over the altar there is still remaining an elegant head of a bishop, of which I made a drawing. Here is a fine monument of [Sir Goddard Oxenbridge] who is represented in complete armour except his head, resting his feet on a lion. Over the figure in the back part of the tomb against the wall is the following date [1537] which seems too modern for the figure probably might have been repaired at that time. Here is also part of an ancient brass.[36] The vault in which the [blank] are deposited is in part fallen in and the rest seems likely to follow.

Mounting our horses we returned to our chaise which had waited for us at the turnpike and proceeding on the Rye Road came to Andere [Udimore] Church which lies the distance of a small field to the right of the road. We went to it but it afforded little worth notice [Sussex views, 167]. There were a few brasses for the Freebodyes, one of whom, the last of the family, is buried in the churchyard. His epitaph recites that he was possessed of an estate which had continued in the family upwards of 400 years. There were also some brasses for the Burdets and Jordens.[37]

Remounting our chaise and within about three miles of Rye resumed our horses and, turning to the right through long winding and dirty roads, reached Winchelsea which is about four miles from the turning off. Here saw several pleasant views among which is the town of Rye situated on a high hill commanding the country all around. [f. 111] Reached Winchelsea and sent our horses to the Bear and on repairing to the church found Mr Webster fully occupied in drawing the fine monuments [SV, 182]. There are five fine ones, three of cross-legged knights, one in particular in what is now the belfry. It is a lady, the other is a priest. Here is also a handsome brass of a priest.[38]

After drawing these and a view of the church, went to see the Priory now fitted up by Mr Holcombe [correctly, Thomas Holford, d. 1783], an apothecary and surgeon [View 197]. South of the chapel is a complete house and some other buildings all evidently formerly belonging to the Priory, as also a fine vaulted cellar. Mr [Holford] has planted before the front of the chapel so that it will be shortly invisible, or at least till one is too near to draw it. Drew a view of the town gate leading to Rye [View 198].

Mounted again and after crossing the river visited [f. 111v] Camber Castle built by Henry VIII. This castle, like most of the others, consists of a number of circular towers; the keep is a great round tower having some low or subterranean works about it. This castle is chiefly built of brick and faced with stone, particularly the inside buildings. Proceeded to Rye and dined at the George, the roads fine and distance only three miles. The evening fine, but for ourselves an election feast at the inn on account of the election of Mr Dickenson.[39]

[Wednesday] 28th [May]. Set forwards in our chaise for Tunbridge. At the turnpike mounted our horses and rode to Beckley Church in which was nothing worth drawing, except a glass window [Sussex views, 17]. Returned to our chaise which waited for us at the turnpike, the distance owing to the winding road upwards of two miles. Proceeded to Peasmarsh, a handsome church of which I made a drawing together with some brass plates. Returned to our chaise and proceeded to Northiam of which I likewise made [f. 113] a drawing, as also of some brasses.[40] From thence proceeded to Sandhurst Green; the roads remarkably fine and the prospects all along extensive and beautiful. At Sandhurst Green mounted our horses and rode to Bodiam. The church is small and situated on a hill on the left hand side of the road [Sussex views, 22], the village a miserable one consisting of a few straggling cottages. Rode on towards the castle which, being situated in a retired place, we dismounted and walked over the fields.

[f. 119] Bodiam Castle stands in a bottom and is encompassed by a stagnant moat overgrown with rushes and chickweed [View 20]. The castle is a magnificent building not unlike Ragland Castle in Monmouthshire. The great front was on the north side over a kind of bridge or causey defended by an advanced tower, the ruins of which are now standing. The front is adorned with three shields of arms [*blank*] and the ancient iron portcullis is still suspended under the chief entrance. There was a bridge with a gate or porter's lodge before it. [f. 119v] NB Bodiam Castle is the property of Sir Whistler Webster.

After making two drawings of this elegant ruin, mounted and returned to Sandhurst, and after eating some bread and butter with some gammon of bacon at the Angel got into the chaise and proceeded on to Tunbridge where we arrived and inned at the Rose & Crown. The ways and prospects in the day's journey were many and elegant.

Passed through Hawkhurst where a tradesman is building a whimsical house. Lamberhurst, a long street with a bridge. Summer Hill, an ancient seat on the pinnacle of a most beautiful and woody hill. The road this day mostly sandy and woody. Tonbridge: at the entrance, see an old chapel turned into a barn and in passing the bridge had an elegant view of the castle, the property of Mr Hooker who has fitted it up with great taste.

Set out on Thursday the 29th at seven o'clock and passed by Knole and through Sevenoaks and Riverhead. In going up Madams Scut [Madamscourt] Hill, got out of the chaise and walked. Saw a most delightful prospect of Sir Jeffry [f. 120] Amherst's Combe Bank [a conflation of Amherst's Montreal and the Duke of Argyll's Combe Bank?] and many other gentlemen's seats. Saw on the left Knockholt Beeches. Arrived about one at Bromley where we baited the horses for two hours at the White Hart - at 3 put to and set out for London and arrived at about 1/2 after 4 at the obelisk in St George's Fields [now St George's Circus at the south end of Blackfriars Road] where I got out and walked to Mr Hooper's [his publisher at 25 Ludgate Hill]. My horses and portmanteau William took to [f. 120v] Wandsworth from the New Cross turnpike.

5.2 The drawings

The following list comprises all the known drawings (and three engravings) which are likely to have originated during this tour, presumably all from Grose's hand, though in some cases copied by others. Simple coats of arms have been excluded. The left-hand column gives the subject; the captions to drawings in the diary seem mostly to have been added by Burrell; ** signifies that the drawing was engraved and published in *The antiquities* and is listed in Document 4. The right-hand column gives the location of copies or of other drawings: '17398' stands for 'BL, Add. MS. 17398', the diary; '5697' for 'BL, Add. MS. 5697', Burrell's church notes; 'c.1' for 'Bodl., MS. Douce c.1', a volume of copies of Grose's drawings made for Francis Douce (1757-1834); and 'SA' for 'Society of Antiquaries, Grose', for which full references are on pages 110-13 above. Not included here are seven pictures by Grose which Burrell owned and listed in BL, Add. MS. 5705, f. 9, and which may have originated from the 1777 tour (Battle Abbey; three of Pevensey Castle; Winchelsea Castle, Church and Priory).

Battle Abbey, three carved stones	5697, f. 9
Battle Church from south	5697, f. 15
Battle Church, brass in middle aisle of William Arnold d. 1435	17398, f. 112. 5697, f. 4
Battle Church, brass of John Wythines, d. 1615, and inscription**	17398, ff. 117, 118. 5697, f. 4. Bodl., MS. Top. gen. e.70, f. 52. SA
Battle Church, canopy over tomb	5697, ff. 3-8, 13-15
Battle Church, capitals of an octagonal and a circular column	17398, f. 114 . 5697, f. 4
Battle Church, crest in the little window of north aisle	17398, f. 115
Battle Church, font	17398, f. 120. 5697, f. 14
Battle Church, north aisle, east end, painted glass of St Christopher	5697, f. 8
Battle Church, north aisle, east end, three lights of female saints	5697, f. 5
Battle Church, north aisle, west end, four-light window, painted glass of Madonna and Child and saints	5697, ff. 6 and 7
Battle Church, north aisle, west end, painted glass of mitred bishop	17398, f. 113.
Battle Church, north aisle, west end, window	17398, f. 116.
Battle Church, Sir Anthony Browne's tomb	5697, ff. 3-8, 13-15
Battle Church, brasses	5697, ff. 3-8, 13-15
Beckley Church, painted glass and arms carved on tombstone	17398, ff. 121, 122.
Bexhill, Church and village from north	5697, f. 19
Bishopstone Church from south	5697, f. 169
Bishopstone Church, font**	5697, f. 169. c.1, f. 6. SA
Bodiam Castle I, from south-west**	engraving in *The antiquities*
Bodiam Castle II, from north**	engraving in *The antiquities*
Bodiam Church, brass inscription to Thomas Grove and wife, with small figure of a child	17398, f. 124.
Bodiam Church, brass plate of a woman in a shroud**	17398, f. 124. 5697, f. 25. Bodl., MS. Top. gen. e.70, f. 48. SA
Bodiam Church, font	17398, f. 123. 5697, f. 24. c.1, f. 6
Bodiam Church?, unidentified coat of arms	17398, f. 118v.
Brede Church, two brasses	5697, ff. 27, 30
Brede Church, bishop painted on glass	5697, ff. 27, 30
Brede Church, escutcheon on the jamb of the pillar which separates the Great Chancel from the south chancel	5697, f. 28
Brede Church, font	5697, ff. 27, 30
Brede Church, Oxenbridge monument	5697, f. 28. c.1, f. 8

Denton Church and old rectory (View 66)	5697, f. 189. BL, K. Top. 42.42. Private coll.
Denton Church, font**	5697, f. 188. c.1, f. 4. SA
Eastdean Church, painted glass of an angel	5697, ff. 194-5. c.1, f. 6. Bodl., MS. Top. gen. e.70, f. 1
Fletching Church, brass	5697, f. 199
Fletching Church, coat of arm of Walter de la Lynde	5697, f. 200
Fletching, Sheffield Place	engraving in *Antiquarian Repertory*, 2 (1779), fc. 204.
Friston Church, exterior	5697, f. 217. Private coll.
Friston Church, monument to Th. Selwyn d.1613	5697, f. 215
Hastings Castle, inside from south west	Bodl., Gough maps 31, f. 32
Hastings Castle, towers	Bodl., Gough maps 31, f. 31
Hastings Castle, view from south west	Bodl., Gough maps 31, f. 32
Hastings Rock and Castle from west	Bodl., Gough maps 31, f. 31
Ifield Church, exterior	Private coll.
Ifield Church, font	c.1, f. 5. Private coll.
Northiam Church from south-east	5697, f. 92
Northiam Church, arms painted on glass	17398, f. 123. 5697, f. 95
Northiam Church, brass of Nicholas Tufton**	17398, f. 123. 5697, f. 94. SA
Peasmarsh Church from south east	5697, f. 99
Pevensey Church from north	5697, f. 286
Pevensey Church, font	5697, f. 285. c.1, f. 5
Pevensey Church, gravestone in the nave near the chancel door**	5697, f. 308. Bodl., MS. Top. gen. e.70, f. 46. SA
Seaford Church, capital	5697, f. 304. c.1, f. 72
Tarring Neville Church, font**	5697, f. 308. c.1, f. 4. Sotheby's, 19 Nov. 1992 (252). SA
Udimore Church, brass inscriptions and two coats of arms	17398, f. 126.
Westdean Church, font	5697, f. 323
Westdean Church, monument to William Thomas	5697, f. 320
Westham Church, female saint on glass	5697, f. 328
Westham Church, font	5697, f. 329
Westham, gravestone in the south cross near the door of the Priesthawe chancel**	5697, f. 346. Bodl., MS. Top. gen. e.70, f. 46. SA
Winchelsea Church	Private coll.
Winchelsea Church, effigy of knight, elevation and plan	5697, ff. 147-8
Winchelsea Church, monument of Sir — Oxenbridge, S side	5697, f. 144
Winchelsea Church, on the capital of a friar's monument	5697, f. 146
Winchelsea Church, tomb of Knight Templar in the belfry	5697, f. 143. c.1, f. 13

6. Two letters from William Burrell

6.1 Dr William Burrell to the Revd William Hayley, 21 April 1778

This letter is known only as printed, undated, by M. A. Lower in 1865. Lower had been lent it by the Revd Burrell Hayley, from amongst the papers of William Hayley. Hayley's drafts of his letters to Burrell have survived in BL, Add. MS. 6359, with a list of the dates of letters received from Burrell; they corresponded from October 1775 to July 1785, at least. Burrell quoted the letter from Hayley to which he was replying. That letter was dated 27 January 1778 and included copious extracts from the parish registers for Brightling, Burwash and Etchingham, along with comments on the incumbents of the latter two and on John Philipot's 1634 visitation of Sussex, and the advice: 'If you should chance to spend a few days at Tunbridge Wells in the course of the next summer, you'll find it an agreeable excursion from thence to either Mayfield or Etchingham. The one is distant about 7 or 8 miles, and the other about 12 or 14. At either or both of which places I shall attend you with pleasure.' The next letter from Burrell in Hayley's list was dated 21 April 1778 - which must be the one printed by Lower. Hayley replied on 3 May: 'I have great acknowledgement to make to you for the many kind communications concerning persons and things which I receive by the favour of your correspondence, in return for my trash.'

The letter provides an interesting conspectus of antiquarian activity in Sussex in the 1770s: Burrell organising the clergy to examine records for him and to measure Lewes Priory, a herald writing the history of Lord Surrey's property, Lord Dacre commissioning drawings of Herstmonceux Castle, Lady Burrell writing verses on Gundrada de Warenne.

'Burwash register' Hayley had borrowed from the incumbent, and had offered to do the same for Salehurst, if the newly arrived curate proved unwilling to make extracts.

'Mr Hare Naylor' was Robert Hare, Rector of Herstmonceux, who adopted the name Naylor on inheriting Herstmonceux Castle from his half-brother in 1775 (Views 111 and 112). His reputation amongst antiquaries was tarnished by his demolition of the castle's interior which had prompted Lord Dacre to commission the Lamberts to make drawings. S. H. Grimm was the 'very eminent artist' who made copies for Burrell.

'Mr Brooke' was John Charles Brooke (1748-94) who had just been appointed Somerset Herald, helped by the Earl of Surrey's recommendation to his father the 10th Duke of Norfolk, Earl Marshal, and the Earl of Effingham, Deputy Earl Marshal. When Surrey succeeded as Deputy in 1782, Brooke became his secretary in that capacity. Brooke had seen Burrell's collection on 24 February 1778 but

From the slight view which [Brooke] had of them he could not discover anything which came immediately to the object of Lord Surrey's enquiries, but still they contain much curious matter which will lead to more minute researches. Mr B. showed the greatest liberality of sentiment, and said his Lordship should be extremely welcome to any of his assistance, but expressed the desire of seeing his Lordship on the occasion, that he might see what he would have, and that they might settle a plan for having them copied for his Lordship's use.

In May, Brooke was to send Surrey a history of Greystoke, his seat in Cumberland, and that seems to have been the limit of the project, which did not develop as Burrell had been led to hope. But Surrey maintained his interest in Burrell's collection, as

Brooke wrote in January 1789, 'I last week spent a day with the Duke of Norfolk [as Surrey had been since 1786], and found it was his Grace's intention, had you been in town to request the favour to pass the morning with you to look over your Sussex collections and drawings; he desired I would write to you to inform thereof ....' After Brooke's accidental death in a crush at the Little Theatre, Haymarket, he was commemorated by a portrait painted on a window in a gallery at Arundel Castle. Brooke and Burrell were two of John Elliot's sponsors for his election as FSA in 1780.[41]

'Gundrada's tomb' is that of the wife of William de Warenne, who together were the founders of Lewes Priory; she died in 1085. At some date unknown, the Revd William Clarke, Rector of Buxted (1695-1771, Essay 2.1) discovered the greater part of the lid of her tomb serving, inverted, as the top of the tomb of Edward Shirley, d. 1550, in the family's chapel in Isfield Church. In 1775 Burrell obtained permission, and paid, for the stone to be removed to St John's Church, Southover, just by the priory ruins, on 2 October. The inhabitants, John Elliot informed the Society of Antiquaries the following month, 'are preparing a proper case or shrine to receive it, and gratify the curiosity of the public.' On 7 December 1776, Hayley told Burrell that 'Last week I had the satisfaction of seeing the inscribed stone of Gundrada's monument.... It is not yet fixed up according to your instructions, but with its one edge on the ground leans against the west pew', but in November 1777 it was 'offered fairly to my view'.[42] The verses were by Burrell's wife, Sophia.

The Revd Robert Austen had already in 1772 provided measurements of Lewes Priory to Francis Grose who published them in 1773 (see Essay 3.1); Hayley was trying to persuade Austen to do (presumably) a more detailed or complete version.

Hayley in his previous letter had responded to Burrell's report of Elliot finding a map, probably George Randoll's of Lewes, 1620: 'The view of the Earl of Dorset's houses one would wish to have preserved, and among the other seats delineated in it, you may perhaps retrieve the memory of some one or other whose very existence is forgot and not a ruin remains. I have not the pleasure of knowing Mr Elliot, but have often heard him spoken of as a gentleman curious in his researches and indefatigable. I love a rummaging disposition which, although it does not always meet with everything it was in quest of, yet will generally find something worth the looking after.'

M. A. Lower, Sussex worthies *(Lewes: Bacon, 1865), 133*

[21 April 1778]

Dear Sir,

The readiness with which you executed my troublesome antiquarian commissions has imposed a silence on me for some time, that I might not appear to trespass too much, and put your goodness to a very severe trial. I have therefore postponed returning thanks (as I ought) for the packet of information you favoured me with so long [ago], I fear I am open to a charge of incivility at least, not to add ingratitude. For the remission of both these sins I must throw myself upon your mercy, and crave something more than a Papal indulgence, I mean a friendly generosity; and allow me now to assure you how much I feel indebted for your many learned and judicious observations, which always throw light upon subjects which without them would remain in utter darkness.

I observe you say, 'In the Burwash register the names of Cruttenden, Polhill and Hepden occur very often, and that you have only mentioned some of the principal of each', but will favour me with the rest if necessary? From the numerous extracts already transmitted I should suppose few remained unnoticed. But the utility derived from parish registers is so great that I should wish to have the remaining names of those families, and that of Oxenbridge, if it can be done without much inconvenience, and to avoid giving you unnecessary trouble, I enclose you the extracts already received, which I have entered in their proper places. From Salehurst I have received no account of the incumbents, nor extracts from the register (the inscriptions I took two years ago);[43] your kind assistance in that respect will much oblige me, as also in the extracts of Ninfield and Herstmonceux. I have no inscriptions or extracts for the parishes of Wartling, Hooe or Westfield. If an acquaintance with the gentlemen who officiate in those parishes should enable you to promise me this information wanted, it will tend greatly to complete my researches in your Rape of Hastings.

My friend, Lord Dacre (whose ancestors, the Fynes and Filliols, made so respectable a figure in former ages) is very anxious to learn whether there are any brasses in Wartling Church, and what remains of that ancient seat of Filliol, called Old Court, in Wartling. I told him I knew but one gentleman in that part of the country capable of satisfying his Lordship's curiosity, of whose readiness to oblige I had so many repeated instances, that I would venture to mention it to Mr Hayley, and did not doubt a successful issue to the application, when he had an opportunity of riding in that neighbourhood. I should suppose the register of Herstmonceux will furnish many curious extracts, though I doubt the attaining them without your kind interposition, as Mr Hare Naylor the Rector's taste will not lead him to dip into musty parchments. Lord Dacre's veneration for the memory of Sir Roger Fiennes has induced him to have exact drawings made, by Lambert, of the different courts of that noble and venerable mansion of Herstmonceux, the great hall, kitchen, etc., at the expense of 110 guineas; he has been so obliged as to allow me to have a copy, upon which I have employed a very eminent artist, and shall be very happy in showing it [to] Mr Hayley, if amusement or business brings him to London.

I am very glad to have the addition of your authority for the reading of Gundrada's inscription 'alabastrum', though I must frankly I could not discern the A as stated. I beg you will continue to remind Mr Austen of his promise to take the measurement and ground plot of the remaining walls of Lewes Priory, and so much of its foundations as still appear; when drawn on paper it may possibly give us some idea of the building, which the frenzy of Reformation destroyed.

I have the pleasure to inform you, the Earl of Surrey has formed a resolution of having an historical account drawn up of all the property descended to him from the late Duke of Norfolk, in which he has employed a very sensible young man of the Heralds' Office, Mr Brooke, who proposes to have drawings of all the monuments at Arundel, the Castle, etc. Lord Surrey applied to me for information on this head. I told him I would communicate everything in my power; though I collected materials for a History of Sussex with a view to publish them, I wished to benefit others, not myself, by such publication, and as I had not the smallest or most distant object to gain, I should be ashamed to wrap my talent in a napkin and, when I had experienced so much kindness from individuals, to withhold information where it might be useful. I doubt not you will agree with me in thinking an Earl of Surrey no mean convert to the love of Antiquity, and wish too, with me, another Arundel may live in Surrey![44]

A lady of my acquaintance has sent me a copy of verses on Gundrada's Tomb, which I send for your amusement, and which may, perhaps, agreeable to the great Lord Bolingbroke, be deemed a grain of sweet, to render palatable a world of bitter, which has flowed from the pen of, Dear Sir,

Your much obliged humble servant,   Wm Burrell

6.2 Sir William Burrell to Charles Gilbert, 27 June 1794

This letter responded to an enquiry from the Lewes lawyer, Charles Gilbert, George Medley's steward, about Langney Grange in Westham. It implies that when Burrell saw Medley's court rolls, in Gilbert's custody (Document 7.2), he did so, not at Gilbert's Lewes office, but at Buxted. The letter has been written by a secretary.

East Sussex Record Office, SAS/ME 22

The Deepdene [Dorking, Surrey], June 27th 1794

Dear Sir,

It is impossible I can so far forget the civility I received from my Sussex friends, particularly from Mr Medley, as to withhold any information that it is in my power to give, but I am sorry to say my ability is not equal to my inclination. I perfectly recollect the building at Langney, and the remains of the chapel,[45] but if <u>you</u> have been unable to find any satisfactory account (of its origin, and what particulars you wish to know) in Mr Medley's papers, you may be assured it is not in my power to give you the information you desire, as the papers whence I made my extracts were at <u>Buxted</u>. I have none of my Sussex books here, and the persons whom I employed in copying my memorandums are dead, therefore my original plan is frustrated; and it would be a difficult task to decipher many parts of those books, even if my health permitted me to continue collecting information respecting antiquities in Sussex. Pray communicate this, with my sincere respects to Mr Medley, and be pleased to assure him, the real pleasure I should have in conversing with him on the subject, if he would honour The Deepdene with a visit, and give an old friend the satisfaction of seeing him.

Your most obedient humble servant,
Wm Burrell

7. 'Books and MSS perused': William Burrell's sources

From an early stage of his research, Burrell kept lists of his sources, separately for the 'books and MSS perused'. The lists were started in the first copy of Thomas Cox's *A compleat history of Sussex* (1730) which he annotated (now BL, Add. MS. 5708); they were transferred to the second copy (now in East Sussex County Library, Eastbourne Reference Library). They are referred to below as the 'earlier' and 'later' lists. He also made a list of views and maps (BL, Add. MS. 5705, f. 9), but its 70 or so items are too slight to warrant printing, as they do not include the pictures he commissioned of the Lamberts and Grimm, but comprise mainly published items mentioned in the Essay, such as Hollar's etchings, the Bucks' engravings, Budgen's map of Sussex, Yeakell and Gardiner's map of Chichester and Lambert's prospect of Brighton. The only notable group are ten original views by Francis Grose, seven of which may date from the 1777 tour (see Document 5.2), the other three being of Boxgrove Priory, the blockhouse at Brighton and Knepp Castle. A detailed list of Sussex views published down to about 1776 is in Gough 1780, 2: 286-96.

7.1 The books

The earlier list comprises 25 books (none published after 1769), apparently entered as they were read. These were transferred to the later list, but arranged alphabetically, with space left for additions. The final tally was 53 books with the latest date of publication of 1782. Burrell identified the books he had perused by the author's surname and one word from the title, e.g. 'Lloyds Worthies', 'Morants Essex', and (in the later list) placed them in a rough alphabetical order, by either author or title, e.g. 'Strypes Annals' is followed by 'Erdswicks Staffordshire'. These descriptions are reproduced here only in cases of doubt, within quotation marks. Rather a fuller bibliographical description is given, in alphabetical order by author with some guesswork as to the edition Burrell consulted. Whether the book was offered in the auction of Burrell's town library following his death, in May 1796, is shown in the form [Sale lot xxx]. The absence of a title from the sale is not proof that Burrell did not own a copy, but he did not move his Sussex collection to The Deepdene, as shown by the letter of 1794 in Document 6.2 and from major titles, such as his enlarged copy of Dugdale's *Monasticon*, being in the sale. That several county histories not in the list below were auctioned suggests that he did not own others.

There are several obvious omissions from the list. First, *Magna Britannia et Hibernia* for Sussex was in the sale as lot 238, 'interleaved, with large additions, prints, etc.', presumably the copy from which the later list is taken. Secondly, Camden's *Britannia*, in Gibson's edition of 1695, reprinted in 1772, was offered as lot 319, and the Sussex section annotated from collections of John Elliot and Edward Clarke is now in BL, Add. MS. 5703. Thirdly, notes from Thomas Fuller's *The history of the worthies of England* (1662) and John Ray's *A collection of English words* (1674, 1691) are in BL, Add. MS. 5705. Other minor omissions are the editions of two medieval chroniclers, Orderic Vitalis and Matthew Paris, which are cited in the manorial volumes.

Archaeologia, or Miscellaneous Tracts relating to Antiquity published by the Society of Antiquaries of London, 1-4 (1770-77)

'Aubreys Berks': probably Aubrey, John, *The natural history and antiquities of Surrey begun in the year 1673 by John Aubrey and continued to the present time*, ed. Richard Rawlinson, 5 vols (1718), but possibly Ashmole, Elias, *Antiquities of Berkshire* (1719)

A new baronetage of England, or a genealogical and historical account of the present English baronets..., 3 vols (1769)

Blomefield, Francis, *Collectanea Cantabrigiensia* (1750)

Blount, Thomas, *Fragmenta antiquitatis. Antient tenures of land, and jocular customs of some mannors, etc.* (1679)

Burr, Thomas Benge, *The history of Tunbridge Wells* (1766). 'A very foolish book.'

Burton, William, *Description of Leicestershire* (1622)

Caraccioli, Charles, *The antiquities of Arundel; the peculiar privilege of its castle and lordships; with an abstract of the lives of the earls of Arundel, from the Conquest to this time* (1766)

Chauncy, Sir Henry, *Historical antiquities* [of Hertfordshire] (1700)

Collins, Arthur, *The baronettage of England: being an historical and genealogical account of baronets, from their first institution in the reign of King James I, etc.*, 2 vols (1720) [Sale lot 213]

Collins, Arthur, *The peerage of England; containing a genealogical and historical account of all the peers of England, now existing, etc.*, 3rd edn, 1 (1741). First published in 1709; 4th edn (1768); 5th edn (1779)

[Ducarel, Andrew Coltee, and John Warburton], *Some account of the alien priories, and of such lands as they are known to have possessed in England and Wales*, 2 vols (1779)

Dugdale, Sir William, *Antiquities of Warwickshire illustrated; from records, leiger books, manuscripts, charters, evidences, tombes, and armes: beautified with maps, prospects and portraictures* (1656)

Dugdale, Sir William, *The Baronage of England, or an historical account of the lives and most memorable actions of our English Nobility, in the Saxons' time, to the Norman Conquest; and from thence of those who had their rise before the end of King Henry the Third's Reign (after the end of King Henry the Third's Reign, and before the eleventh year of Richard the Second)*, 2 vols (1675-6) [Sale lot 480, 2 vols in 1]

Dugdale, Sir William, *Monasticon Anglicanum*, 3 vols (1655, 1661, 1673) [Sale lot 313, 'with Additions in Print and some MS. and a great Number of additional Prints and original Drawings, in further Illustration of that valuable Work, interleaved with large writing paper, in 10 volumes, inestimable'] See Essay 3.5 for the surmise that the prints and drawings are now at the University of Bristol.

Ecton, John, *Thesaurus rerum ecclesiasticarum: being an account of the valuation of all the ecclesiastical benefices... in England and Wales...*(1742)

Erdeswick, Sampson, *A survey of Staffordshire* (1717, 1723)

Farley, Abraham (ed.), *Domesday book seu Liber censualis Wilhelmi Primi Regis Angliae*, 2 vols (1783)

Farmer, John, *The history of Waltham Abbey* (1735)

Gale, Roger (ed.), *Registrum Honoris de Richmond* (1722)

Habingdon, Thomas, *The antiquities of the Cathedral Church of Worcester, to which are added the antiquities of the Cathedral Churches of Chichester and Lichfeld* (1717)

Harris, John, *The history of Kent; ... containing I. an exact topography, ... II. the civil history, ... III. the ecclesiastical history of Kent. IV. The history of the Royal Navy of England. V. The natural history of Kent*, 1 (1719)

Hasted, Edward, *History and topographical survey of the County of Kent*, 4 vols (1778-99). Two volumes listed as perused. [Sale lot 321, 3 vols (1778, 1782, 1790), large paper in Russia with additional plates]

Hearne, Thomas (ed.), *The itinerary of John Leland the antiquary* (1710-12; 3rd ed. 1770)

Howard, Hon. Charles [10th Duke of Norfolk], *Historical anecdotes of some of the Howard family* (1769)

'Journals of the Lords [15 *deleted*] 30 vols' *Journals of the House of Lords* (1771-77) [Sale lot 484, Journals of the House of Lords, 1509-1767, 31 vols]

Kennett, White, *Parochial antiquities attempted in the history of Ambrosden, Burchester and other adjacent parts [Oxon.]* (1695)

Kirby, John, *Suffolk traveller* (1735, 1764)

Lambarde, William, *A perambulation of Kent* (1576)

Lambarde, William, *Dictionarium Angliæ Topographicum et Historicum* (1730)

Le Neve, John, *Monumenta Anglicana; being inscriptions on the monuments of eminent persons deceased in or since 1600 (to the end of 1718)*, 5 vols (1719)

Lloyd, David, *State worthies, or the statesmen and favourites of England, from the Reformation to the Revolution. To this edition is added the characters of the Kings and Queens of England during the above period, etc. (Lives selected from Winstanley's England's worthies) by C. Whitworth* (1766); 1st edn 1670.

Lodge, John, *The peerage of Ireland* (1754)

Madox, Thomas, *The history and antiquities of the Exchequer of the Kings of England,…from the Norman Conquest,… to the end of the reign of K. Edward II. … Together with a correct copy of the ancient Dialogue concerning the Exchequer generally ascribed to Gervasius Tilburensis; and a dissertation concerning the ancient Great Roll of the Exchequer, commonly styled the Roll of Quinto Regis Stephani*, 2nd edn (1711) [Sale lot 486]

Madox, Thomas, *Formulare Anglicanum: or a collection of antient charters and instruments of divers kinds, taken from the originals … and deduced … from the Norman Conquest to the end of the reign of King Henry the VIII* (1702)

Morant, Philip, *History and antiquities of Essex*, 2 vols (1762-8)

Nash, Treadway, *Collections for the history of Worcestershire*, 1 (1781)

Norden, John, *Speculi Britanniae pars; a topographical and chorographical description of Cornwall, with a map of the County and each Hundred* (1728)

'Prynne Papal usurpations': probably Prynne, William, *The fourth part of a brief register, kalendar and survey of the several kinds, forms of parliamentary writs, comprising all writs de expensis militum, civium, et burgensium Parliamenti, extent in the Tower records* (1664) [Why Burrell used this abbreviation, which appears frequently in his manorial notes, is obscure.]

Rotuli Parliamentorum [1278-1503], 6 vols (1767-77) [Sale lot 484]

Rymer, Thomas, *Foedera, conventiones, literae, et cuiuscumque generis acta publica, inter reges Angliae et alios quosvis imperatores, reges*, 20 vols (1726-35) [Sale lot 485]

Salmon, Nathaniel, *Antiquities of Surrey … with some account of the present state and natural history of the County* (1736)

Stow, John, *The survay of London* (1618)

Strype, John, *Annals of the Reformation and establishment of religion and … other occurrences in the Church of England; during the first twelve years of Queen Elizabeths … Reign: … with an Appendix, etc.*, 3rd edn, 4 vols (1725-31)

Tanner, Thomas, *Notitia monastica* (1695)

Thoroton, Robert, *Antiquities of Nottinghamshire* (1677)

Thorpe, John, *Registrum Roffense: or, a collection of ancient, records, charters, and instruments of divers kinds, necessary for illustrating the ecclesiastical history and antiquities of the diocese and cathedral Church of Rochester* (1769) [Sale lot 322]

Weever, John, *Ancient funeral monuments within the United Monarchie of Great Britain* (1631)

Willis, Browne, *A survey of the cathedrals, etc.*, 3 vols (1727-30) [Sale lot 235, 3 vols in 2, 1727-33]

Willis, Browne, *A view of the mitred abbeys with a catalogue of their respective abbots*, 2 vols (1718-19) [Sale lot 204, with MS. additions by Burrell]

Worsley, Sir Richard, *The history of the Isle of Wight* (1781)

Wyndham, Henry Penruddocke, *A gentleman's tour through Monmouthshire and Wales*, 2nd ed. (1781).

7.2 The manuscripts

The list of Burrell's manuscript sources given below is a transcript of the later list, augmented with information, given in <brackets>, from the earlier list and from BL, Add. MS. 5705, a volume of extracts made by Burrell, mainly in 1771-3. There is a close correspondence between the earlier and later lists, down to the point indicated. The correspondence between the lists and Add. MS. 5705 is close enough to confirm that the lists are running ones. The order in which Burrell started notes was: surveys in the office of the Surveyor General of Crown Lands; British Museum, Harleian MSS; Dugdale MS.; Sir Charles Hedges's letters; MSS lent by the Revd William Clarke; Testa de Nevil; John Rowe's MS.; Thomas Marshall's surveys (which were probably amongst the material in the second entry on the list).

Burrell set out the later list of manuscripts in three columns. The left-hand column is usually blank, but Burrell occasionally used it for the date he inspected the manuscript and this date is here placed before the detail of the manuscript, Burrell's middle column. Burrell's right-hand column gives his source of the manuscript. The last few entries of manuscripts are dated from November 1780 to July 1782, with just two outliers from 1784 and 1790/1. His searching the Duke of Norfolk's archives at his London house, indicated by J. C. Brooke in January 1786, is not recorded. Modern identification of a manuscript and editorial comment is given in [brackets]. I have not followed references in the list to the extracts Burrell made and then compared these with the original documents, so the modern identifications are strictly speaking not proven. Those designated as 'now' are nevertheless almost certain, while 'see' points the reader to where the documents may be or to further information. It is noteworthy what a high proportion of the manuscripts still survive, all of them in repositories accessible to the public or (for two in solicitors' hands) published. The manuscripts which Burrell owned may have been destroyed in the fire at Knepp Castle, Shipley, on 18 January 1904, which consumed 'a noble library and valuable MSS'.[46]

Mr Rowe's MS. relative to Lewes Town and several manors belonging to [blank] Ld Abergavenny <Burrell borrowed from Medley and made extracts between 8 June and 2 September 1772> [now with Adams & Remer, solicitors, Lewes; published in Rowe 1928][47]	George Medley, esq.
Several volumes relative to Richard Earl of Dorset's lands [see ESRO, ADA]	Mr William Shadwell <of Ringmer>
Inquisitions temp. Eliz. & James I [prepared for Sir Edward Bysshe (1615?-79), now Bodl., MS. Rawlinson B.433, and calendared in Holgate 1927]	Bodley Library Oxon
Several papers in the possession of:	Revd Edward Clarke
Copy of Testa de Nevil in the Exchequer <Liber Feodorum Militum, from MS. purchased by Earl of Shelburne from library of Philip Carteret Webb, copy of book in the Exchequer called by some Testa de Nevill. Note by Webb 2 July 1761 that original in King's Remembrancer's Office> [published in Public Record Office 1920-31]	Earl of Shelburne
Various MSS <Harleian MSS. 60, 152, 204, 606-8, 892, 1172, 1176, 1178, 1192, 1326, 1557, 5805; Cottonian MS. Claudius A.VI>	British Museum
Harleian MS. State Property No. 708 Escheats [this entry appears in the list of books; now BL, Harleian MS. 708, 'Compendium omnium Eschaetriarum, a tempore R. Henrici III, usque ad annum 21 R. Ricardi II ex Recordis in Turre Londinensi conservatis, extractum.']	[British Museum]
<Dugdale's MSS 43: statutes of Pevensey Marsh> [now Bodl., MS. Dugdale 43; published in Turner 1866]	<Ashmole Museum, Oxon>
<Letters transcribed [in BL, Add. MS. 5705, ff. 82-3, 91-2, 151] from the MSS of Mr/ Sir Charles Hedges, Judge of the [Admiralty Court] relative to the Cinque Ports>[48]	<Wm Macham, LLD, Advocate of Doctors' Commons 1771>
Tower Records, transcripts relative to Sussex <transcribed by Mr Conway for Mr [William] Hay [1695-1755, presumably while he held the sinecure of Keeper of the Records in the Tower, 1754-55], now in the possession of his son>	Col. <Thomas Hay of Glyndebourne>
Original deeds relative to Wiggenholt Manor [see WSRO, Petworth House Archives]	[blank] Swayne, esq. <the owner>
Battle Abbey Registrum, procured me by G[odfrey] W[ebster], esq. <lent me by Sir Thomas and Mr [Godfrey] Webster> [but Sir Thomas died in 1751; probably the transcripts by David Casley, now Henry E. Huntington Library, BA 31 and 32]	Sir W[histler] Webster bt
Original deeds of Sheffield and Warpsbourne [see ESRO, SPK]	Mr [John Baker] Holroyd
Crown surveys by [Thomas] Marshall, 2 vols, 6 Jac. [I] <in the possession of the Revd Mr Michell of Brighton; or, in another place and more likely, William Shadwell, who gave to Burrell>	W. B[urrell].
Crown records in Surveyor General's Office [now Public Record Office, CRES 39/67-74]	Peter Burrell, esq. [Surveyor General of Crown Lands, 1769-75]
Nomina Villarum Sussex as used by the Sheriff 1740 and many years prior thereto [copy now BL, Add. MS. 5701, ff. 2-5], and various deeds	Mr John Elliot

Liber de sancti monasterii de Bello, which is transcribed by Casley into the 2nd volume of Sir Thomas Webster's Registrum de Bello <now in Sir Whistler Webster's possession> [now Henry E. Huntington Library, BA 32]	[British Museum,] Cotton. Lib'y Domitian A.II, f. 7
Observationes quaedam de illustri & antiqua Covertorum familia summa cum fide ex diplomatibus, archivis scriniisque regiis, monumentis et testamentis (e quibus veritas ipsa optima elici potest) collectae et Waltero Covert, Equiti aurato, huius familiae haeredi masculo, veritatis antiquitatis, et amoris ergo datae, dicatae, dedicatae, per Sir Lowe Knyvetorum [title from copy in BL, Add MS. 5701, ff. 21-46]	W.B.
Many curious anecdotes relative to different churches and manors [see Document 6.1]	Revd William Hayley of Brightling
Court rolls of many manors in the custody of: viz. Duke of Dorset's [now ESRO, ADA], Mr [Thomas] Chowne's, Mr [George] Medley's <and ?Henry Shelley's >	Mr Charles Gilbert of Lewes
Court rolls of Lord Gage's manors [see ESRO, SAS/G] <also Mr Richard Hoskyns MSS who was steward to Sir John Gage 1625, lent me by Mr Mitchell steward to Viscount Gage 1775>[49] [now ESRO, SAS/G/ACC 920]	Mr James Michell, Mr [Henry] Burtenshaw [lawyers of Lewes]
Bosham, Yapton, etc. [probably as next entry]	Revd George Farrell[50]
Various inscriptions and extracts from churches in the neighbourhood of Chichester	Revd Mr [Thomas] Durnford, Walter Boisdaune, [John] Buckner, [Bragg] Blagden
Many court rolls of different manors [see WSRO, Sergison MSS]	Francis Warden, esq. [of Butlers Green in Cuckfield]
An account of the manors belonging to the Duke of Norfolk, Sir William Thomas, Earl of Newburgh, Miss Bettesworth and Mr Knight	[Edward] Carleton, esq. [lawyer] of Arundel
A transcript of many deeds relating to the Arundel Estate, the property of Miss [Charlotte] Bettesworth [of Woolavington] [see WSRO, Lavington Estate MSS]	Mr Carleton
Harris and Dobbs survey of manors in Sussex and Hants taken 12 Eliz. by order of the Duke of Norfolk [1570; see Arundel Castle Archives, MD 491, 535 and 718; extracts in Lower 1857b]	Mr Carleton

[This above is the last of the entries corresponding to those in the earlier list. In both lists, Burrell started to list Pelham MSS extracted on a separate page or column, under the heading 'MSS belonging to Lord Pelham in the custody of [Abraham] Bayly Esq.' in the later list. The following entries may therefore relate to material consulted at the same period as material above.]

<Oct 1 1773 [Edward] Austen's Rentals 1717 to 1773 of Hastings Rape [now ESRO, AMS 5735/53, for 1717-25, and 5887 (copy of original in Hastings Museum), for 1731-41, both initialled 'WB'.] Schedule of the Rape of Hastings Inspeximus of James I relative to ditto A Rental of the Tenures held of the Rape of Hastings Various deeds relative to Walderne [Waldron] als Harringdales from 19 Eliz to 39 Eliz & 41 Eliz>	[Lord Pelham in custody of Abraham Bayley]

A collection and transcript taken out of the records in the Tower of all such charters and other evidences as concern the Honor etc. of Richmond and especially touching the Rape, Honor and Castle of Hastings in Sussex being a principal member thereof [now BL, Add. MS. 33189]	ditto
Many ancient deeds and charters in Mr Bayley's custody [see BL, Add. Ch. 30988-32739]	ditto
Account of the Lord Wardens of the Cinque Ports with their arms, done for Villiers Duke of Buckingham [now ESRO, ASH 3199: Philipot 1956]	Lord Ashburnham
Inscriptions at Willingdon	Revd Mr [Owen] Evans
Title deeds and court rolls of North Mundham and Nyetimber manors [court rolls now WSRO, Add. MSS 873, 876]	Mrs Brereton
Bishop Littleton's church notes at: [by Charles Lyttelton, Bishop of Carlisle, now Society of Antiquaries, MS. 153]	the Antiquaries Society
Boundaries of the hundreds of the Duchy of Lancaster within the Rape of Pevensey, taken on inquisition, A.D. 1579 [now ESRO, ASH 1117a or ADA uncat.]	Mr Charles Gilbert [Lewes lawyer]
A visitation taken in about 1634, 1 vol. quarto [now SAS, library accn 336, identified by the signature of a Bristow on the flyleaf; other copies edited in Bannerman 1905]	Mr Bristow [through?] Mr Medley
Segar's Baronies [pedigrees by Sir William Segar (d. 1633) bought by Edmundson at the sale of John Warburton's library and partly published in 1764-84 [Sale lot 479]; now at College of Arms. There is a separate note: 'Mr [John] Nicoll of Court Lodge, Mountfield has Segar's Pedigrees of Sussex.'	Mr [Joseph] Edmundson
Lord Dacre's curious pedigree of Fiennes, a MS. account of Herstmonceux Castle taken 23 Aug. 12 Eliz. belonging to the Revd Mr Hare [see Essex Record Office, D/DL; the latter printed from Burrell's transcript in Parry 1833, 246-8] Leave to copy Lambert's drawings of Herstmonceux Castle [see Document 6.1]	Lord Dacre
Mr John Harrison's title deeds of Birchden and Osenersh manors	John Harrison, esq.
[John] Warburton (Somerset Herald) remarks in his Sussex tour, MSS octavo, rough calf and clasps - a few idle superficial observations in pencil and outlines of houses miserably sketched [now BL, Lansdowne MS. 918]	Earl of Shelburne
Surveys of the manors of Gregory Fiennes Lord Dacre, temp. Eliz. lent me by: [printed from Burrell's transcript in Venables 1851, 198-201]	Revd Mr [Robert] Hare of Herstmonceux
Survey of Ash	Revd Mr Hare
Customs of the free Port reeve, lands and tenements within the Liberty and Port of Pevensey [now Bodl., MS. Rolls Sussex 11, printed in Larking 1851]	Lady Peachey [of Glynleigh in Westham, View 193]
Several inscriptions taken by [blank] Constable of Arundel, bricklayer, from the coffin plates in the north and south vaults of the Norfolk family	[blank] Constable

An accurate account of Ticehurst with many extracts from the parish register	Revd Mr [Christopher] Gawthrop, Minister of Ticehurst
Copy of Lady Margaret Covert's will of Sullington Anno 1366	Mr Stephen Vine of Lindfield
Account of the manors and estates of the Covert family temp, Chas I and II	ditto
Customs of the manor of Cuckfield	ditto
Rental of South Malling and Lindfield	ditto
Copies of decrees relating to Ashdown Forest 1691 and 1693 [other copies in Public Record Office, DL 4/126/1691/2 and 44/1253B; Burrell's copies in BL, Add. MSS 5681, 5705 and 5709; Thomas Wakeham's in ESRO, SAS/ACC 1398]	ditto
Several charters to Lewes Priory, and notes of divers manors, records and various MSS in the British Museum [mainly from the cartulary, BL, Cotton Vesp. F.XV: Salzman 1932-4]	Thomas Willard, esq. [1729-94, but likely in error for John Elliot, as Burrell copied his notes from Lewes Priory documents]

[The entry above is at the bottom of a page. The following five entries may belong here chronologically, as they are at the bottom of the page listing books which Burrell may have used before utilising the rest of the page initially reserved for listing Pelham MSS.]

Several MS. papers relative to Sussex given to me by	Revd Wm & Edw Clarke
Drawing of a piece of mosaic pavement found in the Bishop's garden	[Revd Wm & Edw Clarke][51]
A drawing of an ancient monument at Wiston	Lord de Ferrers
Transcript of Miss Butler's court rolls	John Morgan, esq.
Particulars relative to Jevington [Lewis Bagot resigned the rectories of Jevington and Rye on election as Dean in 1777]	Dean of Christ Church, Dr Bagot
Examined and transcribed 7 Dec. 1780 A very curious MS. supposed to be written about the time of Edward I and containing a particular account of the manors and estates of Richard Earl of Arundel, in Sussex, together with the free and copyholders of the different manors, and their respective tenures. NB this MS. consists of 78 leaves in quarto. (I have transcribed entirely and entered it under the respective manors.) It seems to have descended in regular succession to the late Earl of Halifax, after whose death it was long missing, and after much pains and enquiry found amongst the muniments of Lord Halifax's estate, and very politely lent to me by my worthy friend Francis Earl of Shipbrook, one of Lord H's trustees, the other two trustees were Lovel Stanhope, esq. and [blank] Sedgewick, esq. [now Arundel Castle Archives, published as Book B in Clough 1969, dated to about 1400]	Lord Shipbrook
Transcribed Nov. 1780 MS. inquisitiones post mortem of the estates of the Earls of Arundel from 56 Henry III to 9 Henry V inclusive [perhaps Arundel Castle Archives, MD 239, 1231, 1259, 1303, 1304]	[Duke of Norfolk]
Feb. 1781 Pedigree of Bray. Particulars of lands belonging to Mr Smith's Charity [View 187; see Surrey History Centre, 2840 and 3171], and sundry deeds of Miss Tucker relating to the manors of Codelawe and Changston in Sussex	Mr [William] Bray, attorney at law [of Shere in Surrey, 1736-1832]

June 1782 MSS taken out of a book of heraldry collected by Gregory King, Lancaster Herald, 1689. 'Le livre de la famille de Howard recuillé par Hen. Lilly fut fait par un pursuivant des Armes, demeurant chez le dit Hen. Lilly par accident à l'heure de son mort, fut aprés acheté par Compton Comte de Northampton pour cent livres sterling ore et demeure a cet heure 1684', and with the E. of N. 1782 [Lilly's original of 1638 now in Arundel Castle Library; possibly the document lent by Northampton's agent to Lord Ferrars and seen by J. C. Brooke in 1779: 'the most magnificent work of the kind executed in the kingdom, contains complete historical and genealogical account with paintings of monuments, effigies, etc.']52 — [Earl of Northampton]

The Parliamentary Surveys bound in parchment consisting of 3 rolls, 1st roll consists of 496 pages, 2nd roll of 579 pages, 3rd roll of 616 [now WSRO, Cap. I/30/1-3] — Dean of Chichester

May, June, July 1782 A folio MS. lent me by the Dean of Chichester containing 603 pages in which are transcripts of various muniments relative to the Church of Chichester [now WSRO, Cap. I/12/3] — [Dean of Chichester]

1782 A custumal of the town of Brighton lent me by: [now with Howlett Clarke Cushman, solicitors, Brighton; published as Webb and Wilson 1952] — the Revd Mr [Henry] Michell, Vicar

1784 Finished the inspection of Sir James Peachey's deeds [now at West Dean Estate Office, formerly at WSRO] — [Sir James Peachey of West Dean, View 65]

1790, 1791 the inspection of the family muniments at Cowdray permitted me by the late and present Viscounts Montague [now WSRO, Cowdray MSS]53 — [Viscount Montague]

8. S. H. Grimm's will, 1790

Public Record Office, PROB 11/1247/322

Having obtained his permission, I institute Mr John Webber, painter and member of the Royal Academy, to be the executor of this my last disposition made by me whilst blessed with sound memory and judgement.[54] When my better part is recalled by the Benevolent Almighty Being who lent it me and there appear undoubtful proofs of a real dissolution, the corpse is to be buried, no matter where, in the cheapest and most private manner. Never appeared anything more silly to me than the pomp of an undertaker.

The £306 11s. 3d. put into the Stock March 13th 1783 and set down in the 3 per cent Consolidated for £450 @ 68 1/8 per cent, whereof Messrs Francis & Thomas Wright (now Thomas Wright Esq. & Co.) in Covent Garden have power by letter of attorney, being my own inheritance shall go back to my next heir in blood in Switzerland who is at present Mrs Catherine Trechsel at Burgdorf, Canton of Berne, daughter of my late elder brother Johan Jacob Grimm; or in case of her dying before me without lawfully begotten heirs it shall go to the next heir in blood by the mother's side, being an inheritance from the mother's side, but who is that next heir I know not at present.

The contents of an old book in folio bound in marbled paper with green strings, consisting mostly of sketches from nature, or copies from my sketches from nature, kept loose between the leaves ranged according to counties, the greatest part in octavo size, mostly finished in Indian ink and hitherto not numbered as additions may still occur, shall not be sold separately or by the piece, but shall go altogether to the highest bidder, being in that state worth the attention of a collector, which it would no more be if divided, scattered and garbled. However my worthy friends and employers Sir William Burrell bt in Harley Street, Cavendish Square, or Cornelius Heathcote Rodes Esqr of Barlborough Hall near Chesterfield, Derbyshire, shall have the preference in case it should be their choice. The Revd Sir Richard Kaye bt, Dean of Lincoln, should be here included, had he not already a larger collection of my drawings than all the rest of my employers together, a collection which I shall never be able totally to finish. There are 12 finished coloured drawings framed and glazed in my apartment and several other finished coloured drawings in a large sheet of paper whose number may soon augment, but now consists of 21 pieces of different sizes but mostly folio, kept in a large portfolio of prints; these may be sold, as well as what remains worth any notice and attention of the drawings and rubbish of memorandums of drawings contained in a book of grey paper bound in parchment but much worn, and what is not worth minding shall be burnt. As I never collected prints, the few I have and such as they are, contained partly in a large portfolio of marble paper and partly in a small book of cartoon with torn leaves, consisting of etchings of Weyrotter,[55] Waterloo,[56] Gessner,[57] Rigendas etc. etc., and straggling prints and sketches, are likewise to be sold. There are some sketch books remaining of some unmeaning studies made partly abroad and partly about London, the greatest part much soiled and impaired, but 3 of them (mostly containing ruins in Normandy) are better drawn and contain objects more worthy of attention, as likewise a book of views made in and about Canterbury; these are likewise to be sold, the English together with the foreign ones together.[58] The copper plates in my drawers are without exception to be immediately totally defaced that no more impressions can be taken from them, all the impressions that may be found destroyed and the defaced plates sold for the copper. The books in my possession are to be sold, but all manuscripts, memorandums, old pocket books with their contents, letters, receipts and copies of letters ought to be burnt, the pocket book and account book of the current year excepted.

My clothes, linen, instruments and utensils of my profession, and what may be found of knickknacks of different sorts I leave to my landlady Mrs Susanna Sledge. The ready cash which I may have at my decease or which may happen to be in bankers' hands shall go to the burial expenses and to the liquidation of any running debt I may then have, but if there is not sufficient cash for these purposes the surplus shall be made up from the sale of the above mentioned things, and what remains therefrom from the sale is to go one half to Mrs S. Sledge, as a grateful acknowledgement for the friendly care she always took of me, and the other half to my executor as a remembrance of friendship. But if there be cash sufficient for the liquidation of debts and for funeral expenses in mine or the bankers' hands, the whole of the surplus shall go to the above mentioned Mrs S. Sledge, and the product of the things sold [shall] be equally divided between her and my executor. In case Mrs S. Sledge shall die before me these things above bequeathed to her shall go to the next heir, the above mentioned Mrs Catherine Trexel or her heirs lawfully begotten, or in default of such or in case of her dying before me without any, to the next lawful heir from the mother's side.

N.B. I mentioned in one of my letters to Switzerland Mr Jacob Stakly, carpenter of Burgdorf. But the amount of my drawings, prints [and] books shall, in case of Mrs Sledge's death before me, go to my executor. London May 20th 1790 - Samuel Hieronimus [sic] Grimm. Witness, John Oaksley Clarke, William Wellings.

On the twenty-eighth day of July in the year of our Lord one thousand seven hundred and ninety four, administration (with the will annexed) of all and singular the goods, chattels and credits of Samuel Hieronimus Grimm, otherwise Samuel Jerome Grimm, late of Covent Garden in the parish of Saint Paul Covent Garden in the County of Middlesex, a bachelor, deceased, was granted to George Baker, the lawful attorney of Marie Catherine Trechsel (wife of Jean Trechsel), the niece and next of kin of the said deceased, for the use and benefit of the said Catherine Marie Trechsel now residing in Burgdorf in the Canton of Berne in Switzerland, having been first sworn duly to administer, John Webber, the sole executor named in the said will, dying in the lifetime of the said deceased and no residuary legatee being named therein.

9. References

1 PRO, PROB 11/539. SAS, Budgen Papers, 86/8-19; 88/10-11. ESRO, BAT 4421; AMS 4868; W/INV 2365. Centre for Kentish Studies, U469 P28. Budgen 1730, 23-8. Crossley and Saville 1991, letters 267, 274.

2 Bendall 1997, under names. Kingsley 1982, 59. Marshall 1980, 40. The children of Richard II are confirmed by ESRO, ABE 14F/2. Brent 1993, 11, 126.

3 Kingsley 1982, 57-63. The subscribers' names are conveniently printed in Ellis 1873.

4 Messenger 1951.

5 BL, Add. MS. 32123, ff. 11-14.

6 Mosse 1933, 148-9. Mayhew 1987, 115.

7 For the fraught history of the new harbour at Rye: Farrant 1976b, 5.

8 Mosse 1933, 194-6.

9 Lyttelton: 'I ... regret you not seeing Battle Abbey Register.... I had the same temptation at Lord Chetwynd's: in his glass case in his library at Ingestre I saw the original MS. survey of Staffordshire by Erdeswick and two or three other volumes relating to the antiquities of that county but could not open the door and satisfy my longing.'

10 Completed from '[31]' from Mosse 1933, 25-6. The date of death is blank on the monument.

11 See Stevens 1982, 107, for a more detailed sketch of 1739.

12 See John Elliot's drawing of 1770 in Gilbert 1985, 270. Pye 1965, identifies the same stones as replacements which must therefore predate 1743.

13 Lyttelton: 'The present Mr [Edward] Medley [1719-51] I am a stranger to and his two elder brothers [Thomas (1714-35) and Samuel (1716-41)] we both remember at Eton and Oxford. Their father was steward to the Dukes of Somerset [Dorset?] and pillaged them of all the estate as I have heard.' The reference may properly be to their grandfather Thomas (1645-1728) as well as their father Thomas (1679-1732).

14 Removed to Easebourne in 1851: Mosse 1933, 72-5.

15 Gore 1977 on the picture collection. Lyttelton: 'Your account of old Somerset's way of living is very entertaining and I find he leads just such a life in London as I was informed when I was at Northumberland House.' Cokayne 1910-98, 12: 79.

16 For the effigies: Mosse 1933, 17-20.

17 Davidson-Houston 1935, 63-5.

18 Davidson-Houston 1935, 72-3.

19 Camden 1806, 1: 269. and Dallaway 1832, 200.

20 For the effigies: Mosse 1933, 40-4. In 1740 'in this church are many inscriptions containing accounts of persons buried there, only on paper in a frame, others on wood': Warwickshire County Record Office, CR 2017/TP 1, p. 52. These had been prepared by Richard Bowchier (1661-1723) and were copied by Browne Willis (Welch 1956, 201), but Milles gives a few details not in the copy at WSRO, Cap. I/12/3. Of the 11 bishops' tombs which Milles mentioned, six are today in the same location (or have the same attribution), four have been moved (or have a changed attribution) and one (Ralph Luffa) is unaccounted.

21 Dallaway 1815, 1: 140.

22 Raeburn, Voronikhina and Nurnberg 1995, especially 354-7, 403, 416.

23 Another is published in Grose 1963.

24 ESRO, AMS 6113/1, f. 10. Dawson 1909, 2: 548. Sutton 1946, 84-5.

25 Waddon Court in Croydon, residence of John Parker, whose son John Dewy was with Grose a captain in the Surrey Militia. William West (1770-1854) recollected, from the age of six, that Grose had been a constant guest at Parker's house. West 1830, 9-10, 39-41.

26 VCH Surrey, 3: 258.

27 Mosse 1933, 118-20.

28 Perhaps the son obtained the pews in the church which c. 1770 came from St Margaret's Westminster: VCHS, 6 (3): 62, 70.

29 Probably Sir – Dallingridge and wife: Davidson-Houston 1936, 187-9.

30 Ducarel, Burrell's fellow ecclesiastical lawyer, supported by Michell, must have been conducting the spiritual court for the Peculiar of South Malling, for which the clergy came to Lewes. Brent 1993, 80-3.

31 Captain William Green of Lewes: see Essay 3.1 and Farrant 1993a, 154.

32 Probably meaning Sir William whose father

had purchased, and who rebuilt, Folkington Place: View 85.

33 This and the measurements below refer to the account of the castle with which Green had provided Grose for the plate published in about July 1775 and to the plan published in September 1776, and which may have been based on observations in 1759 when Green oversaw construction of a battery at Hastings: Grose 1772-87, 3: unpag.; Farrant 1993a, 154.

34 Willis 1718-19, 1: 33.

35 Identified as Godfrey, on the strength of 'GW Esq.' gaining Burrell access to the Battle Abbey register: Document 7.2; either the brother (d. 1780) of Sir Whistler, 2nd bt (d. 1779), or perhaps more likely that brother's son, later 4th bt (c. 1749-1800).

36 Mosse 1933, 32-3. Davidson-Houston 1935, 89-90.

37 Davidson-Houston 1939, 128-30.

38 Mosse 1933, 194-6. The brass is of a civilian: Davidson-Houston 1939, 140-1.

39 William Dickinson of Kingweston in Somerset, esq. (1745-1806), was elected MP for Rye at the Hundred Court on 20 May 1777, in succession to his wife's uncle Rose Fuller who had died on 7 May: ESRO, RYE 1/17, Namier and Brooke 1964, 2: 322.

40 Davidson-Houston 1935, 74-80, for Northiam, but none recorded at Peasmarsh.

41 Bodl., MS. Eng. lett. e. 98, ff. 27-33, 104-5; MS. Eng. lett. c. 226, f. 1. Shoberl 1813, 81. Society of Antiquaries, Minute Book XVII, 15 June 1780.

42 Watson 1782, 1: 59-61, probably written by Elliot. Horsfield 1824-7, 1: 115-17. Society of Antiquaries, Ants Papers, 16 Nov 1775. BL, Add. MS. 6359, 7 Dec. 1776, 28 Jan. 1778. Also ESRO, BMW/C 3, for Sir Robert Smyth giving leave for its removal, 18 May 1775. Anderson 1992, espec. Fig. 18 for 'ALABASTR'.

43 On 27 May 1776: BL, Add. MS. 5697, f. 113.

44 'another Arundel', perhaps an allusion to Henry Fitzalan, 12th Earl of Arundel (1511?-80), who amassed an important library of manuscripts and was a member of the Elizabethan Society of Antiquaries.

45 Langney Grange in Westham: Toy 1953, including Grimm's view of 1785.

46 Bodl., MS. Eng. lett. e. 99, f. 34. *West Sussex Gazette*, 21 Jan., 4 Feb. 1904.

47 The Medleys neither owned nor were stewards for manors in Rowe's MS. - which probably passed to Thomas Medley by his marriage to the niece of Edward Raynes, Rowe's successor in practice: see View 12.

48 These are not in the papers of Sir Charles Hedges (c. 1652-1714) in BL, Add. MSS 24102-7.

49 BL, Add. MS. 5681, f. 14.

50 Perhaps George Parker Farhill, Prebendary of Fittleworth, 1773-90.

51 Nichols 1817-58, 3: 555, for undated letter recording this gift.

52 Robinson 1995, 105, 245. Bodl., MS. Eng. lett. e. 98, f. 68.

53 Burrell may have been working on them also in 1781 and 1782: Dibben 1960-4, 1: xxviii, xxxii.

54 Webber (1752-93), a landscape artist, etcher and engraver, was born in London, but was the son of a Swiss sculptor who sent him to Berne at the age of six. His masters were the same as Grimm's, first J. L. Aberli in Berne and then J. G. Wille in Paris, where he must have arrived about the time Grimm left for London. He was ARA at the date of the will, being elected RA in 1791. Like Grimm he was a bachelor. DNB 1998, Waterhouse 1981, 403.

55 Franz Edmund Weirotter (1730-71).

56 Anthonie Waterlo (1609/10-90).

57 Salomon Gessner (1730-88)?

58 See BM, P&D, 1919-7-12, for a sketchbook attributed to Grimm, mainly of views along the Thames west of London.

Ashburnham Place and Park, c. 1730 *Peter Tillemans* Private collection *See View 8*

Beckley Parsonage, 1784 S. *H. Grimm* British Library, Add. MS. 5670, f. 13 [23] *See View 16*

Bodiam Castle, 1782 *James Lambert senior* British Library, Add. MS. 5676, f. 3 [5] *See View 20*

Chichester, East Street Market, *c.* 1808 *Joseph Francis Gilbert* West Sussex Record Office, Fuller PD 478 *See View 54*

Compton, Littlegreen, 1793 *Humphry Repton* West Sussex Record Office, Add. MS. 520, pl. iv *See View 58*

Dallington, Herrings, 1784 *S. H. Grimm* British Library, Add. MS. 5670, f. 67 [123] *See View 63*

The Draught of an Antient Roman tesselated Pavement at East Bourne near Pevensy in Sussex according to the Description of the Learned Dr. John Tabor of Lewis in a Letter of January 16. 1717 to Dr. John Thorpe R.S.t and by him communicated to the Royal Society.

A   The Pavement   B The Bath.   C The Aperture to let the water
    in to the Bath and out again at the East End.
D The Roman Brick wt. wch. brunted the Pavement, this
    flat and toward in the Terras
E The laning place out of the bath and Steps &c.
F The foundations and sides of the bath wch. are also
    continued under the Roman brick wch. bears the
    Pavement.
G The cornes of a large space pavd wth. Roman brick
    and coverd wt. Ashes, Coals, &c.
H Walls supposed round the Bath and pavement &c.
I. K Roman bricks found in the Rubbish

Eastbourne, the Roman pavement and bath, 1717 *Unknown artist, after John Tabor* British Library, K Top 42.39.1 *See View 73*

Ewhurst Place, 1784 *S. H. Grimm* British Library, Add. MS. 5670, f. 12 [22] *See View 79*

Frant, camp on Waterdown Forest, 1780 *James Lambert senior* British Library, Add. MS. 5676, f. 51 [77] *See View 87*

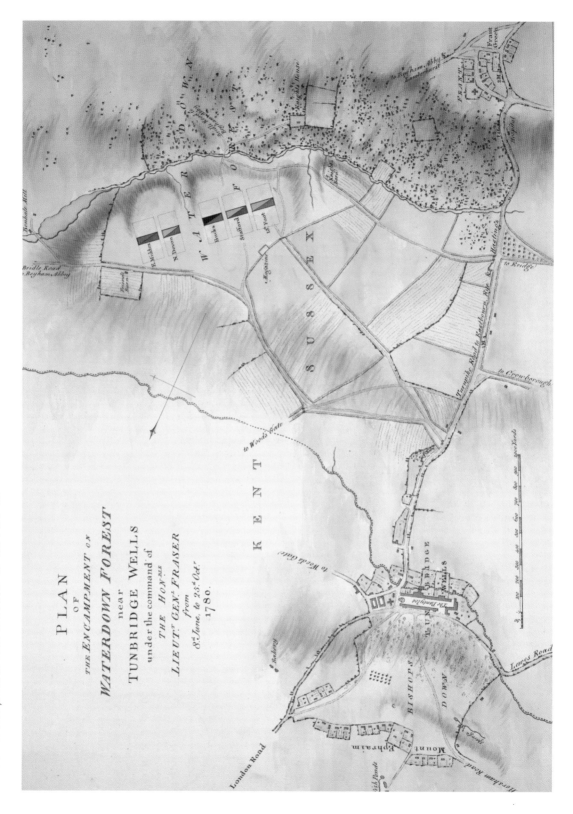

Frant, camp on Waterdown Forest, plan, 1780 *Lieut. Daniel Paterson and Ensign Edward Morrison* British Library, Add. MS. 15533, f. 43 *See View 88*

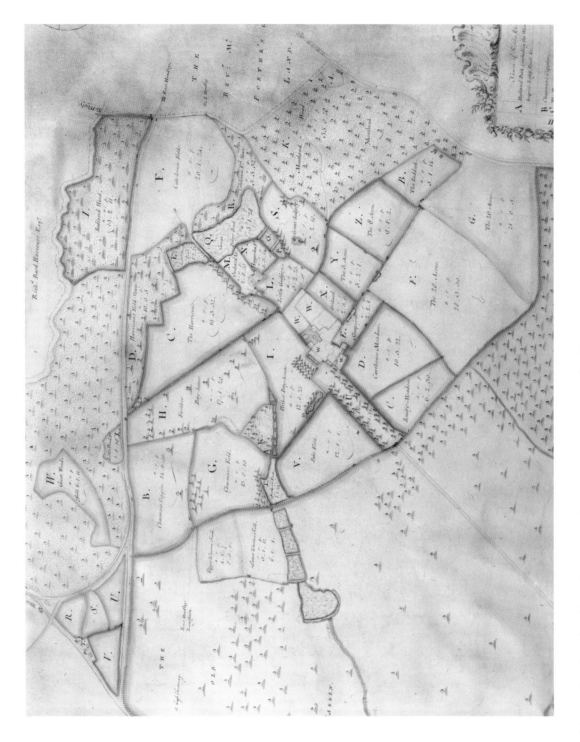

East Hoathly, Halland Park, 1778 *Thomas Marchant* East Sussex Record Office, ACC 3714/2 *See View 114*

South Malling, Southerham chapel, 1780 *James Lambert senior* British Library, Add. MS. 5676, f. 86 [132] *See View 136*

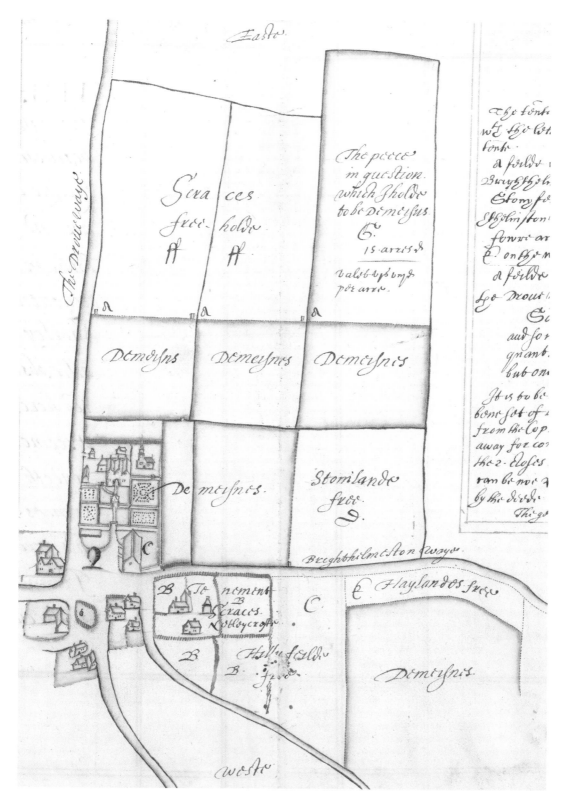

Easte.

The Drineway.

Graces freeholde. A A

The piece in question which sholde to be Demeisnes. C 15. acres d valeb. p. d. vnd. per acre.

Demeisns Demeisns Demeisns

De meisnes.

Stomlande free.

Breghthilmeston waye.

Tenement B Graces. Kobleycroft. C E Flaylandes free.

B Hallafelde free. B. Demeisns

Weste.

The tenb wt the tenb tonb a filde Burghtholm Stony fe Stholmston fowre ar C on th m a foilde ho mout

and for gnanb bub on

It is to be bene set of from the Cop away for con the 2 Clo(es ran be no by the dede The g

Preston Episcopi, Preston Manor and village, 1617 *John Norden* British Library, Add. MS 6027, ff. 115v–116r *See View 149*

Selmeston, Sherrington, 1787 *S. H. Grimm* British Library, Add. MS. 5671, f. 59 [105] *See View 168*

Stopham Church,
painted glass, *c.* 1600
S. H. Grimm after Roelant, 1780

British Library, Add. MS. 5674,
f. 45 [83]
See View 178

Ticehurst, Wardsbrook, 1612 *William Gier* East Sussex Record Office, SAS/CO/D 2 *See View 180*

The Views

Summary list of the artists of the Views

The numbers are of the Views. The artists are also included in the Index, by page number. * signifies that the View reproduced here is by another artist (who is signified by †), after a picture by the artist named.

Artist	Views
Buck, Samuel (1696-1779)	51*, 111
Budgen, Richard (1695-1731)	attributed: 181*
Burchell, William John (1781-1863)	31, 32
Caryll, John Baptist (1718-88)	102
Challen, William (fl. 1770)	82
de Cort, Hendrick Josef Frans (1742-1810)	76-8, 123, 176
de Ward, John (fl. 1618; d. 1625)	194*
Devis, Anthony (1729-1816)	164
Dunstall, John, senior (1584?-after 1644)	attributed: 27
Dunstall, John, junior (c. 1630-93)	195
Farington, Joseph (1747-1821)	106
Gier, William (fl. 1612-47)	180
Gilbert, Joseph Francis (1791-1855)	54
Girtin, Thomas (1775-1802)	198
Grimm, Samuel Hieronymus (1733-94)	all other 116 Views (of which 70†, 178†, 181†)
Grose, Francis (1731-91)	66, 91, 129
Hearne, Thomas (1744-1817)	9, 107, 142, 143
Lambert, George (c. 1700-65)	93
Lambert, James, senior (1725-88)	20, 87, 92, 94, 95, 109, 110, 122, 128, 131, 136, 162†, 163†, 167, 169†, 170, 181, 202
Lambert, James, junior (1744-99)	68, 137, 145, 156, 157, 162*, 163*, 196
Malchair, John Baptist (1729-1812)	130
Marchant, Thomas (1750-90)	114
Morrison, Ensign Edward (fl. 1779-82)	88
Nixon, John (c. 1750-1818)	35-7, 61
Norden, John (1547?-1625)	149
Paterson, Lieut. Daniel (1739-1825)	88
Pattenden, John (fl. 1637-63)	42*
Petrie, Henry (1772-1842)	53
Repton, Humphry (1752-1818)	58, 59, 108
Richards, John Inigo (1731-1810)	177
Roelant (fl. c. 1600)	178*
Rooker, Michael Angelo (1743-1801)	197
Sherwin, John Keyse (1751?-90)	70*
Skinner, the Revd John (1772-1839)	30
Smith, George (1713/14-76)	25
Tabor, Dr John (1667-1729)	73*
Tillemans, Peter (1684-1734)	8
Turner, Joseph Mallord William (1775-1851)	29
Unknown artist	42†, 51†, 73†, 80, 118, 146, 169*
Unknown surveyor of the Buxted estate, 1798	12, 13, 43-9, 90, 97, 158
Van Dyck, Anthony (1599-1640)	161
Warburton, John (1682-1759)	96
Withie, John (fl. 1634)	7

Overleaf James Lambert senior and junior sketching Bramber Castle, ?1782
British Library, Add. MS. 5677, f. 59 [87]

1 Aldingbourne, Nyton, 1791

S. H. Grimm

British Library, Add. MS. 5678, f. 22 [44]

There has probably been a building on this site since at least 1222 when Gilbert English gave his tenement at Neuthon to Boxgrove Priory. After the Reformation it passed into lay hands and, probably as a small farmhouse, provided the seat for the establishment of a cadet branch of the Peckham family. Thomas, fifth son of Richard Peckham of Upmarden, acquired it around the time of the Restoration; and by 1722 there was a house of sufficient elegance to serve as the residence of his descendant, another Thomas, who served as High Sheriff and was knighted in that year.

Grimm's view of the south front shows an established family seat probably built around the turn of the 18th century. It must however have incorporated substantial portions of an earlier building. The interior of the north wing shows 16th-century features and there are two staircases dating from the early and late-17th century respectively. Dallaway in 1815 called it 'handsome and … inclosed in a small park', which by 1835 extended to 16 acres. The Peckham connection continued, though it passed by marriage to the Hewitt Smith family in 1786. It was eventually sold in 1880. Between the World Wars it was owned by the Waley-Cohen family and remained a private house until after World War II with the façade little changed. It is now a residential home. *PMW*

Sources Attree 1914, 228. Dallaway 1815, 2: 78. Fleming 1960, 84-6. VCHS, 4: 134. WSRO, Add. MS. 2074, estate map, 1835. *NGR* SU 935 056 *PDB* 3147

West Court of Amberley Castle

2 Amberley Castle, 1788

S. H. Grimm

British Library, Add. MS. 5674, f. 7 [13]

Amberley Castle is more correctly a fortified manor house, developed over centuries on land which had been given to the bishops of Chichester before 1066. The earliest remaining stone building on the site is a hall built by Seffrid I in about 1140. Licence to crenellate was granted in 1377 to Bishop William Reed, and work was still in progress when he died in 1382. The outside of his walls from the north are shown in *Sussex views*, 2. This view from within the western courtyard looks south towards Reed's walls, once lined with two-storey lodgings, and the main entrance.

Bishop Sherborne (1508-36) was responsible for major refurbishment, and the gables to the left of the entrance may be part of his work. Possibly for Henry VIII's visit in 1526, he commissioned Lambert Barnard to produce suites of paintings, notably nine female 'worthies', of whom eight

survive, at Pallant House, Chichester. The 'Queens' Room' was so named as early as 1636.

Not used by bishops after the Reformation, the castle was leased. In 1643, while it was tenanted by the royalist John Goring, General Waller came from Arundel and dismantled the roofs and destroyed the chapel, making it barely habitable. Later remodelling created a house tenanted by two generations of the Butler family and from 1683 by Sir John Briscoe. In 1751 the bishop leased the castle to James Peachey, and nine years before this drawing, the tenant farmer, William Holman, paid tax on 34 windows. It is now a hotel.   *AFH*

Sources Clarkson 1865. Peckham 1921. Peckham 1928.
Croft-Murray 1956, 118-22.

NGR TQ 027 131   *PDB* 2847

3 Arundel Castle, bird's-eye view, 1781

S. H. Grimm

British Library, Add. MS. 5674, f. 28 [50]

Grimm took this bird's-eye view a few years before the 11th Duke of Norfolk (1746-1815) began large-scale reconstruction of the residential buildings within the castle. The view, notionally from the south-east, therefore showed the castle towards the end of a long period of neglect and piecemeal alteration, for the dukes used it only as an occasional residence during the 18th century: the duke 'passes a few days here sometimes', Jeremiah Milles commented in 1743. It usefully complements published survey drawings made between 1786 and 1801, two large oils by James Canter *c.* 1783, and Grimm's view of the south

bailey and keep (*Sussex views*, 10).

The ruined 12th-century keep stood between the north and south baileys; to its south was the gatehouse, though Grimm omitted the barbican of about 1300, which is visible to the right in View 4. Richard Gough in 1767 described the south bailey: 'You enter it by a bridge and gate narrow and high leading into a spacious court formerly surrounded by buildings. Those on the SW side are ruined; they were the hall and kitchen; a carved pedestal of a beam remains in the wall of the first, and a spacious chimney of the last. The lodgings on the NE and SE side are modern, the first inhabited by the Duke of Norfolk's steward, the other somewhat older consists of a hall, gallery and chapel; in the gallery are several old family pictures, and a beautiful original of the Queen of Bohemia. The N side is ruined and at the NW corner is a keep having on it a very large round tower and the

Grimm 1781

4 Arundel Castle, the inner court, 1781

S. H. Grimm

British Library, Add. MS. 5674, f. 29 [53]

largest dimensions I have seen.'

View 4 offers an unusual view, from the wall walk between the gatehouse and the keep, looking down at the south-east range. The eight-bayed, three-storeyed brick façade was in classical style with two rusticated doorways, and was added to provide corridors for a sequence of rooms created in the older, possibly 12th-century, shell behind. It was probably to this work that John Warburton referred on his visit in 1723, 'the Castle being grown ruinous is in some parts repaired by the present owner', Duke Thomas (d. 1732).

William Gilpin in 1774 recorded how the Duke had hired antiquaries to advise on the castle's original form, so that it might be restored. 'But it is happy for every picturesque visitor that his design

miscarried. He would have defaced a very beautiful ruin, and would have gotten in return a very awkward house. At present, it is by no means fit for the reception of a ducal retinue. There are several good rooms in the house, and a handsome gallery: but you see everywhere a thorough want both of repairs and furniture, and in all parts evident tokens of the contempt of its master.'

As the only Sussex castle commanding a major bridge and continuously inhabited, Arundel attracted travellers from an early date. With the Fitzalan Chapel it received the longest entry of any site in John Norden's 'Description of Sussex' of 1595, and Lieutenant Hammond gave a full account in 1635.

JHF

Sources VCHS, 5 (1): 41-6. Steer 1976. Harris 1979, nos 364 a and b. Bodl., MS Top. gen. e.24, ff. 269, 271 (quoted with compass points corrected); MS. Eng. misc. f. 194, ff. 66-8. Northants RO, Finch Hatton MS. 113. Hammond (Lieut.) 1936, 30-3.

NGR TQ 018 073   *PDB* 2884, 2887

5 Arundel, College of the Holy Trinity, 1780

S. H. Grimm

British Library, Add. MS. 5674, f. 24 [42]

The College of the Holy Trinity was founded in 1380 by Richard Earl of Arundel as a corporate body of secular clergy to offer Masses for the founder and his family and to provide for the needs of the parish. It was built soon after along with the new parish church. Its chapel, the north side of a quadrangle, abutted the east end of the parish church and after the Dissolution was appropriated by the earls as their mortuary chapel.

Grimm's view was taken from the south-west corner. The south range, to the right, apparently included the entrance. Hollar's etching dated 1644 shows the south and east ranges intact, and repairs were being carried out in the 1670s. But it was ruinous by 1743. Richard Gough in 1767 observed that 'On the south side of the church are large remains of the college, walls and some windows of

the cloister on the east side making a kind of passage to a house [north-east of the chapel] inhabited by the widow of a late steward of the Duke of Norfolk who keeps the key to the chancel. I was told of a gateway in the farmyard adjoining, but did not see it. Ruins of walls with windows etc. extend south-west of the church.'

The 11th Duke of Norfolk reconstructed the south range for a Roman Catholic chapel in about 1797; with the London Road now cut into the bank below, the entrance was moved to the south-west corner. Further buildings were added in the 19th century, and today they are used as residences for the elderly and as a theatre.   *JHF*

Sources VCHS, 5 (1): 29-31, 89-90. Elvins 1981. Bodl., MS Top. gen. e.24, f. 267. Steer 1974a, pl. 1, for Grimm's view of the church from the north-east.

NGR TQ 016 072   *PDB* 2876

6 Arundel, Fitzalan Chapel roof bosses, ?1781

S. H. Grimm

British Library, Add. MS. 5674, f. 22 [40]

When Grimm first visited Arundel, in May 1780, he drew the Fitzalan Chapel, showing about half the original ceiling of the late 14th century which must have incorporated some 75 wooden bosses. A central line consisted of angels bearing musical instruments, and lines to north and south of other figures, particularly old men with beards, while over the windows were small single heads, some wearing mitres. The replacement of this ceiling is dated by Tierney to 1782, but maybe work was already under way on Grimm's return in early June 1781, allowing him to draw these bosses close to.

The new ceiling, according to the one known picture a century later, seems not to have incorporated them. But this ceiling was in turn replaced at some time between 1886 and 1902, and 38 medieval bosses were reinstated, some at least having been found in an outhouse in Poling. The bosses at the bottom are different in style to those which Grimm showed in place, and it has been suggested that they came from the Lady Chapel which was added, on the north side, perhaps in the early 15th century. Three of these (angel's heads, leaves and lion's heads) are now in Poling Church. The Fitzalan horse, though, remains in the chapel.

JHF

Source Cave 1932. VCHS, 5 (1): 90-3.

NGR TQ 016 072

PDB 2873

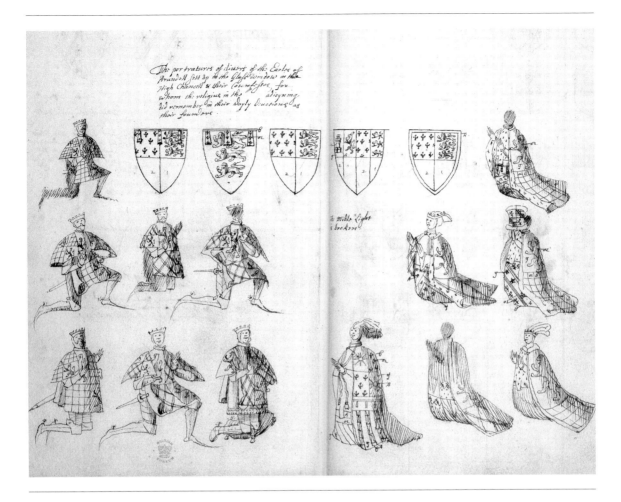

7 Arundel, Fitzalan Chapel, painted glass, 1634

John Withie

British Library, Harleian MS. 1076, ff. 213v-214

John Withie was a herald-painter. He accompanied the herald John Philipot on his visitation of Sussex in 1634, and recorded evidence of local families' right to bear arms. In the Fitzalan Chapel, according to Lieut. Hammond visiting the following year, 'upon the fair east window above the high altar are emblazoned the arms of the earls of that noble family, with their honorable matches, who were the founders' of the college.

From the lower portions of seven lights, Withie sketched the portraits of seven earls of Arundel (on the left) and six countesses (on the right), down to Thomas, 10th Earl (d. 1524). They were shown worshipping Christ in glory in the central light, but

for Withie the point of interest was the arms which each earl bore on his surcoat. Also in the window were the arms of Richard, Earl of Cambridge; Henry, Duke of Lancaster; England; Pedro III, King of Castile; and Thomas of Woodstock, Duke of Gloucester; of Aragon, Portugal, the earls and their wives, and several archbishops of Canterbury.

The windows of the chapel were already 'very much broken' in 1603, and were probably finally destroyed during the Civil War. The glass with Archbishop Thomas Bouchier's arms alone survives today, but not in the chapel.

From the same visitation survive Withie's sketches of arms in Chichester Cathedral and Horsham Church, and of the effigy of Sir Thomas de Braose (d. 1395) in the latter. *JHF*

Sources Hammond (Lieut.) 1936, 33. Elvins 1981, 64-5. VCHS, 5 (1): 91, 94. Wagner 1967, 260.

NGR TQ 016 072 *PDB* 8079

8 Ashburnham
Place and Park, *c*. 1730

Peter Tillemans

Private collection

Colour plate I

Ashburnham Place appears on a map of 1638 as a double-courtyard house of perhaps about 1500, orientated to the south-east. Debts had caused it to be sold out of the family before 1620, but the brothers John (1603-71) and William (d. 1679) Ashburnham, both Royalists, returned at the Restoration to offices at Court, recovered the family estates and built a new house. In 1671 there stood 'a very fair stately palace not quite finished, and so not furnished.'

Commissioned by John, 1st Earl of Ashburnham (1687-1736), Tillemans depicted the resulting house, viewed from behind the main, five-bay front. We see the north-east wing: seven bays under a hipped roof, two storeys of tall sash windows and ground-floor bays at each end, in mellow brick under a white wooden cornice. On the other wing, the crenellated section, with stone

transoms, must surely be part of the old house; indeed between the two wings are larger transoms, such as may have lit a hall, and an unfinished join between old and new building. William's correspondence refers to new rooms adjacent to old. Curiously, then, the 1638 map places the old house south of the church (*SV*, 13), rather than east where the new house was positioned, and a 1717 map appears to show the outer court still standing to the south.

A much longer, 15-bay, main range was added forward of the 1670s front, in 1757-61, as drawn by Lambert and Grimm. After several further campaigns of alteration, demolition in 1958-9 took away two-thirds of the house, including everything of 17th-century and earlier build. The remainder with much new construction continues in use as a Christian conference centre.

The view looks south-east down the approach, cut through Burrage Wood, which ended at the walled court before the house; to the left is the lake formed by damming a stream. This park was reshaped in accordance with 'Capability' Brown's scheme for the 2nd Earl in 1767. The 3rd Earl had Hearne do at least five watercolours of the

9 Ashburnham Park, a waterfall, 1815/6

Thomas Hearne

The National Gallery of Scotland, D.5023/24

resulting landscape. By then it may have gone more 'wild' than Brown would have wished, though Hearne may have heightened its 'sublime' characteristics. This waterfall is not 'the Casade' and has not been located; it may have lain outside the formal gardens.

Thomas Hearne (1744-1817) was introduced to George Ashburnham, the 3rd Earl (1760-1830) by Sir George Beaumont (1753-1827) and George Dance (1741-1825), who were seeking a berth for an ailing artist whose work was falling out of favour. Dance was employed on alterations to the house and also drew members of the family (SAS, pic. coll. 2189-95). Hearne was staying at

Ashburnham in August 1815 (View 107) and in November 1816, maybe earning his keep by giving drawing lessons to Lady Ashburnham. But, he said to Farington, 'the hospitality and kindness of Lord and Lady Ashburnham was great, and the servants seeing their disposition showed him much attention: but still it was not like home, where he could do as he pleased, by a warm fireside.'   *JHF*

Sources View 8 Raines 1978-80. Woodruff 1910, 194. Hussey 1953. ESRO, ACC 2300/8, ASH 159, ASH 4381.

View 9 Morris 1985, 103-5. Morris 1989a, 135-8. Farington 1978-84, 11: 4133, 12: 2485, 13: 4693-4, 14: 4880, 4910, 4967. Farrant 1989, 176. Brandon 1974, 206.

NGR TQ 690 145; TQ 69 14   *PDB* 6032, 3708

10 Ashington, Buncton chapel, 1789

S. H. Grimm

British Library, Add. MS. 5673, f. 34 [60]

Buncton chapel, seen here from the south-east, still stands. Built chiefly of flint and rubble masonry, with fragments of Roman tile, the structure can be dated to the late 11th or 12th century from the north and south doorways and the plain chancel. The lancet chancel windows are later. Both side walls of the chancel are decorated externally with attached Romanesque arcades in elaborately carved ashlar; their purpose is not clear. Grimm failed to notice these, but in 1805 Petrie recorded those on the north wall. The chancel was shortened apparently in the 14th century; the new east wall was built of re-used ashlar masonry from an unknown source, and contains a contemporary two-light window with an ogee quatrefoil above. A bellcote was added in the 19th century, and restoration in 1906 was undertaken discreetly.

Buncton was a parish by 1323, but was united with Ashington some time between 1411 and 1486. This union, and the isolation of the chapel in 1789, and indeed 200 years later, indicate that the community it was built to serve shrank in the later medieval period. Earthworks west and north-west of the chapel have been identified as house platforms. In 1724 and perhaps throughout the 18th century services were held at Buncton monthly.

JHF

Sources VCHS, 6 (2): 64-5, 71-3. Nairn and Pevsner 1965, 120. SAS, Sharpe Coll. 59.

NGR TQ 144 139   *PDB* 2770

11 Ashurst Church and parsonage, 1788

S. H. Grimm

British Library, Add. MS. 5673, f. 30 [51]

The Revd Edward Wilson was instituted as Rector of Ashurst in December 1719 and straightaway set about remodelling the rectory at his own expense. The basically 17th-century timber-framed house gained a five-bayed two-storeyed south front, with three bays on the west. These fronts appear to be stuccoed with brick window quoins. In 1788, Wilson was dead only five years and his son, also Edward (1735-1806), was the incumbent. Further remodelling around 1800 covered part of the building with mathematical tiles. Now called the Old House, it is no longer the rectory.

A garden roller leant again the wall separating the garden from the churchyard. The Church of St James beyond to the north mostly dates from the later 12th and early 13th century, and is built chiefly of flint rubble with freestone dressings and stone-tiled roof; the south-west tower carries a shingled spire.

JHF

Sources VCHS, 6 (2): 81-2.

NGR TQ 176 163

PDB 2762

12 Barcombe, Conyboro House, 1798

Unknown surveyor of the Buxted estate
East Sussex Record Office, ACC 3712, f. 14 [A]

This view shows the formal fronts of the first Sussex mansion to be owned by the Medley family of lawyers. There was a house at Conyboro by 1643, built on land sold off from the demesne land of Barcombe manor in 1581. Edward Raynes, a Lewes lawyer, bought the house, and his niece Susannah married Thomas Medley (1645-1728) in 1672. Medley had acted for the Earls of Thanet and Dukes of Dorset since the late 1660s and was said to have enriched himself at their expense.

The semi-octagonal hall in the south face represents an insertion, probably of the 1760s. The house originally had turrets on the three corners visible in the view. These, with the stone quoins and the keystones above the windows, suggest a house of an earlier generation than Buxted Place which Thomas Medley began in 1726 (View 43).

His youngest son Edward Medley (1680-1754) may have been the builder, in the 1710s or '20s; Mountfield Place, built by James Nicoll at about the same time, provides a close parallel. But alternatively Conyboro may have been an architecturally advanced house built by Edward Raynes or his son John in the 1670s or '80s.

A fine map of 1738 shows elaborate formal gardens, avenues of trees and a deer-park.

After Edward Medley's widow died in 1761 Conyboro was let out to tenants, among them the Archdeacon of Lewes, Thomas D'Oyly. In 1785 he yielded possession to Thomas Kemp, MP for Lewes, who in 1798 rented the house and contents with ten acres of garden and a deer-park of forty acres, for £124 a year. Kemp died at Conyboro in 1811, and the house was demolished in about 1816. In about 1866 John George Dodson, MP (1825-97), later Lord Monk Bretton, commissioned Henry Marley Burton (1813-80) to design a mansion on a new site.   *CHCW*

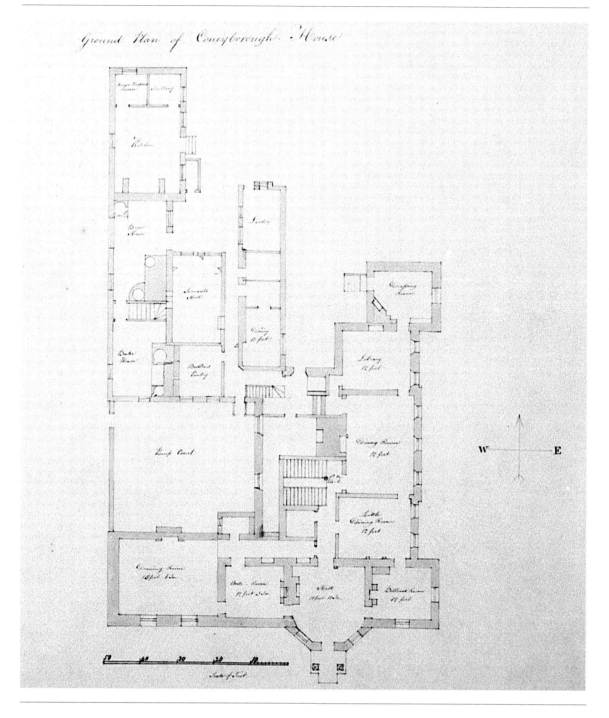

13 Barcombe, Conyboro House, ground floor plan, 1798

Unknown surveyor of the Buxted estate

East Sussex Record Office, ACC 3712, f. 14 [B]

Sources ESRO, HBR 1/1122; MOB 1688; SAS/PN; BMW C4/1. BL, Add MS. 38486 ff. 343-5; 32123, f. 11.

NGR TQ 405 143

PDB 7731, 8070

14 Battle, Mr Worge's house at Starrs Green, 1783

S. H. Grimm

British Library, Add. MS. 5670, f. 33 [62]

George Worge (1705-1765), the son of an Eastbourne landowning family, was in practice as a solicitor in Battle by 1729, when he became steward to the Websters' Battle Abbey estate. He possibly owed his preferment to his father-in-law John Collier, town clerk of Hastings and the Pelham family's political agent in eastern Sussex. Worge seems to have been retained by other Whig landowners, including Spencer Compton.

He initially rented a house from the Websters, but in 1761 a major exchange of land gave him the freehold of the site on which this house was built. Collier had died in the previous year and Worge's wife inherited £2000; that, together with the purchase from the estate of timber worth £99, points to 1761 as the year of erection. Worge was clearly no architectural pathfinder; the classical aspect of his mansion would not have been out of place thirty years before. On his death in 1765, the estate passed to his nephew Thomas Jenner, on condition of changing his name to Worge.

In 1787 Worge let the mansion to Sir Godfrey Webster, whose mother occupied Battle Abbey; the inventory taken lists thirteen rooms and six cellars. The house was tenanted by General Sir Robert Prescott in 1815 and by the Hastings landowner Wastel Briscoe in 1832. After abortive attempts to sell to the Battle Abbey estate, it was sold to Luke Thomas Flood of Fairlight, esq., in 1835 and had been demolished by 1858. The site now forms part of the park of Telham Place.   *CHCW*

Sources ESRO, TDE 158; RAF uncat., deeds of the Telham Court estate; BAT 1442, 2135, 2678; GIL 1/28.

NGR about TQ 757 151   *PDB* 2350

15 Battle
from Starrs Green, 1783

S. H. Grimm

British Library, Add. MS. 5670, f. 34 [64]

Having completed the view of Mr Worge's house, Grimm turned his easel to the right to draw this landscape of Battle, looking to the west. Starrs Green was near Spital Hill, the site of the hospital established by the abbey shortly after its foundation. The hospital formed the eastern boundary of the borough of Sandlake, one of the original administrative subdivisions of the town. Settlement had reached out towards the Spital by 1433, and the view of 1783 probably represents a considerable retreat from the density of medieval occupation. The tower of the parish church is clearly visible in the middle distance and the two windmills at Watch Oak on the horizon.

To the left of the view rise twin towers, the remnants of monastic guest house rebuilt by Sir Anthony Browne in the late 1530s. He was the guardian of Princess Elizabeth and, intending her to reside with him at Battle, began a great range of buildings 197 feet long and 42 feet wide, stretching over two floors. The range, which Samuel Buck found standing in 1736 (but probably roofless, as it certainly was in 1743), had been demolished when Francis Grose sketched in 1761, with the exception of the two octagonal stair-turrets, which were presumably retained to afford tourists a view of the battlefield. The building at the foot of the slope was a tannery.

The scene would be profoundly altered in 1845, when the South-Eastern Railway drove its line past the tannery and built Battle station in the foreground of this view. *CHCW*

Sources: ESRO, BAT 39; QDP 231. VCHS, 9: 105.

NGR TQ 750 158 (church) *PDB* 2352

16 Beckley Parsonage, 1784

S. H. Grimm

British Library, Add. MS. 5670, f. 13 [23]

Colour plate II

The lower, gabled, portion of this house, with its elaborate barge-boards, was built during the incumbency of Thomas Sharpe (*c.* 1587-1644) in 1636; the date can be made out over the porch. It was not, however, built for owner-occupation: Sharpe lived at the much grander Church House, which he had built or substantially improved in 1626. It was probably there, rather than at the rectory, that he and his wife were terrorised by Colonel Morley's troopers in 1643. They both died in the year following and Church House descended in their family.

Subsequent rectors were non-resident until 1699 when Thomas Hooper (1673-1753), whose father Thomas Hooper of Mayfield had acquired the advowson, was presented. Hooper, who became Vicar of Hailsham in 1701 and rector of two Dorset parishes in 1712, lived at Beckley and is certainly responsible for the loftier rear range with its M-roof. In 1752 he was succeeded at Beckley by his grandson Thomas Hooper.

A map of the glebe in 1798 shows the house to have enjoyed an elaborate garden with exotic trees, water-features (possibly incorporating the remains of a moat), a rustic bridge and a ha-ha. It is clear that the oriel window, part of Thomas Hooper's new range, was positioned to provide a vantage-point on some of these horticultural delights.

The building was substantially altered on Thomas Hooper's death in 1804, entirely re-modelled in 1839 and sold into private ownership in 1937.   *CHCW*

Sources ESRO, PAR 237 6/2/1, 12/5 p.186; HBR 1/967. Wolseley 1934. Blaauw 1852, 72-7.

NGR TQ 844 242   *PDB* 2311

17 South Bersted, Bognor Lodge, 1790

S. H. Grimm

British Library, Add. MS. 5675, f. 72 [138]

Sir Richard Hotham (1722-99), a London merchant and former MP who lived at Wimbledon, convalesced at a farmhouse at Bognor, a tithing of South Bersted, in 1784. He later purchased it, rebuilding it as Bognor Lodge, shown here. This first stage in Hotham's creation of a seaside resort was recorded in the South Bersted parish register on 18 January 1787. The house stood between what is now High Street and the south aspect of Hotham Park House. A photograph from the east in Fleming 1949-50 suggests that the original house was orientated north-south, with Hotham's addition east-west. This view is from the south and to the left are the farm outbuildings which included an octagonal barn and a raised granary.

At the sale of Hotham's estate in 1800 the house comprised a drawing room (with domed ceiling and Adam-style reliefs), dining parlour, breakfast parlour, entrance hall and staircase, six bed chambers and a closet. Domestic quarters included kitchen, wash-house, laundry, dairy, china closet and cellarage. Outside were stabling for eight horses, double coach-house, courtyard, gardens and lands totalling 26 acres.

The future Queen Victoria stayed here from 1821 as a summer guest of Lord Arran. Other owners included Sir John Harington (before 1820), William Bray (who named the house 'Darlinghurst', *c.* 1870) and from 1890, George Gatehouse, a Chichester brewer. Bognor Lodge was demolished in 1938 by a speculative builder. The site became a playing field for a nearby Catholic school and was developed for flats in 1987. *RI*

Sources WSRO, SP.2076, lot II; Par. 19/1/1/4, f. 28. Dally 1828, 18. Davis 1807, 77-81. Fleming 1949-50, 2: fc. 556. Young 1983, 11, 112, 239.

NGR SZ 940 993   *PDB* 3069

The Fox Inn at Bognor a Rocks.

S. H. Grimm fecit June 4th 1790

18 South Bersted, The Fox Inn at Bognor Rocks, 1790

S. H. Grimm

British Library, Add. MS. 5675, f. 93 [165]

The Fox Inn was a thatched alehouse near the shoreline at Bognor Rocks, a hamlet within South Bersted parish. Around 1790, Sir Richard Hotham (View 17) began converting it to his new resort's first hotel, three storeys high and comprising by 1800 8 dining rooms, 17 bedrooms, coffee room, bar, parlour and taproom, with stabling for 80 horses and 15 carriages. Its position is best shown on two Quarter Sessions road plans of 1823-4: the site is now occupied by the promenade at the foot of West Street.

From which direction this view was taken is unclear. The thatched inn was apparently retained behind the hotel which faced east-south-east, and both appear on a 1796 sketch reproduced in Fleming 1949-50. Two more views of the hotel, from the east (with a smaller building on a

promontory to the south, housing a subscription room, milliner's shop, library and warm baths) appeared in Dr J. B. Davis's guidebook of 1807 and William Daniell's aquatint of 1823.

In 1792 the proprietor, George Grinder, transferred himself and the name of The Fox to a tavern in Felpham. Richard Pink (1800) and Charles East Walkden (1823) were later landlords at Bognor of what Greenwood's 1825 map of Sussex named as the Royal Hotel. Along with nearby buildings it was destroyed by fire on 26 June 1826.

RI

Sources WSRO, SP.2076, lot XXXVII; QDP/W.47, 53; PM.15. Dally 1828, 22-3. Davis 1807, frontispiece, 77. Fleming 1949-50, 3: cxiii, fc. ccxii. Young 1983, front endpaper, 13, 101.

NGR SZ 932 987   *PDB* 3097

19 Bignor Park, ?1791

S. H. Grimm

British Library, Add. MS. 5674, f. 47 [85]

The Pellatt family of Steyning acquired Bignor in 1580, formerly a deer-park of the earls of Arundel. William Pellatt inherited in 1616, married Bridget Mille of Greatham eleven years later and, as indicated by their initials and arms with the date 1632 on a stone set in a gable of the present house, built a new, or remodelled an existing, house, giving it an E-shape. The Pellatts sold in 1712 to Nicholas Turner, from Stoke near Guildford. In 1779 at St Martin in the Fields, Westminster, Catherine Ann Turner, heir to the estate, married Captain Michael Dorset, probably born in 1753, the son of the vicar of Walberton.

This drawing shows the symmetrical entrance front: a turreted gatehouse flanked by gables and corner turrets. Grimm's view of the garden front, in *Sussex views*, 19, shows gables also, flanking a five-sided extension topped by a turret. The gabled ranges survived from Pellatt's house, while Dorset made the 'Gothick' additions in the 1780s. The grounds seen here with the lake in the foreground suggest deliberate landscaping, perhaps also in the

1780s. His wife and, more so, her elder sister, Mrs Charlotte Smith were in their day poetesses of some repute. John Hawkins bought the property in 1806, and commissioned Henry Harrison to design the present box-like house, 'in a somewhat tame Greek Revival style', in 1826.   *AFH and JHF*

Sources Steer 1959, xii. Phillips 1892, 115, 122-3. Phillips 1894, 74. Colvin 1995, 463, quoted. Horsfield 1835, 2: 150. DNB 1998.
NGR SU 990 155   *PDB* 2919

20 Bodiam Castle, 1782

James Lambert senior

British Library, Add. MS. 5676, f. 3 [5]

Colour plate III

Bodiam Castle was built by Sir Edward Dallingridge in the last decades of the 14th century. To destroy its military potential, it was partly demolished after the Civil War, in about 1650. Materials may have been taken for Ewhurst Place (View 79). So it was a ruin that Sir Thomas Webster purchased in 1723, perhaps out of antiquarian sentiment, as he also bought Battle Abbey and Robertsbridge Priory. He sponsored the Bucks' engraving of it.

His heirs may not have shared the same sentiment, for they did not encourage tourists. John Byng arrived to view in 1788: 'This castle belongs to Sir Godfrey Webster, who has locked up the gate leading to the interior of the square; and from a narrowness of possession does not allow a key to any neighbour; though surely a proper

inhabitant would secure and preserve it, and get a livelihood (or at least much support), from us castle hunters. So I could only walk around the little lake which washes the walls and adds much to the curiosity and safety of the building.' Francis Grose in 1777 also viewed only the exterior (Document 5).

Lambert's view, looking south, shows a cottage built against the postern tower and the castle's interior put to good use for rows of vegetables bordered by fruit bushes. John Fuller of Rose Hill bought the castle in 1829, to forestall, it is said, its final destruction for the materials. Restoration was started in the 1860s and continued particularly under Lord Curzon who bequeathed the castle to the National Trust in 1925.   *JHF*

Sources Thackray 1991, which prints eight of Grimm's ten views of 1784.

NGR TQ 785 256   *PDB* 4006

21 Bosham, Vicarage House and Church, 1782

S. H. Grimm

British Library, Add. MS. 5675, f. 47 [87]

By Grimm's time Bosham was already established on antiquarian itineraries as a major Saxon monument and a collegiate foundation, and for its association with Earl Godwin (Document 3) - though the mythologies claiming King Canute and his daughter had not yet gained currency. The main emphasis in Grimm's depiction of the church from the east-north-east is the lowered (almost flattened) roof. Reputedly the result of decay and neglect around the time of the College's suppression in 1548, it was raised back to its original line in 1865.

Burrell's caption is puzzling: 'View of the Vicarage House (olim the College) & Church of Bosham.' Traditionally the college buildings were believed to have stood at the south side of the church - but all that survived the Dissolution was a small house which became the Vicarage. A separate view of this by Grimm was reproduced in *Sussex views*, 26, and does not resemble the house at the left of our picture. The Vicarage/College building stood opposite the south porch of the church and would appear here to be screened by a row of trees. Other views by Grimm are known to omit trees found in inconvenient places – but not on this occasion.

The house became ruinous and was pulled down in 1840. All now remaining today are a gateway and a length of wall - though some of the College masonry has also been used in nearby buildings.

This picture is badly foxed. *PMW*

Sources Dallaway 1815, 2: 91. MacDermott 1911, 34, 44. Nairn and Pevsner 1965, 112. WSRO, Cap I/25/4.

NGR SU 804 039 *PDB* 3018

22 Boxgrove Priory, guest-house and church, 1781

S. H. Grimm

British Library, Add. MS. 5675, f. 83 [153]

Boxgrove Priory was founded by Robert de Haye who in 1105 bestowed upon the Abbey of Lessay in Normandy the church at Boxgrove. The community of Benedictine monks, nineteen in number at its largest in about 1230, was dissolved in 1537. Then the patron, Thomas West, Lord de la Warr, begged Thomas Cromwell that the church should be left unspoiled; this was granted inasmuch as only the parochial nave was pulled down and the choir, which had formed the monastic church, was with the tower retained as the parish church. Grimm's views of the interior of the church and the de la Warr monument are in *Sussex views*, 27 and 28.

The rest, 'the mansion house and site of the late priory of Boxgrove', was leased to de la Warr. The Crown exchanged it in 1560 with the Earl of Arundel, out of whose family it passed, via the Lumleys, by sale to John Morley in 1587. The 3rd Duke of Richmond bought it with Halnaker (View 22) in 1765. A survey of 1570 recorded 'divers ruinous houses' used as a brewhouse, a barn for the tithes, a stable for 20 geldings, a dove house and 'certain rooms above and under' which with some 'pains-taking' were used as malting floors, there being a kiln but no cistern for steeping the barley.

Samuel Buck in 1736 drew the building in View 22 from the same, north-east, angle, with abutting buildings extending to the north-west, all roofless. The engraving as published in 1737 shows the windows and doors in the east wall as open, but the drawing (British Museum, P&D 1981-12-12-33 (4)) shows them to be blocked and there to be no windows in the south gable - an example of the licence taken by the engraver. By 1781 the walls to the right had nearly all gone, but the other building had been roofed, presumably being used

23 Boxgrove Priory, interior of the guest-house, 1781

S. H. Grimm

British Library, Add. MS. 5675, f. 87 [157]

hall and the undercroft were used as malting floors. Stabilised by the Ministry of Works in 1966, it is in ruins today with only the north and south gable walls standing to their full height.

TJMcC and JHF

as a barn. The interior view, 23, is looking north. It is difficult to know what to make of Francis Grose's statement that some parts of the priory had been converted into dwelling houses - a personal observation, as he was there in March 1761.

Standing separately beyond the cloisters, the building has been identified as the monastic guest-house, probably of the early-14th century. It was two storied, the lower vaulted in five bays and two alleys, and the upper consisting of a great hall, over 60 feet long internally, with, already gone by 1736, a solar 20 feet long to the south and perhaps the stairs and a buttery in the north-west wing. Perhaps the solar had in 1570 been converted to the kiln, while windows would be blocked if the

Sources: Petit 1861. Fleming 1960. Ratcliff 1976. VCHS, 2: 55-60, 4: 140-50. Peckham 1920.

NGR SU 908 075   *PDB* 3084, 3088

24 Boxgrove,
Halnaker House, 1781

S. H. Grimm

British Library, Add. MS. 5675, f. 75 [141]

Halnaker House in Halnaker Park, north of Stane Street in Boxgrove, was a semi-fortified manor house, surrounded by a curtain wall with the gatehouse in the south range and a square tower at the south-west angle, here shown from outside. Grimm's drawings of the six-gabled north range and the east range of an irregular courtyard, and of the panelling in the hall, are reproduced in *Sussex views*, 29 and 30. There may have been another courtyard beyond the north range.

Perhaps first built by Robert de Haye, the founder of Boxgrove Priory in the early 12th century, the surviving remains of the chapel are dated to the 13th century and of the main structure to the 14th with extensive remodelling (and maybe replanning) by Thomas West, Lord de la Warr in the mid-16th (as evident in the upper floor of the gatehouse). It descended through the Lumleys to the Morleys. An inventory of 1701 lists 39 residential rooms with 17 hearths; the incomplete record of the service quarters runs to 12 rooms with three hearths. By then the great hall was sparsely furnished, and the richly furnished rooms were the upper parlour, the withdrawing room, the long gallery, the great chapel chamber and My Lady's chamber. A brick-built range was added, in the south-east corner, a few years later.

After the death in 1752 of the last Morley, the Countess of Derby, Halnaker was allowed to decay. The 3rd Duke of Richmond purchased it in 1765 and absorbed it into the Goodwood estate. In 1812, Thomas Smith reported that part had been taken down by order of the present owner; that in summer 1804 the brick buildings had fallen down; and that it was inhabited by poor people. Still occupied around 1840, it was ruinous by 1900. Carvings, windows, fireplaces and much stonework were taken for The Grange, an early Victorian house in Chapel Street, Chichester, demolished in its turn in 1962, and for The Chantry in Canon Lane, Chichester. *TJMcC and JHF*

Sources André 1900. Godfrey 1941. Smith 1812. Steer 1963b. Walpole 1937-83, 12: 200. Bodl., MS. Rolls Sussex 12 and 13 (copy at ESRO, XA 79)

NGR SU 908 089   *PDB 3072*

25 Boxgrove, the Catacombs in Goodwood Park, *c.* 1750

George Smith

The Trustees of the Goodwood Collection

Both the Catacombs and the Pheasantry were formed under the direction of Charles Lennox, 2nd Duke of Richmond (1701-50), probably in the mid-1740s. Taking advantage of a dell in the High Wood behind Goodwood House, possibly the site of a Neolithic flint mine, the Duke

erected shell houses, grottoes and recesses in a hollow near an entrance to the labyrinth. In 1747 George Vertue described the 'Rock dell with other ruins erected (lately) artfully with stone cells underground and dark recesses or passages subterranean, which are as well contrived as curious, vast stones, porpheryes, sea pebbles etc. variously disposed.' In the same year Lady Newdigate found 'a very particular place called the Stone dell which is a sort of rocky pit near which is the ruins of a church, a hermit's cave, a skittle alley with a Chinese house in it, a Lapland house and two or

26 Boxgrove, the Pheasantry in Goodwood Park, 1782

S. H. Grimm

British Library, Add. MS. 5675, f. 67 [128]

three other odd (and we thought tasteless) buildings much crowded.' The Duke's family buried their smaller pets and animals here with elaborate ceremony, poetic valedictories and memorial inscriptions. According to tradition it was built for a hermit, whom Smith introduced into the picture, but human occupation goes unrecorded before 1838 when a hermit sought permission to live there. At least one tunnel has collapsed and the shell houses and grottoes have decayed, but the roof of the main underground chamber has recently been restored. This picture is unusual amongst the work of George Smith of Chichester (1713/14-76) for being of an identifiable place.

The Pheasantry was situated in the remains of an old chalk-pit, which formed an amphitheatre with steep banks near Carne's Seat. A variety of chinese and other pheasants were raised here, as well as parrots, parroquets and cockatoos. Lady Newdigate in 1747 recorded 'in the woods a building for maccaws which fly about and add infinitely to the beauty of them.' Later a pond stocked with goldfish and silverfish was added. It was surrounded by a high wall falling to a ha-ha on the south which afforded a prospect to those within. The sides were planted with evergreens and cut into paths leading to the summit, around which was a turfed walk. The drawing shows a white pillar of stone surmounted by a vase, which acted as a false chimney for the dwelling-house, an ornament to the park and a guide for mariners. It was taken down shortly after the drawing. The structures included a small dwelling-house, occupied by the keeper, an octagonal wooden building, possibly an apiary, and a wooden seat.

TJMcC and JHF

Sources Vertue 1930-55, 5: 143. Lennox 1911. McCann 1994. Connor 1979, 190. Jaques 1822. Mason 1839. Warwickshire County Record Office, CR 1841/7, p. 26.
NGR SU 887 090, SU 889 094   *PDB* 5407, 3058

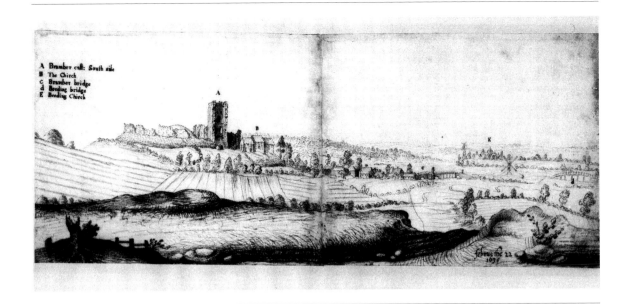

A Bramber cast: South side
B The Chirch
c Bramber bridge
d Beeding bridge
E Beeding Chirch

27 Bramber Castle and Church, 1636

attributed to John Dunstall senior

Leeds Museums and Galleries (City Art Gallery), 13.28b/53

This is one of five drawings dated 1635-6 which may have belonged to Wenceslaus Hollar. Three of the others seem to be the source for Hollar's etchings of Bramber Castle from the west, Wiston Place and Pevensey Castle. But they are dated before Hollar's arrival in England, and they can be attributed to John Dunstall senior (b. 1584?) who was working as a military surveyor in Ireland in 1612, is found as a Chichester stationer in 1644 and probably was the artist of five etchings of Chichester and neighbourhood (see Essay 1.2).

Hollar's three etchings of Bramber Castle are from the east, west and north. The view here completes the circuit, being taken from a vantage point on the Downs to the south. The castle is on the left, with the gatehouse given prominence; Bramber Church is to its right, with the village strung along the road falling to Bramber bridge and, on the far right, Beeding bridge, with the church at Upper Beeding in the distance between them. What this and the related drawings do is to settle that the castle was in a ruinous state before the Civil War and was not therefore slighted by Parliamentarian forces. *JHF*

Sources Camden 1977, 47, and VCHS, 6 (1): fc. 208 for two of Hollar's etchings. Barton and Holden 1977, 15, 21-2.

NGR TQ 185 106   *PDB* 2007

28 Brede Place, 1784

S. H. Grimm

British Library, Add. MS. 5670, f. 18 [34]

Like Bodiam Castle and Ewhurst Place (Views 20 and 79), Brede Place was surplus to its owner's requirements for much of the 18th and 19th centuries, and when Grimm visited it was wearing an air of neglect. Originally known as the messuage 'atte Forde' and by about 1500 as Forde Place, Brede Place was rebuilt or extensively remodelled in Sussex sandstone from about 1400, by members of the Oxenbrigge family. The chapel - covered in ivy in Grimm's view of the west front of the house - may have been founded as late as the 1490s, for it is mentioned in Thomas Oxenbrigge's will of 1496 but seems not to be referred to in two previous Oxenbrigge wills of 1488 and 1493/4. The square-headed two-light window seen through the ivy could be of this date.

Further changes were made in the early-16th century when the projecting bay in the centre of the west front - possibly originally housing a newel staircase - and the porch wing at the north end were added, both in brick. Of a similar date are the six-light windows at ground- and first-floor levels between the projecting bay and the chapel. The blocked arch glimpsed underneath the six-light windows at one time gave access to cellars.

Sir Edward Frewen of Brickwall, Northiam, bought the Brede Place estate in 1708 and it remained in the Frewen family until 1936. The house and chapel were severely damaged by fire in January 1979. *JB*

Sources Austen 1946, 31-2. Godfrey 1935-41, 1: 199-206. VCHS, 9: 165. Warne 1972, 29. ESRO, HBR 1/381.

NGR TQ 836 183

PDB 2322

29 Brightling Park, 1816

J. M. W. Turner

British Museum, P&D, 1958-7-12-411

On acquiring the site in about 1698, Thomas Fuller replaced an existing mansion of about 1550 with the core of the house (to the left, facing north), nine bays with central entrance in red brick and grey headers. John Fuller (1680-1745), ironmaster, came into possession in 1703 and renamed it Rose Hill, in honour of his wife Elizabeth Rose (1681-1728) whose inheritance transformed the family's wealth, status and connections.

Their son John (1706-55) added at the west end a large drawing-room, decorated with elaborate plaster work by Joseph Daw of Lewes in 1746-8. John was also responsible for the service wing to the south. These additions were demolished in 1955. He formed the park between 1748 and 1751 and wanted to 'plant clumps of trees to make it look like a forest'; he certainly erected a Chinese temple. But the main

landscaping was at the instigation of John Fuller III (1757-1834), possibly to a design by 'Capability' Brown. In 1794-7 he more than doubled the park's size to 565 acres. Repton's proposals of 1806 were implemented only in part.

John III was perhaps Turner's principal patron after the Earl of Egremont, though Turner was well established when Fuller first commissioned him in 1810. Eventually Fuller was to own 13 Turner watercolours and two oils. At Fuller's expense four of these were reproduced as coloured aquatints in about 1812, and a further five were engraved and published in 1819 as the first part of *Views in Sussex*. Two other planned parts did not materialise (Essay 4.4).   *JHF*

Sources Martin 1990? Dale 1955. White 1984, 246. Farrant 1989, 172. Salt 1969, 14-15, 17, fc. 21, for Grimm's view, 1784. Shanes 1990, 8-10, 28 for colour reproduction of this view. Shanes 1998. ESRO, AMS 3501.

NGR TQ 683 209   *PDB* 5758

mama 3. 1815.

Brighton Church & Barrows

30 Brighton, St Nicholas's Church and barrows, 1815

John Skinner

British Library, Add. MS. 33649, f. 145.

This drawing supports the contention that the Church of St Nicholas at Brighton was located within, or adjacent to, a pre-existing ritual landscape. Skinner depicts *inter alia* a flat-topped barrow and, in the immediate foreground, a smaller domed one on the hill above the church. A companion sketch (f. 151 'Barrows and remains of a cromlech on the hill above Brighton Church') shows a flat-topped barrow - perhaps that in this view - measuring 13 yards across at the top, three large stones, a rectangular enclosure measuring 20 yards on its longest side, and a circular feature 20 yards in diameter, all within about 100 yards of each other. By 'cromlech', Skinner is probably referring to a stone circle, perhaps of sarsens, the existence of which is suggested also in a drawing by John Nixon engraved in 1802.

On this visit to Brighton, Skinner met the Revd James Douglas and on 4 March they excavated several barrows 'about three miles' from the town (Essay 4.1). In August 1815 Douglas excavated 'the great barrow on the hill close to the church'. On that occasion, he was accompanied by the artist Benjamin Robert Haydon who recorded that an inverted urn containing burnt human bones was discovered - but that Douglas broke it in his excitement to examine the find.

The church is shown with the dormer windows which were inserted to allow light into the galleries. It was largely rebuilt to plans by R. C. Carpenter in 1853.

JB

Sources Grinsell 1940, 210-11. Grinsell 1942, 120, for Skinner's drawing of the Hove barrow. Harrison and North 1937, 153-5. Jessup 1975, 147-8, 164. Haydon 1950, 259-60. VCHS, 7: 259. SAS, pic. coll. 1767.

NGR TQ 306 046   *PDB* 7920

31 Brighton, Town Parade, ?1801

W. J. Burchell

MuseuMAfricA, Johannesburg, 68/1788 [B1616]

Born in Fulham, the son of a nurseryman, William John Burchell (1781-1863) sailed to St Helena in 1805 and moved on to Cape Town in 1810. In five years he amassed 63,000 natural history specimens during expeditions over a vast and varied stretch of the interior. With these he returned to England in 1815 and travelled again only to Brazil in 1825-30. All that he published were his journals up to 1812 as *Travels into the interior of Southern Africa* (1822-4) and he was to be disappointed as others, who had come after him, published their findings and robbed him of the honours for which he had hoped. Since his death, however, his collections, through their detailed annotations, have enriched others' work.

Among over 800 surviving sketches are 19 of Sussex, made in 1799 to 1803. Burchell was then aged between 18 and 21, having already received instruction in landscape drawing from Merigot, a Frenchman who had been a tutor in the Pugin

family, and from the topographical draughtsman John Claude Nattes (1765-1839). Pictures of Brighton dated August 1799 and September 1801 suggest holiday visits, and sketches were made on the road from or back to Fulham via Horsham and Henfield in the latter year. The Rocks at Eridge were visited in 1801 and East Grinstead in 1803.

The first view here was from Town Parade, the northern limit of the town. The Prince of Wales's Marine Pavilion lay south of the Duke of Marlborough's red-brick Grove House, in the centre. To the right was East Street, the main road into the town, and to the left the Steine, the fashionable promenade closed at the seaward end by Russell House. There were at the date of Burchell's visit probably large barracks to his right, between Church Street and North Road, and he sketched some troops drilling. More elaborate military parades were also held here, to the Prince's delight.

The second view is of the Theatre which was built on the north-west part of Duke Street, opened in July 1790 and sold for demolition in 1807. Burchell sketched an exterior view, showing its blind façade of weather boarding, grooved or rusticated in imitation of masonry, fronting the

32 Brighton, interior of the Theatre, 1799

W. J. Burchell

MuseuMAfricA, Johannesburg, 68/1745 [B1576]

street, with a wide porch of Tuscan columns under a pediment giving direct entrance to the boxes. The one other view of the interior is on an engraved benefit card of October 1790. At that date the auditorium was rectangular. It is said to have been remodelled into a horseshoe shape in 1796, though that does not show in Burchell's

sketch which is dated 20 August 1799 and annotated that 'The finished coloured copy of this was given to my uncle Hewett'. It is indeed partly coded for colouring: the panelling in and below the boxes was yellow, framed in lake. The next known picture of the interior of a Brighton theatre, some 50 years later, is by William Alfred Delamotte (Brighton Art Gallery, 100495, 103020).

JHF

Sources Gordon-Brown and Jacot Guillarmond 1972. Kennedy 1971. Dinkel 1983, 20-4, including Spornberg's views of the Steine, 1796. Farrant 1982. Dale 1980, 2-4. Rosenfeld 1954. Steer 1958b, 61 and pl. 12.

NGR TQ 313 043, TQ 307 042   *PDB* 7659, 7644

33 Broadwater,
Cissbury Ring, 1780

S. H. Grimm

British Library, Add. MS. 5672, f. 22 [38]

Grimm's vantage point was from Muntham, north-west of Findon village, which lay in the valley bottom below him. The Ring is the only earthwork on the Sussex Downs which Camden noted in the first edition of *Britannia* (1586): the locals believed Caesar camped there, but the name, he claimed, showed it to be the work of Cissa, the second Saxon king, who had landed with his brother Cimen at Cimenshore, or Old Shoreham, in 477. John Tabor identified 18 hillforts on the Sussex Downs, but Cissbury, from its name, was the only one with evidence of date or purpose. All were used during Saxon conquest: 'the ground was disputed inch by inch: that in the attack, as well as defence of it, the pick-axe and spade, were as much made use of, as the sword.' Excavated pottery now

dates Cissbury to early in the Middle Iron Age, *c*. 400-250 BC, constructed over some 270 Neolithic flint mines.

The Ring lay at the north limit of Broadwater parish and was part of the manorial demesne which in 1780 belonged to the two daughters of James Butler, late of Warminghurst (d. 1775; View 189). Broadwater farm, at over 800 acres, was typical of the big tenanted farms lying on the south flanks of the Downs, with a large sheep flock which grazed on the higher land and was folded for their manure on the arable fields below. The Findon sheep fair seems to have dated from the 1790s. The Ring is now owned by the National Trust.

JHF

Sources VCHS, 6 (1): 29, 70, 74. Tabor 1717, 791-3. Donachie and Field 1994. Hamilton and Manley 1997, 101.

NGR TQ 140 081   *PDB* 2673

34 Broadwater, Warwick House, 1790

S. H. Grimm

British Library, Add. MS. 5678, f. 19 [37]

In the early 1780s John Luther built for himself this marine residence at the corner of High Street and the Broadway in Worthing, its bow facing south to the sea over open ground which was laid out in about 1811 as the Steyne. Luther (1739?-86) was of Myles's, near Ongar, Essex, and MP for that county, 1763-84, but owned an estate at Petworth. In 1789, his representatives sold to George Greville, 2nd Earl of Warwick. Although he retained it for only seven years, his name remained with the house. John William Commerell of Berkeley Street, London, and Horsham, was the owner until 1801, and then Edward Ogle of Clapton, a wealthy stockbroker who laid out the gardens and died in 1824. In their time, it was Worthing's premier house.

Built in squared and faced flint with brick quoins and window reveals, the central block contained a magnificent dining-room on the ground floor, 20 by 30 feet, leading into the bow, a morning room, a smoking room, a hall and other apartments. On the first floor were a drawing room of similar proportions to the dining room, six principal bedrooms, a boudoir, and three servants' bedrooms having a separate staircase. An attic floor under the roof gave two more rooms, one of which opened on to a balcony above the bow window. Domestic quarters were in the connected low west wing and the stables were detached on the east. The central block was almost unaltered externally when the whole site was cleared in 1896.   *JHF*

Sources Smail 1952. VCHS, 6 (1): 97. Namier and Brooke 1964, 3: 63-4.

NGR TQ 151 026   *PDB* 3141

35 Broadwater, Worthing sea front, ?1807

John Nixon

Worthing Museum & Art Gallery, 1974/182

John Nixon (*c*. 1750-1818) was a wealthy London merchant trading with Ireland, and a competent amateur artist. He shared much in common with Francis Grose, first in his conviviality and powers as a raconteur, for the house he shared with his brother and business partner was well known for its liberal hospitality to artists, actors and musicians; secondly for his caricatures, not only of friends (including Grose on the 1791 trip to Ireland on which he died) but also of the ordinary folk; and thirdly for his topographical drawings, though these had a stronger bent to the contemporary scene than to the antiquarian.

He toured extensively, sometimes with other artists (including Thomas Rowlandson); he visited Scotland at least once, and France and the Low Countries in 1783 and 1784, and as soon as they were open again to Englishmen, during the Peace of Amiens in 1802 and in 1814. But most of his sketching was done during summer tours in the south of England, at the seaside resorts and spas. He first visited the Isle of Wight in 1779 or '80 and was to die there. He provided many of the drawings which were engraved for Thomas Pennant's *Journey from London to the Isle of Wight* (1801), including eight in Sussex, mainly of the standard antiquarian sights.

Many sketches by him were sold by the French Hospital of La Providence, Rochester, between 1973 and 1985, and over 100 of Sussex can be identified in the auction catalogues, but only about 15 are in public collections at Worthing Museum and YCBA. Brighton and Hastings feature most frequently. Those dated come from 1783, 1787, 1789-91, 1794, 1801 and 1804-8.

Views 35 and 36 can be confidently dated to 1807. He exhibited at the Royal Academy between 1781 and 1815, and in 1808 submitted 'A morning view on the sands at Worthing' which is now in the Victoria & Albert Museum (P.69-1920) and printed in Chancellor 1926, pl. 74. This features the town crier of whom the preparatory sketch dated 1807 is in private hands. View 35 is replicated in the exhibited picture. To the right of the picture are the Sea House Hotel and the New Hotel, facing each other across the south end of South Street; to

36 Broadwater, Sea House Hotel, Worthing, ?1807

John Nixon

Worthing Museum & Art Gallery, 1974/184

their left is Montague Place. 'At Worthing,' said the author of the first guidebook (1805), 'are two Inns close to the beach - from the windows of which are pleasing views of the ocean. They are kept by two widows of the name of Hogsflesh and Bacon! Looking up at these names on their respective signs - which extending across the road almost touch each other in social amity - many a smile is excited by a coincidence as singular as it is unexpected.' A further inn was then under construction at the bottom of Bedford Row.

The Sea House Hotel (Mrs Hogsflesh) is detailed in View 36. The left-hand house perhaps predated Worthing's development as a resort, serving travellers riding along the beach, the fishermen and the occasional beached cargo-boat, whereas the right-hand one could date from the 1790s, at the very start of building at the beach for visitors. The decade 1801-11 saw the number of houses in Broadwater triple, and the terrace visible on the west side of Montague Place (1802-5) was typical of that period.

The Teville tollgate (View 37) was at the junction of the modern Teville and Broadwater Roads and North Street, at the southern end of the turnpike road to Washington which greatly

37 Broadwater, Teville tollgate, ?1807

John Nixon

Worthing Museum & Art Gallery, 1974/185

improved communication to London. This road was completed in 1804, so the tollgate presumably dated from then. On the tollhouse is a sign headed 'VAGABONDS & THIEVES', while the open gate is inscribed 'NO TRUST', perhaps to inform travellers that the turnpike trust's jurisdiction did not extend any further south. The house was redundant from 1823 when the road to Offington Corner was disturnpiked, and was removed in about 1845. In the right foreground is Teville pond; to the north-west can be seen the Cross Street (or Worthing) mill and in the distance the spire of West Tarring Church and Highdown mill.

JHF

Sources Mallalieu 1977. Christie's, 4 June 1974, 14. Elleray 1998, 120. Evans 1805, 35-6. VCHS, 6 (1): 97-8, 103.
NGR TQ 149 024, TQ 149 024, TQ 147 032

PDB 4913, 4915, 4916

38 Broadwater, Offington, 1780

S. H. Grimm

British Library, Add. MS. 5673, f. 60 [107]

Offington was, with Buckhurst and Cowdray, one of but three great houses in Sussex noted by Camden in 1586, for it was a seat of Lord de la Warr. An inventory of 1554 - now known only from a copy made for William Burrell - identified some 68 rooms. Sold out of the family in 1601, it may have already been reduced in size by 1664, even though it then had 25 hearths.

In 1780 the owner and occupier was John Margesson (1716-85) who had inherited in 1746. Stebbing Shaw ten years later observed that it 'has undergone much alteration, being low and heavy built of stone, and quite plain in front, with two small projecting wings. The ground which surrounds is inclosed in a rough wall, and has the appearance of a small park, with good groups of timber, but no deer.'

The hood-moulds and the plaque over the door, however, suggest that the main, east, range was old, perhaps of the early 16th century. The roof line of the south wing, with the parapet rising above the eaves, indicates an older south range behind. The alterations may have remodelled domestic quarters. The east range was refronted in flint in the mid-19th century. The house was divided into flats after 1935 and demolished in 1963. *JHF*

Sources Smail 1950. VCHS, 6 (1): 71-2. Shaw 1791b, 150. White 2000, 120.

NGR TQ 142 051   *PDB* 2819

Burpham Camp ... S:H: Grimm fecit 1789

39 Burpham Camp, 1789

S. H. Grimm

British Library, Add. MS. 5674, f. 32 [58]

The fortified camp at Burpham occupies a promontory in the floodplain of the River Arun. It extends to about 22 acres, with the most formidable defence on the north at the neck of the promontory where the rampart is 290 yards long and from 20 to 25 feet high. This rampart is in two nearly equal sections which approach each other obtusely, with a narrow entrance in between and a ditch on the outside. Grimm's view - unobtainable today as his sight line is broken by a sports pavilion - is taken from inside the camp looking north through the gateway in the embankment, to the church and village outside the camp.

The camp is nowadays considered to be the site of the Anglo-Saxon *burh* made at Burpham in about 900 as part of the Alfredian plan of defences against the Vikings. It is interesting to note that

Hadrian Allcroft, whilst acknowledging Burpham as one of these Anglo-Saxon burhs, considered the rampart to be Viking in origin. Indeed, it has yet to be established whether the rampart is contemporary with or earlier than the founding of the *burh* - a recent excavation was inconclusive on this point, the archaeologist observing that 'these (fortifications) may still prove to be of the Iron Age period'. Evidence of Anglo-Saxon occupation before 900, however, was found within the area of the camp, which may suggest that the *burh* was planted onto a pre-existing community.

JB

Sources Allcroft 1924, 218-21. Curwen and Curwen 1922, 2. Drewett, Rudling, and Gardiner 1988, 323-6. Hill and Rumble 1996, 195-6. Sutermeister 1976, 206 (quoted).

NGR TQ 039 089   *PDB* 2892

40 Burpham Church, 1789

S. H. Grimm

British Library, Add. MS. 5674, f. 33 [60]

Grimm's view from the north-east looks into the angle between the chancel on the left and the north transept on the right. The upper stage of the plain perpendicular west tower (of about 1400?) with a low pyramidal roof rises behind the north transept. The view today shows some small changes. The top of the staircase head on the tower has been bevelled, the east window of the north transept is new, and the lancet in the gable of the east end, probably coeval (*c.* 1200-20) with the lancets below it, has been rather crudely repaired. Was this window merely a ventilator for the roof space above the vaulted chancel, or did it look into a chamber designed for use? (Compare, for example, St Mary, Broadwater and, further afield, St John, Devizes.)

The 'deceptively demure' exterior masks an impressive interior, a small part of which Grimm

records as an inset. The early-12th-century south transept arch has roll-mouldings on the inner orders and chevron mouldings on the outer - Grimm records only the latter. Stebbing Shaw, visiting in 1790, felt that 'The inside gives a striking idea of cold, from the openness and bad repair of the roof.... The chancel is small but well proportioned, and quite of Gothic structure, rarely met with in a country place.'

Domesday Book records a church at Burpham, and some of the surviving fabric could date from this time. The existence of an earlier church at Burpham, though whether on this site is not known, is presupposed by the founding of an Anglo-Saxon *burh* here in about 900 (View 39).

JB

Sources Harrison and Leeney 1933, 111. Little 1985, 118-19. Nairn and Pevsner 1965, 120-2 (quoted). Roberts 1988, 154-7. Shaw 1790c, 206. Steer 1961a, 3-4.

NGR TQ 039 089   *PDB* 2894

41 Burton Park, 1780

S. H. Grimm

British Library, Add. MS. 5674, f. 50 [88]

In 1826 the house was largely destroyed by fire and the site cleared for a new one which survives today. The walls of the 18th-century kitchen gardens are still standing.   *JHF*

B urton Park is shown within a deer-park on Norden's map of 1595, and the house may have had an Elizabethan hall lying between two courtyards. But a fire led to the building of the east, garden, front seen here, dated to 1738 on the pediment. The client was Richard Biddulph, whose Roman Catholicism may have influenced his choice of architect, Giacomo Leoni (*c.* 1686-1746). Describing himself as a Venetian, Leoni was in England by 1715 and his principal claim to fame was publishing *The architecture of A. Palladio* (1715-20), with translations into both English and French by Nicholas Dubois, who in the 1720s was the architect of Stanmer House and Lewes Bridge.

At Burton Park he took up the style of Inigo Jones. 'All the details of the façade are Jonesian, as is also the general plainness. However, the façade derived a piquant effect from the rather high proportion of the ground floor. The main rooms were on the *piano nobile*, and consisted of a drawing room, and a saloon in the proportion of a cube and a half.' The lawns shown in this view, with a water feature to the right, are consistent with the gardens having been laid out when the house was rebuilt.

Sources Hudson 1975, quotation at 833. Hudson 1994a. Colvin 1995, 323-5, 608-11. Horsfield 1835, 2: 171-2.

NGR SU 968 175   *PDB* 2922

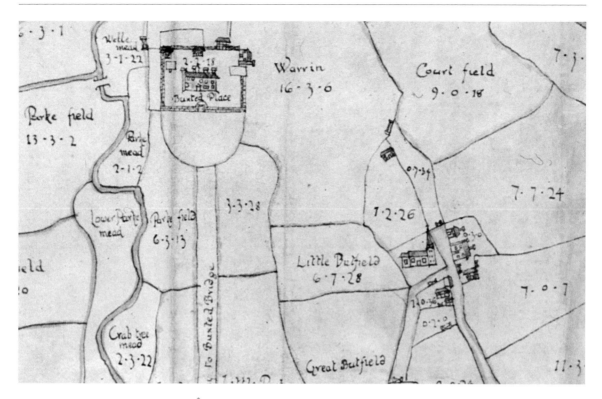

42 Buxted Place and village, 1654
after John Pattenden, c. 1930
East Sussex Record Office, AMS 6362

43 Buxted Place, 1798
Unknown surveyor of the Buxted estate
East Sussex Record Office, ACC 3712, f. 2

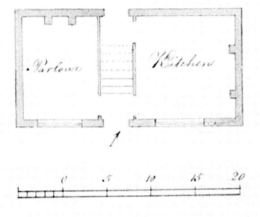

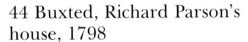

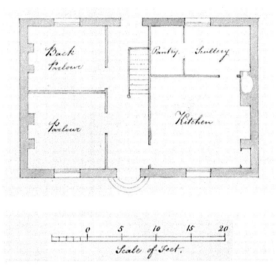

Scale of Feet.

44 Buxted, Richard Parson's house, 1798

Unknown surveyor of the Buxted estate
East Sussex Record Office, ACC 3712, f. 11 [C]

Buxted provides a fine example of a village's changing topography in which the church provides the one fixed point over the past 800 years; and, thanks to a survey of 1798, a rare instance of ordinary houses recorded in both view and plan. House platforms indicate that the medieval village was strung along a street of some 700 yards, west and north-east of the church, and that it was already much reduced by 1654 (View 42; south is at the top). If there was a manor house, it was probably in the same vicinity. Probably in the second half of the 16th century, the Wells family chose a new site some 450 yards south of the church and built a new house. It was assessed at 17 hearths for the 1662 Hearth Tax,

45 Buxted, the Revd Mr Evans's house, 1798

Unknown surveyor of the Buxted estate
East Sussex Record Office, ACC 3712, f. 10 [A]

Edward Benge being the occupier, and was described at about that date as: 'The mansion house [built] with stone, with two stables and a fair brewhouse, one of the stables built with hewn stone containing two fair granaries with two lodging chambers, with gardens and orchards containing four acres of ground encompassed with a fair stone wall.' That wall is not marked by the wall of today's derelict kitchen garden, for the house was immediately north-east of it. Rabbits may have been farmed in the Warren, adjacent to the house, for sport as well as meat and fur.

46 Buxted, the Tap House from the south, 1798

Unknown surveyor of the Buxted estate
East Sussex Record Office, ACC 3712, f. 11 [B]

47 Buxted, the Tap House from the north-west, 1798

Unknown surveyor of the Buxted estate
East Sussex Record Office, ACC 3712, f. 11 [A]

The map was made for Stephen Penkherst of Mayfield who in 1651 bought from the heirs of Edward Lindsey the estate of which Buxted Place was part. His heirs completed its sale to Thomas Medley (1645-1728) in 1724. At some date the Medleys commissioned a further house, on higher ground 250 yards north-west, closer to the church. On the strength of architect's plans reported in 1927 but now lost, Thomas is said to have built the present house in 1726. On the other hand, the avenue of limes, 730 yards long, terminating at the old house was planted around the 1720s; and in 1743 Jeremiah Milles observed that 'Mr Medley', his grandson Edward (1719-51), 'is building a fine seat at a place called Buxted' (Document 3). Maybe the deaths of successive heirs to the property in 1732, 1735 and 1741 meant that construction was repeatedly interrupted.

The north-east front of the house in 1798 appears in View 43: nine bays of three storeys over a basement, in red brick, probably with cornice, blocking-course and window surrounds in stone, the central portion of three bays projecting with a stone portico of six Doric columns. Grimm's view of the south-west front in 1785, in *Sussex views*, 34, showed the flanking service blocks. In 1999 two storeys of the main block, stuccoed, and the west service block survive as part of a hotel. An avenue of fir trees aligned north-east-north from the

house, skirting the east wall of the church yard, was planted in 1777.

Edward was succeeded in 1751 by his brother George on whose death in 1796 the property passed to his niece. Her husband Sir George Shuckburgh Evelyn, bt (1751-1804) commissioned the survey made in 1798 from which Views 43 to 49 are taken. Even though three documents (but not the map) survive from the survey, they give no clue as to the surveyor's identity, though his inability to transcribe the surname of Thomas Marchant, the county's leading surveyor, suggests that he was not from Sussex.

As opportunity allowed, the Medleys bought the freeholds around the church and in 1767 consolidated their ownership. In 1810 Sir George's daughter Julia (1790-1814) married Charles Jenkinson, later Lord Liverpool (1784-1851). They immediately put in hand alterations to the house and ordered the removal of all but one of the houses in 'Buxted Street', so as to enlarge the park and leave in isolation the church and the house immediately west of it (that in View 49).

The 1798 survey recorded ten tenants occupying houses in five plots around the church, at rents of £2 10s. or £3 a year. The two houses backing onto the north side of the churchyard do not appear on the 1654 map because their site was not then part of the estate; the other four plots

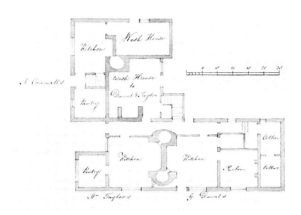

48 Buxted, the Tap House, plan, 1798

Unknown surveyor of the Buxted estate

East Sussex Record Office, ACC 3712, f. 11 [A+B]

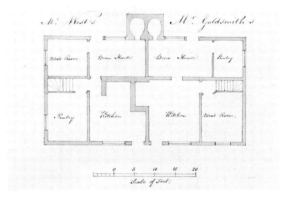

49 Buxted, Joshua Goldsmith's and widow West's house, 1798

Unknown surveyor of the Buxted estate

East Sussex Record Office, ACC 3712, f. 10

correspond to the four on the map. Richard Parson's 17th-century house at the east end had the stocks beside: View 44. It appears, in common with the other houses, to have had a Horsham stone roof. Adjoining was the house of the curate, Mr Evans, as the rector from 1787 to 1815, Matthias D'Oyly, preferred to live in Lewes: View 45. Rebuilt in the mid-18th century, this was the most recent house in the village and the only one in brick.

Facing these houses to the north was the L-shaped Tap House, presumably named after John Tapp, an occupier in 1724 - when it was called the Five Bells: Views 46, 47 and 48. Its core was 17th century or earlier, to which the gabled extension had been added. It had once been in single occupancy; indeed Taylor and Duval shared the wash house and staircase. Joshua Goldsmith and widow West occupied the 17th-century house facing the church spire, which had been divided to make two cottages: View 49. The gate to the left gave access to the grounds of Buxted Place. The survey also illustrates the two houses on the plots to the north, of similar style but smaller.   *JHF*

Sources Tebbutt 1972. Tebbutt 1975. Tebbutt 1979. Farrant 1989, 170-1. Hawkesbury 1904, fc. 108. Phillips 1986. MacDermott 1927. MacDermott 1929, 5. Hussey 1934. ESRO, HBR 1/1243; DYK 615; ACC 5179/9; AMS 3164-8; SAS/PN 37, 81, 84, 106 (calendar); DYK 805; BMW/C4/1 and 2; BMW/C8/1 and 2; TD/E 135.
NGR TQ 484 228 (Buxted Place); TQ 485 230 (church)
PDB 7201, 7704, 7721, 7715, 7719, 7720, 7825, 7716

50 Chailey, The Hooke, ?1787

S. H. Grimm

British Library, Add. MS. 5671, f. 45 [79]

In 1731 a Cheshire gentleman, William Poole (1696-1779), married a daughter of Henry Pelham of Lewes and the following year bought the Hooke, a small estate of 169 acres. By zealously supporting the Newcastle interest, he prospered and built up his lands to some 600 acres, of which he was a progressive farmer. He renovated the late-17th-century house in 1735 but his third marriage, to a Yorkshire heiress, enabled him partially to rebuild it between 1754 and 1756.

This view, from the east, shows the embellishment on the north front: two canted window bays crowned with battlements, reflecting the contemporary vogue for the 'Gothick'. The stables beyond may be of the same date. The Lewes mason John Morris was probably his builder. Bricks were made on the estate and tiles on Ditchling Common, the stone for facing was fetched from Scaynes Hill and the timber imported through Lewes. Slates roof the house today and possibly in the 1780s: they would likely have come from Northumberland. From 1753 the gardens were replanned. In 1757 a canal was filled in and a Chinese house which stood by it was moved across the frozen lake to an island specially constructed for it. A south wing by Decimus Burton added in 1838-44 was largely demolished in 1958.

Poole's cousin Francis had married another of Henry Pelham's daughters and established himself in Lewes; both his sons died without issue. William's son and heir the Revd Henry Poole (d. 1821) also inherited his second cousin's baronetcy but was last of the male line in Sussex. *JHF*

Sources Brent 1976. Colvin 1995, 199.

NGR TQ 383 185 *PDB* 2524

51 Chichester, prospect from the south-west, ?1736

Unknown artist, after Samuel Buck,
1736-8

West Sussex Record Office, F/PD 329 (detail)

Buck's view was taken from the fields outside the city walls which formed part of the Deanery Farm, now the Avenue de Chartres and playing fields for the Prebendal School. The Bishop's Palace, at the left, had undergone restoration in 1725-8, at the same time as the new Deanery, prominent to the right, replaced the one destroyed in the Civil War. The large inked-in building between them may be today's 4 Canon Lane which was restored in the 18th century and totally rebuilt in 1870. Or it may represent the old Treasury which fronted what is now St Richard's Walk. Badly damaged in the Civil War, it was restored in 1686 and demolished in 1834.

This view was published as an engraving in 1738 (Essay 2.2). The presumption is that Samuel Buck made the field sketches in 1736, while also sketching the Sussex antiquities published in 1737.

But the standard of draughtsmanship is superior to his: compare View 111. Therefore another artist was employed to work up his sketches, though he may have added the Deanery and the house to its left. All the people and animals appear in the foreground as engraved, but the drawing does not bear the marks of having been used to transfer an outline to the engraver's plate. A similar working draft is in Bodl., Gough maps 31, f. 2a.

Endorsements show that A. W. F. Fuller bought this picture from a dealer in 1940 for £5 5s.

AMcC and JHF

Sources VCHS, 3: 146-59. McCann 1985. Tatton-Brown 1994.

NGR SU 859 048 (cathedral)   *PDB* 1370

52 Chichester Cathedral, Bishop Stratford's tomb, 1781

S. H. Grimm

British Library, Add. MS. 5675, f. 60 [118]

A cleric in royal service who was twice Chancellor of the Exchequer, Robert Stratford was rewarded with the see of Chichester in 1337, dying in office in 1362. After the destruction of St Richard's shrine in 1538, all knowledge of its whereabouts was quickly lost, and at the time of Grimm's drawing, Stratford's chest tomb behind the choir stalls, facing the south transept, was thought to be St Richard's. The attribution to St Richard was then fairly recent, perhaps from the 1740s, as Jeremiah Milles in 1743 had noted Bishop Stratford's tomb in the 'south cross aisle' and made no mention of St Richard's. But William Clarke in 1753 referred to St Richard's monument, with some remains of its former adornment, on the north side of the paintings of the kings in the south aisle, behind the stalls. 'It was visited,' he said ambiguously, 'by the Papists ever since the Reformation on the 3d of April.'

This location for the shrine was questioned as early as 1810 but was generally rejected only 50 or more years later. In 1860 the sacellum was dismantled and the tomb removed, so both escaped damage from the spire's collapse in the following year. The tomb, which Edward Richardson had restored in 1843, was soon reinstated, but the sacellum not until 1904-7. The sacellum was originally put up by Stratford, perhaps as the pulpitum closing off the choir from the nave, before the Arundel Screen was erected in about 1470. See *Sussex views*, 37-9, for Grimm's drawings of the cathedral's nave and exterior.

TJMcC and JHF

Sources Hay 1804, 384, 413. Camden 1789, 1: 195. McCann 1975. Mosse 1933. Tummers 1994. VCHS, 3: 132. Nairn and Pevsner 1965, 159-60.

NGR SU 859 048   *PDB* 3049

53 Chichester, St Martin's Church, 1804

Henry Petrie

Sussex Archaeological Society, Sharpe Collection 78

Some of the fabric of St Martin's Church may date from as early as the 10th century. When it was demolished in 1906, the remains of a 13th-century wall painting were found, together with evidence of 16th or 17th-century rebuilding. The church was described in 1750 as having a small nave, chancel and north aisle, with two bells in a spire steeple. It was heavily restored in 1802-3 at the expense of Miss Martha Dear, a parishioner and daughter of a former Town Clerk. The restoration was very badly done. The old walls were hidden by a lath and plaster skin, fixed to the wall on battens. The 'pillars' were actually inadequate and re-used beams, encased in wooden panels. By the early 20th century, the building was in a poor state of repair, and no funds were available for the structural work which needed to be done. It was therefore partly demolished in 1906, leaving only the outer walls, which now contain a small public garden. *AMcC*

Sources VCHS, 3: 165. Hay 1804, 389. McCann and others 2000. Street 1907.

NGR SU 861 049   *PDB* 6395

54 Chichester, East Street Market, c. 1808

Joseph Francis Gilbert

West Sussex Record Office, Fuller PD 478

Colour plate IV

This picture was painted between 1792, when the city streets were paved and lit, and 1808, when the Cross was enclosed with railings - but much nearer the later date as the artist was born in 1791. The engraving by M. Duboag published in 1814 achieved considerable popularity and was reissued.

The beast-market was held fortnightly on Wednesdays, and sheep were penned in this part of East Street. Horses, cow, bullocks and other animals were tied up between Little London and East Walls. North Street was used for calves, more sheep, and pigs. Gilbert is looking west from the junction with North Pallant and St Martin's Street. His father occupied premises five properties to the east. On the right was a city property originally called the White Oven and occupied by James Knight, butcher. Beyond, with balcony and hanging sign, was the Swan, a principal inn. Burnt

down in 1819, it was rebuilt on the same site. The butcher's shop on the left was James Gates's, with the Chichester Bank next towards the Cross.

The town crier, to the left, also erected and took down the wattles for the market, and collected the market dues. He was John Baxter, a labourer. The bulky man in the centre foreground featured as 'A person well known in Chichester Market' in Thomas King's engraving published in 1808.

By 1871 the beast-market, which also extended into West Street, was causing major inconvenience to the inhabitants and was removed to a new site outside Eastgate.   *AMcC*

Sources Willis 1928. Steer 1963a. Morgan 1992. Stewart and Cutten 1987, 14. WSRO, Chichester Documentary Research Group record cards.

NGR SU 861 048   *PDB* 2242

55 East Chiltington, Stantons, ?1787

S. H. Grimm

British Library, Add. MS. 5672, f. 19 [33]

Stantons is located about 200 yards south of East Chiltington Church on the east side of the way to Novington. Grimm records from the north a five-bay house with a central two-storey porch and a central chimney stack shared by the two western bays. There is an external stack at each end, that to the east as part of the original five-bay house, that on the west as part of an extension. The house survives today as does the 17th-century barn across the road, glimpsed by Grimm at extreme right.

Nicholas Chaloner (d. 1566) acquired the manor of Chiltington alias Stantons in 1548. His younger son, Nicholas (d. 1612) built (or rebuilt) the main house in 1570, and had a son, Francis (d. 1624), who may have been responsible for the extension at the west end. The date of 1570 appears above the crest in a stone which Grimm detailed (right). With the older branch of the family living at Chapel House next to the church, Stantons continued as the home of the younger branch until 1714 when Nicholas Chaloner, great-grandson of Francis, sold it to Michael Marten, whose family owned it when Grimm visited.

With Wootton and Chapel farms, Stantons was one of the major properties in the parish, and its farmer doubtless was a well-known figure in the locality. For much of the 19th century, however, it was better known for 'the mistress of Stantons Farm', Susannah Hooker, who married the widowed tenant William Stacey in 1832. When she died aged 80 in 1893, her reputation as a wise woman had spread well beyond the confines of the parish.

JB

Sources Davey 1991, 55-6. VCHS, 7: 99-100. Woodward 1939, 116-25.

NGR TQ 371 149   *PDB* 2670

Chithurst place

56 Chithurst Manor, 1791

S. H. Grimm

British Library, Add. MS. 5678, f. 3 [6]

When Grimm drew 'Chithurst Place' from the south-east, the house was recognisable as a fine example of a small manor house, perhaps for yeomanry rather than gentry – very characteristic of north-west Sussex. The south wing at the left of the picture must have formed the original hall house acquired by Peter Bettsworth of Fyning in 1579; and timber and plaster work (and jettied first floor) are clearly discernible. In the 17th century his descendants added the substantial north wing, using local sandstone, and provided the Horsham stone roof.

The Bettsworths sold in 1758 to the Peacheys, Sir James being the owner in 1791. The estate was tenanted and the house eventually descended into cottages. But it was sensitively restored after World War I and a number of windows which had been blocked in Grimm's time were reopened, while tile

hanging was added to the gable ends. It seems at this time to have acquired the name of Chithurst Abbey, perhaps embroidering on the probability that the manor at one time formed part of Durford Abbey's estate, but it is now simply Chithurst Manor.

The house stands to the west of Chithurst church, of which Grimm's view, with the house partly hidden behind by trees, is in *Sussex views*, 46.

PMW

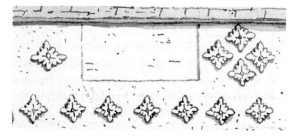

Sources Dallaway 1815, 2: 225-6. Nairn and Pevsner 1965, 187. VCHS, 2: 388, 4: 4-5. Wolseley 1932. WSRO, MP 4281, Wealden Buildings Study Group report, 1997.

NGR SU 842 231   *PDB* 3111

57 Clapham, Michelgrove, 1788

S. H. Grimm

British Library, Add. MS. 5674, f. 1 [1]

The estates of the Michelgrove family came to the Shelley family in 1474. As recorded above the arcade, William Shelley rebuilt the existing house in 1534. The Tudor building was in brick, quadrangular with an open internal courtyard and polygonal towers at the outer angles. An inventory of 1585 names 53 rooms. The south façade, shown here, had a three-bay Doric or Tuscan arcade in stone.

Grimm's view also shows the large alterations made in about 1769. The building was cased in cream-coloured brick, and the internal courtyard was converted into a hall 53 feet by 27, and 40 feet high, rising above the rest of the building, with four square towers at its corners. It was demolished soon after 1827.

James Lambert's view in 1780 showed, east of the house, the stables with a Mannerist south façade decorated with volutes, and grooms leading horses, for which the Shelleys were then famed. The stables were demolished in about 1813.

The family remained faithful to Catholicism until the 4th baronet, Sir John Shelley (1692-1771),

conformed in 1716. He improved the family fortunes further by marrying secondly the sister of the Duke of Newcastle in 1727; he immediately entered the Commons as MP for Arundel and later for Lewes. If the date of 1769 is accurate, the alterations were probably put in hand by his son and heir, John (1730?-83), for whom his uncle secured the lucrative sinecures of keeper of the records in the Tower and clerk of the pipe in the Exchequer in 1755 and 1758.   *JHF*

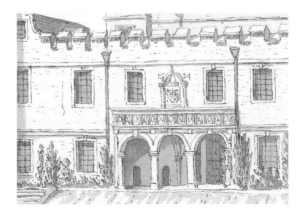

Sources VCHS, 6 (1): 13-14. Whitley 1912. Sedgwick 1970, 2: 419-20. Farrant 1997a, 259. Evans 1814, 2: 46.

NGR TQ 081 083   *PDB* 2836

58 Compton, Littlegreen, 1793

Humphry Repton

West Sussex Record Office, Add. MS. 520, pl. iv
Colour plate V

When Thomas Peckham Phipps inherited in 1793 the small estate of Littlegreen, centred on an unpretentious farmhouse with substantial outbuildings, he must have decided to raise its status. He therefore commissioned Humphry Repton (1752-1818) who produced his report in the form of one of his famous 'Red Books'.

The estate abutted on a far grander neighbour, Uppark, and Repton was at pains to propose a character of 'simplicity and elegance' and to prevent it from being mistaken for 'a farmhouse or steward's residence belonging to the other [i.e. Uppark]'. Using his personal style of 'before' and 'after' views, Repton demonstrated how to achieve 'Gentlemanlike independence'. He proposed, first, that the house should be 'so embosomed by ... large trees that the whole will never be seen from the same point of view, and will appear larger'; and

secondly, that it should be surrounded by lawn or parkland.

Repton's solution necessitated the complete demolition of the original house and outbuildings, and construction of a new house about 50 yards to the north. By 1815 Dallaway could report that the house had been rebuilt 'in a style of modern accommodation and improvement', and the landscaping of the park is recorded on an estate map of 1818. The house, now a school, was substantially revamped by the Reckitt family in the 1920s, when it was provided with an elaborate Tudorbethan interior. It is therefore difficult to establish how much of Thomas Peckham Phipps's building survives, though the exterior appears largely unaltered.

Repton had an extensive list of clients in Sussex. He prepared surviving Red Books for, in chronological order: Phipps at Littlegreen 1793, Francis Newbery at Heathfield Park 1794 (View 108), Earl Camden at Bayham Abbey 1800, Lord George Cavendish at Compton Place 1803 (View 74), the Prince of Wales at Brighton 1805 (having advised since 1797), Lord Whitworth at Stonelands in Buckhurst 1805, John Fuller at Rose Hill in

59 Compton, Littlegreen, proposed improvements, 1793

Humphry Repton

West Sussex Record Office, Add. MS. 520, pl. vi

Brightling 1806 (View 29) and Sir Harry
Fetherstonhaugh at Uppark 1810. There is good
evidence that he advised Lord Sheffield at
Sheffield Park 1789, Richard Walker at
Michelgrove *c*. 1800 (View 57) and Charles Abbot
at Kidbrooke Park 1806-9 (View 93); and slighter
evidence for his advising an unnamed client in
Balcombe before 1807, Captain Peyton at
Wakehurst in Ardingly before 1808, Mrs Board at
Paxhill Park before 1809 (View 132) and Thomas
Erskine at Buchan Hill in Lower Beeding 1812.
Even a Red Book, however, is insufficient evidence
that the landscaping recommended was carried out
in whole or part.   *PMW and JHF*

Sources Dallaway 1815, 2: 179. WSRO, Add. MS. 2066, estate map,
1818. Daniels 1999, 192, 261, 268.

NGR SU 771 157   *PDB* 7810, 7818

60 Cowfold, Oakendene Park, 1788

S. H. Grimm

British Library, Add. MS. 5673, f. 3 [4]

The name of this house describes its original setting - a swine pasture in woodland - and prominent local residents from the 13th century took it as a surname and later as a forename. By the end of the 16th century they had been superseded by the Agate family, and subsequently by Gratwicks and Lintotts; all three had considerable property interests in the neighbourhood.

The A272 road now lies to the north of the house, and very little is apparent of the timber-framed, tile-hung and gabled range to the left of the picture from the south-east. The roof line indicates that it was built in several phases, but the range was completely encased and re-roofed, probably in the early 19th century. It is clear from a mortgage that the house had come to the Lintott family by 1654, and it was John, who married Susannah Dennett in 1742, who was responsible

for the east-facing range to the right which still stands: the stone high on the chimney reads '1744'. The diminutive building to the left, the edging to the pond and the finial in the shrubs to the right suggest attention to the gardens, while what appear to be early lightning conductors top the chimneys. His youngest son, John Henry, who was in occupation in 1788, married Philadelphia Leppard in 1791, and when he died in 1804 the house passed away from the family. It subsequently belonged to the Nortons of Portslade, and was leased for several decades.   *AFH*

Sources VCHS, 6 (3): 181. Deeds in private hands.

NGR TQ 227 226   *PDB 2715*

61 Cuckfield, the King's Head Inn, *c.* 1790

John Nixon

sold at Sotheby's, London, 10 April 1980

Cuckfield owed its coaching trade to the turnpike road between London and Brighton on which a daily service operated from 1784 and which was the predominant route from 1790. A lady is descending from a coach at the centre of the picture. James Lintott, whose name is on the sign at the left, died around the turn of 1795/6, and Nixon's pictures of Brighton dated before then come from 1787, 1791 and 1793. Nixon's vantage point was outside today's 18 High Street, at the corner of Ockenden Lane, looking south to the parish church. The site of the King's Head Inn has long since been redeveloped, but the tile-hung house with carved barge board, to the left, is still standing as The Sanctuary. See View 35 for more on Nixon. Francis Grose and William Burrell stayed at the King's Head on their tour in May 1777 (Document 5).

Thomas Rowlandson also sketched in Cuckfield while on the road. His watercolour, 'Cuckfield, Sussex, at fair time', is taken from about the same spot and is dated 1789. As a finished picture worked up from sketches, it is inaccurate topographically.

JHF

Sources Farrant 1986, 87-8. ESRO, WA 67/225. Coombs 1978, 156, for Rowlandson's view in the Walker Art Gallery, Liverpool, also published in aquatint, 1790.

NGR TQ 303 245   *PDB* 4889

62 Cuckfield, Bridge House, 1787

S. H. Grimm

British Library, Add. MS. 5672, f. 34 [60]

Several generations of Garstons were yeomen of Bridge Farm, near Hammermill Bridge, a mile north of Slough Green. On John Garston's death in 1725 it passed to his daughter who in 1720 had married Thomas Grainger, a London embroiderer. Grainger enlarged the farm, buying at least three copyholds of the manor of Cuckfield amounting to 116 acres in 1725-31. Most likely it was he who refronted the old house in brick, carrying the west elevation up above the eaves and half-hiding the dormer windows, and added the wing at the right. Thomas was succeeded in 1770 by his eldest son John Grainger esq., d. 1797. This house was demolished by 1875 and replaced on a site to the east; as further modified the replacement is now called The Old Kennels.

This view provides a cautionary tale. Grimm has titled it, 'Mr Granger's'. Probably now hidden on the back is a fuller version used by Burrell's clerk to enter on the contents page: 'Mr Granger's near Slaugham Green'. On the strength of that the house shown here has been identified as the core of Ashfold Lodge in Slaugham parish which was rebuilt to George Devey's designs in 1875-84 and demolished in 1956 - and as the house from which Lord Nelson left for the Battle of Trafalgar in 1805. But the clerk, not knowing minor place names, probably read Slough for nearby Slaugham. And Nelson's brother-in-law, George Matcham, first viewed and immediately bought Ashfold on 6 August 1806, perhaps on the strength of the grants paid four days earlier by a grateful Government to the grieving Nelson family.

JHF and CHCW

Sources Dengate 1929, 89. Gérin 1970, 133-4. Allibone 1991, 95-6, 170. OS 1:2500, 1st edn. ESRO, ACC 2953; AMS 6008/2/6. WSRO, Add. MSS 30721-30725, John Grainger's diaries 1787-97; SAS/B 116-125. PRO, PROB 11/611 204.

NGR TQ 282 276   *PDB* 2698

63 Dallington, Herrings, 1784

S. H. Grimm

British Library, Add. MS. 5670, f. 67 [123]

Colour plate VI

Herrings lay on the boundary between
Ashburnham and Dallington, and the first
house on the site was built between the mid-1550s
and 1587. In that year it was owned by John
Glydd, but the house shown by Grimm probably
dates from about half a century later. Between
1716 and his death in 1741 it was owned by Robert
Burnett, Steward of the Household to the Duke of
Newcastle and a principal agent in Sussex of the
all-powerful Pelham family, with whom the Duke of
Richmond and Henry Pelham dined when
canvassing in 1740.

Grimm shows the house from the west in
sombre mood; the funeral hatchment of Burnett's
nephew Robert Randoll of Herrings and Nassau
Street, Westminster, who had been buried at
Dallington on 15 July 1783, still hangs from the
porch-turret a year later as a warning to visitors of
the owner's death. Grimm shows his achievement
of arms, impaled with those of his wife Margaretta
Lane, as an inset. Margaretta died childless in 1791
and the entail created by Burnett's will carried the
estate to his great-nephew Patrick George
Crawfurd of the Paymaster General's office. In
1792 it consisted of a mansion house 'suitable for a
large family', a coach-house and detached stabling
for twenty horses, a hop-oast and other buildings.
It was sold to the Ashburnham estate in 1801 and
the house pulled down between 1805 and 1807.
The stable was converted into a farmhouse for the
tenant of the farmland and the materials sold off –
the vicar of Dallington bought some of the oak
floorboards to improve his parsonage.   *CHCW*

Sources Martin 1991, P13/25. Kelch 1974, 23. McCann 1984, 46.
WSRO, Ep II/5/4, ff. 120-3. ESRO, PAR 302 1/1/2; ASH 2364-6,
L1195-1261; AMS 5702. BL, Add. MS. 39495.

NGR TQ 667 180   *PDB* 2410

64 West Dean, Chilgrove House, 1782

S. H. Grimm

British Library, Add. MS. 5675, f. 33 [58]

Chilgrove House was the home of the Woods family of whom Gilbert White was an occasional guest. The house, here viewed from the south-east, seems to be of two phases, with the three gabled bays on the east side having rounded windows on the ground floor, perhaps of the early 16th century, while the two western gabled bays have mullioned windows, perhaps half a century later.

A feature of the picture is the proximity of barns and outbuildings to the house itself, and of the farmhouse shown in the foreground. These reflect the family's agricultural interests which, with an enthusiasm for meteorology, are well documented in family papers (copies at WSRO).

The house was demolished in 1853. The present house, in Elizabethan style of brick and flint with a tiled roof, was built on the site for Sir John Wickens in the 1860s, and has recently been converted into apartments. *TJMcC*

Sources WSRO, MP 1477-1490, SP 566 and 568.

NGR SU 834 144 *PDB* 2987

65 West Dean House, 1781

S. H. Grimm

British Library, Add. MS. 5675, f. 35 [61]

Built in 1622 by John Lewkenor as Canon House, the manor house of West Dean Canons, West Dean House was acquired by the Peachey family through marriage in 1745. Groom of the Bedchamber to the Prince of Wales from 1751, and Master of the Robes on his accession as King George III in 1760, Sir James Peachey inherited West Dean from his brother in 1765 and took it as his residence. He was created Baron Selsey in 1794.

The Jacobean house was probably built of flint with some stone facing (part can still be seen at the western end of the north front). The line of the south façade in Grimm's view corresponds to that on a block plan of 1673, but by 1781 the house had been improved, perhaps in the early 18th century. A cornice has been added to the upper storey, the entrance turret heightened almost to hide the gable and the entire frontage refenestrated. The 1673 plan shows outbuildings rather incongruously placed forward and east of the house, around a formal garden. These, along with the parterres at the west side, had by 1781 been replaced by more informal tree planting.

In 1804 Lord Selsey commissioned James Wyatt to rebuild and enlarge the mansion house. This work was incomplete on Selsey's death in 1808 and was finished for his son by Francis Sandys. When William James acquired the West Dean estate in 1891, he had the house altered and greatly extended by Sir Ernest George and Harold Peto.

TJMcC and JHF

Sources Simon 1981. Colvin 1995, 849, 1119; also 235. WSRO, West Dean MS. 3154.

NGR SU 862 126   *PDB* 2992

66 Denton Church and parsonage, ?1777

Francis Grose

British Library, K. Top. 42.42

Grose's view is taken from the rectory grounds looking south towards St Leonard's Church, Denton, with the parsonage in the right foreground. Drawings by the Lamberts in 1767 and 1782 include one from the west.

About 10 yards to the north-north-west of the west end of the church survives a small amount of ruinous flint wall with stone quoins and a window opening of about 1300, but it is not clear how this relates to the parsonage recorded by Grose and Lambert. They drew a range of buildings with a central block constructed of stone in chequerwork pattern and exhibiting a window of probably 1450-1500 and a doorway later than about 1200. Lambert's 1767 drawing records a window and doorway of similar respective styles in the west wall of the south part; Grose shows a chimney on its east side and a detached gable end at the south-east corner. The weatherboarded part to the north may be the stable described in 1724 as in good repair. The whole is roofed with thatch in poor condition.

The origin of the parsonage is not known, though in 1341 the rector 'has a messuage newly endowed with a curtilage and garden worth p.a. 10s.' - possibly the parsonage was rebuilt at this time. In 1724 there is 'a small matter wanting to the mansion [rectory] house', and a new rectory was built 'on the foundations of an older building' in about 1817.

The Early-English church was restored in 1865, and a vestry was added to the north side in about 1935.

JB

Sources BL Add. MS. 5676, f. 78 [118], [119]. ESRO, PAR 306/2/1 (quoted). Ford 1994, 166 (quoted). Lower 1857a, 96 (quoted). Nairn and Pevsner 1965, 480.

NGR TQ 455 026   *PDB* 49

67 Ditchling Church, 1787

S. H. Grimm

British Library, Add. MS. 5672, f. 14 [25]

In 1724 the church was reported in good repair though the south chancel wanted paving. In 1748 the local vestry minuted that money collected from the charity lands in the parish should be applied to the church's repair. The fabric of the building as shown by Grimm in 1787 appears to be in decent repair, though the blocked windows of the chancel suggest that this part of the church was not used for liturgical purposes.

Grimm's view from the north-east shows three lancets of about 1260-70 equally spaced in the north wall of the chancel, with contemporary tower and north transept. Views of 1802 and 1850, however, show a larger space, just as there is today, between the centre and the westernmost lancets than between the centre and easternmost. The restoration of 1863 destroyed some of the features shown by Grimm. The roof over the stairwell from the north transept to the belfry in the tower and the bell-ringers' door disappeared with the rebuilding of the north transept. Because the singing gallery was dismantled, the external flight of steps and door leading directly to it (and just visible at the right of the picture) were removed in the rebuilding of the north wall of the nave.

The church occupies a prominent site within the village, and the raised nature of the site is indicated by the level of the roof of a house at the extreme right of the view.   *JB*

Sources Cheal 1901, 62, 66. Ford 1994, 129. VCHS, 7: 106-7. ESRO, PAR 308/12/1/2, f. 15. SAS, Sharp Coll. 112; drawings by W. T. Quartermain (East Sussex), 78.

NGR TQ 325 152   *PDB* 2660

RUINS OF DURRINGTON CHAPEL. 1778.

68 Durrington chapel, 1778

James Lambert junior
British Library, Add. MS. 5677, f. 69 [103]

Throughout the Middle Ages and into the 17th century there was a two-cell chapel at Durrington which, like Heene (View 109), was dependent on West Tarring. A new chancel (and perhaps a nave) was built in 1257, at which time the dedication was changed from St Nicholas to St Thomas Becket. Lambert's view appears to be taken from the north-east, and shows an entirely ruined chancel, a round-headed chancel arch (presumably *in situ* by about 1200 and, therefore, surviving the rebuilding), and a nave beyond with walls rising to eaves level or thereabouts.

Local inhabitants claimed in 1677 that the chapel had been in decay for 26 years, and that 'the ruins thereof were chiefly occasioned by soldiers in the time of the late Wars' as a result of a bitter dispute with their Royalist vicar, William Stanley. In 1680 the inhabitants were excused rebuilding the chapel, and given leave to attend West Tarring Church instead; at the same time, they took materials from the chapel to prevent their further decay. Notwithstanding the local tradition of continuing use for certain services, it is likely that the chapel fell quickly into disrepair. There is no evidence of use in a visitation return of West Tarring parish in 1720, and in 1766 it was reported that 'the chapel has long been fallen to decay [and] I believe nobody now living can remember its being made use of ....'

Some of the ruined walling was incorporated into the new church of St Symphorian, dedicated in 1915.   *JB*

Sources Elleray 1977, pl. 171-2. Fenton 1892, 154-9. Ford 1994, 228. Macray 1882, 135. Springett 1898, 75-6. VCHS, 6 (1): 84-5. Welch 1961, 225-6 (quoted). ESRO, ACC 3632, 1 and 2 July 1766 (quoted).

NGR TQ 118 053   *PDB* 4490

69 Easebourne Priory, 1780

S. H. Grimm

British Library, Add. MS. 5675, f. 8 [14]

The Priory of Easebourne was founded for a prioress and ten Augustinian nuns by one of the de Bohun family of Midhurst in the 13th century, the original endowment including the church of Easebourne. It was suppressed in 1536. *Sussex views*, 52, shows the east front. This drawing shows the remains of the frater or refectory in the south range of buildings, opposite to the church. The frater was a large room (60 feet by 21 feet), entered by a staircase at the east, lit on the west by a three-light window, with cellarage in two large rooms underneath. The west range contained a pantry and buttery communicating via a hatchway with the kitchen now destroyed. It was probably in this room that Queen Elizabeth was entertained on 18 August 1591. In the 17th century a pigeon loft was constructed, large enough to hold one thousand pigeons, by building brick partitions at the east end. By 1780 all the windows were blocked, and the large doorway shown in the drawing enabled the building to be used as a barn. In 1912 the windows were unblocked, the upper floor was turned into a parish room, the pigeon loft into a lobby, and the lower floor into smaller rooms.

TJMcC

Sources Hope 1919. Field 1977.

NGR SU 895 225

PDB 2945

70 Easebourne, Cowdray House, 1781

S. H. Grimm, after John Keyse Sherwin

British Library, Add. MS. 5675, f. 11 [17]

Sir John de Bohun had moved to this site from St Ann's Hill in about 1280 (View 141). Sir David Owen married the Bohun heiress and, probably demolishing the Bohun house, in the 1520s built the east and north ranges, and the west range as far as the gatehouse. Sir William Fitzwilliam completed the quadrilateral plan in the 1530s. Cowdray House remained virtually unchanged until gutted by fire in 1793. By good chance, the Society of Antiquaries had commissioned Grimm in 1786 to copy the Tudor paintings (described in Document 3). Those pictures and the ones made for Burrell are the best surviving record: *Sussex views*, 110-14.

This drawing shows the west range. In the three-storied gatehouse, the double door of oak is surmounted by a white marble slab with the arms of Anthony Browne, 1st Viscount Montague, above that by an 18th-century window of eighteen panes

on top of which is a white marble lunette with splayed eagle crest, and finally over the string course by a high battled parapet with a clock. The flanking three-storied turrets with a parapet at the top are octagonal in plan and the chambers are lit by cross-shaped oillets and small chamfered window-openings, while those behind are slightly taller and semi-octagonal in shape. Either side of the gatehouse are two stories of chambers ending with three-storied blocks with bay windows. Since the fire the ruins have remained open to the elements.

Stabilised in 1908, much of the gatehouse walls, along with the frame of the south range, are standing.

John Keyse Sherwin (1751?-90) was working as a labourer in East Dean when his employer, William Mitford, recognised his artistic talent. He rose to be engraver to both the King and the Prince of Wales, but reckless spending contributed to an early death in poverty.   *TJMcC and JHF*

Sources Hope 1919, 90-2. Roundell 1884. DNB 1998.

NGR SU 891 217   *PDB* 2948

71 Easebourne, Hollest, 1790

S. H. Grimm

British Library, Add. MS. 5675, f. 1 [2]

Hollest was described by James Dallaway in
1815 as 'a good mansion house and estate'. It
had been acquired by the Riggs family in the mid-
17th century. In 1790, it was owned by Henry
Riggs, and occupied by Edward Hide, a farmer, as
his tenant. Grimm's view appears to be taken from
the Easebourne road, as a map of 1784 shows gates
and a courtyard as seen here. The property was
acquired in 1799 by Lord Robert Spencer, from
whom it came to the Ponsonbys. By 1847, the
property was in decline, and the farmer, William
Merritt, did not live there. The buildings around
the farm yard were inhabited by labourers and
paupers. The 1851 census recorded the fact that a
house was being built at Hollist Buildings, and by
1861, William Merritt, farmer of 94 acres, was
living there with his family. The property which
was the Hollest farm house and yard still exists, but
has been extensively altered in recent times to
form several residences.   *AMcC*

Sources Dallaway 1815, 2: 239-40. WSRO, Land Tax returns;
TD/W45; Cowdray MS. 1679; Add. MS. 15245.

NGR SU 881 229   *PDB* 2932

72 Eastbourne, Sea Houses, 1785

S. H. Grimm

British Library, Add. MS. 5671, f. 75 [145]

So called by 1368, 'Sea Houses' owed its existence to fishermen, fowlers on the levels, the occasional cargo, a quarry for Greensand (though long since worked out by the 18th century) and travellers coming off the Downs to follow the shore. 'A small public house' existed in 1717, and Jeremiah Milles noticed several when passing by in 1743 (Document 3).

Grimm visited as Eastbourne was developing as a seaside resort. He took this view from the Round House, immediately north of the landward end of today's pier. Formerly the base of a horizontal mill, it had been remodelled in 1769 into two lodgings. These were the first facilities at the beach for visitors during the season, although people had been bathing and drinking sea water there by 1754. He looked north-east over the field in which

Thomas Willard's workmen had found the Roman bath in 1712 (View 73). At the seaward edge of the field, Willard's great-nephew, also Thomas (1729-94), built for himself the house on the right. It was 'lately erected' at his death, but not mentioned in a transaction of 1735, and by 1811 was called The Field House.

The buildings beyond were outside the field, on land leased from the manorial waste; the box-shaped one may be that referred to as 'Mrs Becket's house' in 1800. Grimm's companion view (*Sussex views*, 54) was taken on the beach from the opposite end of that row of buildings, showing the Ship Inn kept by Mr Webb. This view is not consistent with *Sussex views*, 55, which looks like another artist's work.

The Roman pavement and bath were discovered and excavated in 1712 and 1716 (Essay 2.1). They lay to the rear of the houses on the east side of Cavendish Place, south of Seaside Road. Remains of a villa at the cliff edge about 100 yards away were noted by Burrell in 1781 and sketched by W. H. Brooke in 1850. This drawing was presumably made by a draughtsman from Tabor's

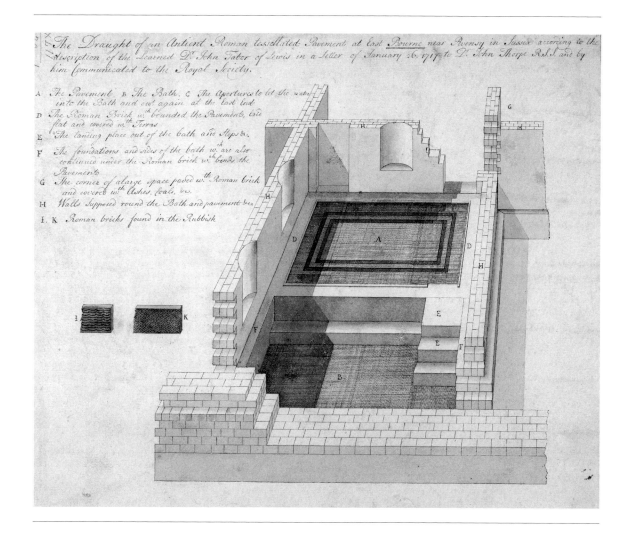

The Draught of an Antient Roman tessellated Pavement at East *Bourne* near *Pevensy* in *Sussex* according to the Description of the Learned Dr. *John Tabor* of *Lewis* in a Letter of January 26. 1717 to Dr. *John Thorpe* R.S.S. and by him Communicated to the Royal Society.

A The Pavement. B The Bath. C The Apertures to let the water into the Bath and out again at the East End.

D The Roman Brick wᶜʰ bounded the Pavements, laie flat and covered wᵗʰ Terras

E The Landing place out of the bath and Steps &c.

F The foundations and sides of the bath wᶜʰ are also continued under the Roman brick wᶜʰ bounds the Pavements

G The corner of a large space paved wᵗʰ Roman brick and covered wᵗʰ Ashes, Coals, &c.

H Walls supposed round the Bath and pavement &c.

I. K Roman bricks found in the Rubbish

73 Eastbourne, the Roman pavement and bath, 1717

Unknown artist, after John Tabor

British Library, K Top 42.39.1

Colour plate VII

field sketches. It was engraved for Tabor's article, with some amendments, particularly to omit the conjectural walls. South is at the top; the pavement of white and brown tesserae (marked 'A') was 17 feet 4 inches by 11 feet.   *JHF*

Sources Mawer and Stenton 1929-30, 2: 427. Stevens 1982, 134-6. Farrant 1993b. Stevens and Gilbert 1973. Budgen 1912, 252-7; pl. XXXIX(a). Milton 1997. WSRO, Cap. II/15A/1. ESRO, GIL 3/44/22. *NGR* TV 617 989   *PDB* 2591, 5453

74 Eastbourne, Compton Place, 1783

S. H. Grimm

British Library, Add. MS. 5671, f. 77 [149]

In 1550 James Burton built a timber-framed hall house with a cross-wing; it had eight rooms and four hearths on the ground floor. By 1625 it had been absorbed into a north-facing, two-storeyed house with an H plan. Perhaps it was William Wilson who, after his purchase in 1644, formed a courtyard house by adding a south range with seven bays across three storeys, and a four-storey porch.

Spencer Compton, Speaker of the Commons and later Earl of Wilmington (1672/3-1743), tenanted 'Bourne Place' from 1717 and bought it in 1724. He retained Colen Campbell in 1726-9 to rebuilt the south façade (shown here) with eleven bays and two storeys faced with ashlar, and to remodel the interior, filling in the courtyard. Amongst the craftsmen employed were James Richards, the King's Master Carver, and Charles Stanley, responsible for 'a ceiling gloriously overdecorated' in the King's Room. But for a visitor in 1735 the old structure yielded ill-proportioned rooms: 'Lord Wilmington has laid out a great sum of money about an old house to inform posterity how much he wants taste: there is a profuseness of gilding and carved work in rooms you can scarce stand right up in.' Jeremiah Milles however admired the setting in 1743 (Document 3).

In 1781, with Lady Elizabeth Compton's marriage to Lord George Cavendish imminent, James Wyatt planned large extensions. These were not executed, but the north front (which Sophia Burrell had drawn shortly before) was remodelled, the whole exterior was stuccoed and some internal refurbishment was undertaken. This was the house as Grimm drew it. In 1808 John Harvey completed the extensive domestic offices and stables added to the east at a cost of nearly £30,000. A language school today leases the house.

JB and JHF

Sources Budgen 1912, 4-5, 37-8. Colvin 1995, 471. Hussey 1965, 87-96. Nairn and Pevsner 1965, 485 (quoted). Wolseley 1928, 42, 46. ESRO, SAS/CP 183, 290-300, 354; SRL 21/4; ACC 3729; AMS 5937 (quoted). SAS, Budgen papers 96/42-5; 117/ 25v-26; 119/ 11-12, 42-3, 47-8. Eastbourne Reference Library, Burrell's copy of *A compleat history of Sussex*, 518-19.

NGR TV 603 985   *PDB* 2594

75 Eastdean, Dipperay's, 1785

S. H. Grimm.

British Library, Add. MS. 5671, f. 79 [152] (detail)

Grimm's view from the east of 'Mr Dipperay's house' could be the pictorial model for a description of the village in a contemporary local guidebook - '...the village of East Dean looks very pretty at a distance, particularly the house and grounds of Mr Dippery.'

James Dippery (1703-91) was a local boy making good. His father (1662/3-1721) became tenant of Birling Manor Farm in 1706, but James, who began to purchase property in Eastdean in 1732, became mortgagee of Birling in 1752 and bought it outright in 1763. He was the owner-occupier until 1769, when he leased the farm to his nephew, Nicholas Willard. He probably then built the house shown here, now called Dipperay's, for in 1786 he referred to 'the new built messuage … wherein I now live', and in 1790 it was described as 'a good modern house near the Green'. The two

full-height bows to be seen today are not shown by Grimm in 1785, and are probably additions made by about 1800. Challen confused this house with 'Underhill', another of James's properties located to the south of the village on the northern flank of Went Hill. By 1837 all the Dippery estate in Eastdean had been acquired by the Davies-Gilbert family of Eastbourne and Trelissick, Cornwall.   *JB*

Sources Royer 1787, 29-30 (quoted). Shaw 1790a, 378 (quoted). Challen 1948/9, 86, 109. ESRO, ELT/East Dean; GIL 1/33/37-54, 56; GIL 1/80/1 (quoted), 4.

NGR TV 556 978   *PDB* 2597

76 Edburton Church and village, *c.* 1794

Hendrick de Cort

West Sussex Record Office, M/PD 258

Hendrick Josef Frans de Cort (1742-1810) studied in Antwerp and worked there, apart for a few years in Paris, until about 1790 when he settled in London for the rest of his life. He built up a sound reputation for views of country houses, castles, cathedrals, and other antiquities. Herrmann describes his work as more reminiscent of his 17th-century than his 18th-century predecessors, and examples of his finished pictures as 'typical of de Cort's precise and lifeless manner, which must certainly have appealed to the more antiquarian-minded lovers of the picturesque.'

On the travels which his clients' commissions necessitated, de Cort made numerous wash drawings. That 32 drawings descended in the Mitford archive does not, however, prove that he worked for the family. They may have been acquired from his studio collection after his death. None is a finished piece of work and, although all of Sussex, none is of a scene clearly connected with the Mitfords. That the one Sussex view he exhibited at the Royal Academy or the British Institution, in 1801, was of a famous oak in Burton Park, makes the Biddulph family a more likely client (View 41). Four of the drawings are dated: 1792, 1792, 1793 and 1799.

Three views of Edburton are reproduced here. With neither gentry influence within the parish nor a good road to connect it with the outside world, an early-18th century rector described Edburton as 'a poor remote place' so that he was

77 Edburton, Shepherd and Dog Inn at Fulking, *c.* 1794

Hendrick de Cort

West Sussex Record Office, M/PD 260

'as it were buried alive'. The distant view of the village looks east and is taken from a point between Truleigh Manor Farm and the medieval parish church of St Andrew. The house in the right foreground may be September Cottage, while amongst the buildings immediately to the right of the church is Michaelmas Cottage - both surviving today as examples of small timber-framed 16th-century cottages with 17th-century additions.

The church was built on the lower slopes of Edburton Hill, and overlooks Edburton spring to the west (towards the view point), which rises about 200 yards south-west and runs into the Adur Levels south of Henfield. It was the ecclesiastical centre of an administratively divided parish. For centuries the eastern part of the parish, including Fulking, was in Lewes rape and Poynings hundred, and the remainder, including the church, was in Bramber rape and Burbeach hundred. In 1889 the

two parts were placed in different counties but were re-united in West Sussex in 1974.

The Shepherd and Dog Inn at Fulking looks markedly different today with alterations and enlargements at both ends, but de Cort's chimney, left door and some windows, though all probably rebuilt, are in position today. The house on the left of the view has not survived, and may have been replaced, perhaps in about 1820, by Old Bakery Cottage which stands today in what appears to be the front part of the house plot.

The hanging sign shows that it was an inn or alehouse in the 1790s; it is not, though, listed in a national survey compiled in 1686. The name, which was certainly in place by 1825, reflects the importance which sheep have played in the local economy for centuries. Not only were there large flocks on the Downs above but, during the early-19th century at least, sheep from a much wider area were brought to Fulking to be washed in the spring adjacent to the inn prior to shearing in June. Sheep washers, immersed for hours in the spring, would walk to the inn 'stiff and scarcely able to move with cold', and the local company of sheep-shearers would enjoy a 'black ram' there at the end of the season. Tithe suppers and club-days

78 Edburton, Perching, *c.* 1794

Hendrick de Cort

West Sussex Record Office, M/PD 259

were also held at the inn.

The first licence to crenellate Perching manor, issued in 1264, is predated in Sussex only by that of 1258 for Sedgwick near Horsham, and was followed by further licences in 1268 and 1329. The standard phrase in most licences, 'to enclose and fortify with fosse and wall of stone and lime', often belies the scale of operation: for example, it was used of Bodiam Castle and its moats. That there were three licences for Perching may indicate operations of some importance. Elements of the manor's ground plan can be traced in earthworks north of the Fulking road. These include a roughly square or rectangular platform on which a major structure must once have stood. This view, unique of the structures at Perching, depicts in the background the ruinous remains of a huge square tower, at least three storeys high, dominating the other domestic buildings. It is possible that this fortified tower was the subject of the licences. Whilst the golden age of keep-building had passed

by the mid-13th century, tower keeps continued to be constructed to the whims of owner and architect. In Sussex, the Ypres tower in Rye exhibits elements common to the keep tradition, and this structure is now dated to the reign of Henry III (1216-72), contemporary therefore with the first two Perching licences. *JB and RJ*

Sources : Green 1996. Herrmann 1973, 128 (quoted). VCHS, 6 (3): 45-51, 7: 202-3. Blaker 1919, 9-11 (quoted), 15, 34, 60. Short and Leslie 1999, 50-1, 68-9. Blaauw 1861, 107, corrected by Public Record Office 1913, 307, 381. PRO, WO 30/48/7788, ff. 437-43 (ex inf. Janet Pennington). SAS, pic. coll. 2859.
NGR TQ 233 115, TQ 247 113, TQ 241 115
PDB 1662, 1664, 1663

79 Ewhurst Place, 1784

S. H. Grimm

British Library, Add. MS. 5670, f. 12 [22]
Colour plate VIII

When Court Lodge (later known as Ewhurst Place) was leased to Nathaniel Powell for 21 years in 1635, it was a triple-gabled house with an L-shaped ground plan. Probably by 1659, when Powell owned the house and was planning an aqueduct 'to bring water to (his) dwelling-house called Ewhurst Court Lodge', it had been entirely refashioned into the house recorded by Grimm - two Dutch-gabled ranges with a central entrance area, which in 1718 contained at least 19 rooms. Some of the materials for the house could have been reused from Bodiam Castle, purchased by Powell in 1645 and thought to have been internally dismantled at about that time (View 20).

Powell was a survivor in difficult times, for he was a Parliamentarian and gunfounder to the Commonwealth yet knighted by Charles II in 1661, and was not averse to attempting tax avoidance. In October 1663, he stopped up chimneys at 'the Courtlodge', and in June 1664, opened them up again. It is not clear from the surviving Hearth Tax returns whether this ploy succeeded.

Powell moved to Kent soon after, and Court Lodge was leased to a succession of tenant farmers, a pattern which remained unbroken when the estate was sold to Thomas Webster of Battle Abbey in 1723. Signs of neglect are apparent in Grimm's view, and it had become labourers' tenements by the 1830s. The house was demolished by 1872. The site was recently field-walked and nothing of the house fabric survives above ground. *JB*

Sources Curzon of Kedleston (Marquis) 1926, 43-4, 73-5. ESRO, BAT 979, 4420; AMS 5691/2/2 and 3. Henry E. Huntington Library, BA 71/4 and 6. Brown 2000. Horsfield 1835, 1: 519. Jones 1999. OS 1:2500, 1st edn. Thackray 1991, 24. Thorpe 1835, 154. VCHS, 9: 264-8.

NGR TQ 795 243   *PDB* 2310.

80 Fairlight, from Friar's Hill, *c.* 1795

Unknown artist

Leeds Museums and Galleries (City Art Gallery), Acc. 5.129/52

As the finger-post tells us, this view was taken on the road between Hastings and Pett - at Friar's Hill (TQ 860 135), looking due south to the sandstone ridge topped by Fairlight village, dominated by its church, standing at over 500 feet above the sea only half a mile further on. This is one of very few 18th-century views of a tract of the Sussex Weald.

The picture has been attributed to James Lambert, but the composition is quite unlike any of his signed work. More probably, it was by one of the professional or talented amateur artists whom the war with France obliged to take their holidays in England and who came to Kent and eastern Sussex, or whose service in the militia found him under canvas nearby on Fairlight Down.

Lambert's drawing of the church in the 1770s is at *Sussex views*, 63.   *JHF*

NGR TQ 860 119   *PDB 4276*

81 Felpham, The Old Rectory, 1790

S. H. Grimm

British Library, Add. MS. 5674, f. 38 [71]

This house stands east-north-east of the Fox Inn in Vicarage Lane. Both this and another view of 1819 are from the south and show the late-18th-century addition to the 17th-century range running north-south behind. This front was later extended westwards and a verandah added.

In 1341, the rectorial estate, owned by Shaftesbury Abbey until its dissolution, consisted of a house, probably on the same site, and over eight acres of land. The six to eight acres of glebe to the east recorded in 1615 may well be the garden and Parsonage Field, owned by the rector in 1844. Grimm called the house 'Mrs Steele's'. She was Elizabeth, widow of Thomas Steele, the Recorder of Chichester who had died in 1775 when the lease passed to his son Robert, named as occupier from 1795. Perhaps William Burrell rented the house

for his summer holidays in 1776 and 1777. From about 1807 the tenant was Dr Cyril Jackson, lately Dean of Christ Church, Oxford. According to Joseph Farington in 1814, he 'lived in elegant retirement.… He passes much time in the open air, 7 or 8 hours walking on the sea beach or in the country, and when he makes excursions from home he drinks nothing but milk.'

From the late 1840s the house was leased to successive vicars of Felpham, until purchased in 1926 by F. G. Penny MP, later Lord Marchwood. Bought by a local trust in 1958, it was converted into flats for elderly people, with a large part of the garden opened to the public.   *RI and JHF*

Sources Bognor Regis Post, 19 July, 13 Dec. 1958. Dally 1828, 63. Davis 1807, 96. Farington 1978-84, 13: 4539. Hudson and Hudson 1988, 13, 36. VCHS, 5 (1), 172-3, 179. WSRO, PD 1006; TD/W 54; QDE/1.

NGR SZ 951 997   *PDB* 2905

82 Ferring, prospect from Highdown Hill, 1770

William Challen

Worthing Museum, X1975/382

William Challen was perhaps an artisan painter whose usual line of business was house painting and shop- and inn-signs. For this prospect of the coastal plain from West Ferring to Worthing, with Beachy Head in the far distance, the client must have been William Westbrook Richardson (1725/6-71): five of the 17 features numbered in the view are identified as his property.

The easy ascent made 'Heydown Hill' a popular excursion for seaside visitors, enhanced by the tomb in the foreground. This was erected in 1766, so the inscription reads, 'for the reception of the body of John Oliver, when deceased, to the will of God.' Saplings were planted at the corners. Twenty-four years later, when Stebbing Shaw visited, Oliver (1709-93), the local miller, spent most of his leisure hours a few yards away in an alcove which, though painted with emblems of death, also served as 'an agreeable resting place for those who walk hither from the adjacent villages, and a very convenient tea-drinking box for company residing at Goring.' At his small house, a quarter of a mile north, 'besides some whimsical figures fixed to a tree or pole in the garden, and

another short motto over the door, here he has prepared a white coffin, on which are inscribed these words, Memento mori. It used to be on castors, and wheeled every night under the bed of its intended possessor. But that ceremony we believe is now dropped, and it hangs in one of his apartments, belonging to the mill.' 'Though neither strong, active, nor particularly cheerful,' he was 'a sincere Christian, and of an exemplary and charitable disposition.'

JHF

Sources Shaw 1790b, 213-14. Dallaway 1832, 29-34.
NGR TQ 096 042

PDB 1593

S.W. front of Muntham house. W.r Franklin.   *S.H.Grimm fecit 1789.*

83 Findon, Muntham House, 1789

S. H. Grimm.

British Library, Add. MS. 5673, f. 57 [102]

Anthony Browne, Viscount Montague, bought Muntham, the Middleton family home for over a century, in 1743 and developed the site apparently as a hunting lodge. By 1754 he had rebuilt or enlarged the existing house, was making great plantations and had brought water there at great expense.

With the profits of a career with the East India Company, William Frankland (1720-1805) purchased the estate from Montague in 1765 and set about creating a gentleman's residence. His probably is the 11-bay, red-brick frontage with central porch and flattened bow on the return seen here. But the roofs behind this frontage surely belong to earlier buildings, and the south-east face of two-storey projections below (?blind) semi-circular windows perhaps dates to Montague's hunting lodge. On the hillside behind, a gothic pavilion embosomed within a stand of young trees, suggests landscaping of the site over the previous

40 years or so, but a yew hedge around the house, a mature feature by 1900, is not apparent.

Having established himself at Muntham, Frankland devoted his time to collecting and operating a variety of mechanical devices. There were rooms given over to lathes, spinning and winding machines ('he makes all his own cloth', a visitor in 1789 noted), printing presses, time pieces 'together with electrifying machines and optical instruments in an almost endless variety', and mechanical musical instruments. This collection was dispersed by sale after his death. By 1794 he had devised, also, a horizontal windmill to raise water for the house from a well measured at 350 feet in 1773.

The house was demolished in 1961 to make way for a crematorium.   *JB*

Sources Banting 1984. Evans 1805, 72-4 (quoted). Hudson 1978. Pike 1910, 118. Pococke 1888-9, 2: 106-7. VCHS, 6 (1): 22, 26. Centre for Kentish Studies, U 1007/F2 ([Polhill, G.], 'A Tour...from Chipstead to Portsmouth, ... Arundel ... Hastings, ...Tunbridge Wells...1789'), f. 3 (quoted).

NGR TQ 110 096   *PDB* 2813

84 Folkington Place from the west, 1783

S. H. Grimm

British Library, Add. MS. 5671, f. 84 [160]

Folkington manor was bought by Sir Richard Sackville in 1542 from Sir Thomas West, Lord de la Warr, whose ancestor had married Olympia de Folkington in the 1240s. There is no indication of a substantial house in a lease of 1562, but in 1623 it was described as a capital messuage. The timber-framed building shown in View 84 must date from around the turn of the century; it is stylistically alien to Sussex, belonging more to a West Midlands tradition. The house must be the work of the Culpeper family, who lived at Folkington as tenants from before 1595 until at least 1639; a beneficial lease from the Sackvilles may have enabled them to invest in a new building.

William Thomas of Westdean bought Folkington for £6120 in 1652 but died at Westdean two years later, and the ambitious mansion shown

in the second view must be the work of his son William Thomas (1640/1-1706). Aged 13 at his father's death, he entered Oriel College in 1659 and was created a baronet on 23 July 1660. He was returned for Seaford in 1661, when he can barely have attained his majority, and sat in Parliament for the rest of his life. He served as a JP from 1668 and a deputy lieutenant from 1670.

The result and perhaps the purpose of the new work was to change the aspect of Folkington Place away from the direction of Wilmington (where Culpepers had lived at the priory) southward towards the Downs. There is no firm evidence allowing us to date the new range in View 85, but it is built in the Artisan Mannerist style fashionable in the middle decades of the 17th century. Folkington was one of the three Sussex houses illustrated in 1707 by Leonard Knyff (1650-1721). The 'stately mansion of Sir William Thomas' is naturally shown from the south, entirely masking the earlier work which had probably been degraded to servants' accommodation. The other two houses, Stansted and Uppark, were each ten years old when Knyff did his fieldwork, and

85 Folkington Place from the south, 1783

S. H. Grimm

British Library, Add. MS. 5671, f. 84 [161]

Folkington's inclusion in *Britannia illustrata* may indicate the scarcity of new and fashionable houses in the Sussex of the 1690s.

Sir William died in 1706 and the estate passed to his nephew William Dobell, who left his family home at Streat Place for Folkington. A comparison of Knyff's view with that of Grimm shows that Dobell had added the pediment and two central pilasters, to bring the building more in line with the classical tastes of the 18th century. Dobell's will encouraged his wife to remain at Folkington, 'and keep the same with the buildings and gardens thereto belonging in such good repair as I have done.' Dobell died in 1752 leaving an only daughter Mary, who was declared insane in 1773. The estate was run by her cousins, the Lanes of

Streat Place, and the house fell into disrepair. On her death in 1796 it passed to Lancelot Harison, and had been entirely demolished by 1824. *CHCW*

Sources ESRO, SAS/M; GWY 3/1. Cokayne 1910-98, 4: 140n.
Attree and Booker 1904. Henning 1983.

NGR TQ 560 040   *PDB* 2606, 2605

86 Framfield, the hall at Hempstead House, 1785

S. H. Grimm

British Library, Add. MS. 5671, f. 103 [197]

Hempstead, usually described as a capital messuage, had for almost two centuries been the residence of the Warnett family when Edward Warnett, the last of his line, died in 1704. It was held of the archbishop of Canterbury's lordship of South Malling; Archbishop John Peckham had freed Robert de Hempstead from serfdom in 1288 and in 1495 John Morton enfranchised the tenure of the land.

Grimm's exterior view, showing the timber-framed kitchen-range and the massive chimney added to it in about 1570, was published in *Sussex views*, 65. The open hall shown here still stands, although the parlour behind the point of view has been demolished. Both were added to the kitchen range, probably in the opening years of the 16th century, by John Warnett, who in 1537 bequeathed

a bell and mass-book at his place at Hempstead to Little Horsted church. By the time of Grimm's view the room had been panelled and hung with at least eleven portraits, each depicting a Greek philosopher – Socrates, Solon, Plato, Democritus, Heraclitus, Pythagoras, Aristarchus, Aristotle and Hippocrates can be made out. Robert Smith of Framfield, whose family tenanted Hempstead and eventually became its owners, established a charity school in the parish in 1720 and it is possible that it had once been conducted in the hall. Grimm also shows a fine staircase, added in about 1600 but since much altered, rising to connect the hall with the rest of the house.

In 1841 Miss Elizabeth Sarah Smith sold the house and over 320 acres in Framfield, Buxted and Uckfield to the Buxted Park Estate.   *CHCW*

Sources Caffyn 1998, 117. Horsfield 1824-7, 2: 107. PRO, PROB 11/27 (ESRO, AMS 6326/72). ESRO, ADA 137 pp. 48, 166, HBR 1/1324; SAS/C 605; SAS/FB 694.

NGR TQ 486 217   *PDB* 2448

87 Frant, camp on Waterdown Forest, 1780

James Lambert senior
British Library, Add. MS. 5676, f. 51 [77]
Colour plate IX

Whenever invasion threatened in the 18th century, at the season of greatest risk, from June to November, the War Office assembled the available Army units in temporary camps to train and to guard the approaches to London and Portsmouth. Sites had to be fairly flat, free from fences and other impediments to movement; dry and well drained; but with adequate fresh water, and wood or furze for fuel. Owners of poor-grade land such as the heathland in the High Weald were willing to rent.

The site of this camp, unsurprisingly chosen in preference to Tunbridge Wells Common, was north-west of the stream feeding the pond of Benhall Mill, today enlarged as Frant Ponds; Lambert was the other side of the stream, depicting the skyline of Tunbridge Wells implausibly close. The regiments were encamped from 8 June to 25 October: one regular, 13th Foot (replaced by 65th Foot in August), and four militia, Staffs, Bucks, Devon and Middlesex, with nominal complements totalling some 3250 men, but fewer

on the ground. Their presence is apparent in the Frant parish register, with ten marriages of soldiers added to, typically, five or six a year - but curiously no baptisms or burials which can be associated with the camp.

Lambert's view shows the regulation layout of a camp. Nearest to him were five groups of six or so tents, these being the quarter guard for each regiment. Beyond them were the parade ground and then long rows of tents, the men's lines. If the regiments were up to strength they each required nine or ten lines, but about six appear here. The officers' tents and the circular field-kitchens were at the far end, with, according to the map (View 88), the magazine beyond. Another, unofficial, map by Ensign J. P. Christian of the 65th Foot also marks the forage yard, east of the stream on the west side of the road leading to Knights House. The layout of the individual elements are shown in more detail on the map of the 1793 camp on Ashdown Forest, reproduced in Margary 1965. It was this camp, pitched for only one week, which distracted Lord Sheffield from attending more fully to the Revd Arthur Young at the start of the latter's agricultural tour of Sussex, Essay 4.1.

A larger camp for 7000 men in 104 lines of tents was laid out in Frant in 1793 at the north-east edge of Broadwater Forest, TQ 565 366 to TQ 556 378, on Lord Abergavenny's land, as in 1780. In

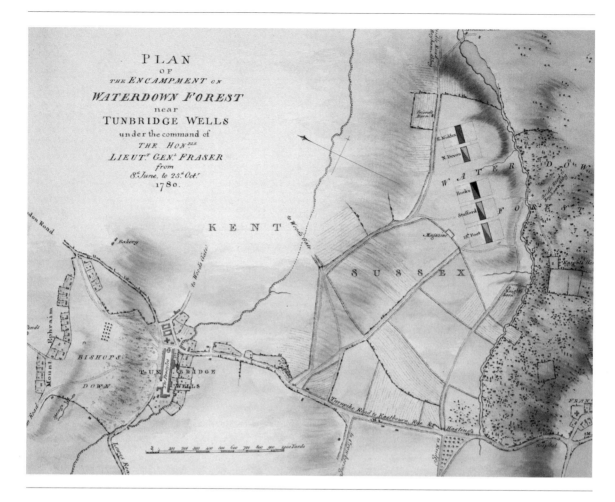

88 Frant, camp on Waterdown Forest, plan, 1780

*Lieut. Daniel Paterson and
Ensign Edward Morrison*
British Library, Add. MS. 15533, f. 43
Colour plate X

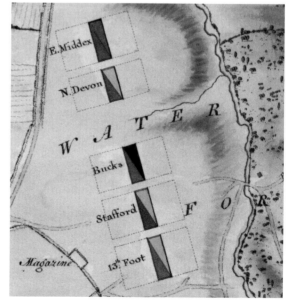

the 1960s traces of the circular field-kitchens were recorded there.

Other camps in Sussex included Playden Heights (1779, 1780, 1781), Fairlight Down (1779), Westfield (1779, 1782) and Wick in Brighton and Hove (1793).   *JHF*

Sources Houlding 1981, 322-32. Margary 1965. Margary 1969. Holden 1970. BL, Add. MS. 60393 B.

NGR front line of camp, TQ 596 368 to 603 373 *PDB* 4061, 8078

Fristone Church & Parsonage house

89 Friston Church and parsonage, ?1785

S. H. Grimm

British Library, Add. MS. 5678, f. 6 [12]

Grimm's view from the south shows the church, the parsonage and, in front of the latter, the remains of two walls. These may be the remnants of the parsonage barn - burnt down in 1722 after being struck by lightning - which stood within the glebe and on the east side of the present way from Friston to Crowlink. No remains survive above ground.

In 1724, the parsonage was described as 'very mean and out of repair', and was not lived in by the incumbent. He was at Eastdean, the other parish of a united benefice where, though the vicarage had also recently burnt down, a parishioner had bequeathed a house to the minister and his successors. Friston parsonage is shown here as two cottages and, like the surviving late-medieval clergy houses at Alfriston and West

Hoathly, timber-framed. A companion view from the north (f. 5 [11]) suggests that the parsonage was on the site currently occupied by Old Vicarage Cottage, though whether any of the timber-framed building is incorporated into the present house is not known.

As to the church, Grimm records a triple lancet at the east end of an apparently lopsided or off-centre chancel. But four other roughly contemporary views from a similar angle all agree that the east window was of two lights only, and that the chancel stood squarely and centrally against the nave. The broach spire seen here had been replaced by a simple bell-turret by 1804.

Francis Grose visited the church in 1777 (Document 5.1) and would have seen the altar piece which James Lambert junior painted three years previous.
JB

Sources Ford 1994, 171 (quoted). Shaw 1792, 3. BL, Add MS 5678, f. 75 [114]. SAS, pic. coll. 2844, 3003; Sharpe coll. 143. Private coll. (view by Francis Grose, 1777)

NGR TV 552 982   *PDB* 3117

Friston House, in the Occupation of George Ulfrey.
(from the South Side) May 14. Feb. 32.

Ground plan of Friston House.

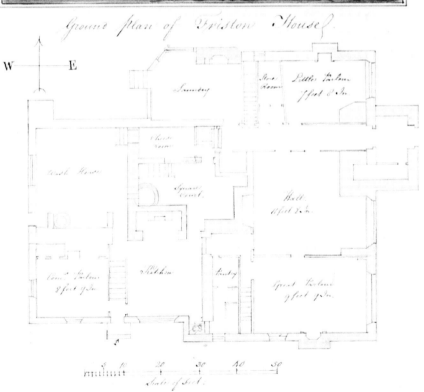

90 Friston Place, 1798

Unknown surveyor of the Buxted estate

East Sussex Record Office, ACC 3712, f. 19 [C]

The east range of Friston Place, to the right of this 1798 view, constituted its original core, a timber-framed 'Wealden' hall-house with jetties on both the east and the west faces. The builder may have been Thomas Selwyn of Sherrington in Selmeston (View 168) (d. 1539). He acquired the estate in about 1500 by marriage to Margery, the daughter of John and Alice Adam. Alice was the heir to the Potman family who for several generations had held the estate, then known as Bechington. The mouldings to the king-post and the principal timbers, and the close studding on the west face, indicate top-quality work.

The Selwyns enlarged the house on several occasions. The earliest addition may have been the two bays west of the service end ('Laundry' in 1798), the chamber having a moulded crown-post. Late in the 16th century, the original solar at south end of the hall was replaced by the present cross-wing, to provide a fairly large parlour and chamber. The west wing, of flint with stone quoins, probably dates to the early 17th century, and certainly before the house was assessed for 13 hearths in 1664. Two date-stones in the east front, 'T S 1613' and 'P S 1634', have been moved at least once, and could be related to it. The fine wall painting in an upstairs chamber, with its theme of hunting, is likely to predate the Civil War. Finally, the east front was rebuilt in brick, a few feet forward of the original façade. The splayed brickwork of the window heads points to a date in the later 17th century. By then the hall had been divided into two storeys. The east front, with elaborate bargeboards decorating its four gables, is what Mrs Sophia Burrell drew in 1781, probably on an excursion while staying at Compton Place.

The male line of the Selwyns failed in 1705, and Thomas Medley of Conyboro in Barcombe (View 12) bought the estate from the heirs in 1705-9. His brothers lived there until 1754 when the farm was let to George Allfrey. His son, another George, succeeded to the tenancy in 1764 and established a reputation as a progressive farmer. Embarking on the report on Sussex for the Board of Agriculture, the Revd Arthur Young arrived at Sheffield Park in August 1793. As Lord Sheffield was preoccupied with a militia review, Young was immediately recommended to Thomas Kemp of Conyboro, John Ellman of Glynde and George Allfrey of Friston. Reaching Friston with a package from the Board's President, though, Young encountered 'a large farmer', the farmer of a large acreage who, 'whatever his motive ... was extremely backward and disinclined to give me the least information, respecting the experience and knowledge upon which the system of his breeding was established.' But he obtained the notes which Allfrey had sent to the President. They perhaps reveal the reason: Allfrey exchanged rams every four or five years with neighbours who had the best flocks, contrary, as he acknowledged, to the maxims of Arthur Young senior, Robert Bakewell and the other advocates of continual breeding-in. Allfrey had seen his father's flock degenerate from breeding the same strain for 20 years. Having farmed for nearly 30 years, Allfrey may have been disinclined to argue with a 24-year-old newly graduated from Cambridge, without practical experience, who knew only his father's opinions.

This George Allfrey died during the following year. The substance of the large Downland tenant farmers is illustrated by his cash bequests of £2500 to his younger son and of £1000 to each of his five daughters. His widow was to have the use of the upper lodging house at Seaford adjoining his wine vaults. It was his son George who was tenant at the time of the 1798 survey. He was leasing 693 acres of which 234 acres were in tillage, some 170 pasture and 281 sheepdown, for an annual rent of £320. He also rented from the Buxted estate, for £39, 87 acres at Months Farm in Hailsham, which gave him an all-important 38 acres of meadow on the marshes for stock fattening. He either owned or leased from other owners several further parcels of land in Friston and four or five other parishes.

Landowners were disinclined to invest in their tenanted houses and John Bodle, the steward, suggested in 1824 that Friston Place was too large for the farmer and should be reduced in size - though that was not acted upon. In 1867 the 6th Duke of Devonshire bought the farm but, after 30 years, the 7th Duke sold it to a gentleman farmer. J. A. Maitland, his son and grandson rescued the house from dereliction.   *JHF*

Sources Aslet 1986. Young 1794, 240-2. Farrant 1992, 203. Allfrey 1804. Hawkesbury 1904. Davey 1991, 87, 127, 222, 245, 246, 254. Wolseley 1936. ESRO, SAS/H 254; AMS 6270/57-59; SAS/PN 370, 372; ELT. Eastbourne Reference Library, Burrell's copy of *A compleat history of Sussex*, 524-5.

NGR TV 548 988   *PDB* 7747

91 Glynde, Mount Caburn, 1762

Francis Grose

Sussex Archaeological Society, picture collection 94 (detail)

This drawing is dated 6 November 1762, when Lieutenant Grose, adjutant and paymaster of the 2nd (western) Battalion of the Surrey Militia, was stationed at Lewes (see also View 129). His view point was probably on Upper Rise (TQ 418 087), in the Brooks south of Lewes, looking east, and his interest, as a military man, was doubtless in the earthworks, clearly delineated on Mount Caburn. John Tabor, the Lewes physician and archaeologist (Views 73 and 131), considered Caburn, like most of the hill-forts on the Sussex Downs, to date from the Britons' resistance to the invading Saxons' eastwards advance (see Cissbury, View 33). The buildings and haystacks of Southerham Farm clustered beneath Caburn, near the River Ouse (View 136).

During six months' sojourn in Lewes, Grose is likely to have read the poem *Mount Caburn*, published by William Hay of Glyndebourne in 1730, which offered a potted local history inspired by the view. It encompasses the former Forest of Anderida, its iron works and oak for the Navy, the ancient Britons' resistance to the Romans, the Saxon invasion, marauding Danes, the Norman Conquest, Battle Abbey, Lewes Priory, the Magnus inscription, and the Battle of Lewes, finishing with Laughton Place and a eulogy to the Duke of Newcastle, to whose duchess the poem is dedicated. As to archaeology, and the 'Bergs or Burying Places' seen on many hill summits:

> The curious Antiquaries with Surprize
> View their odd Armour, and Gigantick Size,
> And us their Modern Pigmy-Race despise.

JHF

Sources Tabor 1717, 793. Drewett and Hamilton 1999, for the most recent discussion of Caburn. Hay 1730. Taylor and Jones 1998, lxi-lxiii.

NGR TQ 444 089

PDB 3406

N:W: View — of Eastgrinsted Church as it appeard after the Steeple fell Down on Saturday the 12 of Novr. 1785.

92 East Grinstead Church, 1785

James Lambert senior

British Library, Add. MS. 71714, no. 27

Dated 16-17 November 1785 and titled 'N:W: View of Eastgrinsted Church as it appear'd after the Steeple fell Down on the Saturday 12th of Novr 1785', this drawing is an interesting complement to the often-reproduced views from opposite directions inside the relatively unscathed eastern end (e.g. *Sussex views*, 56 and 57); these latter are with little doubt also by Lambert, but are known only from copies by Grimm. With Lambert's equally familiar painting of the church from the south-east in 1781 (e.g. *Sussex views*, 55) they give a good idea of the structure and dimensions of the whole building. Lambert's accuracy is confirmed by the appearance of the buildings in the right-hand background, still the same today.

The tower, which had been poorly rebuilt after a lightning-strike in 1683, had been in a dangerous condition for some time before its dramatic collapse at about 1.45 p.m., less than two hours after the school at its base had ended for the week. An eye-witness account by Thomas Wakeham of the Hermitage (View 95) was printed in an edited version in the *Gentleman's Magazine*.

Fund-raising difficulties meant that work on the new building, designed by James Wyatt (1746-1813), did not start until 1789 and was completed in about 1793. The fitting out was not finished until 1808. The tower, redesigned by J. T. Groves, was built in 1811, completing the building we still have today, though internally there have been many embellishments and rearrangements.   *MJL*

Sources Wakeham 1785. WSRO, Acc. 7986, f. 3; Par. 348/4/3-5 and 47.

NGR TQ 396 380   *PDB* 3967

93 East Grinstead, Kidbrooke Park, *c.* 1740

George Lambert

Yale Center for British Art, Paul Mellon Collection, B1981.25.396

The main, east, front of Kidbrooke Park, here shown from the south-east, still has over the entrance 'W.A.A.' and '17[3]4', referring to William Nevill, Lord Abergavenny (*c.* 1697-1744), and his wife. In 1733 he obtained the Act of Parliament to purchase the land on which to build this house. The site was marshy and named from at least the 15th century after the stream running through it, just south-west of Forest Row and west of the East Grinstead to Lewes turnpike. The house, in the local sandstone, consisted of a central block of five bays on two floors with service wings north and south. The clock on the large stable block alongside bears the date 1736. Possibly his brother-in-law, Henry Herbert, 9th Earl of Pembroke, had a hand in the design. A formal parterre perhaps with

fountain fronted the house; a temple embellished a walled garden at the back, adjacent to the kitchen garden; recently planted clumps of trees are in the foreground. On the horizon can be seen the tower of East Grinstead Church before its fall (View 92) and windmills at Ashurst Wood. Presumably it was Nevill who commissioned Lambert (*c.* 1700-65) to paint this view.

In 1803 the Nevills returned to Eridge and sold Kidbrooke to Charles Abbot (1757-1829), who engaged Repton to redesign the grounds between 1806 and 1809. George Dance junior added a colonnade to the south front in 1815, but the central block remains virtually unchanged. Since World War II the house has been a school, by which it is cherished and sometimes opened to the public.   *MJL*

Sources Byford 1984. Colvin 1995, 292. Farrant 1989, 172-3. *NGR* TQ 419 345   *PDB* 3937

SANTHILL *Eastgrinsted*
Belonging to Gibbs Crawfurd Esq.

94 East Grinstead, Saint Hill, *c.* 1782

James Lambert senior

British Library, Add. MS. 5676, f. 39 [60]

This is a view from the south-south-west of the property known from the 1790s as Saint Hill but earlier that century as Santhill, apparently a corruption of Sandhill. The earliest record of its name is on Budgen's map of Sussex, 1724. The house appears to be of ashlar, doubtless local sandstone, with a tiled roof. The tall chimneys, slightly projecting wings and barley-sugar pillars suggest an early-17th-century date. John Crawfurd (*c.* 1697-1762), a Scot who, dispossessed of an inheritance, came south and by 1720 was lord of the manor of Duddleswell on Ashdown Forest. He acquired this house in about 1733. In 1788 John's son Gibbs Crawfurd (*c.* 1732-93, MP for Queenborough) was putting up 'a grand house' in its place. That was the year of Lambert's death, so he probably painted this view in one of the years with which he dated other East Grinstead scenes, 1781, '82, '83 or '85.

The second house was partly pulled down and rebuilt, still on the original site and with the original orientation, in 1890 by Edgar March Crookshank (1858-1928), founder of the first bacteriological laboratory in England. Twentieth-century owners have included the Maharajah of Jaipur and L. Ron Hubbard, the founder of Scientology, who had additional buildings put up. It is still his followers' headquarters and sometimes open for guided visits. *MJL*

Sources Leppard 2000. Crawfurd 1927. Byng 1934, 1: 381.
NGR TQ 382 358   *PDB* 4049

The HERMITAGE *East grinsted* Belonging to M.r Wakeham.

95 East Grinstead, The Hermitage, 1783

James Lambert senior

British Library, Add. MS. 5676, f. 40 [61]

The Hermitage stood about 220 yards south of East Grinstead High Street at the bottom of the rocky defile of Hermitage Lane, immediately after the ancient borough boundary, almost on the road and facing north-west. It was a continuous-jettied timber-framed house of the mid-16th century with Horsham stone roof and apparently with the usual cross-passage between front and back doors and an axial four-flue chimney with a tall stack. By the date of this view, the north-east wall and gable had been cased in brick and tile and the front seemingly plastered. Other typical Georgian embellishments visible are dormers, sash windows with shutters, and a pedimented porch.

No early name is known; the Hermitage seems to have been the choice of Thomas Wakeham (c. 1728-1803), who occupied it from at least 1780. He had property in several parishes and was an attorney and the steward of several prominent Sussex and Surrey landowners. That he was also an antiquary known to Burrell was perhaps the reason for his house being portrayed.

By then enlarged and temporarily renamed South Dene, it was mostly destroyed in 1897 in the fire which killed its wealthy American tenant. The larger successor house kept the same alignment and re-used some old materials. After the death of its last owner, the philanthropist Alfred Wagg, plans in 1969 to convert it for community uses came to nothing and its site and grounds became the housing development Lower Mere.   *MJL*

Sources Wood 1972. Leppard 1972, 7. Davey 1991, 9, 58, 89, 194-5, 226-7.

NGR TQ 397 377   *PDB* 4050

96 West Grinstead Place, 1723

John Warburton

British Library, Lansdowne MS. 918, f. 32

This pencil sketch is the only record of West Grinstead Place before its entrance front was rebuilt after 1749, as drawn by Grimm in 1781. In the early 19th century it was demolished so completely, that its location is now uncertain. In 1723, the building was apparently of 16th- or early-17th-century date. According to the key, the south-facing entrance front, approached through an iron gate, had a three-bayed centre of freestone, the gabled wing to the right in brick, sash windows (except for a transom in stone to the right of the door) and a tiled roof.

The builders were the Shirleys, who held the manor of West Grinstead from 1512, or possibly, after the death of the last Shirley in 1606, his daughter and her husband. By 1637 the manor had passed to the Caryll family. So Warburton found it 'a good old seat situated in a pleasant well wooded and well stocked park belonging to John Carril Esq. a Roman Catholic gentleman of great estate' - except that between 1715 and 1736 the house was sequestered for recusancy and John Caryll was living on his estate at Ladyholt (View 102). That seems not to have prevented the Jesuit mission endowed by the family continuing at West Grinstead, and the chapel closed only when the financial burdens imposed by the Penal Acts forced the next generation to sell the manor to Merrik Burrell in 1749. *JHF*

Sources VCHS, 6 (2): 90-1. McCann 1986. Both reproduce Grimm's drawing of 1781.

NGR TQ 170 216

PDB 7992

Great Maxfield House in the Occupation of Mt. John Gilfin. Map 26. Fig. 13.

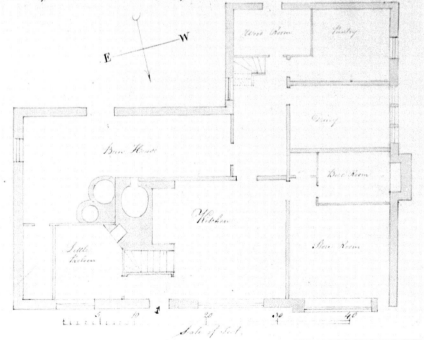

Ground Plan of Great Maxfield House.

97 Guestling, Great Maxfield House, 1798

Unknown surveyor of the Buxted estate

East Sussex Record Office, ACC 3712, f. 22 [B]

The Great Maxfield estate was assembled in the 1230s by Battle Abbey and used to endow the almonry. The monks used the house as a retreat and as a place of business with the men of the Five Ports: it was at Maxfield that the abbot sealed the agreement to found a chantry in Winchelsea Church in memory of Henry Alard in 1319.

The site was moated with a gatehouse, drawbridge and adjoining park and mill. An inventory of 1427-8 provides a list of rooms with their contents: the hall, lord's chamber, chapel chamber, the chamber under the lord's chamber and Saynes Chamber; a chapel, buttery, kitchen, larder and cook's chamber. There were 16 locks with keys on various doors of the buildings within the moat, and one lock on the gate of the moat.

Works at the manor can be charted through the almoner's accounts. A surviving stone chimney was built in 1372-3 at a cost of £13 3s. 4d., partly defrayed by Thomas Clerk's legacy of £5; its octagonal cap resembles those at Bodiam Castle of perhaps 15 years later. Unfortunately the fine timbered cross-wing on the right of the view cannot be dated precisely, but clearly belongs to the decades either side of 1500. It may well be associated with the new building at Maxfield for which timber and stone were carted from Battle in 1502 and 1503.

The farmland was tenanted by the 15th century, and its produce included cheese. In 1474 the new tenant, Thomas Carpenter of Ore, covenanted to find a horse and servant to bring victuals from Winchelsea, Hastings and Battle whenever the abbot and convent took their recreation at Maxfield, rushes to spread in the hall and chambers and straw to make beds. He also undertook to carry a tun of wine from Winchelsea or Hastings to the monastery at Battle every year when required. He was allowed to use all the buildings within the moat, and when the convent was not in residence he was allowed to use the kitchen as well.

In 1539 Maxfield passed to Sir Anthony Browne with the Battle Abbey estate, and was sold to Robert Barham of Boughton Monchelsea in Kent in 1620. In 1663 his son sold it, with 300 acres, to Benjamin Henshaw, citizen and embroiderer of London, and the timber-framed range on the site of the medieval hall was probably built in his time. Traces of blocked flanking-windows, some of the latest on record in the area, can just be made out on the upper storeys, but were present on the ground floor as well.

In 1696 the farm, tenanted by members of the Purfield family for almost a century, passed into the Buxted Park estate when Thomas Medley bought it and a neighbouring property for £2000.

John Gilfin, the tenant when the survey was made, had come to Maxfield in his prime in 1762. In 1798 he held 238 acres of land (worth £12 an acre) and 53 of wood in Guestling, together with 90 acres of marshland in Pett (worth £28 an acre) at an annual rent of £275. His lease, for 21 years from 1791, contained a penalty of £10 an acre for growing flax or hemp and £5 an acre for more than four acres of hops. As well as his tenancy of Maxfield, Gilfin also owned a farm of 133 acres in Pett, which was occupied by his son-in-law Thomas Russell. Gilfin did not see the end of his lease, and died at Maxfield at the age of 77 in 1807.

The Catholic priest and Bible translator Gregory Martin (*c.* 1540-82) is said to have been born at Maxfield. The assertion goes back to at least the late 17th century and has been repeated unquestioned since then, though no evidence from a primary source is known.   *CHCW*

Sources ESRO, AMS 5899; SAS/PN 374-403; BMW C4/1; ELT; PAR 350 1/1/2; W/A 70 126; HBR 1/806. Henry E. Huntington Library, BA 53/1605, BA 152-222.

NGR TQ 834 152   *PDB* 7758

98 Guestling, Broomham, 1783

S. H. Grimm

British Library, Add. MS. 5670, f. 26 [48]

Broomham came by marriage to Richard Ashburnham, a younger son of the main line, in the 1450s, and remained in his family for over 500 years. In 1783 it was a residence of Sir William Ashburnham (1710-97), Bishop of Chichester since 1754.

The oldest part of the house, to the rear of the view, is a stone range incorporating a timber-framed element at its southern end. In the years around 1600, Broomham was extended by north and south wings, in which elaborate panelling and carved work survives. In 1662 it was assessed for the Hearth Tax at 18 flues, suggesting that a courtyard had already been formed by a west range.

But the architecturally ambitious west front which dominates Grimm's view was probably built by Sir William, the second baronet (1677-1755). The road had been diverted to form a park and Sir William's building may have been little more than a façade built to impress passing travellers. Neither he nor his nephew the bishop went on to complete the prospect by relocating the farm buildings. Sir

William's father, Sir Denny (*c.* 1628-97) had sat as MP for Hastings, and left Broomham occupied by a yeoman in 1662. Sir William represented Hastings and Seaford in the Pelham interest between 1710 and 1741; and the bishop, previously dean at Chichester, owed both positions to Newcastle. Perhaps their political preoccupations made them only occasional residents at Broomham, which remained a working farm.

A survey of the estate, by the Herstmonceux schoolmaster William Allfree in 1810, identifies the buildings as an extensive stable and a barn. The latter, though remodelled at the beginning of the 18th century, nevertheless incorporates substantial remains of a 15th-century barn with a crown-post roof. In 1926 the west front was demolished as part of an extensive remodelling of the house, which is now used as a school.

Grimm's composition is enhanced by his depiction of the horizon slightly above the roof-line of the house; the characteristic profile of Udimore church is clearly visible to the left. *CHCW*

Sources ESRO, HBR 1/747, 748. Henning 1983, 1: 551-2. Sedgwick 1970, 1: 421-2. ESRO AMS 6188; ACC 5257; VCHS, 9: 179-80.

NGR TQ 851 151   *PDB* 2336

99 Harting Church, 1782

S. H. Grimm

British Library, Add. MS. 5675, f. 32 [55]

Grimm took this view 'from near the Cold Bath.'
South Harting is located on the Upper
Greensand bench which separates the Chalk and
Hythe Beds to the south from the Gault to the
north. The 'Cold Bath' is probably to be associated
with the ponds in South Gardens to the south of
Harting Church, which are fed from the spring-
line, a characteristic of the Upper Greensand in
this part of Sussex. The 1914 Ordnance Survey
map records a bathing house there. Indeed, a
spring which, in 1870, 'gushes out from the base of
the hill' here was also the motive power for a pump
to supply water to Uppark, 300 feet higher on the
chalk to the south. The spring was probably first
utilised for this purpose by Sir Edward Ford (d.
1670), owner of Uppark and a much-respected
water engineer of his day.

Grimm's view of the church shows a spire,
presumably post-dating the fire of about 1575
which destroyed the roof; it was soon, in 1797-9, to
be replaced by today's strongly-waisted broach
spire. He also shows in the angle of the south
transept and chancel, the mortuary chapel of the
Caryll family, see detail below. It first received the
remains of Sir Edward (d. 1610) and his son Sir
Richard (d. 1616) (Views 100 and 101), but was
taken down almost to the ground in 1860.

This picture is badly foxed. *JB*

Sources DNB 1998, Ford, Edward. Francombe [1983], 6, 8.
Gordon 1877, 5 (quoted). Hunter 1970, 13. VCHS, 4: 16, 18, 20.
Yates 1972, 5, 11.

NGR SU 784 193   *PDB* 2984

100 Harting Church, Sir Edward Caryll's monument, ?1782

S. H. Grimm

British Library, Add. MS. 5675, f. 31 [51]

From a family of lawyers of Warnham and Shipley, Edward Caryll (1538-1610) settled in Harting in 1590 when he purchased the manor of West Harting. He was Attorney of the Duchy of Lancaster to Queen Elizabeth, Sheriff of Sussex in 1571 and a JP 1585-7 and 1591-1610, despite being fined for persistent recusancy. He was knighted in 1603. In about 1610 the family built a chancel with burial vault on the south side of the church. The recumbent figure of Sir Edward, in alabaster, lay beneath the family's arms and beside an inscription recording his three wives and the monument's erection at his youngest son Richard's expense. His sword is suspended by a scarf.

Richard inherited the Harting estates and was knighted in 1615. Dying in 1616, he wished to be buried 'within the Chapel in Harting Church newly built where my father was buried.' The estates he

101 Harting Church, Sir Richard Caryll's monument, ?1782

S. H. Grimm

British Library, Add. MS. 5675, f. 31 [52]

bequeathed to his elder brother Thomas Caryll of Shipley, and in default of heirs to his cousin John Caryll of Warnham, the senior branch of the family, as the inscription records. John erected the monument in gratitude for the bequest.

The monuments remained in the chancel while it was used as a school and then as a carpenter's shop. The roof having fallen in, the chancel was partially demolished in 1860. In 1956 the remains of Edward's monument (head and trunk alone surviving) were brought into the church and re-erected on the south wall. Having been found in five pieces in the church's tool shed in 1948, Richard's memorial tablet was re-erected alongside in 1965.

TJMcC

Sources Gordon 1877. Mosse 1933. Peckham 1955. Godfrey and Steer 1965. Parry 1976. anon. 1948.

NGR SU 784 194   *PDB* 2983, 2982

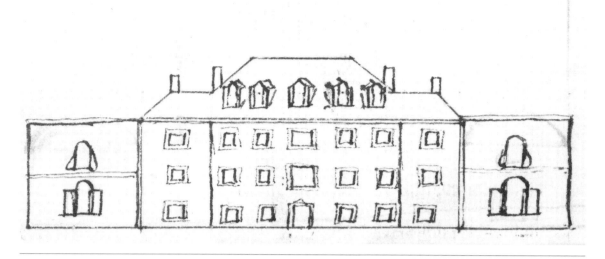

102 Harting, Ladyholt, *c.* 1760

John Baptist Caryll

British Library, Add. MS. 28250, f. 563

The Caryll Papers in the British Library afford no direct evidence of the exact date when Ladyholt was built. It was completed by the beginning of 1680, as a conveyance of 7 January describes the 'new erected mansion house'. Built for John Caryll, later Secretary of State for the exiled James II, and father of John Caryll the author and friend of Alexander Pope, Ladyholt became the home of the senior branch of the family until sold to Sir Matthew Fetherstonhaugh of Uppark in 1767 and demolished. This sketch of the front elevation by John Baptist Caryll, the grandson of Mr Secretary Caryll, is the only known view, and was made when he planned some additions to the original house. However, he was soon forced by mounting debts to sell it.

No 'architect' has ever been associated with the house, and the builder probably designed it, with a north-east-facing symmetrical front of seven bays, a central doorway and two storeys, under a hipped roof with dormer windows and tall chimneys. The wings at each end were the additions planned by Caryll, to include on the south-east a new dining-room with a library above and on the north-west a new kitchen with a Catholic chapel above.

The particulars for the sale in 1767 list the contents of the house after the Carylls had left. They describe some 27 rooms including the blue check room, the red check room, the green closet, the dining parlour, the kitchen, the steward's room, the chintz room and dressing room, the flock room and closet, the white room and dressing room, the drawing room, the little green room, the tapestry room and dressing room, Mr Caryll's dressing room and library, the lobby and stair case, the crimson silk damask bedchamber and dressing room, the gallery, the hall, the yellow closet, the servants hall and pantry, together with store rooms, attic rooms and a cellar. Outside the main house were rooms over the stables, laundry and dairy and a brewhouse and well-house.   *TJMcC*

Sources Erskine-Hill 1975. Gordon 1877. BL, Add. MS. 28250, passim. WSRO, Add. MS. 28770.

NGR SU 754 166   *PDB* 8049

103 Hastings, Dudeney's chapel, west end, 1784

S. H. Grimm

British Library, Add. MS. 5670, f. 31 [59]

The artists who drew this structure gave it several alternative identities:

c. 1780 James Lambert senior, St Mary Magdalen near Hastings (BL, Add. MS 5676, f. 33 [49])

1784 S. H. Grimm, Dudeney's chapel (reproduced here)

1802 Henry Petrie, St Leonard's (SAS, Sharpe Coll. 283 and 284)

1815 Marianne Johnson, The Chapel Barn (Hastings Museum, L.269: Baines 1963, fc. 112)

by 1834 Joseph Powell, St Leonard's Chapel near Hastings (SAS, pic. coll. 4148).

View 103 was engraved and published by 1788 as 'Dudeney Chapel' in Alexander Hogg's *Picturesque views of antiquities of England and Wales*, with the assertion that it was 'situated in the forest

of Ashdown'. The Revd Edward Turner in the 1850s speculated that it had stood in Maresfield. However, the name refers to the Deudney family, agents to the Eversfield family and large tenant farmers in Hastings and St Leonard's both sides of 1800. The structure was either the chapel of the hospital of St Mary Magdalen at Hastings (thought to have been situated in the rear of 9 De Cham Road) or the parish church of St Leonard (of which the graveyard was disturbed when the Wesleyan Chapel was built in Norman Road). The lie of the land towards Hastings Castle, at the right, suggests the former, which is consistent with an account of 1786: near the windmill above White Rock were the foundations of a church or chapel and to the north-west was a barn made out of a chapel dedicated to St Mary Magdalen. 'The west end is entire, in which was a door with a sharp-pointed arch, and over it a long narrow window, both filled up. The walls are built with stones; some round, some thin and flat, some square; the mortar made with small pebbles.'

Neither hospital nor church is recorded until

104 Hastings, Dudeney's chapel, interior, 1784

S. H. Grimm

British Library, Add. MS. 5670, f. 31 [58]

the 13th century, but the building here has features which can be fairly confidently dated to the 12th century at latest. Both were out of use by the end of the 16th century - the hospital probably was dissolved before 1550 and, by that date, the inhabitants of the old parish of St Leonard's had 'time out of mind' attended Hollington church for services. When artists recorded the building, it was in agricultural use. No remains of hospital or church now survive above ground.

The triple arcade between chancel and nave is an unusual though not unknown feature in Sussex. Other examples occur at Pyecombe of which a visitor in 1825 wrote 'The chancel arch Norman, early, and very narrow and a small arch of like form on each side of it - a Sussex arrangement', Patcham (now blocked) and, prior to mid-19th-

century restoration, Bolney. A mid-19th-century picture hints at blocked side arches at Coombes, but the feature at Ovingdean does not appear on a plan of the church in 1869. The arcade at Dudeney's chapel is of similar style to that at Pyecombe, and looks to be unquestionably Romanesque. Petrie's exterior view from the south-east supports that dating - it clearly depicts a round-headed chancel arch on the other side of the wall, and traces of the side arches. *JB and JHF*

Sources Baines 1963, 106-8, 113. Boswell 1786-8, pts 63 and 90. Bullock 1949, 200-13. Cooper and Ross 1862, fc. 67, 69. Dale 1858, 61. Davey 1991, index, 'Deudney'. Ford 1978. Glynne 1963, 58 (quoted). Hills 1869, fc. 40. L. 1786, 852. Nairn and Pevsner 1965, 587. Salzman 1921, 36. SAS. pic. coll. 2578. Turner 1857, 43-4. VCHS, 7: 142-3, 214, 219. VCHS, 9: 86.

NGR TQ 809 089   *PDB* 2346, 2347

105 Hastings, East Cliff House and the beach, 1784

S. H. Grimm

British Library, Add. MS. 5670, f. 30 [56]

The house to the left has been nominated as the earliest known among the first fashionable houses to be built, not just beside the sea, but consciously facing it. Edward Capell (1713-81), Shakespeare scholar, Deputy Inspector of Plays and friend of David Garrick, may have been his own architect. In December 1760 he bought most of the site, the greater part being the redundant East Fort at the bottom of All Saints Street. The house, faced in yellow brick and rusticated stucco, was completed in 1762, and Capell was to spend his summers there, wintering in London at the Middle Temple. Grimm called it 'Mr Capell's house', though Capell had been dead several years; presumably his executors were letting it to tenants.

The sea-facing terrace, formerly the gun platform, had, by 1796, a small gatehouse at the right-hand end giving access to steps to the beach. By 1815 narrow gabled wings had been added to both sides of the house, as well as a balcony to the first floor, French windows being formed in the three central bays. Later all the windows gained external shutters. The shutters have gone and the house's exterior is now (2000) essentially as in 1815. But the fine interior fittings were removed in the 1970s.

The house to the right, with a cupola and two west-facing bows, is now East Hill House in Tackleway, and was built in the 1770s for the Wenham family. From the cupola, Grimm took the view to the north reproduced as *Sussex views*, 75.

JHF

Sources Hunter 1998. Old Hastings Preservation Society 1989, 18. Cornish and Williams 1991, 14 (Hearne's drawing, wrongly captioned). SAS, library accn 9089.

NGR TQ 825 095   *PDB* 2344

106 Hastings, fishing boat under East Hill, 1785

Joseph Farington

Hastings Museum & Art Gallery, T.P.378

Joseph Farington (1747-1814) is chiefly known for the diary he kept from 1793 until his death, which is a prime source of information on the Royal Academy and the art world of London. But he was also a professional topographical draughtsman of much accomplishment. By his early 20s he was already settled into the habit of making summer tours to places of antiquarian or picturesque interest. Hastings was his destination for the first time in 1785, and about a dozen pictures taken there and in the neighbourhood are known (four in Hastings Museum, with others in the Whitworth Gallery and VAM). They doubtless

provided material for the oil paintings of Hastings which he exhibited at the Royal Academy in 1787. Several, like this one, show close observation of the fishermen and their dress, although he seems not to have found figure-drawing easy and usually avoided it. For this view he positioned himself on the beach under East Hill, looking west to the town and Castle Hill.

Later visits are recorded in the diary: for three weeks in September 1797 (a sketchbook in VAM, P84-1921), for 11 weeks between November 1813 to January 1814 and two months in September to November 1818. No pictures from the latter two visits have been identified. *JHF*

Sources Ruddick and Turner 1977. Farington 1978-84, 3: 892-4, 12: 4428-44, 13: 4445-6, 15: 5261-80.

NGR TQ 829 095 *PDB* 2120

107 Hastings, 'Noah's Ark' on the America Ground, ?1815

Thomas Hearne

Hastings Museum & Art Gallery, 953.44.10

The America Ground was the name given seven acres of land between White Rock and Priory Stream, which had been formed by the accumulation of shingle, mainly in the 16th to 18th centuries. The Crown claimed ownership only in 1826, by which time it had been appropriated to a variety of uses: first occasional, fairs and cricket matches, and then continuing, rope-walks, net-stores and small workshops. Permanent habitable buildings followed from about 1806, and a rush to appropriate plots occurred around 1820, with some occupiers paying rents to the Corporation or the Earl of Chichester.

When these buildings - some 195 which housed a thousand people - were surveyed by the Crown in 1830, only one, 'Polymina', derived from the hulk of a vessel, but it was said to have been the first permanent building erected there. This may be what the drawing shows; Castle Hill is to the east behind. The site was cleared in 1835, but only in 1849 did the Crown find a lessee willing to develop what are now Robertson Street and Carlisle Parade.

Hearne visited Hastings with Lady Ashburnham and children in August 1815, and Hastings Museum's group of 13 sketches (1953.44.1-13) probably dates from then. His friend George Dance had found him at Ashburnham in feeble health, but thought the change of residence would be beneficial (see View 9).

JHF

Sources Funnell 1989. Farington 1978-84, 13: 4693-4.

NGR TQ 815 092

PDB 3686

108 Heathfield Park, 1794

Humphry Repton

East Sussex Record Office, AMS 6310

'Bayley Park' was built in 1677-82 for James Plummer, a London merchant, in red brick with stone quoins and window surrounds. It comprised two main floors over a basement, plus rooms in the roof behind a straight pediment. In 1706 Plummer's son was forced to settle debts by conveying the estate to John Turvin who sold to John Fuller of Tanners in Waldron in 1708. It then pass by sale through Raymond Blackmore, a London merchant (1721) and Arthur O'Keefe, a barrister (1742) to Lieut.-General George Eliott (1766). A professional soldier of Scottish descent, Eliott (1717-90) bought the estate with prize money received as second-in-command at the capture of Havana, Cuba. His greatest distinction was to defend Gibraltar under Spanish siege in 1779-82.

On Eliott's death Francis Newbery (1743-1818) used his fortune from publishing books and selling patent medicines to buy the estate of 1378 acres for £17,500. He changed its name to Heathfield Park, built a 55-foot tower to commemorate the defence of Gibraltar and refaced the house in fashionable stucco with triangular pediments. Repton was engaged to landscape the grounds, and this view gives his proposal for the approach to the house, taken from the Red Book (see View 58 for Repton's other work in Sussex).

One of Newbery's sons, William, was an amateur watercolourist who had probably met William Crotch in Oxford where they both studied drawing with John Malchair (View 130). They both made pictures of the park and its environs.

The house was remodelled to the designs of Reginald Blomfield in 1896-8.   *JHF*

Sources Pryce 1996, 41-9, 72-93, 128.
NGR TQ 599 209   *PDB* 5144

RUINS OF HEENE CHAPEL 1778.

109 Heene chapel, 1778

James Lambert senior
British Library, Add. MS. 5677, f. 69 [102]

In 1766, only four years after repair work had been carried out 'at a considerable expense', a faculty was obtained to demolish the chapel at Heene and reuse the materials in repairs to the mother church at West Tarring. About ten years later, Lambert's view recorded a roofless ruin, though with a gable and at least three pointed window openings surviving. A view by Grimm in 1790 (BL, Add. MS. 5673, f. 63 [113]) indicates further demolition and/or natural decay of the fabric.

The decline of the chapel may be traced from at least 1622, when the inhabitants petitioned the bishop for leave to demolish an aisle. At the beginning of the 18th century the chapel saw only one service a week, and by the 1720s or thereabouts had ceased to be used for divine service. Other uses for the building were soon found. It was converted into a carpenter's shop, and a sometime chapel-warden had to endure the seizure of the smuggled rum which he had stored there. The repair work of the early 1760s was presumably undertaken to maintain the building for secular use.

The dedication to St Botolph was recorded in 1534 is shared with only one other church in the diocese, that at Botolphs in the Adur valley. A new church of St Botolph was built on the site in 1873.

JB

Sources Shaw 1792. Secker 1995, 232 (quoted). Salzman 1932-4, 2: 80. VCHS, 6 (1): 91. Bickerton 1963, 15.

NGR TQ 137 028   *PDB* 4206

Henfield Octob: 26 1765

110 Henfield, Ameys, 1765

James Lambert senior

British Library, Add. MS. 71714, no. 9

Henfield parish has over fifty surviving vernacular houses, most of them well off the beaten track. Many can be traced as holdings in the records of Stretham manor, which was situated to the south and had come into the hands of the bishops of Chichester by 1066. Among a group of timber-framed cottages still standing down by the river are two which were thatched until after World War II, one of them being Ameys of which this is probably a view; the barn has long gone. This and nearby Neaves were both built in the mid- to late 16th century as comfortable 'modern' dwellings for smallholders. Only in later centuries did they become overcrowded and sub-standard.

Lambert probably made this sketch as a study for his oil paintings of imaginary landscapes: see, for example, the house at the right in the view dated 1769 of a wide river in wooded terrain, with a ruined castle reminiscent of Herstmonceux on a promontory behind and horned cattle in the foreground (Tate Gallery, 1658). See also the Arcadian composition of Southerham chapel in View 136. It was only from about 1771 that he received commissions for strictly topographical pictures.

AFH

Sources de Candole 1947.

NGR TQ 196 164

PDB 3949

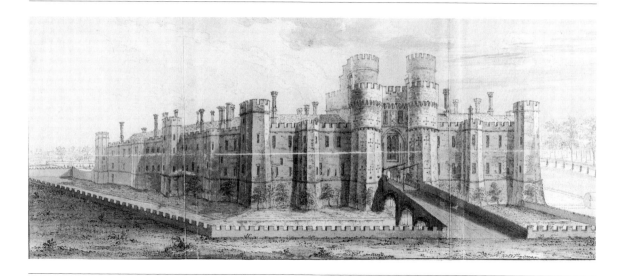

111 Herstmonceux Castle, 1736

Samuel Buck

Yale Center for British Art, Paul Mellon Collection,
B1977.14.1111

Sir Roger Fiennes was granted a licence to
crenellate in 1441 and the outer walls of the
vast mansion house which resulted still stand
substantially unchanged - the oldest brick building
of any note in England. This view, from the south-
west, is the earliest known of the castle and is
Buck's draft for his engraving published the
following year. There are fewer discrepancies
between draft and engraving than in his other
Sussex views: one fewer crenellation to the right-
hand gate-tower and - as Stephen Vine in 1773
confirmed they were - no fruit trees at the foot of
the walls. Vine said that the moat had been kept
dry for many years but could be filled easily by
ponds above it. It was filled in 1736, as was another
channel to the east, reflecting the beech trees for
which the park was famed.

The owner in 1736 was Francis Hare Naylor (d.
1775) to whom the engraving was dedicated and
whose uncle had bought the estate from Fiennes's
descendants in 1708. The family clearly regarded
the castle as a burden. His father advised him in
1740 that: 'The annual expense of the house,
gardens and park is near one third of the clear
produce of the estate whether one live there or
not, which is an insupportable grievance. If you
keep Herstmonceux you must .... resolve to live
like a private gentleman and within compass and
not to support a ridiculous popularity and the
figure of a great house, ruin yourself and be forced
to sell an estate which you would be glad to keep.'

Walpole in 1752 found that the house was
'scarcely furnished with a few necessary beds and
chairs', and a traveller in 1772 noted that it had
not been inhabited for several years, though kept
in good repair.

Naylor's half-brother and heir had most of the
interior demolished in 1777 (it was built anew from
1913). Nor were antiquaries welcome. Visiting in
1788, John Byng found that 'Nothing now remains
but the great shell and the kitchen gardens, into
neither of which, being locked up, could we enter,
nor by any noise bring anyone to assist us.... That
all the interior was in ruins, I could see through
the many windows. Surely at the destruction there
might have been some plunder for the antiquary,
of paintings, carved work, wainscoting, magnificent
chimney-pieces, tapestry, etc. etc. All sold as lumber
and long since burnt! Though sometimes a
curiosity is to be found in a neighbouring cottage,
as a bedstead or an old panel painting nailed over
a hole.'

The picture was painted on three sheets joined
vertically and has been damaged by being folded
horizontally.

JHF

Sources VCHS, 9: 131-4. Vine 1773. Walpole 1937-83, 35: 138.
GM 1772, 42: 562. Byng 1934, 365.

NGR TQ 646 103   *PDB* 1371

112 Herstmonceux Place from the north-east, 1785

S. H. Grimm

British Library, Add. MS. 5670, f. 74 [137]

Herstmonceux Place has at its core a timber-framed building of about 1550. That property, a freehold tenement of Herstmonceux manor called Collins with 20 acres, had been expanded by the end of the 17th century to an estate of 63 acres. The ambitious north façade in View 112 was built for the Revd William Jenkins, who had been presented by his father, the barrister Thomas Jenkins of Rampendene in Burwash, to the living of Herstmonceux in 1714 and who bought Herstmonceux Place from John Foster's heirs in 1719. The rebuilding cost was £3000.

Jenkins died in 1743 and his widow sold Herstmonceux Place to Francis Hare Naylor, the owner of the castle, in 1745. The house nevertheless remained the rector's residence, and in 1772 Naylor sold it to his half-brother Robert

Hare on his induction. The rectory proper, to which much valuable land was attached, was usually rented out to a farmer. On Naylor's death in 1775 the entire estate, including the castle, descended to Robert Hare. He and his wife Henrietta were faced with the choice of moving to the vast brick-built castle (View 111), assessed at 66 flues in 1666, or remaining at their modern house and finding another use for the castle. On the advice of the architect Samuel Wyatt (1737-1807) they opted to remain at Herstmonceux Place, demolish the interior of the castle and employ the materials to improve their own house.

Wyatt's scheme, one of his first recorded commissions, embodied a classical pediment on the east front and twin drums with cupolas on the south, with recesses housing Coade-stone panels between the two stories (View 113). It was clearly to be seen from the castle, which was incorporated into its grounds as a picturesque ruin, and to convince the onlooker that it was a new house. Jenkins's north façade of 1720 was however retained as a rear element, and the north-east view

113 Herstmonceux Place from the south-east, ?1785

S. H. Grimm

British Library, Add. MS. 5670, f. 74 [136]

shows the architect's sleight of hand in transforming the older building's three stories into two floors in the new work with the aid of blank windows on the east façade. The only incongruous note was provided by the demolition of the pediment of the north façade, necessary to bring it down to the level of Wyatt's second storey. Herstmonceux Place remained the rector's residence until 1792, when Hare's son Robert Hare rebuilt the rectory on his presentation to the living.

Antiquaries bemoaned the loss of the castle, and cast scorn on Herstmonceux Place: 'a paltry, Citizen-looking house' according to John Byng in 1788. In 1851 the Revd Edmund Venables thought 'Mr Wyatt's raw white stucco ... a poor substitute for Roger Fiennes' mellow red brick ....' But the need for a scapegoat settled on Robert Hare's second wife Henrietta. Augustus J. C. Hare (1834-1903), writing the life of his great-uncle Francis Hare-Naylor for the *Dictionary of National Biography* in the 1880s, states that Henrietta, the subject's stepmother, having wasted her own assets by constant extravagance, had persuaded her husband to demolish the castle in order to build a modern house, which could then be settled on her own children, only to be thwarted at the last when the land was found to be entailed. This frequently repeated myth seems to have no basis in fact and owes more to family enmity against a stepmother.

CHCW

Sources Martin 1996, P23/1, 2, 62. ESRO, HBR 1/977. Byng 1934, 365.

NGR TQ 639 110   *PDB* 2424, 2425

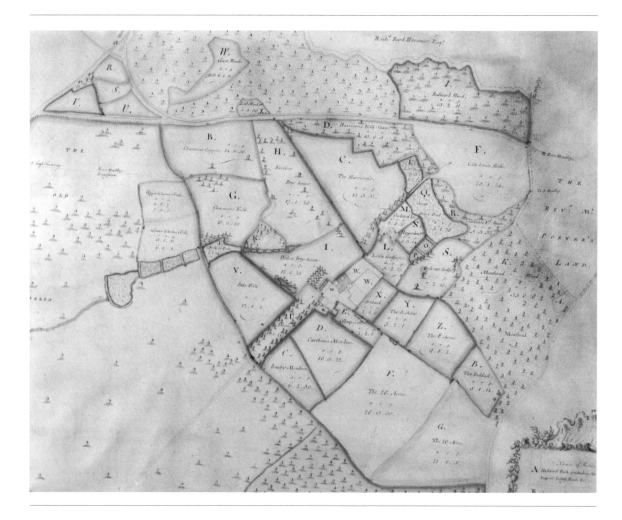

114 East Hoathly, Halland Park, 1778

Thomas Marchant
East Sussex Record Office, ACC 3714/2
Colour plate XI

Halland is best remembered for the entertainments provide by Thomas Pelham-Holles, Duke of Newcastle (1693-1768), to nurture his political interest in Sussex. Thomas Turner, the local shopkeeper, enjoyed, and recorded in his diary, the annual 'public days' and 'rejoicings' at military victories, and the frantic activity for the local tradesmen before the Duke arrived for a brief summer stay. The Duke may have loved his childhood home, but his inheritance of a great fortune, his accumulation of five residences and his elevation to high politics meant that Halland was

neglected. The inventory made on his death reflects a ramshackle house of an earlier generation fleetingly occupied: amongst some one hundred rooms were chambers for the Duke and a few relatives, rooms designated for household officials long dead, a great hall with a boarded parlour and a stone parlour adjacent, rooms unfashionably hung with tapestry or gilded leather, two rooms noted for being hung with paper, two spinning rooms and an armoury. The contents were valued at only £547 (compared with, say, £1069 at Lord de la Warr's 58-room Sheffield Place three years earlier).

The Duke of Newcastle died childless in November 1768, and as Horace Walpole put it, 'the sums he owed were only exceeded by those he wasted'. Newcastle had neglected maintenance and his executors' surveyor reported: 'The house of Halland being so very large and old, would be

115 East Hoathly, Halland, north-west front, 1783

S. H. Grimm

British Library, Add. MS. 5671, f. 47 [82]

wanting much repairs to make it habitable, nor can it be kept in sufficient repair to keep out the weather, without very considerable and constant expense. The out buildings, such as the barns, stables and granary are also very old, but are sufficiently large enough and convenient for the purpose of the farm, nor do they want any very material present repairs to keep them in condition for the use now made of them. The garden walls are also very old, and if kept up will shortly want repairs.' The trees and underwood were overgrown in the neglected 890-acre park.

The timber and deer were sold, in preparation for letting it. The household effects went under the hammer in May 1769. The great brewhouse and the wood house were demolished and 51,400 bricks and other materials were taken for building The Caprons in Lewes. The service quarters in the south corner were fitted up for the tenant farmer and separated from 'the Great House' which was shut up 'in order to save taxes'.

Grimm found the house in June 1783 'fast going to ruin.' John Byng witnessed the end in August 1788: 'the park ... is nearly felled, so that it now exhibits a scene of wildness and waste; the old house has been pulling down all the summer, but a part remains, which will soon come down with the yet-standing avenue trees.' A new farm house was built at the west corner. The coach house, of more recent build, further west was reprieved and was used as a barn until conversion to a residence in about 1999. The outer walls of the house at the north corner and the boundary wall (View 115) survive today to a height of about six feet, and show it to have been built of brick with sandstone quoins.

Laughton Place was the ancient family seat of the Pelhams, and Sir William Pelham (1486-1538) started extensive alterations in the 1530s, but his son Sir Nicholas (1517-60) did not complete them, perhaps reckoning that its low-lying and unhealthy location argued against further investment. In 1557 he bought 'Hall's land' in East Hoathly which had been owned by the Hall family from at least 1401 to 1537 and which adjoined the 1200 acres of common waste enclosed by his father in 1530, mostly for the 'New Park'. It was Sir Thomas Pelham (d. 1624) who built the great house, some three miles north of, and 150 feet above, Laughton Place. He was resident by July 1594, and a stone bearing the date 1595 has been reset over the door

S.H.Grimm fecit 1783

116 East Hoathly, Halland, the Great Court, 1783

S. H. Grimm

British Library, Add. MS. 5671, f. 48 [85]

of today's farm house. In 1662 the house was assessed at 38 hearths, more than any other any other in Pevensey Rape and exceeded in Lewes Rape only by Slaugham Place at 40 hearths (View 172).

Only seven pictures are known of Halland. Of Grimm's five, three are printed here; that of the South Court is in *Sussex views*, 78; the fifth is another view of the Great Court. An anonymous view of 1785 also appears here; a view of the main front from another source is engraved in Horsfield 1835, 1: 358. The map by Thomas Marchant of Lewes (1750-90) helps to interpret them and shows the park.

The entrance front faced north-west, marked out by the ogee gables: View 115. The view of the

Great Court, 116, indicates two phases of building, for the change in the height of the plinth and the partial string course are also evident in the view of the other side. The screen between the wings, on the left in 116, is sufficiently different in style to suggest a third phase, but not many years apart. Heavy borrowing in 1592 and 1602/3 suggests at least two building campaigns. The main entrance was off-centre because it aligned with the door to the hall which was behind and to Grimm's right in 116. The hall range terminated in the larger, central gable of the five on the north-east, or garden, front, at the left in 115. Given this orientation, one wonders whether the approach was originally from the north, through the plots marked H and I on the map. At the right of 118 was the farm house formed in 1769.

The south-east view, 117, is hard to reconcile with the other views and the map. The large range with chimney stacks on both sides perhaps housed the kitchen. The opposite end of it, giving onto the South Court, is in *Sussex views*, 78. At the left, partly hidden by the garden wall, is a derelict timber-

117 East Hoathly,
Halland, south-east front, 1783

S. H. Grimm
British Library, Add. MS. 5671, f. 47 [83]

Detail of house and gardens
from View 114

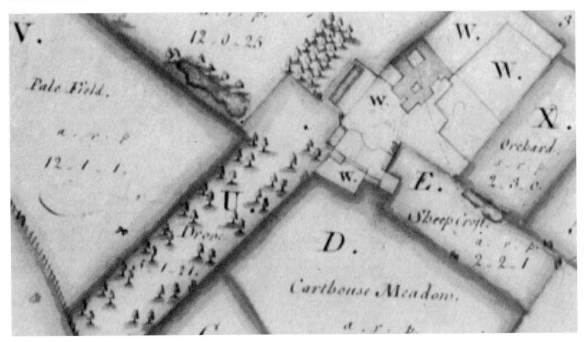

118 East Hoathly, Halland, from the west, 1785

Unknown artist

British Library, K Top 42.30.2.

framed building, perhaps the last remnant of a house on the site before Pelham began building; the free-standing gable and chimney and broken walls, at the far right in the view from the west, 118, may be part of the same structure.

None of the construction in these views looks later than the first half of the 17th century, and that Sir Thomas Pelham was spending on trees, plants and seeds for the garden in 1643 may signal attention turning from the house to its surrounds. If, as his accounts of 80 years later suggest, Newcastle was investing in Halland, it was not in new building. Perhaps he was also spending on the grounds and a new approach to the house. The south-east front in the 1780s gave onto pleasure gardens running down to (so the map suggests) a

terrace with a fine view to the Downs. The drove running to the south-west was of Spanish chestnuts which were still standing in the 1920s, having escaped, against Byng's prediction, the axe in 1788, but it has since been felled. A rectangular stretch of water south-west of the house, called the horse pond in 1769, was presumably a garden feature, but the string of ponds served as fish-stews, stocked with about 100 brace in 1768, and as decoy ponds for fowling.

JHF

Sources Kelch 1974, 12, 189-90. Turner 1984, e.g. 11, 107, 156, 161, pl. 2a. Steer 1956. Brent 1993, 207-8. Byng 1934, 366-7. Farrant et al. 1991, 153, 161. Cliffe 1999, 55. Wolseley 1925, 97. ESRO, AMS 2132, 2133; ACC 6077/22/7, 25; East Hoathly parish register transcript. BL, Add. MSS 33139, ff. 339-41; 33337, ff. 15-18; 5681, f. 364; 5697, f. 237; Add. Ch. 30221, 30244-5, 30247, 30257-62.

NGR TQ 511 159   *PDB* 8076, 2529, 2530, 2527, 44

119 Horsham, Springfield Park, 1789

S. H. Grimm

British Library, Add. MS. 5673, f. 12 [21]

This house was built for Samuel Blunt of Horsham between 1752 and 1758, on land originally called Dyers, which lay within Marlpost, an outlier of the archbishop of Canterbury's manor of Tarring. His great-grandfather was a mercer who had migrated from Bolney. Samuel's first wife Sarah, daughter of Leonard Gale, the ironmaster of Crabbet Park, died young in 1752, and when in 1759 he married Winifred Scawen, the settlement included Newbuildings at Shipley, and the 'newly erected capital messuage' in Horsham, shown on a plan the previous year. It is perhaps the only Georgian house of a single build in Horsham, and as the interests of symmetry were paramount there were several false windows, some glazed, some

merely painted. The almost symmetrical wings of the stable blocks are reminiscent of grander work by Vanbrugh and Francis Smith, but typically of a building in a country town, it was already rather old-fashioned when first erected. An orangery linked the house to one of the stable blocks.

From one of the sons of Samuel and Winifred descended Wilfred Scawen Blunt (1840-1922), explorer, poet and breeder of Arab horses. His daughter married the 3rd Earl Lytton, whose grandson lives at Newbuildings today. Descendants of the Blunts owned Springfield Park until the end of the 1950s, by which time it had been a school for some years. Having stood derelict for several years from 1989, the house and its grounds were refurbished and developed as private dwellings.

AFH

Sources Hughes 1996.

NGR TQ 171 311   *PDB* 2732

120 Horsham, the New Gaol, 1788

S. H. Grimm

British Library, Add. MS. 5673, f. 13 [24]

Horsham had a county gaol from at least 1540, successively on three different sites in the Carfax. After a series of escapes, John Howard made a damning report in 1774, and under the leadership of the Lord Lieutenant, the 3rd Duke of Richmond, the decision was taken to build a new gaol in East Street, to a classical design by William Ride (*c.* 1723-78). When completed in 1779, it was the first model gaol in England, and, it was claimed, the first in the world to have a cell for each prisoner, although it bankrupted the builders. Grimm depicted its front range comprising the governor's house and gatehouses.

In 1782 John Howard could write that he 'found the Gaol as quiet as a private house, the prison is clean, healthy and well regulated.' At that time the gaol was housing an average of 34 prisoners. It was enlarged in 1819, and from 1820 executions were carried out in front of it. The last to hang there was John Lawrence, murderer of the Chief Constable of Brighton, in 1844.

After 1830, the Assizes were no longer held at Horsham, so the prison population declined, the prison was closed and in 1845 the land and buildings were sold to Henry Michell, the brewer. He subsequently demolished the prison and the materials were reused for a police-lock-up and a brewery in Horsham, a parchment factory in Steyning, private houses, and works on the railway line from Three Bridges to Horsham. See Views 147 and 148 for Petworth House of Correction completed in 1789.

AFH

Sources Albery 1947, pt 4. VCHS, 6 (2): 133-4. Colvin 1995, 817. *NGR* TQ 175 304   *PDB* 2734

121 Horsted Keynes, Broadhurst House, 1785

S. H. Grimm

British Library, Add. MS. 5671, f. 108 [206]

The landholding called Broadhurst is first mentioned by name in 1121 among the endowments of Lewes Priory, and over a hundred years later it passed into the hands of the Lewkenor family. In 1567 Thomas Lewkenor conveyed the manor to Richard Michelborne of Ditchling who and whose son Sir Richard (d. 1638) lived there. It is very likely that they were responsible for building the range which still survives. Sir Richard's son William sold in 1652 to Edward Lightmaker, brother-in-law to the Archbishop of Glasgow, Robert Leighton, but when Grimm drew the house it had been recently sold by wealthy ironmasters, the Pigotts, to Viscount Hampden.

Pictured here from a field on the east, the range of four bays with its three large chimney stacks has unusual stair 'hatches', comparable to those at Hangleton Manor near Hove. It contains a fireback dated 1658. Two of the outbuildings also survive, and the one still thatched is thought to have served some non-agricultural function. By the end of the 19th century Broadhurst had been purchased by John Stephenson Clarke, and he was responsible for major rebuilding and restoration in the 1920s after a disastrous fire destroyed earlier buildings to the north. The fireplaces and chimneys of the old range are carefully echoed in the new building, as are the mullioned windows and stone roof.

AFH

Sources Eardley 1939. Wolseley 1925, 61-78. Dell 1964, 198-203.
NGR TQ 387 330 *PDB* 2457

HOVE

122 Hove Church, 1776

James Lambert senior

British Library, Add. MS 5677, f. 37 [53]

In 1586 the churchwardens at Hove reported that 'our church is in such decay that we are not able to amend it.' One hundred years later the porch roof had fallen down, the walls, windows, doors and floors wanted repair, and the steeple walls and floors were 'much decayed'. The impression gained by these descriptions is of a settlement in crisis, a view amply confirmed by John Warburton, herald and antiquary, in 1723: 'I passed through a ruinous village called Hove which the sea is daily eating up and is a fair way of being quite deserted; but the church being large and a good distance from the shore may perhaps escape.'

So it did, but only in much reduced part. In 1724 the nave was in 'tolerable repair', but the top of the tower was ruinous and there was no chancel. Furthermore, a few years later, the aisles fell into disrepair and the tower was demolished, the masonry being taken for Carne's Seat, a sham ruin built as a prospect house in the park at Goodwood in 1743 (Views 25 and 26). When Lambert took his view in 1776, showing the ?12th-century chancel arch and 13th-century nave arcade blocked up, the few services held were confined to the four eastern bays of the nave. By 1804 the porch had been reroofed, and the church was rebuilt in 1836.   *JB*

Sources Ford 1994, 39, 143 (both quoted). Nairn and Pevsner 1965, 229. Renshaw 1910, 3 (quoted). VCHS, 7: 267, picture fc. 268 by John (not Russell) Skinner, 1804. BL, Lansdowne MS. 918, f. 90v (quoted); Add. MS. 5698, f. 64.

NGR TQ 286 048   *PDB* 4171

123 Iping Bridge, *c.* 1792

Hendrick de Cort

West Sussex Record Office, M/PD 266

This bridge over the western Rother is among the nine or so most ancient in West Sussex. The medieval structure, as de Cort saw it and as it survives today, reflects the results of major repair in 1650 when it had become 'very much in decay so that a cart could not cross.' De Cort's skilfully chosen view, looking south east and downstream towards the bridge epitomises its picturesqueness and rural tranquillity - almost certainly in contrast with scenes of noise and bustle immediately behind the artist. For behind him was the unpicturesque Iping Mill, which since 1725 at latest had developed, as Dallaway records, into a 'manufactory of writing and printing paper of the finer sorts, which employs about a hundred persons, principally women and children.' In the 1790s the proprietor was John Bigg who, having been a tenant, bought the mill from Lord Egremont in 1785/6. In 1800 it boasted 'three water-wheels and six white vats, presses, frames, stuff chests, fixtures and every apparatus for carrying on a trade of the first consequence.' It supplied the 19th-century *Times* and continued in operation until it was burnt down in 1925.

Beyond the bridge can be seen Iping House, which was acquired early in the 19th century by Admiral Sir Charles Hamilton (1767-1849), and remained the family seat until World War I. The exterior remains virtually unchanged. *PMW*

Sources Dallaway 1815, 2: 226. Challen 1944. Shorter 1951, 170-2. Nairn and Pevsner 1965, 250. VCHS, 2: 238, 4: 63-4. WSRO, QTD/W 71; QAB/3/W 1 f. 78; MF 642.

NGR SU 853 229   *PDB* 1670

124 Itchingfield, Muntham House, 1788

S. H. Grimm

British Library, Add. MS. 5673, f. 7 [10]

Muntham House stands almost in the centre of Itchingfield parish, and its history is included in the articles on the parish by Percy S. Godman in the 1890s. These owed much to documents in the private possession of the Chitty family, owners from 1817 to 1878. To summarise, Muntham paid dues to Thakeham manor in the 14th century, and is probably identical with the three-hide manor listed in Domesday, held by Morin from William de Braose. In the top left-hand corner of Grimm's drawing are details of a stone that was let in over the door of the front range: 'T [?J] M 1371 Rebuilt by Jo Merlott 1741'. This refers to a tradition that the first house on the site was built by John de Mundham, who alienated the manor in 1372. His wife was a Merlott, the family who were then owners until the 19th century, and William Merlott

married a niece of Archbishop Juxon in 1649. It is possible that the framed rear wing shown in 1788 contained remains of that earlier house.

Godman demolished the Merlott house after 1880, although a plan in his article of 1896 suggests that a small portion still may be encased. The Merlott date-stone is said to be fixed over a fireplace in the library of the school which now occupies the site.

AFH

Sources Godman 1896. Godman 1898. VCHS, 6 (2): 10-11.
NGR TQ 124 275   *PDB* 2722

125 Lamberhurst, Scotney, west front, ?1783

S. H. Grimm

British Library, Add. MS. 5670, f. 1 [2]

Prior to 1894 Scotney was in the Sussex portion of the parish of Lamberhurst, as it had been for centuries. The medieval castle developed there by Roger de Ashburnham in the late 1370s shows marked similarity with that of Bodiam, built only ten years later, also on the profits of the French Wars. Both castles exhibit an essentially rectangular ground plan, moated, with four corner-towers and a gatehouse set into the curtain wall. One of these corner-towers, the so-called Ashburnham tower (surviving today), is seen in Grimm's view from the west (View 125), and the bases of two further towers can be seen on the extreme right of the view from the north-east (View 126).

The south wing (immediately to the left of the Ashburnham tower in View 125) was reconstructed in about 1580 by Thomas Darell, whose family had acquired the property through marriage in the early 15th century. From the late 16th century may date, also, the timber-framed stable block, prominently centre-right in View 125, but since largely demolished. It was located on the smaller of the two islands in the moat - the site of Ashburnham's castle was on the larger which was, and remains, accessible only from the smaller. Effectively, therefore, the smaller island became the outer ward of the castle.

By 1650, the east range had been rebuilt, probably by William, grandson of Thomas Darell, to form an elegant front (View 126) and a somewhat more prosaic, four-gabled rear (View 125). It was planned as fifteen bays, whereas Grimm shows only seven with another one or two out of site behind the porch. Some medieval walling was incorporated into this rebuild, but it is likely that other parts of the old castle were demolished when this development took place.

126 Lamberhurst, Scotney, north-east front, 1783

S. H. Grimm

British Library, Add. MS. 5670, f. 1 [1]

The Darell family's association with Scotney ended in 1774 when debts forced a sale. The auction particulars describe the house as having been 'lately substantially repaired', though exactly what had been done is not clear. Edward Hussey, non-practising barrister and grandson of a local ironfounder, bought the castle in 1778. It remained in the family for almost 200 years until bequeathed to the National Trust by Christopher Hussey (1899-1970).

Within 60 years of Grimm's record of the castle, it had been deliberately ruinated, particularly in respect of the east range. A new house to a design by Anthony Salvin was built on the hill above the old castle, the site being chosen after consultation with the artist and landscape gardener (and nephew of the Revd William), William Sawrey Gilpin. It was built of stone from the site, the consequent quarry being part of the planned landscape and allowing a view from the new house of the ruined castle below. The picturesque nature of the old castle within the landscaped grounds of the new house is generally acknowledged. 'The grey and rust-coloured castle tower in the lily-moat reflecting sky, trees and ruined mansion against a steep wilderness of quarry and flowers, to-day makes an exquisite picture. If ever ruin-making has justified itself, this has' (Rose Macaulay writing in 1953).

JB

Sources anon. 1989, passim (quoted). Hussey 1970, 1, quoting Macaulay. Newman 1969, 487. Stevens 1928, 40-1.

NGR TQ 689 352

PDB 2289, 2290

127 East Lavant, West Lavant Place, *c.* 1780

S. H. Grimm

British Library, Add. MS. 5675, f. 17 [33]

West Lavant Place was the seat of the Miller family. Gilbert Miller came to Chichester from Wrotham in Kent at the end of the 16th century. The family soon purchased property at West Lavant and probably built the house represented in this view by the central section of five bays and the wing of two bays to the right (west), both of two storeys, the central section with dormers: these can be dated to about 1600. On the left was probably a balancing wing which was, perhaps a century later, enlarged by the three-storey extension. Various outhouses to the east are hidden by the trees.

Three members of the family were elected as MPs for Chichester, Thomas Miller in 1688 and 1690, John Miller in 1698, 1701, 1702 and 1710 and Thomas Miller in 1714 and 1722, the last receiving a baronetcy in 1705. Sir John Miller, a fellow planter of trees and close friend of the 2nd Duke of Richmond, briefly canvassed the city in 1741; he was mayor in 1748. The family purchased Froyle Place near Alton, Hants in 1770. In 1785, Lady Miller had some land in the parish in hand, but West Lavant Farm was tenanted by John Sadler. The 3rd Duke purchased the West Lavant house in 1791 and ordered its demolition.

TJMcC and JHF

Sources VCHS, 4: 102. WSRO, Goodwood MSS E 491-5; MP 3424. Readman et al. 2000, 150. *NGR* SU 851 083   *PDB* 3138

128 Lewes, Westgate, 1772

James Lambert senior, 1774

Sussex Archaeological Society, LEWSA 1997.7 21

The Anglo-Saxon *burh* of Lewes was defended on the west by a substantial earthwork across the spur; this was augmented in about 1275 by a stone wall and the 'westgate' in Greensand. It consisted of two rectangular towers with circular fronts to the west. The whole structure was 68 feet across and 30 feet in depth, with the gate itself 10 feet wide. On his map of 1620 John de Ward showed the Westgate still with crenellations and its archway across the road. But by the time the master of the nearby grammar school, the Revd Robert Austen (Essay 3.2), drew it from the west, both towers had been reduced to below the springing points of the arch, and vegetation was taking hold. He made his drawing (later copied by

the Lamberts) when removal of the inner walls was imminent, allegedly for a wager, but more likely for road widening: at the end of October 1763, 'The Westgate is almost down,... and Mr Webb's house very much exposed to the wheels of the carriages, if not good care taken.' A ground plan by the Lewes mason John Morris in 1777 was probably commissioned by John Elliot (Essay 3.2), as was the view reproduced here which is known in several copies, the earliest dated 1772. This was taken looking into the south bastion, with the entrance to Westgate Chapel and the west wall of Bull House, to the left. Number 93 High Street which now stands on the site was built in 1790; its east wall incorporates reused Greensand stone.   *JHF*

Sources VCHS, 7: 7, 11-12. Brent 1995, front cover. Lambert 1956. ESRO, SHR 939 (quoted). Dunvan 1795, 349. Houghton 1997, 74.

NGR TQ 412 099   *PDB* 4322

129 Lewes Priory dovecote, ?1762

Francis Grose

Sussex Archaeological Society, picture collection 3590 (detail)

The cruciform dovecote was located in the south-west corner of the priory precincts, on a site now occupied by the pavilion of the Southdown Club. Its date is not known but is generally considered to be of the late medieval period. Grose's view is from the north-east, and the second reredorter of the priory, built in about 1200 as a larger replacement to the original 11th-century reredorter, appears on the right of the picture.

Substantial ruins of the reredorter survive but nothing remains above ground of the dovecote - it was demolished in the early years of the 19th century and the materials used in road-building and for other construction work. Its walls had stood 30 feet from ground to eaves. The crop-mark of the foundations appeared during the dry summer of 1895, and the exterior measurements were recorded as 81 feet 3 inches from north to south and 80 feet 3 inches from east to west.

The interior space appears to have been organised into four rectangular compartments, the two on the north/south axis being the larger. Access for the birds was at the top of each of the four gables. The dovecote is said to have had 3228 nest-holes ('ingeniously constructed of hewn chalk'), which would make it one of the largest ever recorded in England. More usually dovecotes were round, square or octagonal in plan, with fewer than a thousand nest-holes.

Grose's view is undated, but a companion is, to 2 August 1762, while the Surrey Militia was billeted on Lewes. That view is of the Lord's Place, formed out of the Prior's Lodging but torn down soon after 1668 (BL, K. Top. 42.42l). *JB*

Sources Brent 1993, 110. Brent 1995, 35. Brunskill 1987, 88. Johnston 1901, 162. Lyne 1997, 33, 55. Mantell 1846, 431-2 (quoted). Sawyer 1896, 271.

NGR TQ 412 094.   *PDB* 3407

130 Lewes, the Castle and the High Street, 1755-6

J. B. Malchair

Ashmolean Museum, Oxford, DBB 1107

John Baptist Malchair (1730-1812) came to England from his home town, Cologne, via Nancy, in about 1754. He was in Lewes for a year from August 1755 as a musician in an Army regiment, and returned in July 1757. Living in Oxford for the rest of his life, he may have made later visits. But on stylistic grounds, this view can be dated to 1755-6. His one other view of Lewes shows soldiers on guard duty on the north side of the Castle (Corpus Christi College, Oxford, MS. 443.II.35). His vantage point for this picture was The Mount (TQ 415 096), south-east of the town. At the right and centre were St Martin's Lane and Green Lane. The nearer buildings were on the south side of Steward's Inn Lane; those beyond were on the south side of the High Street. Several of the latter appear as substantial multi-bay houses, though by the 1750s were sub-divided. The Castle keep sported, on its east, the summer house which Thomas Friend had built at some date since 1732.

Well might the traveller John Macky in 1713 admire the 'gentlemen's seats joining to one another with their gardens up hill and down hill.' Large houses with adjacent gardens were more in evidence further east in the High Street (View 131). The gardens in this view were occupied with the houses on the High Street from which they were separated by Steward's Inn Lane.   *JHF*

Sources Farrant 1997a, 253. Harrison 1998, 11. Farrant 1996a, 173. Houghton 1989. Macky 1714, 1: letter IV.

NGR TQ 413 101   *PDB* 6077

HENRY HUMPHREY Esq.   JOHN FULLER Esq.

HOUSES in LEWES

131 Lewes, two houses on School Hill, 1783

James Lambert senior
British Library, Add. MS. 5677, f. 3 [5]

As the administrative, commercial and social centre for eastern Sussex, Lewes's High Street incorporated the substantial houses of its 'urban gentry'. These two on the south side of School Hill reflect the good fortunes of its physicians. The right-hand house, now number 33, School Hill House, had its red-brick front stack added in 1715 by Dr Peter White (d. 1725) who had lived there since 1683. The design came from the combined efforts of White, his bricklayer (perhaps Arthur Morris, *c.* 1685-1744) and Peter Courthope who purchased and shipped materials from London. White's grandson, John Fuller (1732-1804), a Wealden landowner, was owner and occupier in 1783.

Henry Humphrey, a barrister, lived at number

32, Lewes House. The owner in 1625, John Coulstock, gained a grant of waste, 30 by 15 feet, probably for the porch; perhaps the façade of the house was rebuilt at the same time, in Caen stone salvaged from the Priory. In 1699 Dr John Tabor (1667-1729), archaeologist (View 73) as well as physician, married the widowed owner's daughter. He or his son-in-law William Kempe refaced the garden front; certainly he acquired land to the south-west and diverting the twitten, to form, at two acres, the largest garden within the town. The present three-storied street frontage was added between 1783 and 1799. The house just visible to the left was the poor-house of the parish of All Saints.

Lewes District Council owns both houses and occupies number 32; number 33 is appropriately used as a doctors' surgery.   *JHF*

Sources Houghton 1989. Dunvan 1795, 481. ESRO, SHR 1641-53; ACC 2953/7.

NGR TQ 416 101   *PDB* 4129

132 Lindfield, Paxhill Park, ?1787

S. H. Grimm

British Library, Add. MS. 5672, f. 35 [63]

Paxhill Park still stands on rising ground north-east of the village of Lindfield. Grimm drew the main, west, front. The spandrels of the entrance are inscribed '1606 NB', recording that the house was built, in local sandstone, for Ninian Boord (or Board) who died in that year. Extensive oak panelling and decorated plaster moulding survive inside. Ninian's father came from Cuckfield to Lindfield.

William Board who was in possession when Grimm took this view was to be the last male heir, and on his death in 1790 Paxhill passed by a daughter's marriage to Gibbs Crawfurd, son of John Crawfurd of Saint Hill (View 94). A north

wing was added for Northall Laurie in 1865 (but has since been demolished) and a south wing for William Sturdy in 1877. The west front is changed only in details, as weathered stone has been replaced and finials added on the parapet. Paxhill Park is now a residential home for the elderly.

This picture illustrates how Grimm's views were trimmed (his title at the bottom left being cut) and mounted on a secondary sheet of paper on which were added decorative borders of ruled ink lines and bands of watercolour wash. Burrell or his clerk squeezed a title into the space between the first and second borders. This practice hid any notes which Grimm had made on the back of the picture and in at least one case may have contributed to misidentification in the new title, as in View 62. *JHF*

Sources anon. 1978. Donnithorne 1995.

NGR TQ 359 265 *PDB* 2700

ve yaldings house on Black down near Fernhurst.

wy 1640 Y

S.H.Grimm fe.t . c. 27th 1790

133 Lodsworth, Blackdown House, 1790

S. H. Grimm

British Library, Add. MS. 5675, f. 1 [1]

'Mr Yalding's house' stands today as Blackdown House, sporting the alterations of 1844-6, by Anthony Salvin, and of 1891. Grimm's view of the north front shows the 'handsome plain stone manor house' of 1640 which clearly recalls an earlier, 16th-century, style. The 'WY' of the date stone was presumably William Yalden, Roundhead and friend of Cromwell's, successful ironmaster, steward to Viscount Montague, and MP for Midhurst in 1659. The family had been at Blackdown since at least the late 16th century.

Of special interest in this view is the landscaping. The house and grounds are framed by woodland. In the foreground a terrace or ha-ha within gardens is separated from the house by walls and the drive. Behind the house, a grass slope steps up the hillside to a small shelter and, higher up, a wall with a porched gate giving onto an avenue of trees. The relics of this landscaping survive today. Grimm has also recorded a circular field monument just below the summit of the Downs.

Grimm may have been no stranger to the Yalden family, as in 1776 Gilbert White wrote of the artist visiting the Revd Yalden of Newton Valence, a parish adjacent to Selborne and only a handful of miles from Blackdown, to take a view of the vicarage.

JB and JHF

Sources Dallaway 1832, 363. Cleere and Crossley 1995, 333, 342, 346, 360. Cochrane 1967, 46. Fletcher 1975, 28. Kenyon 1952, 235. Leconfield (Lord) 1954, 101-3. Nairn and Pevsner 1965, 106 (quoted). VCHS, 4: 72 and n.6. Holt-White 1901, 1: 319-20, 328.
NGR SU 916 286   *PDB* 2933

134 Lyminster, Pynham Priory, 1781

S. H. Grimm

British Library, Add. MS. 5674, f. 12 [22]

The house of Augustinian Canons dedicated to St Bartholomew at Pynham, also known as Calceto, was founded before 1151 by Adeliza, second wife of Henry I (d.1135) and subsequently wife of William de Albini, lord of the honor of Arundel. It was a small foundation of only two or three regular priests who were obliged to serve the chapel of the house, undertake the repair of the causeway and the wooden bridge across the river on the south east side of Arundel, and maintain a hospital or hostelry for poor travellers. (St Bartholomew was a popular dedication for hospitals throughout the medieval period.) It was suppressed in 1525 and its revenues were granted to Cardinal Wolsey's new college in Oxford. After Wolsey's disgrace the estate of the priory was resumed by the Crown until, in 1607, it was granted to Sir Anthony Browne, Viscount Montague.

Grimm's view from the north records no obvious sign of medieval antiquity unless, perhaps, it is in the buttress - Stebbing Shaw visited the site in 1790 and considered that 'only a remaining buttress or two against a small square building now point out [the priory's] former existence.' The small square building, apparently derelict when Grimm visited but renovated by 1793, survives today as the core of a house. A two-storey domestic extension replaces the lean-to shown by Grimm, and all but the top few inches of Grimm's buttress has been hidden from view (or demolished) by another extension. The window under the eaves in the 'shadow' wall survives; that in the 'sunlit' wall is blocked but can be traced in the stonework.   *JB*

Sources Binns 1989, 31. Nairn and Pevsner 1965, 94. VCHS, 2: 80. Horsfield 1835, 2: 144. Shaw 1790c, 202 (quoted). Smith 1793.
NGR TQ 025 063   *PDB* 2856

135 Madehurst, Dale Park, 1791

S. H. Grimm

British Library, Add. MS. 5674, f. 31 [55]

Madehurst Place, as Grimm called it but better known as Dale Park, was a south-facing three-storied house of seven bays with asymmetrical two-storied wings, here seen from the south-east. The four eastern bays were fronted by a colonnade, as was the east wing. A lodge gave entrance to the as-yet unfinished gardens, for the house was newly built, designed by Joseph Bonomi the elder (1739-1808) and constructed in 1784-8. In Sussex Bonomi also worked on Stansted House with James Wyatt in 1786-91.

The client was Sir George Thomas, 3rd baronet (*c.* 1748-1815), son and heir of Sir William Thomas of Yapton Place and Madehurst. The Thomas fortune was established by his grandfather, sometime Governor of the Leeward Islands - which office Sir George sought unsuccessfully three times in the 1790s. Disinherited for marrying a foreigner, he nevertheless succeeded to estates in Antigua under his father's marriage settlement, and by several purchases acquired the whole of Madehurst parish. He was MP for Arundel 1790-7, Colonel of the Sussex Fencible Cavalry 1795-9 and a cousin of George White Thomas of Watergate in Up Marden, the lawyer and MP for Chichester, 1784-1807 (View 138). His house was later owned by Thomas Read Kemp, while briefly MP for Arundel in 1823-6; by John Smith of the Smith family of London bankers, whose son John Abel Smith, the local MP, sold it to the Duke of Abercorn; and by John Charles Fletcher, High Sheriff of Sussex in 1863. Described by Pevsner as 'a plain and ugly house', it was demolished in 1959 and the present Dale House built on the site.

TJMcC

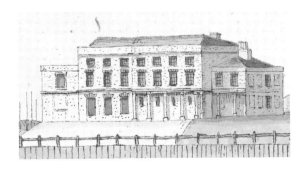

Sources Colvin 1995, 141-3. Nairn and Pevsner 1965, 268. Pike 1910, 182. Thorne 1986, 5: 365.

NGR SU 974 101

PDB 2889

136 South Malling, Southerham chapel, 1780

James Lambert senior
British Library, Add. MS. 5676, f. 86 [132]
Colour plate XII

The earliest reference to a chapel at Southerham occurs in a late-14th-century copy of the Taxation of Pope Nicholas of about 1291, where it is recorded as an appendage to the benefice of the rectory of St Thomas in the Cliffe next Lewes. By the 1530s the chapel, dedicated to St Mary Magdalen, had fallen into disrepair and, probably, disuse, but in 1540 it was 'then newly erected', that is, renovated as a dwelling, and let as copyhold of the manor of Ranscombe. Thus, in 1549/50, Edward Brown was paying a rent of 4d. a year for 'the messuage sometime the chapel of Sothram', and in 1631, Peter Browne was admitted to a building 'once a chapel'.

Over the next 200 years or so it appears regularly in manorial documents described as a tenement, but Hussey, writing in 1852, notes that 'every vestige of the ancient building was removed in 1837.' The thatched cottage viewed from the north-west by Lambert was probably on the site of the chapel. Other views show two ruined walls slightly inset extending from the east side of the cottage. They could very plausibly be the remains of a chancel. The shepherd and sheep occupying the rough pasture in the foreground, and the flowering shrubs near the cottage, are reminiscent of the pastoral paintings of Lambert's master, George Smith of Chichester.

This and the following view of Upper Stoneham Farm allow comparison of the work of the two Lamberts. *JB*

Sources BL, Add. MS. 5677, f. 28 [37]. ESRO/SAS/G 8/46 (quoted), 34/36 (quoted), 78. Farrant 1997a, 254-7. Hussey 1852, 255 (quoted). Peckham 1946, 322. SAS, LEWSA 1999/36.
NGR TQ 427 092   *PDB* 4111

137 South Malling, Upper Stoneham Farm, 1781

James Lambert junior
British Library, Add. MS. 5676, f. 91 [139]

New and Old Stonehams (nowadays Upper and Lower, respectively) were created in 1693 by the partition of the 1000-acre medieval demesne of Stoneham with East Gote in South Malling and Ringmer. The focal point of the demesne is thought to have been at Old Stoneham, and, though there may have been some ancillary agricultural buildings at New Stoneham, there is no record of a dwelling there until the partition. Probably from that time dates the rather plain, 3½-bay house with projecting cross-wing, here shown from the south-east; another late-18th-century view shows what may be an outshot at the back. The house today presents a very different appearance, having been remodelled and refronted, possibly in the early 19th century.

Its owner in 1781 was Dr William Burrell, Lambert's client, hence the carefully finished view of a modest tenanted farmhouse. In 1806 the property was described as a farm house, yards, gardens, a cottage and five barns along with 375 acres of arable land, 126½ acres of meadow and pasture, 179 acres of sheepdown, including a chalk quarry, and 8½ acres of woodland.

A major Roman road from London passes the site of Upper Stoneham about 100 yards west, and the lane in front of the house is a putative Roman road running across the Downs from a bridging point at Glynde to a junction with the London road. Finds of Roman roofing tile are recorded from within the area of the medieval demesne.

JB

Sources ESRO, AMS 5763/33; SAS/FB 17. Margary 1948, 150-3, 198. Scott 1993, 59.
NGR TQ 427 117   *PDB* 4463

138 Up Marden, Watergate, 1791

S. H. Grimm

British Library, Add. MS. 5675, f. 96 [171]

In the first decade of the 17th century, John Drury purchased the Watergate estate in Up Marden and Stoughton and built Watergate House for his son. After Drury's death, the house was successively owned by Thomas Lodger, the Cotton family of Warblington in Hampshire, and John Page, MP for Chichester, 1741-79. John Page's daughter Frances married George White Thomas, a lawyer and MP for Chichester 1784-1807 - the owner at the time that Grimm drew it.

Shortly afterwards the Jacobean house in the drawing was demolished and replaced by a substantial brick and flint cemented new house in the Greek style, with two principal fronts embellished with Ionic columns, for many years attributed to Sir John Soane. Thomas's daughter married Major General Sir John Gustavus Crosbie of Donnington, who erected the formal geometric garden at the rear of the stable block. Watergate passed to the Hall family and by the 1881 census the house was uninhabited. In 1882 the Georgian house was rebuilt by Richard Christy. The house was occupied by the Canadian army in 1939 and was totally destroyed by a chimney fire in 1942.

TJMcC

Sources WSRO, Add. MSS 30472-5; MP 3106; SP 1543.
NGR SU 784 119   PDB 3102

139 Maresfield Park, *c.* 1787

S. H. Grimm

British Library, Add. MS. 5671, f. 94 [179]

Roger Pratt's Coleshill in Warwickshire (1655) set a trend for classical buildings surmounted by a belvedere within a pilastered enclosure. Eagle House in Mitcham, built in 1705 for Queen Catherine of Braganza's physician, differs from 'Mr Newnham's house' (as Grimm called it) only by the addition of a pedimented front. The Newnhams came to Maresfield in the 1660s, when John Newnham (d. 1691) occupied the ironworks. His son John (d. 1737) was pricked as sheriff in the year of his father's death, and this house could have been built as a fashionable place to entertain the county elite in his shrieval year.

At the time of Grimm's visit, the residence of his descendent John Newnham (1746-1814) was known as the Cross House. It became Maresfield Park only later, as the roads from which it took its name were diverted away from it. Sir John Shelley inherited the estate from his uncle in 1814 and commissioned extensive remodelling by Benjamin Dean Wyatt in 1816. It has always been assumed that the Dutch gables, employed by Wyatt for the new work, mimicked existing features of 17th-century origin. But the dentilated eaves-course and the key-stones above the ground-floor windows can be made out from a view of 1839, and it seems likely that Wyatt also augmented the house shown here by the addition of gables to heighten a rather low structure. The house was largely demolished in 1921.

CHCW

Sources Cherry and Pevsner 1983, 443. Colvin 1995, 1104-5. Shelley 1912-13, 2: fc. 68 and 220. PRO, PROB 4/18887. ESRO, SAS/G 13/50; AMS 5558; PAR 420 26/1.

NGR TQ 463 243 *PDB* 2624

140 Mayfield Place, 1783

S. H. Grimm

British Library, Add. MS. 5671, f. 36 [62]

By 1783 much of the former palace of the archbishops of Canterbury was in ruins and the remainder turned into a tenanted farm.

The great hall (*Sussex views*, 106) and western range were built by Archbishop Islip (d. 1366), but this view shows the courtyard of the eastern part of the palace (*Sussex views*, 105). The facing range with its staircase turret is 15th-century work; that on the right was built in the early 16th century by Archbishop Warham, whose arms appeared in one of its rooms. In 1571 the financier Sir Thomas Gresham refurbished Warham's range, and is said to have entertained Queen Elizabeth at Mayfield two years later.

The manor passed to the Baker family of ironmasters, who in 1724 sold the lordship but retained the house. Late in the 1740s Michael Baker (1716-50) moved the family's main residence to the Lower House, de-roofed the great hall and may have lowered at least two of these ranges. Baker designed a monument for the relics of St Dunstan's encounter with the devil - an anvil, hammer and tongs - at the house, and celebrated his improvements in verse:

By Dunstan's first, and last by Baker's hands
Groves, water, visto's grace these lofty lands;
One from the curse of thorns relieved the soil,
The other freed it from the plowman's toil.

Further degradation had occurred by 1841, when the herald William Courthope of Wadhurst undertook a detailed survey. In 1863 the Duchess of Leeds purchased the site and transformed the ruins into a convent to Edward Welby Pugin's designs.

CHCW

Sources Hoare 1849. Cooper 1869. Roberts 1867. ESRO, KIR 8/12-15, 9/2-6, 29/43-49. College of Arms, Courthope MS. 23 145-92 (microfilm at ESRO, XA 38/2).

NGR TQ 587 271

PDB 2507

141 Midhurst, St Ann's Hill, 1785

S. H. Grimm

British Library, Add. MS. 5675, f. 22 [33]

St Ann's Hill or Castle Hill is just east of the
Market Square in Midhurst, in the angle of the
River Rother. It appears behind the church in
Grimm's prospect of Midhurst in *Sussex views*, 107.
It is traditionally the site of a chapel dedicated to St
Dennis and the original home of the de Bohun
family, described in an inquisition post mortem of
1273 as a hall and other houses with a curtilage
and garden. Dr William Burrell noted, probably in
1776, that the site 'has three fosses, the lowest of
which was formed by the river which runs on the
east side of the hill; the foundations were
discovered a few years since by Sir Herbert
Mackworth in cutting through the north side of the
hill to make a walk.' Excavations in 1913 revealed
what were identified as a keep, hall and chambers,
kitchen and chapel, all within a walled enclosure.

The de Bohuns seemed to have abandoned the
site in about 1280, in favour of Cowdray on level
ground on the other side of the river (View 70).
The old house was pulled down by 1311, except
that the chapel 'in a place called Courtgreene' was
still standing in 1367.   *TJMcC*

Sources Hope 1919, 2-4, 90. Turner 1868. Public Record Office
1938, 102.

NGR SU 889 215   *PDB* 2963

142 Mountfield, a lime kiln, 1815/16

Thomas Hearne
Private collection

Other than fishermen on the beach (for example, View 105), working people and scenes were of interest to few artists, and these two views on the Ashburnham Estate by Thomas Hearne are a rare survival. Arthur Young viewed the Earl of Ashburnham's lime-works in 1788 and pronounced him 'the greatest lime burner in England'; what he described was a perpetual-draw kiln. Shown here is a periodic kiln, such as his son, the Revd Arthur Young (1769-1827), saw in summer 1793. The description and plan, provided by the superintendent, of a kiln in the wooded valley in Orchard Wood, in the south-east corner of Mountfield parish, match the picture closely.

This design was called a tunnel kiln and was built into a bank. The first stage of operation was to construct the arches, by extending the 'throats' in the front wall to the back. The space above was filled from the bank behind, with the larger pieces of stone, the size of a man's head, going in first. The tunnels were packed with faggots cut in the Earl's woods, and the kiln was fired, being thoroughly heated after 15 hours and kept fired

143 Mountfield, a stone quarry, 1815/16

Thomas Hearne
Private collection

for a further unspecified time (elsewhere given as 24 hours); after cooling for 30 hours, the kiln was emptied. The lime was mainly used for manure. The stone came from a mine higher up the valley and some 80 feet deep; it was blasted with gunpowder, conveyed to the shaft on a railway and hauled to the surface where it was stacked to weather before being burnt. The lime-works were disused in 1830, perhaps having ceased operation in the mid-1820s due to falling demand during the agricultural depression. The tenant at Glaziers Forge Farm (TQ 650 214), John Westover, though, was still burning lime in 1830, renting rights to raise limestone from a shaft of 100 to 130 feet depth.

What Hearne drew was a surface quarry,

location unknown, for building stone. The machine on the left seems to have been for dragging away from the working face of the quarry, large stones which had been separated from their bed along bedding planes and joints. They were then broken into smaller pieces by driving in a line of wedges.

Quarries were, just at the time of Hearne's drawing, acquiring an added interest for the geological strata revealed and fossils discovered (Essay 4.1). The frontispiece to Mantell's *Geology of Sussex* shows two gentlemen supervising workmen chiselling out an antler in a quarry in Tilgate Forest.

JHF

Sources Young 1789, 246-7. Young 1793, 33-37. Young 1794, 266-8. ESRO, ASH 1173, ff. 21-2; 1172; 4471 (plot 904); 1835-82 for accounts of the lime-works 1786-1812. Holt 1971, 25. Marshall 1798, 2: 179-83, for lime-burning at Petworth, 1791. Mantell 1827.

NGR in the vicinity of TQ 742 185   *PDB* 8082, 8081

144 North Mundham Church, 1782

S. H. Grimm

British Library, Add. MS. 5675, f. 48 [89]

In this view from the north-east Grimm captures the church at an interesting moment in its evolution. The simple east wall formed the end of the nave: the medieval chancel which had once continued beyond it had been demolished at an unknown date after the Reformation. Stebbing Shaw in 1790 found the church in good repair: the inside 'makes a very creditable appearance ... [and] affords many relics for the antiquarians, particularly in a fine old altar tomb.' But the Georgian additions within the church had not quite reached their final point: within the next half century a gallery would be built in the north aisle and a dormer window would appear in the roof to light it. Some of Grimm's detail is puzzling: for instance what appears to be a round Norman doorway in

the north wall was later described as a 'simple chamfered and pointed door'. Drastic restoration by A. W. Blomfield in 1883 preserved some superficial similarities by re-using the stonework of the arches, windows and doors - but only after the north, south and east walls had been completely demolished and rebuilt. Additionally a complete new chancel was added. Only the tower remained relatively unscathed.

The building at the left is Pigeon House Farmhouse - though the angle from which it drawn seems slightly wide. Although the building as it stands today is old, it is virtually unrecognisable against Grimm's version: it would appear that the simple Georgian portion at the left has been demolished.

PMW

Sources Dallaway 1815, 2: 62. Fleming 1944. Nairn and Pevsner 1965, 275. Shaw 1791b, 252. VCHS, 4: 164. WSRO, Par. 141/7/12. *NGR* SU 875 022   *PDB* 3020

Charity School Newick Place 10 July 1779

Endow'd by the Hon. Louissa Barbara Vernon AD 1771 Two Widdows Liveing in the house and the Education and I think Cloaths of 10 Children (Girles)

145 Newick, Lady Vernon's charity school, 1779

James Lambert junior

West Sussex County Council Library Service
(Worthing Library)

The second line of Lambert's note gives the inscription on the plaque over the door. With her husband George Venables Vernon, later 2nd Baron Kinderton (1735-1813), the Hon. Louisa Barbara Vernon (1733-86) endowed the school with a rent-charge of £50 a year. Of that £15 was for the schoolmistress who was to live in the recently erected house and instruct 12 poor girls of Newick in reading, writing and needlework, to make them useful servants; £15 was for clothing the children, and £15 for maintaining, boarding and instructing a girl who would assist the mistress. The remaining £5 could be used for fuel and repairs. The schoolhouse survives, much altered, as a private residence, and the charity's substantial assets continue to benefit girls in the parish. Lady Vernon also had Lambert make views of her late-17th-century house, its lodges (though not those standing today) and of Rottingdean.

The fair copy of this draft sketch made for Burrell is a mirror image, suggesting that Lambert drew one or other with an optical device. The sketch is numbered and priced in the bottom right-hand corner, 'N 108 6d', perhaps for the sale of Lambert's effects after his death in 1799.   *JHF*

Sources Caffyn 1998, 206.

NGR TQ 419 199   *PDB* 4640

146 Petworth, Old Petworth House and Stables, *c.* 1680

Unknown artist

Collection of the Duke of Northumberland

This view of the stables of Petworth House must pre-date about 1688, when Charles, 6th Duke of Somerset, began rebuilding the house in the background. The Honour of Petworth had belonged to the Percy family since the mid-12th century, and the Duke had married the Percy heiress in 1682.

In 1635 Lieutenant Hammond enthused about 'the stately, lofty, fair-built stables' constructed for the 9th Earl of Northumberland in 1623-5, 'the like whereof I am sure not a subject in all England hath to show', 80 of his paces in length, housing 120 horses, in freestone from the Earl's own quarry, paved and covered in similar 'white slate'. The riding house filling one wing, and the storerooms another, were complemented by 'a fair large armoury for horse and foot', and handsome lodgings for the gentlemen of the horse and the

servants. In 1680 were enumerated a riding barn, coach house, saddle house, forge, and bedrooms for thirteen servants, as well as the stables themselves. When John Macky visited in September 1713, the stables had been demolished to open the vista from the new house to the formal gardens laid out in the French style in 1702-10, though not to good effect in Milles's opinion in 1743 (Document 3). New stables slightly to the south were completed in 1716. These were in their turn demolished and replaced with the western range of the present stables, which were built to the designs of Matthew Brettingham in 1756-63.

Petworth House descended from the 7th Duke to the Wyndham family, by whom it was given to the National Trust in 1947.   *AMcC and JHF*

Sources Rowell 1997. Jackson-Stops 1977. Stroud 1977, fig. 3 for John Norden's sketch of 1625. McCann 1999. Hammond (Lieut.) 1936, 36-7. Macky 1714, 1: letter VI. WSRO, PHA 438-439, 3577, 6261, 6375, 6618. Harris 1995, no. 14, for colour reproduction.
NGR SU 971 218   *PDB* 391

Petworth Jail

147 Petworth House of Correction, exterior, 1791

S. H. Grimm

British Library, Add. MS. 5678, f. 11 [22]

Houses of correction were a creation of Tudor social policy. The first opened in 1556, at Bridewell in London, and about 200 followed in the next 150 years. Unlike gaols, which only imprisoned, houses of correction were intended also to reform by imposing a strict regime of work on inmates. By the time Grimm visited Petworth, however, this distinction had largely disappeared in all but name.

The house at Petworth was opened in about 1630; other houses in Sussex appeared at Battle (by 1647), Chichester (by 1617), Horsham (by 1586), Lewes (1612), and Rye (?by 1580). A house opened at Arundel in 1650 was intended to take over the role of the three houses in western Sussex, but it was redundant by 1700 and its functions

returned to the three earlier houses.

The penal reformer John Howard in the mid-1770s considered Petworth bridewell thoroughly inadequate to its purpose: it had only two rooms and was 'too small for the general number of prisoners'. Furthermore, there was no chimney, no yard, no water and no employment. Notwithstanding local protests, but with the enthusiastic support of the 3rd Duke of Richmond, Quarter Sessions ordered a new house to be built to a design by James Wyatt, who was later to work for Richmond at Goodwood. This 32-cell house was built in two stages between 1785 and 1789, being completed just ten years after the new county gaol had opened at Horsham (View 120) and four years before the new house of correction (also 32-cell) at Lewes, both, again, built with the close involvement of Richmond.

Petworth was built to a rectangular ground plan with arcades on either side of a central entrance block containing store rooms and turnkey's offices. Two vagrants' rooms and a mill were built into the end of the arcade to the right of the central block

Petworth Jail from the Court   S.H. Grimm fecit 1791

148 Petworth House of Correction, interior, 1791

S. H. Grimm

British Library, Add. MS. 5678, f. 11 [21]

(View 148), while the cells, chapel and infirmary rooms were on the two upper floors. Access was through the keeper's house which, flanked by gardens at either side, fronted the high wall (View 147). Prisoners were kept in solitary confinement, and the chapel was designed such that the 32 pews had 'sides so lofty that the prisoners cannot see each other; though they are all in the view of the chaplain'. Exercise in one of the four 'airing grounds' or yards laid out around the prison block was taken alone.

In 1816, following concern expressed in Parliament about the severity of Petworth's system of solitary confinement, Quarter Sessions discussed whether the building could be modified to facilitate a relaxation of the system. As a result, the arcades were enclosed into three workrooms, a day room (all with stoves) and a lobby containing two looms, where prisoners worked together during daytime in the production of woollen goods.

The Petworth house was demolished in 1882. Some of the materials were reused in two new buildings on the site, Belle Vue House which originally was the residence of West Sussex's Chief Constable and is today the police station, and the Red House which has been demolished. Some warders' cottages survive in Grove Road.   *JB*

Sources Arnold 1864, 95-6. Brent 1993, 70-1. Brent 1995, 49. Dallaway 1832, viii. Historical Manuscripts Commission 1892, 72. Jerrome 1990, 128-30. McConville 1981, 30, 42-8, 95. Morgan 1991, 174. Royall 1999, 7, 14, 16, 24, 161. Topp 1991, 23, 28-35. VCHS, 5 (1): 15. VCHS, 6 (2): 134.

NGR SU 979 214   *PDB* 3127, 3128

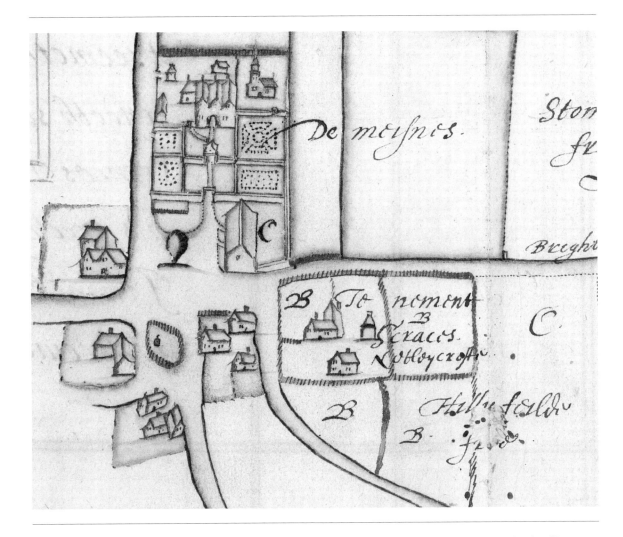

149 Preston Episcopi, Preston Manor and village, 1617

John Norden

British Library, Add. MS 6027, ff. 115v-116r

Colour plate XIII

When surveying the manor of Preston for the Crown in 1617, Norden judged that Anthony Shirley was claiming part of the demesne, which his family had leased since 1569, as his freehold, and to prove the point drew a plan of the manor house, the village and the surrounding fields: View 149. East is at the top. Norden described the house as 'well built with stone, two green courts at the entry, with convenient outhouses, orchards, gardens, dower house and curtilage.' Thomas

Marshall's survey of 1608 had listed a dwelling house, two yards, two orchards, two gardens, barn, stable, dovecot and other buildings. Features in the cellars point to construction in about 1600 of a building facing west down the slope to the Brighton road and to the village in the valley bottom; no evidence of an earlier building survives. Norden depicted a three-gabled, double-pile mansion, of advanced design and probably built in flint with brick and stone dressings. It was assessed at 18 flues for the 1662 Hearth Tax. Shirley probably by 1600 held a lease for the demesne running to 1660, long enough to justify new building; only in 1628 did his grandson acquire the lordship of the manor.

In 1712 the manor of Preston passed to Thomas Western, a London merchant of Rivenhall in Essex. His son, Thomas (1714-66), largely

150 Preston Episcopi, Preston Manor and village, 1782

S. H. Grimm

British Library, Add. MS. 5672, f. 20 [35]

demolished the old house and in 1738, according to a stone plaque, built the central five bays in View 150. The old house was aligned to the west, the new one to the north. This view is looking down the road towards Brighton. Shown in an early view by Lambert dated 1763, though possibly added at different times, the two flanking wings gave the house a fashionable Palladian appearance. Grimm shows the church correctly orientated: Norden had turned the nave to face west.

The Westerns were letting 'Preston Place' by 1767, and in 1782 the tenant was Thomas Kemp esq., MP for Lewes and a substantial landowner in Brighton. His brother Nathaniel had taken over the tenancy by 1791. When Charles Callis Western put the manor up for auction in 1793, the house comprised, on the ground floor, a kitchen, servants' hall, butler's pantry, housekeeper's room, mangle room, laundry, bake house, larder, wine and beer vaults; on the principal floor, a drawing room, hall, dining parlour, library, small drawing room and stucco room; and, reached by two staircases, eight bed chambers and closets on the first floor and seven rooms for servants in the attics. Outside were stabling for 13 horses, a coach house for three carriages, granary, stable, yard, bowling green, three large enclosed gardens, pleasure grounds, plantations, and several pieces of adjoining land. The main structure of the 18th-century house survived the remodelling of 1905 which gave the house its present shape. Brighton & Hove Council maintains it as a museum.

In 1782, the houses in the village were clearly aligned, not with the road to Brighton, but with the east-west droveway crossing the combe. Marshall's survey lists 14 cottages in Preston parish - the same number of buildings shown by Norden outside the manor house's curtilage, some 10 of them with chimneys (the enclosure in the street may be around a well). The 1670 Hearth Tax indicates 19 houses in the village, the 1801 Census 28. The additions came by forming a third street to the north of the two shown in 1617. Marshall recorded 12 copyholders with yardlands in the common fields; by 1782 a few yardlands had passed to the lord of the manor and the rest accumulated by Bartholomew Smithers. But the aggregation into two farms seems not to have depopulated the parish.

JHF

Sources Brighton Reference Library, SB9 P92 (accn 62136). Martin 1999. VCHS, 7: 270. Beevers 1999, 24-5, 29-30. Caffyn 1998, fc. 1. SWA, 29 July 1793. Farrant and Farrant 1975.

NGR TQ 303 063   *PDB* 7809, 2671

151 Pulborough, 'Upper mount', 1780

S. H. Grimm

British Library, Add. MS. 5674, f. 44 [80]

This must be the hill now known as Park Mound, lying west of the parish church (Sussex views, 130), and looking south over the water meadows of the Rother towards the site of the Roman posting station at Hardham. The water bailiff to the Earl of Arundel described it thus in 1637: '... the old demolished Fort, at this day called Lodg-hill in Pulborough Park, the ancient inheritance of Alarde la Flemminge (a knight's fee sometimes belonging to the Honour of Arundel)....'

By 1244 Adelard (or Alard) le Fleming held two knights' fees in Pulborough and was made a grant in 1252: '... as his houses in his manor of Puleberg were lately burned by accident that they may rebuild in his park of Puleberg where his ancestors used to inhabit as he thinks best, without crenel-lating.' John Maunsell, who signed the grant as 'chancellor of the Exchequer' to Henry III, was Adelard's brother-in-law.

Whereas the mound was probably the site of a timber motte-and-bailey, the rebuild seems to have been on what is now the site of Old Place, nearer the church. Stebbing Shaw in 1790 described this as 'the remains of an ancient mansion ... now only a farm.' There is a 16th-century house close to the mound called, at least since 1825, Park Farm. *AFH*

Sources Fowler 1929, 21. Shaw 1791a, 354. Steer 1961b, 39.
NGR TQ 037 189
PDB 2916

152 Pyecombe, Wolstonbury Hill, 1780

S. H. Grimm

British Library, Add. MS. 5672, f. 23 [39]

Grimm's view of Wolstonbury Hill in Pyecombe is taken from Hurstpierpoint churchyard nearly two miles to the north. The isolated house in the right middle distance may be Wanbarrow Farm.

Early-19th century antiquaries interpreted the embanked feature on the summit of Wolstonbury Hill as a British (i.e. Iron Age) camp. Later archaeologists followed this interpretation, though Curwen noticed that the bank was outside the ditch, an arrangement which 'seems little likely to increase the defensibility of the site'. Recent research into prehistoric enclosures in south-east England suggests, however, that the site may be of Bronze-Age date and may stand in the tradition of ceremonial or ritual enclosures, rather than being a fortified settlement enclosure.

The grave-boards drawn by Grimm are reminders that wood, a locally abundant material, was widely used in Sussex during the 18th and, indeed, well into the 19th centuries for churchyard memorials - yet sufficiently distinctive for the well-travelled John Warburton in 1723 to note the churchyard at Horsham as 'near covered with frames of wood' over the graves (Essay 2.3; see also View 92). The form was commonly a board supported between two posts, though Hurstpierpoint churchyard (as depicted by Lambert in 1777, *Sussex views*, 83) contained an example of four boards supported in rectangular plan by four posts. In about 1800, May and Parsons, stonemasons of Lewes, were selling a typical Sussex head and foot-stone with linking stone grave rail of Portland stone for £4 to £5 (plus costs of transport). Though no accounts for their erection are known to survive, wooden grave-boards are likely to have been considerably cheaper.

JB

Sources Burgess 1979, 117-8, 273. Curwen 1930, 237 (quoted). Drewett, Rudling, and Gardiner 1988, 70. Hamper 1806, 900.
NGR TQ 284 138 from TQ 279 165   *PDB* 2675

153 Racton Tower and Church, 1789

S. H. Grimm

British Library, Add. MS. 5675, f. 40 [73]

'Stansted Tower', as Grimm called it, and Maidenhead Town Hall are the sum of the known work of Theodosius Keene, son of the more famous Henry. It was commissioned by George Montague Dunk, 2nd Earl of Halifax, proprietor of the Stansted estate – for whom the father provided a Gothick spire at Westbourne in 1770 (while the mother was reputed to provide more personal services). It was built around the same date as a gazebo and picnic house, principally offering a viewpoint for Chichester Harbour. Having no necessity to build for a practical function, Keene was able to adopt a triangular plan – a conceit or game played by several 18th-century architects when given a free hand with ornamental buildings, as a triangular building shows the observer greater changes in profile than conventional plans. Hiorn's

Tower of 1790 at Arundel is a more sober and better preserved example. The elder Keene was the architect of the Vandalian Tower at Uppark built in 1773-4.

Racton Tower was reported to have cost £10,000, and was dismissed by Horace Walpole as 'a very ugly tower' which was 'by no means proportional to the prodigious expense.' Grimm's view is from the south-east, with Racton Church in the right foreground. By then it had already gained an unsavoury reputation as 'a resort of ladies and gentlemen of ill fame' and in 1815 Dallaway described it as 'having been neglected, now in ruins.' Only the brick core remains today, with all the original flint facings long gone. Perhaps some of its associations endure – as it was a haunt for Hell's Angels in the 1970s and reputedly a witches' coven in the 1980s. *PMW*

Sources Arnold 1871, 18-19. Arnold 1888. Ponsonby and Aslet 1984. Colvin 1995, 571-4. Dallaway 1815, 2: 153. White 1985.

NGR SU 776 094   *PDB* 3004

154 Racton House, 1782

S. H. Grimm

British Library, Add. MS. 5675, f. 42 [76]

Racton, on the western border of the county, is one of the smallest and least populated parishes in West Sussex, but it contained within its boundaries two important houses - Racton House and Lordington, the seat of the Pole family and the reputed birthplace of Cardinal Pole (*Sussex views*, 131). Of Racton Manor, only the church and a few cottages survive. Racton House, south of the church and on the other side of the River Ems, stood at the south side of the junction where the Funtington road meets the road to Petersfield. Here its owner Colonel George Gunter organised Charles II's escape to the Continent in 1651. Reputedly built in the early 15th century by Roger Gunter, it was the family seat until the early 18th.

By the time Grimm took this view from the south, the house was owned by William Legge, 2nd Earl of Dartmouth who in 1755 had married Frances Nicholl, the last of the Gunters. Along with a considerable acreage in Racton and Westbourne it was tenanted in 1785 by John Painter. The eastern part of the house appears to have been modernised to provide the farmhouse. But the western portion retained its older character and presumably contained the large hall in View 155, some 30 foot square, with carved oak wainscot, painted light blue and ornamented with scrolls and armorial bearings, similar to that at Halnaker House (View 24).

Writing in 1871, the Revd Frederick Arnold recorded that the structure had been dismantled about 30 years before and had been large, low and irregular, built of flint walls at least three feet thick with such excellent mortar that ordinary tools proved useless in removing it. Some timber, and the arms and crest of Sir Charles Gunter Nicholl, were taken and incorporated into the replacement house in Westbourne for Racton Park Farm.

The hatchment in the hall may be that of Catherine, daughter of Sir Laurence Hyde of

155 Racton House, interior of the hall, 1782

S. H. Grimm

British Library, Add. MS. 5675, f. 42 [77]

Salisbury and wife of George Gunter; she died in January 1684 and was buried at Racton

TJMcC and PMW

Sources Arnold 1871, 16-18. Bradley 1967. Dallaway 1815, 2: 156. Readman et al. 2000, 186, 238. VCHS, 4: 113.

NGR SU 782 093   *PDB* 3008, 3007

Col. BLOUNTS at Ringmer near LEWES.

156 Ringmer, Delves House, south-east view, 1783

James Lambert junior
British Library, Add. MS. 5676, f. 83 [128]

For much of the 18th century Delves House was owned and occupied by the Snooke family, and it was in the garden here, during visits to his aunt Rebecca, widowed since Henry Snooke's death in 1763, that Gilbert White recorded the lifestyle of Timothy the tortoise. Rebecca died in 1780, Gilbert took Timothy to live with him in Selborne, and the Delves estate followed the entail in her husband's will to Henry (also Harry) Blunt. Harry (b. 1735) was 'of Ringmer' and a colonel when he married Mary (d. 1822), only child of Ferdinando Askew of Lydiard Millicent in Wiltshire, in December 1768.

In the years immediately following 1780, Harry

and Mary Blunt rebuilt and landscaped with enthusiasm. The view of 1783 shows a newly refronted house - very similar to the existing frontage of Hill Lodge in Lewes, rebuilt probably in the 1770s - which is surely the work of the new owners rather than of the aged Rebecca Snooke. Also, new work in the grounds around the house can be identified in the wider views of 1787 (a companion piece from the south is also at Yale and reproduced in Plumb 1980, 66). A date stone 'H. and M.B. 1784', surviving in 1900 on an ancillary building, confirms their development of the site.

The view of 1783 probably shows the 'court before the house' where Timothy was kept for at least 30 years, and the rough grazing 'just before the house', where Mrs Snooke lost a coach-horse during a thunderstorm in July 1775. Neither of these features is apparent in 1787 - the walled enclosure in front of the house has disappeared, a

157 Ringmer, Delves House, east view, 1787

James Lambert junior

Yale Center for British Art, Paul Mellon Collection, B1986.29.572

coach-drive now sweeps up to the front door, and the rough grazing has been incorporated into an area of lawn. Additionally, a number of young shrubs and trees can be seen in the later views, and the cart shed behind the house in 1783 seems to have disappeared by 1787.

The two views of 1787 must be house portraits for the proud owners made at the end of a period of rebuilding and landscaping, the immaculately kept ponds in the foreground of both views reflecting their sensibilities. The ponds were of irregular outline in the early 18th century, and their use for water supply by neighbours during the dry summer of 1778 when all the usual sources in the village had dried up suggests that they were

not then the manicured landscape features which they had become by 1787.

The Blunts sold in 1893 to Aubrey de Putron who refronted in brick and extended the service area at the rear. In the mid-1930s Delves House was bought by John Christie of Glyndebourne and was demolished in 1936 when a new house was built. That house survives today and, with recent additions, serves as sheltered accommodation for the elderly.

JB

Sources Legge 1900, 10. Ringmer History Study Group, 1983, 10: 2; 1983, 14: 1; 1993, 97: 3. White 1981, 120-1, 132-3, 214-15. White 1931, 68, 108 (both quoted), 155-6, 169. ESRO, AMS 5799/2.

NGR TQ 446 126

PDB 4107, 4435

Ground Plan of the Green Man

158 Ringmer, The Green Man Inn, 1798

Unknown surveyor of the Buxted estate
East Sussex Record Office, ACC 3712, f. 18 [A]

The building shown here, located at Broyle Gate and perhaps of late-medieval origin, had substantial additions made in 1837 and was demolished in the 1930s to make way for the present Green Man Inn. Having run an ale house in nearby Broyle Lane since at least 1756, William Dicker had opened the Green Man here in the mid-1760s. He died in 1792 and was succeeded by

Richard Dicker, probably his son, who was the Buxted estate's tenant in 1798.

The inn is situated on the edge of the Broyle, a 2000-acre medieval deer-park enclosed for agriculture in 1767, and probably derives its name from the association of the green (or wild) man with woods and parkland areas. William Dicker's father and grandfather had been keepers of the park.   *JB*

Sources Kay 2000. Ringmer History Study Group, 1985, 28: 3; 1988, 54: 2-3; 2000, 154: 4. Simpson and Roud 2000, 154, 391. Turner 1984, 44.

NGR TQ 456 128   *PDB* 7741

159 Rogate, Durford Abbey, 1782

S. H. Grimm

British Library, Add. MS. 5675, f. 29 [47]

The Premonstratensian house of Durford Abbey was founded by Henry Hussey, Lord of Harting, in about 1160 on lands close to the border of Sussex and Hampshire, north of the River Rother in Rogate. At its dissolution in 1536, the community comprised eight canons, a novice, twelve domestic and twelve agricultural servants. The Crown sold the site and the demesne in 1544 to Sir Edmund Mervyn who resided there for only a few years. In 1613 Mervyn's son sold it to Thomas Bilson, Bishop of Winchester, through whose family it descended to Henry Bilson Legge who became Lord Stawell in 1780.

The buildings were not modified to form a gentry residence, rather parts were incorporated in Durford Farm. Grimm made three drawings. The views from the east and the south are printed in *Sussex views*, 136 and 137. This view was from the west. The house shown was replaced two years later, in 1784, by Lord Stawell, for the tenant farmer, William Egger. This successor stands today and is likely to have medieval footings. Medieval fragments are still visible in the stable shown to the right of the house. Numerous pieces of worked stone are found around the garden and built into walls; they are Hythe Bed sandstone and perhaps came from the quarry given to the Abbey by a Chithurst family. No one has proposed how the standing buildings relate to the conventual layout.

TJMcC and JHF

Sources Blaauw 1856. Lloyd 1996. VCHS, 4: 22-6. Yates 1980. Readman et al. 2000, 186. Aldsworth 1979a.

NGR SU 778 233

PDB 2978

160 Rotherfield, Walshes, ?1785

S. H. Grimm

British Library, Add. MS. 5671, f. 22 [36]

Walshes manor house, shown on the left, was built in 1551 by Alexander Fermor, who had purchased the rights of the Knight family in the previous year. The moated site of the original Walshes can still be identified in a neighbouring field. The manor was referred to as Walshes otherwise Sipses, perpetuating the names of the two families which had owned neighbouring land two centuries before. The two houses shown by Grimm may well owe their origins to that division.

Although a squat and rather unassuming building, Walshes exhibits some marks of its status as a manor-house. Close studding is visible on the gabled end, which also carries an oriel window; a wing at right angles can be seen to the rear, possibly heated by the larger stack at its junction with the main range. The hall is lit by a tall window, and to the left, perhaps beneath the parlour, a cellar window can just be made out. The roof appears to be tiled, but whether the front was brick, stone, tile-hanging or shingle remains unresolved by Grimm's monochrome. Walshes burnt down on the night of 26 February 1893 and this view, along with a distant photograph by the Crowborough antiquary-physician Charles Leeson Prince, is the only image of the home of the Fermors.

The house to the right is a much more ambitious building of about 1600. An overhanging gable supported by console brackets, rather than a tiled pentice, weathers the oriel, which is itself supported on four large brackets. In the background between the two houses huddles a group of thatched farm-buildings.

At the date of the view the estate was owned by the trustees of Sir Henry Fermor who had been born, probably at Walshes, in 1667. He died in 1734, endowing a school and chapel at Crowborough which were built in 1744 and drawn by James Lambert in 1776 (*Sussex views*, 50).

CHCW

Sources Pullein 1928, 336-73. Caffyn 1998, 223-4.

NGR TQ 525 287   *PDB* 2482

161 Rye Church and Watchbell Street, 1634

Anthony Van Dyck

Gabinetto disegni e stampe Uffizi, Florence, 762P

Van Dyck arrived in England in 1632 and was appointed Principal Painter to the King and Queen. He returned to Antwerp in the early months of 1634, but was back in London a year later. Rye was a principal port for passenger traffic to the Continent, and it may therefore have been while waiting to sail on that journey, that he made this drawing. Indeed, all his five drawings of known locations in England are of Rye, as may be another three. The one other which is dated, on 25 August 1633 - and which Hollar copied for a 1659 map of Kent - Van Dyck may have made when meeting his brother. Rye's cargo carriage with France and with Dieppe in particular was booming for about a dozen years from the early 1630s; and in 1631 a Paris correspondent sent some fruit trees 'by the ordinary weekly passage boat'. Disruption on the Continent caused by the Thirty Years' War was funnelling French and Italian luxury textile goods destined for England through Lyons and the Normandy ports.

The view was taken from the deck of a boat in the harbour beneath the town, where now there is dry land. The Church of St Mary is seen from the south-east, the pinnacles on the west front standing much higher than when James Lambert junior drew the church in 1781 (*Sussex views*, 142). In the foreground are the gardens and backs of the houses on the south side of Watchbell Street. The archway to the right gave onto the Upper Gun Garden, the Ypres Tower being just out of sight (but shown in a companion picture now in the Fitzwilliam Museum, Cambridge).   *JHF*

Sources Royalton-Kisch 1999, 86-99. Hipkin 1999, 124-37. Farrant 1980, 8.

NGR TQ 921 202   *PDB* 7768

162 Salehurst, Robertsbridge Abbey, 1783

James Lambert senior, after James Lambert junior

British Library, Add. MS. 5676, f. 18 [27]

The Cistercian Abbey of St Mary was founded by Alvred de St Martin, Sheriff of the Rape of Hastings, in or about 1176. It is thought to have been originally located within the vill of Robertsbridge in the parish of Salehurst but, possibly as early as 1210, to have removed to a more remote site in the same parish.

Very little of Robertsbridge Abbey survives above ground today. Apart from the ruinous refectory, View 163, the only medieval fabric still standing (including a crypt which may have been part of the abbot's house) is incorporated into the farmhouse. Of the church and the other conventual buildings, and of the 'great' western

and 'little ... inner' (?eastern) gatehouses, nothing remains to be seen, though a ground plan can be partially reconstructed with the aid of aerial photographs.

The two-storey masonry building recorded by Lambert, View 162, is obviously of medieval origin. It was located about 30 yards south-west of the farmhouse and 40 yards north of the west gate, on a site now occupied by an oast house. Previously identified as the refectory, it is now thought to have been the guest house. James Moore's view of 1785 engraved in Grose's *Antiquities* shows the same building from the north-west - the wooden extension, the west end of which is shown by Lambert, seems to have had single-door access to the ground floor and dormer access by a fixed ladder with handrail to the first floor.

The building referred to by Lambert as 'the chapel', View 163, is now identified as the refectory. His view is taken from the north-west and, looking into the ruined building, shows some of the window openings of the south wall. The wall

163 Salehurst, Robertsbridge Abbey, the refectory, 1783

James Lambert senior, after James Lambert junior

British Library, Add. MS. 5676, f. 18 [28]

in the foreground is the north wall of the refectory, which also marks the southern extent of the cloister. Some of the fabric recorded by Lambert is still standing, but it has degraded considerably since his day. Drawings by Grimm, 1783 (*Sussex views*, 144) and D. T. Powell, *c.* 1810, confirm much of what Lambert records, and, though not so apparent in Lambert's views, they show many round-headed windows and door arches. This goes some way towards confirming an early-13th century *terminus ante quem* for the relocation of the abbey to this site.

Both these views are signed by James Lambert senior as 'from J. L. junr'. The latter's views are in the same volume of Burrell's collection. Salzman used these to contrast the two artists' work: 'The elder man was the better artist; the younger tended to a certain woolliness and was weaker in the handling of animals and trees.... The re-drawn version in each case is superior, and in the first instance [View 162] the uncle has actually shifted the angle of lighting, so as to bring out the tracery of a window which the nephew had left in shadow.'

JB

Sources D'Elboux 1946, 125 (quoted). Hodson 1914, fc. 30, Moore's view wrongly dated to 1776. Knowles and St Joseph 1952, 134-5. Martin 1966. Martin 1967?, fig. 3. Martin 1971? SAS, library accn 9089, f. 31. Godfrey and Salzman 1951, xi (quoted). VCHS, 2: 71.

NGR TQ 754 238   *PDB* 4022, 4021

164 Seaford Head from Newhaven, *c.* 1765

Anthony Devis

British Museum, P&D, 1944-10-14-87

Anthony Devis (1729-1816) came to London from Preston in Lancashire in about 1742, first assisting his brother Arthur, the portraitist. From 1760 he worked independently by painting for their owners views of country houses and parks, and copies of Old Masters to decorate the interiors. He explored the Channel coast extensively and a large number of views, mainly in pen and wash, survive, most dating from after 1780. He considered buying a house at Fairlight before settling in 1780 for Albury, near Guildford, Surrey. His house there in six acres suggests that he made a better living than did his contemporaries Grimm and the Lamberts from similar work. A Sussex commission was at Kidbrooke Park. John Trower (*c.* 1755-*c.* 1840) of Muntham Place, Findon, was reputedly a substantial patron who on Devis's death bought the contents of his studio; these were dispersed in about 1937 by his granddaughter, Mrs

Hubert Powell of Hill Lodge, Lewes.

This view may be from a tour well before 1780 because the tidemills at Bishopstone do not feature - though they could be hidden by the drop of the cliff. The mills were authorised by Act of Parliament in 1761 and were standing in 1768, on a dam across the lagoon behind the shingle spit to the left. The lagoon had been the course of the River Ouse before the mouth of 1538 beneath Castle Hill was reopened in 1733.

Devis's viewpoint was on Castle Hill, Newhaven, eastwards, with the fort of 1759/60 in the left foreground and perhaps exaggerated undulations on the site of the 1860s fort on the right, Seaford town in the middle distance and Seaford Head beyond. Similar views are in the Harris Art Gallery, Preston, and the Towner Art Gallery, Eastbourne.

JHF

Sources Pavière 1950, 73-97. Whittle 1993. Farrant 1975.

NGR from TQ 449 001   *PDB* 1987

165 Seaford town from the beach, 1785

S. H. Grimm

British Library, Add. MS. 5671, f. 82 [157]

Jeremiah Milles had little to say of Seaford in
1743: 'a poor miserable village situated on the
sea shore, but there is no port to it, the fisherboats
are drawn up upon the beach for security.' He was
echoed by Thomas Pennant in 1793: a small town
'seated in a low plain, defended from the sea by an
enormous beach of pebbles, which at this time was
covered with boats employed in the mackerel
fishery.' Regrettably a 12-foot shark was cut up
before the famed naturalist could get a proper look
at it.

From the shingle bank separating it from the sea,
Grimm's vantage point in late May 1785 was
below Church Street, looking north to the parish
church, the clock on which was moved from the
east to the south face of the tower later that year.
From the shingle bank separating it from the sea,
he showed the lagoon which was the remnant of
the outfall of the River Ouse before the cut at 'the

New Haven' in 1538. A few fishermen and their
boats are in the foreground; the timber stacked
beyond was doubtless freighted on vessels beached
on the high tide. The physical fabric of Seaford at
this date was scarcely yet touched by resort
development. The buildings are those of a long-
decayed port, minor market town and pocket
borough, still within its medieval bounds. As a
unnamed visitor five years later observed, 'This as
almost every other seaport is becoming a watering
place, not however very commodious for bathing.
The sands not good and the accommodation very
indifferent.'

JHF

Sources Taylor 1937, 55, 75. Pennant 1801, 2: 59-60. University of
London, Goldsmiths' Library, MS. 491, f. 98.

NGR SV 482 991

PDB 2602

166 Selham Church, 1791

S. H. Grimm

British Library, Add. MS. 5678, f.32 [63]

Grimm's Selham Church, taken from the north-west, consisted of an 11th-century chancel and nave with a 15th-century window in the west wall, south chapel, probably 14th-century, a corner of which is seen beyond the west end, and north porch. The ground plan is very similar today, though the porch, chapel, and west wall of the nave have been rebuilt. In 1849 a weathervane graced the west end. In 1860, when some restoration is said to have been undertaken, Quartermain recorded today's bellcote in its place, but no decorative barge-board on the porch. The assertion by Cartwright that the church once had a west tower may be based on its representation on a map of 1629, though there is no supporting archaeological evidence.

The accuracy of the 1629 map is further questioned by showing a two-storied, multi-gabled 'parsonage house' on the rectory plot, where Grimm records only a single-storied vernacular cottage with roughly plastered walls. With windows and door opening into the churchyard, it could have served as a church house (often a single storey building) or as a dwelling for the parish clerk. Alternatively it may have housed servants attached to the rectory. By 1850 it had lost its west facing windows and door, probably beneath a brick facing, and all three chimneys, though it had acquired a window in the north gable and a chimney stack added to the west wall at the south end. The lower part of this stack appears to survive, and the building is used today for accommodation and garaging.   *JB*

Sources anon. 1998. Cartwright 1830, 296. Cowley 1970, 39, 53. Harrison 1920, 178. SAS, drawings by W. T. Quartermain (West Sussex), 229. VCHS, 4: 81. WSRO, Mitford MS. 998; PD 2011/2, f. 110.

NGR SU 933 206   *PDB* 3167

167 Selmeston, Mays House, 1783

James Lambert senior
British Library, Add. MS. 5676, f. 61 [91]

Mays House was already described as a capital messuage in the will of Thomas Wenham in 1596; it had been his residence for over 40 years. The house shown by Grimm may have been built by Wenham towards the end of his life, but is more likely to be the work of the ironmaster William Crowe, tenant of the Gage ironworks in Maresfield, who bought Mays from Thomas Wenham's son William in the first decade of the 17th century. After Crowe's bankruptcy Mays passed to Sir William Russell, a courtier, who probably sold it to the Revd John Nutt, Vicar of Berwick, who was living here in 1651.

The view shows only a fragment of Crowe's mansion, which had been assessed at 14 flues for the Hearth Tax of 1662. It must have been down-sized for occupation by tenants, possibly after Sir Thomas Nutt's death in 1674, when his estate passed to his two daughters and their husbands. Sir Thomas Dyke of Horam in Waldron bought out his brother-in-law in 1704, and Sir John Dixon Dyke's farmer when Grimm visited Mays in 1783 was Matthew Mannington, a strict nonconformist who was prepared to ride every Sunday as far as Heathfield to attend the independent Calvinist chapel.

In 1786 Sir John sold Mays to John Bean of Clapham in Litlington, whose son sold it to Joseph Fuller of Arlington in 1803, after a chancery cause, brought to protect the interests of his cousin Barbara Bean Bayly, had ordered funds to be raised. It was Fuller who built the present house on a new site to the south-west, before he in turn sold to the Gage estate in 1822. Some footings of the old house remain in the farm buildings. *CHCW*

Sources ESRO, AMS 535-8, 5923/8, 6454/20; SAS/GA 307-34, 374-80; SAS/G 41/20; SAS/G/ACC 929; SAS/BB 65, 66; ACC 4299/7/4, 10/16, 18. PRO E179/258/16; RG 4/3107. BL, Add. MS. 5682, f. 17. Horsfield 1835, 1: 334.

NGR TQ 521 079 *PDB* 4071

168 Selmeston, Sherrington, 1787

S. H. Grimm

British Library, Add. MS. 5671, f. 59 [105]
Colour plate XIV

Grimm's view shows the impressive remains of what must have been a major medieval moated site. The artist has ignored the south or garden front, partly rebuilt in brick in the 1720s, to provide a rare glimpse of the rear range. Two timber-framed structures, both probably medieval and that to the left jettied, flank a central brick range which is all that survives today. That on the left forms the main range of the house – a crosswing can be seen behind the chimneys – and that to the right conceivably represents a once detached kitchen, subsequently linked to the main house by the central range. The present house occupies only a portion of the moated enclosure, but substantial earthworks around the platform hint of something yet more impressive.

In the middle of the 14th century John Selwyn married Katherine, the heiress of Simon Sherrington, and the Selwyns remained at Selmeston until the beginning of the 16th century, when Thomas Selwyn chose to live on the estate at Friston (View 90) which his wife had inherited from her grandfather John Potman.

In 1626 Sherrington was purchased by Matthias Caldecott, a favourite of the Earl of Dorset, to whom he was known as Matti. His arms, impaling those of his wife Ann Apsley, appear above the view (in Colour plate XIV), probably copied from glass remaining at the house in 1787. The family degenerated to the rank of farmers; in 1800 Matthias Caldecott of Sherrington (1755-1808) was fined for evading the tolls of Lewes Market by an illicit purchase of chickens.

Matthias ignored his brothers' children and bequeathed Sherrington to Mary Hawes, who married James Skinner, an Alfriston surgeon, in 1811. Mary died in 1819 and James was farming Sherrington by 1831. He died in 1873, when the manor was inherited by his daughter Mary, wife of Richard Henry Billiter of the Barcombe oil-mills. In 1881 she listed her occupation as 'Lady of the Manor'. Only the central portion survived extensive rebuilding in 1874, and in recent years the house and outbuildings have grown yet further.

CHCW

Sources Huxford 1982. Smith 1969, 95-6. Dunkin 1914-15, 2: 392. ESRO, SAS/G 5/35; W/A 70 232; LT; PAR 230 1/1/3; PAR 482 1/5/1; XA 27/13.

NGR TQ 506 074   *PDB* 2550

169 Shermanbury Place, 1750

James Lambert senior, ?1779

British Library, Add. MS. 5677, f. 64 [95]

The descent of this manor and the owners and occupants of Shermanbury Place are admirably covered in the *Victoria County History*. The tenancy was in the hands of the de Buci family, which links it with Kingston near Shoreham. The earliest reference to a manor house (with a small deer-park) is in 1361, but the drawing shows a rebuild of the late-16th/early-17th century, a timber-framed house of two storeys forming three sides of a square, approached from the north. This was probably built by the Comber family, who held the lease by 1542 until it passed to two married daughters in 1635. The site is adjacent to Shermanbury Church, which must occupy the site of the small church or 'ecclesiola' mentioned in Domesday.

In 1753, Henry Farncombe, who had married the heir Cassandra Lintott, bought the freehold. By 1779, when Lambert drew it, his son-in-law, John Challen (d. 1794) replaced the timber-framed house with a three-bay brick building of two-storeys over a basement, flanked by lower wings. Much of this remains today. For the recently demolished house, with its topiary and box-edged beds in front, Lambert must have relied on a picture which Challen showed him, perhaps in the margin of a 1750 map by a local surveyor, as a formal house prospect in oils is unlikely at that date.

AFH

Sources VCHS, 6 (3): 192-3.

NGR TQ 214 188

PDB 4200

GATE WAY at Ewhurst near SHERMANBURY

170 Shermanbury, Ewhurst Manor gatehouse, 1783

James Lambert senior

British Library, Add. MS. 5677, f. 62 [90]

Ewhurst Manor stands a small moated site north-west of Shermanbury Place. In 1795 it was approached from the south, from the drive to that house, although the gatehouse is on its north. From 1243, the tenancy of Ewhurst manor included control of Mockbridge over the Adur (to the south) which was famously contested by Thomas Peverell (then tenant) with Sele Priory in 1303. The 1536 will of Eleanor West of Broadwater mentions the hall, chapel and chapel chamber 'of Ewhurst', and as the manor was within Shermanbury parish, this may account for a reference in 1405 to 'the church of Ewhurst'. In 1554, Thomas West left furniture in the 'great chamber' at Ewhurst. The present L-shaped house, called a capital messuage in 1748, cannot be dated before the end of the 1500s, and is probably the work of William Comber, who also held Shermanbury, early in the following century.

Nothing remains of the earlier house on the site, except some possible foundations and a stone carved as a head. The latter is very similar to two others reset in Shermanbury Church when it was considerably 'renovated' in the early 1700s. The length and height of the church were reduced, and the tops of the old windows must have resembled the carved heads in openings on the gatehouse. Perhaps the gatehouse was a contemporary 'reconstruction', combining materials remaining from the earlier house and from the church - rather than dating from the late 13th century, as Wolseley suggested in 1929. *AFH*

Sources VCHS, 6 (3): 193-4. Wolseley 1929.
NGR TQ 211 190

PDB 4196

171 Old Shoreham, Old Erringham chapel, 1787

S. H. Grimm

British Library, Add. MS. 5673, f. 47 [81]

Old Erringham is a mile north of Old Shoreham, and in about 1300 was only slightly less populous than the latter. By 1524 the village had shrunk to a single farmstead. The manor house there, of which the east front in 1787 appears in *Sussex views*, 149, survives today as a flint and brick-rubble house with brick and stone dressings. Its main range is possibly of the late 16th century, with a small west wing build up against it and an early-17th-century north range. An externally-projecting chimney breast in the south face carries a dated stone of 1710, and is built of flint, Caen stone dressings and bricks. Holden concluded that the Caen stone came from the quoins at the west (right-hand) end of the chapel and was replaced by bricks similar to those in the chimney. Hence the nave (internally some 50 by 17 feet) was standing in 1710 but demolished by 1787.

The outline which Grimm sketched comprised mortar on the chalk, as the walls had been built without foundation trenches. The 1957 excavation did not confirm the south doorway and found the internal walls to have been post-medieval. Burrell in 1782 recorded the chancel in use as a stable by the farmer.

That the structure, which lies at the south-west corner of the house's garden, was a chapel is solely evidenced by its layout, as no documentary references have yet been found. Holden suggested a broad date-range of 1025-1125.   *JHF*

Sources Holden 1980, 262-7, 280. VCHS, 6 (1): 144, 152.
NGR TQ 205 077   *PDB* 2792

172 Slaugham Place, 1787

S. H. Grimm

British Library, Add. MS. 5672, f. 1 [1]

Grimm's three drawings are, alas, the earliest views of what must have been a fine house. Its original construction, for Richard Covert (d. 1579), is dated to about 1560, but major changes in layout were designed by John Thorpe (c. 1565-?1655) for Sir Walter Covert (1543-1632), a substantial landowner and active representative of the Crown in Sussex during three reigns. Built in local sandstone, Slaugham Place comprised a courtyard about 80 feet square surrounded by ranges some 25 to 30 feet wide, with domestic offices to the south-west. The great hall was in the west range, but Thorpe moved the principal entrance to the north, garden, front where the arcade shown here gave onto a single-storeyed loggia. Grimm exaggerated its height. The piers - three of which are still standing and visible from a public footpath - have attached fluted pilasters with Doric capitals and bases on tall enriched pedestals; in the reveals are shell-headed niches. In the spandrels of the arches and along the frieze are many shields of arms. There was a large outer area of gardens and courts, the boundary walls having bastions and corner-turrets.

The house and estate passed from the Coverts in the 1670s, probably sold to pay debts. In about 1730 they were acquired by the Sergisons of Cuckfield who had no need of the house as a residence and who fairly soon dismantled most of it. Thomas Sergison, a leading county Tory, took the main staircase to embellish The Star, the venue in Lewes for his party's assemblies and, rebuilt, now the Town Hall.   *JHF*

Sources VCHS, 7: 182-3. Colvin 1995, 979. Thorpe 1966, 26, 104, pls 109-11. Cooper 1904, 129-39. Cooper 1905. Brent 1993, 137.

NGR TQ 260 278   *PDB* 2638

173 Slindon House, 1781

S. H. Grimm

British Library, Add. MS. 5674, f. 40 [74]

Formerly within the archbishop of Canterbury's peculiar jurisdiction of Pagham and Tarring, Slindon House was once an archiepiscopal seat, supposedly the residence of Stephen Langton and John Peckham. The house was probably built or rebuilt by Antony Kempe or his son Sir Garret Kempe, members of a Catholic family who owned the estate in the 16th and early 17th centuries. In 1781 the house belonged to James Bartholomew Radcliffe, Earl of Newburgh, who had married Barbara Kempe. The 16th-century west front (at the left) had a two-storied projecting entrance between two projecting bays, surmounted by an attic storey with blind windows and above that eight dormer windows. To the south six plain 18th-century bays between a pair of circular turrets were surmounted by four dormer windows. These turrets were later crenellated. A two-storey wing projected from the north-west corner of the house.

A chapel in the house was the centre of the Catholic mission in the area until the building of St Richard's Church Slindon in 1864. The registers date from 1697 and the mission was staffed by Jesuit chaplains until the end of the 18th century. The chapel disappeared when Charles Leslie, the owner, had the house repaired in 1870. Mervyn Macartney, Mr Wootton Isaacson's architect in 1914-21, stripped out much of the interior, inserted an extra storey on the west front, made the turrets octagonal and changed the shape of the windows, with the result that nothing is now quite as it seems. The house was bequeathed to the National Trust in 1949 and is now an independent school.

TJMcC

Sources VCHS, 4: 234. Nairn and Pevsner 1965, 327-8. Wolseley 1928b.

NGR SU 960 085

PDB 2908

174 Slinfold Church, 1788

S. H. Grimm

British Library, Add. MS. 5673, f. 8 [13]

The parish church of Slinfold, here seen from the south-east, enters the documentary record in about 1230, and the arrangement and style of windows recorded by Grimm in the chancel could date to that time. It is not known whether there was already a church at Slinfold, but the herring-bone work apparent in the south wall of the chancel recalls an earlier, perhaps 12th-century, date. The windows in the nave are a mixture of later-medieval lancets and post-medieval domestic with glazing bars. By 1848 all the windows in this wall are recorded as domestic. The east end of the chapel of the manor of Dedisham is visible beyond the chancel.

The building was in tolerably good condition in 1724, but underwent repairs in 1779 which 'have excluded all the discriminating remains of antiquity [though] the church has gained by them the praise of superior neatness.' It is not clear exactly what these repairs were, but by 1795 there were reported 'dilapidations and want of repair', particularly to the furniture.

The weatherboard tower was supported by four upright beams of a length and diameter 'very seldom seen'. In his will of 1533, Thomas Hall, of the neighbouring parish of Warnham, bequeathed some timber 'to the making of the steeple of Slinfold'. Both the tower and timber porch were demolished when the church was rebuilt ('proud and uncompromising but not unsympathetic') by Benjamin Ferrey in 1861. In 1969 Ferrey's broach spire was declared unsafe and taken down. James Dallaway, the historian of west Sussex, was non-resident vicar from 1804 to 1834.

JB

Sources Dallaway 1832, 395 (quoted). Ford 1994, 87. Godfrey 1935-41, 4: 141 (quoted). Nairn and Pevsner 1965, 328. Smith 1979, no. 304. Steer 1965, fc. 16. SAS, drawings by W. T. Quartermain (West Sussex), 209. WSRO, Ep. I/40/33 (quoted).

NGR TQ 117 316   *PDB* 2725

175 Stanmer village, 1787

S. H. Grimm

British Library, Add. MS. 5672, f. 12 [21]

To take this view from the north-west, Grimm sat on or near the former 'West Street' of Stanmer, and the ridges he drew in the foreground suggest that he had noticed old house-platforms. For Stanmer was a shrunken settlement. Sir Richard Michelborne (d. 1633) bought the manor in 1616 and set about buying up and extinguishing the copyholds, as was achieved, bar 1½ acres, in his grandson's time in 1659. The 27 houses which had stood in 1608 were reduced to about a dozen, located on the far side of 'the street' in the combe bottom, just visible at the left. Those which had stood in the foreground were cleared.

Henry Pelham (*c*. 1656-1721) bought the estate in 1712/13. His sons Henry (*c*. 1684-1725) and Thomas (*c*. 1696-1737) built a new house in fashionable Palladian style, beyond the trees in the centre and probably to the south of the demolished old house - of which the pigeon house at the right was perhaps a survival. At Grimm's visit in 1787,

Thomas, Baron Pelham of Stanmer (1728-1805), was the resident owner and was in the process of giving the gardens and park to the south the general form they have today. He kept the farm in hand, and his steward lived in the house to the left. The church (*Sussex views*, 150) was rebuilt in 1838.

JHF

Sources Warne 1989. Farrant 1979.

NGR TQ 336 095

PDB 2657

176 Stedham Mill, 1792

Hendrick de Cort

West Sussex Record Office, M/PD 276

Situated at the top of a meander in the Rother above Midhurst, the mill de Cort drew in 1785 may have been on a Domesday site: it has been listed among the half dozen most ancient mills in West Sussex. In the 18th century Stedham Mill formed part of the estates of the Peachey family of West Dean, passing in the 19th to the Hamiltons of Iping (View 123).

It was probably the mill's picturesque quality rather than its antiquity which attracted de Cort's attention. Despite its slightly dilapidated appearance, however, it continued to operate as a flour mill throughout the next century. Subsequently it was burnt down, but rebuilt to continue producing flour until 1929. Now the mill house has gone, while a brick and concrete sluice replaces its wooden predecessor. *PMW*

Sources Dallaway 1815, 2: 299. Tupper *c*. 1950. VCHS, 2: 394, 4: 82-4. WSRO, Add. MSS 20806-21, 28204-12; PH 10816-17.

NGR SU 864 232 *PDB* 1680

177 Steyning High Street, ?1797

John Inigo Richards

Yale Center for British Art, Paul Mellon Collection,
B1977.14.5570

Richards's view of Highdown mill in Ferring is dated 1797. Perhaps on the same tour he made this drawing of the crossroads in Steyning, taking a view from the White Horse Inn south-east down the lower High Street, then known as Singwell Street. The elevated pavement and railings on the left, at the corner of Church Street, remain today, as does the complex of part-Wealden house and cottage (1, 3, 5 High Street) in the centre. The 15th-century Grammar School buildings in Church Street are hidden but the former cooper's premises known today as Chatfields, part of its classrooms, can be seen next to the Wealden house. The level of Singwell Street as shown was considerably lower - the basement entrance and cellar window to the house on the corner can no longer be seen. These houses were occupied by tradesmen and craftsmen.

The chimney on the extreme right of the picture is part of the present Orwell Cottage. The only building no longer visible is the barn or stable shielding this house. Its site is now occupied by a parking area and part of a wide grass verge in front of the Grammar School's side entrance and by late-Victorian housing.

Steyning's weekly market was held in the streets. The muddy condition of the highway bears witness to its regular use by large numbers of cattle, horses and sheep. This pastoral scene, with its hint of the South Downs in the background, gives a romanticised view of a busy little market town.

JP and JS

Sources Lacey and Lacey 1974. Pennington and Sleight 1992.

NGR TQ 176 111   *PDB* 5146

178 Stopham Church, painted glass, *c.* 1600

S. H. Grimm after Roelant, 1780

British Library, Add. MS. 5674, f. 45 [83]
Colour plate XV

Armorial glass in the east window is inscribed to the effect that it was reinstalled there in 1638. Maybe it came from the Barttelots' house, as perhaps did also this early-17th-century enamelled glass window in the north wall, an extremely rare example of figural glass of that period. The glazier, Roelant (not Roeland, as Grimm read) is not otherwise known. The right-hand light portrays William de Stopham, d. 1372/3, and his three daughters by his wife Joan, in costume and in a setting appropriate to a tomb design of about 1600: compare for example the six daughters on the brass in the church to Mary Barttelot, d. 1626. The left-hand light is the more interesting as Roelant has attempted to portray Sir Brian de Stopham, d. 1273, son of Ralph and father of Ralph, in chain mail and a 'quite impossible' surcoat of the late 14th century, presumably by copying a brass or a stone effigy.

Extensive restoration in 1853 introduced glass from another window, of a kneeling civilian, above the capital between the two putti on the left and wrongly changed the year of Sir Brian's death from 1273 (2 Edward I) to 1277. Grimm's drawing confirms the extent of restoration and also that he was broadly accurate but not in every detail.

JHF

Sources Davidson-Houston 1939, 105. Marks 1993, 234-5. Robinson 1877, 61-2 , fc. 62. Round 1912, 24-5, amends the pedigree. Steer 1958a, 10-11 (quoted).
NGR TQ 026 189   *PDB* 2917

179 Thakeham Place, 1789

S. H. Grimm

British Library, Add. MS. 5673, f. 36 [65]

Grimm's viewpoint was the churchyard, to the north of Thakeham Place - from which in turn he took a distant view of the church. The main, south-facing, range is of 17th-century date and still standing with two storeys and attics over a basement, across five bays. Stucco now covers the original material on the front, but the west wall is of stone with a brick chimney inserted later. In 1789, at right angles to its north-east corner, stood an older detached timber-framed range, also of two storeys with attics. In 1477 the manor house had included a great chamber and other rooms, and a gatehouse. If Cartwright was reliably informed in the 1820s that there had been a courtyard house with an entrance gateway and a chapel and a hall on opposite sides, which had been demolished in about 1770, then it may have been in fact only partially demolished by 1789. The range shown here was demolished only during the following 30 years and replaced by a parallel range added on the north face of a remodelled south range.

Outhouses today stand on similar alignments to the thatched farm buildings and cottage shown here west of the house.

In the 1360s or '70s the manor of Thakeham was partitioned between two daughters. Thakeham Place, the manor house, passed with the Apsley moiety and remained in the family until the failure of male heirs in 1651. In 1673 it passed by marriage to the Butler family. At least from the time, around 1710, that the Butlers established themselves at Warminghurst (View 189), Thakeham was probably tenanted, Edward Chatfield being the farmer in 1785. With the partition of the Butler inheritance in 1789, the way was open for sale and in 1805 the Duke of Norfolk acquired the house and lands along with Warminghurst. The Norfolk trustees sold Thakeham Place in 1925.   *JHF*

Sources VCHS, 6 (2): 35-6. Readman et al. 2000, 224.
NGR TQ 111 171   *PDB* 2775

180 Ticehurst, Wardsbrook, 1612

William Gier

East Sussex Record Office, SAS/CO/D 2

Colour plate XVI

This house portrait appears in the lower margin of William Gier's map of Anthony Apsley's 467-acre estate in Ticehurst and Etchingham, surveyed in 1612. Apsley had inherited the estate in 1604 on the death of his brother-in-law Herbert Randolph, whose grandfather had probably built the house shown by Gier. With its bay windows, porch, garderobe and back range built round a courtyard, Gier showed an impressive building – so impressive, in fact, that the surviving house, which lacks any ambitious features, seemed to suggest exaggeration. But in 1993 the building was entirely overhauled, and it became clear that a radical downgrading had taken place in about 1700. Once stripped back to its frame, the house revealed the

evidence for its former grandeur, and for the accuracy of Gier's representation – the extensive rear ranges had been dismantled and reassembled close against the front range, which had been shorn of all its high-status features in preparation for its future life as a farmhouse. Only a kitchen-range remained, converted into an oast house.

William Gier, of Hawkhurst, may have been a lawyer – he acted as trustee of Sir Henry Baker's estate in 1615 – but he was certainly well-read. The *vanitas* and *memento mori* symbols with which he has surrounded the representation of Wardsbrook are closely based on an engraving made in 1594 by Hendrik Goltzius of Haarlem, whose prints could be bought in Pope's Head Alley in London. Apsley cannot have taken the cartographer's warning too seriously – in 1614 he had Gier enrich the border of another map with a portrait of himself. *CHCW*

Sources ESRO, SAS/CO/D 3; HBR 1/723. Hastings Museum, Priory Charters 110. Marchant 1986.

NGR TQ 687 290   *PDB* 7884

181 Ticehurst, Whiligh House, 1722

James Lambert senior, c. 1780

British Library, Add. MS. 5676, f. 53 [79]

The mansion of the Courthope family in 1722 - perhaps drawn in a map's margin by Richard Budgen (Document 1) - presented a deceptively uniform appearance. Whiligh came to the Courthopes by marriage in 1512, and once their title had been secured by three decades of litigation they seem to have embarked upon a progressive rebuilding of the house.

Probably in the 1550s, the main range was rebuilt, the open medieval hall yielding to a ground-floor hall with a chamber above. In 1586 a cross-wing, heated by a massive stone chimney, was built at the east end of the hall, to the right of this

view. Either then or perhaps a decade later, a jettied and gabled projection was grafted onto the western end, giving the impression of a double cross-winged building. During the early 17th century an impressive splay-sided bay window, stretching over two floors and capped by a jettied gable, was inserted into the centre. This work, which involved major structural adjustments, also allowed the insertion of a plaster ceiling and panelling into the hall chamber.

Whiligh was assessed for 14 flues in 1662, and a detailed inventory of 1715 confirms that the house, with its kitchen garden, orchard and (at the left) pleasure garden, had been extended around a rear courtyard. That range was obliterated by rebuilding in 1836.

CHCW

Sources ESRO, HBR 1/52.

NGR TQ 656 312

PDB 4063

182 Tillington, Pitshill, 1785

S. H. Grimm

British Library, Add. MS. 5675, f. 23 [35]

William Mitford bought the property, then known as New Grove, in 1760 and built up an estate around it - partly with the proceeds of his post as Receiver General for Assessed Taxes for Sussex, an office which was subsequently occupied by two further generations of his family. The house remained the family seat until 1959. Grimm's view shows the east front of the original house substantially as Mitford had acquired it 25 years earlier: an attractive building, in a local style, with similarities to 17th-century buildings such as Somerset Lodge in Petworth. Other examples of Dutch gables are in Views 79 and 192.

By 1794 the view would have become quite unrecognisable. Mitford's son (also William and something of an amateur architect) embarked on ambitious alterations which must have amounted to virtual rebuilding. He created a new façade of three storeys and seven bays with no projecting porch, and appears to have built a totally new roof structure. Working in collaboration with the Petworth Estate architect, John Upton, and with some contribution from Sir John Soane, he produced what Ian Nairn calls 'a fine-drawn late-18th-century house'. Dallaway was even more enthusiastic: 'The general effect of the elevation is an ornamental simplicity combined with taste and judgement, not often seen in an equal degree in the works of professional architects.'

Further alterations in the 1840s meant that the west front provided the main entrance, but otherwise the exterior of the house remains substantially the same today.   *PMW*

Sources Dallaway 1832, 298. Nairn and Pevsner 1965, 352-3. Readman et al. 2000, 12-16. Steer 1961b, v-vii. WSRO, Mitford MSS 1274, 2280; QTD/W 127.

NGR SU 949 229   *PDB* 2966

183 Tortington Priory, 1782

S. H. Grimm

British Library, Add. MS. 5674, f. 37 [68]

The house of Augustinian canons at Tortington was founded in about 1180 and dissolved in 1536, when the surviving buildings became part of Priory Farm - which in 1785 the owner, William Mill Leeves, had in hand.

In this view from the south-east, Grimm described the barn in the middle distance as the refectory. The barn is now thought to have been constructed within the exterior angle of the nave and north transept of the priory church - thus, the wall-shafts and stumps of fan vaulting above them were on the interior north wall of the nave, and the east wall of the barn was the west wall of the transept. Grimm's view records four wall-shafts in 1782; Thomas Smith's view of 1793 in the *Gentleman's Magazine* shows three; by 1995 only two survived; and only traces now remain of the large blocked window opening recorded by Grimm

between the two shafts to the right of the barn doors. Notwithstanding the evidence of relatively ornate and expensive fan vaulting, the priory was never a large or wealthy establishment, and a visitation in 1527 reports the house in bad repair.

Limited excavation in 1998 within the area of the yard shown on the south side of the barn found evidence of human interment. In 1787 was discovered a vault containing a skeleton 'as some men were taking up dung in the yard opposite the barn doors.' These interments were presumably burials within the nave of the church. *JB*

Sources Johnson 2000. Readman et al. 2000, 229. Smith 1794 (quoted). VCHS, 2: 82. VCHS, 5 (1): 219.

NGR TQ 006 059   *PDB* 2902

184 Tortington Park, 1782

S. H. Grimm

British Library, Add. MS. 5674, f. 35 [64]

'Torton Place' as Grimm called it, was built shortly before 1699, perhaps by Carew Weekes, MP for Arundel in 1701-5, to replace as his residence the original manor house at Priory Farm (View 183). That build was probably the lower range depicted behind the grander north-facing range of five bays with a central pediment which was added in front in, if a date stone is to be relied upon, 1739. The north range survives, remodelled in the early 19th century, at the same time as the east range was replaced. Further additions and alterations have been made since then. Oliver Weekes sold in 1706 to William Leeves of Arundel, whose descendents sold to the Duke of Norfolk in 1790. North-west of the house, the stable block, around three sides of a courtyard, was probably recently built when Grimm drew it; much of the structure remains.

Known as Tortington House in the 19th century, the house became a Catholic girls school called Tortington Park between 1922 and 1969, and from 1971 until the late 1990s the English campus of New England College at Henniker in New Hampshire. The buildings are (in 2001) being converted to apartments and houses, and the development retains the name Tortington Park.

TJMcC

Sources VCHS, 5 (1): 218.

NGR TQ 003 053

PDB 2898

185 Uckfield, Copwood, 1784

S. H. Grimm

British Library, Add. MS. 5671, f. 98 [188]

As early as 1617 Drew Ellis's house called Ludsham at Copwood had an estate of 172 acres; the house lay at the centre of a bondhold tenement of 37 acres, suggesting that its high status was of relatively recent origin. In 1670 the estate was inherited by Elizabeth Ellis, aged 19, who married Gabriel Egles two years later; it was then described as a capital messuage. He died in 1707 and in the following year his son John Egles settled at Copwood on his marriage with Mary Goring.

The house shown by Grimm was probably built by John Egles; the grant to him in 1727 of half an acre of wasteland in front of the house, with ten oak trees growing on it, may well mark the date of erection, and his sale of a farm in Ewhurst the following year the source of finance. Of three storeys over a basement and containing seven bays, it is seen from the Uckfield to Isfield road which then lay to the north. The whole is surmounted by a pediment with stone balls, but the house was undoubtedly of brick, perhaps burnt in the kiln shown, just behind the point of view, on a map of 1766. To the right of the view, and perhaps contemporary with the house, is an elaborate pedimented coach-house and stables; its height is augmented by a weather-vane set on an octagonal cupola, its Chinese style perhaps indicating a later addition. As well as farm buildings behind the house, the map shows a string of ponds and, nearer the house, a more formal rectangular lake.

John Egles died in 1750, leaving an only daughter Mary; on her death in 1789, Copwood was inherited by her nephew Richard Thomas Streatfeild of Bletchingley. He had bought The Rocks in Uckfield in 1784, had little use for Copwood and demolished it, leaving only the coach-house standing, perhaps to house his gamekeeper. It survives today, shorn of its pediment and cupola, but sufficiently intact to reveal the slight inaccuracy in Grimm's depiction. Only the fine rubbed bricks and lime-putty pointing of the door-arch and windows suggest the vanished grandeur of John Egles's house.   *CHCW*

Sources ESRO ADA 116-21, 137; ACC 6497/10, 212; AMS 1207, 1214, 6546.

NGR TQ 460 210   *PDB* 2632

Walberton Place

186 Walberton Place, 1790

S. H. Grimm

British Library, Add. MS. 5678, f. 28 [55]

Walberton Place, the home of the Nash family, Lords of the Manor of Walberton between 1677 and 1801, stood north of the present house, and faced the lane leading to the parish church. Grimm's drawing shows a house with a main, west, front of late-17th-century character with seven bays, the central three being recessed with a pedimented entrance, and a south front with a central Venetian window and flanking two-storeyed canted bays, which apparently belong to a mid-18th century refacing. To the east is a lower range, presumably the domestic offices, which may have incorporated earlier work. A map of 1756 shows that the house was approached through a walled forecourt entered from the lane. It also shows large formal gardens to the south and south-east, including two square-plan areas each with diagonal paths and a pond, shrubberies and a kitchen garden.

Having purchased it from Gawen Richard Nash, General John Whyte rebuilt and greatly enlarged the house in about 1803. Whyte's son Alexander in 1817 sold to Richard Prime. Partly because of its faulty construction, Prime immediately replaced the house with a larger building on a different site in plain Greek Revival style by Sir Robert Smirke. Now renamed Walberton Park, that house, stripped of the western section of the original colonnade and the eastern bay of its southern section, and with a new entrance lobby, is divided into apartments. *TJMcC*

Sources VCHS, 5 (1): 232. WSRO, Add. MS. 1802.

NGR SU 972 057

PDB 3159

187 Warbleton, Iwood, 1785

S. H. Grimm

British Library, Add. MS. 5670, f. 71 [131]

Although Iwood was demolished in 1796 we know a remarkable amount about the building, shown here by Grimm as a tenanted farmhouse in terminal decline. The view shows a brick house consisting of a central hall-block with projecting crosswings to the north and south. A central bay is depicted without a gable, which may have been removed during alterations. The main entrance was at the southern end of the hall, and an inventory of 1616 shows that the parlour was contained in the northern crosswing and a little parlour or study in that to the south. One of the lofts was used to store apples and the offices, invisible behind the house, included a brew-house, coal-house and well-house.

The date of 1591, then above the gateway into the garden, would suit the building perfectly. The ironmaster Thomas Stollion, described by his gentry neighbours as 'so wealthy and wilful a yeoman', bought the manor of Warbleton from his partner Herbert Pelham in 1586. He then lived in Warbleton, and was certainly at Iwood by 1595. Stollion's bankruptcy in 1616 forced the sale of his estate to his mortgagee Henry Smith, whose charitable foundation retained Iwood until 1986.

In 1722 the house was in a ruinous state, and the trustees ordered that it should be 'lessened and fitted for a farmhouse'. It is clear from the view that all the flanking-windows and all but two of the lights in the northern wing were blocked, perhaps to save window-tax and to convert the rooms to storage. In 1796 the house, 60 feet square, contained eight large rooms on the ground floor, some 20 feet long. The whole was so totally decayed as to be unfit for habitation; it was demolished and the materials used to build 'a new and commodious house', the present Iwood Place, for the tenant Stephen Waters, who had come to Iwood in the year in which the view was taken.

CHCW

Sources Bray 1800. Farrant 1977, 71. ESRO, HBR 1/1001. PRO, C 239/85; C 54/1239.

NGR TQ 631 167   *PDB* 2419

188 Warbleton, Marklye, 1785

S. H. Grimm

British Library, Add. MS. 5670, f. 72 [133]

In 1646 Marklye, with 36 acres of land, was bought for £290 by Thomas Jenner (c. 1610-68), whose father-in-law Geoffrey Glydd perhaps ran Rushlake Furnace in the valley below the house; he certainly owned the neighbouring Charne Mill. Captain Jenner, briefly a JP during the Commonwealth, was purged from the bench with other radicals in July 1659. In 1692 Marklye was purchased by Ann Hawksworth (1654-1737), who left it to her kinsman Edward Hawes (1709-69).

Grimm shows from the south-east a large, low-eaved and profoundly unassuming house, with fairly extensive timber-framed outbuildings. Probably in the time of Edward Hawes – the brick corbels are typical of the middle of the 18th century and the plants had not grown far up the walls – attempts had been made to improve Marklye's appearance. The original house, probably timber-framed, was encased in brick and two tall windows inserted to light the first-floor rooms; the eaves have been raised to accommodate

them. The half-hipped roofs of the front elevation suggest a more substantial internal remodelling, perhaps to gain height in the ground-floor rooms.

Grimm's view of 1785 provides a last glimpse of the old house. Burrell's note within the following few years that 'Mr Parsons is building a large new brick house on a declivity a little to the north [of Rushlake Green]', fits the present Marklye perfectly - Parsons presumably being the contractor and Edward's son Robert Hawes (1747-1817) the client. This campaign replaced the left-hand and central ranges. Having bought Marklye with its contents in 1819, John Darby (1751-1834), an irascible Anglo-Irish merchant, changed the house's orientation by adding today's seven-bay entrance front, originally stuccoed, and diverted the highway eastwards to gain land for a long private drive, from Rushlake Green, hiding the house behind a high stone wall. The right-hand wing was demolished in 1957.

CHCW

Sources Martin 1988?, P45/66, 112. Cleere and Crossley 1995, 343. Fletcher 1975, 317. DNB 1998, Jenner, Thomas. ESRO, AMS 6146-9, 6320; ACC 4919; DUN 8/11, 15; ASH 525. PRO, PROB 11/326 (copy ESRO, AMS 6326/117). BL, Add. MS. 5682, f. 128.
NGR TQ 625 187
PDB 2421

189 Warminghurst Place, 1789

S. H. Grimm

British Library, Add. MS. 5673, f. 35 [62]

For some 30 years, William Penn, the Quaker founder of Pennsylvania, owned the (tithe-free) Warminghurst estate, but after numerous mortgages sold it in 1707 to James Butler (1679/80-1741), grandson of a London merchant, and MP for Arundel, 1705-8, and for Sussex, 1715-21 and 1728-41. Butler demolished the existing manor house and by 1710 on a new, adjoining, site had built this double-pile house, with three storeys above a southern basement. Both north and south fronts were of 11 bays with a pediment over the middle three.

Grimm greatly foreshortened this view of the north front, perhaps through using a camera obscura: between the front wall with espaliers and the house was the entrance court with a circular drive. To the south terraces ran down to the great

pond, as shown in the companion view reproduced in VCHS - which likewise gives the impression that the buildings in the background were closer to the house than they actually were.

Passing by in 1723, John Warburton noted that it was 'situated on a gentle rising bank and has an opening to the north [south?] and through the South Downs to the sea ... with the fine park, garden and other beauties.' In 1775 the estate passed to the builder's great-granddaughters who married brothers in 1780, and thereafter the house was normally let. Hence Grimm described it as 'Mr Richardson's'. Having been bought by the Duke of Norfolk in 1805, it was demolished by 1810. *JHF*

Sources VCHS, 6 (2): 52-3; fc. 96. BL, Lansdowne MS. 918, ff. 21, 34. Booker 1965, pl. II, for another view of 1789, from the south-west.

NGR TQ 116 166 *PDB* 2772

190 Warnham Place, 1788

S. H. Grimm

British Library, Add. MS. 5673, f. 5 [7]

One morning, two weeks before Christmas 1540, 'Dorothy Carill was in a chamber in the house of John Carill esq. at Warnham' where she hanged herself from 'a beam called a rayle.' That house was the earliest known 'manor' house of Fusts or Feists. The first Caryll to settle in Warnham was John Caryll (d. 1523), sergeant-at-law, and Dorothy was his youngest daughter, still a spinster at time of her suicide and living with her brother. The Carylls went on to build up large landholdings in Sussex, particularly at West Grinstead (View 96), Shipley and Harting (View 102), although they remained staunchly Roman Catholic and suffered the consequences.

In 1686 'Warnham Place originally Fusts' was settled on Henry Yates of Ends (or Edes) in Warnham, but in 1737 the family sold it on to Edward Shelley of Field Place; for a time it was home to Timothy, great-grandfather of the poet. The old house was demolished by his son, Bysshe, so that the only remains of the original manor house of Fusts in 1788 was the chimney stack shown to the left of the drawing. He was responsible, shortly before 1772, for the box-like building, of two storeys over a basement, drawn from the south-east by Grimm. Less than thirty years later this was demolished in its turn, and its materials used towards the building of Shelley's new house at Castle Goring near Worthing.   *AFH*

Sources VCHS, 6 (2): 210. Hunnisett 1985, 32.
NGR TQ 167 329   *PDB* 2718

191 Washington, Highden House, 1789

S. H. Grimm

British Library, Add. MS. 5673, f. 56 [100]

The inquisition following the death of John Bellingham in 1577 mentioned a house at Highden, with a garden and dovecot; it was sizeable, with 14 hearths taxed in 1664. The style of Highden House as Grimm saw it in 1789, and the positioning of the chimneys, suggest that the house shown here was built around that earlier house in the late 17th or early 18th century.

A freehold tenement of Washington manor, Highden had been in the Goring family since at least 1610; Sir Henry Goring who succeeded to the family estates in 1655 and died in 1702 is the most likely candidate for builder, perhaps for his term as Sheriff in 1681. Grimm drew the symmetrical south façade of nine bays and two storeys under a hipped roof, which, like the east façade, was built in brick with stone quoins.

The house remained the Gorings' seat until they sold the estate in 1887 to General R. T. Godman whose widow lived there until at least 1930. It passed to Sir Richard Denman who in 1934 sold the house and park to Windlesham House School. Large additions, including an extra storey, were made before the school removed from Brighton in the following year. The school still occupies the site, and a new Highden House was built for Denman in 1936.

JHF

Sources VCHS, 6 (1): 251. Hare 2000, 11-14.
NGR TQ 113 112

PDB 2811

192 Washington, Rowdell House, 1789

S. H. Grimm

British Library, Add. MS. 5673, f. 55 [98]

From its style, the regular nine-bay east façade of Rowdell House, with mullioned and transomed windows, Dutch gables and tall chimneys, is likely to have been a rebuild, or a new front to an older house, of the early 17th century. At that period the owners were John Byne (d. 1600) and his son Sir John (d. 1641), whose grandson John (d. 1661) was the last in the male line. At his death, the family estate extended over some 530 acres in West Grinstead, Ashurst and Shipley. At its centre was the mansion house, which had 15 hearths in 1664 and was leased in 1669 with the South Barn, stall, stables, dovehouse, granaries, hay-houses, outhouses, three gaterooms or yards, gardens, orchards, hop grounds, coppices and 38 acres of land.

It passed through female heirs until it was sold to James Butler (d. 1741) in 1710. In the year of Grimm's view, 1789, the inheritance of James Butler of Warminghurst (d. 1775) was partitioned between his two daughters. The estate of Rowdell passed to Patty, the widow of Richard Clough. Her less accomplished drawing of the east front includes also a walled entrance court. She sold the house in 1799 to Charles Goring, a nabob of Henley in Arden, Warwickshire, not of Wiston, who by 1814 had replaced it by a plain stuccoed building. That, with its Victorian extensions, was demolished in the late 1950s.

JHF

Sources VCHS, 6 (1): 252-3. Booker 1965, pl. II. Booker 1975, 237. Evans 1814, 2: 158, 162. Hare 2000, 11. ESRO, SAS/A 201-2 (calendar).

NGR TQ 113 129   *PDB* 2809

193 Westham, Glynleigh, 1783

S. H. Grimm

British Library, Add. MS. 5671, f. 54 [95]

The Almon family from nearby Pevensey built up an estate at Glynleigh, and the house shown from the south in Grimm's view was probably built by one of the sons of Thomas Almon, who died in 1559, with fashionable onion-domes on corner octagonal turrets. All the sons died childless and in 1591 Glynleigh passed to his nephew Thomas Meeres; the house was described as a capital messuage on his death six years later. His great-grandson John Meeres left it to his widow Elizabeth, who in 1694 married Thomas Fagg of Wiston; he died in 1705 and she enjoyed a second widowhood of sixteen years. In 1717 a Presbyterian congregation of over 100 met under her roof.

Her son Thomas Meeres Fagg settled Glynleigh on his only daughter Elizabeth on her marriage to Sir John Peachey of West Dean, bt, in 1752. Fagg died in 1769 and Lady Peachey, already a widow, lived mostly at Tunbridge Wells. In about 1785

Glynleigh was described as 'a very comfortable house, always left in perfect order, though not inhabited by her ladyship. A fine grove of trees in front, fish-ponds and woods behind; a good kitchen-garden and pleasant views.' Lady Peachey died in 1804 and the house perhaps fell victim to the need for building-materials for barracks; it was described as 'much diminished in size' in 1835. Shortly after his purchase in 1872 Captain William Taylor enlarged the house, which remained of sufficient interest to be visited by the Sussex Archaeological Society in 1907. Today it is a hotel.

CHCW

Sources Caplan 1977, 117. Horsfield 1835, 1: 303. Kelly, 1878 edn. anon. 1908, xvi. ESRO, ACC 2327/2/4/1-2.

NGR TQ 604 086

PDB 2541

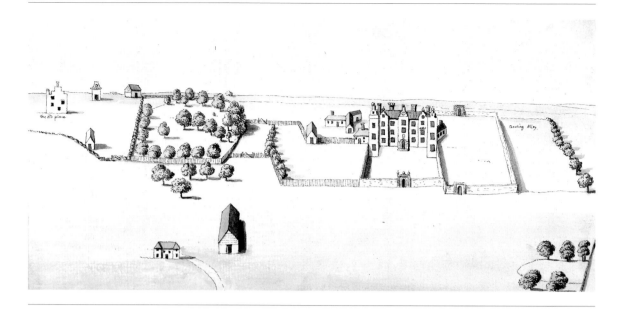

194 Westham, Priesthawes, 1621

S. H. Grimm after John de Ward, ?1783

British Library, Add. MS. 5671, f. 56 [99]

The Eastbourne surveyor John de Ward surveyed the estates of John Thatcher of Priesthawes in 1621. The map from which Grimm copied is lost, but the book of reference survives: 'The mansion or capital house is fair and sumptuous, and newly built with free stone, and covered with Horsham stone, and consisteth of one fair garden with divers sorts of trees of good and principal fruit, one fair kitchen-garden and one fair court, and the garth or site thereof consisteth also of divers convenient buildings and all offices thereunto belonging, with divers ponds well stored with fish, and a fair and large warren well stored with coneys.' The survey also included the Old Place, 'being now for the most part ruinated', with a dove-house and two barns, at the left in the view above. The bowling alley is to the right.

At three storeys high and with stepped gables, two outer wings, a porch-turret and turrets in the angles, Priesthawes was typical of the prodigy houses of the 1590s. Built by James Thatcher (d. 1613), it was reputed to have cost £5000. His son William's father-in-law was Sir Thomas Tresham of Rushton in Northamptonshire, the builder and probably the architect of several startlingly innovative houses, and it is tempting to see his hand in the design of the rather staid but nonetheless ambitious Priesthawes.

A leading Catholic recusant in Sussex, James Thatcher had his other son John educated at Douai before many years in service in Rome. Aside from lands forming the endowment of a secret Catholic charity, the estate descended to John's eight sisters on his death without issue in 1649. It was partitioned, after extensive litigation, in 1699, and Thomas Medley of Buxted Park purchased the mansion in 1705.

James spent £5 on 600 loads of stone from Pevensey Castle in 1592. By the time Grimm drew it in 1783 (*Sussex views*, 178), Priesthawes had itself served as a quarry for other buildings: a mere fragment of his house remained, with only roofless ranges and jagged walls to suggest its former magnificence.

CHCW

Sources ESRO, AMS 6270/38-48, de Ward's survey at 38, ff. 4v–7. BL, Harleian MS. 6806, f. 218. Urquhart 1967.

NGR TQ 606 058   *PDB* 2544

John Dunstall fecit.

195 Westhampnett Place and a pollard oak, *c.* 1660

John Dunstall junior

British Museum, P&D, 1943-4-10-1

Dunstall's viewpoint was from the north-east, with a half-timbered mill over the course of the River Lavant and, beyond, Westhampnett Place, a gabled 16th-century house in brick. Chichester Cathedral, with its detached bell-tower, has been repositioned from right of the mill to the centre. The house's ownership is poorly documented and no client for construction can be suggested. Sir Hutchins Williams added a new front in about 1720, and his son sold the estate in the 1750s or '60s to the 3rd Duke of Richmond. By 1815 the house was leased as the Westhampnett Union Workhouse; it burnt down in December 1899.

Employing a traditional technique of opaque watercolour on vellum, the artist was probably the son and pupil of John Dunstall senior, former military surveyor, and by 1644 stationer of Chichester (View 27). The son married in Chichester in 1655, but died in 1693 in London, having moved there by 1661 when he was established as a drawing master. He etched many sets of drawings, among them five views around Chichester, including Westhampnett Place as shown here, probably from drawings by his father in the 1630s. Most of the etchings were of natural history subjects, and were sold as copybooks for amateur artists and for craftsmen such as silversmiths and embroiderers. With the tree is its central feature, Dunstall may have composed this picture in London, as an exemplar of his work, rather than as an accurate topographical view for a local client.

TJMcC and JHF

Sources VCHS, 4: 177. Dallaway 1815, 2: 117. Johnson 1998, 61-7. Stewart and Cutten 1987. Bodl., Gough maps 31, f. 42b. Essay 1.2.

NGR SU 879 060   *PDB* 2008

WARTLINGTON.

196 Whatlington Church, 1779

James Lambert junior

British Library, Add. MS. 5676, f. 20 [31]

St Mary Magdalene's Church served the smallest rural parish (1260 acres) in the Rape of Hastings. During the early 19th century it was well suited to its purpose, for in 1801 the population of the parish was 211, and in 1851, before any significant alterations had been made to the fabric or ground plan, the capacity of the church was about 200.

The style of the east window and, possibly, the lancet in the nave is of the later 13th century; the plainer lancet in the chancel may be of about 1230. The church and chancel were considered to be 'in sufficient repair' in 1686, but in 1724, though the chancel was 'in good order', the steeple was 'much out of repair' and the roof was in a bad condition. It is not clear whether the weatherboarded bell turret shown here was that steeple or a replacement. The turret was removed during S. W. Tracy's refashioning in 1862 when a steepled tower was built where the porch had stood and an apsidal vestry was added to the north side.

The known early history of Whatlington Church is similar to that of many others in the diocese. Probably only archaeology could now supply evidence for an Anglo-Saxon or immediate post-Conquest church here. When it first appears in the documentary record in the 12th century it is referred to as a chapel rather than a church; by 1268 it was a parish church. The dedication, not a common one in the Middle Ages, is known only from a modern source.   *JB*

Sources Davey 1991, 219. Ford 1994, 50, 119 (quoted). Nairn and Pevsner 1965, 628-9. Orme 1996, 31, 41. Salzmann 1908, no. 747. VCHS, 2: 222-3; 9: 113. Vickers 1989, 23.

NGR TQ 760 182   *PDB* 4446

197 Winchelsea, chapel of the Greyfriars, ?1791

Michael Angelo Rooker

Yale Center for British Art, Paul Mellon Collection, B1975.4.1718

These remains of the Greyfriars' chapel are dated to about 1290, soon after New Winchelsea was laid out. In the 1780s and '90s the Holfords were the owners, and the cells (to the left), from at least 1785 converted into a family house, were occupied by the Luxfords. John Byng visited on 18 August 1788: 'At a small distance is the old friary, now fitted up as a smart villa, with a beautiful sea view, still in parts showing much antiquity, and on one side of the garden remains the shell of their chapel whose inner walls are weakened and disfigured by the nailing of fruit trees upon them. On the eastern and semicircular end, towards the sea, and where the altar stood was an eagle chained (to distress by his misery, dirt and clamour) and at the western end is a noble arch, well shaded by ash trees, which the gardener is for removing, and has also recommended to his master the pulling down one side of the chapel and fitting up the other as a greenhouse, which glorious advice will probably be followed; as the general wish of all possessors of old buildings is to put them to some gardening or farming use, or else to pull down the materials for the repairing of pigsties or the roads. The tower has been a stand for custom house officers.'

For Gilpin in 1774, it was picturesque: 'Its walls are nearly complete - its proportions are just - its architecture elegant; and its situation among lofty trees, on a projecting knoll, sets it off to advantage.'

Sussex views, 183, shows the interior (and eagle) in 1784.   *JHF*

Sources VCHS, 2: 96, 376. Stell 1794, 102. Byng 1934, 1: 355-6 (quoted). Gilpin 1804, 61-2 (quoted).

NGR TQ 905 170   *PDB* 5172

198 Winchelsea, Strand Gate, ?1795

Thomas Girtin

Yale Center for British Art, Paul Mellon Collection, B1975.3.1164

This view of the 14th-century Strand Gate and adjacent houses was taken from the north-east, from where the sea once lapped the cliffs and ships berthed. Winchelsea's history - its foundation by Edward I, the over-ambitious plan, the retreat of the sea and its partial desertion - was often recounted by visitors (for example by Jeremiah Milles in Document 3), drawn by its proximity to Tunbridge Wells and, later, Hastings which was so attractive to artists.

Some 15 pictures on or near the coast between Rye and Pevensey by Thomas Girtin (1775-1802) are known, two only being dated, 1795 (Pevensey) and 1796 (Winchelsea). Several of them can be

paralleled by drawings by James Moore, an affluent London linen-draper (1762-99) with strong antiquarian interests, who had impecunious professional artists work up his sketches for his books, for example *Monastic remains and ancient castles in England and Wales*, 1 (1792). Of his 28 Sussex pictures the dated ones are 1784 (Bodiam), 1785 (Battle, plus Crowhurst and Salehurst (Views 162 and 163) as engraved for Grose's *Antiquities*), 1793 (Henfield and Lewes, his view of the castle matched by Girtin's) and 1795 (Icklesham, the tour on which Girtin may have accompanied him). But the view here is not so much topographical as taken for the artistic effect, and Girtin perhaps made it for his own pleasure.

JHF

Sources VCHS, 9: 64-7. Girtin and Loshak 1954, 26-8. Brown 1982, 334-5, 468-75.

NGR TQ 906 174

PDB 2254

199 Wisborough Green, Loxwood chapel, 1791

S. H. Grimm

British Library, Add. MS. 5678, f. 35 [69]

The chapel of St John the Baptist at Loxwood was built in 1404/5. As they lived 'distant from their parish Church three long miles deep and miry and full of moorish woods so that in rainy and winter seasons the access to their parish Church … is too tiresome and long', several parishioners joined Walter Whitchurch, Vicar of the mother parish of Wisborough Green, to petition Robert Praty, Bishop of Chichester, to license the building of a chapel. He allowed that they could 'build and make one oratory or chapel in some meet and convenient place at Loxwood' in which masses and purifications should be celebrated, excepting on certain festival days in the year, when the parishioners would be expected to attend the parish church of SS Peter and Paul at Wisborough

Green. Grimm's view makes clear that Loxwood chapel, like its neighbour at Plaistow, survived in the half-timbered vernacular style into the late 18th century.

Various endowments were made to the chapel during the first half of the 16th century, and the fabric seems to have been kept in tolerably decent repair; in 1724 the only complaints of any substance made by the incumbent at the visitation were that the floor of the chancel wanted paving and that a bell needed replacing. By about 1820, however, the nave had fallen into disrepair and was rebuilt in brick and slate. A new church was built on a different site in 1898, and the old chancel and rebuilt nave of the earlier church were demolished around 1900.   *JB*

Sources Brandon and Short 1990, 45. Buckwell 1914, 176-7 (quoted), 185. Dallaway 1832, 2(1): 378. Ford 1994, 93. Godfrey 1935-41, 4: 385. Nairn and Pevsner 1965, 265.

NGR TQ 038 314   *PDB* 3173

Lodge in Whiston Park S. H. Grimm fecit 1789

200 Wiston, the Round House, 1789

S. H. Grimm

British Library, Add. MS. 5673, f. 34 [59]

The Round House, as it is called today, stands on a knoll giving fine views to Wiston House and the Downs to the south, and Wolstonbury Hill to the east. A garden ornament to be seen from Wiston, it may have been built when the latter was remodelled in the 1740s and a stone mullioned window and decorated doorway were taken from the 1570s house and incorporated into it. The date of 1790, with the initials JS, crudely incised in one of the south-facing pillars is implausible, given the drawing here. The pale yellow decorative brickwork is finely moulded, though some parts are quite worn. The roof is of Horsham slab, except for the tile-hung curved section over the dormer window. The house can be glimpsed from the road which now separates it from the former deer-park, in which deer, no longer hunted, roam freely, while some land is sheep pasture.

In the past it has been called the ranger's cottage and may at one time have been lived in by a falconer. It had ceased to be used in conjunction with the estate by 1928 when Viscountess Wolseley reported that 'it has recently been converted into a charming miniature house of two bedrooms and one living-room, and the walls, being circular, give a very distinctive and pleasing character to the interior.' The Round House probably acquired that name then and continues to be tenanted. Windows and doors have been inserted between the pillars and small additions made to the west and north.

JP

Sources VCHS, 6 (1): 262. Wolseley 1928c, 114.
NGR TQ 157 134
PDB 2771

201 Withyham Church and parsonage, 1783

S. H. Grimm

British Library, Add. MS. 5671, f. 10 [14]

Withyham Church was severely damaged by lightning in June 1663, but, according to the date on a reset stone sundial in the modern (1841) porch, had been rebuilt by 1672. The walls of the 14th-century tower survived relatively intact, but the burnt-out spire was not replaced. The bells hanging in the tower were melted by the heat, and two new ones were hung in 1674 and a further four in 1715. The two pits in the churchyard noted in the 1686 church inspection, 'one whereof is very dangerous', must have been the bell-founder's.

In 1724 the parsonage was being repaired from a very bad condition. Here seen from the west, it was rebuilt by Sackville Spencer Bale, rector 1749-77, 'in a very elegant manner' with a situation rendered pleasant 'by a fine open prospect in

front, which is extended a great many miles over a well improved country.' It was renovated in about 1800 'as well in the house as in the gardens and grounds' by Bale's son and heir, Sackville Stephens Bale, rector 1778-1836. With further work of about 1918, the parsonage survives and is a Listed building.

The building shown straddling the churchyard wall may have been a church house *cum* lych gate, an early-16th century example of which survives at the south-west corner of the churchyard in the neighbouring parish of Hartfield. It had gone by 1799 when a map (in common with one of 1842) shows buildings ranged along only the outside of the churchyard wall; no buildings were mapped there in 1874.

JB

Sources Amsinck 1810, 162 (quoted). Burr 1766, 265 (quoted). Ford 1994, 41 (quoted), 184. Nairn and Pevsner 1965, 517. Sutton 1902, 29, 34, 37. OS 1874, 1:2500. ESRO, PAR 512/4/2; DLW 562/16; TD/E 138.

NGR TQ 494 355   *PDB* 2441

WOODMANCOTE

202 Woodmancote Church, 1777

James Lambert senior

British Library, Add. MS. 5677, f. 67 [100]

Woodmancote Church is located due south of Woodmancote Place and about a mile east of Henfield. Lambert records from the south-east a two-cell church with rendered exterior walls, south porch and weatherboarded bell turret. The roofing is mainly of Horsham Stone, with shingles on the turret cap. The two double lancets in the south wall look to be of the mid- to late 13th century, while the single lancet in the chancel is probably about a century earlier. The east window is Perpendicular and could well be coeval with the window referred to in the will of Sir William Percy, 1406-7, 'which is now begun on the north side of the said church.' The entrance to the porch has distinctive springers and key stone - more apparent in views by Petrie, 1802, and Quartermain, 1859 - to the round-headed arch and a triangular feature in the gable, all of which could date 1650-1750.

Most of this was swept away when the church was restored and refenestrated between 1869 and 1873 to designs by Henry Woodyer. The chancel was lengthened, the cap of the bell turret was replaced by a broach spire, and the porch was rebuilt.

The church was the setting for an etching of about 1850 by H. Smith of 'Old Penniket' playing the anthem 'Awake, thou that sleepest' on his clarinet to a slumbering congregation.   *JB*

Sources MacDermott 1919, 27-8. Godfrey 1935-41, 4: 411. VCHS, 6(3): 167. SAS, drawings by W. T. Quartermain (West Sussex), 286. SAS, Sharpe Coll. 363.

NGR TQ 231 150   *PDB* 4204

203 Woolbeding House, 1782

S. H. Grimm

British Library, Add. MS. 5675, f. 24 [37]

Grimm drew Woolbeding House from the Midhurst road to the south-west, showing the church to the south, which was linked by a paved path. The view from this angle is broadly unchanged today, but Grimm has foreshortened the distance between the house and the church.

This stone house appears on a map of about 1690 as built about a central courtyard, perhaps being essentially a 16th-century H-shaped house with an east range added later. The ancient features are a Tudor fireplace behind the 17th-century chimney on the south range and a moulded string course on that wall. The plastered west front, 58 feet in length, recessed in the middle and fitted with Ionic columns to form a shallow portico, has been dated to about 1700 (it appears thus on a 1724 map); the diamond may be a hatchment. In 1791 the house still surrounded an open court yard between the hall on the west front and the offices on the longer east front. By 1838 the courtyard had been roofed over to take the

main staircase. Grimm placed the doorway in the south face, but the maps, both previous and later, show a formal entrance court before the west front - which by 1838 was extended across the road by an avenue of trees to the river. The wall at the left screened the outhouses beyond.

In 1785 the owner and occupier was the Revd Sir Charles Mill bt whose family had acquired the manor by marriage in the mid-17th century, but he sold it to Lord Robert Spencer (1747-1831) in 1791. Spencer immediately commissioned John White to make alterations to the house, and Joseph Bonomi to prepare an (unexecuted) design for a new wing. There were Victorian additions on the north front, most of which were removed in the 1950s. The Lascelles family were bequeathed the house by Lord Laverton in 1893, and they continued to inhabit it until a few years ago, although they passed it to the National Trust just after World War II. The house is now occupied by the Sainsbury family.   *TJMcC and JHF*

Sources VCHS, 4: 84-5 , Nairn and Pevsner 1965, 385. Readman et al. 2000, 252. Colvin, 143, 1043. WSRO, Add. MSS 1052, 13418-22; TD/W 152; Acc. 12225.

NGR SU 874 227   *PDB* 2967

204 Worth, Fen Place, 1787

S. H. Grimm

British Library, Add. MS. 5671, f. 109 [208]

Two details in this drawing of the west front are of significance for the history of the building. First, to the left can be seen part of an earlier timber-framed house, the subject of an old painting. Secondly, Grimm also drew the doorway in the porch in detail to show the date 1596 flanked by the initials JB and MB, for John and Mercy Bysshe. It was at about this date that the old house of the atte Fennes was superseded by the new Bysshe mansion. Both the atte Fenne and atte Besche families were resident in the area from the late 13th century, and appeared in the records of the archbishop's South Malling estate.

The marriage of John Shelley to Helen Bysshe in 1692 brought the house into the family who were to own it until the mid-1800s. In 1761 the custody of John Shelley of Turners Hill, who in 1743 had been 'found to be a lunatic and not enjoying lucid intervals', was granted to his sister Margaret Payne of East Grinstead. The income from the estate appears to have been devoted to his care until his death in an asylum in 1772, and the Shelleys continued to lease out the house until the middle of the 19th century. In 1785 the occupier was Sarah Nicholls

Parts of the house drawn by Grimm still survive in the Alexander Hotel, now on the site. But none of the diamond patterning on the façade remains to confirm that it was formed by lines scored in a thin layer of freshly applied rendering.   *AFH*

Sources ESRO, SAS/DD 813. Comber 1932, 64-8. Davey 1991, 228. *NGR* TQ 353 361

PDB 2459

Bibliography

Albery, W. 1947. *A millennium of facts in the history of Horsham and Sussex 947-1947*. Horsham: Horsham Museum Society.

Aldsworth, F. G. 1979a. Durford Abbey. *Sussex Archaeological Collections* 117: 251.

Aldsworth, F. G. 1979b. 'The Mound' at Church Norton, Selsey, and the site of St Wilfrid's church. *Sussex Archaeological Collections* 117: 103-7.

Aldsworth, F. G., and E. D. Garnett. 1981. Excavations on 'The Mound' at Church Norton, Selsey, in 1911 and 1965. *Sussex Archaeological Collections* 119: 217-21.

Allcroft, A. H. 1924. *Downland pathways*. 2nd edn. London: Methuen.

Allen, D. C. G. 1992. Artists and the Society in the eighteenth century. In *'The virtuoso tribe of arts and sciences.' Studies in the eighteenth century work and membership of the London Society of Arts*, eds J. L. Abbott and D. C. G. Allen, 91-119. Athens: Univ. of Georgia Press.

Allfrey, G. 1804. Description of the Southdown sheep. *Annals of Agriculture* 41: 509-16.

Allibone, J. 1991. *George Devey architect, 1820-1886*. Cambridge: Lutterworth Press.

Amsinck, P. 1810. *Tunbridge Wells and neighbourhood*. London: William Miller.

Anderson, F. 1992. 'Uxor mea': the first wife of the first William of Warenne. *Sussex Archaeological Collections* 130: 107-29.

André, J. L. 1900. Halnaker House. *Sussex Archaeological Collections* 43: 201-13.

Andrews, J. H. 1960a. Defoe and the sources of his 'Tour'. *Geographical J.* 126: 268-77.

Andrews, J. H. 1960b. Defoe's 'Tour' and Macky's 'Journey'. *Notes and Queries* 205: 290-2.

anon. 1777. *A catalogue of the pictures at Cowdray House, the seat of the Right Honourable Lord Viscount Montague, near Midhurst, Sussex*. Portsmouth: R. Carr.

anon. 1908. Report for 1907. *Sussex Archaeological Collections* 51: xv-xvii.

anon. 1927. Knepp and Sedgwick Castles. *Sussex County Magazine* 1: 344-8.

anon. 1948. The Caryll Chapel, Harting. *Sussex Notes and Queries* 12 (3): 64.

anon. 1978. Paxhill Park. *Conservation. The Journal of the Society for the Preservation of Lindfield* 11: 3-8.

anon. 1989. *Scotney Castle Kent*. London: National Trust.

anon. 1998. *St James Church Selham. A church guide*. s.l.: s.n.

Arnold, F. H. 1864. *Petworth: A sketch of its history and antiquities*. Petworth: Bryant.

Arnold, F. H. 1871. Racton. *Sussex Archaeological Collections* 23: 1-19.

Arnold, F. H. 1888. Racton Tower and some other similar structures in West Sussex. *Sussex Archaeological Collections* 36: 89-94.

Aslet, C. 1986. Friston Place, East Sussex. *Country Life*, 19 June, 1748-52.

Aston, M. 1973. English ruins and history: the Dissolution and the sense of the past. *J. Warburg and Courtauld Institutes* 36: 231-55.

Attree, F. W. T., ed. 1914. *Post Mortem Inquisitions in Sussex 1 Henry VII to 1649 and after*. Sussex Record Society 14.

Attree, F. W. T., and J. H. L. Booker. 1904. The Sussex Colepepers. *Sussex Archaeological Collections* 47: 47-81.

Aubin, R. A. 1936. *Topographical poetry in XVIII-century England*. New York: MLAA.

Aubrey, J. 1980. *Monumenta Britannica or A miscellany of British antiquities, by John Aubrey*, eds R. Legg and J. Fowles. Sherborne: Dorset Publishing Co.

Aubrey, J. 1986. John Aubrey's excursion into Sussex in 1692, ed. J. Greenwood. *West Sussex History* 34: 22-4.

Austen, E. 1946. *Brede the story of a Sussex parish*. Rye: Adams and Son.

Baines, J. M. 1963. *Historic Hastings*. Hastings: J. F. Parsons.

Baker, G. F. R., and A. H. Stenning. 1928. *The record of Old Westminsters*. 2 vols. London: Chiswick Press.

Bannerman, W. B., ed. 1905. *The visitations of Sussex 1530 and 1633-4*. Harleian Society 53.

Banting, D. R. 1984. *William of Muntham: a nabob of Sussex*. Worthing?: author?

Barton, K. J., and E. W. Holden. 1977. Excavations at Bramber Castle, Sussex, 1966-67. *Archaeological J.* 134: 11-79.

Beevers, D. 1995. *Brighton revealed through artists' eyes c. 1760 - c. 1960*. Exhib. cat. Brighton: Royal Pavilion, Art Gallery & Museums.

Beevers, D. 1999. *Preston Manor*. Brighton: Brighton & Hove Council.

Bendall, S. 1992. *Maps, land and society: a history, with a carto-bibliography of Cambridgeshire estate maps, c. 1600-1836*. Cambridge: Cambridge Univ. Press.

Bendall, S. 1997. *Dictionary of land surveyors and local map-makers of Great Britain and Ireland 1530-1850*. 2 vols. London: British Library.

Berry, S. P. 2000. Pleasure gardens in Georgian and Regency seaside resorts: Brighton, 1750-1840. *Garden History* 28 (2): 222-30.

Bickerton, L. M. 1963. *Worthing: a brief account of the history of the town from Neolithic times to the present day*. 3rd edn. Worthing Museum Publications 3.

Binns, A. 1989. *Dedications of monastic houses in England and Wales 1066-1216*. Woodbridge: Boydell Press.

Blaauw, W. H. 1852. Passages of the Civil War in Sussex, from 1642 to 1660. *Sussex Archaeological Collections* 5: 29-104.

Blaauw, W. H. 1856. Dureford Abbey, its fortunes and misfortunes. *Sussex Archaeological Collections* 8: 41-96.

Blaauw, W. H. 1861. Royal licenses to fortify towns and houses, in Sussex. *Sussex Archaeological Collections* 13: 104-17.

Blaker, N. P. 1919. *Sussex in bygone days*. Hove: Combridges.

Blencowe, R. W. 1849. South-down shepherds and their songs at the sheepshearing. *Sussex Archaeological Collections* 2: 246-56.

Blencowe, R. W. 1858. Extracts from manuscripts ... at Danny and ... Charlton House. *Sussex Archaeological Collections* 10: 1-52.

Booker, J. M. L., ed. 1965. *The Clough and Butler archives. A catalogue*. Chichester: West Sussex County Council.

Booker, J. M. L. 1975. *The Wiston archives, a catalogue*. Chichester: West Sussex County Council.

Boswell, H. 1786-8. *Historical descriptions of new and elegant picturesque views of antiquities of England and Wales*. London: Alexander Hogg.

Bradley, R. 1967. The deserted medieval village of Racton. *Sussex Notes and Queries* 16 (10): 328-9.

Brandon, P. 1974. *The Sussex landscape*. The making of the English landscape. London: Hodder and Stoughton.

Brandon, P. 1998. *The South Downs*. Chichester: Phillimore.

Brandon, P., and B. Short. 1990. *The South-East from AD 1000*. Harlow: Longman.

Bray, W. 1800. *Collections relating to Henry Smith, esq., some time alderman of London, the estates by him given to charitable purposes, and the trustees appointed by him*. London: printed by John Nichols.

Brent, C. 1993. *Georgian Lewes 1714-1830. The heyday of a county town*. Lewes: Colin Brent Books.

Brent, C. 1995. *Historic Lewes*. Lewes: Lewes Town Council.

Brent, J. A. 1976. The Pooles of Chailey and Lewes: the establishment and influence of a gentry family, 1732-1779. *Sussex Archaeological Collections* 114: 69-80.

Bridson, G. D. R., V. C. Phillips, and A. P. Harvey. 1980. *Natural history manuscript resources in the British Isles*. London: Mansell.

Bridson, G. D. R., and J. J. White. 1990. *Plant, animal and anatomical illustration in art and science. A bibliographical guide from the 16th century to the present day*. Winchester: St Paul's Bibliographies.

Brown, D. B. 1982. *Ashmolean Museum Oxford catalogue of the collection of drawings, IV*. Oxford: Clarendon Press.

Brown, R. H. 2000. Notes from the Office of the Ordnance: the 1650s. *Wealden Iron* 2nd s., 20: 39-55.

Brunskill, R. W. 1987. *Traditional farm buildings of Britain*. Rev. edn. London: Gollancz.

Buck, S. 1979. *Samuel Buck's Yorkshire sketchbook*, ed. I. Hall. Wakefield: Wakefield Historical Publications.

Buckwell, J. C. 1914. Stories of Loxwood. *Sussex Archaeological Collections* 56: 161-91.

Budgen, R. 1730. *The passage of the hurricane from the sea-side at Bexhill in Sussex, to Newingden-Level, the twentieth day of May 1729*. London: John Senex.

Budgen, W. 1912. *Old Eastbourne, its church, its clergy, its people*. London: Sherlock.

Bullock, F. W. B. 1949. *A history of the 'Church-in-the-Wood' Hollington, Sussex*. St Leonard's-on-Sea: Budd and Gillatt.

Burgess, F. 1979. *English churchyard memorials*. First pb. edn. London: SPCK.

Burr, T. B. 1766. *The history of Tunbridge Wells*. London: M. Hingeston, etc.

Burrell, S. 1793. *Poems*. 2 vols. London: Leigh & Sotheby.

Burrell, T. 1850. Extracts from the journal and account-book of Timothy Burrell ... of Ockenden House, Cuckfield ... 1863 to 1714, ed. R. W. Blencowe. *Sussex Archaeological Collections* 3: 117-72.

Burrell, W. 1885. *Reports of cases determined by the High Court of Admiralty and upon appeal therefrom, temp. Sir T. Salusbury and Sir G. Hay, Judges, 1758-1774. By Sir W. Burrell ... With extracts from the books and records of the High Court of Admiralty and the Court of the Judges Delegates, 1584-1839. And a collection of cases and opinions upon Admiralty matters, 1701-1781*, ed. R. G. Marsden. London: W. Clowes & Sons.

Burrell, W. 1997. *Sir William Burrell's northern tour, 1758*, ed. J. G. Dunbar. Sources in Local History 6. East Linton: Tuckwell Press.

Burton, J. 1752. Οδοιπορουντος μελετηματα *[Hodiporountos meletemata] sive Iter Surriense et Sussexiense. Praemittitur de linguæ Gracæ institutionibus quibusdam epistola critica*. London: J. and J. Rivington.

Burton, J. 1856. Extracts from the 'Iter Sussexiense' of Dr John Burton, ed. W. H. Blaauw. *Sussex Archaeological Collections* 8: 250-65.

Burton, J. 1916. An eighteenth century journey through Surrey and Sussex, ed. H. E. Malden. *Surrey Archaeological Collections* 29: 34-48.

Butler, M., M. Luther, and I. Warrell. 1989. *Turner at Petworth. Painter and patron*. London: Tate Gallery.

Byford, E. C. 1984. Kidbrooke over two hundred years. *Forest Row: Historical Aspects and Recollections* 1 (3): 4-16 and (4): 2-15.

Byng, J. 1933. A tour into Sussex (1788), ed. C. B. Andrews. *Sussex County Magazine* 7: in six parts.

Byng, J. 1934. A tour into Sussex 1788. In *The Torrington diaries: containing the tours through England and Wales of the Hon. John Byng (later fifth Viscount Torrington) between the years 1781 and 1794, 1*, ed. C. B. Andrews, 339-78. London: Eyre & Spottiswoode.

Caffyn, J. 1998. *Sussex schools in the 18th century*. Sussex Record Society 81.

Camden, W. 1586. *Britannia. Siue florentissimorum regnorum, Angliae, Scotiae, Hiberniae, et Insularum adiacentium ex intima antiquitate chorographica descriptio, etc.* London: R. Newbery.

Camden, W. 1695. *Camden's Britannia, newly translated into English : with large additions and improvements*, ed. E. Gibson. London: A. Swalle.

Camden, W. 1789. *Britannia*, ed. R. Gough. 3 vols. London: T. Payne and Son.

Camden, W. 1806. *Britannia*, ed. R. Gough. 2nd edn. 4 vols. London: J. Stockdale.

Camden, W. 1977. *Camden's Britannia, Surrey & Sussex*, ed. G. J. Copley. London: Hutchinson.

Caplan, N. 1977. Religious dissent in Sussex in 1717. *Sussex Archaeological Society Newsletter* 21: 116-17.

Caraccioli, C. 1766. *The antiquities of Arundel; the peculiar privilege of its castle and lordships; with an abstract of the lives of the earls of Arundel, from the Conquest to this time*. London: author.

Cartwright, E. 1830. *History of the western division of the County of Sussex, 2, pt 2, Rape of Bramber*. London: J. B. Nichols & Son.

Cave, C. J. P. 1932. The wooden roof bosses in the Fitzalan Chapel, Arundel and in Poling church. *Sussex Archaeological Collections* 73: 1-11.

Challen, W. H. 1944. Iping Mill House. *Sussex Notes and Queries* 10 (1): 19-20.

Challen, W. H. 1948/9. Sussex entries in London parish registers. *Sussex Notes and Queries* 12 (4): 83-6 and (5): 109-10.

Challen, W. H. 1952. Baldy's Garden, the painters Lambert and other Sussex families. *Sussex Archaeological Collections* 90: 102-52.

Chancellor, E. B. 1926. *Life in Regency and early Victorian times*. London: Batsford.

Cheal, H. 1901. *The history of Ditchling in the county of Sussex*. Lewes: Lewes and South Counties Press.

Cherry, B., and N. Pevsner. 1983. *The buildings of England. London 2: south*. Harmondsworth: Penguin Books.

Christie's. [Sale catalogue for date given]. London: Christie's.

Clarkson, G. A. 1865. Notes on Amberley, its castle, church, etc. *Sussex Archaeological Collections* 17: 185-239.

Clay, R. M. 1941. *Samuel Hieronymus Grimm of Burgdorf in Switzerland*. London: Faber.

Cleere, H., and D. Crossley. 1995. *The iron industry of the Weald*. 2nd edn. Cardiff: Merton Priory Press.

Cliffe, J. T. 1999. *The world of the country house in seventeenth-century England*. New Haven and London: Yale Univ. Press.

Clough, M., ed. 1969. *Two estate surveys of the Fitzalan earls of Arundel*. Sussex Record Society 67.

Coad, J. G. 1984. *Battle Abbey*. London: English Heritage.

Cochrane, L. 1967. Linch and its iron resources. *Sussex Archaeological Collections* 105: 37-48.

Cokayne, G. E. 1910-98. *The complete peerage of England, Scotland, Ireland, Great Britain and the United Kingdom, extant, extinct or dormant*. 14 vols. London: St Catherine's Press.

Cole, W. 1951. *William Cole, A journal of my journey to Paris in the year 1765*, ed. F. G. Stoke. London: Constable.

Colvin, H. 1995. *A biographical dictionary of British architects 1600-1840*. 3rd edn. New Haven and London: Yale Univ. Press.

Comber, J. 1932. *Sussex genealogies, Ardingly centre*. Cambridge: W. Heffer.

Conner, P. 1984. *Michael Angelo Rooker 1746-1801*. London: B. T. Batsford.

Connor, T. P. 1979. Architecture and planting at Goodwood, 1723-1750. *Sussex Archaeological Collections* 117: 185-93.

Coombs, D. 1978. *Sport and the countryside in English paintings, watercolours and prints*. Oxford: Phaidon.

Cooper, J. H. 1900. Cuckfield families III [Burrell]. *Sussex Archaeological Collections* 43: 1-43.

Cooper, J. H. 1902. The vicars and parish of Cuckfield in the seventeenth century. *Sussex Archaeological Collections* 45: 1-33.

Cooper, J. H. 1904. The Coverts, part II. *Sussex Archaeological Collections* 47: 116-47.

Cooper, J. H. 1905. The Coverts, part III. *Sussex Archaeological Collections* 48: 1-15.

Cooper, N. 1999. *Houses of the gentry 1480-1680*. New Haven and London: Yale Univ. Press.

Cooper, W. D. 1869. Mayfield. *Sussex Archaeological Collections* 21: 1-23.

Cooper, W. D., and T. Ross. 1862. Notices of Hastings, and its municipal rights. *Sussex Archaeological Collections* 14: 65-118.

Cornish, L., and V. Williams. 1991. *Turner to Burra*. Exhib. cat. Hastings: Hastings Museum and Art Gallery.

Cowley, P. 1970. *The church houses: their religious and social significance*. London: SPCK, for the Alcuin Club.

Cox, T. 1730. *A compleat history of Sussex*. London: Thomas Cox.

Crawford, G. P. 1927. A settler in Sussex. *Sussex Notes and Queries* 1 (7): 208-10.

Croft-Murray, E., and P. Hulton. 1960. *Catalogue of British drawings. I. XVI and XVII centuries*. London: British Museum.

Croft-Murray, P. 1956. Lambert Barnard: an early English renaissance painter. *Archaeological J.* 113: 108-25.

Crossley, D., and R. Saville, eds. 1991. *The Fuller letters 1728-1755. Guns, slaves and finance*. Sussex Record Society 76.

Currie, C. R. J., and C. P. Lewis, eds. 1994. *English county histories: a guide*. Stroud: Alan Sutton.

Curtis, L. P. 1966. *Chichester towers*. New Haven and London: Yale Univ. Press.

Curwen, E., and E. C. Curwen. 1922. Notes on the archaeology of Burpham and the neighbouring downs. *Sussex Archaeological Collections* 63: 1-53.

Curwen, E. C. 1930. Wolstonbury. *Sussex Archaeological Collections* 71: 237-45.

Curzon of Kedleston (Marquis). 1926. *Bodiam Castle Sussex*. London: Jonathan Cape.

D'Elboux, R. H., ed. 1946. *Survey of the manor of Robertsbridge . . . 1567-1570*. Sussex Record Society 47.

Dale, A. 1955. Brightling Park. *Sussex County Magazine* 29: 462-9.

Dale, A. 1980. *The Theatre Royal Brighton*. Stockfield: Oriel Press.

Dale, J. 1858. Notice of the south doorway of the church at Bolney. *Sussex Archaeological Collections* 10: 59-62.

Dallaway, J. 1815. *History of the western division of the County of Sussex, 1, Rape of Chichester*. 2 vols. London: T. Bensley. *Plates, additament and sheets to be cancelled of volume I* was issued in 1819, comprising another map of Chichester Rape; portrait of John Buckner dated 1817, to go in pt. 1 at p. 91; cancels at pp. cxlv-clxviii (including 'Observations on geological phenomena' by John Hawkins) to replace cxlv-clxvi in pt 1, and pp. 177-8 and 227-8 in pt 2; 18 pages of 'Additions and corrections': WSRO, Mitford Library 195, for all components (except pp. 227-8) in the printer's wrapper, WSRO, Library 8344-6, for volumes with all bound in, and Steer 1959, 17, for date.

Dallaway, J. 1819. *History of the western division of the County of Sussex, 2, pt 1 [Rape of Arundel]*. London: Bensley and Son.

Dallaway, J. 1832. *History of the western division of the County of Sussex, 2, pt 1, Rape of Arundel*, ed. E. Cartwright. London: Nichols and Son.

Dally, R. 1828. *The Bognor, Arundel and Littlehampton guide*. Chichester: William Mason.

Daniels, S. 1990. Goodly prospects: estate portraiture, 1670-1730. In *Mapping the landscape*, eds N. Alfrey and S. Daniels, 10-12. Exhib. cat. Nottingham: Univ. of Nottingham Art Gallery.

Daniels, S. 1999. *Humphry Repton. Landscape gardening and the geography of Georgian England*. New Haven and London: Yale Univ. Press.

Davey, R., ed. 1991. *East Sussex Land Tax 1785*. Sussex Record Society 77.

Davidson-Houston, C. E. D. 1935. Sussex monumental brasses. *Sussex Archaeological Collections* 76: 46-114.

Davidson-Houston, C. E. D. 1936. Sussex monumental brasses, part II. *Sussex Archaeological Collections* 77: 130-94.

Davidson-Houston, C. E. D. 1939. Sussex monumental brasses, part V. *Sussex Archaeological Collections* 80: 93-147.

Davies, J. C., ed. 1972. *Catalogue of manuscripts in the Library of the Honourable Society of the Inner Temple*. 3 vols. London: Oxford Univ. Press.

Davis, J. B. 1807. *The origin and description of Bognor, or Hothamton*. London: Samuel Tipper.

Dawson, C. 1909. *History of Hastings Castle*. 2 vols. London: Constable.

de Candole, H. 1947. *The story of Henfield*. Hove: Combridges.

Dean, D. R. 1999. *Gideon Mantell and the discovery of dinosaurs*. Cambridge: Cambridge Univ. Press.

Defoe, D. 1724-7. *A tour thro' the whole island of Great Britain*. 3 vols. London: G. Strahan.

Delap, J. 1792. *The Royal Pavilion, an ode*. Lewes: W. Lee.

Dell, R. F. 1964. *The Glynde Place archives*. Lewes: East Sussex County Council.

Dengate, W. A. 1929. *Slaugham, a parish in Sussex*. s.l.: s.n.

Desmond, R. 1994. *Dictionary of British and Irish botanists and horticulturalists*. London: Taylor and Francis.

Dibben, A. A., ed. 1960-4. *The Cowdray archives*. 2 vols. Chichester: West Sussex County Council.

Dinkel, J. 1983. *The Royal Pavilion Brighton*. London: Philip Wilson.

DNB. 1998. *Dictionary of national biography on CD-ROM*. 1.1 edn. Oxford: Oxford Univ. Press. Originally published 1885-1993.

Donachie, J. D., and D. J. Field. 1994. Cissbury Ring. A survey by the Royal Commission on the Historical Monuments of England. *Sussex Archaeological Collections* 132: 25-32.

Donnithorne, A. 1995. Media, paper, watermarks and mounts. In *Views of Windsor. Watercolours by Thomas and Paul Sandby*, ed. J. Roberts, 138-43. London: Merrell Holberton.

Douglas, D. 1951. *English scholars 1660-1730*. 2nd edn. London: Eyre & Spottiswoode.

Douglas, J. 1818. The ancient barrows observable on the South Downs near Brighthelmstone. *The Gleaner's Portfolio, or Provincial Magazine [Lewes]* 1 (1): 1-5.

Drewett, P., and S. Hamilton. 1999. Marking time and making space. Excavations and landscape studies at the Caburn hillfort, East Sussex, 1996-98. *Sussex Archaeological Collections* 137: 7-37.

Drewett, P., D. Rudling, and M. Gardiner. 1988. *The South-East to AD 1000*. Harlow: Longman.

Dunkin, E. H. W., ed. 1914-15. *Sussex manors, advowsons, etc., recorded in the feet of fines ... (1509-1833)*. Sussex Record Society 19, 20.

Dunvan, P. 1795. *History of Lewes and Brighthelmston*. Lewes: William Lee.

Eardley, F. S. 1939. *Horsted Keynes Sussex. The church and parish of St Giles*. London: Macmillan.

East Sussex Record Office. 1986. The Domesday tradition. Surveys and maps in East Sussex, 11th to 20th centuries, Captions for an exhibition.

Elleray, D. R. 1977. *Worthing a pictorial history*. Chichester: Phillimore.

Elleray, D. R. 1998. *A millennium encyclopaedia of Worthing history*. Worthing: Optimus Books.

Ellis, W. S. 1873. Budgen's unofficial heraldic visitation of Sussex, 1724. *Sussex Archaeological Collections* 25: 85-100.

Elvins, M. A. 1981. *Arundel Priory, 1380-1980. The College of Holy Trinity*. Chichester: Phillimore.

Erskine-Hill, H. 1975. John Caryll, 2nd Baron Caryll of Durford, 1667-1736. In *The social milieu of Alexander Pope*, ed. H. Erskine-Hill, 42-102. New Haven and London: Yale Univ. Press.

Evans, J. 1805. *A picture of Worthing; to which is added an account of Arundel and Shoreham, with other parts of the surrounding country*. London: John and Arthur Arch.

Evans, J. 1814. *A picture of Worthing; to which is added an account of the adjacent villages, and of the rides and excursions in its vicinity*. 2 vols. Worthing: William Phillips.

Evelyn, J. 1955. *The diary of John Evelyn*, ed. E. S. de Beer. 6 vols. Oxford: Clarendon Press.

Fant, H. B. 1942. John Burton, DD, one of the founders of the Colony of Georgia. *Oxoniensia* 6: 70-83.

Farington, J. 1978-84. *The diary of Joseph Farington*, eds K. Garlick, A. Macintyre and K. Cave. 16 vols. New Haven and London: Yale Univ. Press.

Farrant, J. H. 1972. The evolution of Newhaven Harbour and the Lower Ouse before 1800. *Sussex Archaeological Collections* 110: 44-60.

Farrant, J. H. 1973/4. Civil engineering in Sussex around 1800, and the career of Cater Rand. *Sussex Industrial History* 6: 2-14.

Farrant, J. H. 1976a. The dates of John Burton's journeys through Surrey and Sussex. *Sussex Archaeological Collections* 114: 337-8; also 1979, 117: 263.

Farrant, J. H. 1976b. *The harbours of Sussex 1700-1914.* Brighton: author.

Farrant, J. H. 1977. Noblemen and gentry in Sussex in 1595. *Sussex Family Historian* 3 (3): 69-72.

Farrant, J. H. 1978. John Norden's 'Description of Sussex', 1595. *Sussex Archaeological Collections* 116: 269-75.

Farrant, J. H. 1980. Passenger travel between Sussex and France in the eighteenth and early nineteenth centuries. *Sussex History* 1 (10): 8-13.

Farrant, J. H. 1983. Visitors to eighteenth century Sussex. *Sussex Genealogist and Local Historian* 5 (2): 44-51.

Farrant, J. H. 1985. The rise and decline of a south coast seafaring town: Brighton, 1550-1750. *Mariner's Mirror* 71: 59-76.

Farrant, J. H. 1988. Building practices in the eastern Weald around 1700. *Sussex Archaeological Collections* 126: 248-50.

Farrant, J. H. 1992. 'Spirited and intelligent farmers': the Arthur Youngs and the Board of Agriculture's reports on Sussex, 1793 and 1808. *Sussex Archaeological Collections* 130: 200-12.

Farrant, J. H. 1993a. The making of Francis Grose's Antiquities: evidence from Sussex. *Sussex Archaeological Collections* 131: 152-8.

Farrant, J. H. 1993b. Visitors to Eastbourne in the early eighteenth century. *Eastbourne Local Historian* 89: 17-22.

Farrant, J. H. 1995a. A drawing of the Long Man of Wilmington, East Sussex, by the Revd D. T. Powell. *Sussex Archaeological Collections* 133: 282-4.

Farrant, J. H. 1995b. The travels and travails of Francis Grose, FSA. *Antiquaries Journal* 75: 365-80.

Farrant, J. H. 1996a. 'A garden in a desert place and a palace among the ruins': Lewes Castle transformed, 1600-1850. *Sussex Archaeological Collections* 134: 169-77.

Farrant, J. H. 1996b. Pictures by or associated with Francis Grose, FSA (1731-91). Lewes: author. Copy in Society of Antiquaries Library.

Farrant, J. H. 1997a. James Lambert, senior and junior, landscape painters of Lewes. *Sussex Archaeological Collections* 135: 249-63.

Farrant, J. H. 1997b. A working list of pictures by James Lambert, senior and junior, of Lewes. Lewes: author. Copy in SAS Library.

Farrant, J. H. 1999. Sussex views in SA. *Sussex Past and Present* 89: 8.

Farrant, J. H. forthcoming. [Articles on Sussex antiquaries]. In *New dictionary of national biography*, eds H. C. G. Matthew and B. Harrison. Oxford: Oxford Univ. Press.

Farrant, J. H., and S. Farrant. 1975. *Preston in the 17th and 18th centuries.* Univ. of Sussex Centre for Continuing Education Occasional Papers 3.

Farrant, J. H., M. Howard, D. Rudling, et al. 1991. Laughton Place: a manorial and architectural history, with an account of recent restoration and excavation. *Sussex Archaeological Collections* 129: 99-164.

Farrant, S. P. 1975. Bishopstone tidemills. *Sussex Archaeological Collections* 113: 199-202.

Farrant, S. P. 1979. The building of Stanmer House and the early development of the park c. 1720 to 1750. *Sussex Archaeological Collections* 117: 195-9.

Farrant, S. P. 1982. The physical development of the Royal Pavilion estate and its influence on Brighton (E. Sussex) 1785-1823. *Sussex Archaeological Collections* 120: 171-84.

Farrant, S. P. 1986. The development of coaching services from Brighton to London, c. 1750-1822. *Sussex Genealogist and Local Historian* 7 (3): 85-92.

Farrant, S. P. 1989. The development of landscape parks and garden in eastern Sussex c. 1700-1820: a guide and gazetteer. *Garden History* 17: 166-81.

Fenton, A. J. 1892. Some extracts, relating to Sussex, from the Exchequer Special Commissions... in 1584 and other years.... *Sussex Archaeological Collections* 38: 141-59.

Field, M. C. 1977. *Easebourne: its church and priory.* Easebourne: Parochial Church Council.

Fiennes, C. 1949. *The journeys of Celia Fiennes*, ed. C. Morris. Rev. edn. London: Cresset Press.

Finberg, A. J. 1927. *An introduction to Turner's Southern coast.* London: Cotswold Gallery.

Fleming, L. 1944. North Mundham Church restoration. *Sussex Notes and Queries* 10 (3): 52-4.

Fleming, L. 1949-50. *History of Pagham in Sussex.* 3 vols. Ditchling: Ditchling Press.

Fleming, L., ed. 1960. *The chartulary of Boxgrove Priory.* Sussex Record Society 59.

Fletcher, A. 1975. *A county community in peace and war: Sussex 1600-1660.* London: Longman.

Flower, S. J. 1986. The Smiths - a biography. In *The Smith brothers of Chichester.* Exhib. cat. Chichester: Pallant House Gallery.

Ford, T. D., and H. S. Torrens. 1989. John Farey (1766-1826) an unrecognised polymath. In J. Farey, *General view of the agriculture and minerals of Derbyshire* 1: unpag. Sheffield: Peak District Mines Historical Society.

Ford, W. K. 1978. The Reverend Joseph Dale and the extension of Bolney church. *Sussex Archaeological Collections* 116: 401-2.

Ford, W. K., ed. 1994. *Chichester diocesan surveys 1686 and 1724.* Sussex Record Society 78.

Foster, J. 1887-92. *Alumni Oxonienses.* 4 vols. Oxford: Parker.

Fowler, J., ed. 1929. *A description of the high stream of Arundel*. Nature and Archaeology Circle, Littlehampton, Extra Publication 1.

Francombe, D. C. R. [1983]. *The parish church of St Mary and St Gabriel, Harting: a guide and history*. Harting: Parochial Parish Council.

Freeman, J., and R. A. E. Wells. 1991. Jasper Sprange, printer of Tunbridge Wells. In *A common tradition. Popular art of Britain and America*, eds A. Durr and H. Martin, 28-34. Exhib. cat. Brighton: Brighton Polytechnic.

Frew, J. 1980. An aspect of the early Gothic Revival: the transformation of medievalist research, 1770-1800. *J. Warburg and Courtauld Institutes* 43: 174-85.

Funnell, B. 1989. *The America Ground*. Hastings: Hastings Area Archaeological Research Group.

Garraty, J. A., and M. C. Carnes, eds. 1999. *American national biography*. 24 vols. New York and Oxford: Oxford Univ. Press.

Gérin, W. 1970. *Horatia Nelson*. Oxford: Clarendon Press.

Gibbs, D. F., and J. H. Farrant. 1970/1. The Upper Ouse Navigation 1790-1868. *Sussex Industrial History* 1: 22-40.

Gilbert, R. 1985. Another look at Magnus. *Sussex Archaeological Collections* 123: 268-70.

Gilpin, W. 1804. *Observations on the coasts of Hampshire, Sussex, and Kent, relative chiefly to picturesque beauty: made in the summer of the year 1774*. London: T. Cadell and W. Davies.

Girtin, T., and D. Loshak. 1954. *The art of Thomas Girtin*. London: Adam & Charles Black.

Glynne, S. 1963. Glynne on Sussex churches, ed. V. J. Torr. *Sussex Notes and Queries* 16 (2): 53-62.

GM. *Gentleman's Magazine*.

Godfrey, W. H., ed. 1935-41. *Transcripts of Sussex wills...by the late R. Garraway Rice*. 4 vols. Sussex Record Society 41-3, 45.

Godfrey, W. H. 1939. Sussex domestic wall paintings. *Sussex Notes and Queries* 7 (5): 150-1.

Godfrey, W. H. 1940. Sketches of Sussex churches. *Sussex Notes and Queries* 8 (3): 76-7.

Godfrey, W. H. 1941. The la Warr family and Halnaker House. *Sussex Archaeological Collections* 82: 59-64.

Godfrey, W. H. 1942-3. Gallops, Albourne. *Sussex Archaeological Collections* 83: 1-14.

Godfrey, W. H., and L. F. Salzman, eds 1951. *Sussex views selected from the Burrell Collections*. Sussex Record Society Jubilee volume.

Godfrey, W. H., and F. W. Steer. 1965. *Guide to the church of St. Mary and St. Gabriel, Harting*. Rev. edn. Sussex Churches 14. Harting: Parochial Church Council.

Godfrey, W. H., A. Wagner and H. S. London. 1963. *The College of Arms*. London Survey Committee Monograph 16. London: the Committee.

Godman, P. S. 1896. Itchingfield. *Sussex Archaeological Collections* 40: 79-130.

Godman, P. S. 1898. Itchingfield. *Sussex Archaeological Collections* 41: 95-158.

Gordon, H. D. 1877. *The history of Harting*. London: author.

Gordon-Brown, A., and A. F. M. G. Jacot Guillarmond. 1972. Burchell, William John. In *Dictionary of South African biography*, 2: 104-6. Cape Town: Tafelberg-Uitgewers.

Gore, S. J. 1977. Three centuries of discrimination. *Apollo* 105: 346-57.

Gough, R. 1780. *British topography*. 2nd edn. 2 vols. London: T. Payne.

Green, R. 1996. Cort, Hendrick Josef Frans de. In *The dictionary of art*, 34 vols, ed. J. Turner, 7: 900. London: Macmillan.

Greenslade, M. W. 1994. Introduction: county history. In *English county histories: a guide*, eds C. R. J. Currie and C. P. Lewis, 26-31. Stroud: Alan Sutton.

Griffiths, A. 1998. *The print in Stuart Britain 1603-1689*. Exhib. cat. London: British Museum Press.

Grinsell, L. V. 1940. Sussex barrows: supplementary paper. *Sussex Archaeological Collections* 81: 210-14.

Grinsell, L. V. 1942. Sussex barrows: supplementary paper no. II. *Sussex Archaeological Collections* 82: 115-23.

Grose, F. 1772-87. *The antiquities of England and Wales*. 6 vols. London: S. Hooper.

Grose, F. 1934. A Sussex tour in 1777, ed. J. Playford. *Sussex County Magazine* 8: 702-6.

Grose, F. 1963. Francis Grose's tour in Glamorgan, 1775, ed. T. J. Hopkins. *Glamorgan Historian* 1: 158-70.

Gunther, R. W. T. 1934. Letters from John Ray to Peter Courthope. *J. Botany* 72: 217-23.

Gunther, R. W. T. 1937. *Early science in Cambridge*. Oxford: author.

Hall, A., etc. 1720-31. *Magna Britannia et Hibernia, antiqua et nova*. 6 vols. London: Thomas Cox, etc.

Hall, M. 1985. *Bosham and its Berkeley barons. A medieval manor 1483-1919*. Bosham: author.

Hamilton, S., and J. Manley. 1997. Points of view. Prominent enclosures in 1st millennium BC Sussex. *Sussex Archaeological Collections* 135: 93-112.

Hammond (Lieut.). 1936. *Relation of a short survey of the western counties... in 1635*, ed. L. G. W. Legg. Camden Miscellany 16. Camden Society 3rd s., 52.

Hamper, W. 1806. Hurstpierpoint. *Gentleman's Magazine* 76 pt II: 897-900.

Hardie, M. 1966-8. *Water-colour painting in Britain*. 3 vols. London: Batsford.

Hare, C. 2000. *The Washington story. The forgotten history of a downland village*. West Chiltington: Washington Parish Council.

Harris, J. 1979. *The artist and the country house. A history of country house and garden view painting in Britain 1540-1870*. London: Philip Wilson.

Harris, J. 1995. *The artist and the country house from the fifteenth century to the present day*. London: Sotheby's.

Harrison, C. 1998. *John Malchair of Oxford, artist and musician*. Exhib. cat. Oxford: Ashmolean Museum.

Harrison, F. 1920. *Notes on Sussex churches*. 4th edn. Hove:

Combridges.

Harrison, F., and O. H. Leeney. 1933. The church of St
Mary, Broadwater. *Sussex Archaeological Collections*
74: 99-130.

Harrison, F., and J. S. North. 1937. *Old Brighton, old
Preston, old Hove*. Brighton: printed by J. S. North.

Harting, J. E. 1890. On an unpublished manuscript of
William Markwick on the birds of Sussex. *Zoologist*
14: 335-45, 379.

Harvey, P. D. A. 1993. *Maps in Tudor England*. London:
Public Record Office and British Library.

Haskell, F. 1985. The British as collectors. In *The treasure
houses of Britain. Five hundred years of private patronage
and art collecting*, ed. G. Jackson-Stops, 50-9.
New Haven and London: Yale Univ. Press.

Hawkesbury (Lord). 1904. Catalogues of portraits at
Compton Place and at Buxted Park, in Sussex.
Sussex Archaeological Collections 47: 82-108.

Hay, A. 1783. *The Chichester guide: containing an account of
the ancient and present state of the City of Chichester and its
neighbourhood*. Chichester: C. Jaques.

Hay, A. 1794. *The Chichester guide: containing an account of
the ancient and present state of the City of Chichester and its
neighbourhood. Together with all that's worthy of notice in
the neighbouring places, noblemen and gentlemen's seats,
and the fashionable and elegant watering place of Bognor*.
Chichester: J. Seagrave.

Hay, A. 1804. *History of Chichester*. Chichester: Joseph
Seagrave.

Hay, W. 1730. *Mount Caburn. A poem humbly inscribed to Her
Grace the Duchess of Norfolk*. London: J. Stagg.

Haydon, B. R. 1950. *The autobiography and journals of
Benjamin Robert Haydon (1786-1846)*, ed. M. Elwin.
London: Macdonald.

Hearne, T., ed. 1727. *Adami de Domerham Historia de rebus
gestis Glastoniensibus ... Guilielmi Malmesburiensis librum
de antiquitate ecclesiae Glastoniensis, et Edmundi Archeri
excerpta ... è registris Wellensibus, praemisit*. Oxford: at
the Sheldonian Theatre.

Henning, B. D. 1983. *The House of Commons 1660-1690*.
3 vols. The History of Parliament. London: Secker &
Warburg.

Henshall, S., and J. Wilkinson, eds. 1799. *Domesday ...
number 1, the counties of Kent, Sussex and Surrey*.
London: authors.

Heron-Allen, E., and H. K. James. 1940. The first
'Chichester Guide'. *Sussex County Magazine* 14: 162-5.

Herrmann, L. 1973. *English landscape painting of the
eighteenth century*. London: Faber.

Hill, C. 1994. *Puritanism and Revolution*. London: Secker &
Warburg.

Hill, D., and A. Rumble, eds 1996. *The defence of Wessex:
the Burghal Hideage and Anglo-Saxon fortifications*.
Manchester: Manchester Univ. Press.

Hills, G. M. 1869. The church of West-hampnett, Sussex,
chiefly in reference to its Roman remains.
Sussex Archaeological Collections 21: 33-43.

Hipkin, S. 1999. The maritime economy of Rye, 1560-

1640. *Southern History* 20/21: 108-42.

Historical Manuscripts Commission. 1892. *Thirteenth
report, Appendix, part IV. The manuscripts of Rye and
Hereford Corporations*. London: HMSO.

Hoare, H. R. 1849. Historical and architectural notices of
Mayfield Palace. *Sussex Archaeological Collections*
2: 221-46.

Hobbs, M., ed. 1994. *Chichester Cathedral. An historical
survey*. Chichester: Phillimore.

Hodson, D. 1984-97. *County atlases of the British Isles
published after 1703. A bibliography*. 3 vols. Welwyn;
London: Tewin Press; British Library.

Hodson, L. J. 1914. *A short history of the parish of Salehurst
(Sussex)*. Robertsbridge: author.

Holden, E. W. 1970. Militia camps in Sussex, 1793, and
the situation of 'Wick' church. *Sussex Archaeological
Collections* 108: 82-5.

Holden, E. W. 1980. Excavations at Old Erringham,
Shoreham, West Sussex: part II: the 'chapel' and
ringwork. *Sussex Archaeological Collections* 118: 257-97.

Holgate, M. S., ed. 1927. *Sussex inquisitions*. Sussex Record
Society 33.

Holland, T. R. 1957. The Yeakell and Gardner maps of
Sussex. *Sussex Archaeological Collections* 95: 94-104.

Hollar, W. 1674. *Animalium, ferarum, et bestiarum, florum,
fructuum, muscarum, vermiumque icones variae, omnes ad
vivum delineatae*. 2nd edn. London: P. Stent.

Holt, M. 1971. Lime kilns in central Sussex.
Sussex Industrial History 2: 23-30.

Holt-White, R. 1901. *The life and letters of Gilbert White of
Selborne*. 2 vols. London: Murray.

Hope, T. J. 1974a. John Sibthorp's last expedition to the
Balkans: the accounts of Sibthorp and Dallaway about
their travels in 1794. *Revue des Etudes Sud-Est
Européennes* 12 (1): 87-102.

Hope, T. J. 1974b. The travels of the Rev. James Dallaway
in the Ottoman Empire: some unpublished
correspondence with Robert Liston.
Sussex Archaeological Collections 112: 9-14.

Hope, W. H. St J. 1919. *Cowdray and Easebourne Priory in
the County of Sussex*. London: Country Life.

Horsfield, T. W. 1824-7. *The history and antiquities of Lewes
and its vicinity*. 2 vols. Lewes: J. Baxter.

Horsfield, T. W. 1832. *Supplement to The history and
antiquities of Lewes and its vicinity*. Lewes: J. Baxter.

Horsfield, T. W. 1835. *The history, antiquities, and topography
of the County of Sussex*. 2 vols. Lewes: J. Baxter.

Houghton, J. 1989. *Property and land ownership in
Lewes*. Typescript in ESRO and Sussex
Archaeological Society Library.

Houghton, J. 1997. *Unknown Lewes. An historical geography*.
Horam: Tartarus Press.

Houlding, J. A. 1981. *Fit for service. The training of the
British Army, 1715-1795*. Oxford: Clarendon Press.

Hudson, T. P. 1975. A Venetian architect in England.
Country Life, 3 April, 830-3.

Hudson, T. P. 1978. Muntham well, Findon. *Sussex
Industrial History* 8: 2-4.

Hudson, T. P. 1994a. Burton Park, Sussex: a further note. *Recusant History* 22 (1): 26-8.

Hudson, T. P. 1994b. Sussex. In *English county histories: a guide*, eds C. R. J. Currie and C. P. Lewis, 385-95. Stroud: Alan Sutton.

Hudson, T. P., and A. Hudson, eds 1988. *Felpham by the sea. Aspects of history in a Sussex parish*. Bognor: T. P. Hudson.

Hughes, A. F. 1996. *Seven Horsham houses*. Horsham: author.

Hunnisett, R. F. 1977. *Editing records for publication*. Archives and the User 4. London: British Records Association.

Hunnisett, R. F., ed. 1985. *Sussex coroners' inquests, 1485-1558*. Sussex Record Society 74.

Hunt, W. H., ed. 1909. *The registers of St Paul's Church, Covent Garden, London, 5*. Harleian Society, Register Section 37.

Hunter, M. C. W. 1970. *The restorations of Harting church, 1796-1876*. Harting Papers 2. Harting: Harting Society.

Hunter, M. C. W. 1975. *John Aubrey and the realm of learning*. London: Duckworth.

Hunter, M. C. W. 1982. *The Royal Society and its Fellows 1660-1700. The morphology of an early scientific institution*. Chalfont St Giles: British Society for the History of Science.

Hunter, M. C. W. 1995. *Science and the shape of orthodoxy. Intellectual change in late seventeenth-century Britain*. Woodbridge: Boydell Press.

Hunter, M. C. W. 1998. The first seaside house? *The Georgian Society Journal* 8: 135-42.

Hussey, A. 1852. *Notes on the churches in the counties of Kent, Sussex, and Surrey*. London: John Russell Smith.

Hussey, C. 1934. Buxted Park. *Country Life*, 21 and 28 April, 404-7, 432-7.

Hussey, C. 1953. Ashburnham Place, Sussex. *Country Life*, 16, 23 and 30 April, 1158-60, 1246-50, 1334-8.

Hussey, C. 1965. *English country houses. Early Georgian 1715-1760*. Rev. edn. London: Country Life.

Hussey, C. 1970. *A short history of Scotney Castle*. s.l.: s.n.

Huxford, J. F. 1982. *Arms of Sussex families*. Chichester: Phillimore.

Hyde, R. 1994. *A prospect of Britain. The town panoramas of Samuel and Nathaniel Buck*. London: Pavilion Books.

IGI. *International genealogical index*. Salt Lake City: Church of Jesus Christ of Latter-day Saints. On-line database at (in 2001) http://www.familysearch.org. Also published on microfiche and CD-ROM.

Inderwick, F. A., and R. A. Roberts, eds 1896-1936. *A calendar of the Inner Temple records*. 5 vols. London: Masters of the Bench.

Jackson-Stops, G. 1977. The building of Petworth. *Apollo* 105: 326-33.

Jaques, D. 1822. *A visit to Goodwood*. Chichester: Dennett Jaques.

Jeake, S. 1988. *An astrological diary of the seventeenth century: Samuel Jeake of Rye 1652-1699*, eds M. Hunter and A. Gregory. Oxford: Clarendon Press.

Jeake, S. 1999. *A radical's books. The library catalogue of Samuel Jeake of Rye, 1623-90*, eds M. Hunter, G. Mandelbrote, R. Ovenden and N. Smith. Woodbridge: D. S. Brewer.

Jerrome, P. 1990. *Tread lightly here*. Petworth: Window Press.

Jessup, R. 1975. *Man of many talents: an informal biography of James Douglas 1753 - 1819*. Chichester: Phillimore.

Johnson, C. 2000. [Tortington Priory]. Pers. comm.

Johnson, W. H. 1998. *Sussex disasters in the last two centuries*. Seaford: S. B. Publications.

Johnston, P. M. 1901. Notes on an early map of Atherington Manor. *Sussex Archaeological Collections* 44: 147-66.

Johnstone, H., and F. W. Steer. 1961. *Alexander Hay historian of Chichester*. Chichester Papers 20.

Jones, G. 1999. [Field-walking at Ewhurst]. Pers. comm.

Joyner, P. 1983. *Samuel Hieronymus Grimm. Views in Wales*. Exhib. cat. Cardiff: National Museum of Wales.

Kay, J. 2000. The Broyle Enclosure 1767-1771. *Sussex Archaeological Collections* 138.

Keane, J. 1995. *Tom Paine. A political life*. London: Bloomsbury.

Kelch, R. A. 1974. *Newcastle. A duke without money: Thomas Pelham-Holles 1693-1768*. Berkeley and Los Angeles, CA: Univ. of California Press.

Kelly. *Kelly's directory of Sussex*. Title varies; 27 editions, 1845-1938.

Kendrick, T. D. 1950. *British antiquity*. London: Methuen.

Kennedy, R. F. 1971. *Catalogue of pictures in the Africana Museum, 6, Supplement A-G*. Johannesburg: Africana Museum.

Kenyon, G. H. 1952. Wealden iron. *Sussex Notes and Queries* 13 (11/12): 234-41.

King, E. 1801. *Munimenta antiqua; or, Observations on antient castles...* London: W. Bulmer.

Kingsley, D. 1982. *Printed maps of Sussex 1575-1900*. Sussex Record Society 72.

Kitchen, F. 1987a. Sussex in 1595: John Norden's Speculum Britanniae, pars Sussex. *Sussex History* 23: 2-6.

Kitchen, F. 1987b. Sussex towns in 1595. *Sussex History* 24: 12-17.

Kitchen, F. 1992. Cosmo-choro-poly-grapher: an analytical account of the life and work of John Norden, 1547?-1625. Brighton: University of Sussex DPhil thesis.

Kitchen, F. 1997. John Norden (c. 1547-1625): estate surveyor, topographer, county mapmaker and devotional writer. *Imago Mundi* 49: 43-61.

Knowles, D., and J. K. S. St Joseph. 1952. *Monastic sites from the air*. Cambridge: Cambridge Univ. Press.

Knyff, L. 1984. *Britannia illustrata. Knyff & Kip*, eds J. Harris and G. Jackson-Stops. Bungay: Paradigm Press.

Kuist, J. M. 1982. *The Nichols file of the Gentleman's Magazine*. Madison: Univ. of Wisconsin Press.

L. 1786. Corrections and additions to The account of Hastings. *Gentleman's Magazine* 56: 852-4.

Lacey, H. M., and U. E. Lacey. 1974. *The timber-framed buildings of Steyning*. Worthing: authors.

Lambert, J. 1956. Remains of the West Gate, Lewes. *Sussex County Magazine* 30: 105.

Lambert, J., and W. Green. 1776. An account of a very extraordinary effect of lightening on a bullock, at Swanborow, in the parish of Iford near Lewes, in Sussex. *Phil. Trans. Royal Soc.* 66: 493-503.

Larking, L. B. 1851. The custumal of Pevensey, as delivered to the Lord Warden at Dover Castle, in 1356. *Sussex Archaeological Collections* 4: 209-18.

Le Neve, J. 1964. *Fasti Ecclesiae Anglicanae 1541-1851, 7, Chichester Diocese*, ed. J. M. Horne. London: Athlone Press.

Leconfield (Lord). 1954. *Petworth Manor in the seventeenth century*. Oxford: Oxford Univ. Press.

Leeney, O. H. 1947. References to ancient Sussex churches in *The Ecclesiologist*. *Sussex Archaeological Collections* 86: 154-86.

Legge, W. H. 1900. Delves House, Ringmer, with some account of Gilbert White and his relatives there residing. *Reliquary and Illustrated Archaeologist* n.s. 6 (1): 1-14.

Leland, J. 1906-10. *The itinerary of John Leland in or about the years 1535-1543*, ed. L. T. Smith. 5 vols. London: George Bell.

Lennox, C. G. 1911. *A Duke and his friends. The life and letters of the second Duke of Richmond*. 2 vols. London: Hutchinson & Co.

Leppard, M. J. 1972. The Hermitage. *East Grinstead Society Bulletin* 9: 7.

Leppard, M. J. 2000. The place-name Saint Hill. *East Grinstead Society Bulletin* 71: 7.

Leslie, K., and B. Short, eds. 1999. *An historical atlas of Sussex*. Chichester: Phillimore.

Levy, F. J. 1967. *Tudor historical thought*. San Marino, CA: Huntington Library.

Litten, J. 1991. *The English way of death. The common funeral since 1450*. London: Robert Hale.

Little, B. 1985. *Architecture in Norman Britain*. London: Batsford.

Lloyd, L. 1996. *Durford Abbey*. Rogate: Rogate Society.

London, H. S. 1947. John Philipot, MP, Somerset Herald 1624-1645. *Archaeologia Cantiana* 60: 24-53.

Lower, M. A. 1857a. Notes on the churches of Newhaven and Denton. *Sussex Archaeological Collections* 9: 89-101.

Lower, M. A. 1857b. Notes respecting Halnaker, Boxgrove, etc. *Sussex Archaeological Collections* 9: 223-6.

Lower, M. A. 1862. Parochial history of Chiddingly. *Sussex Archaeological Collections* 14: 207-52.

Lower, M. A. 1865. *Worthies of Sussex*. Lewes: Bacon.

Lyles, A., and R. Hamlyn. 1997. *British watercolours from the Oppé collection*. Exhib. cat. London: Tate Gallery.

Lyne, M. 1997. *Lewes Priory: excavations by Richard Lewis, 1969-82*, ed. M. Gardiner. Lewes: Lewes Priory Trust.

MacDermott, K. H. 1911. *Bosham Church, its history and antiquities*. Chichester: J. W. Moore.

MacDermott, K. H. 1919. Sussex church music in the past. *Sussex Archaeological Collections* 60: 1-33.

MacDermott, K. H. 1927. The Medley family at Buxted. *Sussex Notes and Queries* 1 (5): 161.

MacDermott, K. H. 1929. *Buxted the beautiful*. Brighton: Pell and Son.

Macky, J. 1714. *A journey through England in familiar letters from a gentleman to his friend*. London: T. Caldecott.

Macky, J. 1940. A letter from Sussex in Queen Anne's reign, ed. C. B. Andrews. *Sussex County Magazine* 14: 57-9.

Macray, W. D. 1882. *Notes from the muniments of St Mary Magdalen College, Oxford, from the twelfth to the seventeenth century*. Oxford: Parker.

Mallalieu, H. 1977. John Nixon and his circle. *Country Life*, 12 May, 1260-1.

Mallalieu, H. L. 1976-90. *The dictionary of British water-colour artists up to 1920*. 3 vols. Woodbridge: Antique Collectors' Club.

Mandler, P. 1997. *The fall and rise of the stately home*. New Haven and London: Yale Univ. Press.

Mantell, G. A. 1822. *The fossils of the South Downs; or, Illustrations of the geology of Sussex*. London: Lupton Relfe.

Mantell, G. A. 1827. *Illustrations of the geology of Sussex*. London: Lupton Relfe.

Mantell, G. A. 1846. A few remarks on the discovery of the remains of William de Warren, and his wife Gundrad, among the ruins of the priory of Saint Pancras, at Southover, near Lewes, in Sussex. *Archaeologia* 31: 430-2.

Marchant, H. 1986. A memento mori or vanitas emblem on an estate map of 1612. *Maplines* 44: 1-4.

Margary, I. D. 1948. *Roman ways in the Weald*. London: Phoenix House.

Margary, I. D. 1965. Military field kitchens of the eighteenth century. *Sussex Archaeological Collections* 103: 60-6.

Margary, I. D. 1969. Militia camps in Sussex, 1793, and a lady's fan. *Sussex Archaeological Collections* 107: 135-6.

Marks, R. 1993. *Stained glass in England during the Middle Ages*. London: Routledge.

Markwick, W. 1791. On migration of certain birds. *Trans. Linnean Soc.* 1: 118-30.

Markwick, W. 1798. Aves Sussexiensis, or A catalogue of birds found in the county of Sussex, with remarks. *Trans. Linnean Soc.* 4: 1-30.

Marshall, D. W. 1980. Military maps of the eighteenth century and the Tower of London drawing room. *Imago Mundi* 32: 21-44.

Marshall, W. 1798. *The rural economy of the southern counties*. 2 vols. London: G. Nicol.

Martin, D. 1971? The foundation of Robertsbridge village. *Recologea Papers* 3 (3): 44-5.

Martin, D. 1988? Warbleton tenement analysis. Robertsbridge: Rape of Hastings Architectural Survey. Typescript in ESRO.

Martin, D. 1990? Brightling tenement analysis. Robertsbridge: Rape of Hastings Architectural Survey. Typescript in ESRO.

Martin, D. 1991. Dallington tenement analysis. Robertsbridge: Rape of Hastings Architectural Survey. Typescript in ESRO.

Martin, D. 1996. Herstmonceux tenement analysis. Robertsbridge: Rape of Hastings Architectural Survey. Typescript in ESRO and SAS Library.

Martin, D. 1999. Preston - Preston Manor. London: University College London. Copy at ESRO, HBR 1/1346.

Martin, D., and B. Martin. 1999. A re-interpretation of Hastings Castle, Hastings, East Sussex. London: Archaeology South-East, Institute of Archaeology, University College. 3 vols. Typescript in ESRO.

Martin, J. 1966. Cloistral remains, Robertsbridge Abbey. *Recologea Papers* 1 (5).

Martin, J. 1967? Robertsbridge Abbey precincts. *Recologea Papers* 2 (2): 13-14.

Mason, W. H. 1839. *Goodwood its house park and grounds.* London: Smith, Elder & Co.

Mawer, A., and F. M. Stenton. 1929-30. *The place-names of Sussex.* 2 vols. English Place-Name Society 6, 7. Cambridge: Cambridge Univ. Press.

Mayhew, G. 1987. *Tudor Rye.* Univ. of Sussex Centre for Continuing Education Occasional Paper 27.

McCann, A. 1975. *A short history of Chichester Cathedral.* Prints from the Past, Set 3. Chichester: West Sussex County Council.

McCann, A. 1983. A private laboratory at Petworth House, Sussex, in the late eighteenth century. *Annals of Science* 40: 635-55.

McCann, A. 1985. *A short history of Chichester and its Cathedral.* Chichester: West Sussex County Council.

McCann, A. 1999. The history of Petworth Park. In *An historical atlas of Sussex*, eds K. Leslie and B. Short, 100-1. Chichester: Phillimore.

McCann, A., and others. 2000. *2000 years of Chichester.* Chichester: West Sussex County Council.

McCann, T. J., ed. 1984. *The correspondence of the Dukes of Richmond and Newcastle 1724-1750.* Sussex Record Society 73.

McCann, T. J. 1986. West Grinstead: a centre of Catholicism in Sussex, 1671-1814. *Sussex Archaeological Collections* 124: 192-212.

McCann, T. J. 1994. 'Much troubled with very rude Company ...:' The 2nd Duke of Richmond's menagerie at Goodwood'. *Sussex Archaeological Collections* 132: 143-9.

McCann, T. J. 1995. *'Restricted grandeur', impressions of Chichester, 1586-1948.* 2nd edn. Chichester: West Sussex County Council.

McConville, S. 1981. *A history of English prison administration, 1, 1750-1877.* London: Routledge and Kegan Paul.

McKisack, M. 1971. *Medieval history in the Tudor age.* Oxford: Clarendon Press.

Mendyk, S. A. E. 1989. *'Speculum Britanniae'. Regional study, antiquarianism, and science in Britain to 1700.* Toronto: Univ. of Toronto Press.

Mercer, D. 1977. The Deepdene, Dorking. *Surrey Archaeological Collections* 71: 111-38.

Messenger, A. W. B. 1951. An eighteenth century dean of Exeter and his family. *Trans. Devonshire Assoc. for Advancement of Science, Literature and Art* 83: 22-33.

Millburn, J. R. 1973. Martin's Magazine. The General Magazine of Arts and Sciences, 1755-1765. *Library* 5th s., 28: 221-39.

Milton, R. 1997. The 18th century Ship Inn at Sea Houses. *Eastbourne Local Historian* 106: 9-12.

Morgan, R. R. 1991. Chichester's Civil War scars. *Sussex Archaeological Collections* 129: 253-5.

Morgan, R. R. 1992. *Chichester: a documentary history.* Chichester: Phillimore.

Morley, J. 1984. *The making of the Royal Pavilion, Brighton. Designs and drawings.* London: Philip Wilson.

Morris, D. 1985. *Thomas Hearne 1744-1817, watercolours and drawings.* Exhib. cat., Bolton, Southampton, Bath. Bolton: Bolton Museum and Art Gallery.

Morris, D. 1989. *Thomas Hearne and his landscape.* London: Reaktion Books.

Moss, W. G. 1824. *The history and antiquities of the town and port of Hastings.* Kennington: W. G. Moss.

Moss, W. G. 1825. *The history and antiquities of the Rape of Hastings, part 1.* London and Kennington: R. Jennings and W. G. Moss. Copy in ESRO, AMS 6113/5.

Mosse, H. R. 1933. *The monumental effigies of Sussex (1250 to 1650).* 2nd edn. Hove: Combridges.

Mowl, T. 2000. *Gentlemen and players; gardeners of the English landscape.* Stroud: Sutton.

Mullens, W. H. 1922. William Markwick. A biographical sketch and notes on his natural history manuscripts now in the Hastings Museum. *Hastings and East Sussex Naturalist* 3 (5): 179-98.

Mullens, W. H., H. K. Swann and F. C. R. Jourdain. 1919. *A geographical bibliography of British ornithology from the earliest times to the end of 1918 arranged under counties: being a record of printed books, published articles, notes and records relating to local avifauna.* London: Witherby.

Murphy, R. C. 1959. Robert Ferryman, forgotten naturalist. *Proc. American Phil. Soc.* 103: 774-7.

Murray, K. M. E. 1980. Francis William Steer. *Sussex Archaeological Collections* 118: 359-61.

Nairn, I., and N. Pevsner. 1965. *The buildings of England. Sussex.* Harmondsworth: Penguin Books.

Namier, L., and J. Brooke. 1964. *The House of Commons 1754-1790.* 3 vols. The History of Parliament. London: HMSO.

Newman, J. 1969. *The buildings of England. West Kent and the Weald.* Harmondsworth: Penguin Books.

Nichols, J. 1812-16. *Literary anecdotes of the eighteenth century.* 9 vols. London: Nichols, Son, and Bentley.

Nichols, J. 1817-58. *Illustrations of the literary history of the eighteenth century.* 8 vols. London: Nichols, Son, and

Bentley.

Nightingale, J. 1818. *The history and antiquities of the Parochial Church of St. Saviour, Southwark, illustrated by a series of engravings ... from drawings by W. G. Moss.* London: W. G. Moss.

North, J. S. 1926. The Bartholomews property, Brighthelmston, 1547 to 1592. *Brighton and Hove Archaeologist* 3: 81-104.

Nurse, B. forthcoming. Petrie, (Frederick) Henry. In *New dictionary of national biography*, eds H. C. G. Matthew and B. Harrison. Oxford: Oxford Univ. Press.

Old Hastings Preservation Society. 1989. *Old Town walk.* Hastings: OHPS.

Orme, N. 1996. *English church dedications with a survey of Cornwall and Devon.* Exeter: Univ. of Exeter Press.

Parry, A. 1976. *The Carylls of Harting.* Harting: Harting Society.

Parry, J. D. 1833. *An historical and descriptive account of the coast of Sussex.* Brighton: Wright and Son.

Pavière, S. H. 1950. *The Devis family of painters.* Leigh-on-Sea: F. Lewis.

Peckham, W. D. 1920. The conventual buildings of Boxgrove Priory. *Sussex Archaeological Collections* 61: 1-19.

Peckham, W. D. 1921. The architectural history of Amberley Castle. *Sussex Archaeological Collections* 62: 21-63.

Peckham, W. D. 1928. Amberley Castle. *Sussex Archaeological Collections* 69: 226-7.

Peckham, W. D., ed. 1946. *The chartulary of the high church of Chichester.* Sussex Record Society 46.

Peckham, W. D. 1955. The Caryll Vault at Harting. *Sussex Notes and Queries* 14 (7/8): 129-30.

Pennant, T. 1801. *A journey from London to the Isle of Wight.* 2 vols. London: Edward Harding.

Pennington, J., and J. Sleight. 1992. Steyning town and its trades 1559-1787. *Sussex Archaeological Collections* 130: 164-88.

Pennington, R. 1982. *A descriptive catalogue of the etched work of Wenceslaus Hollar 1608-1677.* Cambridge: Cambridge Univ. Press.

Petit, J. L. 1861. *The architectural history of Boxgrove Priory.* Chichester: William Hayley Mason.

Petiver, J. 1862-3. Local botany in the eighteenth century. Journal of a botanical tour from London to Dover ... [1714]. *Phytologist* [n.s.] 6: 114-120.

Philipot, J. 1956. *John Philipot's Roll of the Constables of Dover Castle and Lord Wardens of the Cinque Ports 1627*, ed. F. W. Steer. London: G. Bell and Sons.

Phillips, B. 1986. Lime avenue at Buxted. *Sussex Archaeological Society Newsletter* 49: 500.

Phillips, J. 1844. *Memoirs of William Smith, LLD.* London: J. Murray.

Phillips, M. 1892. Pedigree and genealogical memoranda relating to the family of Pellatt, pt I. *Sussex Archaeological Collections* 38: 99-128.

Phillips, M. 1894. Pedigree and genealogical memoranda relating to the family of Pellatt, pt II.

Sussex Archaeological Collections 39: 55-93.

Phimister, E. J., S. Wiles and C. D. Denison. 1992. *Sketching at home and abroad. British landscape drawing 1750-1850.* New York: Pierpont Morgan Library.

Pike, W. T., ed. 1910. *Sussex in the twentieth century. Contemporary biographies.* Brighton: W. T. Pike & Co.

Platt, C. 1994. *The great rebuildings of Tudor and Stuart England   revolutions in architectural taste.* London: UCL Press.

Pleasants, J. H. 1943. Four late eighteenth century Anglo-American landscape painters. *Proc. American Antiquarian Society* 52: 189-324.

Plumb, J. H. 1980. *Georgian delights.* London: Weidenfeld & Nicolson.

Pococke, R. 1888-9. *The travels through England of Dr Richard Pococke successively Bishop of Meath and of Ossory during 1750, 1751 and later years*, ed. J. J. Cartwright. 2 vols. Camden Society, 2nd s. 43, 44.

Ponsonby, F., and C. Aslet. 1984. *Enchanted forest: the story of Stansted.* London: Weidenfeld and Nicolson.

Poole, H. 1993. View of Lewes by Dominic Serres, RA, 1760. *Sussex Archaeological Society Newsletter* 69: 4.

Pryce, R. 1996. *Heathfield Park. A private estate and a Wealden town.* Heathfield: author.

Public Record Office. 1913. *Calendar of the Patent Rolls, Henry III, 1258-66.* London: HMSO.

Public Record Office. 1920-31. *Liber Feodorum. The Book of Fees, commonly called Testa de Nevill.* 3 vols. London: HMSO.

Public Record Office. 1938. *Calendar of inquisitiones post mortem* 12. London: HMSO.

Pullein, C. 1928. *Rotherfield: the story of some Wealden manors.* Tunbridge Wells: Courier Printing and Publishing Co.

Pye, D. W. 1965. The Magnus inscription. *Sussex Notes and Queries* 16 (6): 181-4.

Raeburn, M., L. N. Voronikhina and A. Nurnberg, eds 1995. *The Green Frog Service.* London: Cacklegoose Press.

Raines, R. 1978-80. Peter Tillemans: life and work, with a list of representative paintings. *Walpole Society* 47: 21-59.

Ratcliff, R. 1976. *The story of Boxgrove Priory.* Boxgrove: Parochial Church Council.

Raven, C. E. 1950. *John Ray naturalist. His life and works.* 2nd edn. Cambridge: Cambridge Univ. Press.

Rawlinson, R. 1720. *The English topographer.* London: T. Jauncy.

Ray, J. 1674. *A collection of English words, not generally used, with their significations and origin.* London: H. Bruges, for T. Burrell.

Readman, A., L. Falconer, R. Ritchie, et al., eds. 2000. *West Sussex Land Tax 1785.* Sussex Record Society 82.

Redgrave, S. 1878. *Dictionary of artists of the English school.* New edn. London: G. Bell.

Rees, S. 1998. *The Charlton Hunt. A history.* Chichester: Phillimore.

Relhan, A. 1761. *A short history of Brighthelmston.* London:

W. Johnston.

Rennert, J. 1975. *William Crotch (1775-1847) composer, artist, teacher*. Lavenham: Terence Dalton.

Renshaw, W. C. 1910. East Sussex churches in 1586. *Sussex Archaeological Collections* 53: 1-4.

Ringmer History Study Group. *Newsletter*. Ringmer: RHSG.

Roberts, E. 1867. Mayfield in Sussex. *J. British Archaeological Association* 23: 333-69.

Roberts, R. 1988. *Twelfth-century church architecture in Sussex*. Lewes: Book Guild.

Robinson, C. J. 1877. Stopham. *Sussex Archaeological Collections* 27: 37-68.

Robinson, J. M. 1995. *The Dukes of Norfolk*. Rev. edn. Chichester: Phillimore.

Rogers, P. 1975. Defoe at work: the making of *A Tour thro' Great Britain*, vol. 1. *Bull. New York Public Library* 78: 431-50.

Rosenfeld, S. 1954. Duke Street theatre, Brighton, 1790-1806. *Theatre Notebook* 8 (3): 60-1.

Round, J. H. 1912. The Stophams, the Zouches, and the Honour of Petworth. *Sussex Archaeological Collections* 55: 19-34.

Round, J. H. 1929. The origin of the Finches. *Sussex Archaeological Collections* 70: 19-31.

Roundell, C. M. 1884. *Cowdray: The history of a great English house*. London: Bickers & Son.

Rowe, J. 1928. *The book of John Rowe, steward of the manors of Lord Bergavenny, 1597-1622*, ed. W. H. Godfrey. Sussex Record Society 34.

Rowell, C. 1997. *Petworth House*. London: National Trust.

Royall, M. 1999. *The Petworth House of Correction: A history of the West Sussex Bridewell*. s.l.: author.

Royalton-Kisch, M. 1999. *The light of nature. Landscape drawings and watercolours by Van Dyck and his contemporaries*. Exhib. cat. London: British Museum Press.

Royer, J. 1787. *Eastbourne, being a descriptive account of that village in the county of Sussex, and its environs*. London: Hooper.

Ruddick, W., and M. G. Turner. 1977. *Joseph Farington, watercolours and drawings*. Exhib. cat., Bolton, Hastings, Oxford. Bolton: Bolton Metropolitan Borough Arts Dept.

Sabatier, W. 1963. *Roman military works near Chichester*, ed. F. W. Steer. Chichester Papers 41.

Salt, M. C. L. 1969. The Fullers of Brightling Park III. *Sussex Archaeological Collections* 107: 14-24.

Salzman, L. F. 1921. *The story of the English towns: Hastings*. London: SPCK.

Salzman, L. F. 1928. The early heraldry of Pelham. *Sussex Archaeological Collections* 69: 53-70.

Salzman, L. F., ed. 1932-4. *The chartulary of the Priory of St Pancras of Lewes*. 2 vols. Sussex Record Society 38, 40.

Salzman, L. F., ed. 1946. *The Town Book of Lewes, 1542-1701*. Sussex Record Society 48.

Salzman, L. F. 1952. Sussex drawings by John Buckler. *Sussex Notes and Queries* 13 (11/12): 257-8.

Salzman, L. F. 1967. Horsfield's History of Sussex.

Sussex Notes and Queries 16 (10): 336-7.

Salzmann, L. F., ed. 1908. *An abstract of the feet of fines relating to the county of Sussex from 34 Henry III to 35 Edward I*. Sussex Record Society 7.

Sawyer, F. J. 1896. The 'great pigeon-house' of the Cluniac priory of St Pancras, Lewes. *Sussex Archaeological Collections* 40: 270-1.

Scott, E. 1993. *A gazetteer of Roman villas in Britain*. Leicester: Leicester Univ. Archaeological Research Centre.

Secker, T. 1995. *The Speculum of Archbishop Thomas Secker*, ed. J. Gregory. Church of England Record Society 2. Woodbridge: Boydell Press.

Sedgwick, R. 1970. *The House of Commons 1715-1754*. 2 vols. The History of Parliament. London: HMSO.

Shanes, E. 1990. *Turner's England 1810-38*. London: Cassell.

Shanes, E. 1998. *Turner in 1066 Country*. Exhib. cat. Hastings: Hastings Museum & Art Gallery.

Shaw, S. 1790a. Excursion from Lewes to Eastbourn, in Sussex, with an account of the late shipwrecks near Beachy Head. *Topographer* 3: 364-86.

Shaw, S. 1790b. History of Ferring. *Topographer* 2: 156-63, 209-14.

Shaw, S. 1790c. Journal of a short excursion up the river Arun, with an account of Batworth Park, Warningcamp, and Burpham. *Topographer* 3: 201-9.

Shaw, S. 1791a. An account of Pulborough. *Topographer* 4: 353.

Shaw, S. 1791b. Excursion from London to Littlehampton, 1790. *Topographer* 4: 129-54.

Shaw, S. 1792. Collections for the County of Sussex. *Topographical Miscellanies* 1: 3-104.

Shelley, F. 1912-13. *The diary of Frances Lady Shelley*, ed. R. Edgcumbe. 2 vols. London: John Murray.

Sheppard, F. H. W., ed. 1980. *Survey of London, 40: The Grosvenor Estate in Mayfair. Part 2. The buildings*. London: Athlone Press.

Shoberl, F. 1813. Sussex. In *The beauties of England and Wales* 14. London: Vernor & Hood.

Shorter, A. H. 1951. Paper-mills in Sussex. *Sussex Notes and Queries* 13 (8): 169-74.

Simon, N. 1981. *The Edward James Foundation*. West Dean: Edward James Foundation.

Simpson, J., and S. Roud. 2000. *A dictionary of English folk-lore*. Oxford: Oxford Univ. Press.

Skelton, R. A., ed. 1970. *Two hundred and fifty years of map-making in the county of Sussex*. Lympne: Harry Margary.

Skinner, J. 1984. *The journal of a Somerset rector 1803-1834*, eds H. Combes and R. Combes. London: Oxford Univ. Press.

Sloan, K. 2000. *'A noble art'. Amateur artists and drawing masters c. 1600-1800*. Exhib. cat. London: British Museum Press.

Smail, H. 1950. *Notable houses of Worthing 2: Offington, Broadwater Manor, Charmandean*. The Worthing Pageant. Worthing: Aldridge Bros.

Smail, H. 1952. *Notable houses of Worthing 5: Warwick*

House. The Worthing Pageant. Worthing: Aldridge Bros.

Smith, T. 1793. [Pynham Priory]. *Gentleman's Magazine* 63: 17 and plate.

Smith, T. 1794. Torkington Priory. *Gentleman's Magazine* 64: 785, fc. 793.

Smith, T. 1812. Halnaker House, Sussex. *Gentleman's Magazine* 72 pt. 1: 409.

Smith, V. 1969. The Lewes Market. *Sussex Archaeological Collections* 107: 87-101.

Smith, V., ed. 1973. *The Town Book of Lewes, 1702-1837*. Sussex Record Society 69.

Smith, V. 1979. *Sussex churches. The Sharpe collection of watercolours and drawings 1797-1809 mainly by Henry Petrie FSA*. Lewes: Sussex Archaeological Society.

Somner, W. 1693. *A treatise of the Roman ports and forts of Kent*. Oxford: printed at the Theatre.

Sotheby's. [Sale catalogue for date given]. London: Sotheby's.

Spershott, J. 1962. *The memoirs of James Spershott*, ed. F. W. Steer. Chichester Papers 30.

Sprange, J. 1780. *The Tunbridge Wells guide*. Tunbridge Wells: J. Sprange.

Springett, W. D. 1898. Durrington Chapel. *Sussex Archaeological Collections* 41: 73-8.

Sprinzels, F. 1938. *Hollar handzeichnungen*. Vienna: Rolf Passer.

Squibb, G. D. 1977. *Doctors' Commons*. Oxford: Clarendon Press.

Steer, F. W. 1956. A Sussex mansion in the eighteenth century. *Sussex Archaeological Collections* 94: 13-34.

Steer, F. W. 1958a. Heraldic glass in Stopham Church. *New England Historical and Genealogical Register* 112: 308-12.

Steer, F. W. 1958b. Sources of information on 18th and early 19th century theatres in Sussex. *Theatre Notebook* 12 (2): 58-64.

Steer, F. W., ed. 1959. *'I am, my dear Sir.' A selection of letters written mainly to and by John Hawkins, FRS, FGS, 1761-1841*. [Chichester]: author.

Steer, F. W. 1961a. *Guide to the church of St Mary the Virgin, Burpham*. Burpham: Parochial Church Council.

Steer, F. W. 1961b. *The Mitford archives, a catalogue*. Chichester: West Sussex County Council.

Steer, F. W. 1962. *A catalogue of Sussex estate and tithe award maps*. Sussex Record Society 61.

Steer, F. W., ed. 1963a. *Common Council minute book, 1783-1826*. Sussex Record Society 62.

Steer, F. W. 1963b. *A short description of Halnaker House*. 2nd edn. Chichester: Mrs Redmond McGrath.

Steer, F. W. 1965. Memoir and letters of James Dallaway, 1763-1834. *Sussex Archaeological Collections* 103: 1-48.

Steer, F. W., ed. 1966. *The letters of John Hawkins and Samuel and Daniel Lysons, 1812-1830*. Chichester: West Sussex County Council.

Steer, F. W. 1967. Memoir and letters of James Dallaway, 1763-1834. A postscript. *Sussex Archaeological Collections* 105: 62-9.

Steer, F. W., ed. 1968. *A catalogue of Sussex maps*. Sussex Record Society 66.

Steer, F. W. 1971. Louis Francis Salzman, 1878-1971. *Sussex Archaeological Collections* 109: 1-3.

Steer, F. W. 1974a. *The Fitzalan Chapel, Arundel. A guide and a short history*. 4th edn. s.l.: s.n.

Steer, F. W. 1974b. Introduction. In T. W. Horsfield, *The history, antiquities, and topography of the County of Sussex* 1: [iii]-[vii]. Dorking: Kohler & Coombes.

Steer, F. W., ed. 1976. *Plans, elevations and particular measurements of Arundel Castle in Sussex*. Arundel: the Duke of Norfolk.

Stell, J. 1794. *The Hastings guide*. Hastings: J. Stell.

Stevens, F. B. 1928. The boundary between Sussex and Kent. (ii) The Lamberhurst area. *Sussex Notes and Queries* 2 (2): 38-41.

Stevens, F. B. 1961. Walter H. Godfrey, CBE, FSA. *Sussex Notes and Queries* 15 (8): 283-6.

Stevens, L. 1982. Some windmill sites in Friston and Eastbourne, Sussex. *Sussex Archaeological Collections* 120: 93-128.

Stevens, L., and R. Gilbert. 1973. *The Eastbourne Roman villa*. Eastbourne: Crane Services.

Stewart, B., and M. Cutten. 1987. *Chichester artists 1530-1900*. Canterbury: Bladon Press.

Street, E. E. 1907. St. Martin's church, Chichester. *Sussex Archaeological Collections* 50: 47-60.

Strong, R. 2000. *The artist and the garden*. New Haven and London: Yale Univ. Press.

Stroud, D. 1977. The gardens and park [of Petworth House]. *Apollo* 105: 334-9.

Stukeley, W. 1724. *Itinerarium curiosum. Or, an account of the antiquitys and remarkable curiositys in nature or art, observ'd in travels thro' Great Brittan*. London: printed for the author.

Stukeley, W. 1887. *The family papers of the Rev. William Stukeley, 3*, ed. W. C. Lukis. Surtees Society 80.

Sutermeister, H. 1976. Burpham: a settlement site within the Saxon defences. *Sussex Archaeological Collections* 114: 196-206.

Sutherland, L. S., and L. G. Mitchell, eds. 1986. *The history of the University of Oxford, volume V, The eighteenth century*. Oxford: Clarendon Press.

Sutton, C. N. 1902. *Historical notes of Withyham, Hartfield and Ashdown Forest*. Tunbridge Wells: Baldwin.

Sutton, T. 1946. The library and museums. *Sussex Archaeological Collections* 85: 77-112.

SWA. *Sussex Weekly Advertiser*. Lewes.

Sweet, R. 1997. *The writing of urban histories in eighteenth-century England*. Oxford: Clarendon Press.

Tabor, J. 1717. An account of a tessellated pavement, bath, and other Roman antiquities, lately discover'd near East Bourne, in Sussex. *Phil. Trans. Royal Soc.* 30 (351): 549-63; (356): 783-802.

Tate Gallery. 1984. *George Stubbs 1724-1806*. Exhib. cat. London: Tate Gallery.

Tatton-Brown, T. 1994. The buildings of the Bishop's Palace and the Close. In *Chichester Cathedral, An historical survey*, ed. M. Hobbs, 225-46. Chichester: Phillimore.

Taylor, J. 1940. John Taylor's tour in Sussex in 1653, ed. J. B. Caldecott. *Sussex Archaeological Collections* 81: 19-30.

Taylor, J. G. 1937. *The parish church of St Leonard, Seaford*. London: George White.

Taylor, S., and C. Jones, eds 1998. *Tory and Whig. The parliamentary papers of Edward Harley, 3rd Earl of Oxford, and William Hay, MP for Seaford 1716-1753*. Parliamentary History Record Series 1. Woodbridge: Boydell Press.

Tebbutt, C. F. 1972. Two newly-discovered medieval sites. *Sussex Archaeological Collections* 110: 31-6.

Tebbutt, C. F. 1975. Old Buxted Place. *Sussex Archaeological Collections* 113: 51-3.

Tebbutt, C. F. 1979. Buxted medieval village site. *Sussex Archaeological Collections* 117: 261-3.

Thackray, D. 1991. *Bodiam Castle*. London: National Trust.

Thompson, P. 1885. A journey from Poole to Brighton in 1760. *Antiquarian Magazine and Bibliographer* 7: 178-81.

Thompson, R. 1974. Some newly discovered letters of John Ray. *J. Soc. Bibliogr. Natural Hist.* 7: 111-23.

Thorne, R. G. 1986. *The House of Commons 1790-1820*. 5 vols. The History of Parliament. London: Seker and Warburg.

Thorpe, J. 1966. *The book of architecture of John Thorpe*, ed. J. Summerson. Walpole Society 40.

Thorpe, T. 1835. *Descriptive catalogue of the . . . muniments of Battle Abbey*. London: T. Thorpe.

Tibble, R. 1989. The Revd John Mossop MA (1756-1794). *Sussex Family Historian* 8 (8): 368-72.

Tierney, M. A. 1834. *The history and antiquities of the Castle and Town of Arundel; including the biography of its earls from the Conquest to the present time*. 2 vols. London: G. and W. Nicol.

Tomlin, R. S. O. 1997. Reading a 1st-century Roman gold signet ring from Fishbourne. *Sussex Archaeological Collections* 135: 127-30.

Topp, J. 1991. A history of Sussex prisons. Typescript in ESRO.

Torrens, H. S. 1998. Coal hunting at Bexhill 1805-1811: how the new science of stratigraphy was ignored. *Sussex Archaeological Collection* 136: 177-91.

Toy, S. 1953. Langney Grange, Westham. *Sussex Archaeological Collections* 91: 125-33.

Trail, R. R., and F. W. Steer. 1963. *Dr. John Bayly of Chichester*. Chichester Paper 34.

Tummers, H. A. 1994. Church monuments. In *Chichester Cathedral: An historical survey*, ed. M. Hobbs, 203-24. Chichester: Phillimore.

Tupper, M. E. *c.* 1950. *History of Stedham and its church*. s. l.: s. n.

Turner, E. 1857. The free chapels of Maresfield and Dudeney. *Sussex Archaeological Collections* 9: 41-4.

Turner, E. 1866. The statutes of the marshes of Pevensey and Romney; and the custumal of the town, port and leege of Pevensey. *Sussex Archaeological Collections* 18: 42-53.

Turner, E. 1868. St. Anne's Hill, Midhurst. *Sussex Archaeological Collections* 20: 175-9.

Turner, E. 1872. A brief sketch of the history of John Rowe. *Sussex Archaeological Collections* 24: 85-98.

Turner, T. 1984. *The diary of Thomas Turner 1754-1765*, ed. D. Vaisey. Oxford: Oxford Univ. Press.

Urquhart, M. J. 1967. A Sussex Recusant family. *Dublin Review* 512: 162-70.

Ussher, J. 1658. *The annals of the World ... collected from all history, as well sacred, as prophane, and methodicaly digested*. London: J. Crook and G. Bedell.

VCH Surrey. *Victoria County History of Surrey*. 5 vols.

VCHS. *Victoria County History of Sussex*. Volumes published to date: 1 (1905) natural history, geology, pre-medieval archaeology, the Domesday survey, and political history; 2 (1907) ecclesiastical, maritime, social and economic history, population 1801-1901, industries, agriculture, forestry, architecture, schools and sport; 3 (1935) Romano-British Sussex, and the City of Chichester; 4 (1953) the Rape of Chichester; 5 (1) (1997) south-western part of the Rape of Arundel; 6 (1) (1980) southern part of the Rape of Bramber, (2) (1986) north-western part, (3) (1987) north-eastern part; 7 (1940) the Rape of Lewes; 9 (1937) the Rape of Hastings; Index (and corrigenda) to vols 1-4, 7 and 9 (1984).

Venables, E. 1851. The castle of Herstmonceux and its lords. *Sussex Archaeological Collections* 4: 125-202.

Venn, J., and J. A. Venn. 1922-54. *Alumni Cantabrigienses*. 10 vols. Cambridge: Cambridge Univ. Press.

Vertue, G. 1930-55. *Vertue note books*. 6 plus index vols. Walpole Society 18, 20, 22, 24, 26, 29, 30.

Vickers, J. A., ed. 1989. *The Religious Census of Sussex 1851*. Sussex Record Society 75.

Vine, S. 1773. [Herstmonceux Castle]. *Gentleman's Magazine* 43: 63.

Wagner, A. 1967. *Heralds of England. A history of the office and College of Arms*. London: HMSO.

Wakeham, T. 1785. [Fall of the tower of East Grinstead church]. *Gentleman's Magazine* 55: 913-14.

Walpole, H. 1937-83. *Horace Walpole's correspondence*, ed. W. S. Lewis. 48 vols. London: Oxford Univ. Press.

Wark, R. R. 1969. *Early British drawings in the Huntington Collection 1600-1750*. San Marino, CA: Huntington Library.

Warne, H. 1989. Stanmer: a restructured settlement. *Sussex Archaeological Collections* 127: 189-210.

Warne, H. M. 1972. *A catalogue of the Frewen archives*. Lewes: East Sussex County Council.

Waterhouse, E. 1981. *The dictionary of British 18th century painters in oils and crayons*. [Woodbridge]: Antique Collectors' Club.

Watson, J. 1782. *Memoirs of the ancient Earls of Warren and Surrey, and their descendents to the present time*. Warrington: William Eyres.

Webb, C., and A. E. Wilson, eds 1952. *Elizabethan Brighton. The Ancient Customs of Brighthelmston 1580.* Brighton: John Beal.

Welch, C. E. 1956. An early plan of Chichester Cathedral. *Sussex Notes and Queries* 14 (11/12): 199-203.

Welch, C. E. 1961. The end of Durrington Chapel. *Sussex Notes and Queries* 15 (7): 224-8.

Weller, L., and J. Warren. forthcoming. *West Sussex country houses.* Chichester: Phillimore.

Wellesley, H. 1850. Catalogue of drawings relating to Sussex by S. H. Grimm in the Bodleian Library. *Sussex Archaeological Collections* 3: 232-8.

Wellesley, H. 1852. On two engravings by John Dunstall of 'A temple by Chichester'. *Sussex Archaeological Collections* 5: 277-80.

West, W. 1830. *Fifty years' recollections of an old bookseller.* Cork: author.

Whaley, J. 1945. A tour through Sussex in 1735, ed. V. J. Torr. *Sussex County Magazine* 19: 253-8.

White, G. 1931. *Journals of Gilbert White*, ed. W. Johnson. London: George Routledge.

White, G. 1981. *The illustrated Natural history of Selborne*, eds R. Davidson-Houston and J. E. Chatfield. Exeter: Webb and Bower.

White, R. 1984. Wiston House remodelled. *Architectural History* 27: 241-8.

White, R. 1985. Mere conceit or whimsy: 18th century triangular towers. *Country Life*, 31 Jan., 254-6, 258.

White, S. 2000. *Worthing past.* Chichester: Phillimore.

Whitley, H. M. 1912. An inventory of the goods and chattels of William Shelley of Michelgrove, 1585. *Sussex Archaeological Collections* 55: 284-98.

Whittick, C. forthcoming. Caraccioli, Charles. In *New dictionary of national biography*, eds H. C. G. Matthew and B. Harrison. Oxford: Oxford Univ. Press.

Whittle, S. 1993. *Anthony Devis (1729-1816), a 'picturesque traveller'.* Exhib. cat. Preston: Harris Museum & Art Gallery.

Williamson, G. C. 1903. *Andrew and Nathaniel Plimer, miniature painters. Their lives and their works.* London: George Bell & Sons.

Williamson, T. 1995. *Polite landscapes: gardens and society in eighteenth-century England.* Stroud: Alan Sutton.

Willis, B. 1718-19. *An history of the mitred parliamentary abbies, and conventual cathedral churches.* 2 vols. London: R. Gosling.

Willis, T. G. 1928. *Records of Chichester.* Chichester: author.

Wilson, D. 1985. *The Bayeux Tapestry.* London: Thames and Hudson.

Wilson, R., and A. Mackley. 2000. *Creating Paradise. The building of the English country house 1660-1880.* London: Hambledon and London.

Wolley-Dod, A. H., ed. 1937. *Flora of Sussex.* Hastings: Kenneth Saville.

Wolseley, F. 1925. *Some of the smaller manor houses of Sussex.* London and Boston: Medici Society.

Wolseley, F. 1928a. Compton Place, Eastbourne. *Sussex County Magazine* 2: 42-7, 59.

Wolseley, F. 1928b. Slindon House. *Sussex County Magazine* 2: 426-32.

Wolseley, F. 1928c. *Sussex in the past.* London and Boston: Medici Society.

Wolseley, F. 1929. Ewhurst Manor, Henfield. *Sussex County Magazine* 3: 747-52.

Wolseley, F. 1932. Chithurst Abbey nr. Rogate. *Sussex County Magazine* 6: 411-16.

Wolseley, F. 1934. Church House, Beckley. *Sussex County Magazine* 8: 536-40.

Wolseley, F. 1936. Friston Place. *Sussex County Magazine* 10: 294-301.

Wood, R. H. 1972. The Hermitage, East Grinstead. Unpub. notes in private hands in East Grinstead.

Woodruff, C. E. 1910. A survey of the Sussex estates of the Dean and Chapter of Canterbury taken in 1671. *Sussex Archaeological Collections* 53: 192-7.

Woodward, M. 1939. *The mistress of Stantons Farm.* 2nd edn. London: Heath Cranton.

Wratten, N. 1974. *Index to Hay's History of Chichester (1804).* Lists and Indexes 8. Chichester: West Sussex County and Diocesan Record Office.

Wyndham, H. P. 1779. Observations on an ancient building at Warnford, Hampshire. *Archæologia* 5: 357-66.

Yates, E. M. 1972. *A history of the landscapes of the parishes of South Harting and Rogate.* Chichester: Phillimore.

Yates, E. M. 1980. *Durford Abbey and its lands.* Harting Papers. Harting: for Harting Society.

Yates, E. M. 1982. Vernacular buildings on early maps of the Weald. *Trans. Ancient Monuments Society* 26: 210-26.

Young, A. 1771. *The farmer's tour through the east of England.* 4 vols. London: W. Strahan.

Young, A. 1789. A tour through Sussex by the Editor. *Annals of Agriculture* 11: 170-304.

Young, A. 1793. *General view of the agriculture of the county of Sussex, with observations on the means of its improvement.* London: J. Nichols.

Young, A. 1794. A tour through Sussex 1793. *Annals of Agriculture* 22: 171-334, 494-631.

Young, A. 1808. *General view of the agriculture of the county of Sussex*, ed. A. Young. London: Richard Phillips.

Young, G. 1983. *A history of Bognor Regis.* Chichester: Phillimore.

SUSSEX ARCHÆOLOGICAL SOCIETY.

PROPOSED RECORD SOCIETY.

DEAR SIR,

A strong feeling has been growing of late years as to the importance of printing Local Documents with a view to preserving their contents and making them accessible to Students of all branches of our National History.

It is impossible to effect this without the establishment of a County Record Society as a Branch of the Parent Society, as there is manifestly no room in the present volumes of our "Collections" for such matter, including, as it must, a great variety of subjects. Moreover, a Record of any importance is sufficient to fill an annual volume, and Calendaring and Indexing, which to be of any service must be very exhaustive, would be beyond the scope of our "Collections."

There are stores of County, Ecclesiastical, Borough and Parochial Documents which are at present practically inaccessible, but which would, if printed, be of great value for students of the history of our County. The Public Record Office and the British Museum and other Depositories are also rich in documents relating to the County which can only be studied by skilled experts.

The Scheme has been in its broad outlines approved by the Committee of the Society, who will afford every assistance in their power.

In order to cover the expense of transcribing and printing sufficient materials for an annual volume, a sum of at least £100 a year will be required, and it will not be desirable to commence operations until this sum is assured.

The Annual Subscription will be £1. 1s., and it is hoped that a sufficient number of Subscribers will signify their intention to support the project and so enable the County of Sussex to imitate the example already set with excellent results by Yorkshire, Somerset and other counties.

It will give me much pleasure to add your name to the List of Members.

The following Gentlemen have already promised their cordial support :—

THE LORD BISHOP OF CHICHESTER.
REV. W. D. PARISH, M.A., *Chairman of Committee.*
J. LEWIS ANDRÉ, F.S.A.
REV. CANON COOPER, M.A.
REV. T. S. COOPER, F.S.A.
PERCY S. GODMAN.

HAMILTON HALL, F.S.A.
W. H. ST. JOHN HOPE, M.A.
REV. W. HUDSON, F.S.A.
R. GARRAWAY RICE, F.S.A.
L. F. SALZMANN.

H. MICHELL WHITLEY,

Hon. Sec.

THE CASTLE, LEWES,
July 14th, 1900.

above The circular of 1900 initiating the formation of the Sussex Record Society, and *opposite* a minute of the Annual Meeting on 26 February 1901. ESRO, SRS 1/1

The draft Rules proposed were read by the Hon:
Secretary. pro. tem: and the same were unanimously
adopted and ordered to be entered in the Minutes

Sussex Record Society

Rules

1. The Society shall be called the "Sussex Record
Society" and its object shall be to transcribe and
publish documents relating to the County

2. The affairs of the Society shall be managed by a
Council which shall consist of a President, Vice-
Presidents, the Secretary, Literary Director, the
Treasurer and 12 Members all of whom shall be
elected at the Annual General Meeting. 3 Members
of the Council shall form a quorum.

3. Every candidate for membership on being
nominated by a Member to whom he is personally
known shall be admitted by the Secretary on
payment of his subscription.

4. The Council shall have power to elect as an
Honary Member outside the County any person
likely to promote the interests of the Society

The Sussex Record Society,
1901-2001

The editors of the Society's Jubilee volume of 1951, *Sussex views*:
above left Louis Francis Salzman (1878-1971) was a signatory to the circular initiating the Society's formation, was elected to the Council in 1901 and remained a member until his death, giving 45 years' service as Literary Director and editing 11 other volumes.
above right Walter Hindes Godfrey (1881-1961) joined the Society in 1923 and served on the Council for 33 years, for 25 of them as Chairman and 17 as Literary Director jointly with Salzman. He edited five other volumes.

Left Miss Verena Smith (1903-93) supported the Society unstintingly for 30 years and her legacy has made this Centenary volume possible. For many years she organised the Sussex Archaeological Society's visits and this picture shows her conducting members around Twineham Church in 1974.

Photographs: Sussex Archaeological Society

Notes towards a History
Compiled by Andrew Foster, Leslie Lloyd and Peter Wilkinson

In celebration of its jubilee in 1951, the Sussex Record Society issued *Sussex views*, edited by Walter Godfrey and Louis Salzman, based on material in the Burrell Collections held in the British Museum. The editors devoted less than three pages of their introduction to a typically terse and modest history of the Society.

It is fitting that the Society should now celebrate its centenary with another volume of views, whilst also reissuing the celebrated Jubilee volume which has been long out of print. These notes towards a history of the Society pick up the brief story set out in the Jubilee volume and also provide details of those who have served as officers of the Society over the past hundred years, together with a full listing of members and publications during that period. Further research on the Society's history has now been made possible by the deposit of its archives for 1900-74 in the East Sussex Record Office (catalogue mark SRS 1-6).

The series of lists that have been compiled draws heavily on the pioneering work of Alan Dibben, who first saw the need for an authoritative record of the Society's principal office holders. They cover past Presidents, Secretaries, Treasurers and Literary Directors. No list has been produced for the office of Vice-President; election to this post has largely been used as an honour to recognise members who have already made an important contribution to the Society's work. There is, however, a list of those important individuals who have been elected annually to chair Council meetings, and therefore carried considerable burdens of office without recognition as such in the constitution. In this centenary year it has also seemed appropriate to put on record all the Society's members, both individuals and institutions, over the past hundred years. To complete the account we have given a full listing of all the Society's publications with details of all the editors. In compiling these lists we have found it surprisingly difficult to render personal names and titles in the consistent style we would demand from the editors of our texts. As a compromise all names have been given in the form which people held at the end of their careers, or that by which they were most widely known - and with the inclusion of any distinctions acquired en route.

The publishing of over 80 volumes has been the achievement of a large and dedicated team; and it is invidious to single out the work of individuals. But there is one giant in the landscape. Paramount is the contribution of Louis Salzman who dominated the work of the Society from its foundation until his death in 1971, a role he typically understated in the brief history he produced for the Jubilee volume. Salzman edited far more volumes than any other individual, and almost monopolised the key posts on the Council, serving as Literary Director 1905-20, 1941-71, Secretary 1941-71, Treasurer 1946-49, 1950-66 (with a year as President 1961-62). In his last years he was given invaluable support by Verena Smith; and she continued to play a vital role in the decade after his death. Her final contribution has been the generous legacy that has made possible the production of this centenary volume. Her lifelong interest in the visual arts has made it especially appropriate.

When we look back over the Society's publications it is interesting to see how the emphasis of the subjects and sources has shifted in the last 50 years. In its first half-century the Society catered for two parallel readerships. On the one hand were those who wanted information from relatively inaccessible medieval sources with mainly topographical or ecclesiastical themes - such as Feet of Fines and Inquisitions post Mortem. On the other were those who wanted the classic genealogical sources: Parish

Registers and Marriage Licences. The second half-century has seen far greater diversity. While medieval topographical and ecclesiastical texts have retained an important, if diminished role, genealogy disappeared for 40 years at least. Only in the last decade - with the explosion of interest in family history - has it started to regain a significant place in the publication programme. New themes have been taken up - for the most part from the modern rather that the medieval period. The records of the two county towns and of the local courts, catalogues of maps, personal and business correspondence, accounts, have all provided volumes. And the opening of the new century is scheduled to see the Society's first publication of 20th century material: two volumes on World War I.

Whether this new diversity is cause or effect of a shift in choice by the editors is hard to say; but for the most part they have turned their attention away from the great national record series in the Public Record Office (which provided a good third of the volumes in the first half century). Instead they have turned to more specifically local collections in the County Record Offices and elsewhere. At the same time the Society has deliberately encouraged a change in the editing style as it has become necessary to provide fuller introductions to explain sources, and to offer help to those who use our volumes in education.

The diversity of texts is accompanied by changes in the personnel involved in their publication - in Council members and editors. In the last fifty years the impact of the local record offices and their staff has been most apparent. It is probably safe to say that without the support of people like Francis Steer, Alan Dibben, Roger Davey, Philip Bye and Peter Wilkinson, the Society would not have survived the vicissitudes of the past fifty years. And indeed, at one time, it looked as if the record offices themselves might be asked to take responsibility for the work of the Society. Professional academics have also played a more active role in the Society, taking up the mantle left by those who had previously been of independent means or had substantial leisure for research. Whilst almost two thirds of the titles produced in the first half century were edited by antiquaries, almost half of those in the second half were by academics or archivists. The days of the antiquary, the clergyman with time for research, the man of independent means prepared to sponsor as well as edit a volume, have long gone.

The membership of the Society was relatively stable throughout its first fifty years, when it perhaps could have been said to have been dominated by the county gentry. 105 members were recorded in 1903, the same figure as that noted in 1946. A real spurt in membership came with the 1950s, possibly coinciding with the opening of county record offices. Membership had climbed to 150 by 1952, and then jumped again to 205 by 1957. The then Vice-President T. Gurney Stedman was credited with much of this success in what seems to have been a one-man recruitment drive. It was not until 1975 that membership passed the 250 mark, at which date there were 150 individual members and 110 institutional members. This latter figure had grown significantly in the years after the War; and North American and Australian universities have provided its continuing level up to the present day. The Society still stands at about 250 members as it enters a new century.

This success, whilst laudable, is put in perspective when one remembers that the Sussex Archaeological Society had already reached a membership of over 1000 members by 1946 and has always been the dominant partner in a symbiotic relationship over the century. The much older Archaeological Society has always provided the Record Society with support; and indeed at various stages over the past century there has been talk of merger. Many members of one society also hold membership of the other. The Archaeological Society's Barbican House at Lewes serves as the Record Society's headquarters. Yet it is still clear that the Record Society performs a distinct and particular function which should not be subsumed under the range of activities performed so valuably by the larger county society. Significantly, the most successful record publication programmes in other counties have been achieved through the work of independent record societies; and the Council takes pride in the fact that only a handful of counties can match the quantity of published texts provided in Sussex.

As a publishing society, SRS has had to learn that it cannot stay in an ivory tower, untouched by market forces and with its deliberations confined to scholarly debates on the selection and editing of historical sources. The 1980s in particular confronted the Council with major problems caused by the rapidly increasing costs of printing and book production. These difficulties were exacerbated by a dearth of editors and texts - and by two ambitious publications which had attempted (and largely failed) to reach a wider reading public beyond the Society's membership. As in so many activities, the solution, or at least the catalyst, came when we grasped the nettle of Information Technology. The transition was encapsulated in the production of Volume 74, Dr Hunnisett's Coroners' records - where the last text to be received in hand-written form was the first to be printed from computer disk. All subsequent volumes have been printed from some form of digital copy; and this has checked, and to an extent reversed, the escalation of printing costs. While print-runs have been kept modest, it has become apparent that the sought-for wider readership does exist. There is a large market of people interested in local and regional history, as the growth of local history societies testifies. Family historians have also increased far beyond anyone's prediction. The Society has gradually succeeded in maximising sales by identifying and targeting the special interest groups who might respond to the specific and special content of each volume. Such a policy has helped to put the Society on a stable financial footing, and also facilitated the welcome project of producing relatively inexpensive reprints of SRS volumes long out of print.

As we look forward to the new century, perhaps the most encouraging trend is the reappearance of a strong contingent of non-academic members, who have brought in formidable expertise built up through their own researches. They play a key part in the core activities of editing and in serving as Council members and officers. It is this situation that will guarantee that the Society continues to fulfil its role, and that it produces volumes that are wanted by the public. Whilst the emergence of professionals has been vital to the Society over the past fifty years, a great debt is still owed to those far-sighted founding fathers of 1901, and to those, like George Holleyman, Kenneth Dickens, Philip Park and Robert Gold, who have maintained the original traditions of the Society.

Officers of the Society

President

1901	Henry Fitzalan-Howard, 15th Duke of Norfolk
1917	Charles Gordon-Lennox, 7th Duke of Richmond and Gordon
1928	Edward Turnour, 6th Earl of Winterton
1929	Henry Nevill, 3rd Marquess of Abergavenny
1938	The Right Reverend George K. A. Bell, Bishop of Chichester
1959	Henry Gage, 6th Viscount Gage
1961	Louis F. Salzman
1962	Ivan Donald Margary
1964	G. D. Johnston
1966	Kenneth W. Dickins
1968	F. Bentham Stevens
1969	Dr Francis W. Steer
1972	Dr Marie Clough
1974	Dr K. M. E. (Betty) Murray
1978	Dr Peter Brandon
1979	Kenneth W. Dickins
1983	The Right Reverend Eric W. Kemp, Bishop of Chichester

Treasurer

1901	Major Harold Parminter Molineux
1923	F. B. Whitfield
1924	Barclays Bank, Lewes
1946	Louis F. Salzman
1949	Lieutenant Colonel D. MacLeod
1950	Louis F. Salzman
1966	G. L. Remnant
1974	Miss Verena Smith
1980	Philip F. Park
1987	Miss Carol A. Hazleden
1988	Robert Gold
1994	Frederick Horne
1996	Leslie Lloyd

Secretary

1901	H. Michell Whitley
1902	The Revd William Hudson
1904	Percy Godman
1911	Colonel Frederick W. T. Attree
1920	R. Garraway Rice
1929	The Revd Walter Budgen
1941	Louis F. Salzman
1971	G. L. Remnant (also Treasurer)
1974	Miss Verena Smith (also Treasurer)
1980	Alan A. Dibben
1981	Peter Wilkinson

Literary Director

The constitution allows for more than one Literary Director and the post was usually held jointly between 1905 and 1979. Between 1921 and 1940 no formal appointment was made, and the work was done by members of the Council, most probably the Revd Walter Budgen, Louis F. Salzman, R. Garraway Rice and Walter Godfrey.

1901-20	The Revd William Hudson (with Salzman 1905-20)
1905-20, 1941-71	Louis F. Salzman (with Hudson 1905-20, Godfrey 1940-57, and Steer 1957 71)
1940-57	Walter Godfrey (with Salzman)
1957-78	Dr Francis Steer (with Salzman 1957-71, then with Brandon 1971-78)
1970-79	Dr Peter Brandon (with Steer 1971-78, then with Clough for one year)
1979-85	Dr Marie Clough (with Brandon for one year)
1985	Dr Andrew Foster

Chairman of Council

Not technically an officer of the Society, but a key post

1900	Canon James H. Cooper
1909	Walter Renshaw
1919	Colonel Frederick W. T. Attree
1925	J. Edwin Couchman
1927	Sir Charles Thomas-Stanford
1931	R. Garraway Rice
1932	Walter Godfrey
1957	Ivan D. Margary
1970	Dr K. M. E. Murray
1974	George A. Holleyman
1991	Derek S. Rawlings

Members of the Society

Individual members

1951-73	Abbey, Maj. J R
1929-38	Abergavenny, Marquess of
1960-83	Adorian, P
1982-	Adsett, R
1954-75	Agate, R C
1977-	Ainsworth, Maj. J F
1957-60	Airey, J
1957-73	Airey, K W
1993-	Allday, Mrs K J
1982-	Allen, J C
1901-24	Allfrey, Miss K E
1978-85	Almond, A P
1901-02	Andre, J L
1920-35	Anscombe, A
1937-43	Arnold, The Revd H E B
1960-	Ascott, K F
1950-79	Ash, C D
1945-54	Ashburnham, Lady C
1974-	Askew, I V
1909-12	Athill, C H
1901-27	Attree, Lt Col. F W T
1930-33	Aylmer, Capt A L
1973-77	Bachmann, Mrs P
1974-77	Baker, E W
1996-	Baldwin, R
1993-	Balkwill, Miss P M J
1962-74	Ball, W A
1924-31	Ballard, Lt Col. J A
1975-	Ballard, Mrs I V
1901-10	Bannerman, W B
1901-04	Barchard, F
1901-14	Barham, G
1996-	Barham, Mrs J B
1945-55	Barker, E E
1946-87	Barnard, G L
1960-64	Barnes, Miss M I
1957-61	Barnes, The Hon. R G
1974-82	Barr-Hamilton, A
1983-	Barr-Hamilton, M
1950-58	Barron, W A
1901-04	Barwell, The Revd A H S
1932-35	Bateson, H
1956-77	Batho, G R
1901-	Bax, A R
1949-57	Baxendale, H L
1969-	Baxendale, T D
1957-73	Baxendale, Mrs E S
1958-73	Bayley, The Revd T D S
1991-	Beattie, Dr A M
1959-66	Beaumont, Miss G G
1951-68	Beaver, Sir H
1945-00	Beck, R T
1953-60	Becker, W F
1901-43	Beckett, A W
1971-97	Beech, Mrs L

1960-63	Bell, S
2000-	Bell, T I
1995-	Benjamin, Prof. P R
1989-	Bennett, W J
1907-25	Bennett, The Revd Canon F G
1907-14	Bennett, The Revd H
1916-28	Bernau, C A
1983-	Berry, Dr S
1982-	Beswick, Mrs M
1901-17	Bevan, R A
1944-51	Blaber, W H
1978-	Bleach, J
1962-73	Body, Miss L M
1901-38	Boger, J I C
1974-80	Bolton, W J M
1966-80	Bolton, Miss A
1902-05	Booker, The Revd J L
1901-24	Borradaile, C
1923-32	Bothamley, H H
1901-07	Bowden, The Revd J
1911-40	Bowyer, P A
1928-73	Boxall, A B
1901-05	Boxall, W P G
1901-15	Boyson, A P
1987-	Bradford, B H
1974-85	Bradford, H T
1937-40	Braham, H V
1974-90	Braid, D K
1945-76	Brand, M C
1959-	Brandon, P F
1901-19	Breach, W P
1988-96	Bridger, D F
1928-43	Bridger, P D
1924-30	Bridgman, C F
1924-26	Bridgman, P F
1974-	Bright, Mrs S
1951-73	Brightwell, H
1951-63	Bristow, L B
1934-46	Brooke, Lt Col. N P
1968-77	Brooklyn, Miss M
1998-	Brooks, B G C
1901-10	Brown, J E
1973-81	Brown, Miss S F
1985-92	Brunkhorst, F
1955-77	Buckley, The Hon. R B
1907-51	Budgen, The Revd W
1910-31	Bull, Sir W
1946-48	Bullock, G W
1960-92	Burch, J W
1949-66	Burder, E R
1901-43	Burdon, The Revd Canon R J
1957-	Burgess, A J
1927-77	Burgess, H
1901-02	Burrell, Sir R
1989-	Bye, P
1984-00	Byford, E C

1994-	Caffyn, J M
1923-27	Callard, E
1966-73	Calvert-Lee, M J
1952-66	Campbell, Maj. Gen. H M
1948-51	Camplin, W H
1958-68	Carcas, Miss E C J
1999-	Carter, C
1955-57	Cash, Miss M E
1946-92	Catt, Col. P
1982-	Catt, Miss M J
1955-77	Cattermole, E C
1950	Cave, C J P
1906-10	Cavis-Brown, The Revd J
1991-96	Chalklin, Dr C W
1954-58	Challen, F K
1923-28	Chalmers, C H
1935-43	Chambers, T F
1936-39	Chambers, Miss A
1962-64	Chaming, A R G
1967-90	Champion, H W
1927-35	Chance, Sir W
1950-74	Chandler, R
1937-50	Chandler, T H
1972-82	Chandler, Miss H M
1990-	Charman, J C
1984-	Chatwin, Mrs D M
1928-31	Cheney, H I
1955-73	Chevallier, C T
1914-15	Chichester, Archdeacon of (E L Elwes)
1901-08	Chichester, Bishop of (E R Wilberforce)
1908-19	Chichester, Bishop of (C J Ridgeway)
1937-58	Chichester, Bishop of (G K A Bell)
1981-	Chichester, Bishop of (E W Kemp)
1982-90	Chidson, Mrs V J
1987-93	Child, T G
1974-77	Chillingworth, Miss E A
1976-82	Chittleborough, R J
1972-	Church, T S
1901-27	Clarke, S
1901-35	Clarke, C B O
1901-09	Clarke, R S
1905-52	Clarke, Col. R S
1988-97	Clarke, Miss C D
1975-77	Clements, Miss G M
1962-	Clough, Dr M
1901-15	Codrington, The Revd Canon R H
1954-58	Coleman, Dr M B
1921-25	Coles, The Revd L H
1950-73	Collingridge, Miss R
1901-31	Comber, J
1969-77	Combes, P D
1984-	Combes, Mrs P

1963-73	Coomber, Dr C	1931-33	Duke, F	1987-	Gearing, A W
1928-51	Cooper, Miss M H	1901-15	Dunkin, E H W	1982-90	Gibson, The Hon. C
1901-10	Cooper, The Revd Canon J H	1915-45	Dunkin, Mrs R	1957-63	Gill, The Hon. Mrs P D
1901-14	Cooper, The Revd T S	1991-92	Dunlop, A C	1956-64	Gillett, Sir E
1950-52	Cordle, J H	1979-	Durant, H P	1964-73	Gillham, L D
1943-73	Corfield, Dr C	1992-	Durrant, Dr P	1959-73	Gillingham, The Revd P L
1975-77	Corner, Miss E P	1956-73	Dwyer, P G	1973-90	Glasswell, Mrs D M
1991-	Cornes, C N	1974-77	Eacott, M	1934-50	Glover, H J
1952-	Cornwall, J C K	1982-85	Earl, B J	1951-89	Glover, Mrs D J
1901-37	Cotching, J F A	1901-08	Eden, The Revd A	1923-62	Godfrey, W H
1995-	Cotes, D V	1990-	Eldridge, Mrs E D	1901-24	Godman, C B
1907-33	Couchman, J E	1974-77	Elleray, R D	1901-10	Godman, F du C
1916-55	Courthope, Lord	1949-77	Elliott, R H	1901-24	Godman, P S
1928-74	Courthope, Miss E J	1969-	Elliott, V P	1901-03	Godman, Maj. Gen. R T
1970-80	Courthope, The Hon. D	1992-95	Ellis, H H V	1982-95	Gold, R
1958-63	Courtney, Cdr A T	1986-	Elvy, J F	1921-37	Goldsmith, Mrs D
1901-27	Cowdray, Lord	1926-35	Emmet, T A	1975-80	Gooday, Mrs E M
1959-63	Cowper, F H	1960-66	Endeman, H	1952-56	Goodwin, H S
1916-19	Crawfurd, R P	1949-56	Esdaile, Dr, A	1974-	Goring, Dr J
1947-54	Crook, Miss B M	1995-	Evans, Mrs T E	1932-52	Gorringe, W H
1982-	Crow, Mrs W J	1930-46	Evans, The Revd A A	1981-	Goss, D
1991-92	Crowhurst, L J	1945-48	Evelyn, J	1951-80	Graebe, R E
1939-79	Cumberlege, G F J	1960-73	Falconar, H G R	1912-17	Gravely, C E
1979-00	Cumberlege, Mrs V	1957-73	Farley, C A	1918-33	Graves, A F
1997-	Cumbrill, A	1951-73	Farncomb, Rear Adm. H B	1901-05	Gray, G G
1944-77	Cunnington, L W	1901-14	Farncombe, J	1945-50	Gray, Col J V
1980-90	Cunnington, R W	1964-85	Farncombe, L G	1953-56	Greaves, Sir E
1955-62	Curnow, P W	1995-	Farrant, J H	1981-	Greenhill, Miss L J
1906-07	Curtis, J	1909-10	Fearon, F	1901-43	Greenwood, J A
1951-73	Curtis, Miss W J	1901-03	Felton, W V	1981-95	Gregory, D I
1933-50	Curwen, E	1950-73	Field, C W	1956-61	Gregory, A H
1947-58	Cutts, A T	1955-	Field, Maj. E H	1901-12	Gregory, H E
1944-60	D'Elboux, R H	1961-77	Filby, P W	2000-	Grieves, K
1958-77	Dalrymple-Hay, Sir J B	1965-68	Finch, Miss M E	1998-	Grinsted, C
1958-62	Daniel, The Revd M G	1969-73	Firrell, R	1959-73	Gullick, C D
1913-19	Dann, H C	1954-58	FitzRandolph, Mrs M D	1984-94	Guthrie, D
1948-51	Darbyshire, W L	1931-66	Fleming, L	1901-15	Gwynne, J E A
1956-73	Davenport, Mrs C M	1901-41	Fletcher, W H B	1915-24	Gwynne, R S
1982-	Davey, C R	1974-86	Fletcher, Miss G E	1924-63	Gwynne, Col. R
1901-15	Davey, The Revd Canon H M	1972-85	Flight, Miss E V	1956-80	Haddock, F F
1989	Davies, R W	1973-81	Fooks, Mrs E M	1901-16	Haines, C R
1984-89	Davis, P E H	1928-31	Ford, J H	1958-62	Hall, The Revd C A
1983-83	Davis, Lt Col. H D	1970-96	Ford, W K	1974-82	Hall, M K
1901-06	Dawson, C	1974-76	Foster, G L	1901-31	Hall, W H
1958-77	Dawson, Mrs I V	1982-	Foster, Dr A W	1956-62	Hamblin, Miss F A
1909-37	Dawtrey, J	1901-17	Freeland, W B B	1958-62	Hamnett, The Revd H A
1954-60	de Burkett, Mrs S	1975-86	Freeman, W A D	1909-44	Hannah, I C
1941-73	de Candole, Bishop H	1970-90	French, B	1901-10	Harben, H A
1901-21	Deedes, The Revd Canon C	1913-37	Frewer, The Revd G E	1901-12	Harben, Sir H
1929-33	Demetriadi, Lady	1979-85	Frost, A	1921-24	Harding, G
1901-07	Devonshire, Duke of	1998-	Frost, A J	1901-24	Harley, J
1954-84	Dibben, A A	1967-	Fryer, J A	1984-95	Harper, R S
1955-99	Dickins, K W	1901-29	Fuller, The Revd A	1948-89	Harris, A L
1992-	Dickinson, Mrs J E	1945-84	Fuller, A R B	1928-31	Harrison, F
1953-76	Doak, Sir J H	1997-	Fuller, B J	1956-62	Hart, G F W
1937-43	Dobson, E J	1977-82	Fuller, L M	1988-	Harwood-Smart, P
1927-49	Downey, J H	1916-60	Fynmore, A H W	1927-37	Haviland, The Revd E A
1994-	Downham, Mrs J E	1958-84	Gage, Viscount	1909-31	Hawes, G C
1997-	Drake, R F	1946-60	Gardner, Miss E M	1902-05	Hawkesbury, Lord
		1974-89	Gates, W E	2000-	Hawkins, J M
		1997-98	Gayford, M R D	1954-73	Hay, M C

1982-89 Hazelden, Miss C A	1968-77 Jansen, C de W	1981-86 MacDermot, Mrs V
1993-96 Headley, W R	1944-61 Jenkinson, Sir H	1949-55 Macleod, R D
1959-73 Heaton, T G	1953-73 Jennings, Sir R W	1925-64 Macleod, Lt Col. D
1982-93 Hellyer, P	1964-77 Jepson, S	1966-73 Mander, A S
1960-62 Helme, A T	1967-77 Jessup, V C	1968-73 Manley, J B S
1974-88 Hemsley, D T	1942-73 Johnston, G D	1934-43 Mann, P
1970-77 Henderson, A A	1901-12 Johnston, P M	1955-68 Manvell, F
1959-66 Henderson, D H	1948-73 Johnston, Mrs E J	1974-82 Marchant, D A
1975-77 Henshaw, J C	1943-61 Johnstone, Dr H	1934-77 Margary, I D
1901-17 Henty, E	1954- Jones, J R	1912-44 Margesson, Col. E W
1901-13 Henwood, R	1946-50 Jones, The Revd H H	1902-06 Markwick, Col. E C
1911-43 Heron-Allen, E	1993- Kelly, Mrs J D	1911-25 Markwick, Col. E E
1958-66 Herringshaw, E A	1995-97 Kemp, P G	1970-77 Marriott, H W G R
1946-50 Hewett, Maj. W G O'C	1901-05 Kemp, Capt W	1969- Marshall, A E
1953-56 Heymer, E	1901-07 Kempe, C E	1902-08 Marshall, Dr G W
1987- Hilder, I	1999- Kent, T	1953-60 Marshall-Cornwall, Sir J H
1910-33 Hills, W H	1946-78 Kenyon, G H	1916-28 Marten, A E
1986-97 Hoad, A H	1958-77 Kidner, J C	1901-07 Martin, C
1999- Hobbs, C	1975- Killick, B N E	1966-81 Martin, H S
1953-87 Hobbs, H C	1994- Killick, Miss E A	1993-99 Martin, P
1963- Hodsoll, Miss V M	1956-58 King, C S	1958-73 Mason, Sir D H
1919-40 Holgate, Miss M S	1985-87 King, Mrs P	1953-55 Matthews, Miss M
1993- Holkham, T	1978-86 Kingsley, D	1929-44 Maxse, The Hon. Lady M
1966-77 Holland, C G	1991- Kinnison Bourke, Mrs J A	1982-97 Mayhew, Dr G J
1965- Holleyman, G A	1990- Kyle, Mrs H	1994- Maynard, Mrs S D
1956-61 Holman, Miss A C	1918-35 Lacaita, C C	1901-25 McAndrew, J
1901-17 Holmes, G P	1981- Lacey, Mrs K	1981- McCann, T J
1971-99 Holt, Mrs M	1972-80 Lamb, Mrs V B	1951-55 McCarthy, The Revd J
1938-39 Homer-Saunders, T	1926-31 Lambarde, Brig. Gen. F	1998- McDiarmid, Mrs H
1945-68 Homewood, Miss F M	1914-31 Lambert, A U M	1981-88 McGrath, Mrs H
1981- Honeyman, I R	1967-77 Lampard, Miss J	1928-33 McLean, D
1901-19 Hope, Sir W H St J	1974-81 Landymore, V	1969-79 McQuillan, Mrs O M
1966-73 Hordern, P	1951-54 Langdon, The Revd P G	1974-82 Mead, C
1980-98 Horne, F H	1951-52 Leach, C	1984-88 Melanson, Mrs V A
1972- Houghton, J	1952-63 Leconfield, Lord	1965-73 Melhuish, R E
1964-00 Houghton, Mrs L	1987- Leeson, F L	1951-56 Mersey, Viscount
1902-09 Hovenden, R	1983- Leighton, Mrs C A	1929-54 Messell, Col. L
1971-77 Howard, R D	1976-80 Lelliott, L A	1916-23 Michell, H
1964-77 Howden, D G B	1975-95 Leonard, N J	1973-77 Michell, R B
1974-77 Howden, Mrs D	1970- Leppard, M J	1982-94 Miller, C L
1982- Hudson, Dr T P	1981- Leslie, K C	1998- Miller, D
1901-33 Hudson, The Revd W	1901-06 Levy, L	1992- Miller, Mrs P M
1992- Huggett, D J	1901-06 Lewes, Archdeacon of (R	1956- Milner, G
1974-95 Hughes, Capt D T	Sutton)	1907-27 Mitchell, H P
1998- Hughes, Dr A F	1992- Lindfield, A G	1914-16 Mitchell, W W
1982- Humphreys, Miss E P	1970-85 Lindsay, Scott, Capt A W	1901-24 Molineux, Maj. H P
1952- Hunnisett, Dr R F	1959-68 Lintott, B R	1951-76 Monk Bretton, Lord
1959-64 Hunt, H C	1976-81 Little, Mrs E N	1978- Moon, R K L
1959-68 Hunt, Lt Col. S	1901-07 Liverpool, Earl of	1974-81 Moore, P
1964-77 Hunter, M C W	1993- Lloyd, L G	1961-66 Moore, J
1901-03 Hurst, R H	1925-33 Lloyd, N	1974-80 Moore, P D R
1949-63 Hurst, Sir C J B	1970-73 Lloyd-Williams, F N	1947-58 Moorman, Bishop J R H
1991- Hussey, R L	1955-63 Locke, M C	1953-60 Moran, P C
1955-58 Hutchinson, R M	1907-34 Loder, G W E	1982-90 Morgan, R R
1901-37 Huth, E	1958- Lodge, J H	1954-56 Morley, L R
1977- Iden, J R	1995- Loveys, M J C	1962-64 Morris, Miss R E
1968-77 Jackson, W E	1934-40 Loyd, L C	1970-77 Moseley, Mrs P
1901-05 Jackson, The Revd A A	1901-07 Lucas, C J	1930-43 Mosse, H R
1974-77 Jacob, K W	1973-77 Lucas, C J F	1952-98 Murray, Dr K M E
1987- Jacobson, M C	1921-28 Lucy, The Revd W C	1975-77 Napper, Miss L
1901-12 James, W	1901-10 Maberly, Maj. T A	1911-13 Napper, Miss L L

1990-	Nelson, I A
1901-16	Newington, Mrs C
1993-	Newton, J W
1970-77	Newton, S C
1921-25	Nicholls, A E
1999-	Nicholls, D R
1958-68	Nisbet, R V
1964-73	Noakes, A H
1901-17	Norfolk, 15th Duke of
1961-76	Norfolk, 16th Duke of
1981-	Norfolk, 17th Duke of
1913-46	North, J S
1941-63	Odell, W H
1974-76	Offer, Miss E M
1907-44	Oke, A W
1902-19	Oliver, E
1914-	Orme, The Revd J B
1956-62	Osborne, G F
1963-77	Oulds, R G
1926-48	Packham, A B
1992-	Padgham, D C
1901-05	Padwick, H
1956-68	Palmer, O E
1951-56	Palmer, P E
1901-48	Pannett, A R
1948-60	Parish, C W
1901-04	Parish, The Revd W D
1972-92	Park, P F
1975-77	Park, Mrs D
1986-95	Parker, Miss H J
1901-05	Parkin, T
1972-92	Parks, The Revd Canon P F
2000-	Parrott, W
1975-81	Parson, D L
1901-02	Parsons, L
1956-77	Parsons, W S
1960-68	Patterson, Miss W
1967-73	Pavitt, A H
1973-	Pavitt, D H
1927-29	Payne, C R S
1962-65	Payne, Mrs D B
1981-85	Pearce, C J
1946-77	Pearmain, H F
1924-65	Pearson, The Hon. C
1965-77	Pearson, The Hon. Mrs C
1928-33	Pearson, The Revd W A
1924-79	Peckham, W D
1968-86	Pedley, W J
1947-60	Pegge, P W
1928-35	Pelham, The Hon. Mrs A
1975-95	Pelling, G
1909-41	Penfold, F B
1901-02	Penfold, H
1911-48	Penfold, The Revd Canon E W
1913-15	Penfold-Dixon, The Revd W T
1964-73	Penner, A G
1949-54	Penney, S E
1987-	Pennington, Mrs J V
1956-73	Pepler, R H

1974-	Perry, K L W
1993-96	Peskett, Mrs S A
1971-81	Pettitt, J
1975-	Philcox, R A
1954-97	Phillimore, Lord
1983-	Phillips, B K
1966-73	Phillips, D H
1963-73	Phillips, R D
1972-76	Phipps, Bishop S W
1962-64	Pickering, E C
1982-	Pilbeam, Mrs M N
1978-82	Pilmer, Miss J G
1914-17	Plowman, Miss L P
1958-62	Plumridge, Lt Col. J H
1956-63	Pocock, A L
1919-46	Ponsonby, 1st Baron
1968-77	Ponsonby, 2nd Baron
1947-63	Ponsonby, Dowager Lady
1962-77	Pope, R D
1954-61	Poulton, A S
1925-43	Powell, T B
1996-	Pratt, M N
1994-	Pratt, The Revd Canon W R
1960-	Pulford, J S L
1951-58	Pyke, L H
1901-05	Raffety, J H
1901-39	Raper, W A
1901-05	Raper, Sir R
1995-	Rapley, M W
1946-47	Ratcliffe, S C
1982-	Rawlings, D S
1921-51	Ray, J E
1999-	Rea, J
1965-77	Read, J D
1995-	Read, Miss J A
1984-	Reader, K M
1984-85	Reed, Miss T J G
1954-66	Reid, P R
1959-81	Remnant, G L
1982-	Rendall, W F
1901-24	Renshaw, W C
1915-33	Renton, J H
1960-66	Rewell, R H
1962-73	Rewell, Capt A V
1966-96	Rewell, Dr R E
1901-33	Rice, R G
1934-37	Rice, Mrs C E
1917-31	Richmond & Gordon, Duke of
1924-33	Rickards, A W
1933-54	Ridge, C H
1975-77	Ridge, Dr J
1959-73	Ring, K G
1991-	Ritchie, Mrs R
1993-95	Roberts, B J
1982-95	Robinson, T O
1913-33	Roemer, Maj. C H de
1961-63	Rogers, A J
1949-76	Rolston, Dr G R
1998-	Rose, T
1901-29	Round, J H

1988-	Rouse, W R
1916-37	Rudkin, Maj. H E
1991-	Saigeman, F L
1962-80	Salt, M C L
1901-71	Salzman, L F
1963-82	Sanders, R A
1978-	Saville, Dr R V
1928-34	Saxby, T C
1909-10	Sayer-Milward, The Revd W C
1962-73	Scrivener, Dr J P
1956-77	Seago, H
1960-77	Searle, Mrs L T
1926-63	Secretan, S D
1933-60	Selmes, Mrs E M
1994-95	Seymour, A
1988-	Shalit, D M
1975-	Sheffield, R D
1993-	Shepherd, Miss L A
1926-31	Shoosmith, E
1993-	Short, Professor B M
1928-35	Simmonds, The Revd M J
1990-	Simmons, C G W
1951-66	Slyfield, G N
1967-79	Smail, H C P
1948-73	Smart, J E
1958-60	Smart, The Revd J O
1972-93	Smith, B C
1979-94	Smith, Lt Col. M C M
1976-98	Smith, M J
1901-05	Smith, W J
1994-95	Smith, Miss N
1962-93	Smith, Miss V
1969-80	Snelling, H J
1901-19	Snewin, H E
1956-77	Solomon, Maj. J B
1927-37	Somers-Clarke, Col. C
1953-60	Spence, D G C
1994-	Spencer-Richard, J S
1983-90	Spens, The Hon. Miss P S
1933-51	Spokes, P S
1925-39	Spokes, S
1954-60	Srinks, F O
1907-43	Standen, G
1923-44	Standfield, F
1954-62	Stedman, J A
1914-76	Stedman, T G
1954-77	Steer, Dr F W
1901-03	Stenning, A
1901-21	Stenning, J C
1922-33	Stenning, J R
1989-	Stevenage, P H
1954-61	Stevens, A G
1909-68	Stevens, F B
1974-90	Stevenson-Watt, N W
1992-	Stoner, P H
1932-41	Straker, E
1958-77	Stray, S A
1901-33	Streatfeild, R J
1911-14	Street, E E
1956-56	Strievennys, J W A G

1915-37	Stubbs, C		1957-77	Watson, M D C
1969-73	Style, D H		1952-68	Watson, R C
1974-80	Suggers, L C		1944-62	Webb, C
1974-	Susans, H R		1990-	Webb, Mrs P

1915-37 Stubbs, C
1969-73 Style, D H
1974-80 Suggers, L C
1974- Susans, H R
1938-73 Sutton, Col. T
1959-77 Swann, Miss A V
1993-94 Sweatman, Mrs S
1944-58 Talmey, Miss E
1935-42 Taylor, J G
1974-85 Tebbutt, C J
1998- Teeder, Mrs N M
1971-96 Teesdale, E B
1951-54 Tetlow, M R M
1995- Teviot, Lord
1935-37 Thacker, Capt N
1901-33 Thomas-Stanford, Sir C
1996- Thompson, D N
1906-24 Thompson, J M
1966- Thorne, G A
1982-93 Tibble, R B
1912-13 Tollhurst, J G
1991- Tomsett, R
1907-15 Tower, W E
1987-89 Tribe, J
1960-77 Tribe, W S
1965-77 Tribe, The Revd J
1901-11 Trist, G A
2000- Tritton, Mrs J
1965-93 Tritton, Mrs V M
1951-73 Trory, E W
1967-91 Trown, R C
1985- Tsushima, Mrs J E
1992- Tubb, A P
1901-24 Tubbs, Mrs L C
1928-33 Tuck, Mrs D F
1992- Tulley, A R
1992-99 Tuppen, A E
1968-77 Turner, A A
1909-12 Twining, H H
1928-33 Tyacke, G A
1959-73 Tyler, V W
1966-77 Urquhart, M
1935-43 Vallance, W H A
1956-73 Vernon, E W
1901-12 Vernon, M A
1982- Verrall, M S
1941-58 Vivian, Sir S
1986- Voice, A J
1901-26 Wagner, H
1907-37 Wakehurst, Lord
1946-73 Walden-Aspey, The Revd F C
1968-82 Waldy, J R E
1956-60 Wallbridge, J M
1980-87 Wallisfurth, Miss C
1984-98 Walters, Mrs A K
1953-75 Ward, J L
1975- Ward, Mrs N
1998- Warne, Mrs H
1963-77 Warren, S E
1950-56 Warren, Col. J R

1957-77 Watson, M D C
1952-68 Watson, R C
1944-62 Webb, C
1990- Webb, Mrs P
1967-77 Webster, Mrs E
1901-07 Wedgewood, R H
1973-98 Wedgwood, Dame Veronica
1991- Weir, Mrs N S
1954-73 Welch, C E
1969- Weller, W L
1990- Weller, Miss B P
1953-73 Welti, E R
1997-99 West, L F
1959-68 Westcombe, L G
1942-43 Whistler, H
1945-50 Whistler, The Hon. Mrs
1946-87 White, H L
1992- White, Mrs D J
1901-05 Whitley, H M
2000- Whittle, Miss H M
1975-90 Whittle, Mrs F G
1966-73 Whitty, A
1965-73 Wickham, G B
1967- Wigan, Mrs M
1980- Wilkinson, P M
1982- Wilkinson, Miss M
1945-64 Wilkinson, The Revd D F
1959-62 William, Miss N
1958-60 Williams, J C
1974- Willis, Miss I M
1990- Wilmot, R T D
1959-77 Wilson, A E
1966-77 Wilson, B M E
1928-62 Winterton, Earl of
1901-05 Wisden, Col. T
1929-87 Wishart, E E
1914-16 Withington, L
1924-37 Wolseley, Viscountess
1921-28 Wood, F L
1957-60 Woodford, The Revd H
1928-33 Woodland, H A
1905-39 Woollan, J H
1986-88 Worsfold, G R
1968-77 Worssam, B C
1973- Wright, F S
1945-50 Wright, R B
1995- Wright, S H
1979-92 Wright, Miss M
1901-39 Wyatt, H R P
1907-25 Wyatt, J A P
1947-55 Wyatt, Brig. R
1982- Yarnold, J R J
1984-97 Yeldham, R E D
1974-85 Yeoman, Mrs J
1973- Young, Miss D E
1982- Yoward, A

Institutional members

1968- Aberdeen University
1973- Adelaide University
1973- Allen County Public Library [Fort Wayne Library]
1991- University of Saint Andrews
1906- Society of Antiquaries of London
1979- University of Arizona
1909- The College of Arms, London
1965-96 National Library of Australia
1991- Australian Institute of Genealogical Studies
1953- Battle and District Historical Society
1941- Birmingham Public Libraries
1948- Birmingham University Library
1912-37 Bodleian Library, Oxford
1953-77 Bognor Regis College of Education
1979-87 Bognor Regis Public Library
1901- Brighton Public Libraries
1949-61 Brighton & Sussex Students Library
1970- Brighton University
1953-63 Royal Institute of British Architects
1969-77 University of British Columbia
1966-93 The British Library
1941-90 Buffalo & Erie County Public Library
1979-87 Burgess Hill Public Library
1955-77 Cache County Genealogical Library
1962-83 University of California, Berkeley
1956- University of California, Los Angeles
1930-35 Cambridge University Library
1960-77 Chatham Public Libraries
1921- Chicago University
1971-83 Chicago Circle, University of Illinois
1942- Chichester Cathedral Library
1945- Chichester Diocesan Board of Finance
1951- University College Chichester

1970-97 Clemson University
1933-83 Cleveland Public Library
1960-77 Collyers School, Horsham
1976- Concordia University Libraries
1913- Library of Congress
1915- Cornell University Library
1978-87 Crawley Branch Library
1956-93 Delaware University Library
1935- Detroit Public Libraries
1969- Duke University Library
1979-87 East Grinstead Public Library
1942- East Sussex County Library
1950- East Sussex Record Office
1906-07 Eastbourne Central Library
1913-87 Eastbourne Public Libraries
1949- Edinburgh University
1984- Emory University
1993- English Heritage
1970- Exeter University Library
1993- Family History Library
1982- Marc Fitch Fund
1992- Society of Genealogists
1968- Georgia University
1941- Glasgow University Library
1941-56 Grosvenor Library
1913- Guildhall Library
1908- Harvard College Library
1946- Harvard Law School Library
1924-87 Hastings Corporation Museum & Library
1948- Hastings Public Museum
1934-95 Haverford College Library
1979-87 Haywards Heath Public Library
1992- Institute of Heraldic & Genealogical Studies
1961- Johns Hopkins University [Enoch Pratt Library]
1961- Horsham Museum
1979-87 Horsham Public Library
1901-87 Hove Public Library
1937- Henry E Huntington Library
1935- University of Illinois
1949- Iowa State University Library
1974-92 Lakehead University
1964- Lambeth Palace Library
1978- Lancing College Library
1960-98 Leeds City Libraries
1943- Leeds University
1960- Leicester University Library

1949-87 Lewes Area Library
1901-49 Lewes Public Library
1902-40 Lincoln's Inn Library
1948-77 Littlehampton District Council Museum
1948-87 Littlehampton Public Library
1944-90 Liverpool Public Libraries
1959- Liverpool University
1948- London Library
1936-60 London & Middlesex Archaeological Society
1977-84 Polytechnic of North London
1933- London University Library
1935- London University Institute of Historical Research
1933- Lund Royal University Library
1915- John Rylands University Library of Manchester
1936- University of Michigan, Ann Arbor
1964- Michigan State University Library
1958- Minnesota University Library
1949- Missouri University
1971- Montana University
1966-77 National Central Library
1914- New England Historical & Genealogical Society
1909- New York Public Library
1941- Newberry Library, Chicago
1957- Nottingham University
1961- Ohio State University
1921-90 University of Pennsylvania
1982- Portsmouth Central Library
1953- Princeton University Library
1907- Public Record Office
1901-05 Messrs Raper & Freeland
1970- Reading University
1967- Rochester University Library
1936- Royal Historical Society
1933- Family History Library, Salt Lake City
1967- Sheffield University Library
1978-87 Shoreham Public Library
1952- Southampton University Library
1965- Stanford University Libraries
1901- Sussex Archaeological Society

1977- Sussex Family History Group
1964- Sussex University
1982- University College Swansea
1971- Texas University
1953-77 General Theological Seminary
1956- Tohoku University Library
1971- Toronto University
1968- The United Library [Seabury Weston Theological Seminary]
1966- Vanderbilt University [Joint Universities Library]
1958-97 Vassar College Library
1962- Victoria State Library
1953-92 Virginia State Library
1984- Virginia University
1966- Wake Forest University Library
1926-90 National Library of Wales
1970- Warwick University
1986- Washington Memorial Library
1961- Washington State University Library
1967- University of Western Australia
1941- West Sussex County Library
1946- West Sussex Record Office
1994- Western Australian Genealogical Society
1952-85 Westminster City Libraries
1970-83 University of Windsor, Ontario
1967- Wisconsin University
1913-87 Worthing Public Libraries
1968-91 Wyoming University Library
1931- Yale University Library
1963- York University Library

Publications

Where the publication date is not stated in the volume, it has been given in square brackets.

1 *Calendar of Sussex marriage licences recorded in the consistory court of the bishop of Chichester for the archdeaconry of Lewes, August 1586 to March 1642/3.* By Edwin H. W. Dunkin. 1902

2 *An abstract of feet of fines relating to the county of Sussex, from 2 Richard I to 33 Henry III.* Compiled by L. F. Salzman. 1903

3 *A calendar of post mortem inquisitions relating to the county of Sussex, 1 to 25 Elizabeth.* Abstracted and translated by L. F. Salzman. 1904

4 *Miscellaneous records:*
Ecclesiastical returns for 81 parishes in East Sussex, made in 1603. Edited W. C. Renshaw.
A poll for the election of members of parliament for the county of Sussex in 1705.
A calendar of entries relating to Sussex in the Harleian manuscripts. Edited L. F. Salzman.
Extracts from the episcopal register of Richard Praty, Bishop of Chichester, 1438-1445. Edited Cecil Deedes. 1905

5 *West Sussex Protestation returns, 1641-2.* Transcribed, edited and indexed by R. Garraway Rice. 1905

6 *Calendar of Sussex marriage licences...for the archdeaconry of Lewes, August 1670 to March 1728/9, and in the peculiar court of the archbishop of Canterbury for the deanery of South Malling, May 1620 to December 1732.* By Edwin H. W. Dunkin. 1907

7 *An abstract of feet of fines....from 34 Henry III to 35 Edward I.* Compiled by L. F. Salzman. 1908

8 *The episcopal register of Robert Rede, ordinis predicatorum, lord bishop of Chichester, 1397-1415. Part 1.* Summarised and edited with explanatory notes by Cecil Deedes. 1908

9 *Calendar of Sussex marriage licences... for the archdeaconry of Chichester, June 1575 to December 1730.* By Edwin H. W. Dunkin. 1909

10 *The three earliest subsidies for the county of Sussex in the years 1269, 1327, 1332. With some remarks on the origin of local administration in the county through 'borowes' or tithings.* Transcribed and edited by William Hudson. 1910

11 *The episcopal register of Robert Rede.... Part 2.* 1910

12 *Calendar of Sussex marriage licences recorded in the peculiar courts of the dean of Chichester and the archbishop of Canterbury: deanery of Chichester, January 1582/3 to December 1730; deaneries of Pagham and Tarring, January 1579/80 to November 1730.* By Edwin H. W. Dunkin. 1911

13 *The parish registers of Cuckfield, Sussex, 1598-1699.* Edited by W. C. Renshaw. 1911

14 *Notes of post mortem inquisitions taken in Sussex, 1 Henry VII to 1649 and after.* Abstracted and translated by F. W. T. Attree. 1912

15 *The parish registers of Bolney, Sussex, 1541-1812.* Edited by Edward Huth. 1912

16 *Abstracts of star chamber proceedings relating to the county of Sussex, Henry VII to Philip and Mary.* Transcribed and edited by Percy D. Mundy. 1913

17 *The parish registers of Ardingly, Sussex, 1558-1812.* Edited by Gerald W. E. Loder. 1913

18 *The first book of the parish registers of Angmering, Sussex, 1562-1687.* Edited by Edward W. D. Penfold. 1913

19 *Sussex manors, advowsons, etc., recorded in the feet of fines, Henry VIII to William IV, 1509-1833. Volume 1: A-L.* Alphabetically arranged and edited by Edwin H. W. Dunkin. 1914

20 *Sussex manors, advowsons, etc., recorded in the feet of fines... Volume 2: M-Z.* 1915

21 *The parish register of Horsham in the county of Sussex, 1541-1635.* Transcribed, edited and indexed by R. Garraway Rice. 1915

22 *The parish register of Cowfold, Sussex, 1558-1812.* Edited by P. S. Godman. 1916

23 *An abstract of feet of fines relating to the county of Sussex from I Edward II to 24 Henry VII.* Compiled by L. F. Salzman. 1916

24 *The parish register of East Grinstead, 1558-1661.* Edited by R. P. Crawford. 1917

25 *Calendar of Sussex marriage licences... for the archdeaconry of Lewes, and in the peculiar court of the archbishop of Canterbury for the deanery of South Malling, 1772-1837. Part 1 A-L.* Compiled by Edwin H. W. Dunkin and edited by E. W. D. Penfold. 1917

26 *Calendar of Sussex marriage licences...for the archdeaconry of Lewes, and...for the deanery of South Malling, 1772-1837. Part 2 M-Z.* 1919

27 *An abstract of the court rolls of the manor of Preston (Preston Episcopi).* [1562-1702] By Charles Thomas-Stanford. 1921

28 *Sussex apprentices and masters, 1710 to 1752.* Extracted from the apprenticeship books and edited and indexed by R. Garraway Rice. 1924

29 *Abstracts of Sussex deeds and documents from the muniments of the late H.C. Lane, esq., of Middleton Manor, Westmeston, Sussex.* [Mainly 1500-1900] Edited by W. Budgen. 1924

30 *The parish register of Glynde, Sussex, 1558-1812.* Edited by L. F. Salzman. 1924

31 *Thirteen custumals of the Sussex manors of the bishop of Chichester, and other documents, from Libri P and C of the episcopal manuscripts.* [Mainly 1300-1400] Translated and edited by W. D. Peckham.1925

32 *Calendar of Sussex marriage licences...for the archdeaconry of Chichester, January 1731 to December 1774.* Compiled by Edwin H. W. Dunkin and edited by D. MacLeod. 1926

33 *Sussex inquisitions. Extracts from Rawlinson Ms. B.433 in the Bodleian Library, Oxford, described as inquisitiones post mortem relating to Sussex.* [1541-1616] Edited by Mary S. Holgate. 1927

34 *The book of John Rowe, steward of the manors of Lord Bergavenny, 1597-1622, comprising rentals of twenty-seven manors in Sussex, manorial customs and information concerning the borough of Lewes, the* hundreds within the rape of Lewes, etc. Edited by Walter H. Godfrey. 1928

35 *Calendar of Sussex marriage licences...for the archdeaconry of Chichester, January 1775 to December 1800. Index to volumes 32 and 35, 1731-1800.* Compiled by Edwin H. W. Dunkin and edited by D. MacLeod. 1929

36 *Sussex chantry records, extracted from documents in the Public Record Office relating to the dissolution of the chantries, colleges, free chapels, fraternities, brotherhoods, guilds and other institutions.* [1535-1652] Edited by John E. Ray. 1931

37 *Lathe court rolls and views of frankpledge in the rape of Hastings, 1387 to 1474.* Edited by Elinor Joan Courthope and Beryl E. R. Formoy. [1934]

38 *The chartulary of the priory of St. Pancras of Lewes. Part I.* [11th -14th centuries] Edited by L. F. Salzman. [1933]

39 *The Buckhurst terrier, 1597-1598.* Epitomised by Ernest Straker. [1934]

40 *The chartulary of the priory of St. Pancras of Lewes. Part II.* [12th -14th centuries] [1935]

41 *Transcripts of Sussex wills as far as they relate to ecclesiological and parochial subjects up to the year 1560. Volume I: Albourne to Chichester.* Transcribed and classified by R. Garraway Rice and edited by Walter H. Godfrey. [1935]

42 *Transcripts of Sussex wills... Volume II: Chiddingly to Horsham.* [1938]

43 *Transcripts of Sussex wills... Volume III: Horsted Keynes to Pyecombe.* [1939]

44 *Records of the barony and honour of the rape of Lewes.* [1265-1465] Edited by Arnold J. Taylor. [1940]

45 *Transcripts of Sussex wills... Volume IV: Racton to Yapton.* [1941]

46 *The chartulary of the high church of Chichester.* [13th-16th centuries] Edited by W. D. Peckham. [1941]

[-] *The chartulary of Lewes priory. The portions relating*

to counties other than Sussex. [Draws from material published by other societies, hence not part of SRS numbered series] 1943

47 *Surveys of the manors of Robertsbridge, Sussex, and Michelmarsh, Hampshire, and of the demesne lands of Halden in Rolvenden, Kent, 1567-1570.* Edited by R. H. D'Elboux. [1946]

48 *The town book of Lewes, 1542-1701.* Edited by L. F. Salzman. [1947]

49 *Churchwardens' presentments (17th century). Part I: Archdeaconry of Chichester.* Edited by Hilda Johnstone. [1949]

50 *Churchwardens' presentments (17th century). Part II: Archdeaconry of Lewes.* [1950]

51 *Record of deputations of gamekeepers.* [1781-1928] Edited by L. F. Salzman. [1951]

[-] *Sussex views selected from the Burrell collections. Being the jubilee volume of the Sussex Record Society.* [Reproductions of drawings by Samuel Hieronymus Grimm and James Lambert] Edited by Walter H. Godfrey and L. F. Salzman. 1951

52 *The acts of the dean and chapter of the cathedral church of Chichester, 1472-1544 (the white act book).* Edited by W. D. Peckham. [1952]

53 *The manor of Etchingham cum Salehurst.* [1597-1865] Edited by Sir Sylvanus P. Vivian. [1953]

54 *Quarter sessions order book, 1642-1649.* Edited by B. C. Redwood. [1954]

55 *Ministers' accounts of the manor of Petworth, 1347-1353.* Edited by L. F. Salzman. [1955]

56 *The lay subsidy rolls for the county of Sussex, 1524-25.* Transcribed and edited by Julian Cornwall. [1957]

57 *Custumals of the Sussex manors of the archbishop of Canterbury.* [c. 1285-c. 1330] Edited by B. C. Redwood and A. E. Wilson. 1958

58 *The acts of the dean and chapter of the cathedral church of Chichester, 1545-1642.* Edited by W. D. Peckham. [1960]

59 *The chartulary of Boxgrove priory.* [12th-14th centuries] Translated and edited by Lindsay Fleming. 1960

60 *Custumals of the manors of Laughton, Willingdon and Goring.* [1292-1321] Translated and edited by A. E. Wilson. [1962]

61 *A catalogue of Sussex estate and tithe award maps.* [c. 1600-1884] Compiled by Francis W. Steer. 1962

62 *Minute book of the common council of the city of Chichester, 1783-1826.* Edited by Francis W. Steer. 1963

63 *The book of Bartholomew Bolney.* [c. 1460] Edited by Marie Clough. 1964

64 *Rye shipping records, 1566-1590.* Edited by Richard F. Dell. 1966

65 *The cellarers' rolls of Battle abbey, 1275-1513.* Edited by Eleanor Searle and Barbara Ross. 1967

66 *A catalogue of Sussex maps.* [1620-1888] Edited by Francis W. Steer. 1968

67 *Two estate surveys of the Fitzalan earls of Arundel.* [c. 1300-1464] Edited by Marie Clough. 1969

68 *The journal of Giles Moore.* [1655-1679] Edited by Ruth Bird. 1971

69 *The town book of Lewes, 1702-1837.* Edited by Verena Smith. [1973]

70 *The town book of Lewes, 1837-1901.* Edited by Verena Smith. [1976]

71 *Accounts of the Roberts family of Boarzell, Sussex, c.1568-1582.* Edited by Robert Tittler. [1979]

72 *Printed maps of Sussex, 1575-1900.* By David Kingsley with an introduction by Helen Wallis. 1982

73 *The correspondence of the Dukes of Richmond and Newcastle 1724-1750.* Edited by Timothy J. McCann. 1984

74 *Sussex coroners' inquests 1485-1558.* Edited by R. F. Hunnisett. 1985

75 *The Religious Census of Sussex 1851.* Edited by John A. Vickers. 1989

76 *The Fuller letters 1728-1755. Guns, slaves and finance.* Edited by David Crossley and Richard Saville. 1991

77 *East Sussex Land Tax 1785.* Edited by Roger Davey. 1991

78 *Chichester diocesan surveys 1686 and 1724.* Edited by Wyn K. Ford. 1994

79 *Saint Richard of Chichester. The sources for his life.* Edited by David Jones 1995

80 *The Ashdown Forest dispute 1876-1882. Environmental politics and custom.* Edited by Brian Short. 1997

81 *Sussex schools in the 18th century: schooling provision, schoolteachers and scholars.* Compiled by John Caffyn. 1998

82 *West Sussex Land Tax, 1785.* Edited by Alan Readman, Lionel Falconer, Rosie Ritchie and Peter Wilkinson. 2000

83 *Mid-Sussex Poor Law records, 1601-1835.* Edited by Ian Nelson and Norma Pilbeam. 2001

84 *World War I: the Sussex Home Front.* Edited by Keith Grieves. [In preparation]

85 *Sussex Depicted. Views and descriptions 1600-1800.* By John H. Farrant. 2001

Principal Editors

The following list of all who edited two or more titles provides an indication of those who have made the greatest contribution to the publication programme.

Clough 63, 67	**1964-69**
Deedes 4, 8, 11	**1905-07**
Dunkin 1, 6, 9, 12, 19, 20, 25, 26, 32, 35	**1902-29**
Garraway Rice 5, 21, 28, 41, 42, 43, 45	**1906-41**
Godfrey 34, 41, 42, 43, 45	**1928-41**
Johnstone 49, 50	**1949-50**
MacLeod 32, 35	**1926-29**
Peckham 31, 46, 52, 58	**1925-60**
Penfold 18, 25, 26	**1913-19**
Renshaw 4, 13	**1905-11**
Redwood 54, 57	**1954-58**
Salzman 2, 3, 4, 7, 23, 30, 38, 40, 47, 51, 55	**1903-57**
Smith 69, 70	**1973-76**
Steer 61, 62, 66	**1962-68**
Wilson 57, 60	**1958-62**

Index of persons and places

Page references in bold type indicate subjects or artists of Views. Other text illustrations are indicated by italics, and colour plates by upper-case Roman numbers. Sussex places are indexed under ancient ecclesiastical parishes (except for urban parishes where the town - Chichester, Hastings or Lewes – is given). Authors mentioned in captions to Views are indexed only where quoted extensively. Pages 361-76, 'The Sussex Record Society, 1901-2001' are not included in the index.